The
PIANIST'S
GUIDE TO
STANDARD
TEACHING
and
PERFORMANCE
LITERATURE

*An Invaluable Resource of Piano Literature
from Baroque through Contemporary Periods
for Teachers, Students and Performers*

JANE MAGRATH

Alfred Publishing Co., Inc.
P.O. Box 10003
Van Nuys, CA 91410-0003

Project Editor: Kevin M. Mitchell
Cover Design: Tanya Maiboroda
Interior Design/Production Coordinator: Pat Eichhorst, Shepherd, Inc.

ISBN No: softcover 088284-655-8
          hardcover 088284-654-X
Library of Congress Catalog Number: 95-75642

CONTENTS

Preface

Pianists have direct access to what is possibly the greatest solo literature composed for any instrument. This is true of the concert repertoire as well as of the extensive body of teaching literature often studied in preparation for playing the standard advanced repertoire. The purpose of this book is to provide information on a wealth of serious piano solo teaching literature which can pave the way to musical and technical advancement.

A second purpose is to bring to light the abundance of serious literature for pianists who are not yet able to perform the Chopin *Études*, the Beethoven *Sonatas* or the Copland *Variations*. Literature examined here is that which is generally considered to be easier than the Bach *Well-Tempered Clavier*, the moderate-level Beethoven *Sonatas* and the more difficult Chopin *Nocturnes*. This easier "black hole" literature often corresponds to the period in a student's study when he or she may seem to be remaining static in terms of progression, and yet is in need of new challenges at the same difficulty level.

It is also hoped that this book will document much of the fine keyboard literature that is regrettably becoming less readily available or even out-of-print, while at the same time fostering the study and performance of this repertoire.

The book is aimed toward the piano instructor, but also may be used with benefit by the keyboard student or the amateur performer looking for suitable literature to play. Only solo literature is included, some of it written for concert performance and some for teaching purposes. Multiple-composer anthologies are omitted, although single-composer collections are included when appropriate.

Composers are grouped first by historical period and then alphabetically within their period. For the purposes of this book, composers listed in the Baroque section flourished between 1600 and 1750. Composers in the Classical period flourished between about 1750 and 1825. Similarly, the Romantic period is deemed roughly 1825–1900, and the 20th-century era is self-explanatory.

Generally only compositions originally written for piano solo (or for harpsichord/clavichord for earlier music) are included. Occasionally transcriptions are included, but are confined to such well-known music as the *Viennese Sonatinas* of Mozart or the Haydn *Minuets*. Compositions are normally in print and available from publishers. However, frequent changes in the publishing field do create difficulties. Works often get deleted from a catalogue due to low sales, or appear to have been deleted due to the wholesale transfer of a catalogue from one publisher or agent to another. Some worthy works not in print are listed here in an effort to provide a relatively complete listing of the teaching works of a specific composer, and in the hope that these works will not be lost and forgotten.

Descriptions of works are in general as objective as possible, although naturally the experience and opinions of the author may reveal themselves. Every effort has been taken, however, to provide information to guide the teacher and others to make their own informed decisions about a work, i.e., to lead them directly to the score itself.

I have included almost exclusively scores which I have examined myself, and I have taken virtually every precaution to insure the accuracy of information provided. Those scores not examined are listed under the section "Additional Works for Study." Due to the enormous amount of data involved, some discrepancies may occur. I would appreciate being informed of them through the University of Oklahoma School of Music, Norman, Oklahoma, that I might amend this book for successive editions.

Works and movements are graded from Level 1 to Level 10, and a detailed explanation of the grading system is given following the acknowledgments. The use of 10 increments is meant to reinforce the point that the even and systematic development of technical and musical growth is an intricate process that requires careful pacing and sequencing of literature. Naturally some individuals may disagree with the levels assigned to specific pieces or movements, but the inclusion of levels allows teachers to gain a sense of the relative difficulty of a particular piece in comparison to standard works from the piano repertoire. One can take exception to individual categorizations, but it is hoped that the leveling will be used in the spirit in which it is intended, as a general reference and comparison rather than a factual grading.

Finally, I sincerely hope that use of this volume can help foster the continued study and performance of both teaching and concert keyboard literature; that it documents much of the repertoire that is becoming less readily available to the public; and that it will encourage the republishing of worthy works that have gone out of print.

Jane Magrath
Norman, Oklahoma
March, 1995

General Information

This annotated bibliography includes pieces ranging from elementary teaching pieces included in keyboard treatises of such composers as Clementi, Türk and others to moderate-level standard piano works. Thousands of works have been evaluated, with individual information provided concerning stylistic interpretation, unique characteristics, technical requirements, musical concepts and potential problems, as well as the pedagogical situation in which a piece might be used, a grading for each work, and identification of publishing sources.

Arrangement of entries

The *Guide* is organized by historical period, with entries grouped into Baroque, Classical, Romantic and 20th-century categories. Within each period, composers are listed alphabetically. For many of the more important works, all appropriate movements are annotated separately, especially works from Levels 6–10. For other selections, the work as a whole is annotated, though in some instances reference to a specific movement is provided, to direct the reader in further investigation. When known, the date of composition is provided after the title of the work.

Descriptions

Descriptions are usually limited to general style characterizations of the works or movements, with some consideration given to possible pedagogical uses of a work. At times more subjective reference is made in an effort to note a particularly fine composition or a special teaching issue. Editorial strengths or weaknesses of a particular edition or anthology generally are not mentioned. Often it is impossible to list all publishers of a standard work, in which case the indication "Many standard editions" is given, or one or two publishers are noted along with the reference ". . . and other publishers."

Order of Works Listed

Each individual composer presented his or her own set of problems in the ordering and listing of works, and in each instance a certain ordering system seemed most appropriate. Compositions are therefore given in one of several possible orders: by opus number (or the composer's numbering system); chronologically by date of composition; by level of difficulty from easiest to more advanced works; alphabetically by the first major word in the title; by genre; or, rarely, in some other logical ordering system. Major works are listed first, and anthologies are always listed last.

SAMPLE ENTRY

Work title

General information on the work. (Publisher.) Suggested level.

Movement

> In some instances, descriptions are given of selected movements, or of all movements of a work. When a grade is provided for all the separate movements of a complete work, no grade is assigned overall to the work. When a publisher or grade is not provided, that information was not available for inclusion.

Miscellaneous Volumes

Listed here are anthologies of works by the composer. The editor and/or compiler's last name also is given, along with the publisher and general level for the entire volume.

Additional Works for Study

> Works listed in this section were not examined, but may be appropriate for study at some point for pianists working between Levels 1–10. In some instances, publishers are given.

Acknowledgments

This book has benefited from the efforts and talents of so many individuals. I am indebted to all of them for their support and tireless efforts toward my goal of compiling this guidebook and arranging it in an accessible format.

Particular appreciation is due to the many students in my courses who encouraged this project through their thirst for knowledge of this music.

A special word of thanks goes to music store owners Ray A. Freeman and Jacqueline Freeman of Oklahoma City, who opened their invaluable and unique collection in The Full Score to me for so many months for my study. Their generosity and interest in this project helped make it possible, and their support sustained me through numerous years of research and probing. My days playing through scores and writing at The Full Score hold fond memories.

Many students and friends have provided special assistance with this project through various help with portions of the text. Such credit and thanks go to Kelli Birdsong, Jackie Edwards, Young Eun Kim, Anna Kwa, Naegeli Metcalf, Mary Frances Reyburn and Kim Watson, as well as others. Their watchful eyes did much to help support the project.

The writing was sustained through busy times with the assistance of Yvette Varela, whose devotion to the project evidenced itself by the exceptionally high quality of her work. I'm also grateful for the excellent work of Peter Mose, who provided his musical and editing expertise as a copyeditor.

Beth Levy has provided invaluable research and editorial assistance. Her attention to detail, strong research skills and thirst for knowledge have aided me and the project far beyond any expectations. Her brilliant work anticipates a bright career as a researcher/scholar.

The individuals at Alfred Publishing foster a wonderful working situation. Their commitment to this formidable project has been unstinting, and their attention to detail and penchant for accuracy has made the later stages of this book's genesis a complete pleasure. The warmth and sincere interest expressed by Morton and Iris Manus must be unique in the publishing industry. The dedication of this effort, long hours and genuine enthusiasm for this project contributed by Kevin Mitchell have provided an indelible mark on the final volume. I express to him and the entire staff at Alfred Publishing Company my most gracious appreciation.

Finally, sincere gratitude and appreciation goes to my wonderful family, colleagues and administration personnel of the School of Music at the University of Oklahoma, friends and students for faithfully helping me sustain this project to its conclusion.

Leveling of Literature

Reference Chart for Grading

Levels 1–10, Beginning to Early-Advanced Levels

Level 1 Bartók *Mikrokosmos*, Vol. 1

Level 2 Türk *Pieces for Beginners*

Level 3 Latour Sonatinas; Kabalevsky *Pieces for Young People*, Op. 39

Level 4 *Anna Magdalena Bach Notebook*; Gurlitt *Album for the Young*, Op. 140; Tchaikovsky *Album for the Young*, Op. 39

Level 5 *Anna Magdalena Bach Notebook*; Sonatinas by Attwood, Lynes; Menotti *Poemetti*

Level 6 Clementi *Sonatinas*, Op. 36; Burgmüller *25 Progressive Pieces*, Op. 100

Level 7 Kuhlau and Diabelli Sonatinas; Bach easier *Two-Part Inventions*; Bach *Little Preludes*; Dello Joio *Lyric Pieces for the Young*

Level 8 Moderately difficult Bach *Two-Part Inventions*; Beethoven easier variations sets; Field Nocturnes; Schumann *Album Leaves*, Op. 124; Schubert Waltzes; Turina *Miniatures*

Level 9 Easier Bach *Three-Part Inventions*; easiest Haydn Sonata movements; easiest Mendelssohn *Songs Without Words*; easiest Chopin Mazurkas

Level 10 Bach *Three-Part Inventions*; easiest Chopin Nocturnes; Beethoven *Sonatas*, Op. 49, 79; Mozart *Sonata*, K. 283; Muczynski *Preludes*

Abbreviations

Anh. Anhang (Appendix of a thematic catalogue, generally used for works of uncertain authorship)

b. born

B. B. numbers represent the numbering in the thematic catalogue of Handel's works by A. Craig Bell

Bach When mentioned in the text, refers to the works of J. S. Bach unless other initials appear

BWV Bach Werke Verzeichnis or Bach Catalogue of Works, the numbering system for J. S. Bach's works

c. circa

D. D. numbers refer to works by Schubert indexed in Otto Erich Deutsch, *Schubert: Thematic Catalogue of All His Works in Chronological Order*

ed. edited

G. G. numbers refer to the numbering of the works of Handel by Anthony Hicks in the *New Grove Dictionary of Music and Musicians*, 1980

Hob. Hoboken, Anthony van, *Joseph Haydn: Thematisch-bibliographisches Werkzeichnis*, the thematic catalogue of Haydn's works

K. When associated with the works of Mozart, K. refers to Köchel, Ludwig von, *Chronologisch-thematisches Verzeichnis sämtlicher Tonwerke Wolfgang Amadé Mozarts*, the chronological catalogue of Mozart's works

K. When associated with the sonatas of Scarlatti, K. refers to Kirkpatrick, Ralph, the definitive biographer of Scarlatti, who ordered the sonatas and published them in facsimile edition

KK. KK refers to the Chopin catalogue by Krystyna Kobylanska *Frédéric Chopin's Thematisch-bibliographisches Werkverzeichnis*

L.   Longo numbers, an earlier ordering system for the Scarlatti sonatas (see Kirkpatrick above); after Alessandro Longo

Op.   Opus

PWM   Polskie Wydawnictwo Muyczne (Polish Music Publishers); see Index of Music Publishers

S.   S. numbers in connection with pieces by Liszt refer to the listing of Liszt's works by Humphrey Searle in *Thematic Catalogue of the Works of Liszt*

W.   Numbering of Tcherepnin's works in chronological order, taken from *Alexander Tcherepnin, A Bio-Bibliography* by Enrique Alberto Arias

WoO   Without Opus Number, referring to works by Beethoven in Georg Kinsky and Hans Halm *Das Werk Beethovens: Thematisch-bibliographisches Verzeichnis seiner sämtlichen vollendeten Kompositionen*

Wq.   Wotquenne, Alfred, *Thematisches Verzeichnis der Werke von Carl Philipp Emanuel Bach*, the thematic catalogue for the works of C.P.E. Bach

Z.   Refers to the numbering of Purcell's music by Franklin Zimmerman in *Henry Purcell, 1659–1695: An Analytical Catalogue of his Music*

BAROQUE LITERATURE

A

JOHN ALCOCK (1715–1806) Great Britain

Alcock was known during the 18th century as both an organist and composer.

Six Suites of Easy Lessons

Suites of three or four movements with writing generally in two voices. The style is graceful but highly florid, and the large number of ornaments makes these works more difficult than they initially appear. See especially suites Nos. 4 and 5. (Associated Board of the Royal Schools of Music.) Level 8.

THOMAS ARNE (1710–1778) Great Britain

Arne composed at approximately the same time that J. C. Bach introduced the new pianoforte in London. Arne wrote relatively few works for keyboard (primarily the *Eight Sonatas*), in comparison to his vast output in other areas.

Eight Sonatas

These works contain surprisingly fresh and inviting movements. The textures are generally thin, often in two voices, and the writing is tuneful. Although they range from two to four movements, most of the sonatas are in three movements, often corresponding to the Baroque binary dance forms. Especially suited for performers who might otherwise believe that they do not enjoy playing Baroque music. (Kalmus and other editions.)

Sonata No. I in F Major

> The opening, singing *Andante* and the final lilting *Allegro* in 3/8 are connected by an *Adagio* cadential flourish of three chords. The entire sonata (suite) is approximately five pages in print. Interesting writing and an effective program opener. Level 8.

Sonata No. II in E Minor

> A lyrical *Andante* is followed by a 13-measure *Adagio* and concludes with a short *Allegrissimo*. The brevity of the movements makes it possible for a typical student to learn the entire sonata for performance. The musical material is unexpectedly interesting and rewarding to the ear. Level 9.

Sonata No. III in G Major

Improvisatory opening *Prelude* is followed by a concerto-like *Allegro*. The concluding *Minuet* with two variations is elegant. Strong writing. Level 9.

Sonata No. IV in D Minor

One of the more difficult sonatas in this set. The short *Siciliano-Largo* leads to a three-voice fugue, highly rhythmic and straight-forward. The final three-voice *Allegro* is also imitative. Level 10.

Sonata No. V in B-flat Major

By contrast with the other sonatas discussed here, this is the easiest and one of the shortest. The minuet-like first movement precedes a charming gavotte. Level 8.

Sonata No. VI in G Minor

Another short, two-movement sonata with slow-fast tempos. See especially the final *Gigue*. Level 9.

Sonata No. VII in A Major

Fast-slow-fast. Strong contrast between the movements. One of the best sonatas. Level 9.

Sonata No. VIII in G Major

Minuet and variations. Writing is not as strong as in the other sonatas. Level 9.

Miscellaneous Piece

A Keyboard Allegro

A tuneful concerto movement which first appeared as the third movement of Arne's *Concerto No. 1 in C Major*. This four-page work bubbles with Baroque rhythmic vitality and tuneful writing. Appropriate for the performer ready to play the Bach *Two-Part Inventions*, or for the pianist who thinks Baroque music is not his or her favorite. (Oxford.) Level 8.

B

JOHANN SEBASTIAN BACH (1685–1750) Germany

Bach's works brought Baroque music to its highest perfection and for this reason most historians date the end of the era with his death. His family played a significant role in German music for over 150 years. Bach was well known during his lifetime as a composer and organist. German musicologist Wolfgang Schmieder catalogued Bach's music under the title *Systematic Thematic Index of the Musical Works of J. S. Bach.* BWV numbers (*Bach-Werke-Verzeichnis,* or *Bach Work-Catalogue*) are used here to identify individual works.

Notebook for Anna Magdalena Bach (1722/1725)

The Bach family collected and produced three notebooks which together comprise a kind of family album. They are the *Clavierbüchlein für Wilhelm Friedemann Bach* (1720) and the two *Musical Notebooks* (1722/1725), which J. S. Bach compiled for the use of his second wife, Anna Magdalena. The two blank notebooks, a gift from J. S. Bach to his wife, were filled over the course of about five years with the easy pieces which so many pianists play today along with preludes, suites, chorales and both sacred and secular songs.

The Notebook opens with the J. S. Bach *Partitas in A Minor* and *E Minor* and is followed by compositions of various composers including J. S. Bach, not arranged in any particular order. Also found in the notebooks are two *French Suites, D Minor* and *C Minor.* Due to their size, these works, along with the partitas, are not included here. We know that the notebook was filled with favorite selections of the members of the Bach circle, and some were in J. S. Bach's handwriting as well as in the writing of his children. Many of the compositions in the notebooks were intended for use in the musical instruction of Bach's own children, and compositions by composers other than J. S. Bach are included, such as C.P.E. Bach and four anonymous composers. Teachers usually refer to the *Anna Magdalena Bach Notebook* as a source of the most accessible keyboard works of J. S. Bach for teaching.

Complete editions of the *Anna Magdalena Bach Notebook* include Hofmeister, Henle, Kalmus, Peters and others. Selected pieces from the *Anna Magdalena Bach Notebook* are offered by Alfred, Associated Board of the Royal Schools of Music, International, Kalmus, Masters Music, Peters, Willis and others.

Minuet in F Major, BWV 113

This binary-form minuet is not frequently found in collections, perhaps due to the disjunct nature of the two voices. Many different rhythmic values are featured. Level 6.

Minuet in G Major, BWV Anh. 114

Perhaps the best known of the *Anna Magdalena Bach Notebook* minuets, with an ascending G Major five-finger pattern in the right hand. Especially suitable for helping a student develop an even legato sound. The minuet's true authorship is unknown. Level 4.

Minuet in G Minor, BWV Anh. 115

Lyrical writing requiring a slightly better-developed legato than the previous minuet. Deserves its popularity and its prominent position as a teaching piece. Level 4.

Minuet in G Major, BWV Anh. 116

The opening ascending G Major broken chord distinguishes this work from the other well-known *Minuet in G Major*. Appropriate for helping a student begin to feel octave stretches, and for work on expansion and contraction of the hand. Two-voice writing. Level 4.

Polonaise in F Major, BWV Anh. 117a

Much more difficult than the surrounding compositions due to its highly ornamented melody. This piece could substitute for a two-part invention if one wants a shorter work. Many different rhythmic values. Level 7.

Minuet in B-flat Major, BWV Anh. 118

An infrequently heard work, perhaps due to the disjunct nature of the right-hand melody. This piece may help a student develop a feeling for contrapuntal playing in a work that is not excessively difficult. Level 6.

Polonaise in G Minor, BWV Anh. 119

The tuneful nature of this polonaise contributes to its popularity. Composed in two independent lines, this binary work is in three sections of 4+6+6 measures and opens with the strong feeling of a procession. Will require attention to various articulations. Level 6.

Minuet in A Minor, BWV Anh. 120

Two-voice work with many canonic passages, especially appropriate for developing independence between the hands. Level 5.

Minuet in C Minor, BWV Anh. 121

Highly chromatic writing in which a skillful legato is needed as well as a good sense of harmonic direction. This well-known minuet is one of the best of the shorter pieces. Two-voice counterpoint and sequential passages. Level 5.

Marche in D Major, BWV Anh. 122

Attributed to C.P.E. Bach. The tuneful melody and cheerful character make this work a student favorite. Careful attention to articulation is required, and the feeling of one pulse per measure is important. Left-hand detached walking bass. Level 4.

Polonaise in G Minor, BWV Anh. 123

Attributed to C.P.E. Bach. The right-hand sixths and thirds provide the primary technical difficulty for younger intermediate pianists with small hands. Strong dance-like character is required in performance. Level 7.

Marche in G Major, BWV Anh. 124

Attributed to C.P.E. Bach. Vigorous two-voice march with prominent repeated notes. Needs subtle inflection without stressing the repeated notes. The interpretation must be confident and bold. Level 6.

Polonaise in G Minor, BWV Anh. 125

Attributed to C.P.E. Bach. Recognition of the back-and-forth dialogue in this work is a key to its musical understanding. Especially suited for the student who enjoys robust music. Rapid motive shifts between hands. Level 7.

Musette in D Major, BWV Anh. 126

Cheerful, bright and deserving of its popularity. The music provides opportunity for work on contraction and expansion of the hand at the elementary level. The quick shifts in hand position must be executed precisely in tempo. Level 4.

Marche in E-flat Major, BWV Anh. 127

The musical and technical difficulties of this piece stem from the large number of different ideas. The juxtaposition of duple and triple rhythm and the long-spun phrases make its musical comprehension more challenging than surrounding works. Requires a steady pulse and independence between the hands. Some complex fingerings. One of the most difficult pieces in the *Anna Magdalena Bach Notebook*. Level 7.

Polonaise in D Minor, BWV Anh. 128

Highly florid melody above a continuo-like and somewhat static lower part. Features a contemplative and sad mood. Many different rhythmic values are used. Level 7.

Polonaise in G Major, BWV Anh. 130

Seldom heard, but would make a fine contrapuntal study for the performer playing intermediate-level Bach inventions. Level 7.

Präeludium in C Major, BWV 846

The justifiably familiar prelude of the *Prelude and Fugue in C Major, Well-Tempered Clavier* is found in the *Anna Magdalena Bach Notebook* as a separate piece. It is an excellent study for hearing harmonic rhythm. Level 6.

Minuet in F Major, BWV Anh. 131

Originally untitled, this selection appears under a myriad of titles including *Minuet, Chorale, Air* and others. One of the most accessible short works. Level 4.

Minuet in D Minor, BWV Anh. 132

Deservedly one of the most popular of the shorter pieces in the *Anna Magdalena Bach Notebook*. The wide skips in the melody call for careful execution. Level 4.

The Little Notebook for Wilhelm Friedemann Bach (Clavierbüchlein) (1720)

J. S. Bach supervised the compilation of a notebook for his son Wilhelm Friedemann. This notebook probably existed more as instruction for W. F. Bach's compositional development than for his keyboard development, and is almost entirely in the handwriting of either J. S. Bach or Wilhelm Friedemann. Included in it were seven of the *Short Preludes* (also known as the *Little Preludes* or the *Small Preludes*), the *Two-Part Inventions*, 14 of the *Three-Part Inventions* or *Sinfonias*, 11 of the preludes that would become part of the *Well-Tempered Clavier*, Book I, and other miscellaneous works. Most of these works are annotated here with the entire body of the genre (such as the *Short Preludes* and *Two-Part Inventions*). Some of the less musically significant works from the *Notebook* are not listed separately in this section.

Publishers of the complete *Notebook for Wilhelm Friedemann Bach* (Clavierbüchlein) include Kalmus and others. Publishers of the *Short Preludes* include Alfred, Associated Board of the Royal Schools of Music, Breitkopf, Carl Fischer, Henle, Kalmus, Peters, G. Schirmer, Willis and many others.

Applicatio in C Major, BWV 994

The first work in the *Clavierbüchlein* is this short piece, intended as an application of ornamentation principles of Bach's time. It is especially significant in that the ornaments are assuredly by J. S. Bach and are fingered by him as well, thus providing direct insight into performance practice of the time. The music requires the crossing of the third finger over the fourth, a reference to Baroque practices, while at the same time it requires the use of the thumb in a more innovative way than even earlier. Most significant from a historical point of view. Level 7.

Short Preludes (Little Preludes, Small Preludes)

The *Short Preludes* are sometimes grouped as *18 Short Preludes*, and are also referred to as the *Little Preludes* or *Small Preludes*. These preludes foreshadow two of Bach's principal compositional genres, the suites and the preludes and fugues. In the *Short Preludes* are various dance forms, contrapuntal works (inventions and even fughettas), preludes or fantasias, toccatas and free forms.

Short Preludes from the Clavierbüchlein
for Wilhelm Friedemann Bach

These six preludes were gathered from various parts of the *Wilhelm Friedemann Bach Notebook* and grouped together. They were collected by Griepenkerl, an editor for Peters, in the middle 1800s and grouped with the six from the Kellner collection as a set of 12.

Prelude in C Major, BWV 924

A prelude built on broken chords in the right hand. Suspensions and dissonance are created from the moving voices of the right hand chords against the accompaniment. This work is more difficult than it appears. Left-hand mordents may present problems, and the pacing of the cadenza-like passage will need attention. Level 5.

Prelude in D Minor, BWV 926

Built on broken chords with consistent eighth-note motion throughout. A study in control of rhythm and evenness of passagework. The ornaments, although not technically difficult, present some coordination problems, and the cadenza needs interpretative maturity. Level 7.

Prelude in F Major, BWV 927

This fine toccata-like work is one of the most famous of the short preludes. Performers should listen for the harmonic intensity and suspensions. Alberti-like figures appear in both hands. Suitable for developing coordination between hands and control of even sixteenths. Level 5.

Prelude in G Minor, BWV 930

Several short motives based on chord outlines are tossed back and forth between the two voices. This work was fingered in the autograph. Numerous ornaments present the primary difficulties. One of the most cumbersome of the set. Level 8.

Prelude in F Major, BWV 928

Dance-like with bold, vertical writing, a piece especially appropriate for the aggressive performer. Musically easy to comprehend, with many short, square phrases. Level 9.

Prelude in D Major, BWV 925

Essentially a fughetta, this work contains continuous sixteenths against two-voice suspensions, with frequently alternating dialogue between the hands. An especially appropriate work for developing the playing of three voices. Level 9.

Six Small Preludes from Johann Peter Kellner's Collection

These preludes were found scattered in manuscripts owned by Kellner, a German organist contemporaneous with Bach. Some scholars feel that Nos. 1–4 were not composed by Bach, but by one of his pupils. Nos. 5 and 6 undoubtedly are by Bach. These six preludes are sometimes combined with the six preludes from the *Short Preludes* from the *Clavierbüchlein for Wilhelm Friedemann Bach* to make what is referred to as the *12 Short Preludes*.

Prelude in C Major, BWV 939

This well-known prelude is best performed with two pulses per measure. It is an excellent elementary work for illustrating chordal structures within a composition. Level 4.

Prelude in D Minor, BWV 940

Expressive writing, particularly appropriate for study before the *Invention in G Minor* because of its long lines and the nature of the ornaments. One of the most accessible three-voice preludes, with much dialogue between the hands. Many differing note values may make rhythm tricky. Level 7.

Prelude in E Minor, BWV 941

One of the most beautiful of the short preludes, providing another fine introduction to three-voice playing. Suspensions in the soprano and alto may help a student listen for dissonance and resolution. Prominent chordal outlines make this work easy to comprehend harmonically. This elegant prelude can help a student work on contraction and expansion of the hand as well as on contrapuntal voicing. Level 6.

Prelude in A Minor, BWV 942

Gigue-like, two-voice work concluding with scale and chordal flourishes. More difficult than it appears in terms of coordination. Level 8.

Prelude in C Major, BWV 943

Essentially a fughetta, requiring finger substitution for legato. Level 9.

Prelude in C Minor, BWV 999

Composed originally for lute, this prelude portrays an easier version of the toccata-style preludes from the *Well-Tempered Clavier*. Students with agile fingers will enjoy this broken-chord study. Careful attention to areas of harmonic pull and strong rhythmic drive are necessary for an effective interpretation. Level 6.

Six Small Preludes for Beginners on the Clavier

This collection contains some of the most accessible preludes of the *Short Preludes*. They were probably arranged by Bach in systematic order according to key and difficulty. These are the most highly developed works of the three groups of preludes. All are in binary form.

Prelude in C Major, BWV 933

The tuneful character of this concerto-like piece and its appealing sequential passages can help students surpass the technical difficulties. Mordents in the right-hand chords present the major technical problems, and mordents in the inner voices can help in developing a student's finger independence. Needs a strong sense of rhythm, and should be played with one pulse per measure. In some respects, this work sounds more difficult than it is. Level 7.

Prelude in C Minor, BWV 934

Dance-like work and one of the most easily manageable of the early-intermediate level *Little Preludes*. Texture generally involves passagework in eighths in the right hand against quarters in the left.

Especially appropriate for a student playing the easiest Bach inventions. Students will need to maintain a light thumb and play the appoggiaturas without distorting the rhythm. Level 6.

Prelude in D Minor, BWV 935

Essentially a two-part invention in binary form, similar to but slightly easier than the *Two-Part Invention in D Minor*. The texture consists primarily of sixteenths against eighths. Some of the sixteenth-note patterns have slightly unusual turns. Level 7.

Prelude in D Major, BWV 936

An elegant, lyrical work featuring contrapuntal dialogue between soprano and alto above a continuo bass. One of the most musically satisfying of the set. An excellent study in voicing and in accurate holding of note values. Sustained notes occur against moving lines. Level 8.

Prelude in E Major, BWV 937

This uncomplicated dance-like work with running sixteenth notes is a rewarding substitute for a Bach two-part invention. Baroque sound and style are easily achieved in the performance of this piece. In many respects it is similar in character to the *Courante* of the *French Suite in G Major*. A busy sixteenth-note figure is tossed between the hands in this binary form work. Especially appropriate for the student with strong fingers, or for building finger-strength. Evenness in passagework, expansion and contraction of the hands, and hand independence required. Level 8.

Prelude in E Minor, BWV 938

Two-voice writing featuring lyrical lines in an invention-like texture with some imitation between the hands. Mordents and short trills should be played gently and without excessive hand tension. The many sequences and the clear dialogue between the hands can help the performer present a clear interpretation. A good piece for learning about ornaments. Level 8.

Small Fugues

Except for the two-voice third fugue, all are in three voices. The short fugues are most easily available in the Lemoine or the Vienna Urtext editions.

Fugue in C Major, BWV 953

This joyful work should be played with vitality. The figurations approach the quick finger shifts required in more advanced Bach. An excellent selection for study prior to the fugues of the *Well-Tempered Clavier*. Often only two of the three voices are heard. Level 9.

Fugue in C Major, BWV 952

Careful attention should be taken to avoid accenting the thumb in this three-voice fughetta, which approaches the level of the easiest fugues in the *Well-Tempered Clavier*. Requires holding sustained notes in one part of the hand while playing quick sixteenths in the same hand. The hands generally remain contracted. Level 10.

Fugue in C Minor, BWV 961

Gigue-like writing in two voices. This would be an appropriate substitute for one of the gigue-like inventions such as the *Two-Part Invention in G Major*. Level 10.

Short Preludes with Fugues (Small Preludes and Fugues)

These four works, pointing toward the *Well-Tempered Clavier*, vary in quality but provide prospective alternative literature for study. The exact body of repertoire known as the *Short Preludes and Fugues* is sometimes confusing. Many individuals think that they are the volume published originally by G. Schirmer as *18 Little Preludes and Fugues* of Bach and still in print. In reality, however, this is not an authentic grouping. It stems instead from the late 1800s when the editor Buonamici took the *18 Short Preludes* of J. S. Bach and put them with six short fugues of J. S. Bach and 12 fughettas of Wilhelm Friedemann Bach. Obviously this pairing was not created by J. S. Bach. The works listed below can serve as excellent preparatory studies to the *Well-Tempered Clavier*. (Many standard editions.)

Prelude in G Major, BWV 902 (902a),
Fughetta in G Major, from BWV 902

One of the easiest prelude and fugue pairings. Two different preludes in G Major—BWV 902 and BWV 902a—appeared in different sources with the fugue, BWV 902. Performance of either prelude with the fugue is correct. The first *Prelude in G*, BWV 902, was composed in Leipzig and perhaps was intended to be included in the second book of the *Well-Tempered Clavier*. Its lyrical nature and many suspensions require careful attention to voicing, sustaining notes for their proper length, and legato playing. It is an excellent preparatory study to any of the lyrical preludes in the *Well-Tempered Clavier*. Careful matching of tones is required. The second *Prelude in G*, BWV 902a, is the more commonly performed prelude with this fugue. It features driving toccata-like rhythms and sixteenths switching from hand to hand. The fugue is an early version of the one from the *Well-Tempered Clavier II*. This version makes it one of the most accessible of the short fugues and perhaps the most rewarding. Level 9.

Prelude and Fughetta in D Minor, BWV 899

Lyrical prelude with captivating suspensions and dissonances. An excellent study in contrapuntal playing between the hands in both the prelude and the fugue. One of the most accessible four-voice contrapuntal works available. Fugue in triple meter. Level 9.

Prelude and Fugue in E Minor, BWV 900

The fast passagework in this prelude borders on bravura. The long three-voice fugue is built on a subject which is sectional and sequential. Level 9.

Prelude and Fugue in A Minor, BWV 895

Short declamatory prelude and bold fughetta with a repeated-note motive in eighths in the fugue subject. Level 9.

Two-Part Inventions, BWV 772–801

The *Two-Part Inventions* were composed from 1720 to 1723 as teaching pieces and written while Bach was living in Cöthen. Each in only two voices, they appear in ascending order by pitch, starting with C, and use only those major and minor keys which employ no more than four sharps or flats. The inventions exhibit remarkable economy of material. Most are sectional, with parts clearly defined by conclusive cadences or by recurrence of material. A common mistake is to teach the *Two-Part Inventions* too early in a student's musical development. Fine alternatives at easier levels exist in the *Short Preludes*.

Publishers of the *Two- and Three-Part Inventions* under one cover include Alfred, Associated Board of the Royal Schools of Music, Bärenreiter, Dover, Henle, Kalmus, Vienna Urtext and many other standard editions.

Invention No. 1 in C Major, BWV 772

One of the most frequently played inventions, in which some form of its short, stepwise motive permeates all but a few measures of the piece. Passagework is more intricate than in the *Inventions in D Minor* and *F Major*. Bach added triplets to the autograph at a later stage, perhaps to demonstrate a valid type of melodic ornamentation. Level 7.

Invention No. 2 in C Minor, BWV 773

Long, lyrical lines encourage independence of the hands in phrase shaping. Inflection of motives within the phrase is essential to a successful performance. Constructed largely in strict canon. Level 7.

Invention No. 3 in D Major, BWV 774

Based on scalewise passages more than arpeggiation, this invention demands a moving tempo and careful coordination of some difficult ornaments in the countermotive. The motive fits the hand well and fingering should not be a problem. Natural phrase contours from the shape of the motive are obvious. Level 8.

Invention No. 4 in D Minor, BWV 775

Extended trills are the primary technical consideration in this otherwise accessible work, which is an almost perfect example of invention technique, brimming with clear examples of contrapuntal devices. Deservedly popular. Level 7.

Invention No. 5 in E-flat Major, BWV 776

Perhaps the most difficult of the set, but also one of the most musically satisfying. The ornaments present a considerable musical and technical challenge. This invention is constructed in invertible counterpoint and in three main sections. Level 8.

Invention No. 6 in E Major, BWV 777

Features examples of invertible counterpoint and musically constructed in rounded binary form with an obvious return to the original key near the end. Requires a refined legato and cantabile. A graceful and dance-like work with many notated mordents. One of the more technically accessible inventions. Levels 7–8.

Invention No. 7 in E Minor, BWV 778

Lyrical, with long lines. The frequent ornaments must not interfere with flow of the line. This invention has more varied melodic material and technical demands than most of the inventions. Level 8.

Invention No. 8 in F Major, BWV 779

Perhaps the best-known and one of the most approachable of the inventions in which few rhythmic difficulties exist and the harmonic outlines are clear. Passages fit the hand well but require strong fingers. Appealing to students perhaps because a fast speed can be achieved without excessive coordination problems. Level 7.

Invention No. 9 in F Minor, BWV 780

The long lyrical lines need to be sustained while the eighth-note leaps require *detaché*. The physical negotiation of some of the passages on the black keys is awkward. Constructed primarily in double counterpoint. Level 8.

Invention No. 10 in G Major, BWV 781

Actually a gigue based on broken chords, with several articulation choices possible for the rollicking eighths. Securing a proper tempo and coordinating the hands are important considerations. Level 7.

Invention No. 11 in G Minor, BWV 782

The long motive is in three parts, punctuated by skips of a seventh. This work is lyrical and highly expressive, with some interesting harmonic progressions that require mature musicianship. Level 9.

Invention No. 12 in A Major, BWV 783

Lively and rhythmic theme that is treated fugally. The level of difficulty is close to one of the more difficult *French Suite* movements. Ornaments here can sometimes be awkward. Level 9.

Invention No. 13 in A Minor, BWV 784

Based on broken-chord patterns that appear in many variations. The three short themes are linked, each growing out of its predecessor. Often considered to be one of the most accessible of the inventions. Level 7.

Invention No. 14 in B-flat Major, BWV 785

Based on a simple broken chord with elaboration. This invention's prevalent thirty-second notes must speak clearly and evenly, never interrupting the flow of the musical line. Level 7.

Invention No. 15 in B Minor, BWV 786

Presents three pairs of entries that structurally define this symmetrical work. Precision in playing the many mordents is needed. One of the most difficult inventions in the set. Level 9.

Sinfonias or Three-Part Inventions

These challenging works might be regarded as fugue-like, although here the first announcement of the theme is accompanied by counterpoint or a countersubject. All but the C Minor and the D Major were part of the *Clavierbüchlein*. Nos. 1, 3, 4, 6 and 15 are recommended as starters. (Many standard editions. See the entry for the *Two-Part Inventions*.)

Sinfonia No. 1 in C Major, BWV 787

A monothematic work, based on an ascending scalewise passage and containing many instances of overlapping entries. Structurally constructed in three large sections. The subject appears throughout most of the piece. Levels 9–10.

Sinfonia No. 2 in C Minor, BWV 788

Gigue-like work that opens with imitation at the octave. Contains lilting eighth-note movement as well as stepwise and scalewise passages in sixteenths. Level 10.

Sinfonia No. 3 in D Major, BWV 789

Especially appropriate preparation for fugal playing. The three voices are florid, with some passages of double thirds and sixths which require skilled voicing within a single hand. Level 9.

Sinfonia No. 4 in D Minor, BWV 790

A highly expressive work with a subject that contains a wide upward leap. Features some intricate voice-leading. Especially suitable for the musically sensitive performer. Level 10.

Sinfonia No. 5 in E-flat Major, BWV 791

A beautiful and highly ornamented Baroque cantilena is found throughout over an accompanimental bass. Requires musical maturity and insight. Level 10.

Sinfonia No. 6 in E Major, BWV 792

A gigue-like and rollicking work with lilting rhythm throughout. The counterpoint calls for skillful voicing and finger substitution within a hand. Some awkward intervallic playing. Level 9.

Sinfonia No. 7 in E Minor, BWV 793

A lyrical work, with the opening motive outlining a triad. Requires a seamless legato. Level 10.

Sinfonia No. 8 in F Major, BWV 794

Dance-like character is abetted by the short trill in the motive. Would be an appropriate choice for a pianist who has already played easier three-voice works or easier sinfonias. At times the short trill in the motive may be difficult to execute because of the placement of the motive as it shifts from voice to voice. Fingering will need careful planning. Level 10.

Sinfonia No. 9 in F Minor, BWV 795

Highly sophisticated writing with rich chromaticism, short motives, many modulations and elided cadences. This slow work should be reserved for musically mature performers. A true masterpiece. Level 10.

Sinfonia No. 10 in G Major, BWV 796

A brilliant and forceful sinfonia, one of the most effective, suited for a performer with natural facility and strong fingers. Several awkward crossings appear, and finger substitution is required. Appropriate for students who are playing their first fugues. Level 9.

Sinfonia No. 11 in G Minor, BWV 797

Beautiful, lyrical, *andante* melody. The performer needs musical maturity, a rich singing tone and the ability to listen carefully. Long musical ideas require careful attention. Level 9.

Sinfonia No. 12 in A Major, BWV 798

Dance-like, with an infectious rhythmic lilt throughout. One of the most immediately appealing sinfonias, although not easy. Level 10.

Sinfonia No. 13 in A Minor, BWV 799

Bubbly writing with a relatively thin texture. The piece unfolds in even, four-measure units. Cadences or cadence-like progressions appear at measures 3–4, 7–8, 11–12 and 15–16. Level 10.

Sinfonia No. 14 in B-flat Major, BWV 800

An infrequently heard work, with a subject based on descending scalewise movement through an octave. A meditative and fugue-like work with four *strettos* disguised in the texture. Some difficult fingerings and expanded hand positions may cause coordination problems. Level 10.

Sinfonia No. 15 in B Minor, BWV 801

This virtuosic work needs technical facility and strong musicianship to avoid a tiresome "sewing machine" effect. Strong coordination between the hands is required and a strong sense of rhythm is needed to achieve continuity of tempo amidst the changes from sixteenths to thirty-seconds. This work can help students learn to hear harmonic rhythm. Level 9.

French Suites, BWV 812–817

The first five, and perhaps all six, *French Suites* were originally part of the *Anna Magdalena Bach Notebooks*. It appears that they represented a middle level in keyboard playing for Bach's students, occupying a place between the inventions and sinfonias and the first book of the *Well-Tempered Clavier*. The *French Suites* consist of baroque dance movements arranged in the order *Allemande, Courante, Sarabande*, an optional dance movement or movements, and *Gigue*. Selected movements from the *French Suites* that are relatively accessible for performers in Levels 7–9 and appropriate for mention in the scope of this book are the *Allemande, Courante,* and *Gavotte* from the *French Suite No. V in G Major; Sarabande* from the *French Suite No. 1 in D Minor; Air* from *French Suite No. II in C Minor; Anglaise* from the *French Suite No. III in B Minor;* and the *Minuet* from the *French Suite No. VI in E Major*. On the whole, *French Suite No. 2 in C Minor* and *No. 3 in B Minor* are the most accessible. Publishers include Alfred, Associated Board of the Royal Schools of Music, Bärenreiter, Breitkopf, Dover, Henle, Kalmus, Vienna Urtext and many others.

Miscellaneous Pieces

Suite in F, BWV Anh. 823

Little-known work in three movements, including a *Prelude, Sarabande en rondeau* and *Gigue*. The *Prelude* is probably the most difficult of the movements. Level 9.

Gigue

Graceful work from the *Suite in F*, BWV 823 with a strong rhythmic swing. A fine choice for most students ready to study three-voice works. It is considerably easier than the fugues of the *Well-Tempered Clavier*. The voicing will be challenging for many students. Level 8.

Miscellaneous Volumes

At the Piano with J. S. Bach, ed. Hinson

Presents a cross-section of Bach's works including several of the *Short Preludes*, an invention, a sinfonia, the *Fantasia in C Minor* and other works. (Alfred.) Levels 4–10.

J. S. Bach: An Introduction to His Keyboard Music, ed. Palmer

A practical collection of the approachable works of Bach for the young student, including the most accessible teaching pieces and many of the short preludes. Excellent preparatory information concerning ornamentation and other historical performance practices. (Alfred.) Levels 3–8.

J. S. Bach: The First Book for Pianists, ed. Palmer

Presents the most accessible pieces from *J. S. Bach: An Introduction to His Keyboard Music*. Many of the well-known first minuets can be found here. A practical first Bach book. (Alfred.) Levels 3–7.

First Lessons in Bach, Carroll-Palmer, Books 1 and 2

Carroll, a prominent English music educator, presents here a practical collection including the most accessible of the pieces from the *Anna Magdalena Bach Notebook*. The Bach-Carroll books have been used by countless students through the century and are still in wide use today. Book 2 is substantially more difficult than the better-known first volume. The selections are thoroughly edited by Carroll. (Alfred, Carl Fischer, G. Schirmer and others.) Levels 3–5.

Dances of J. S. Bach, ed. Hinson

A compilation of various dance movements from such works of Bach as *French Suite No. 2; Suite in F*, BWV Anh. 80; *Overture in F; French Suite No. 5; French Suite No. 6; English Suite No. 3; Partita in A Minor* and others. Many of these selections are printed on one page. (Alfred.) Levels 7–9.

The First Bach Book, ed. Lipsky

Contains many of the easiest pieces from the *Anna Magdalena Bach Notebook* and eight of the *Little Preludes*. Many fingerings included, large print. (Kalmus.) Levels 4–8.

Bach for Beginners, Volumes 1 and 2, ed. Vincent

Large print. Highly edited and fingered thoroughly. (Boosey.) Book 1, Level 4; Book 2, Levels 6–8.

J. S. Bach: Easiest Piano Pieces

Stylistic editing and an attractive selection of pieces included. This would serve well as a student's early Bach book. Wide range of levels of difficulty. (Peters.) Levels 4–8.

Young Pianist's Guide to J. S. Bach, ed. Novik

Eleven of the easiest pieces from the *Anna Magdalena Bach Notebook*. (Studio P/R.) Level 5.

The Very First Bach Studies, ed. Teöke

Selections range in difficulty from the easy minuets to six *French Suite* movements. According to the editor, essential phrasing and articulation has been added. (Editio Musica.) Levels 4–10.

Bach: Master Series for the Young, ed. Hughes

A fine variety of the best-known teaching pieces are included, but the edition has many inauthentic slurrings and articulation markings. (G. Schirmer.) Levels 3–7.

Bach: 19 Easy Pieces, ed. Canino

Taken from the *Anna Magdalena Bach Notebook*, this volume consists mostly of the intermediate pieces from that collection rather than the easiest ones. Edited and fingered. (Ricordi.) Levels 6–8.

JOHN BLOW (1648–1708) Great Britain

Blow composed suites, individual dance movements and short pieces such as chaconnes, as well as important church music.

The Second Part of Musick's Hand-Maid, ed. Dart

Consists of 35 easy keyboard pieces, mostly by John Blow and Henry Purcell, first published in 1689 and re-issued in 1705. This volume is a sequel to *Musick's Hand-Maid: New Lessons and Instructions for the Virginals or Harpsichord of 1660*. The second part of *Musick's Hand-Maid* contains mostly dance movements, chaconnes and marches. Although the music is highly ornamented and performance practice considerations need careful attention, the excellent notes by the editor carefully guide the aspiring performer. This volume is of primarily historical significance. (Stainer and Bell.) Levels 8–10.

John Blow. The Contemporaries of Purcell, Volume II, ed. Fuller-Maitland

Contains miscellaneous pieces such as dance movements, preludes, fugues and ayres for the intermediate pianist. Many of the ornaments have been written into the score by the editor, who also added dynamic indications. (Chester.) Levels 7–9.

GEORG BÖHM (1661–1733) Germany

Keyboard Suites

Böhm composed 11 keyboard suites, many of which are appropriate for the early-advanced performer. Hopefully the easier suites, those less difficult than the Bach *French Suites*, will eventually appear in performing editions. (Breitkopf.) Levels 9–10.

WILLIAM BYRD (1543–1623) Great Britain

Byrd was one of the dominating English keyboard composers of his time, and considered the founder of the English virginal school of writing. Some standard teaching anthologies include one or two of his shorter works.

The Carman's Whistle

Based on a popular song of the day, and consisting of a lively theme and eight inviting variations. Deserving of its relative familiarity today. (Many standard editions.) Level 7.

Popular Pieces

Pieces are selected and edited to make Byrd more accessible. Regrettably, ornaments are written into the score with no indications of the original symbol. Useful primarily for the enthusiast. Included are some preludes, pavanes with variations, galliards, the well-known *Sellenger's Round* and *The Carman's Whistle*. (Kalmus.) Level 9.

Three Anonymous Keyboard Pieces Attributed to William Byrd, ed. Neighbour

A beautiful edition with excellent commentary. These three short pieces can provide the performer with a taste of Byrd's writing through a fine edition that allows the performer to see the composer's markings. (Novello.) Level 7.

C

THOMAS CHILCOT (c. 1700–1766) Great Britain

Six Suites of Lessons for the Harpsichord or Spinet

Surprisingly accessible literature with few ornaments and generally clear-cut phrases. The writing is not extremely contrapuntal and the textures are relatively thin. The last five suites follow closely the ordering of *Allemande, Corente, Saraband, Jig* and *Minuet*. The first suite, however, opens with a large two-section overture and includes an unusual siciliano. Dance music that is less complex than much from the Baroque period. These movements could be appropriate predecessors to the Bach *French Suites*. (Heugel.) Levels 7–9.

JEREMIAH CLARKE (c. 1673–1707) Great Britain

Clarke was an English composer and organist in the Chapel Royal in London, who committed suicide after a hopeless love affair.

Selected Works for Keyboard, ed. Barsham

Elementary teaching pieces, somewhat easier than those in the *Anna Magdalena Bach Notebook*. Most are in the English Baroque tradition, with dotted rhythms, syncopated displacements of melody, and thin texture. Interesting writing in these ornamented pieces. (Oxford University Press.) Levels 3–5.

Additional Works for Study:
1700 Choice Collection of Ayres
1711 Choice Lessons for Harpsichord or Spinet

ARCANGELO CORELLI (1653–1713) Italy

Well known as an Italian violinist and composer, Corelli also is regarded the founder of violin technique.

24 Pieces, Volumes I and II

Various dance movements and other pieces at the intermediate and upper-intermediate levels appear in this highly edited volume. Interesting writing, worth investigating. (Kalmus.) Levels 7–9.

CARLO COTUMACCI (1698–1785) Italy

14 Toccatas

Italian Baroque pieces that may serve as preparation for Bach inventions. All are one printed page in length, and worthwhile. See especially *Toccatas Nos. 2* and *4*. (Berben.) Levels 7–8.

FRANÇOIS COUPERIN (1668–1733) France

Composer of over 230 piano pieces in 27 *ordres* in less than 30 years, Couperin was the most distinguished member of an influential family of musicians. The earlier pieces have traces of the usual dance forms such as the allemande and sarabande, but programmatic titles are used instead. In fact, most of Couperin's works are program pieces, conjuring a mood or idyllic picture. Although much of his music looks easy on the page, it is actually more difficult to perform, due to the detailed ornamentation needed. Couperin's treatise *The Art of Playing the Keyboard Instrument* is of musicological significance and provides helpful instruction on how to perform his music.

The Art of Playing the Keyboard Instrument

Important as a chief 18th-century book on music instruction, containing information on performance style, fingering, phrasing and ornamentation. As part of the treatise, Couperin includes eight preludes and an allemande which illustrate the principles covered in his manual. The Margery Halford edition published by Alfred contains an extensive introduction clarifying some aspects of Couperin's tradition in music writing, the variable-length dot, rhythmic inequality, ornamentation, fingering, phrasing and articulation, expression and style, and provides a concise summary of Couperin's rules. (Many standard editions.) Levels 9–10.

Miscellaneous Pieces

The miscellaneous pieces appear in many different standard editions. See especially the volume *Selected Harpsichord Music*, ed. Marlowe published by G. Schirmer for practical information on authentic performance.

Allemande, D Minor

Slightly easier than the Bach inventions. Two-part contrapuntal playing with ornamentation, calling for expansion and contraction of the hand. Scale patterns alternate with broken chords. Level 7.

Les Coucous, B Minor

Highly descriptive writing, perhaps representative of some of the earliest character pieces. Generally features even sixteenths throughout. Level 3.

Le Petit Rien, D Major

Popular work that can be played with *notes inégales*. Many patterns and repeated sections. Sometimes printed in anthologies in an abbreviated form. Level 4.

Les Moissonneurs, B-flat Major

"The Reapers" is a *gavotte en rondeau* with three episodes alternating with the initial rondeau theme. Performance of this work should include the practice of playing *notes inégales*. Depicted in the music is the swing and swish of the reapers' scythes. Level 10.

Le Moucheron, E-flat Major

A light, fast Italian gigue depicting the buzzing of a gnat, with vividly biting ornaments. Witty writing. Level 10.

Le Réveil-Matin, F Major

An amusing virtuosic Italian-style gigue which suggests the tinkling of an alarm clock. Level 10.

Le Tic-Toc-Choc, F Major

May refer to the ticking of a clock or to the tinkling tines of a music box. Originally composed for harpsichord with two keyboards, consequently the hands often overlap. Level 10.

La Bandoline, A Minor

Probably a portrait of a lady from the southern French town of Bandol. Level 10.

D

LOUIS-CLAUDE DAQUIN (1694–1772) France

Daquin's most celebrated book, *Pièces de Clavecin* (1735) contains numerous individual pieces in suites, many of which contain descriptive titles.

Le Coucou, E Minor

Frequently taught, and requiring agile fingers. One of the earliest keyboard program pieces featuring obvious bird sounds. Effective in performance and highly popular. (Many standard editions.) Level 8.

F

JOSEPH-HECTOR FIOCCO (1703–1741) Belgium

Born in Belgium of an Italian family, Fiocco worked in Brussels and Antwerp as a church musician.

Eight Keyboard Pieces

Eight movements that illustrate the influence of the French composers of the day, particularly Couperin. These movements use a wide variety of different kinds of ornaments, making their study especially helpful for the scholar of Baroque keyboard music. Titles include *La Villageoise, L'Italienne, La Musette* and *Allegro*. (Associated Board of the Royal Schools of Music.) Levels 8–9.

G

BALDASSARE GALUPPI (1706–1785) Italy

See the listing in the Classical Period.

H

GEORGE FRIDERIC HANDEL (1685–1759) Germany

In many respects, Handel is one of the least known of the great composers. Most of his keyboard works were composed during the first part of his creative life. Handel enjoyed fame as a performer and improviser on the harpsichord and organ and took part in the practice common at the time of borrowing thematic material from his own and other composers' writing. Selected movements from the 16 keyboard suites are often effective for teaching. These works may be especially appropriate for a student who feels that he or she does not enjoy Baroque music. Identifying numbers are assigned as "G" numbers, compiled by Anthony Hicks for the latest *New Grove Dictionary of Music and Musicians*, 1980. "B" numbers represent the numbering in the thematic catalogue of Handel's works by A. Craig Bell. H. or B. numbers are given below when available. Additional miscellaneous movements from the suites suggested for study include *Sarabande in D Minor (Suite XI)*, B.60/12, G. 110; *Courante in G (Suite XIV)*, B.60/16, G. 213; *Allegro in G Minor (Suite VII)*, B.60/7, G/33; *Gigue in D Minor (Suite X)*, B.60/11, G. 121; *Prelude in E Major (Suite XIII)*, B.60/15, G. 145; and *Gavotte in G Major (Suite XIV)*, B.60/16, G. 217. (Many standard editions.)

Suites

Handel composed what are commonly called the *Eight Great Suites*, in addition to approximately 15 miscellaneous complete suites and some unfinished suites. The suites usually are comprised of four or five pieces each, but are not limited to the allemande-courante-sarabande-optional dance-gigue format of the Bach suites. Variation movements, chaconnes, passacaglias, dance movements and airs with and without "doubles" appear commonly. The keyboard music generally is less elaborate than that of Bach. Some suggested movements are listed on the next page.

Air with Variations, G. 36 (from Suite in B-flat Major)

This set of five figural variations is based on the same theme that Brahms later used to create the *Variations on a Theme of Handel*. The figurations tossed from one voice to the other fit the hands well. This movement is especially effective. Level 6.

Sarabande in D Minor, G. 110 (from Suite in D Minor)

A well-known movement with two variations in a slow walking tempo. The contrapuntal demands are not difficult. Level 4.

Gigue in D Minor, G. 111 (from Suite in D Minor)

A movement in triplet sixteenths with rollicking broken-chord figures tossed from hand to hand. Triadic writing in an 11-measure piece. Level 5.

Allemande, G. 211 (from Suite in G Major)

The strong dotted figure lends charm to this movement. All fast passagework occurs in the right hand, with the left hand playing mainly eighths and quarters. Accessible two-voice writing for the student not ready to play Bach inventions. Level 6.

Allegro, G. 212 (from Suite in G Major)

The texture consists of broken chords and descending arpeggiation. The small quantity of fast passagework occurs in the right hand. Level 6.

Courante, G. 213 (from Suite in G Major)

A bold and energetic two-voice work. The eighth-note passagework in the right hand is not difficult. Right-hand extension and contraction are required. Level 6.

Air in G Major, G. 214 (from Suite in G Major)

One of the most popular teaching pieces by Handel. A short work, in two voices, with several sequential patterns. Especially appropriate for working with an intermediate student on contraction of the hand. Level 6.

Passacaglia and Variations, G. 255 (from Suite VII in G Minor)

An assertive movement saturated with dotted rhythms, especially pianistic and effective in performance. Double-note writing, octaves, scales and broken chords appear in the various variations. Level 8.

Miscellaneous Short Pieces

Air in B-flat Major, G. 39

An imitative composition in two-part counterpoint that should be played at an easy *allegretto* tempo. Might provide fine preparation for more complex contrapuntal works such as the inventions of Bach. Level 6.

Sonatina in B-flat Major, G. 40

A well-known piece in two voices, with imitation between the hands. The large amount of sequential material in this work makes it easy to learn. Level 5.

Sonata in C Major, G. 59

Opens with a descending C Major scale, stated first in the soprano and then in the bass. Recurring patterns and sequential writing abound. This piece sounds more difficult than it is. Level 9.

Fantasia in C Major (Sonata in C Major), G. 60

The enchanting sequences are a large part of the appeal of this popular composition. Effective in performance. Level 8.

Minuet in D Minor

Short binary movement in 3/8 with both hands moving in nearly identical eighth-note rhythm. Highly patterned work, elegant in performance. Level 2.

Minuet in G Minor

A charming and stately work with three independent lines simulating two violins and a left-hand continuo. This piece provides an especially fine introduction to the playing of three voices, and deserves to be better known. Level 6.

Gavotte in G Major

Continuous left-hand quarter notes underpin short right-hand phrases requiring detailed articulation. An appealing teaching piece due to the contrast between the continuo part and a rhythmically varied melody. Level 4.

Passepied in C Major

Cast in the form of a *passepied*, a spirited French dance in triple meter, this piece is primarily a two-voice texture. It could provide a student's first introduction to the playing of contrapuntal Baroque literature. Level 2.

Aria in D Minor

A simple aria, with both hands generally playing in quarter notes. Level 4.

Carillon in D Major

A repetitive but exciting work of rich sonorities, filled with broken chords and loud broken octaves. Level 7.

Impertinence

A simple two-voice contrapuntal work in binary form with thin texture. The primary challenge involves consistency of articulation between the hands. Level 4.

Courante in F Major

Frequently found in repertoire anthologies. A tuneful melody based on descending and ascending scale passages in sixteenths, and skips and broken chords in eighth notes. Level 5.

Entrée in G Minor

Strong rhythmic drive is inherent in this vibrant work with many sequential patterns and scales. Level 6.

Fughettas

Six miscellaneous small fugues. While the first two or three are relatively accessible, the remaining ones seem to be unnecessarily complex and uninspired. Perhaps best used as a study of fugal form. More difficult than they initially appear. (Peters.) Levels 8–10.

Miscellaneous Volumes

Handel: A First Book, ed. Lucktenberg

Contains an attractive variety of single-movement pieces, many of which are difficult to find elsewhere. (Alfred.) Levels 4–6.

Handel: An Introduction to His Keyboard Works, ed. Lucktenberg

Contains the same pieces as *A First Book* along with several more that are slightly more difficult. An excellent selection of some better literature of Handel. The editorial articulation markings are stylistic and helpful. (Alfred.) Levels 4–8.

A Handel Anthology, ed. Heath

Features various movements from suites and interesting additional keyboard works. The Grove identifying numbers are provided in this edition and the text contains no editing other than fingerings, leaving articulation and phrasing to the discretion of the performer. (FJH.) Levels 5–8.

Handel-Selected Keyboard Works, Book 1

Presents selections from the suites of 1720 and 1727 and some of the sonatinas. (Associated Board of the Royal Schools of Music.) Levels 5–8.

A Handel Album: The Easiest Piano Pieces, ed. Scholtz

A fine selection of 17 of the very easiest works by Handel. (Universal.) Levels 3–6.

Händel Büchlein, ed. Herrmann

An attractive collection of the easiest pieces of Handel. (Schott.) Levels 3–7.

CONRAD FRIEDRICH HURLEBUSCH (1696–1765) Germany

According to Agi Jambor in his preface to the sonatas published by Elkan-Vogel, Hurlebusch ". . . had a difficult, unbending character, which was probably guided by strong convictions and a paranoiac tendency. Furthermore, his style of writing was so progressive that it may have aroused controversial reactions among his contemporaries. Hurlebusch seemed to be searching for new harmonies, strange modulations, lyricism and pathos, and application of German, French and Italian musical styles."

Keyboard Sonatas, Volumes 1 and 2, ed. Jambor

Intriguing writing in the many dance movements and sonata movements. The textures are thin and few double-notes appear in the fast passages. Some of these pianistic selections would be welcome additions to a modern anthology for teaching. (Elkan-Vogel.) Levels 7–9.

K

JOHANN PHILIPP KIRNBERGER (1721–1783) Germany

Kirnberger was a student of J. S. Bach and a friend of C.P.E. Bach. He composed several treatises and numerous pieces for teaching purposes.

A Miscellany of Dances

Kirnberger stated in his preface to this work that he wrote these pieces to help students develop a good sense of time and rhythm. According to Richard Jones in the introduction to the Associated Board of the Royal Schools of Music publication, "Kirnberger mixes pieces in the traditional French dance style—somewhat old-fashioned by the 1770s—with others in a more up-to-date pre-Classical style. . . . Nos. 1–18 are a sequence of short dances in D Major/Minor, prefaced by an *Entrée* and concluding with a *Marche*. . . . Nos. 19–26 are eight pieces in various keys, all but two of which have fanciful titles, according to the French fashion of the 18th century." Although many of the pieces use ornaments, others are straightforward and provide fine pre-Classic teaching pieces. They are at approximately the same level of difficulty as the most accessible of the Bach *Short Preludes*. (Associated Board of the Royal Schools of Music.) Level 7.

Eight Fugues

These accessible fugues take their place along with the Handel fugues for their teaching value in preparing students for playing the major fugues of J. S. Bach. The quality of writing may be higher in the Kirnberger works. Ranging from one to three pages in length, these fugues are in two or three voices and feature figurations that are idiomatically written. Valuable teaching literature. (Schott.) Level 8.

Kirnberger Collection, ed. Jonas

One of the most practical sources of elementary dance pieces by Kirnberger. The short movements included here are minuets, polonaises, bourrées, and one each of a gavotte, rigaudon, presto allegro and rondo. The writing is tuneful and interesting. (Summy.) Levels 5–7.

JOHANN KUHNAU (1660–1722) Germany

Kuhnau is remembered primarily as Bach's predecessor as cantor and organist at the Thomaskirche in Leipzig. He was well acquainted with J. S. Bach and exerted a considerable influence on Bach and other European composers. His programmatic *Six Biblical Sonatas*, the last of his keyboard works, each contained a collection of short, related movements with an Italian caption describing the action taking place. The sonatas were given such titles as *Saul Cured Through Music by David (No. 2)*, *Jacob's Wedding (No. 3)* and *Gideon, the Deliverer of Israel (No. 5)*.

Biblical Sonata No. 1, The Battle Between David and Goliath

The story of the fight between David and Goliath is depicted in the sections of this work, one of the earliest examples of keyboard program music. The movements depict *The boasting and ranting of Goliath, The trembling of the Israelites and their prayer to God at the sight of the horrible enemy, The courage of David, His eager desire to crush the giant's proud defiance, His childlike trust in the help of God* and so on through the continuing sections of the piece. These short musical scenes are highly descriptive. This *Biblical Sonata* requires a performer with the insight and skill to adhere to the historical performance practice traditions dictated by this style. (Alfred.) Levels 9–10.

L
LEONARDO LEO (1694–1744) Italy

Leo composed many works for the church, the stage and various instrumental ensembles. He served as an organist in Naples.

14 Toccatas

Short works on small thematic cells in a *gallant* style, somewhat typical of the Neopolitan School and in the vein of Scarlatti. Some virtuoso and contrapuntal passages. The writing is generally based on triadic outlines and fits the hands well. The music is effective and accessible. Worth investigating. (Carisch.) Levels 7–9.

MATTHEW LOCKE (c. 1622–1677) Great Britain
Melothesia (1673)

A collection of pieces and of writing on music containing "the first rules ever published in this kingdom on the subject of continued or thorough-bass" according to Sir John Hawkins of England in 1778. The highly ornamented music found here consists of suites for the harpsichord and organ by Locke and other masters of the day. (Oxford.) Levels 9–10.

JEAN-BAPTISTE LOEILLET (1680–1730) Belgium
Ten Keyboard Pieces, ed. Barsham

The Baroque dances found here were taken from *Lessons for the Harpsichord or Spinet*, c. 1712 or *Six Suites or Lessons for the Harpsichord or Spinet*, 1723. The dances are winsome, similar in level of difficulty to the *Little Preludes* of J. S. Bach. Ornaments abound, but suggested realizations are presented above the text in this edition. The writing is generally in two or three parts and is slightly less difficult than that of the dances in the Bach *French Suites*. The pieces in this volume are based on first editions and are edited tastefully. (Associated Board of the Royal Schools of Music.) Levels 7–8.

Additional Work for Study:
Six Suites of Lessons for the Harpsichord or Spinet

M
BENEDETTO MARCELLO (1686–1739) Italy
Sonatas pour clavecin

These sonatas are within the technical and musical grasp of early-advanced students. The textures are thin (usually two voices), the phrasing relatively predictable, and the writing often contains dialogue back and forth from one voice to another. Although none of these sonatas is presently in the teaching repertory, any of the 12 would be a welcomed addition. (Heugel.) Levels 8–9.

GIOVANNI BATTISTA MARTINI (1706–1784) Italy

Martini was a friend of kings and princes, and as such did a good deal to help further the career of Mozart.

Six Sonatas

Many are written in two voices and the number of movements varies. Interesting works, if not profound. (Kalmus.) Levels 9–10.

P
JOHANN PACHELBEL (1653–1706) Germany

Pachelbel was a leading German composer of his time and also an organist at several cathedrals in Germany. His *Canon in D* is ubiquitous.

Fughette in C Major

Useful as a student's early introduction to fugal writing and suitable for developing independence of the hands. (Many standard editions.) Level 6.

Gavotte with Two Variations

Presents a regal effect, especially appropriate for the musically mature student. The ornaments may pose some problems, but the writing is particularly interesting. A little-known Baroque composition. (Frederick Harris and other editions.) Level 7.

BERNARDO PASQUINI (1637–1710) Italy

Pasquini was renowned in his day as a keyboard virtuoso, and is considered to be the most important Italian keyboard composer between Frescobaldi and Scarlatti.

Miscellaneous Pieces

Toccata

Single-movement work of approximately four pages. Some bravura passages are integrated into a texture comprised of motivic counterpoint. Level 8.

Variationi sopra la Follia

Set of variations based on the *Folia*, which was originally a dance-song of Portuguese provenance. The dance rhythm is prominent throughout this short work. Level 8.

GIOVANNI BATTISTA PESCETTI (1704–1766) Italy

Pescetti was a composer, organist and harpsichordist who spent time in London as director of an opera company.

Sonate per Gravicembalo

Nine sonatas with two to four movements each, most often three. They blend the bipartite sonata form with the dance spirit, and should be better known. (Ricordi.) Levels 7–10.

Sonata in C Minor

The well-known final movement, *Presto*, is a favorite teaching piece. All fast passagework appears in the right hand. The many patterns and idiomatic figuration make it especially easy to learn. (Alfred and many standard editions.) Level 7.

HENRY PURCELL (c. 1659–1695) Great Britain

Purcell is considered the greatest English composer of the Baroque period and is best remembered for his orchestral and vocal works. His keyboard music includes the *Eight Suites* and some shorter pieces that are taken primarily from *The Second Part of Musick's Hand-Maid* (1689), which contains 35 pieces by Blow, Purcell and others. Also sometimes attributed to

Purcell is *The Second Book of the Lady's Banquet* (1706), which now is thought to contain only several pieces that are considered to be authentic. "Z." numbers refer to the authoritative Zimmerman catalogue of Purcell's works.

Eight Suites

These pieces were originally found in the first part of *A Choice Collection of Lessons*, a work that grouped pieces by key to form eight suites. These suites were then followed by six independent pieces which are in fact transcriptions. The suite movements vary in degree of difficulty, ranging from elementary to early-advanced, although practically none are as advanced technically as are most of the movements of the Bach *French Suites*. The pieces generally are in two or three voices and have quite simple textures. Many of the preludes to these suites would provide fine alternatives for the Bach inventions. (Chester, Stainer and Bell.)

Suite No. 1 in G Major, Z. 660

> The shortest and least difficult of the suites, only three printed pages in some volumes. The *Prelude* appears in many anthologies, popular for its simple imitation between the hands and clear chordal outlines. The *Allemande, Courant* and *Sarabande* which follow the *Prelude* are also accessible to the young student. Level 6.

Suite No. 2 in G Minor, Z. 661

> See especially the two-page *Prelude*, a fine substitute for a Bach invention. Continuous sixteenths, strong harmonic foundation. Other movements are highly ornamented. Level 8.

Suite No. 3 in G Major, Z. 662

> The *Prelude* is especially fine and is infrequently played, and again, is an appropriate alternative with the teaching repertoire for a Bach invention. Tuneful writing with little rhythmic variety. The *Allemande* and *Courante* that complete the set are also interesting, but need careful attention to execution of ornaments and rhythmic conventions. Level 8.

Suite No. 5 in C Major, Z. 666

> The *Prelude* of this suite, appearing often in anthologies, is tuneful, chordal, and lacks rhythmic intricacies, making it an appealing opening. The remaining three movements are less difficult technically but require patience in working out the ornamentation. Level 8.

Suite No. 6 in D Major, Z. 668

The tuneful *Prelude* is short, more similar to the scope of the *Prelude* in *Suite No. 1*. Appealing and not frequently heard. The concluding *Hornpipe* is an attractive one-page movement that would be accessible to the early-intermediate student. Level 6.

Suite No. 8 in F Major, Z. 669

See especially the little-known one-page prelude which could be an excellent introduction to imitative writing for the early-intermediate student. The concluding three movements are more difficult. Level 6.

Miscellaneous Works

Air in D Minor

A highly patterned work with a repeated rhythmic motive throughout and an excellent study in playing legato and in moving out of stationary hand positions. Level 3.

Hornpipe in E Minor

A hornpipe was a lively English dance that derived its name from a primitive instrument using a pipe made from the horn of an animal. Infectious in its spirit and character. Level 3.

Hornpipe in B-flat Major

Three strong cadences separate the three sections of this work. Repetitions of a rhythmic motive appear throughout which should be performed in double-dotted fashion. Level 4.

Minuet in A Minor

This lyrical and elegant minuet will encourage the study of legato playing. Level 3.

Trumpet Piece in C Major

Appealing primarily due to the attractive, trumpet-like motive in the main theme. Assertive music. Level 5.

Miscellaneous Volumes

Purcell Complete Harpsichord Music, Book Two, ed. Kite

Found here are a series of short pieces including thirteen pieces from *The Second Part of Musick's Hand-maid*, five miscellaneous pieces, some transcriptions, pieces of doubtful authenticity and some incepts to organ works. The selections appear simple to play in terms of numbers of notes on the page. However, suggestions for realizing the Baroque rhythmic conventions are notated in the margin above the staves. Detailed information concerning ornamentation is also provided. The writing is tuneful and appealing. (Chester.) Levels 6–10.

Miscellaneous Keyboard Pieces, ed. Ferguson

Some of the pieces included here are quite elementary, although most are at the intermediate level. Purcell's music displays pronounced rhythmic character and a noble tunefulness that is characterized by strongly diatonic melodies. This scholarly edition notes rhythmic alterations that are desirable and also indicates the origins of some tunes or transcriptions. The music is fresh, providing attractive repertoire choices for students who do not think that they like Baroque music. The works included are taken from *A Choice Collection of Lessons* (1696/99), *The Second Part of Musick's Hand-maid* (1689) and various other sources. (Stainer and Bell.) Levels 4–8.

Henry Purcell Selected Pieces, ed. Drath

Contains some of the more accessible movements for the intermediate student, including several of the preludes to Purcell's suites. Fingerings and suggested realizations of ornaments are given. A practical performing edition, well-edited. (PWM.) Level 8.

Purcell Album II, ed. Máriássy

Within this volume of movements from suites and other single works by Purcell, no dynamic markings are added, although suggested realizations of ornaments are provided in the margins above. A wide variety of levels of difficulty appear here. (Editio Musica.) Levels 5–9.

Purcell Selected Pieces

Contains miscellaneous movements from the *Choice Collection Of Lessons* and *Musick's Hand-maid, II* in a highly edited volume. Small print. (Kalmus.) Level 9.

R

JEAN-PHILIPPE RAMEAU (1683–1764) France

Rameau composed numerous keyboard pieces for the harpsichord, and many of his easier works appear in teaching anthologies today. Most are flecked with ornaments, making their performance somewhat more difficult than it first appears. The selections include lyric pieces, dances, pieces imitative of nature, and dramatic pieces, and they comprise some of the earliest keyboard character pieces. Only the best-known teaching pieces from the *Premier Livre de Pièces de Clavecin, Pièces de Clavecin* and *Nouvelles Suites de Pièces de Clavecin* are listed here. (The miscellaneous pieces appear in many different standard editions.)

Miscellaneous Pieces

Menuet en Rondeau

Also known as *Rondino*, this popular composition is highly idiomatic and provides a fine technical workout for the right hand while emphasizing expansion and mobility of the left hand. Level 2.

Premier Rigaudon

Calls for hand independence and shifting positions on the keyboard. Tuneful writing. Level 3.

La Joyeuse

A fleet, joyful work, filled with scale passages in various keys. Impressive in performance. Level 5.

Gavotte with Variations

The dance variations embellish the melody with scales, counterpoint, skips and repeated notes. Level 7.

Les Tendres Plaintes

Tender Sorrows is a melancholy piece with a rondeau theme recurring after each of the two episodes. Slurred eighths in the left hand should be played as *notes inégales*. Effective and highly expressive. Level 8.

La Triomphante

The Triumphant One is a character piece with interesting chromatic writing. This bold work contains scales and arpeggiated passages in eighths in a relatively uncomplicated texture. Level 8.

La Timide

Containing a theme that ascends timidly throughout the piece. Requires a refined legato and technical ease in playing the ornaments. Levels 8–9.

La Villageoise

The Village Girl is a lively and beautiful work, filled with good humor as well as with refined writing in sixteenths. Level 9.

Les Sauvages

> *The Savages* depicts a dance of Louisiana Indians (interestingly, Rameau had encountered this at the Italian theatre in Paris). Level 8.

Tambourin

> The tambourin is a long and narrow drum that was struck by one hand while the other hand played a flute. This animated dance features an ostinato bass. Level 6.

Les Cyclopes

> *Cyclops* is a dramatic work which features large arpeggios and is Scarlatti-like in the use of many wide intervals. Level 9.

Miscellaneous Volumes

The Graded Rameau, ed. Motchane

Based on first editions published by Rameau himself, this volume contains a wide variety of pieces, especially suited for the teacher who wants to become more familiar with Rameau's teaching output. (Belwin.) Levels 7–10.

The Easier Rameau, ed. Barsham

Interesting collection that includes a useful table of ornaments. A practical performing edition. (Elkin.) Levels 6–10.

S

GIUSEPPE SARTI (1729–1802) Italy

Sonata I

A one-page free prelude featuring broken and arpeggiated chords between the hands is followed by a delightful binary *Allegro* of four pages, primarily in two voices. Excellent repertoire choice to precede the Haydn sonatas. Not complex technically. (Ricordi.) Level 7.

Sonata II

A *Preludio*, an *Allegro* and an *Allegretto*, written in the *stile galante* with all movements in the key of C. The last two movements present a monothematic, bipartite form with the recapitulation in the dominant. Trills in the second and third movements might cause technical problems. (Ricordi.) Level 8.

Sonata III

Opens with a *Preludio* followed by two binary allegro movements. Clear-cut phrasing, live rhythms and interesting contrasts. (Ricordi.) Level 8.

DOMENICO SCARLATTI (1685–1757) Italy

Domenico Scarlatti was born in Naples where his father was *maestro di cappella* for the Royal Chapel there. Scarlatti composed for various courts in Italy before moving to Madrid, Spain, in 1728, where he lived and composed until his death. The vast number of sonatas composed by Domenico Scarlatti makes it difficult for a teacher or performer to seek out the best of them. One is urged in any case to employ Scarlatti editions dedicated to textural fidelity. Alessandro Longo arbitrarily numbered and edited 545 of the sonatas around the turn of the last century. His contribution was the collection and rediscovery of these works, but the text of his editions cannot be fully trusted and unfortunately remains the basis of many modern editions. In the 1950s Ralph Kirkpatrick, American musicologist and harpsichordist, numbered the sonatas based on manuscript copies (rather than original sources) and advocated their performance in pairs.

The system of assigning K. numbers to the sonatas based on Kirkpatrick's listing has gained wide acceptance. Kirkpatrick also solved many textural problems that had pervaded these works. In 1967 George Pestelli listed the sonatas based on common stylistic criteria. Both Kirkpatrick and Longo numbers are given below. There are many standard editions of these works, but particular editions are listed when a work may be difficult to find.

Sonata in D Minor, K. 1, L. 366

A charming sonata, easy to comprehend musically, that does not require extensive finger work in the left hand. Worth investigating. Level 9.

Sonata in G Major, K. 2, L. 388

Suited for a student with quick fingers and facility. Based on broken octaves and broken chords. Large leaps. Level 9.

Sonata in A Minor, K. 3, L. 378

Looks much easier on the page than it is due to the quick tempo. The fleet quality, with its little opening and closing sixteenth-note descending figures, makes it effective with an audience. Requires a performer who can maintain its electricity. Level 10.

Sonata in F Major, K. 6, L. 479

An elegant sonata filled with interesting harmonies. The trills may pose some problems. Resist taking this sonata too fast. Level 9.

Sonata in D Minor, K. 9, L. 413

This well-known sonata, often referred to as the "Pastorale," requires a refined legato. Scales in thirds must be played precisely together. The many short melodic units call for inflection and shaping. Level 9.

Sonata in C Minor, K. 11, L. 352

Lyrical work that could be a fine recital opener. Attention to the legato left-hand double notes is needed. Appropriate for the sensitive performer. Level 9.

Sonata in D Major, K. 29, L. 461

Toccata-like piece with fast sixteenth-note passages in both hands. Appropriate for the student with agility and drive. Level 10.

Sonata in D Minor, K. 32, L. 423

Often referred to as "Aria," this lyrical and elegant brief work offers many possibilities for color changes. Sounds simple, but requires a degree of maturity to create its gracefulness. Level 7.

Sonata in D Minor, K. 34, L.S. 7

Short work, one of the most accessible sonatas, though seldom played. The left hand plays only quarter notes under a lyrical melody which requires a fine legato. More approachable than some of the Bach *Short Preludes*. Level 7.

Sonata in G Major, K. 63, L. 84

Sometimes known as "Capriccio," this chordal piece can be used to motivate pianists who believe that they do not enjoy playing pre-Classical music. Fits the hand well and presents some obvious echo effects. The wide skips contribute to its capricious character. Level 9.

Sonata in D Minor, K. 64, L. 58

One of the more approachable of the spirited sonatas, with the left-hand often in blocked triads. Appropriate for performers who may not have natural facility. The tempo and flavor of a gavotte should be maintained throughout. Level 8.

Sonata in C Major, K. 73b, L. 217

A lyrical and quite accessible sonata that progresses through a series of sequences and harmonic shifts. The harmonic changes demand a feeling of one pulse in each measure. One of the easiest of the sonatas yet one of the most beautiful. Level 3.

Sonata in A Major, K. 74, L. 94

Appealing, winsome melodies with a dance-like character. Primarily comprised of single notes in the right hand, but needs careful inflection. Appropriate for a student who enjoys "fingery" music. Level 9.

Sonata in B Minor, K. 87, L. 33

An excellent program opener. Strong dissonance and resolution pervade this lyrical and probing work. A masterpiece, requiring maturity and sensitivity. Level 10.

Sonata in C Major, K. 95, L. 358

The frequent right-hand crossings over left-hand triplets are not excessively difficult, and make this fun for performer and audience. Best-suited for a student who enjoys flamboyant literature. Level 8.

Sonata in D Major, K. 96, L. 465

This well-known sonata opens with hunting horn calls. A compendium of Scarlatti effects including repeated notes, wide skips, brilliant octave passages and Spanish color. More difficult than often perceived, but highly effective and deserving of its popularity. Level 10.

Sonata in A Minor, K. 109, L. 138

Lyrical and beautiful writing that would provide an effective contrast to faster sonatas. Requires adept voicing between the hands. Level 9.

Sonata in A Major, K. 113, L. 345

One of the best known of the Scarlatti sonatas, perhaps because of the potentially brilliant hand-crossings and passagework. A dazzling showpiece for a performer with strong, agile fingers. Level 10.

Sonata in A Minor, K. 149, L. 93

Typical Scarlatti characteristics abound such as repeated notes and many sixteenth-note passages, but the difficulties are confined to the right hand. Level 8.

Sonata in C Major, K. 159, L. 104

Contains simulated horn calls in the opening, ornaments suggesting castanets, and Spanish rhythms. One of the best known of the Scarlatti sonatas, not excessively difficult. Coordination of small finger movements is required. A deserved favorite. Level 9.

Sonata in E Major, K. 163, L. 63

Bright, dance-like and cheerful character in 3/8 meter. Typical Scarlatti features include large leaps and several trills. A fine introduction to the style. Level 9.

Sonata in F Minor, K. 185, L. 173

Fine lyrical writing with much of the melodic work appearing in the left hand. This little-known work might be a suitable choice for the expressive performer. Level 10.

Sonata in A Major, K. 208, L. 238

One of Scarlatti's most beautiful sonatas. The highly lyrical writing requires sensitivity and an ear for melodic tension. Level 9.

Sonata in F Major, K. 274, L. 297

One of the few upper-intermediate sonatas that is also in a spirited tempo. Imitative writing, horn-call effects. No fast passagework required. Level 7.

Sonata in A Major, K. 322, L. 483

Bright and sparkling with some repeated notes, ornaments and scale passagework. One of the more accessible of his faster sonatas. Level 8.

Sonata in B Minor, K. 377, L. 263

A pianistic work which sounds more difficult than it is. Generally two-voice texture with some octave skips and effective repeated notes. The passagework, including some sixteenth-note scales, is not excessively difficult. Level 9.

Sonata in G Major, K. 391, L. 79

Sometimes referred to as "Minuet." Graceful triplet writing with many repeated phrases in one of the most frequently taught of the intermediate sonatas. The performer needs an agile right hand to handle the passagework. Level 8.

Sonata in B-flat Major, K. 393, L. 74

An elegant minuet in which the primary technical difficulties are the control of the musical line and inflection of the right-hand motives. No fast finger-work is required, but the performance needs finesse. Level 9.

Sonata in D Major, K. 415, L.S. 11

Subtitled "Pastoral" because of its gentle 12/8 rocking feeling. Contains many right-hand shifts, but the patterns fit the hand well. Will require careful attention to phrasing. Appropriate for study of the inflection of small musical units. Level 9.

Sonata in G Minor, K. 426, L. 128

An *Andante* with rich textures, appropriate for a performer who is innately musical. Requires fine attention to phrasing to make the most of the sudden dramatic silences. Level 10.

Sonata in D Major, K. 430, L. 463

Marked "Tempo di Ballo": in the tempo of a dance or ballet. Requires careful inflection of the small musical units. One of Scarlatti's finest. Level 10.

Sonata in G Major, K. 431, L. 83

This popular sonata is easier than it sounds although it requires a performer with agility. Right-hand triplets predominate. Level 8.

Sonata in B-flat Major, K. 440, L. 97

Gentle flowing "minuet" which later breaks into rapid sixteenth-note scale passages. Level 8.

Sonata in F Major, K. 446, L. 433

Also known as "Siciliano" or "Pastorale." A fine legato is called for within this moderate 12/8 work. A primary musical consideration is the matching of melody tones to avoid unplanned accents. Level 9.

Sonata in F Minor, K. 481, L. 187

Lyrical, cantabile sonata with a rich texture. A suitable choice for opening a program or for working specifically on legato and phrasing. Level 9.

Sonata in E Major, K. 496, L. 372

A triplet rhythmic motive permeates this work. This is one of the few fast sonatas that does not require a great deal of intricate finger-work, although the left-hand triplets sometimes can be awkward. Level 9.

Sonata in D Major, K. 511, L. 314

Lively writing with a minimum of technical problems. Features propelling sequences that are highly idiomatic, and musette-like pedal points which create interest. Especially appropriate for a student playing his first mature Scarlatti sonatas. Level 9.

Sonata in F Major, K. 525, L. 188

Strong propulsive rhythms that could tempt a performer to rush. Suitable for the pianist who enjoys energetic works and who can remain physically relaxed during rapid repeated-note passages. Level 10.

Miscellaneous Volumes

At the Piano With Scarlatti, ed. Hinson

The first 25 pages in this book consist of historical background on Scarlatti and performance practice suggestions for the sonatas and the Baroque period in general. Sixteen interesting sonatas are found here. (Alfred.) Levels 9–10.

Scarlatti: An Introduction to His Keyboard Works, ed. Halford

A valuable collection containing some of the easier works of Scarlatti. (Alfred.) Levels 4–8.

Scarlatti: The First Book for Young Pianists, ed. Halford

This short volume contains nine of the easiest sonatas available in a collection. (Alfred.) Levels 3–7.

The Scholar's Scarlatti, Volumes 1–3, ed. Lincoln

The editor has compiled three volumes of Scarlatti sonatas grouped by key and mood and designed to help the pianist develop Baroque technique in the context of fine music. According to the editor in his preface, "You will become 'scholars' of Scarlatti and enjoy many of the same lessons that [his student and patroness, the Queen of Spain] Maria Barbara worked on. Your training, like hers, will be thorough in both its technical and musical aspects." Volume 1 contains accessible sonatas at the moderate level, arranged in sets. Preceding each set is detailed commentary on the sonatas in the group, analyzing their technical problems and suggesting approaches to interpretation. The sonatas in Volume 2 are moderately difficult, and deal with leaps and cross-hand playing. The sonatas in Volume 3 are still more difficult, although not the most difficult that Scarlatti wrote. Each set of sonatas is planned so that it can be played as a recital group. An excellent source of lesser-played Scarlatti works in a scholarly performing edition, clearly printed with informative notes, and appropriately grouped into sets. (Novello.) Levels 7–10.

Piano Sonatas, Volumes 1 and 2, ed. Hinson

Collections of 14 and 13 sonatas respectively, many of them little known. Valuable preface with information pertaining to ornamentation. (Alfred.) Levels 9–10.

Domenico Scarlatti, ed. Schwerdtner

An exceptionally fine selection of 48 sonatas, arranged in progressive order of difficulty and based on manuscripts and first prints. Fingerings are included but little other editing is present. Unfortunately, K. or L. numbers are not indicated. (Schott.) Levels 8–10.

Domenico Scarlatti Selected Sonatas, ed. Banowetz

An interesting combination of lesser-known and more familiar sonatas for the early-advanced student. Editorial suggestions are provided in red to differentiate them from the composer's markings. Extensive and valuable preface. (Kjos.) Levels 7–10.

Scarlatti Selected Sonatas, ed. Hinson

Another fine selection of sonatas based on authentic sources. Fifteen sonatas are provided, some familiar and others that are more unusual. (Alfred.) Levels 7–10.

Five Pairs of Sonatas, ed. Rosenblum

For the upper-intermediate to early-advanced pianist. Interesting and fresh literature in a scholarly edition grouped by consecutive K. numbers (E. C. Schirmer). Levels 8–10.

The Five Fugues, ed. Jones

Contains the *Cat's Fugue*, K. 30, the culmination of the Essercizi of 1738, three other early fugues that probably pre-date the Essercizi, K. 41, K. 58, and K. 93, and a late fugue, K. 417. Counterpoint lies well under the hands. Some octave doublings in the left hand are used to good effect. (Associated Board of the Royal Schools of Music.) Level 10.

The Graded Scarlatti, ed. Motchane

Excellent variety is incorporated in the selection of sonatas. Forty sonatas are provided here, many well-known and some less known. The early-advanced sonatas are especially valuable for teaching. Text is based on the Longo edition. (Colombo.) Levels 6–10.

Nine Sonatas, ed. Ferguson

A scholarly student edition in which the text is edited and fingered, but the suggestions are excellent. The ornament realizations are provided in the margin above the staves. Several lesser-played sonatas are included. (Associated Board of the Royal Schools of Music.) Levels 9–10.

Twelve Easy Scarlatti Sonatas, ed. Mirovitch

An excellent selection of twelve accessible and attractive works for the intermediate pianist. Unfortunately this text is based on the Longo edition. (Marks.) Levels 7–9.

SAMUEL SCHEIDT (1587–1654) Germany

Bergamasca

Theme and five continuous variations, somewhat reminiscent of the Pachelbel *Canon* since intensity is created through rhythmic diminution. Sustained notes against moving notes within a single hand could challenge students. Perhaps appropriate as a substitute for the well-known Pachelbel *Canon*, but generally more difficult. Level 8.

CARLOS de SEIXAS (1704–1742) Portugal

Seixas was the most important Portuguese keyboard composer of the 18th century. It is possible that he was a student of Domenico Scarlatti. Seixas composed numerous sonatas and toccatas in a mold similar to those of Scarlatti, and used the term sonata and toccata interchangeably. See especially the toccatas and sonatas.

Minuet

A graceful piece that is found in some teaching collections. Left-hand accompaniment is relatively active, helping prepare the performer for contrapuntal textures. A good choice for an advancing student. Level 3.

Toccata in C Major

A fine Baroque "finger piece" with repeated motives that may be treated with terraced dynamics. Fingering will need careful planning. Note the rhythmic shifts from duple to triple. Level 9.

PADRE ANTONIO SOLER (1729–1783) Spain

A pupil of Scarlatti, Soler composed over 300 sonatas which display rhythmic vigor, fondness for wide leaps and extreme ranges, and harmonic surprises.

Sonata in D Major, R84

Dance-like work with a repeated note figure that recurs frequently. Brilliant writing in an interesting harmonic framework. Some left-hand passages appear in parallel octaves. (Alfred.) Level 10.

T

GEORG PHILIPP TELEMANN (1681–1767) Germany

Telemann was one of the most prolific, versatile composers of his time, although his work leans toward superficiality. In his writing he aimed to avoid technical difficulty.

Fantasies (Three Dozen)

Grouped by Telemann into three sets of 12 with the first and third sets in the Italian style with Italian titles and tempo markings, and the second dozen with markings in French. The Italian fantasies are in three movements with a brief slow movement in a related key, and a third movement which is a repeat of the first. The second dozen, the French fantasies, are in four movements. Those of the first dozen are the most practical for performance today and are the most frequently heard. (Associated Board of the Royal Schools of Music, Bärenreiter, Dover, Kalmus and other publishers.)

Fantasie No. 2 in D Minor (from First Dozen)

Perhaps the most widely heard of the Telemann *Fantasies* because of its attractive theme and the tuneful working-out of material. More accessible than similar-level Bach pieces. Levels 7–8.

Fantasie No. 5 in F Major (from First Dozen)

Since the writing is more homophonic, this jovial work is good for a student who is not fond of playing more contrapuntal Baroque period music. Based on buoyant, strong and driving rhythms. A student playing a selection at the level of the Bach *Invention in C Minor* might also study this work. Left-hand chords in the *Largo* may be arpeggiated. Level 8.

Fantasie No. 7 in G Major (from First Dozen)

Presents many possibilities to use terraced dynamics and features left-hand broken octaves and much detached playing. One of the most accessible of the fantasies. Level 7.

Fantasie No. 10 in A Major (from First Dozen)

An appealing work. The music calls for much interplay between the hands and some wide leaps in the left hand. Special attention is needed for voicing the *Largo* movement. Level 7.

Suite in A

This work was included in the *Wilhelm Friedemann Bach Notebook* compiled by J. S. Bach for his son. The *Allemande* contains sixteenth-note passages which are transferred from hand to hand. It is especially effective when performed by a student with strong fingers. Levels 6–7.

Miscellaneous Pieces

Gigue in G Major

Also known as *Gigue a l'Angloise,* this work is spirited and vivacious. The performer needs a strong sense of pulse to avoid rushing the eighth-note figures. Level 8.

Miscellaneous Volumes

Easier Keyboard Pieces, ed. Walter

Included are a little-known fantasy from the second book of 12, separate movements from suites, and a fugue. The collection is an interesting one. Suggested phrasings and articulations are provided at the bottom of the page. (Breitkopf.) Levels 7–8.

Z

DOMENICO ZIPOLI (1688–1720) Italy

Zipoli was an Italian organist and composer.

Suite in G Minor

See especially the *Giga* movement with its continuous right-hand triplets. Especially appropriate for the student with agile fingers and natural left-hand finger independence. Overlapping suspensions create interest. Level 7.

CLASSICAL LITERATURE

A

MATEO ALBÉNIZ (1760?–1831) Spain

Sonata in D Major

Lively, spirited and engrossing both to play and to hear. It is easy to imagine the sounds of flamenco in this lively and energetic work. Musically substantial, reminiscent of Scarlatti. (Union Musical.) Level 8.

SEBASTIAN ALBERO (1722–1756) Spain

Thirty Sonatas

Pre-Classic one-movement sonatas, mostly in binary form. Many are suitable for early-advanced students and the writing is of high quality. (Union Musical.) Levels 8–10.

JOHN ALCOCK (1715–1806) Great Britain

Six Suites of Easy Lessons

Suites of three or four movements with writing generally in two voices. The style is graceful but highly florid, and the large number of ornaments makes these works more difficult than they initially appear. See especially suites Nos. 4 and 5. (Associated Board of the Royal Schools of Music.) Level 8.

(JOHANN) ANTON ANDRÉ (1775–1842) Germany

Sonatinas, Op. 34

The first in C Major and the third in G Major are the most frequently found in teaching collections. Level 5.

Additional Work for Study:
Op. 23 12 Short Pieces for Pianoforte

RAFAEL ANGLÉS (1731–1816) Spain

Two Sonatas

The influence of Haydn is present although both sonatas (four and five pages respectively) are filled with spirited technical clichés such as broken octaves and scales. Not rhythmically intricate. See especially the second, *Sonata in F Major*. Suggested for students who are not yet ready for the easy Haydn sonata movements. (Union Musical.) Level 8.

JUAN CRISÓSTOMO ARRIAGA (1806–1826) Spain

Estudios o caprichos

Three movements, *Allegro assai, Moderato mosso* and *Risoluto (presto)*. Highly pianistic. Those looking for interesting and unusual character music from the Classic period might look here. (Union Musical.) Level 9.

THOMAS ATTWOOD (1763–1838) Great Britain

Attwood was an English organist and composer who held appointments in the royal patronage.

Easy Progressive Lessons

Four classic sonatinas, the first three containing three movements and the last consisting solely of a theme and seven variations. These works provide some of the easiest sonatina literature available for the young student. Most of the writing is in two voices, with one part substantially more active than the other. These pieces should be widely used. The first three are much easier than the last. (Associated Board of the Royal Schools of Music.) Levels 3–5.

Sonatina No. 1 in G Major

A highly accessible and tuneful sonatina, practical as a first sonatina for the elementary pianist. The second movement is the easiest, but both outer movements are strong, and all offer a fine study in classical sonatina playing. Level 3.

B

CARL PHILIPP EMANUEL BACH (1714–1788) Germany

The second surviving son of J. S. Bach and court composer and accompanist to King Frederick the Great. He is sometimes known as "the Berlin Bach" since he spent much of his adult life in Berlin. While he led the way for the development of the Classical sonata, another of his greatest contributions is the monumental *Essay on the True Art of Keyboard Playing* (1753). While much of his music does not appear to be of great technical difficulty, a primary challenge to the performer lies in the proper realization and improvisation of ornaments. W. numbers for Alfred Wotquenne who organized the music of C.P.E. Bach in the *Thematic Catalogue of the Work of C.P.E. Bach* are used for identification. In this thematic index, music is organized by performing medium rather than chronologically.

Sonatas

Six Collections of Sonatas, Free Fantasies and Rondos for Connoisseurs and Amateurs ("Kenner und Liebhaber") (1779–1787)

Original and intriguing writing. Works below are listed and numbered according to the six volumes from the Breitkopf and Härtel edition. (Breitkopf and others.)

Sonata I in C Major (Volume I)

Sparkling *Presto* first movement with passagework and arpeggiations divided between the hands. Sounds more difficult than it is. Lyrical, expressive *Andante* and a cheerful last movement. Entire sonata is six pages. A performer with little experience in playing the music of this period could master this work. Level 8.

Sonata VI in A Major (Volume I)

Robust, concerto-like first movement with broken octaves and strong bass lines. Florid *Adagio* leads to a bright concluding *Allegro*. Level 9.

Rondo in C Major (Volume II)

Highly patterned, somewhat reminiscent of a Baroque harpsichord concerto. Level 9.

Rondo in D Major (Volume II)

Extended passagework in concerto style. Sparkling passages that are easier than they sound. Level 9.

Sonata in F Major (Volume II)

An elegant and expressive slow first movement leads to a robust *Presto*. Entire sonata is only four pages in this volume. Level 9.

Rondo in E-flat Major (Volume VI)

Expressive and melodic with good potential as an opener for a recital. Level 9.

Sonata in D Major (Volume VI)

Three-movement work in only four printed pages. Light-hearted first movement with limited passagework, expressive *Allegretto* and short bucolic *Presto di molto*.

Six Sonatas for Clavier, Wq. 51, ed. Rose

Conservative harmonies. (Theodore Presser.)

Sonata in D Minor, Wq. 51/4

More fully developed than the sonatas listed from the collections for "Kenner und Liebhaber." Three contrasting movements, fast-slow-fast. Effective performed as a whole, perhaps to open a recital. Level 9.

Sonata in F Major, Wq. 51/5

Interesting writing for the pianist capable of playing the easiest Haydn sonatas. Level 9.

Six Sonatas for Keyboard, ed. Friedheim

Excellent edition containing six sonatas that were previously unavailable. Provides an extensive introduction to the volume and to each sonata, giving valuable information on performance practice and on the realization of ornaments. (State University of New York/Galaxy.)

Sonata in G Major, Wq. 62, No. 19

Characteristic jumps from one part of the keyboard to another appear in the first movement. The second movement is less complex than many slow movements of C.P.E. Bach, and the final movement dances with lively skips and running passages. One of the most accessible of the sonatas, with only moderate technical difficulties in its fast outer movements. Level 9.

Sonata in D Minor, Wq. 52, No. 2

Begins with a beautiful slow movement, is followed by another slow movement and a concluding concerto-like Allegro. Musical difficulties outweigh technical considerations. The performance-practice considerations are not overwhelming. Level 10.

Miscellaneous Volumes and Pieces

**Short and Easy Piano Pieces
with Varied Recapitulations, ed. Jonas**

In these works, the repeats were written out in full by the composer rather than indicated by repeat signs. C.P.E. Bach added the ornaments he expected to be performed in these pieces. The Jonas edition is a scholarly performing edition of the highest caliber. The text presents intermediate keyboard pieces with structural information concerning the varied repeats. Editorial commentary, table of ornaments, fingering and notes on the sources are provided. Many of these pieces also appear in other collections. (Universal.) Levels 5–8.

Variations on "Ich Schlief, Da Träumte Mir," Wq. 118/1

A catchy theme provides a fruitful basis for the ensuing eight variations, based on a German folk song constructed of broken chords in eighth notes. Interesting writing for the intermediate performer.

24 Pieces, ed. Vrieslander

Contains miscellaneous pieces such as *Alla Pollacas, Minuets* (presented in alternating pairs), *Solfeggios, Fantasias* and sonatina movements. While the volume as a whole might not be used for study except in special cases, many of these pieces should appear in anthologies. (International.) Levels 6–8.

Selected Keyboard Works, Book I, Short and Easy Pieces, ed. Ferguson

A well-researched and beautifully edited volume containing various pieces such as fantasias, an *alla polacca*, a presto, the *Sonata in C*, Wq. 53/5 and the *Six Sonatinas* from the *Essay on the True Art of Playing Keyboard Instruments*. The extensive introduction is useful because of its substantial emphasis on ornamentation. Valuable for pedagogical and historical reference. (Associated Board of the Royal Schools of Music.) Levels 5–8.

Sonata in C Major, Wq. 52/5

> While it is not C.P.E. Bach's most interesting writing, this sonata is short and is accessible to a performer not yet ready for the easy Haydn sonatas. The first movement provides the opportunity to perfect the playing of legato double notes. Level 8.

Selected Keyboard Works, Book II, Miscellaneous Pieces, ed. Ferguson

Contains longer and more difficult selections than those in *Book I*. For the advancing pianist. Most are at the same level or slightly harder than the well-known *Solfeggietto in C Minor*, Wq. 117/2 , which is also included. Some interesting extractions may be made for repertoire study and development. (Associated Board of the Royal Schools of Music, Peters and other standard editions.) Levels 6–9.

Solfegietto in C Minor, Wq. 117/2 (Solfeggio)

> Deserving of its popularity with both students and teachers. The arpeggiations divided between the hands provide ample opportunity for the student to work on fast, clean passage playing. Level 6.

Allegro in A Major, Wq. 116/16

Elegant writing. Generally the melody appears in the right hand with repeated chords serving a continuo function in the left. Moderate technical facility is required. Level 6.

Rondo in E-flat, Wq. 61/1

Musical writing within an extended movement. For the performer with sophisticated taste and a good legato. Level 8.

Presto in C Minor, Wq. 114/3

For the energetic performer, this lively movement would be a fresh substitution for the frequently played *Solfegietto in C Minor*. The writing is musical and filled with patterns, lacks ornaments, and features a great deal of alternation between the hands. Deserves further investigation. Level 7.

Selected Keyboard Works, Book IV. Six Keyboard Sonatas from the *Essay*, ed. Ferguson

Accessible sonatas in a fine edition that includes realization of the ornaments and fingering. (Associated Board of the Royal Schools of Music.) Levels 8–10.

Sonatas and Pieces, ed. Herrmann

The miscellaneous pieces found here are especially interesting. Several appear in other collections although some such as *Allegro in G Major*, *Allegro in E Major* and *Allegro in A Minor* are less familiar. Wotquenne numbers are not provided. (Peters.) Levels 8–10.

Allegro in G Major

A lively dance-like movement in 3/8 meter. Level 8.

Allegro in A Major

Cheerful with buoyant rhythms and occasional right-hand passagework in triplets. Level 8.

Allegro in C Major

Continuous sixteenth-note passagework with many patterns in the right hand. Good for the pianist with agile fingers and effective in performance. Level 8.

Short Pieces by the Sons of Bach, Volume II

All pieces in this book are easy teaching pieces by C.P.E. Bach. This short book of six attractive solos could be studied by a young student as he or she plays the easy pieces of W. A. Mozart and Haydn. (Chester.) Level 3.

Leichte Spielstücke für Klavier

Contains some of the very easiest teaching pieces of C.P.E. Bach. Some of these are interesting and not found in other volumes. (Hug.) Level 3.

Musikalisches Mancherlei

Found here are *Menuett I* and *II, Sonata per il Cembalo solo, Polonaise* and two *Allegros*. Several selections are of doubtful authenticity since they cannot be found in the Wotquenne listing. Nevertheless, this volume provides interesting intermediate literature that is not especially well-known. (Otto Heinrich Noetzel Verlag/Peters.) Levels 5–7.

Additional Works for Study:
W. 65/22, 33, 11 and *14 Four Leichte Sonaten*
Kurze und Leichte Claviersücke
W. 63 18 Probestücke

JOHANN CHRISTIAN BACH (1735–1782) Germany

After studying with his brother C.P.E. Bach in Berlin, and after briefly living in Italy, J. C. Bach spent the last 20 years of his life living and composing in England. Known as the "London Bach," J. S. Bach's youngest surviving son cultivated the Italian style of vocal and instrumental composition. He contributed greatly to the evolution of the Classical style, especially the sonata form. J. C. Bach was an expert in the cantilena singing style.

Introduction to the Piano (with F. P. Ricci) (1768)

A keyboard method in which most of the music is composed by Christian Bach and the introductory treatise to the method is written by Ricci. Found here are 100 musical gems not now part of the standard teaching literature. Contains movements such as minuets, preludes, allegrettos, rondos, ariosos and others. This method book (introductory treatise plus the sequence of 100 pieces) was designed to take a beginner quickly through the beginning/elementary stages to the early-advanced level. (Novello.) Levels 1–7.

Fourteen Pieces (J. C. Bach and F. P. Ricci), ed. Hinson

A practical collection of some of the best selections from the *Introduction to the Piano*. Fingering, dynamics and articulation are added in this edition. (Hinshaw.) Levels 5–6.

JOHANN CHRISTOPH FRIEDRICH BACH (1732–1895) Germany

Of the children of J. S. Bach, Friedrich was most capable at the keyboard. J.C.F. Bach first studied law, later accepting a position as a court musician at Bückeburg. His music is known for its deep, sincere feeling.

Musical Leisure Hours (Musikalische Nebenstunden)

In 1787–88 J.C.F. Bach published a four-volume collection of his keyboard music, songs and cantatas under the title *Musikalische Nebenstunden*. They are miniatures, intended for light entertainment. Many are popular dance forms of the day including the minuet, Schwäbisch (Swabian dance), musette and march. Several look back to the *Two-Part Inventions* of Bach while others are reminiscent of *Preludes* from the *Well-Tempered Clavier*, Book I. J.C.F. Bach's mature style is also reflected. The keyboard collections published by Schott and the Associated Board of the Royal Schools of Music provide a selection from the *Musical Leisure Hours*. This is lesser-known music that is interesting and of historical significance. Worth investigating. (Associated Board of the Royal Schools of Music, Schott and other editions.) Level 6.

Variations on "Ah, vous dirai-je maman"

Idiomatic to the keyboard, these eighteen variations on a familiar theme are effective in performance. This work is less ornamented, less sophisticated and slightly easier than the set by Mozart on the same theme. (Schott.) Level 8.

Aria in A Minor with 15 Variations

Musical writing that is more Baroque than pre-Classic in style. Would make an interesting and effective recital opening. Level 9.

Six Easy Sonatas, ed. Ruff and Bemmann

Attractive works that could be played by the performer who is almost ready to study the easier Haydn sonatas. All six are in three movements and of equal quality. They seem most appropriate for the mature musician, college age and older. The first sonata in C Major and the last in E-flat Major may be the easiest. The collection as a whole deserves investigation. (Schott.) Level 9.

Miscellaneous Pieces

Schwäbisch (Swabian Dance) in F Major

This folk dance is based on a type found in Bavaria. A rollicking one-page work built on a lilting motive and a strong rhythmic framework. Appealing writing for the elementary student. Level 3.

WILHELM FRIEDEMANN BACH (1710–1784) Germany

The oldest son of J. S. Bach, often called the "Halle" Bach because he spent so many years in that German city. W. F. Bach was possibly the greatest performer on the organ in Germany after the death of his father. His music combines the *empfindsamer* style with polyphonic elements learned from J. S. Bach. W. F. Bach preferred free, quasi-improvisatory forms with interesting thematic treatment. His music is characterized by rich melodies and a varied harmonic palette.

Leichte Spielstücke für Klavier

Contains some lesser-known teaching pieces for the lower-elementary and intermediate performer. More of these works should appear in anthologies to increase their availability. (Hug.) Levels 2–4.

Nine Sonatas

In three volumes of three sonatas each and presenting a mixture of Baroque and Classic tendencies. Some intricate subdivisions of rhythms and highly ornamented passages appear. (Kalmus, Nagels.) Level 10.

Polonaises

Some are highly ornamented and rhythmically elaborate and seem more appropriate for the connoisseur of *empfindsamkeit* than for the student performer. The slow polonaises are the highest in quality. (Universal.) Level 10.

LUDWIG VAN BEETHOVEN (1770–1827) Germany

A musical giant who, by the time he was 30, was one of the most renowned pianists and composers in Europe. Although he adhered to Classical forms, his music was highly innovative from the beginning. He adopted a legato style as the basic touch for keyboard playing, as had Clementi. (Many standard editions. Particular editions are listed when a work may be difficult to find.)

Dances

These short works are often overlooked as teaching pieces. Strong writing appears in works of manageable length. Interesting groups of dances may be created.

Country Dances

The spirited country dance originated in England around the 16th century and was usually danced by a line of men and a line of women facing each other. The music was based on folk tunes, often in eight-measure phrases. The sets of *Country Dances* are as follows: *Seven Country Dances*, WoO 11, *Six Country Dances*, WoO 14 and *Six Country Dances*, WoO 15. Many are actually *Ländler*. From the set of *Six Country Dances*, WoO 14 come the three dances that were freely transcribed from Beethoven's version by Isidor Seiss and have become well-known in that version as *Beethoven: Contra-Dances for the Piano* (G. Schirmer). Those transcribed are No. 1, No. 6 and No. 12. The Seiss arrangement of Beethoven's country dances is more difficult than the original Beethoven version. Levels 4–6.

German Dances

A *German Dance* was a fast, triple-meter dance for couples, a forerunner of the waltz. The sets of *German Dances* for keyboard are as follows: *12 German Dances*, WoO 8, *12 German Dances*, WoO 13 and *Six German Dances*, WoO 42. Thick accompaniments are a feature of many of these works, and many appear frequently in anthologies. Levels 3–7.

Écossaises

The *Écossaise* was a popular dance in 2/4 and was related to the country dance from the British Isles. Several of Beethoven's écossaises have been popular standards in the teaching repertory. The *Écossaise in G Major*, WoO 23 has become a favorite for elementary performers because of its charm and jovial nature. Also a favorite is the set of *Six Écossaises in E-flat Major*, Op. 83 or WoO 16, a work to be played as one continuous selection. The *Écossaise in E-flat Major*, Op. 86 is one of Beethoven's most accessible works, with a simple single-note melody and a broken chord accompaniment. Levels 3–7.

Écossaise in G Major, WoO 23

Charming elementary work with "wrong-note" writing, jovial octave passages and predictable phrases. Level 2.

Six Écossaises, WoO 83

These dances are delightful to many performers, partly because the second phrase in each is always the same—a catchy sequential passage with octave leaps in the left hand that adds to the overall appeal of the piece. It should be performed in its entirety. Level 7.

Écossaises in E-flat, WoO 86

Simple binary form work with question-answer structure. Oom-pah left-hand accompaniment and right-hand single-note melody. One of Beethoven's easiest compositions. Level 3.

Minuets

The Beethoven *Minuets* consist primarily of a miscellaneous *Minuet in F Major* (Anh.), the more popular *Minuet in E-flat Major*, WoO 82 and the set of *Six Minuets*, WoO 10. This last set has gained some popularity, with many of the individual movements appearing in anthologies. See especially *No. 1 in C Major, No. 2 in G Major* and *No. 5 in D Major* from the *Six Minuets*, WoO 10. Levels 4–8.

Minuet in C Major, WoO 10, No. 1

Uses full chords to achieve rich sonority, a feature that may be exciting to a student performing at this level. Requires expansion and contraction of the hands in a work with strong and dramatic writing. Level 5.

Minuet in G Major, WoO 10, No. 2

Another popular minuet in which the thirds and dotted rhythms in the opening measures provide an inviting theme as well as a vehicle for technical development. An all-time favorite. Level 7.

Minuet (and Trio) in E-flat Major, WoO 82

Another perennial favorite, especially appropriate for the student adept in playing full-chorded, quasi-orchestral pieces. Some rhythmic difficulties exist in this work and the several lines of the texture need adept voicing. More challenging than it appears. Level 8.

Waltzes

Includes miscellaneous waltzes composed at different periods of Beethoven's life such as *Waltz in E-flat Major*, WoO 84, *Waltz in D Major*, WoO 85 and others as well as the *Six Waltzes for Klavier*, Anh. 14. The latter are relatively insignificant and little-known works. The other waltzes appear periodically in anthologies. Levels 3–7.

Waltz in E-flat Major, WoO 84

This fine work with a beautiful legato line over an oom-pah-pah accompaniment should be better known. The Trio harkens back in style to Rameau and Couperin. An especially suitable choice to precede the Beethoven bagatelles. The waltz melody needs careful fingering. Level 6.

Sonatinas

The works known as the Beethoven *Sonatinas* consist of the *Two Easy Sonatinas*, Anh. 5 (*G Major* and *F Major*), the three works also known as the *Bonn Sonatas*, and two unfinished works, one in *F Major* and one in *C Major*. The *Bonn Sonatas* are so titled because Beethoven composed them in Bonn when he was 13 years old.

Sonatina in G Major, Anh. 5, No. 1

This popular work is in two movements, with the first untitled. Each movement can fit on one page and may serve as a student's introduction to the playing of sonatinas. The first movement should be played in 4/4 rather than 8/8. Two-note slurs need careful attention. The second movement *Romanza* in sonata-allegro form is a graceful, dance-like piece with a few extensions in each hand. Level 3.

Sonatina in F Major, Anh. 5, No. 2

The first movement is one of the most frequently played teaching pieces by Beethoven, perhaps due to the energetic scale passages and the rapid broken-chord accompaniment. It is cheerful in nature and is in rounded-binary form with Coda. Sixteenth notes proceed from hand to hand, and the scale passages and Alberti bass present the main technical challenges. The second movement, *Rondo*, is carefree and somewhat romantic. Level 4.

Two Movements of a Sonatina in F Major, WoO 50

These are works of lesser value and inspiration. Level 6.

Sonatina in C Major, WoO 51

The first movement is worth investigating, with interesting and beautiful modulations in its development. Level 7.

Bonn Sonata in E-flat Major, WoO 47, No. 1 (Sonatina in E-flat Major)

The first movement is the strongest, featuring a pedal note in the bass at times and containing strong dynamic contrasts. Some double-note passages add to the difficulty of this movement. The last movement is little known, and requires brilliant fingerwork. Level 8.

Bonn Sonata in F Minor, WoO 47, No. 2 (Sonatina in F Minor)

One of the most gratifying of the *Bonn Sonatas*, this work presents many similarities to the much later *Sonate Pathétique*, including an opening with a short, pathetic *larghetto*, and a slow recurring section filled with strong emotional effect. The first movement would provide an appropriate and more accessible substitution for the *Pathetique Sonata*, Op. 13, with sudden dynamic changes and frequent alternation between fast, almost furious passagework and slow chordal, full-bodied sounds. Tremolo patterns call for a strong left-hand. The last movement also contains exciting and urgent passagework. Level 8.

Bonn Sonata in D Major, WoO 47, No. 3 (Sonatina in D Major)

The most difficult and probably the least known of the three *Bonn Sonatas*, approaching the difficulty of Beethoven *Sonata in F Minor*, Op. 2, No. 1. Haydnesque in its tunefulness, this sonata could serve as an interesting pre-Haydn work. The first movement is especially good for a performer with strong fingers and who enjoys playing literature with rapid sixteenth note figures. The musically sophisticated *Menuetto* of the second movement features a sostenuto theme and six rather extended variations. The *Scherzando* final movement again calls for rapid scale playing. Level 9.

Bagatelles

The bagatelle (French, meaning "trifle") is a light, short piece. As a musical form, it was first used by F. Couperin, who included a rondeau entitled *Les Bagatelles* in his 10th *ordre* published in 1717. Although the term was used around 1753 by the French publisher Borvin for a collection of dances, Beethoven first gave the term its fame with his three sets, Op. 33, 119 and 126, and the additional miscellaneous bagatelles without opus numbers. Beethoven's bagatelles have been greatly influential. Some consider the bagatelles of Beethoven to herald the beginning of the 19th-century character piece.

Bagatelles, Op. 33

The witty, energetic works in this set are generally more difficult technically than those in either of the other two collections. (Op. 126 is not dealt with in this book, since it is reserved for advanced players.) The influence of the folk idiom is apparent in several pieces of Op. 33. Many also exhibit large leaps, off-beat accents, a lack of development of thematic material and snatches of virtuosity. Levels 8–10.

Bagatelle in E-flat, Op. 33, No. 1

A fine example of a concise sonata-rondo form and excellent preparation for playing Beethoven sonata movements. This bagatelle contains many written-out ornaments over a simple broken-chord bass. Various rhythmic values develop along with the several variations of the first theme and some right-hand scalewise passages that are cadenza-like. Especially good for a performer who is innately expressive. Clearly in the Mozartian tradition. Requires a variety of touches. Level 9.

Bagatelle in C Major, Op. 33, No. 2

Scherzando work with quick changes of mood, humorous *sforzando* and a tempestuous Trio. Calls for rapid movement around the keyboard. Level 10.

Bagatelle in F Major, Op. 33, No. 3

A 6/8 work in the character of a Haydn *Allegretto,* filled with harmonic surprises. This might be a student's first experience with the music of the mature Beethoven, and possibly could be studied in preparation to playing one of the easier sonata movements. Requires a musician sensitive to harmonic change and surprise. Should be better known. Level 8.

Bagatelle in D Major, Op. 33, No. 6

Lyrical and elegant work in a moderate tempo, calling for careful voicing of the melody over the thicker textures. Marked by Beethoven to be performed with "a speaking expression." Level 8.

Bagatelle in A-flat Major, Op. 33, No. 7

Driving work with pulsating chords and repeated melodic figurations. Contains an exciting close with resonant chord repetitions. Requires dramatic flair. Level 10.

Bagatelles, Op. 119

It has been suggested that Beethoven wrote each of the bagatelles in this set as an experiment, or as a solution to a compositional problem. Some scholars also feel that Beethoven composed the last five pieces of Op. 119 to be included in Friedrich Starke's *Wiener Pianoforte Schule.* At any rate, these bagatelles were written and published at different times throughout Beethoven's life and were clearly not composed as a cycle. Eventually the entire set was published by Clementi in 1823. Some are quite short, and many display dance-like features. Note the conspicuous absence of dynamics throughout the entire opus. Levels 7–9.

Bagatelle in G Minor, Op. 119, No. 1

This selection should be played with one pulse per measure to avoid a heavy, almost lethargic effect. The melodic eighth-note passages at the end need careful inflection of many two-note phrases. Not particularly effective in performance, and in some ways, more difficult than it sounds. Level 7.

Bagatelle in D Major, Op. 119, No. 3

Marked to be played *"a l'Allemande,"* this work features much repetition and requires a strong sense of dance and an inner pulse. Effective and rewarding, with a true economy of material. Level 7.

Bagatelle in C Minor, Op. 119, No. 5

The dotted rhythms and grace notes give this piece its character, but also can serve as the source of minor technical problems. This is a robust work, shorter than many of the others. Level 7.

Bagatelle in A Minor, Op. 119, No. 9

The melody of this short piece is built of broken chords and calls for much extension and contraction of the hand. Waltz-like, with an oom-pah-pah bass. More difficult than it initially appears. Level 6.

Bagatelle in B-flat, Op. 119, No. 11

Fine preparation for slow movements of sonatas, this bagatelle is a study in voicing legato melody above detached quarter-note chords. It features a short cadenza-like section and is especially good for students who are beginning to play expressively. Level 8.

Sonatas

The Beethoven *Sonatas* are landmark works in the pianist's repertoire. Three early sonatas, the *Bonn Sonatas,* written while the composer was still in Bonn, are not found below, but are listed under the *Sonatinas.* All three are dramatic works, and one or two movements of them should precede a student's study of a Beethoven sonata.

Sonata in F Minor, Op. 2, No. 1

A work in four movements, all of which are accessible. The first movement opens with a "Mannheim" rocket theme, an upward-leaping broken chord which encompasses almost two octaves. The final movement, perhaps the most difficult, calls for the playing of quick broken-chords, triplets and resonant chords played with full arm weight. Often this sonata is attempted too early in a student's development. Level 10.

Sonata in C Minor, Op. 10, No. 1

The first movement features a strong broken-chord figure with dotted rhythms that must be played precisely, and not as triplets. The energy of the music in the first movement is appealing but the performer needs to pay close attention to the myriad details in the score to avoid being overcome with excitement. The slow movement is lovely and lyrical. The finale is perhaps the most accessible movement of this sonata, and requires humor. Level 10.

Sonata in F Major, Op. 10, No. 2

The first movement displays sophisticated humor that must be projected in the performance. The performer needs to be skillful in playing resonant, full chords with proper arm involvement. More difficult to interpret than initially apparent. The *Allegretto* second movement in the form of a minuet and trio replaces the slow movement in this sonata. It is appealing in its reserved character and in the primarily chordal writing. The lively *Presto* finale is contrapuntal and conversational, appropriate for the performer with strong rhythm and good finger agility. Level 10.

Sonata in C Minor, Op. 13 "Pathétique"

The name "Pathétique" was one of only two titles given by Beethoven to his sonatas. This first movement is one of the most popular sonata movements in his output. The opening *Grave* section requires interpretative insight and fine skill in executing the complex rhythms with exactness. The movement itself, with the recurring traces of the opening *grave* and the numerous surprises, is more difficult than many performers realize. The familiar second movement is a beautiful hymn-like work in rondo form. Careful attention to voicing the thick textures is required. The final movement is driving and energetic, with long phrases that can easily become sing-song unless carefully inflected. The performer needs strong fingers and a fine sense of articulation in the complex phrases of this dramatic movement. Level 10.

Sonata in E Major, Op. 14, No. 1

Not frequently heard, although a fine repertoire choice for an advancing performer. The slow movement is one of the more accessible movements in the Beethoven *Sonatas*, forming a perfect link between the two outer movements of this powerful sonata. The final *Rondo* sparkles with rapid scales and broken chords. It is lilting, spontaneous and refreshing. Level 10.

Sonata in G Major, Op. 14, No. 2

The first movement is constructed on broken chords that fit the hand well but are somewhat difficult to read initially. The fine, march-like *Andante* is constructed as a theme and four variations. The final movement, *Scherzo*, is light and dance-like. The thin texture of this bucolic movement is enriched with fast scale passages. Performers with strong fingers will especially enjoy it. Level 10.

Sonata in C-sharp Minor, Op. 27, No. 2
"Sonata quasi una fantasia"

This sonata is in reality a sophisticated experiment on the part of Beethoven. The title "Moonlight" was assigned by the publishers rather than by the composer. The first movement is magical in its harmonic journeys. It calls for a highly expressive performer and strong attention to the details of the score. The final movement requires a mature pianist and presents enormous technical difficulties. Level 10.

Sonata in G Minor, Op. 49, No. 1 "Sonata Facile"

Some authors call the Op. 49 Sonatas "sonatinas" because of their relative lack of complexity compared to neighboring works. The *Andante* first movement contains many different ideas and some intricate figurations, making it a movement more difficult musically than many perceive. A well-worked out legato is necessary. The *Rondo-Allegro* requires fine facility for execution of rapid staccato passages and fast sixteenth-note accompaniment. Effective writing at the upper-intermediate level. Level 8.

Sonata in G Major, Op. 49, No. 2

A work also in two movements, this sonata is perhaps the most accessible of all of the Beethoven sonatas. The triplet figurations found in both hands in the first movement need careful musical inflection and a fine sense of style. Note the unpredictable beginning of the development in the key of D Minor rather than D Major. The final movement, *Tempo di minuetto*, is no more difficult than the easier Kuhlau sonatina movements. Capturing the graceful character of this elegant movement is perhaps its most important requirement. Levels 7–8.

Sonata in G Major, Op. 79

One of the most attractive of the easier sonatas and one that is not heard sufficiently often. The theme of the first movement is taken from the Austrian *ländler* dance, and should be played with a folk quality. The cuckoo-like calls in this movement are vivid. The second movement in

9/8 is almost a barcarolle, with a lyrical double-note melody and a rocking left-hand accompaniment. It is beautiful, romantic writing and rewarding to study. The final movement, *Vivace*, is a lively rondo calling for strong fingers and a rollicking dance tempo. Level 9.

Variations

Six Variations on a Swiss Song, WoO 64

A charming and popular work featuring a theme and six variations. Interesting writing and effective in performance. W. Palmer has discovered the song *Dursli and Babeli* upon which this variation set is based. (Many standard editions.) Level 7.

Six Variations on a Duet by Paisiello, WoO 70

Based on an enchanting Italian song, this work gives the performer opportunities to work through various technical challenges as evidenced in the many variations. Often one technical figuration pervades a single variation. Effective in performance. Level 9.

Six Easy Variations on an Original Theme, WoO 77

A popular set, less difficult than the *Paisiello Variations*. Level 8.

Miscellaneous Pieces

Rondo in C Major, Op. 51, No. 1

This work could easily substitute as a repertoire choice for a Beethoven sonata movement. The wide variety of ideas are unified masterfully in the formal structure of this work. The cadenza passage and florid figurations make it rewarding to study and to perform. Level 8.

Two Russian Folk Songs, Op. 107

These pieces are transcriptions taken from a chamber work for flute (or violin) and piano. Both folk songs appear frequently in anthologies, the one in *G Major* being especially attractive. The *A Minor* work is also titled *Little Minka* or *"Air Russe."* Levels 3–4.

Happy and Sad (Lustig, Traurig) (Bagatelle), WoO 54

Alternating sections obviously portraying emotion. A fine programmatic work at the intermediate level. Levels 5–6.

Für Elise, WoO 59

Perhaps Beethoven's most popular piano work. Dedicated to "Elise," the daughter of Beethoven's physician, but possibly originally intended for a friend named Thérèse, and misread by the publisher. Can be considered as a rondo with two episodes. The overall tempo must be determined by the tempo at which the thirty-second note passages will be played. Level 7.

Allemande in A Major, WoO 81

Dance-style work with many arpeggiations in the right hand. Note the quick changes of direction within the arpeggiations. Level 7.

Adieu to the Piano in F Major, Anh. 15

A waltz-like sentimental work with a trio. Lyrical writing that calls for fine distinction between melody and accompaniment within the right hand. Beethoven's biographer Thayer considered this to be Beethoven's last piano composition and named it *Adieu*. Levels 7–8.

Contra-danses, trans. Seiss

Robust and thick-textured arrangements, these works are filled with the folk idiom and are highly rhythmic. See the earlier section on the Beethoven *Country Dances*. Useful more for motivational study than as serious repertoire works. These were orchestral dances by Beethoven, transcribed for piano by Beethoven, and, later, by Seiss for piano. (Alfred, G. Schirmer.) Levels 8–9.

Works for Additional Study:
WoO 52 Bagatelle in C Minor
WoO 56 Bagatelle in C Major
WoO 60 Bagatelle in B-flat Major

Miscellaneous Volumes

Dances of Beethoven—Pieces to Play Before His Sonatinas, ed. Hinson

Contains a selection of familiar works combined with some infrequently heard pieces that should be better known. Minuets, country dances, German dances, waltzes, allemandes and similar pieces. (Alfred.) Levels 4–8.

At the Piano with Beethoven, ed. Hinson

Familiar and unfamiliar works are included. The volume contains *Seven Variations on "God Save the King,"* WoO 78, the *Sonata in G Major,* Op. 79

and other shorter pieces. A wide range in levels of difficulty exists in this volume. The extensive preface and commentary on performance practice are quite valuable. (Alfred.) Levels 5–10.

Beethoven: Piano Music from His Early Years, ed. Hinson

Extensive and valuable preface. Works included are *Rondo in C Major*, WoO 48, *Variations on a March by Dressler*, WoO 63, *Variations on a Swiss Song*, WoO 64, *Sonatina in F Major*, WoO 50 and others. Many of these works are seldom heard. (Alfred.) Levels 6–8.

Beethoven: Piano Music Inspired by Women In His Life, ed. Hinson

Contains *Für Elise, Klavierstück*, WoO 60, *Sonatina in C*, WoO 51, *Sonata in C-sharp Minor*, Op. 27, No. 2 and more. An intriguing theme joins the pieces in this collection. (Alfred.) Levels 6–10.

Beethoven: An Introduction to His Piano Works, ed. Palmer

An attractive volume, due largely to the inclusion of a variety of easier works including several of the bagatelles from Op. 119, country dances, écossaises, menuets and the *Variations on a Swiss Song*, WoO 64. Excellent choices and a fine cross-section of Beethoven's easier works. (Alfred.) Levels 3–8.

Beethoven: The First Book for Young Pianists, ed. Palmer

Presents the easiest pieces from *Beethoven: An Introduction to His Piano Works*, ed. Palmer. This volume includes three *Country Dances*, three minuets, the second movement of the *Sonata in G*, Op. 49, No. 2, and the *Sonatina in G*. (Alfred.) Levels 3–8.

Beethoven: 13 of His Most Popular Piano Selections

Contains the most popular pieces of Beethoven, including the first movement of the *Sonata*, Op. 27, No. 2, *Sonata in G*, Op. 49, No. 2, *Sonatina in F*, Anh. 5, No. 2 and *Six Variations on a Swiss Folk Song*, WoO 64. (Alfred.) Levels 7–9.

Seven Easy Pieces

An interesting combination of less frequently heard pieces by Beethoven for the advancing pianist are included in this highly edited volume. Included are the *Rondo in A, Variations in C on "Une fièvre brûlante," Bagatelle in E-flat*, Op. 33, No. 1, *Bagatelle in C Major*, Op. 33, No. 2, *Bagatelle in E-flat*, Op. 126, No. 3, *Variations in G* and the *Sonata in G Major*, Op. 79. (Kalmus.) Levels 9–10.

A Book of Dances, WoO 81-86, ed. Ferguson

A variety of excellent literature is found here in easy but representative Beethoven pieces. Included are *Allemande in A, Menuet in E-flat, Six Écossaises, Waltz in E-flat, Waltz in D* and *Écossaise in E-flat.* These are different from the other "Beethoven dances" usually studied by intermediate students in that they are original compositions of Beethoven for piano, not transcriptions. This collection should be better known. (Associated Board of the Royal Schools of Music.) Levels 5–6.

Easy Piano Compositions

Contains eight bagatelles, several of the dances, the *Rondo in C* and other miscellaneous pieces. Highly edited. Extensive ranges of difficulty. (Kalmus.) Levels 5–9.

A First Beethoven Book

This volume includes two German dances, an écossaise, an allemande, two ländler, the *Six Easy Variations* and sonatina movements. (Kalmus.) Levels 6–7.

My First Beethoven, ed. Rattalino

This teaching volume was compiled to present some little-known compositions of Beethoven. While some interesting selections are provided such as *Two Little Pieces, Canon in A-flat, Two Bagatelles* and an *Easy Sonata (1796)*, no distinguishing numbers are given. The printed text is quite small. In general, the editor's frequent editorial markings are distinguished from Beethoven's original indications. (Ricordi.) Level 7.

The Beethoven Sketchbooks, arr. for piano and ed. by Werner, Volumes 1-6

The editor has arranged and presented many of the musical drafts from the *Beethoven Sketchbooks* for the student pianist, in approximate order of difficulty. (MSM.) Levels 3–8.

The Young Pianist's Guide to Beethoven, ed. Novik

Teaching volume that is highly edited containing miscellaneous Russian folk dances, écossaises, German dances, ländler, minuets and other pieces. A recording of the editor performing the selections is provided as a model. (Studio P/R.) Levels 5–6.

Beethoven Album, Volumes I and II

Both volumes contain a wealth of material for the early-advanced pianist. Selections in Volume I include the *Bagatelles,* Op. 33, *Rondo,* Op. 51, No. 1, two sets of variations, écossaises, two minuets and three contra-danses. Volume II includes the *Rondo,* Op. 51, No. 1, the *Bagatelles,* Op. 119 and 126, the *Rondo a Capriccio,* Op. 129 and an *andante.* (Editio Musica Budapest.) Level 10.

Beethoven Easiest Piano Pieces

A cross-section of familiar intermediate works, including two écossaises, *Happy and Sad, Three German Dances,* two minuets, a waltz, a contradance, an allegretto and others. (Peters.) Levels 5–6.

Beethoven Easier Favorites

A potentially valuable collection of upper-intermediate and early-advanced selections. Sample works included are *Seven Country Dances, Three German Dances, Theme and Six Variations* and *Air Autrichien.* (Peters.) Levels 6–8.

Beethoven. Master Series for the Young, ed. Hughes

Highly edited but well-conceived collection of pieces at the upper-intermediate to early-advanced level. Encompasses six bagatelles, three of the easier movements from the sonatas, the *Six Easy Variations on a Swiss Song,* several attractive minuets and others. (G. Schirmer.) Levels 7–10.

Beethoven Easy Compositions for Piano, ed. Lebert and von Bülo

A highly edited volume that presents two variation sets, a rondo, the *Bagatelles,* Op. 33 and three sonatas. (G. Schirmer.) Level 10.

Little-Known Piano Pieces, compiled and edited by Zeitlin and Goldberger

Interesting compilation, valuable especially for teachers looking to expand the variety of works by Beethoven which they teach. Some miscellaneous piano pieces, rondos, bagatelles and other works are found here. (Boston.) Levels 7–9.

GEORG ANTONIN BENDA (1722–1795) Bohemia

Benda was a close friend of C.P.E. Bach, and his music did much to prepare the way for the Classicism of Beethoven. Stylistic characteristics found in Benda's works include the occasional use of Mozartian melodies, strongly discernible folk elements, and bold harmonies. His keyboard output consists of sonatas and over 30 sonatinas. Accessible teaching collections of Benda sonatinas include those published by the Associated Board of the Royal Schools of Music and by Brodt Music Company.

Sonatinas

Sonatinas Nos. 1–34

Benda composed approximately 34 one-movement sonatinas, most of which are tuneful and fresh. They may be in binary or ternary form, or are rondos or variations, and show the influence of Scarlatti and of C.P.E. Bach. The complete sonatinas of Benda in this edition are highly edited. (Artia.) Levels 4–8.

Sonatina No. 3 in A Minor

A possible repertoire choice for students who like invention/toccata literature. The tuneful theme makes it inviting. Contains broken chords and hand crossings. Some performers may tend to rush the tempo in the exciting passagework. Level 5.

Sonatina No. 10 in F Major

This work opens with broken F-Major chords played in inversions in the right hand. The rhythm continually shifts from triplets to eighths, making rhythmic steadiness the chief problem in this attractive piece. One of the easiest of the Benda sonatinas. Level 4.

Sonatina No. 11 in C Major

In the style of a minuet and requiring a consistent tempo, especially in the variation on the theme. Effective in performance and definitely worth investigating. Level 7.

Sonatina No. 16 in G Minor

More similar to a *bourrée* than to a Classic-period sonatina. Could possibly serve as appropriate preparation for early Bach. A fine study in ornamentation. Level 6.

Sonatina No. 17 in D Major

A lively and cheerful work with right-hand sixteenths that often appear in descending five-note patterns. The hand position changes, and occasional leaps create excitement as tension builds through the repeated sequences. Level 5.

Sonatina No. 34 in D Major

This vivacious and effective sonatina calls for even finger work, with most of the rapid passagework being played by the right hand. The central "B" section requires inflection of the disjunct melody. Level 6.

12 Sonatinas, ed. Jones

A selection of 12 of the best of these imaginative and effective one-movement sonatinas. The sounds are refreshing and some works contain virtuosic flourishes that can help develop style for playing cadenzas. This literature should be better known. (Associated Board of the Royal Schools of Music.) Levels 6–8.

Seven Sonatinas, ed. Kreutzer

This volume presents a selection of seven of the most accessible of the Benda works. (Brodt Music Company.) Levels 5–6.

JOHANN DANIEL BERLIN (1714–1787) Germany

Johann Daniel Berlin learned to play the keyboard from his father. In 1730 Berlin moved to Norway where he composed, performed and wrote about music.

Sonatina

Five short movements, *Capricetto, Arietta, Gavotta, Menuet* and *Giga.* Tuneful writing with an absence of complex rhythms. The *Capricetto* is concerto-like and calls for agile fingerwork. Much of this sonatina sounds more difficult than it is. A talented young student might want to perform the entire work. Consider adding this to a required repertoire list for competitions. (Norsk Musikksamling/Peters.) Level 6.

PIETER JOSEPH VAN DEN BOSCH (1736–1803) The Netherlands

Sonatine in G

Three-movement work similar to the Clementi Op. 36 sonatinas. The last movement, *Allegro giocoso*, is especially charming with its easy rapid scales and dotted rhythms. Interesting writing that could stand beside any of the traditional teaching sonatinas in quality. Level 5.

C

BENJAMIN CARR (1768–1831) Great Britain

Organist, pianist and singer Benjamin Carr followed Reinagle's example and settled in Philadelphia after coming to America in 1793. He became well-known as a music publisher and retailer.

Federal Overture (1794)

A series of popular tunes including *Yankee Doodle* as the opening number, *The Marseillaise,* and other Revolutionary songs. The score provides an interesting study of works from our American heritage. Easy to read for the advancing intermediate student. The style is reminiscent of orchestral reductions for piano. Level 8.

Additional Works for Study:
The Maid of Lodi
Musical Journal
Musical Miscellany

DOMENICO CIMAROSA (1749–1801) Italy

Although his fame rests on his success as an operatic composer, Cimarosa wrote 32 single-movement sonatas in a homophonic style, often with single notes in the right hand and cliché accompaniment figures. Some scholars have placed the number of his sonatas as high as 80 or 90, but many of these are unavailable today. Cimarosa's works are generally light and buoyant. Characterized by clear textures and elegance, they make fine teaching material, providing unusual selections for the student who enjoys agile fingerwork. The best source of these sonatas is in one of the larger volumes described below.

Sonatas, rev. Sacchetti

Contains six sonatas, almost all of which use Alberti-bass accompaniments. While not musically profound, these pieces encourage the technical development of Classical-style fluency. Few double-note passages are found here. (Edizioni Musicali Bèrben.) Levels 6–7.

11 Sonatas, Volume 1, eds. Ligelijn and Ruperink

These selections present a variety of characters and textures. The musical quality is surprisingly high and the brevity of these works might make them even more attractive. (Broekmans.) Level 8.

32 Sonatas, Volumes 1–3, ed. Boghen

These volumes present a fine variety of sonatas in an edition that is extensively edited. Provides a good source of this difficult-to-find material. (Max Eschig.) Levels 8–9.

Cimarosa Album

A well-edited and well-researched volume. Contains unusual sonatas, some of which are not duplicated in other volumes. The print is unfortunately small, making reading the score more difficult than it should be for such a fine edition. (PWM.) Levels 8–9.

Miscellaneous Pieces

Sonata in B-flat Major

Comfortable to play, this sonata consists primarily of sixteenths in the right hand and eighths in the left. The theme is based on alternating thirds. Level 7.

Sonata in G Major

The passagework occurs primarily in the right hand in this energetic and lively work. One of the best of the Cimarosa works, it sounds more difficult than it is. Level 7.

Sonatina in D Minor

Lyrical and sustained work that calls for sudden contrasts of dynamics and matching of tones in the melodic line. Effective and highly expressive, especially appropriate for the sensitive performer. Levels 7–8.

Sonatina in E-flat Major

Repeated notes in the left-hand represent the sound of the continuo accompaniment in Baroque chamber music. One of the best. Level 8.

MUZIO CLEMENTI (1752–1832) Italy

His 80-year life spanned the transition from Classicism to 19th-century Romanticism, although his musical language remained essentially that of Classicism. Clementi is considered to be the originator of the modern étude and the founder of the modern legato school of piano technique. He had a great influence on Beethoven, especially in the use of *sforando*. The main part of his compositional output lies in the sonatas for keyboard.

Sonatas

During his life, Clementi moved from a brilliant virtuosic style to the use of more chromatic harmonies and more lyric expression in his some 64 solo sonatas. The first movements are typically in sonata-allegro form. The slow movements are frequently florid adagios, often deeply expressive. The final movements usually are rondos.

Six Sonatas, Op. 4

Actually titled *Six Sonatas with an Accompaniment for the Violin or Flute,* these works were erroneously known for many years as the piano *Sonatinas,* Op. 37 and Op. 38. It was thought that their study should directly follow the *Sonatinas,* Op. 36. In fact, the Op. 4 works are much more difficult. All consist of two movements rather than the traditional three movements as more customarily found in Classical sonata form. (Alfred.) Level 8.

Sonata in D Major, Op. 4, No. 1

> The substantial first movement of this sonata, *Allegro assai,* might be appropriate for those who are ready to play easy Haydn sonata movements. This work is exciting and almost concerto-like in its forceful *crescendi* and strong *fortes.* The second movement *Menuetto* calls for fine attention to details of inflection and phrasing. Level 8.

Sonata in B-flat Major, Op. 24, No. 2

> This work concentrates on technical display, especially in the first movement, which is based on a theme from the overture to Mozart's *Magic Flute.* The entire development section consists of a propulsive sixteenth-note motive moving through the circle of fifths. A pause on a tonic 6/4 chord after a brief passage resembling an orchestral tutti invites an improvised cadenza. The slow movement resembles a light operatic aria. A cheerful rondo features broken octaves, broken chords, scale passages and fast finger work. Level 10.

Sonata in D Major, Op. 26, No. 3

> First movement needs even triplets in both hands. The slow movement is an elegant study in legato and singing right-hand lines. The final *Rondo* requires some dexterity in the light pianistic figurations. Levels 8–9.

Didactic Works

Introduction to the Art of Playing on the Pianoforte, Op. 42 (1801)

One of the first piano method books and widely popular in its day, this book was issued in 11 English editions by Clementi's music publishing firm and translated into several languages. The book is in two parts, the first presenting a discussion (with examples) of the elements of music and comments on fingering. Elements included are the presentation of the staff, clefs, names of notes, intervals, note values and tempo terms. The method also contains examples of scale fingerings, trill exercises and double-note exercises. Part II, Op. 43 was the *Appendix to the 5th edition of Clementi's Introduction to the Art of Playing on the Pianoforte* and consists of 50 lesson-pieces, many of which are prefixed by a prelude composed by Clementi. The lessons themselves are by various composers such as Couperin, Rameau, Haydn, Mozart and Handel. One of the first important pedagogical attempts to make use of already existing pieces. (Da Capo and other editions.) Levels 5–8.

Preludes from Introduction to the Art of Playing on the Pianoforte, Op. 43

(See also above.) These piano works are essentially improvisations by Clementi. They present a mature and full sound, and require a student with some musical insight. See especially Nos. 4, 5, 6, 8, 12, 17, 18, 19, 23, 34 and 35. (Carl Fischer.) Levels 5–7.

Six Sonatinas, Op. 36

Clementi published many editions of these familiar sonatinas. The sixth version in 1820 was his final one, and he stated that it contained "considerable improvements by the author." This edition (available today from Hinshaw, ed. Hinson and Bishop) makes many changes in the works, including the use of higher octaves and the thickening of textures. Clementi's first edition of the Sonatinas, not the sixth, is the one printed in almost all anthologies and collections.

Sonatina in C Major, Op. 36, No. 1

Perhaps the most popular of the Clementi Sonatinas. A bright, cheerful character makes the first movement a student favorite. Its pedagogical value lies in the good finger workout provided for the right hand through the consistent running eighths in scales. The opening phrase of the *Andante* slow movement requires a *crescendo* in the left hand. This movement must be played in 3/4 and not in 9/8. The final, contrapuntal is a favorite. This work is actually more similar in level of difficulty to sonatinas of Lynes, Andre and Lichner than to the other Clementi *Sonatinas*. Level 4.

Sonatina in G Major, Op. 36, No. 2

Perhaps the most accessible sonatina in this set after the Op. 36, No. 1. The first movement provides a fine opportunity to work on inflection of two-note slurs and short motives. The *Allegretto* middle movement, with its catchy dotted rhythms, is enjoyable for a student not normally inclined to play slow movements with sensitivity. The last movement consists primarily of single-note passagework in the right hand above broken-chord accompaniment. The writing is effective and sounds more difficult than it is. Level 5.

Sonatina in C Major, Op. 36, No. 3

An intermediate sonatina gratifying to play and musically substantial. Spirited and playful first movement that fits the hands well. Idiomatic right-hand rapid scales. A brief and beautiful *Adagio* precedes a light-hearted and jovial *Allegro* finale. A light Alberti bass is needed in the left hand. Level 7.

Sonatina in F Major, Op. 36, No. 4

This work is slightly more difficult than it appears on the page. Avoid accenting the broken octaves in the first movement. The central *Andante con espressione* is one of Clementi's most beautiful. Rapid passagework in sixteenth-note triplets needs ease of rotation. The writing is jovial but somewhat difficult to execute musically. Level 6.

Sonatina in G Major, Op. 36, No. 5

The first movement is generally based on broken-chord triplet accompaniment figurations calling for rotation technique. Appropriate balance between melody and accompaniment is a potential problem in this busy movement. The last movement is much less difficult than the first, comparable more to the *Sonatina in G Major*, Op. 36, No 2. Most of the passagework lies in the right hand. This movement may be taught separately to an elementary student. Level 7.

Sonatina in D Major, Op. 36, No. 6

A consistently strong work of more fully developed proportions than the earlier sonatinas, especially in the lengthy first movement. The second and final movement is a rondo marked *Allegretto Spiritoso*. Its bubbly character and effective passagework are appealing. Level 6.

Sonata in D Major, Op. 25, No. 6

A happy-go-lucky mood pervades the first movement, with rollicking triplets and spirited passagework. This movement fits the hand well. The second movement, marked *un poco andante,* is a simple and beautiful lyrical statement. The final movement is a spirited and light-hearted rondo. The passagework is not extensive. The entire sonatina is worth investigating. Level 9.

Preludes and Exercises

Subtitled "school of scales," this volume consists of one or more preludes in a particular key, followed by an exercise or technical study in that key. Some of the preludes contain surprisingly interesting writing but the exercises are, almost without exception, rather tedious and technical. Many of the preludes are quite short. (Kalmus, Ricordi and other standard editions.) Levels 8–10.

18 Monferrine, Op. 49

The *monferrina,* a dance from the Italian state of Monferrato, was popular briefly in the late 18th and early 19th centuries. While the dance is in 6/8 with rhythms based on the eighth-note figure, Clementi's monferrine display a wide variety of rhythms. Most are in three-part ABA or ABA' form and have predictable phrase lengths. Almost all are happy and light, in contrast to the profound late sonatas of Op. 50 that Clementi was working on at the same time. The monferrine uses the middle and upper range of the piano more than the lower register. Each selection can be fitted on two pages in most volumes, and these works can serve as interesting alternatives to his standard Op. 36 Sonatinas. Editions include an excellent and scholarly volume of all 18 monferrine edited by Riccardo Allorto for Ricordi. Six are included in a volume edited by Pietro Spada for Bèrben. (Bèrben, Ricordi and others.) Levels 6–8.

24 Waltzes, Op. 38 and Op. 39

Trivial works from his late period, composed with accompaniment parts for triangle and tambourine. (Curci and other standard editions.) Levels 9–10.

Gradus ad Parnassum

Consists of 100 compositions in two volumes, in essence a kind of compendium of technical possibilities during the early 1800s. Many of the studies are quite difficult but others are intriguing and accessible character pieces. Compositions found here include fugues, canons, sonata movements and études. (Da Capo and other editions.) Level 10.

Miscellaneous Volumes

Clementi Rediscovered Masterworks, Volumes 1–3, ed. Mirovitch

Contains seven of the monferrine, two waltzes and three miscellaneous pieces in the first volume. A practical literature source for teaching some of the monferrine (see above). Those who are seeking an alternative to the traditional sonatinas of Clementi might look in this volume. The later volumes contain more advanced works of Clementi. (Marks.) Levels 5–7.

Clementi Easiest Piano Pieces, ed. Ruthardt

Using large-print type, this volume presents some of the easiest movements from Clementi's sonatinas for study by the young student. Included are the *Sonatinas*, Op. 36, Nos. 1 and 5 and two additional short pieces. (Peters.) Level 5.

Clementi: An Introduction to His Piano Works, ed. Schneider

Interesting collection of accessible works by Clementi, many of which are little known. This volume provides a good place to begin investigating intermediate works other than the sonatinas. (Alfred.) Levels 4–9.

Clementi: The First Book for Pianists, ed. Schneider

Contains the most accessible selections from the volume *Clementi: An Introduction to His Piano Works* (ed. J. Schneider). Most of these pieces are one or two printed pages, and were taken from his method *An Introduction to the Art of Playing on the Pianoforte* or from his supplement to the method *Second Part of Clementi's Introduction to the Art of Playing on the Pianoforte*. (Alfred.) Levels 4–6.

Additional Works for Study:
Op. 23, No. 1 Sonata in E-flat Major
Op. 23, No. 2 Sonata in F Major
Op. 23, No. 3 Sonata in E-flat Major
Op. 25, No. 2 Sonata in G Major

Op. 25, No. 3 Sonata in B-flat Major
Op. 10, No. 1 Sonata in A Major
Op. 10, No. 2 Sonata in D Major
Op. 37, No. 3 Sonata in D Major

CARL CZERNY (1791–1857) Austria

The prolific Czerny composed over 1,000 works, many of them for piano pedagogical purposes. He is considered by some as the founder of modern piano technique, and was known for his brilliant technique and sensitive playing. Czerny pupils included Liszt, Kullak and Leschetizky.

For many students it is most practical to play from a Czerny anthology that contains selected études of progressive difficulty. A brief sketch of many of the opuses is provided below, followed by a listing of some of the more practical anthologies. Czerny did not believe in methods for piano, and instead wrote a keyboard treatise, *Klavierschule* or *Complete Theoretical and Practical Piano Forte School* that was published in four volumes. Czerny is considered by some to be the founder of modern technique.

Keyboard School (Klavierschule), 1839

The *Keyboard School* is Czerny's keyboard treatise, published in four volumes. Volume I contains nineteen lessons devoted to fundamentals and beginning technique. Volume II contains sixteen chapters devoted to the problem of fingering. Volume III is devoted to interpretation and expression. The twenty chapters explore such topics as dynamics, improvising, melody playing, memory, public performance, sight reading, style, touch and so on. Found in Volume IV is a discussion of the interpretation of Beethoven's works and fugal playing as well as Czerny's characterization of the six styles of piano playing during his time. Many exercises, études and short pieces are included in the volume. Much of the wisdom contained herein was passed on to Leschetizky. See Études Opp. 299, 300, 335, 355, 399, 400 and 500.

First Instruction in Piano-Playing, ed. Ruthardt

Subtitled "100 Recreations," the pieces in this volume are Czerny's easiest works for pianists and are intended as repertoire, not études. Many are arrangements or adaptations of popular tunes of that time or of themes by other composers. A fine source of very easy Classical-period teaching pieces. (G. Schirmer.) Levels 1–3.

Études

100 Progressive Studies for the Piano, Op. 139

One of the few entire opuses from which intermediate students could work. Études are primarily shorter than one page. Although scale passages are present, fewer are found here than in his other collections. Many of these études are highly melodic, although most are also repetitious. (Many standard editions.) Levels 3–7.

125 Exercises for Passage-Playing, Op. 261

Short studies in various kinds of passage-playing. A useful collection. (Many standard editions.) Levels 8–10.

The School of Velocity, Op. 299

One of the most frequently studied opuses of Czerny's works. In contrast to Op. 139, the pages of this opus are filled with sixteenth and thirty-second notes, providing practice in development of finger agility through countless scales, broken chords, arpeggios and other passages. Études found here are generally two printed pages, though some are more extended. (Many standard editions.) Levels 8–10.

40 Daily Studies, Op. 337

Studies generally printed on two pages and divided into many sections by repeat signs. The sections are intended to be repeated over and over, according to the number of times indicated at the beginning of the study. (Alfred, Peters, G. Schirmer and other standard editions.) Levels 9–10.

Practical Method for Beginners, Op. 599

Another preferred opus in some teaching circles. The 100 short exercises are divided into sections with specific technical purposes such as "the first exercises for the thumb," "exercises exceeding an octave," "exercises in sharps and flats," "exercises in velocity" and so forth. The rate of progression is rapid. Some of the studies, especially from the middle of this opus to the end, could prove helpful to the young student who reads well and who is striving to develop agility. (Many standard editions.) Levels 2–7, mostly levels 5–7.

Preliminary School of Finger Dexterity, Op. 636

For the Czerny proponent working with an early-advanced student, many of these studies could prove helpful in developing facility and agility. (Many standard editions.) Level 9.

24 Studies for the Left Hand, Op. 718

For two hands, but the right hand generally plays only an accompanimental role. (Alfred, G. Schirmer and other standard editions.) Level 10.

The Art of Finger Dexterity, Op. 740

Set of extended études composed to develop facility. This is one of the most widely used sets of Czerny studies. Each deals with a specific technical problem named at the head of the piece, such as "chord passages," "stretches of great strength" and "light movement of the left hand." For the advanced performer. (Many standard editions.) Level 10.

Five-finger Studies, Op. 777

Short études for elementary students in which the right hand remains in set five-finger positions while the left-hand accompaniment features diatonic chords. This collection could be used for a beginning student to work on developing facility while simultaneously enhancing sight-reading skills. (Kalmus.) Levels 2–3.

160 Eight-Measure Exercises, Op. 821

Valuable for the advancing pianist, these brief studies provide the opportunity for concentrated work on a specific technical problem. One of the most practical of Czerny's advanced collections. (Alfred, Peters, G. Schirmer and other standard editions.) Level 10.

The Little Pianist, Op. 823

This useful volume contains exercises for beginners, although the music progresses rapidly to the intermediate level. This book can help develop a feel for playing common patterns in piano literature. (Alfred, Kalmus and other standard editions.) Levels 2–7, mostly levels 6–7.

30 New Studies in Technique, Op. 849

Intended as preparatory to the *School of Velocity*, Op. 299. The emphasis in this book is on the playing of scales, arpeggios and passagework through two-page études. (Alfred, Curci, Peters and other standard editions.) Level 8.

Miscellaneous Volumes

Czerny Selected Piano Studies, arranged in systematic order by Heinrich Germer, Volumes I and II

Germer, who was alive when Czerny was still writing, systematically organized many of the études into three volumes for teaching purposes.

He drew from many opuses including Op. 139, 261, 636, 829 and 849. This is one of the most practical volumes of Czerny works to use for teaching since the rate of progression is carefully paced, and many of the selected studies are short. (Alfred, Boston and others.) Volume I: Level 8; Volume II: Levels 9–10.

Selected Czerny Studies, Volumes I–III, ed. Liebling

Arranged in progressive order. (Presser.) Volume I: Levels 7–8; Volume II: Levels 9–10; Volume III: Level 10.

D

ANTON DIABELLI (1781–1858) Austria

Diabelli, a Viennese composer and music publisher best remembered for his connection to Beethoven, developed a profitable firm that published many of Franz Schubert's works. In his own writing he employed most of the compositional techniques of the Classic period. Although not surveyed here, the duets of Diabelli including *Pleasures of Youth (Sonatinas on Five Notes)*, Op. 163 and *Melodious Pieces*, Op. 149 should not be neglected for teaching purposes.

Sonatinas, Op. 151

Four works, important for the intermediate student and leading generally toward the playing of Beethoven's music. These works should occupy a stronger position within the standard sonatina literature. (Many standard editions.)

Sonatina in G Major, Op. 151, No. 1

The best known of the Diabelli sonatinas and one of the most useful in developing a right-hand legato and singing tone. The second movement *Scherzo* is a short and appealing work while the final *Rondo*, characterized by scales in both hands and chords in various positions, is the most difficult. Level 5.

Sonatina in F Major, Op. 151, No. 3

Jovial first movement *Allegro moderato* featuring a bright theme and many melodic embellishments. The dotted eighth-sixteenth motive must be played strictly to maintain its vitality. The slow movement presents a song-like melody above the sixteenth-note Alberti bass. The pastoral *Rondo* closing movement contains extensive right-hand crossings, and expanding and contracting hand positions. This movement needs facility. Level 7.

Sonatina in C Major, Op. 151, No. 4

The last movement, with its tarantella rhythm, is the most inspired. Levels 6–7.

Sonatinas, Op. 168

Seven works are contained in this opus. These sonatinas are perhaps slightly more difficult than those of Op. 151 but both collections provide fine Classical sonatina study material. (Many standard editions.)

Sonatina in F Major, Op. 168, No. 1

The graceful first movement presents a wide variety of articulations and an especially appealing "cuckoo" passage. The second movement, *Andante cantabile*, is aria-like, with a beautiful melody that appears in the left hand. The finale is the most motivating, featuring right-hand crossovers with crushed appoggiaturas. The performer needs to be able to play a rapid staccato melody. An enjoyable work to practice. Levels 6–7.

Sonatina in C Major, Op. 168, No. 3

The writing is highly sequential and easy to read, making this a possible repertoire choice as a student's first sonatina. Level 6.

Sonatina in D Major, Op. 168, No. 5

The opening *tempo di marcia* is an appealing movement, with dotted rhythms and block chords that need a full, rich sound. The second movement may help develop rhythmic accuracy and facility in chordal playing. The concluding *Rondo militaire* requires articulate passagework. Level 7.

Miscellaneous Volumes

Piano Pieces—Anton Diabelli, compiled and edited by Hinson

Contains pieces ranging from the very easy to intermediate levels. To be noted especially are the easy, ornamented *10 Short Pieces*. Also found in this collection is the famous waltz upon which Diabelli solicited variations from other composers, as well as a sonatina from Op. 168 and a duet. (Hinshaw.) Levels 2–6.

FRANZ DUSSEK (1731–1799) Bohemia

Franz Dussek was one of the first of the traveling piano virtuosos, and also eminent as a composer.

Eight Sonate

Easy to comprehend musically, these three-movement fast-slow-fast works are akin to the classical sonatinas of Kuhlau and Clementi. Many deserve to be better known and will provide fresh teaching literature from the Classical period. (Musica Antiqua Bohemica.) Level 6.

JAN LADISLAV DUSSEK (1760–1812) Bohemia

Piano virtuoso Jan Dussek, who knew C.P.E. Bach and met Clementi and Haydn, is considered to be one of the first players who could produce a true "singing" tone on the pianoforte. With an output consisting of over 50 piano sonatas and a number of shorter pieces, Dussek is also reputed to be the first concert artist to think of placing the grand piano sideways in front of the audience. He published the *Pianoforte Method* in 1800 and also the treatise *Dussek's Instructions on the Art of Playing the Pianoforte or Harpsichord* (1796).

Douze Leçons progressives danoises (Melodic Studies), Op. 16

Twelve single-movement "lessons" that actually resemble four three-movement sonatinas. (Musica Antiqua Bohemica.)

Six Sonatinas, Op. 19

These two-movement works are sometimes listed as Op. 20. The Lionel Salter edition for the Associated Board of the Royal Schools of Music has corrected many of the errors that have come down to us. The first three sonatinas are the best known. (Associated Board of the Royal Schools of Music, Kalmus, G. Schirmer and other standard editions.) Level 7.

Sonatina in G Major, Op. 19, No. 1

Tuneful writing and full sounds in the short first movement make this enjoyable for students who want to play more "advanced sounding" pieces. The left-hand Alberti bass changes frequently on the last beat of the measure, potentially creating technical problems. The last movement *Rondo* features an easy broken-chord accompaniment beneath an elegant melody requiring careful inflection. Effective writing, somewhat reminiscent of the moderately difficult Kuhlau sonatinas. Level 6.

Sonatina in E-flat Major, Op. 19, No. 6

The first movement especially provides a good stepping-stone to Kuhlau's works. The sound in both hands is fuller than in Clementi, almost Beethoven-like. An interesting and unusual selection. Level 7.

Sonate

The eight works in this collection are generally easier than the Haydn *Sonata in D Major*, Hob. XVI/37 and provide little-known alternative Classical-era literature. (Orbis.) Levels 7–8.

The Sufferings of the Queen of France, Op. 23

Interesting work in 10 sections expressing the feelings of the imprisoned Marie Antoinette. (Alfred.) Levels 8–9.

G

BALDASSARE GALUPPI (1706–1785) Italy

Galuppi's keyboard works were well-known in their day. His sonatas represent an important mid-stage in the development of sonata form, namely that period between the late-Baroque and Classical. Although Galuppi composed numerous sonatas (some say as many as 123), severe problems with their ordering exist. The determination of the correct movements even within each sonata is still a matter of debate.

Six Sonatas for Keyboard Instruments, ed. Woodcock

This volume presents an interesting combination of sonatas extracted from the numerous works of Galuppi. The textures are generally thin and the technical demands encompass scales, arpeggios, trills and some hand crossings. (Galaxy.) Levels 9–10.

H

CHARLES-LOUIS HANON (1819–1900) France

The Virtuoso Pianist

One of the best-known and most widely used sets of exercises ever composed. Pattern études that move up and down the keyboard, composed to help students acquire speed and strength. Constructed only on the white keys and easily learned by rote. (Many standard editions.) Levels 7–10.

JOHANN WILHELM HÄSSLER (1747–1822) Germany

Acquaintance of C.P.E. Bach and Mozart, and composer of many teaching pieces for amateurs. Hässler's works are less highly ornamented than the early teaching pieces of L. Mozart, W. A. Mozart and Haydn.

50 Pieces for Beginners, Op. 38 (Der Tonkreis)

Selections in Classical-era idiom and composed in a variety of keys, progressing rapidly in level of difficulty throughout the volume. The performer needs to pay careful attention to the many different articulations present. These works are primarily of historical significance. (Associated Board of the Royal Schools of Music.) Levels 1–8.

Six Easy Sonatas

Short, three-movement works. The middle movements present potential rhythmic complications. These works are appropriate for students who are not yet ready to play Haydn sonatas. Although not profound, these sonatas can help students gain additional finger facility to prepare for more difficult sonatas. See especially *Sonata No. III* which is only six pages long and is well written. (Peters.) Levels 8–9.

Five Sonatas, ed. Oberdoerffer

Included are works from *Six Easy Sonatas for Clavier or Pianoforte*, Parts III and IV, *Six Easy Sonatas*, Part II, and *Six Clavier Soli*, half easy, half difficult. (Peters.) Levels 9–10.

Additional Work for Study:
24 Studies in Waltz Form

FRANZ JOSEPH HAYDN (1732–1809) Austria

For many years, Haydn was in the service of the cultivated Hungarian Prince Esterházy, and was a successful example of a royal court musician. Anthony van Hoboken catalogued Haydn's music in *Joseph Haydn: Thematic-bibliographic Catalogue of Works*. Hoboken or "Hob." numbers identify the specific works. The Roman numeral represents the part of the catalogue covering a specific genre (XVI represents the piano sonatas) and the Arabic number indicates the particular sonata in that grouping. (Many standard editions. Particular editions are listed when a work may be difficult to find.)

Sonatinas

Works often considered to be sonatinas are those numbered Hob. XVI/4, 7, 8, 9, 10 and 11. All are early Haydn, composed before 1768. They were conceived for the harpsichord; however, the first publication around 1790 specified them for either harpsichord or pianoforte. The works Hob. XVI/4, 7 and 8 were originally titled *Divertimentos*. The works Hob. XVI/9, 10 and 11 were originally called sonatas. All of these works sometimes are grouped together and called sonatinas because of their brevity and lack of technical difficulties. However, due to their categorization by Hoboken, they are annotated here under the heading "Sonatas." These six works are Haydn's easiest in the Hoboken grouping XVI.

Sonatas

Haydn's *sonatas* reveal the evolution of the artistic development which spanned his life. His earliest multi-movement compositions were titled *Divertimentos* or *Partitas* and are included here.

Sonata in C Major, Hob. XVI/1

The first movement consists primarily of a left-hand Alberti-bass accompaniment in sixteenths against right-hand quarter notes with rapid ornaments. The final *Minuet* consists of sparse textures and elegant writing. A good choice for a performer with strong fingers and a sense of style. Not difficult. Levels 7–8.

Sonata in C Major, Hob. XVI/3

Left-hand triplet broken chords permeate the first movement while the final *Minuet and Trio* is more inspired. Levels 7–8.

Divertimento [Sonata] in D Major, Hob. XVI/4

Strong opening movement with rhythmic and musical interest. Worth investigating. Level 8.

Sonata in G Major, Hob. XVI/6

This sonata is in a different category from the earlier, more sonatina-like works. Opening with a descending triplet broken triad, this sonata contains many different rhythms in the first movement. The fourth movement finale is one of the easiest and most brilliant movements in the sonatas. The fast passagework is effective. Level 8.

Divertimento [Sonata] in C Major, Hob. XVI/7

The three movements are quite brief, the first comprising only 23 measures and opening with fanfare-like block chords. The *Minuet* and *Trio* are elegant and feasible for students with modest technical ability. Level 6.

Divertimento [Sonata] in G Major, Hob. XVI/8

Again the wide variety in rhythmic values used makes this movement more difficult than it first appears. However for a student with a strong sense of pulse and agile fingers, the changes from duplets to triplets can be exciting. The dotted figures of the main theme and the off-beat punctuations in the second theme are engaging. The *Minuet* and *Andante* are both charming and easy. The brief final *Allegro* is ebullient and presents no potentially tricky rhythms or passages. It is often found separately in anthologies. Level 7.

Sonata in F Major, Hob. XVI/9

The diminutive first movement opens with a full chordal sound and dotted rhythms. The many quick trills add to the difficulty. The last movement is heard frequently and is known as *Scherzo in F*. It contains no rhythmic complexities and the continuous sixteenths make it effective in performance. Level 7.

Sonata in C Major, Hob. XVI/10

Again diversity of rhythms in a short first movement augments this work's complexity. The appealing and playful figure in the opening measures permeates the entire texture. The following two brief movements are also accessible. Level 7.

Sonata in G Major, Hob. XVI/11

Three-movement work, printed on four pages in some editions. Brief *Presto* 3/8 first movement opens with spirited right-hand sixteenth notes above left-hand octaves. Difficulties in this short popular movement lie primarily in the coordination of the fast passagework and the many mordants that are to be played quickly. Sophisticated *Andante* slow movement follows. A charming *Menuet and Trio* requires refined inflection and phrasing in the interpretation. This frequently heard work is especially well-suited for a mature performer. Level 7.

Sonata in A Major, Hob. XVI/12

Opening with a beautiful *Andante* featuring flowing triplets and a naturally expressive cantilena melody, this work is especially appropriate for the advancing performer who is sensitive. The *Trio* forms a strong contrast to the elegant *Minuet* in the second movement, and the third movement is another perpetual motion in 3/8 with lively sixteenth-note passagework that fits the hand well. Strong rhythmic propulsion through the movement. Level 7.

Sonata in E Major, Hob. XVI/13

Interesting writing in a rhythmic first movement that is boldly announced by a full E-Major chord. The *Minuet* and *Trio* are attractive, and Haydn's humor and good nature come through clearly in the driving *Finale*. This effective movement sounds more difficult than it is. Level 8.

Sonata in F Major, Hob. XVI/23

An effective sonata especially when performed in its entirety. The first movement is intriguing harmonically, and the passagework in the development fits the hand well. The *Adagio* features a beautiful cantilena melody in an extremely moving and well-written movement, while the *Finale* is lively and energetic with disjunct two-note slurs making up its theme. Levels 9–10.

Sonata in G Major, Hob. XVI/27

Opening with ornamental turns around G and then B in the opening measure, this movement features a development section that is particularly dramatic and achieves convincing use of Alberti basses and broken octaves. The *Minuet* and *Trio* also are effective while the propulsive *Finale* is written primarily in eighths with some sixteenth-note passages to lend even more drama. A good choice as a performer's first major Haydn sonata. Levels 8–9.

Sonata in E Minor, Hob. XVI/34

An accessible and popular sonata. The sixteenth-note passagework and octaves lend a sense of festivity to the opening *Presto* movement, in which the double-note passages require true legato. The *Adagio* requires sensitivity, while the *Molto vivace* finale is rollicking and lively. Level 9.

Sonata in C Major, Hob. XVI/35

The first movement, with its incessant triplet accompaniment in broken triads, is one of the best-known of the Haydn sonata movements. In many ways it is more difficult than it appears, since the triplet accompaniment needs technical endurance and the extended form requires a performer with a sense of its overall structure. The *Finale* is much more accessible and is one of the most approachable of the Haydn finales. Level 8.

Sonata in D Major, Hob. XVI/37

Perhaps Haydn's best-known first movement. The opening grace note introduces the character of this cheerful movement that requires overall endurance and attention to articulation. More difficult than it is usually perceived to be. The brief but moving *Largo e sostenuto* requires careful attention to rhythmic complexities, while the *Finale*, accessible although not profound, is filled with high spirits. Level 8.

Sonata in G Major, Hob. XVI/39

The first movement is similar to the *Scherzando* from the *Sonata*, Hob. XVI/36 although the Hob. XVI/39 movement is more extended. This movement is especially appropriate for the performer with an ear for detailed inflection. The final movement features syncopated right-hand passagework. Level 9.

Sonata in G Major, Hob. XVI/40

The first movement, *Allegretto innocente*, consists of a theme with variations that contain rapid passagework and requires a strong musical conception. The second and final movement, *Presto*, is a lively rondo, with repeated notes and rapid scale passages that fit the hand well. Level 9.

Variation Sets

Arietta with 20 Variations, Hob. XVII/2

A-Major theme with 19 variations, calling for rapid fingerwork. Levels 7–8.

Arietta with 12 Variations, Hob. XVII/3

This fine variation set, featuring interesting harmonies and chromaticism, is stronger in quality than XVII/2. The music requires attention to voicing as well as to details of articulation and phrasing. Appropriate for the musical performer. Level 10.

Dances

Many of the minuets, German dances and other similar pieces in this section are transcriptions. Some are originally composed by Haydn and some are of doubtful origin but attributed to him. The dances were originally composed for orchestra or military bands and often were heard at private occasions of the wealthy. Many were later transcribed for keyboard. While some of the transcriptions may be from Haydn himself, some were transcribed by others unknown. Of the dances, Hob. IX/4a, IX/10, IX/13, IX/21 and IX/22 are doubtful or spurious.

German Dances

Haydn composed numerous works with this title, many of which appear in anthologies. These include the allemandes and such works as *12 German Dances*, Hob. IX/11 and *12 German Dances*, Hob. IX/12 (transcribed at the request of the Empress). These works have become popular teaching pieces. Levels 4–7.

Minuets

Like the *German Dances*, these works are primarily transcriptions from instrumental scorings such as those in *12 Minuets*, Hob. IX/3 for two violins, bass, flute, two oboes, bassoon and two horns. An excellent teaching edition of the *Minuets* is the *24 Minuets*, Hob. IX/8 and Hob. IX/10 in the Associated Board publication. Additional groupings of the *Minuets* include *Six Minuets*, Hob. IX/4a, *12 Minuets*, Hob. IX/8, *Six Minuets*, Hob. IX/9, *12 Minuets*, Hob. IX/11 and *12 Minuets*, Hob. IX/21. All were transcriptions of now-lost orchestral originals. The writing is sometimes awkward rhythmically and technically. (Associated Board of the Royal Schools of Music and other editions.) Levels 5–8.

12 Short Pieces

Well-known teaching pieces, many of which have appeared in early-intermediate anthologies. All are transcriptions. (Alfred.) Levels 4–8.

No. 2 Allegro Scherzando (from String Quartet, Hob. III/75/4)

One of the most popular and good-natured of Haydn's teaching pieces. A witty and lively movement with sudden dynamic contrasts. Needs careful attention to articulation. Level 8.

No. 11 Vivace Assai (from Symphony No. 89)

A vigorous work with rapid Alberti bass and driving rhythms. Especially suitable for the energetic performer. Level 7.

Miscellaneous Pieces

Pieces for Musical Clock

Both Haydn and Mozart created many works for the Flötenuhr or musical clock, a then-popular device rather like a cross between a self-playing small organ and a timed music box. Many of these short pieces are effective today on the modern piano. They feature ornaments and some complex rhythms, but predominantly are light and winsome, and mostly confined to the treble clef in both hands. The Associated Board of the Royal Schools of Music volume has selected 16 of the 32 Haydn composed. These could work well on an electronic keyboard set to simulate the flute sound of the original musical clocks. (Associated Board of the Royal Schools of Music.) Levels 7–8.

Miscellaneous Volumes

At the Piano With Haydn, ed. Hinson

Contains an interesting cross-section of works by Haydn including many lesser-known works such as a song Hob. XIX/19, *Scherzo* ("The Coffee Party") and others. Begins with a fine preface containing information about dynamics, ornamentation and phrasing in Haydn. (Alfred.) Levels 4–9.

Haydn: An Introduction to His Keyboard Works, ed. Lucktenberg

Extensive notes on biography and performance practice. Works found here include *Allegro Moderato in C Major*, Hob. XVI/7, *Arietta and Variations in A Major*, Hob. XVII/2, *Finale* from *Sonata in A Major*, Hob. XVI/12, *Menuet and Trio* and *Finale* from *Sonata in A Major*, Hob. XVI/26, and *Minuet and Trio in C*, Hob. XVI/3. Practical performing edition with an excellent variety of literature. (Alfred.) Levels 3–10.

Haydn: The First Book for Pianists, ed. Lucktenberg

Contains the most accessible pieces from *Haydn: An Introduction to His Keyboard Works* (ed. Lucktenberg). (Alfred.) Levels 3–7.

Eight Selected Sonatas, ed. Raymar

Features some of the more accessible and best sonatas for the early-advanced student. A source of some fresh works for teaching. Among others, the following sonatas appear: *C Major*, Hob. XVI/15, *A Major*, Hob. XVI/30, *D Major*, Hob. XVI/24, and *D Major*, Hob. XVI/14. (Associated Board of the Royal Schools of Music.) Level 9.

Selected Keyboard Sonatas, Volumes 1–4, ed. Ferguson

An excellent teaching edition, with the editorial suggestions differentiated from the original text by brackets. Suggested realizations of ornaments are provided. The volumes are affordable and contain respectively nine, five, five and four sonatas. (Associated Board of the Royal Schools of Music.) Levels 9–10.

The Easier Haydn, ed. Barsham

Contains 19 pieces, most of which are easier movements taken from the sonatas. The editor's markings appear as dotted lines, in brackets or are otherwise differentiated from original markings. This is a good source for the teacher seeking easy Haydn sonata movements. (Elkin.) Levels 6–8.

JAMES HEWITT (1792–1827) Great Britain

James Hewitt was a professional organist and violinist in London before settling in America when he was 22.

Selected Compositions, ed. Wagner

A scholarly volume that contains attractive intermediate-level compositions by this early American composer. Some of these intriguing selections may be found in other anthologies. (Recent Researches in American Music—A-R Editions, Inc.) Levels 7–9.

JAMES HOOK (1746–1827) Great Britain

A highly prolific composer and one of the most popular organists in England in the 18th century.

12 Sonatinas, Op. 12, ed. Salter

The sonatinas in this collection are of high quality. Most of the first movements are quite short (many occupy the space of one printed page) and are in abbreviated sonatina form. See especially *No. 6 in G Major*. The *Sonatina No. 9 in F Major* is also of interest. (Associated Board of the Royal Schools of Music.)

Sonatina No. 5 in B-flat

Two-movement work, each movement one page long, with strong contrast between the *Allegro* of the first movement and the *Allegretto* of the rondo movement. Level 6.

Sonatina No. 6 in G Major

Fine preparation for the Clementi sonatinas in a work that features interesting and concise writing. The full chords at the beginning of the first movement lend a pompous air and help make this a student favorite. This movement calls for fine inflection of melodic passages in the right hand. Level 6.

Guida di Musica, Parts I (1785) and II (1794)

Part I is an instruction book for beginners, with 24 progressive lessons. Part II contains fingering examples and exercises. Primarily of historical significance. (Broude.)

JOHANN NEPOMUK HUMMEL (1778–1837) Austria

Hummel was a contemporary of Beethoven, famous in Europe as a virtuoso pianist. His studies are polished and facile.

Pianoforte School

A massive keyboard tutor containing over 2,200 musical examples and a wealth of information. Hummel foreshadowed the modern system of fingering. Many of the works included were mere exercises, but the longer ones are appealing and delightful miniatures. The well-known *Scherzo in A (Klavierschule, No. 45)* appears in many anthologies. Levels 5–9.

Six Pièces Très Faciles, Op. 52

These works were composed around 1815 (and published as part of Hummel's series *Répertoire de musique pour les dames*). See especially No. 3 *Tempo di Menuetto*, No. 4 *Romance: con dolcezza*, No. 5 *Écossaise* and No. 6 *Rondo-vivace*. Four pieces from the entire set appear in Hummel's *16 Short Pieces* (Associated Board of the Royal Schools of Music, ed. Roberts) and are short Classical-style works, generally in two voices with single-note melody and broken-chord accompaniment. Level 7.

Allegro in C Major, Op. 52, No. 2

Features Scarlatti-like playfulness, changes of register and appealing staccato passages. Interesting and unusual as a repertoire choice. Level 6.

Miscellaneous Volumes

16 Short Pieces, ed. Roberts

The most practical of the currently available collections of Hummel's accessible works for teaching. Contains four pieces from *Six Very Easy Pieces*, Op. 52 and 12 pieces from the *Keyboard School*. (Associated Board of the Royal Schools of Music.) Levels 7–9.

Allegretto in C Major, Klavierschule, No. 50

Sonatina-style work in ABA form. Animated and lively writing. Level 7.

Additional Work for Study:
Op. 67 (or 63) Preludes in all Major and Minor Keys

FRANZ HÜNTEN (1793–1878) Germany

Nine Rondos, Opp. 21, 30, 48

Light selections, several of which bear titles, often featuring broken-chord accompaniments and lively, single-note melodies. (Ricordi.) Levels 8–9.

K

FRIEDRICH KUHLAU (1786–1832) Germany

While born in Germany, Kuhlau spent most of his years living and composing in Denmark where he served as a royal court composer. He is widely known for his compositions for flute, as well as for the piano sonatinas.

Sonatinas, Op. 20

The first movements of these three works have become standards of the sonatina literature, but the other movements are little known. Appropriate pieces to succeed some of the more difficult sonatinas from Clementi Op. 36, and as a whole perhaps slightly more difficult than the Kuhlau *Sonatinas*, Op. 55. (Many standard editions.)

Sonatina in C Major, Op. 20, No. 1

The first movement is especially appropriate for performers with facility in playing an Alberti bass and for those who have a dramatic flair. Requires fast fingerwork. The slow movement is much shorter than many at this level; its rhythmic complexities will need special attention. The rondo is essentially light, with facile passagework in the right hand and rapid Alberti basses in the left. Level 6.

Sonatina in G Major, Op. 20, No. 2

The change from duplets to triplets in the first movement calls for a strong rhythmic sense. The repeated notes should not sound harsh. More difficult than it appears on the page. The *Adagio* is an especially beautiful movement that calls for musical maturity of a level beyond the technical requirements of this sonatina. The infrequently heard final movement, *Allegro scherzando*, is the strongest of the set and requires musical and interpretative maturity. It could be performed by the student with flair and finesse who is not quite ready to tackle the Haydn sonatas. Level 7.

Sonatina in F Major, Op. 20, No. 3

The effective first movement is relatively well known, perhaps because of the drama in the *sforzando* and the attractive hand crossings. The changes from eighth notes to triplets to sixteenth notes require a secure rhythmic sense. The *Larghetto* provides fine preparation for the student to play Haydn sonata slow movements. The final *Allegro polacca* requires agile fingerwork and a strong sense of rhythmic drive. It is toccata-like, with many clichés. Level 7.

Sonatinas, Op. 55

The first three sonatinas of this set of six are well known, while the last three are difficult to find in modern editions. (Standard editions.) Level 7.

Sonatina in C Major, Op. 55, No. 1

This two-movement sonata is justifiably one of the most popular. Its cheerful and well-constructed opening movement is highly melodic.

The *Vivace* movement calls for strong fingers, and sounds more difficult than it really is. Strong and consistent writing throughout. Level 6.

Sonatina in G Major, Op. 55, No. 2

Another good-natured work. A brief cantabile slow movement is sandwiched between a strong opening movement and a *Scherzando* finale. Level 6.

Sonatina in C Major, Op. 55, No. 3

A popular sonatina that consists of only two movements. The first movement features right-hand parallel sixths and rapid scales. The *grazioso* final movement is heard less frequently, but is charming. Level 6.

Sonatina in D Major, Op. 55, No. 5

The dotted rhythms in the march-like first movement lend appeal, while the second movement requires typical fast fingerwork without Alberti bass accompaniments. Level 7.

Sonatina in C Major, Op. 55, No. 6

One of the most Mozartian of the sonatinas, featuring elegant writing and displaying a strong affinity to a chamber work. Level 7.

Sonatinas, Opp. 59 and 60

Each opus contains three sonatinas. The Op. 60 sonatas are slightly more interesting. All of these works provide appropriate preparation for the playing of Haydn sonatas. (G. Schirmer and other standard editions.)

Sonatina in F Major, Op. 60, No. 1

Two-movement work in which the first movement is a jovial *Allegro* in 6/8 with effective passagework and numerous dramatic effects. The last movement is a theme and four variations, based on a march-like tune of Rossini, and builds to a brilliant conclusion. Level 8.

Sonatina in A Major, Op. 60, No. 2

Another two-movement work, again concluding with a variation set on a theme of Rossini. This effective last movement is perhaps more difficult technically than any other movement of the Kuhlau sonatinas. Level 9.

Sonatina in C Major, Op. 60, No. 3

Intriguing writing in the first movement where the figuration changes dramatically for each section of the exposition. The development begins with chorale-like writing in long note values, which is then integrated into the first theme. Level 9.

Sonatinas, Op. 88

Four sonatinas are contained in this fine opus. These works have considerably fewer ornaments than the early Haydn sonatas and provide interesting repertoire alternatives. (G. Schirmer and other standard editions.)

Sonatina in C Major, Op. 88, No. 1

Sparkling, highly patterned writing in a first movement that is filled with scales, often in the left hand. Short and accessible slow movement. The final *Rondo* is vigorous and exciting. It contains a boisterous accompaniment in broken chords. A viable alternative to one of the easier Haydn sonata movements. Level 7.

Sonatina in G Major, Op. 88, No. 2

The highly lyrical first movement is devoid of sixteenth-note passages with the only rapid passagework occurring in the triplet arpeggiated chords. Suitable for the performer who plays lyrical writing well. The virtuosic final *Rondo* contains quick right-hand figuration. Worth investigating. Level 7.

Sonatina in A Minor, Op. 88, No. 3

The final movement, *Allegro burlesco*, is a performer's favorite because of its dazzling chromatic passages and irresistible *acciaccaturas*. Level 8.

Sonatina in F Major, Op. 88, No. 4

Note the final movement, *Alla polacca*, with the syncopations and *risoluto* writing. Contains some rather difficult sequences of quick two-note slurs. This movement might serve as an interesting substitute to the *Allegro burlesco* movement of the Op. 88, No. 3 sonatina. Levels 7–8.

Additional Work for Study:
Op. 40 Six Easy Rondos

L

JEAN THEODORE LATOUR (1766–1837) France

While born in France, Latour became the pianist and composer to King George IV of England.

Four Sonatas (Sonatinas)

Generally known as "sonatinas," these highly accessible works provide ideal pre-Clementi study material. The writing is idiomatic and the movements generally are short (often one printed page). The absence of double notes and the abundance of typical classical figurations make this a collection that should be better known. Less rhythmically intricate than many of the easiest Mozart teaching pieces. See especially *Sonatina No. 1 in C* and *Sonatina No. 2 in G*. (Elkan.) Level 4.

Sonatina No. 1 in C Major

The best known of the set and appears in many anthologies. The first movement employs extensive use of the C Major scale, with the left hand generally restricted to C five-finger patterns with extensions. The *Pastorale* is a graceful aria in 6/8 in which the left hand features an Alberti bass throughout. The concluding *Rondo* provides a left-hand workout for evenness and control. In all, a good sonatina to be studied in its entirety. Level 3.

Sonata No. 2 in G Major

The first movement can be played by a student who is facile in playing an Alberti bass. One of the easiest sonatina movements in the repertoire. Level 3.

CHRISTIAN LATROBE (1758–1836) Great Britain

Three Sonatas, Op. 3

Haydn-like characteristics in a work that is easy to read and contains relatively thin textures. These works would provide an intriguing substitute for some of the Haydn sonatas. Most of the movements are fairly short. (Boosey.) Level 9.

HENRY LEMOINE (1786–1854) France

Études Enfantines, Op. 37

Two books of charming études for the upper-intermediate student. They could substitute for the Czerny-Germer études. See especially *Études* Nos. 3, 6, 8, 14, 17, 34, 35, 36 and 44. (Kalmus, G. Schirmer.) Levels 7–8.

FRANCISZEK LESSEL (1780–1838) Poland
Three Sonatas, Op. 2

Interesting Classical writing that is less highly ornamented than that of Haydn or Mozart, and features long cantabile lines. (PWM.) Levels 9–10.

M

FRANZ XAVIER MOZART (1791–1844) Austria

See listing under the Romantic period.

LEOPOLD MOZART (1719–1787) Austria, born Germany

One of the finest and best-known violinists in Europe, Leopold Mozart was also a composer and theorist, to say nothing of being father to Nannerl and Wolfgang Mozart. After 1758 Leopold Mozart devoted himself to the education of his children. In the process of educating Wolfgang, he served as teacher, copyist and proofreader for his son's early compositions. Leopold's famous treatise *Fundamentals of Violin Playing* (1756) is on the par with Quantz's *Treatise on Playing the Traverse Flute* and C.P.E. Bach's *Essay on the True Art of Playing the Keyboard Instrument*.

Notebook for Nannerl (1759)

This collection of pieces for Leopold's daughter Nannerl is akin to the *Anna Magdalena Bach Notebook*, in that it is a didactic collection intended for family use. The *Notebook for Nannerl* served not only to provide pieces for her study but also provided some pieces for her little brother, Wolfgang, who was then not yet four. The original notebook contained 20 minuets, one polonaise and 20 other pieces not in dance form (such as andantes, scherzi, marches and allegros) as well as several original pieces by young W. A. Mozart.

The *Notebook for Nannerl* progresses in level of difficulty from the level of easy minuets to that of more difficult sonatinas. Frequent ornaments such as turns, trills and appoggiaturas as well as occasional passages in thirds present challenges to the less-experienced player. The Universal edition, edited by Hans Kann, contains a selection of 41 pieces (excluding those of W. A. Mozart). The Associated Board of the Royal Schools of Music, ed. by Lionel Salter, contains 21 pieces. The shorter Schott edition is also a good study edition. (Associated Board of the Royal Schools of Music, Schott, Universal and other editions.) Levels 2–7.

WOLFGANG AMADEUS MOZART (1756–1791) Austria

Wolfgang Amadeus Mozart was perhaps the greatest of musical geniuses, dying at the early age of 35 but leaving a heritage of unique beauty. Ludwig von Köchel, an Austrian scientist who pursued music as a hobby, was led to catalogue the composer's works because of his love of Mozart's music. Alfred Einstein, German musicologist and cousin of Albert Einstein, revised Köchel's catalogue in 1937 and again in 1947. Original K. (Köchel) numbers are given with revised K. numbers in parentheses. (Many standard editions. Particular editions are listed when a work may be difficult to find.)

(Earliest original compositions)

Mozart's earliest attempts at composition include an andante and an allegro composed at age five, four *Minuets* K. 1, 2, 4 and 5, and an *Allegro*, K. 3. These works were notated in the *Notebook for Nannerl* and are often a student's first Mozart compositions. Level 4.

Sonatas, K. 6–8

Some of these curious early works by Wolfgang had violin accompaniments added to them, perhaps by his father, Leopold. Several movements appear in anthologies such as the *Minuet I* and *Minuet II* of the *Sonata in C*, K. 6 and the *Minuet I* of the *Sonata in D*, K. 7. Levels 6–7.

London Musical Notebook, K. 15

This work contains 42 pieces composed by Mozart at the age of eight, during the time the Mozart family spent in London, 1764–65. Actually many of the pieces were composed in nearby Chelsea, where the family often stayed during this time because of Leopold's health problems. Thus this notebook is sometimes referred to as the "Chelsea Notebook." The works probably were written without Leopold's supervision. Many of these pieces are only sketches, and the manuscript contains numerous oversights including missing notes, dots, rests and mistakes in barring. Included in the *London Notebook* are *allegros, andantes,* dance movements and movements of sonatas. Many of the works in the notebook appear to be sketches for orchestral works, and indeed it was at this time that Mozart's earliest symphonies were written. The works are numbered in the Köchel catalogue from 15a to 15qq and are at least as interesting from a historical perspective as they are important in today's teaching repertoire. Many appear in teaching collections and anthologies. Levels 6–7.

Six "Viennese" Sonatinas, K. Anh. 229 (K. 439b)

These works are part of the very few teaching works which are transcriptions from instrumental compositions but still accepted into the standard teaching literature. Mozart originally composed them in 1738 as *Wind Divertimenti*, K. 439b for two bass horns and bassoon. (At that point in time, 13 of the 19 solo keyboard sonatas had been composed.)

The piano arranger is unknown, although some feel that it may have been Ferdinand Kauer. The order of movements was not the same as in the original: some of the trios were exchanged, and some of the recapitulations shortened. The first edition of the arrangement was published in 1803 by the Viennese firm of Artaria. These sophisticated pieces make a fine introduction to Mozart's keyboard music.

Viennese Sonatina No. 1 in C Major

The first movement is perhaps the most popular movement from all of the sonatinas. It is fanfare-like, with several short contrapuntal passages within a true sonata-allegro form. The strong contrast between its many ideas needs to be emphasized in performance. Needs careful attention to detail. The *Menuetto* contains inspired writing also and would be especially appropriate as a model of Mozart's minuet-and-trio style. A brief ornamented *Adagio* of typical Mozartian expressiveness and transparency leads to a sprightly *Allegro* which requires a singing legato and careful execution of many different articulations. Robust writing with rapid hand shifts. Level 8.

Viennese Sonatina No. 2 in A Major

The *Allegro* first movement contains elegant writing that demands a sensitive, mature performer with the ability to inflect small groups of notes. This could be a good predecessor to the *Sonata in G Major*, K. 283. It is more difficult musically than technically. Both the *Menuetto* and *Adagio* contain strong writing. The concluding *Rondo*, with its quick tempo and good-humored passagework should also be noted. This entire sonata represents some of Mozart's strongest melodic inspiration. Level 9.

Viennese Sonatina No. 3 in D Major

Shorter and less well known than the other sonatinas. In three movements, this work would be most interesting to a student whose musical intellect exceeds his technical ability. Level 8.

Viennese Sonatina No. 4 in B-flat Major

The first movement, *Andante grazioso*, is frequently found in anthologies. It features inspired melodic writing that calls for a fine legato, especially in the double-third passages. The variety of note values in the last movement, *Romanze-Andante*, demands rhythmic security. Level 8.

Viennese Sonatina No. 5 in F Major

The opening *Adagio* contains some of the most easily grasped lyrical passages in the *Viennese Sonatinas*, with little contrast of ideas. The extended *Menuetto* leads to a short spirited *Polonaise*, perhaps the shortest movement in the sonatinas, and one of the most accessible. This sonatina is often found in anthologies and collections. Level 7.

Viennese Sonatina No. 6 in C Major

This sonatina is one of the best known and some of Mozart's most elegant writing is found here. The *Allegro* requires a clean and precise technique, and the ability to deal with several complicated concepts. The brief third movement *Adagio* can aid in the development of a singing legato while the concluding *Polonaise* is as vivacious as the opening. Strong fingers are needed for double-note passages in both hands. Level 8.

Sonatas

Generally the keyboard sonatas are more difficult musically and technically than they appear on the page. Within them, Mozart explores the expressive qualities of the piano. The most approachable ones are listed here.

Sonata in F Major, K. 280 (189e)

The opening *Allegro assai* is the most frequently encountered. The various rhythmic values that are juxtaposed require a performer with a strong rhythmic sense. The slow movement is especially beautiful. Level 10.

Sonata in E-flat Major, K. 282 (189g)

A three-movement work and the only Mozart sonata with an *Adagio* first movement. The middle-position *Menuetto I* and *II* are easy. The closing *Allegro* is spirited and Haydn-esque, and should be more frequently heard. Level 9.

Sonata in G Major, K. 283 (189h)

The gallant first movement is not much more difficult than some movements of the *Viennese Sonatinas*. The second movement calls for a sensitive performer, and the last movement can be technically awkward with its double-third passages. Level 9.

Sonata in A Major, K. 331 (300i)

A popular work, consisting of a first-movement theme and variations, a minuet and finally the famous *Alla turca* rondo. The broken octaves concluding the sonata can provide a technical gauge of difficulty, though in general the earlier two movements are much more difficult. Level 10.

Sonata in C Major, K. 545 "Sonata Facile"

The most immediately recognizable of the Mozart sonatas. Fingering considerations and evenness of passagework play an important role in the study of the first movement. The second and third movements are equally strong. The third movement is perhaps the easiest technically of all Mozart sonata movements. It is spirited, yet gracious and rewarding for the intermediate performer. This sonata should be performed in its entirety more often. Levels 7–8.

Sonata in B-flat Major, K. 570

The first movement is especially suited for a sensitive, lyrical performer. A finely honed legato is a requirement for the slow movement, while the concluding rondo needs good finger technique. The entire sonata requires musical maturity. Level 10.

Variations

Mozart composed 14 variation sets that survive complete. They were likely conceived for his own concert use, and tend to be based on popular themes of the day.

Seven Variations on "Willem Van Nassau," K. 25

This is based on what was in essence a Dutch national anthem, a highly popular work at Mozart's time. An appealing set that is not exceptionally long and might provide an interesting change of fare. Level 7.

12 Variations on "Ah, vous dirai-je, Maman," K. 300e (265)

Based on the same tune as "Twinkle, Twinkle, Little Star," this endearing variation set is recognized instantly. More difficult than most realize, but eminently appealing. Level 8.

Miscellaneous Works

Sonata in G Minor, K. 312 (K. 189a)

A single-movement work, not especially substantial, but available separately or in several collections. Similar in difficulty to the *Viennese Sonatinas*. Level 7.

Eight Minuets and Trios, K. 315a (315g)

Composed in 1779, these works may be an orchestral reduction by Mozart. Most of them use double notes in the right hand, which comprise the primary technical problems. Shorter and less difficult than the *Viennese Sonatinas*. Nos. 1, 3 and 4 are the most frequently heard. Especially suited for the older student with stronger hands who seeks an introduction to Mozart's sophisticated writing. (Henle and others.) Level 7.

Adagio for a Glass Harmonica in C Major, K. 356 (K. 617a)

A highly expressive work, originally composed for a now virtually obsolete instrument. Right-hand double notes will need careful voicing. Level 7.

Fantasy in D Minor, K. 397 (385g)

Strongly contrasting sections, calling for mature interpretation and characterization. The opening is clearly suggestive of Mozart's improvisational style. Careful attention should be paid to the inflection of short motives, especially in the melancholy section that follows the opening. The work was left unfinished, and the last 10 measures were added in 1806 by an unknown composer who was, according to Willard Palmer, possibly A. E. Müller, the author of a popular piano method. Much more difficult than it appears, this fantasy is often assigned before students are truly ready. (Many standard editions.) Level 10.

Marche Funebre del signor maestro contrapuncto in C Minor, K. 453a

Humorous work composed by Mozart for his student Barbara Ployer after she had just studied the *Concerto in G Major*, K. 453. Needs control of touch in the changes from large chordal writing to thinner duet textures. Orchestrally conceived with an adventurous harmonic scheme. Level 8.

Rondo in D Major, K. 485

The most accessible of the rondos, although by no means an easy work. The main theme was originally used by Johann Christian Bach and also appears in Mozart's *Piano Quartet in G Minor*, K. 478. Arguably a monothematic sonata-allegro movement; appropriate as the opening work for a solo recital. (Many standard editions.) Level 10.

German Dances

These several sets were originally scored for instrumental ensembles. Many appeared first in piano arrangements in Artaria and Co. editions. Köchel listings include *Six German Dances*, K. 509, *Six German Dances*, K. 567, *Six German Dances*, K. 600, and *Four German Dances*, K. 602. Generally the individual dances are spirited and provide fine student study material at the intermediate level. Many appear in anthologies and collections. Levels 7–9.

Miscellaneous Volumes

Wolfgang Mozart: Piano Music From His Early Years, ed. Hinson

Excellent biographical and stylistic information. This volume includes several minuets and country dances. (Alfred.) Levels 3–5.

At the Piano With Mozart, ed. Hinson

Contains an interesting selection, including pieces from the *London Musical Notebook* and miscellaneous teaching pieces. Valuable preface contains information about Mozart as a teacher and performer, and concerning Mozart and the 18th-century keyboard. (Alfred.) Levels 3–9.

W. A. Mozart: An Introduction to His Keyboard Works, ed. Palmer

The introductory material includes biographical and performance practice information. Works found here include several minuets, two contradances and movements from the *Sonatas* K. 282 and K. 545. (Alfred.) Levels 3–8.

Mozart: The First Book for Young Pianists, ed. Palmer

Excellent. Includes minuets, contradances and other works. (Alfred.) Levels 3–5.

My First Mozart: The Classics for Young Pianists

A scholarly anthology that presents pieces written by Mozart between the ages of five and 12. The first 10 pieces were from Mozart's first composition notebook, while Nos.11–15 come from the *London Musical Notebook*.

Fingering is editorial, and other markings by the editor are distinguished from the original text. These short minuets, andantes and other movements are more difficult than they appear. (Ricordi.) Levels 6–7.

Easy Keyboard Pieces from the London Notebook

Found here are nine selections for intermediate students taken from the *London Musical Notebook*. The text is edited appropriately for study by young students. Included are various movements such as minuets, allegros and other works. (Breitkopf.) Levels 6–7.

The Young Mozart

Contains some of the easiest original pieces composed by Mozart when he was six to eight years of age. Most are from the *London Musical Notebook* although several are Wolfgang's works taken from the *Notebook for Nannerl*. (Schott.) Levels 4–6.

Additional Works for Study:

K. 24 Variations on "Laat ons juichen" by Graaf (1766)

K. 180 Variations on "Mio caro Adone" by Salieri (1773)

K. 179 Variations on a Minuet by Fischer (1774)

JOSEF MYSLIVEČEK (1737–1782) Bohemia

The musical style of Mysliveček closely resembles that of Mozart, even to the point that Mozart was credited with a work that Mysliveček composed. The latter died in poverty in Rome, even though his works enjoyed enormous success. Since his name was so difficult to pronounce, Italians called him "the divine Bohemian."

Six Easy Divertimentos, ed. Salter

All are in one movement, generally two to four printed pages with da capos. Elegant Classical literature. (Associated Board of the Royal Schools of Music.)

Divertimento No. 1

Alberti bass, might substitute for a Clementi sonatina. Features a wide variety of rhythmic values. Several of the fingerings may be awkward. Level 6.

Divertimento No. 2

Fits the hand well but contains many different subdivisions of the beat. Intriguing modulations. Level 6.

Divertimento No. 6

More difficult than *Divertimento No. 2*. Humorous and dramatic mood, especially suited for the extrovert. Level 6.

P

GIOVANNI PAISIELLO (1740–1816) Italy

Paisiello was a productive composer with a charming, spirited style and a fresh melodic gift.

Six Sonatas

All in one movement and part of a collection of *19 Sonatas for Harpsichord*. Rococo works, especially appropriate for the student not ready to play Haydn sonatas but who plays Alberti bass and other broken chord accompaniments. The reading is relatively easy and study of these sonatas provides a fine introduction to stylistic playing of classical works. Generally four to six printed pages. (Masters Music, Mills and other editions.) Levels 7–8.

PIETRO DOMENICO PARADIES (PARADISI) (1707–1791) Italy

Paradies was known especially for his two-movement sonatas which were admired by Clementi, Cramer and Mozart. Various movements from these works can supply fine teaching material, and several are identified below.

Toccata (from Sonata in A Major)

Paradies' best-known teaching work, often found in single edition or sheet versions. Especially good for a student who enjoys playing "fingery" works. Continuous sixteenths are featured in the right hand against detached eighths in the other, with evenness a primary consideration. Broken chords are used throughout. This piece can help teach the concepts of sequence, analysis of chords, and structural cadences. Requires a substantial amount of contraction/expansion. Effective in motivating almost any type of student. (Alfred, Schott and other editions.) Level 7.

Presto (from Sonata in D Minor)

Brilliant figuration, mostly confined to the right hand. Strictly two-voice playing, often featuring broken triads and terraced dynamics. Would make an effective recital opener. (Many standard editions.) Level 8.

GIOVANNI BATTISTA PESCETTI (1704–1766) Italy

See entry under Baroque period.

GIOVANNI BENEDETTO PLATTI (c. 1690–1763) Italy

Twelve Sonatas

Platti composed 12 pre-Classical sonatas that are highly accessible and would be interesting in recital. Most are in four movements. (Belwin, Breitkopf and Ricordi.) Levels 9–10.

IGNAZ JOSEPH PLEYEL (1757–1831) Austria

Pleyel, a one-time student of Haydn, was a prolific and competent composer. He eventually settled in France where he started a successful piano manufacturing company.

Sonatina in C Major

An interesting alternative to the standard sonatina fare. This good-natured work is in two movements. The repeated notes need changes of fingering. Several tricky sixteenth-note passages and written out turns appear. Worth investigating. (Alfred.) Levels 3–4.

Sonatina in D Major

A two-movement work, the first movement featuring a lyrical melody in longer note values accompanied by triplet broken chords in the left hand. The writing is highly sequential. The concluding *Rondo* is light and spirited and features Alberti-bass patterns, chords and terraced dynamics. (Alfred.) Levels 2–3.

Sonatina in F Major

The first movement is especially tuneful. The left-hand accompaniment consists primarily of diatonic chords in quarter notes. The second movement *Menuetto* is filled with triads, while the third movement displays a sparkling character with attractive dotted-note patterns. (Alfred.) Levels 3–4.

R

ALEXANDER REINAGLE (1756–1809) England

Born in England, Reinagle spent most of his childhood and early adult years in Scotland. Reinagle eventually settled in Philadelphia where he taught, composed, managed concert series and performed often on the pianoforte. He is considered to be America's first professional pianist.

Five Scots Tunes

Scottish tunes that are presented in straight-forward or ornamented settings. Titles include *Moss Plate, Maggie Lauder, Locheil's March, Mount Your Baggage* and *Dainty Davie*. (Hinshaw.) Levels 8–9.

Six Scots Tunes

Some of the earliest serious American compositions, though significant more from a historical standpoint than from a musically substantive perspective. Study of some of these pieces could be incorporated into an elementary student's American history projects. Study of a movement or two might substitute for a movement of a classical sonatina. (Hinshaw.) Level 6.

24 Short and Easy Pieces

Pieces at the level of the easiest Türk selections and composed for Reinagle's pupils in England and Scotland. The composer brought these pieces with him in 1786 to use for his teaching in America. Thought to be the best book for beginners of its day, and some of the easiest standard teaching pieces available. (Alfred.) Levels 2–3.

Mount Vernon Set

A delightfully easy pre-sonatina set of pieces, yet providing "serious" sounds. Especially good for the student who is not ready for *First Lessons in Bach*, Volume 1, ed. Carroll and who needs variety and work on the development of independent hands.

ABATE DE ROSSI ROMANO (n.d.) Italy

Six Sonatas

These early Classical *sonatas* might be appropriate for study prior to some of the Haydn sonatas. The fast movements are relatively short and rhythmic, using typical accompanimental figurations. (Curci.) Level 9.

ANTONIO ROSETTI (c. 1750–1792) Bohemia

Rosetti was a composer of mostly orchestral and chamber music. Baroque and Classical elements can be found in his work, and his style is similar to that of the young Haydn. A popular composer of his day, Rosetti's talents were placed in the same class as Haydn and Mozart.

12 Pieces

Significant collection of well-crafted, light-hearted and little-known teaching pieces. Straightforward phrase structures and typical figurations, strongly idiomatic to the keyboard. Could serve as fine substitutions for any of the Haydn *German Dances.* Excellent shorter studies in Classical style. (Eulenberg.) Levels 5–6.

S

DANIEL STEIBELT (1765–1823) Germany

Six Sonatinas for Piano, Op. 49

Pre-Classical works in two movements, featuring idiomatic writing and tuneful melodies. Unusual repertoire choices can be extracted from this literature. (Ricordi.) Level 7.

T

WENZEL JOHANN TOMASCHEK (1774–1850) Bohemia

A prominent Prague pianist, Tomaschek was in touch with such men as Beethoven and the writer Goethe. He was one of the first composers to write in a decidedly lyrical vein, before the nocturnes of John Field or Chopin.

Eclogues, Opp. 35, 39, 47, 51, 63, 66, 83

Among Tomaschek's more important compositions for piano, the *Eclogues* are in seven volumes of six pieces each. An eclogue in literature is a pastoral poem, and here a light and lyrical composition with uncomplicated textures and modest technical demands. The themes often switch from minor to major and vice versa. The music is filled with parallel thirds and sixths and mystical effects. Selected movements would be appropriate for advancing performers. See especially *Eclogue,* Op. 35, No. 6 and *Eclogue,* Op. 47, No. 5. (Musica Antiqua.) Levels 8–9.

DANIEL GOTTLOB TÜRK (1756–1813) Germany

Türk's *Keyboard-School* (1789) was of great significance as one of the most important treatises written for keyboard players, ranking in importance with the C.P.E. Bach *Essay on the True Art of Keyboard Playing.* Türk also was one of the first to write instructional piano pieces for children. His main work as a teacher was the two-volume set of 120 pieces, 60 in each volume, *Handstücke feur angehende Klavierspieler,* from which most of the very easy teaching pieces that appear in modern teaching anthologies have been extracted. His *Keyboard-School* works are mainly pedagogic in nature and include both sonatas and pieces for beginners. He also published 48 additional sonatas for keyboard, few of which are readily available today.

60 Pieces for Aspiring Players, Book I (1792), Book II (1795)

The 120 pieces here were planned for use with his *Keyboard-School*, the most influential keyboard instruction manual of its day. The pieces in each volume progress from easy to advanced, and each volume is divided into four parts. Part I consists of "Short and very easy pieces in two parts," Part II of "Somewhat longer pieces, but still only in two parts," Part III of "Pieces in three and more parts" and Part IV of "Miscellaneous Pieces" including one with the amusing title, "Dedicated most humbly to the right-hand little finger."

The 120 pieces, all titled, have been compared to Schumann's *Album for the Young* in concept. Choice of dynamics is often left to the performer. This work is of major historical significance. (Associated Board of the Royal Schools of Music, ed. Howard Ferguson; Editio Musica, ed. Sármai and Zoltán.) Levels 1–7.

49 Pieces for Beginners at the Piano

Compilation of some of the easier works from the two books of *60 Pieces*. They are arranged in progressive order. Many are highly ornamented and probably reflect C.P.E. Bach's influence. (Kalmus.) Levels 3–6.

Horn With Echo

Perhaps the most popular of the Türk selections. A robust hunting song in which the single-note bass and treble melodies move in parallel motion a third or a fifth apart. Possibly the greatest challenge for the early elementary student will be to play the dotted rhythms correctly and to finger the extended positions correctly. Level 2.

The Actor

Expressive character piece, *andante patetico e vigoroso*, that uses a full dynamic range. Some hand position shifts and stretches may be difficult. Level 4.

Gavotte

Filled with many ornaments and appoggiaturas and expanding and contracting left-hand passages. An appropriate introduction to dance forms, in which the performer can explore two-note slurs and left-hand *detaché*. Level 5.

Sad and Beautiful

Highly ornamented writing that will need strong consistency of pulse. Double notes must be played exactly together and melodic tones must be carefully matched. Level 6.

Joke

Frequent dynamic changes provide the joking effects in this 16-measure binary form work. Lively and appealing. Level 4.

The Dancing Master

Also known as *The Ballet*, this delicate and popular piece should be played lightly. This piece uses the outer fingers of the right hand, with eighth-note passagework representing "twists" and "twirls." Level 2.

Carefree

Simple work featuring a left hand primarily in whole notes and a right hand in quarter notes. A fine introduction to the reading of independent lines. Could serve as a student's first "classic." Level 1.

12 Pieces for Instruction (appendix to *Klavierschüle*)

Illustrative pieces for the Türk *Klavierschüle* which appear as an appendix to the treatise. Virtually every note is fingered. Level 5.

Sonata in A Minor for Keyboard

The sound of the first movement is full and orchestral. The predictable harmonies and straightforward writing here may be attractive for pianists not as adept in handling the more subtle inflection of an easy Haydn sonata. The second movement is sustained and ornamented, with somewhat complex rhythms, while the last movement is a rollicking finger piece with triplet scalewise passages moving in parallel motion between the hands. Interesting and different. (Kistner and Siegel/Novello.) Level 7.

Sonata in D Major for Keyboard

Siciliano opening movement with an elegant melody above single-note accompaniment. Especially appropriate for the pianist who is able to voice melody and accompaniment well. Short ornamented slow movement prepares for the robust *Balletto* final movement, characterized by leaping melodies. (Kistner and Siegel/Novello.) Level 6.

Miscellaneous Volumes

Leichte Stücke für Klavier, ed. Dolfein

Short collection contains 29 of the more interesting short pieces of Türk. (Schott.) Levels 4–7.

Zwölf Handstücke zum Gebrauche beym Unterrichten

Contains 12 interesting selections from the two books of *60 Pieces*. (Litloff.) Levels 4–5.

W

JOHANN BAPTIST WANHAL (1739–1813) Bohemia

Last name also spelled Vanhal, van Hal, Vanhall, etc. A prolific composer and teacher, he spent most of his life in Vienna.

Sonatina No. 2 in F Major

The left-hand accompaniment can be tricky since it requires the holding of a low F while playing an Alberti figure. Right-hand single note melody. Interesting writing and a fine contrast to better-known easy sonatina literature. (Alfred and other standard editions.) Level 4.

CARL MARIA von WEBER (1786–1826) Germany

See entry under the Romantic Period.

SAMUEL WESLEY (1766–1837) Great Britain

Samuel Wesley was a nephew of the famous Methodist John Wesley and a prolific composer of choral music, hymns, songs and keyboard music.

12 Sonatinas, Op. 4, ed. Roberts

According to Timothy Roberts, this set of sonatinas reveals Wesley's style of "mixing the modern 'Viennese' style with a decidedly Baroque, and especially Handelian, flavor." Twelve single movements which are closely related to character pieces. The writing is interesting if not profound. (Associated Board of the Royal Schools of Music.) Level 7.

ERNST WILHELM WOLF (1735–1792) Germany

Wolf, a little-known composer of the 18th century, composed seven books of six sonatas each, betraying debts to C.P.E. Bach.

Five Sonatas, ed. Oberdoerffer

This volume shows delightfully *galant* writing. A work from this collection might make an interesting opening for a recital. The general level of difficulty is comparable to the easier Haydn sonatas. (Peters.) Levels 8–9.

JOHANN HUGO WORŽISCHEK (1791–1825) Bohemia

The notable if unfamiliar compositions of Woržischek demonstrate the transition from Beethoven to the Romantics.

Six Variations, Op. 19

Short set of variations featuring strong contrast between variations. Dotted rhythms. (Henle.) Level 9.

Impromptus, Op. 7

These are works that strongly influenced Schubert's *Impromptus* and *Moments Musicaux*. Would provide an interesting addition to a recital program. (Henle, Musica Antiqua Bohemica.) Level 10.

ROMANTIC LITERATURE

A

ISAAC ALBÉNIZ (1860–1909) Spain

Albéniz was a brilliant pianist and a prolific composer. His music is intensely emotional and often pictorial.

España, Op. 165

Set of six pieces, primarily in moderate tempi, all of which are accessible to the advancing pianist. The syncopated rhythms help define the Spanish character here. The best-known are *Tango* and *Zortzico*. (Many standard editions.)

No. 1 Prelude

Somewhat improvisatory, featuring lively triplet rhythms. Level 8.

No. 2 Tango

Appealing and popular dance of Spanish rhythms and repeated ideas. Frequent use of two against three and many changes between duple and triple meter. (Carl Fischer.) Level 9.

No. 3 Malagueña

The title refers to a Spanish dance from the province of Málaga. Filled with Spanish clichés and similar to the popular *Malagueña* of Lecuona but less difficult. Much emotion. Level 9.

No. 6 Zortzico

A *zortzico* is a Spanish (Basque) folk dance in 5/8 time. This work contains repetitive rhythms, but displays strong character. Level 10.

Mallorca, Op. 202

Subtitled "Barcarola," this ABA slow-fast-slow piece is filled with Spanish flavor. A good work to develop a smooth, even legato. Some passages are awkward for a small hand. (International.) Level 10.

Serenade Espagñole, Op. 181

Pleasant sonorities and generally thicker texture than in the other Albéniz works listed. Students capable of playing some of the Chopin nocturnes could play this six-page work with ease. (Kalmus and other standard editions.) Level 10.

Suite Española

Eight pieces are found in the volume, several of which are accessible to the pianist ready to play the easiest Chopin waltzes. Strong Spanish flavor. (Kalmus, Union Musical Española and others.)

Granada

This allegretto "serenata" is primarily music for diversion. A large reach is helpful to play the many blocked chords. Not difficult reading. Level 9.

Cataluna

For those who play large chords easily. An easier alternative to Rachmaninoff's *C-sharp Minor Prelude.* Level 9.

Asturias

Highly rhythmic with much rapid alternation between the hands. Requires flair, but sounds more difficult than it is. Level 9.

Castilla

Captivating Spanish flavor, and easier to play than it looks. Level 10.

Cuba (Notturno)

Marked *allegretto,* this is an appealing, easy to read work featuring Spanish rhythms. Melody is presented in octaves. Level 9.

Travel Impressions (Recuredos de viaje)

Set of high-quality works with several movements playable at the early-advanced level. (International, Kalmus, and other editions.)

Dawn

Impressionistic atmosphere but the Spanish flavor is always present. Requires imagination and color. Lyrical melodic writing and left-hand arpeggiations. Level 10.

Malagueña

Most popular of the set, featuring inviting rhythms. Level 10.

On the Beach

Lyrical and melodic, and generally different in character from Albéniz's highly rhythmic, dance-like works. Level 9.

Songs of Spain, Op. 232

Set of five worthwhile solos. See especially *Prelude* (No. 1), *Cordoba* (No. 4) and *Seguidillas* (No. 5). (Many standard editions.) Level 10.

No. 1 Prelude

Rapid hand alternations, primarily in sixteenths, makes this an impressive perpetual-motion piece. Improvisatory middle section in this ABA format lends contrast. Economy of material. Some of the rapid skips are difficult. Level 10.

Miscellaneous Volumes

Isaac Albéniz Masterpieces

Contains several accessible pieces including *Cadiz, Seguidillas, Sevilla* and *Tango (In D)*. (Marks.) Levels 9–10.

Albéniz: His Greatest Piano Solos, ed. Bayas

Found here are some of the most popular of Albéniz's works. Unfortunately identifying opus numbers are not included. (Copa.) Level 10.

CHARLES HENRI VALENTIN ALKAN (1813–1888) France

Alkan, though comparatively unknown today, was one of the great keyboard titans of the mid-19th century, and part of Chopin's circle.

25 Preludes, Op. 31

Worth investigating. Levels 8–10.

Esquisses, Op. 63

Four volumes of 12 pieces each. "Esquisse" means a sketch or draft. These are character pieces with individual titles. Attractive groupings for performance can readily be put together from any volume. Levels 9–10.

Les Mois, Op. 74

Twelve interesting character pieces, one for each month of the year. Levels 9–10.

Miscellaneous Volumes

Alkan in Miniature, ed. Smith

Provides a fine overview of the myriad of styles used by this French romantic composer. While some of the pieces are too difficult for mention here, several pieces are accessible, such as the five selections from the "Preludes." For a highly motivating, rhythmic selection, see especially the *Air á 5 temps* in which Alkan imitates the zortzico, a Basque dance with five beats to the bar. (Billaudot.) Levels 9–10.

ANTON ARENSKY (1861–1906) Russia

Almost all of the music of this Russian composer is pianistic and much is in salon style.

24 Character Pieces, Op. 36

Contains some of Arensky's most interesting writing. All of the character pieces are titled. (Kalmus.)

No. 1 Prelude

Could provide a student's first experience in playing expansive romantic pieces. Arpeggiated left hand and rich, *forte* diatonic chords. Four printed pages. Level 9.

No. 5 Consolation

Lyrical and appealing work with a texture similar to some of Brahms' piano works. Technical difficulties lie in achieving effective voicing. Level 10.

No. 12 Intermezzo

While not profound, this tuneful selection provides practice in voicing a left-hand tenor melody while the right-hand plays double-note figurations. Appealing and potentially satisfying. Level 9.

No. 16 Elegie

Beautiful melodic writing in a work that needs a fine cantabile and skilled ability to project inner voices. Level 10.

No. 21 Marche

Rich chords and occasional open octaves, especially suited to the student who enjoys full-sounding pieces. Level 9.

12 Preludes, Op. 63

See especially No. 4 and No. 10. (Peters.) Level 9.

Arabesques, Op. 67

Set of six effective pieces. See especially No. 2 (*Vivace*), No. 3 (*Tempo di valse*) and No. 4 (*Andantino*). Each is two pages long. (Peters.) Level 9.

12 Études for Piano, Op. 74

Several are suitable for the advancing pianist. Each is in a different key. (Marks.)

No. 1 Étude in C Major

Moderato work with broken chords against single-note melody. Pianistic, and good for developing facility. Level 10.

No. 5 Étude in D Major

Marked *andante con moto*, this work features descending arpeggiation broken between the hands, with melody appearing in the top note of the right hand. Level 9.

No. 7 Étude in E-flat Major

An *andantino* study in voicing an octave melody accompaniment in the same hand. Best played by performers with wide hand spans. Level 10.

No. 11 Étude in A-flat

Broken chords and melody in the right hand, double notes and counter-melody in the left. *Andante.* Level 10.

JOÃO MARCELLINO ARROYO (1861–1930) Portugal

Histoire Simple, Op. 3

Romantic, nocturne-like solo with traditional harmonies and rich sonority. Interesting writing. (Sassetti.) Level 7.

B

MILY BALAKIREV (1837–1910) Russia

Russian pianist and composer, member of the nationalist group known as "The Five." Unfortunately, most of his piano works are best suited for advanced players.

Selected Piano Pieces I, ed. Rüger

Contains primarily romantic character pieces such as a polka, three mazurkas, a lullaby, two waltzes and a toccata. (Peters.) Level 10.

Nocturne in B Minor

Varying accompaniment patterns including wide arpeggiations and triplet repetitions of two-note patterns. Expansive romantic writing. Deserves performance by the advancing amateur as well as the professional. Level 10.

Mazurka in C-sharp Minor

Pleasant two-page work. Level 9.

Lullaby in D-flat Major

This gentle work allows the pianist to perfect a legato arpeggiated accompaniment. Opening mood similar to the well-known Grieg *Nocturne*. Level 9.

Nocturne in D Minor

Expansive left-hand arpeggiations above chordal right hand melody. This fine piece should be better known. Level 10.

AMY MARCY CHENEY (MRS. H.H.A.) BEACH (1867–1944) USA

Brilliant pianist and prolific Romantic composer who wrote for almost every musical medium. She was much heralded in her day in both Europe and the United States, and her music is nowadays undergoing a revival.

Children's Carnival, Op. 25 (1894)

Eight pieces which present the characters of the Italian Renaissance pantomime that became popular in America late in the 19th century. The pieces found here include *Promenade, Columbine, Pantalon* and *Harlequin*. (Alfred.) Levels 5–6.

Children's Album, Op. 36 (1897)

Collection of five pieces with dance titles. The pieces are somewhat reminiscent of the Baroque suites that Mrs. Beach studied as a child and are notated in treble clef for both hands. Thin textures. (Alfred, Schmidt.)

No. 1 Minuet

A good introduction to the Romantic dance style. Features occasional double notes and running passages. Level 5.

No. 2 Gavotte

Predictable phrase lengths with tuneful writing and staccato passages in a highly pianistic work. Level 5.

No. 3 Waltz

Romantic, light and excellent preparation for playing Chopin waltzes. Few left-hand skips, but the oom-pah-pah accompaniment prevails. Sounds more difficult than it is. Level 5.

No. 4 March

Reminiscent perhaps of carnival music. Most of the playing occurs above middle C. Level 6.

No. 5 Polka

Light, *scherzando* movement. Level 5.

Five Improvisations for Piano, Op. 148

Nostalgic writing in a series of five two-page pieces. Accessible musically and technically for the student able to play the easiest Chopin mazurkas. Should be better known. (The Composers Press.) Level 8.

The Life and Music of Amy Beach, ed. G. Smith

Amy Beach and her music are profiled in this volume that includes a kind of family "scrapbook" section with many photos and a short biography, many of her easier piano works, and some of her intermediate and advanced piano pieces. Four of the selections had never been published before. Some music of surprisingly high quality found here. (Creative Keyboard Publications.) Levels 5–10.

PAUL BEAUMONT (n.d.) Great Britain

Con Amore

Much of Beaumont's music is salon-like, but this piece would be valuable for teaching. The melody is presented in octaves. Central flourishes of arpeggiations played with alternating hands gives the student a chance to experience cadenza-like material at an early level. A nocturne-like piece, with lyrical octaves. (Carl Fischer, G. Schirmer.) Level 6.

Tarantelle

A flashy "finger piece"—a potential pupil saver. Especially effective Coda. Worth investigating. (Alfred, Carl Fischer, G. Schirmer.) Level 7.

HERMANN BERENS (1826–1880) Germany

School of Velocity, Op. 61

The pieces are long and academic, showing the result of his study with Czerny. Many are studies with little musical value. (Kalmus and others.) Level 10.

50 Piano Pieces for Beginners, Op. 70

Short études, mostly in the key of C, designed to develop coordination between the hands and a feeling for common piano accompaniments. These short pieces could easily be an elementary student's first études. (Kalmus, G. Schirmer and others.) Levels 1–3.

20 Études for Beginners, Op. 79

Longer than the pieces in Op. 70 and less inspired. (Kalmus and others.) Level 7.

Additional Work for Study:
Op. 81 Six Children's Sonatas

HECTOR BERLIOZ (1803–1869) France

Piano Works, ed. Hinson

Contains the complete piano works of Berlioz—three solo pieces. (Hinshaw.) Levels 7–9.

Rustic Serenade

In four brief sections, slow-fast-slow-fast, this three-page piece with some religious connotations is based on a well-known theme. This would be an appropriate selection for a student needing a short romantic work. Much of the writing here is hymn-like and lyrical. Level 7.

Hymne

Fugue-like, later breaking into octave passages. Perhaps intended originally to be used in the Catholic Mass. Level 9.

Toccata

Contrapuntal writing with two voices in the right hand above running left-hand scale figures. This piece would be an appropriate selection to abet the teaching of voice leading. Level 9.

HENRI BERTINI (1798–1876) England

Bertini taught and concertized in Paris, after a career as a child prodigy on the piano. His études are not especially profound but may be useful.

24 Studies, Op. 29

One- and two-page études written to be "preparatory to the celebrated studies of J. B. Cramer." They feature conventional keyboard patterns. Strong writing. (Many standard editions.) Levels 8–9.

24 Studies, Op. 32

Composed as a sequel to Op. 29, these études are similar in purpose and scope to the earlier set. Many of the studies deal with rotation and passing under of the thumb and in general with fingerwork. (Many standard editions.) Level 9.

25 Studies, Op. 100

Appropriate for small hands, since these studies do not contain octaves. Longer and slightly more difficult than Op. 29 and Op. 32. Generally pedantic études, often based on scale passages. (Many standard editions.) Levels 7–8.

24 Melodious Pieces, Op. 101

Romantic character pieces, some of surprisingly high quality. Bertini's reputation as a composer of études has perhaps kept this collection of teaching pieces from being better known. Similar in many ways to the Burgmüller Op. 100 pieces, though slightly harder. Level 7.

A Progressive and Complete Method for the Pianoforte

Bertini wrote particular pieces to emphasize or illustrate a point. Primarily of historical significance, but could be used in developing technical dexterity. (Ditson.)

Miscellaneous Pieces

Andante in A Major

Lyrical work calling for legato Alberti bass against highly detailed articulation. May help a student develop skills in phrase shaping, balance between the hands, and the playing of two-note slurs. Level 5.

Chord Study, Op. 166, No. 6

This harplike piece is based on a harmonic progression of chords. The performer must carefully match the tone quality between the hands as one hand takes over from the other. An overlapping finger legato is needed here. Level 3.

Additional Work for Study:
12 Little Pieces and Preludes

FERDINAND BEYER (n.d.)

Elementary Instruction Book for the Pianoforte

(Also known as *Preparatory School*, Op. 101.) Method book for beginners containing many academic and somewhat boring exercises. Most early activities are on C and G in a method that stresses learning to play the piano through exercises and academic pieces in one style. (Kalmus, Peters, G. Schirmer and others.) Levels 1–3.

ALBERT BIEHL (1835–1899)

The Elements of Piano Playing, Op. 30

Consists of many patterns to be played in C position while later exercises in the book call for holding down a single note while the other fingers move in sixteenth notes. Pischna-like studies, somewhat pedantic. Better studies are available. (G. Schirmer.) Levels 4–9.

25 Easy and Progressive Studies, Op. 44

Many of the studies are somewhat useful since the figurations appear first in one hand and then in the other hand, thus exercising both hands equally. Published in a series of three volumes. (G. Schirmer.) Levels 4–8.

Four Sonatinas, Op. 57

The best known of Biehl's works and probably the most useful for teaching. All of the sonatinas are in two movements. No. 4 probably is the most accessible of the group.

Joy of Youth, Op. 130

Three melodic and instructive sonatinas. See especially No. 3 in three movements.

ALEXANDRE PIERRE FRANÇOIS BÖELY (1785–1858) France

Anthologie de Piéces pour Piano

Contains various pieces, most distinguished only by tempo indications and opus numbers. The writing is pianistic and surprisingly interesting, given the composer's relative obscurity. (Editions Choudens.) Levels 9–10.

ALEXANDER BORODIN (1833–1887) Russia

Borodin was a member of the Russian Five, a group of Russian nationalistic composers whose piano works remain relatively unknown.

Petite Suite

These are appropriate study pieces to precede Chopin, although the quality is not as good. Highly romantic writing, usually lyrical and nostalgic. Seven movements. See especially *In a Convent, Reverie, Serenade* and *Nocturne.* (Kalmus, Leduc and G. Schirmer.) Levels 9–10.

Borodin: Album for Piano

Contains the complete *Petite Suite* and the *Scherzo.* Romantic and lyrical writing. The *Scherzo* is substantially more difficult than the selections in *Petite Suite.* (Editio Musica.) Levels 9–10.

(MARCO) ENRICO BOSSI (1861–1925) Italy

Kinder-Album

Set of six intermediate pieces in a salon-like style, appealing for their carefree character and lightness. Titles include *Petit Valse, Barcarola, Serenata, Polka, Notturnino* and *Tarantella*. (Hug.) Level 4.

Raccolta

Light Romantic pieces for the intermediate student. Many are remarkably similar to teaching pieces by American contemporary composers in their use of patterns and repetitions. (Curci.) Level 6.

JOHANNES BRAHMS (1833–1897) Germany

Brahms was hailed as the successor to Beethoven and composed in a Romantic style with Classical tendencies. His late piano pieces hold a secure place among the greatest keyboard literature. Almost all of Brahms' music is for mature pianists with accomplished technique and advanced musicianship. Many standard editions are available of all of these works.

Ballade in D Minor, Op. 10, No. 1

Based on the gruesome Scottish ballad "Edward" about a son killing his father, as the son reveals his deed in a conversation with his mother. The opening contains a somber melody in dialogue with another melody in the parallel Major. The central section builds to an impassioned climax before returning to a variant of the "A" section, this time with accompaniment in triplets. Level 10.

Waltzes, Op. 39

Originally composed as piano duets and later arranged by Brahms for solo piano. He also created a simplified piano version, graded here. Many of these waltzes make interesting repertoire studies for the advancing pianist, and since little music by Brahms is truly "accessible," these waltzes in the simplified version offer some of the most practical repertoire by Brahms for many performers. See especially Nos. 2, 3, 4, 8 and 15. (Many standard editions.) Levels 8–10.

Intermezzo in A Major, Op. 76, No. 6

Strong rhythmic interest is exhibited in this two-section work with codetta. Musical tension results from the rhythmic juxtaposition of four against six. It is easy to overdo the rubato, resulting in a performance that starts and stops excessively. Full of sentiment and serenity. Level 10.

Intermezzo in A Minor, Op. 76, No. 7

Brahms first inscribed this work as a "Romance for two sweet lady-voices." Indeed, the work contains two themes, both highly vocal in character. Again, care should be taken not to indulge in excessive rubato. Much of the writing is chordal. Level 9.

Rhapsody in G Minor, Op. 79, No. 2

This popular fiery sonata-allegro movement contrasts march-like themes with more lyrical writing. Difficult to play well, due to thick textures. Undue fluctuations of tempo should be avoided. Level 10.

Intermezzo in A Minor, Op. 116, No. 2

Opens with a calm lyrical melody in a two against three texture with question and answer phrases. The central section offers ethereal passagework which shifts between registers. Careful fingering is a necessity in this middle section. Level 10.

Intermezzo in E Major, Op. 116, No. 6

Needs close attention to voicing, especially in the opening two measures. Chromatic writing pervades this lovely ABA' work. The central trio contains intriguing hemiolas. Level 9.

Intermezzo in E-flat Minor, Op. 117, No. 1

The most accessible of the three Intermezzos in this set. The publisher Simrock originally wanted to call this Intermezzo "Cradle Song," whereupon Brahms suggested "Cradle Song of an Unhappy Mother." It is based on an old Scottish folk song and calls for skillful voicing of inner melodies, especially in the right hand. The B section should be played slightly slower than the A sections, not slightly faster. The A sections require fine voicing of inner lines and avoidance of excessive ritards. Attention to sustaining long phrases is necessary in the D Major section. Level 10.

Intermezzo in B-flat Minor, Op. 117, No. 2

A flowing and highly figured work with broken chords interchanged between the hands. Intricate, lyrical writing and highly pianistic with delicate interplay of sound. Level 10.

Intermezzo in A Major, Op. 118, No. 2

Immensely popular due to its placid feeling. Contains a series of eight-measure phrases of intense emotional expression and quick-changing harmonies. Needs careful attention to voicing and avoidance of excessive rubato. Level 10.

Romanze in F Major, Op. 118, No. 5

A pastoral work, highly lyrical, and requiring fine voicing of inner lines. Long, sustained phrases are necessary in the D-Major section. Level 10.

Intermezzo in C Major, Op. 119, No. 3

The melody is found in the alto in this *grazioso* piece that displays interesting modulations. Requires fine attention to voicing and articulation to elicit the appropriate sound from the staccato chords. Level 10.

Two Sarabandes (A Minor and B Minor)

Brief works from Brahms' youth. The first is a 16-measure piece with a florid soprano line and double notes in the right hand. It is perhaps the least technically difficult work that Brahms wrote. The second sarabande features double notes in thirds or sixths in the right hand. Level 9.

Gavotte(s) and Sarabande

Two Gavottes, one in A Minor and one in A Major, were first published as recently as 1976 in the journal *Music and Letters* (Oct. '76). Their history suggests that it is conceivable that Brahms intended one or both of them to be performed with the *A-Minor Sarabande* mentioned above, as a little suite. (See *Kleine Stücke*, ed. Robert Pascall, published by Doblinger.) Level 9.

Miscellaneous Volumes

Selected Pieces, ed. Cortot

Includes *Capriccio in B Minor*, Op. 76, No. 2, *Intermezzo in A Major*, Op. 118, No. 2, *Ballade in G Minor*, Op. 118, No. 3, *Intermezzo in E-flat Minor*, Op. 118, No. 6, *Intermezzo in C Major*, Op. 119, No. 3, and *Rhapsody in E-flat Major*, Op. 119, No. 4. Each piece is preceded by detailed practice instructions and commentary. (Curci.) Level 10.

Dances of Brahms, ed. Hinson

This practical volume includes the complete *Waltzes*, Op. 39 as well as some miscellaneous works including the *Hungarian Dances*, Nos. 1, 3, 5,

7, Gavotte in A Minor, and *Sarabande in B Minor.* Extensive and valuable preface. (Alfred.) Level 10.

At the Piano With Brahms, ed. Hinson

An interesting cross-section of music including six of the *Waltzes,* Op. 39 and several of the short piano pieces. The first 20 pages of this volume consist of extensive material about Brahms as pianist and composer. (Alfred.) Levels 9–10.

Brahms Selected Works, ed. Levine

Includes the *Ballade in D Minor,* Op. 10, No. 1, two works from Op. 117, three selections from Op. 118, the *Rhapsodies,* Op. 79, and other selections. Excellent variety. (Alfred.) Level 10.

MAX BRUCH (1838–1920) Germany

Six Piano Pieces

Composed in his youth, these pianistic and lyrical pieces will appeal to the teacher who is searching for distinctive romantic literature for an intermediate performer. Surprisingly high quality. (Breitkopf.) Level 9.

JOHANN FRIEDRICH BURGMÜLLER (1806–1874) Germany

Burgmüller was a popular pianist in the 19th century, especially in the Paris salons, where his light and intimate style of playing won him many admirers. His ability to improvise tuneful selections is reflected in the hundreds of teaching pieces he wrote, many of which are still popular.

Rondo alla Turca, Op. 68, No. 3

This is an extended work with repetitions of thematic material throughout. The music is lively and highly motivating. The left-hand repeated chords must be carefully balanced so that the single-note melody can be heard prominently. The central section in A Major provides a sustained melody, forming a lyrical contrast to the short motives and lively passagework of earlier sections. Level 7.

25 Progressive Pieces, Op. 100 (25 Études)

Some of the most important teaching literature from the Romantic school, now experiencing a revival. Although classified as études, they are in essence character pieces. For many years they were considered to be dated, and only recently has their rediscovery brought about their more frequent use. The most popular selections include *No. 2 Arabesque, No. 3 Pastorale, No. 6 Progress, No. 9 The Chase, No. 15 Ballade, No. 19 Ave Maria* and *No. 21 Harmony of the Angels*. This set is known under several names including *25 Études*. Accompaniments by Alfred Butler are available in the volumes *25 Études Arranged for Two Pianos, Volume I Études 1–14, Volume II Études 15–25* (Boston). Many editions of Op. 100 are available including those issued by Alfred, Willis, Kalmus, Associated Board of the Royal Schools of Music, G. Schirmer, Heuwekemeijer and others. Levels 3–6.

No. 1 Sincerity

Emphasizes legato playing and inflection. Lyrical writing in a moderato tempo. Level 4.

No. 2 Arabesque

Students often want to play this ABA work. Rapid five-finger patterns in each hand provide the main technical concerns. The melody is infectious in its tunefulness. Position shifts are not difficult. Level 3.

No. 3 Pastorale

Dreamy and elegant writing in a nocturne-like work. ABA with Coda. Needs a somewhat subdued accompaniment. Level 4.

No. 4 The Little Party

An étude in thirds and sixths, requiring a relaxed wrist. Level 5.

No. 5 Innocence

Requires technical proficiency that includes the playing of scales, finger changes, slurs, phrases of different lengths, evenness of bass trill patterns and an even touch. This pleasant and carefree miniature is based on sequential units making it relatively easy to learn. Facilitates the development of right-hand facility. Level 4.

No. 6 Progress

Scale passages in tenths permeate the opening of this one-page piece. Several different articulations are used throughout, requiring careful attention to detail. Rewarding writing. Level 4.

No. 7 The Clear Stream

Needs technical evenness and calls for voicing within the right hand. The murmuring effect in this perpetual motion piece is not easy to achieve. Level 4.

No. 8 Gracefulness

This character piece actually is a delicate study in playing right-hand turns. Level 5.

No. 9 The Chase

A dramatic hunt is depicted with horn calls and echo effects in this rondo. Every section is based on a repetitive motive consisting of broken octaves and two-note slurs. Highly effective, perhaps sounding more difficult than it is. Avoid rushing the faster passages. Needs loose wrists for the repeated chords. Level 7.

No. 10 Tender Flower

Built on the principle of the two-note slur. Performer will need supple wrists and the ability to inflect tonal levels. Level 6.

No. 11 The Young Shepherdess

Character piece that requires facility in getting around the keyboard, and in chord inversions. A study in *leggiero* and repeated-note playing. Level 6.

No. 12 The Farewell

Appropriate for a performer wanting a virtuoso-sounding étude or for a performer with natural facility. Begins with a recitative-like introduction followed by an ABA form with rapid right-hand figuration in the A sections. Large leaps in both hands. Level 7.

No. 13 Consolation

Holding a note with the thumb and playing an even trill above is the primary difficulty. The passage beginning in measure 24 is similar to the Schumann *Melody* from *Album for the Young*, Op. 68. Level 6.

No. 14 Austrian Dance

Good preparation for the style of the Chopin mazurkas, waltzes and polonaises. Level 4.

No. 15 Ballade

A mysterious and dramatic work for a young student. Rapid sixteenths in the left hand provide the primary technical consideration. Strong contrast in the melodic B section. Highly patterned and predictable writing. Excellent for recital or competition performance. Level 4.

No. 16 Sorrow

Arpeggiated, melodic patterns. Level 6.

No. 17 The Chatterbox

Fast repeated notes in both hands provide a study in changing fingers. Level 6.

No. 18 Inquietude

A depiction of restlessness, calling for fast fingerwork. Requires fine coordination to play the left-hand chord on the downbeats followed by three sixteenth-notes in the right hand. Only in the Coda do the hands play together. Helps to develop facility for rapid playing and a lightness of touch. Right hand fingering needs careful planning. Level 5.

No. 19 Ave Maria

Hymn-like opening, followed by variations. Nocturne-like work that emphasizes chordal playing. Level 4.

No. 20 Tarantella

Dramatic tarantella in rondo form. More of an étude than a character piece. Good for building facility in rapid playing, mostly in the right hand. Level 6.

No. 21 Harmony of the Angels (Angels' Voices)

A piece that is built on rising and falling broken chords divided between the hands. Appropriate for developing an even and legato sound. Requires fine coordination between the hands and is gratifying to perform. Level 5.

No. 22 Barcarolle

An introduction precedes a dance-like work with a singing melodic line. Strong romantic sound. Level 6.

No. 23 The Return

A perpetual-motion piece that depicts the excitement of an individual's return through the playing of repeated notes. Left-hand melody in the B section is comprised primarily of arpeggiated chords. The performer must work for smooth changes of position. Some double thirds and sixths for the right hand are present. Effective romantic writing for the upper-intermediate student. Not as difficult as it sounds. Level 7.

No. 24 The Swallow

Dramatic hand-crossings which occur in every measure lend excitement to this interesting work. The many broken chords help develop a sense of keyboard topography as well as evenness in playing sixteenth-note passages. Requires a singing tone and careful listening for clear pedal changes. Level 6.

No. 25 The Knight Errant

Strong bravura aspects make this piece appealing. Combines most of the technical requirements found in the previous pieces. More difficult than the other works in this volume. Level 7.

12 Brilliant and Melodious Studies, Op. 105

Generally more difficult and less significant than the works in Op. 100 and Op. 109. Untitled selections which frequently focus on a single technical problem. Most valuable as études in romantic passage-playing. (Alfred, Kalmus, G. Schirmer and other editions.) Level 9.

18 Characteristic Studies, Op. 109

Composed as a sequel to the *25 Progressive Pieces*, Op. 100 and dedicated to Heller. More difficult than the *25 Progressive Pieces of Burgmüller* but substantially less difficult than his *12 Brilliant and Melodious Studies*, Op. 105. Several works here should be better known. They fit into an upper-intermediate level of musical and technical development for which little Romantic-era repertoire is known. The best-known ones include *No. 1 Confidence*, *No. 7 Berceuse* and *No. 13 The Storm*. Fine material to study prior to the preludes and waltzes of Chopin. (Alfred, Kalmus, G. Schirmer and other editions.) Levels 7–8.

No. 1 Confidence

Captivating melody with broken-chord accompaniment in the right hand. One of the most inspired in the set. Excellent for teaching voicing of a melody within a single hand. Level 6.

No. 2 The Pearls

Could depict pearls capturing the glimmering sunlight. Primarily a study in right-hand scale playing. Needs attention to clarity and evenness in passagework. Étude-like. Level 7.

No. 3 The Shepherd's Return

Depicts a joyous, lilting character. The left hand plays a moderate oom-pah-pah figure under an eighth-note melody. Could serve as fine preparation to one of the easier Chopin waltzes. Careful attention is needed for the various touches. Level 7.

No. 4 The Gypsies

Vigorous chordal writing and rich sonorities. Appropriate for the student needing practice in playing chords. Level 8.

No. 5 The Spring

Right-hand broken-chord passagework throughout simulates the sounds of a bubbling spring. A miniature version of the Chopin *Étude in A-flat Major*, Op. 25, No. 1 (Harp). Level 8.

No. 6 Light-Hearted Maiden

A study in right-hand double notes. Needs a relatively large span. Level 8.

No. 7 Lullaby

Lyrical *Berceuse*, somewhat reminiscent of Chopin. Needs fine voicing of melody over accompaniment in a single hand. One of the best in the set. Level 7.

No. 8 Agitato

Energetic writing featuring rapid alternation of sixteenths between the hands. For a student with flair who is well coordinated. Fits the hand well. Level 7.

No. 9 Matin Bell

Frequent left-hand crossing over the right to "ring" the bell-like treble sound. Some playing of countermelodies occurs in the right hand. Expressive and lyrical writing in a strong romantic vein. Level 7.

No. 10 Velocity

Highly patterned and rapid right-hand passagework above repeated chord accompaniment. Sounds much more difficult than it is and can be learned rather quickly. Worth investigating. Level 7.

No. 11 Serenade

Grazioso feeling with the simulation of strummed chords on a guitar. Grace-notes. Level 9.

No. 12 Awakening in the Woods

Rapid broken octaves in both hands. Dramatic and virtuostic writing. The repeated full-note chords should not overpower the single-note melody. Level 9.

No. 13 The Storm

Exciting, three-page depiction. Helpful in developing a student's control of soft playing and brilliant passagework. Highly motivating writing that fits the hand well. Appropriate for a student who can build dynamic levels quickly. Level 7.

No. 14 Lay of the Gondolier

Andantino con moto. Lyrical right-hand line with broken chords in the left. Level 8.

No. 15 Sylphs

Exuberant writing with rapid light right-hand figures that fit the hand easily. Looks more difficult on the page than it is. Level 8.

No. 16 Parting

Sometimes agitated writing in a primarily chordal work. Left-hand octaves add resonance to the sonority. Especially good for a strong player. Level 8.

No. 17 March

Full chords and vigorous writing. Has a certain rhythmic and melodic sameness. Level 8.

No. 18 At the Spinning Wheel

Right-hand sixteenth-note passages fit the hand well. A fine study in passage-playing. Level 8.

FERRUCCIO BUSONI (1866–1924) Italy

A fascinating post-Romantic figure who maintained a residence in Berlin most of his life, Busoni was one of the great composer-philosophers of music history, as well as a virtuoso pianist.

Macchiette Medioevali, Op. 33

Six romantic pieces of moderate length, written when Busoni was about 16 years old. They are based on figures from the *commedia dell'arte* and given the titles (in English) *Lady, Knight, Page, Warrior, Astrologist* and *Troubadour*. Interesting, little-known writing. (Breitkopf.) Level 9.

Five Character Pieces

Published posthumously, these pieces were written when Busoni was 12 years old. Surprisingly accomplished writing. Titles include *The Hunt, Song of a Fresh Summer Morning, Village Bustle, The Return* and *Evening Prayer.* (Breitkopf.) Level 8.

C

CÉCILE CHAMINADE (1857–1944) France

Chaminade is recognized as perhaps the most famous French female composer. Her music is characterized by expressive melodies and sparkling rhythms, although her output is often held to be "salon music." She wrote over 200 compositions, some of which were standard fare for many years.

Miscellaneous Pieces

Minuetto, Op. 23

Not significant musically. Slightly harder than the *Sérenade*, Op. 29. Level 9.

Sérénade, Op. 29

Pleasant writing although predictable in phrase structure. Needs adroit voicing of right-hand melody above syncopated accompaniment also in the right hand. Especially suitable for the leisure-time reading of an amateur pianist. Level 8.

Scarf-dance, Op. 37, No. 3

Chaminade's most well known piano work, due in part to its rhythmic and tuneful melody. Contains chromatic passagework. A repetitious parlor piece, once immensely popular. Level 9.

ERNEST CHAUSSON (1855–1899) France

Four Dances, Op. 26

Shows the influence of Franck. Interesting and little-known writing that is accessible to the advancing performer. Movements include *Dédicace, Sarabande, Pavane* and *Forlane*. (Kalmus.) Level 9.

No. 1 Dédicace

Short tranquil selection featuring alternating figures between the hands. Requires the ability to voice a melody over double notes. Appropriate for the student who enjoys dreamy and pensive music. Short and Impressionistic. Level 8.

Paysage, Op. 38

This four-page, slow lyrical solo could be taught to a student who wants to play the Debussy *Arabesque No. 1* but is not yet ready. More romantic than Impressionistic. The flowing arpeggiations and lyrical melody help convey the pensive feeling of viewing a beautiful landscape. (Salabert.) Level 9.

Poem of Love and of the Sea

This two-page solo, slightly easier than *Paysage*, Op. 38, could serve as an Impressionistic selection for a student not yet ready to play the major

Impressionistic works of Debussy and others. Primarily lyrical and flowing in mood. (Salabert.) Level 8.

FRÉDÉRIC CHOPIN (1810–1849) Poland

Chopin arguably composed the most pianistic music in the entire repertoire. Moreover, he was one of the few truly great composers to achieve distinction solely by writing piano music. Even during his lifetime, the popularity of some of the mazurkas, waltzes, nocturnes and polonaises brought Chopin great fame. KK numbers represent entries in the catalogue of Chopin's works by Krystyna Kobylánska in the *Frédéric Chopin Thematisch-bibliographisches Werverzeichnis* of 1979, the most reliable catalogue of Chopin's works; the numbers are given here for miscellaneous works which can be difficult to place and identify. Many standard editions of the works of Chopin are available.

Preludes

The *Preludes* are often considered to be Chopin's most masterful works. They include one in each major and minor key, a plan inspired undoubtedly by the *Well-Tempered Clavier* of J. S. Bach. Many stories surround the completion of the *Preludes* on the island of Majorca, some of them told by Chopin's companion George Sand who was there with him during the violent winter when they were written. While often the *Preludes* are thought of as generally accessible works, many of them are étude-like. Tempo indications are provided since a wide range of possibilities exists.

Prelude in E Minor, Op. 28, No. 4

Largo. Melancholy work, musically sophisticated. The shaping and coloring of the slow sustained right-hand melody is dependent on the harmonic tension created by the chromaticism in the left-hand accompaniment. The climax in measure 17 requires careful pacing of the wide leaps to create tension. Exceptional example of the interdependence of melody on harmony and of harmony on melody. Level 6.

Prelude in B Minor, Op. 28, No. 6

Lento assai. Left hand features a beautiful cello-like melody based on a rising broken chord. Right hand generally accompanies, with a continuous eighth-note repeated figure. Musically sophisticated. Level 6.

Prelude in A Major, Op. 28, No. 7

Andantino. Perhaps the most popular of the preludes; a nostalgic poem. Requires careful pacing of the phrasing as well as adept voicing. A touching work that should be played with a feeling of improvisation. Level 6.

Prelude in E Major, Op. 28, No. 9

Largo. Calls for a big sound and an ear for resonance. Melody is found in the fourth and fifth fingers of the right hand, requiring skillful voicing. Intriguing modulations. Level 8.

Prelude in F-sharp Major, Op. 28, No. 13

Lento. This elegant prelude requires the sustaining of a long melodic line. A work that demands mature musicianship. A fine study in the interplay of melody and accompaniment, and in slow playing that should not drag. Needs careful voicing toward the top of the right hand. Level 10.

Prelude in D-flat Major, Op. 28, No. 15 ("Raindrop")

Sostenuto. Slightly easier than the easiest Chopin nocturnes, this lyric prelude features a beautiful melody in the A section that needs tonal control and inflection. A dark middle section in C-sharp Minor follows. The many repeated notes in the accompaniment should be treated with care to avoid overpowering the other voices. Musical maturity is needed to sustain the long melodic lines, balance the three levels of sound, voice the individual chords and achieve the overall dramatic effect. Level 9.

Prelude in A-flat Major, Op. 28, No. 17

Allegretto. Unpredictable phrase lengths. Interesting harmonic modulations that require calculated color. Level 10.

Prelude in C Minor, Op. 28, No. 20

Largo. A somber work that is popular with pianists of all ages. The piece is a true study in tone color and pacing of *crescendo* and *diminuendo*. All notes in the chords must be played absolutely simultaneously. The last note in the soprano of measure three is purported to be an E-flat since Chopin noted this in the copy of one of his students. Many editions print an E-natural in this place. Level 7.

Prelude in B-flat Major, Op. 28, No. 21

Cantabile. Practically an étude in playing legato left-hand double notes. Long sustained melodic lines that calls for a mature performer. Requires imaginative pedaling. Level 10.

Prelude in G Minor, Op. 28, No. 22

Molto agitato. Dramatic work with resonant left-hand octaves and full sonorities. Study for playing *forte* without harshness. Level 10.

Mazurkas

Chopin's mastery of intimacy is displayed in the mazurkas, which have been referred to as "dances of the soul." In a sense they represent the saying about Chopin that "his heart is sad, his mind is gay." The mazurkas are sad, sweet, dreamy, joyous and more. Many are based on or are a combination of the *mazur, kujawiak* and the *oberek*.

Mazurka in F-sharp Minor, Op. 6, No. 1

Allegro. Strong characterization and flair required. Several different ideas in a work that uses a wide dynamic range. Some right-hand double notes. Level 10.

Mazurka in B-flat Major, Op. 7, No. 1

Vivace. This is one of the most effective of the easier mazurkas. Rhythm is easy to execute. Texture consists generally of right-hand melody above oom-pah-pah accompaniment. Skill in negotiating the left-hand jumps is needed. Level 9.

Mazurka in A Minor, Op. 7, No. 2

Vivo ma non troppo. Another accessible work in which the primary difficulties occur in the brief double-note section for the right hand. ABA da capo form, highly expressive. Rich, romantic sounds are required as fine inflection of the melodic lines. Level 8.

Mazurka in C Major, Op. 7, No. 5

Vivo. The briefest and least fully developed of all of the mazurkas. This work is probably a fragment, and it contains no ending but rather the da capo repeats indefinitely. Level 7.

Mazurka in E Minor, Op. 17, No. 2

Lento ma non troppo. Especially good for a student needing to develop inflection in the right hand. Plaintive writing requiring a mature musician. Level 9.

Mazurka in A Minor, Op. 17, No. 4

Lento ma non troppo. One of the most beautiful mazurkas, requiring a fine sense of rubato and a sensitive ear for harmonic and melodic tension and chromaticism. Chopin at his best. Level 10.

Mazurka in G Minor, Op. 24, No. 1

Lento. Angular melody over a thick oom-pah-pah accompaniment. Harmony is less chromatic than in some mazurkas. Level 9.

Mazurka in B Minor, Op. 30, No. 2

Allegretto. Calls for fine inflection of short motives. Intriguing harmonic writing with an especially interesting chromatic progression that is repeated. Less difficult than it sounds. Level 9.

Mazurka in F Minor, Op. 63, No. 2

Lento. An eerie melancholy permeates the beautiful melody of this work. The theme of the middle section is dance-like, but the performer should avoid playing it too fast. An especially beautiful, little-heard and yet accessible mazurka. Level 10.

Mazurka in G Minor, Op. 67, No. 2

Cantabile. One of the best mazurkas to use as an introduction to this genre and one that is easy to bring off. Grace-notes and voicing considerations occur as well as an oom-pah-pah bass and some double-note writing in the right hand. Calls for a sensitive performer. Level 8.

Mazurka in A Minor, Op. 67, No. 4

Moderato animato. One of the most effective of the moderately fast mazurkas. Calls for subtle use of rubato and fine inflection of the right-hand melody. The passagework here fits the hand very well. Level 9.

Mazurka in A Minor, Op. 68, No. 2

Lento. Another especially beautiful work with a certain nostalgic quality. A solemnity pervades, although the middle section should be played in a slightly faster tempo, suggesting a dance. The economy of material renders this work relatively easy to learn. Level 9.

Mazurka in F Major, Op. 68, No. 3

Allegro ma non troppo. Primarily block-chord writing. One of the most popular mazurkas for teaching, it can become rhythmically monotonous unless phrased in large units. The melody with the drone accompaniment in the B section needs to move forward musically. Some left-hand intricacies appear such as the holding of notes while others in the same hand move. Level 7.

Nocturnes

Irish composer-pianist John Field is considered to be the originator of the Romantic piano composition known as the nocturne ("night-piece"), which became a highly expressive form for Chopin. All of Chopin's nocturnes feature an expressive cantilena melody and wide range of emotion, and are among his most inspired compositions.

Nocturne in E-flat Major, Op. 9, No. 2

Andante. Some feel that this familiar work is the best of the nocturnes. The ability to execute the filigree passagework and to change tone color is essential. Bass notes need resonance. The form is essentially a theme and variations. This is a selection that is often assigned before a student is fully prepared for its difficulties. (Many standard editions.) Level 9.

Nocturne in G Minor, Op. 15, No. 3

Lento. Features an unadorned, languid melody of descending intervals that makes it seem to "sigh." The accompanimental chords must be played quietly. Chorale-like central section calls for skillful voicing. Perhaps the easiest of the nocturnes. Level 9.

Nocturne in B Major, Op. 32, No. 1

Andante sostenuto. Unpredictable changes in similar passages, increasing the difficulty in memorization. Needs a supple rhythmic flow. Highly dramatic ending but the central section is on a small scale. Level 10.

Nocturne in G Minor, Op. 37, No. 1

Andante sostenuto. A deep melancholy permeates this beautiful piece. Some relatively easy florid figures unfold in the right-hand melody. A haunting chorale-like passage forms the middle section. Level 9.

Nocturne in F Minor, Op. 55, No. 1

Andante. Needs careful balance between melody and chords. The performer must sustain the tension in the melodic line to avoid rhythmic monotony. An animated triplet central section provides change in the mood while the final triplet section, which propels to the end, is the most difficult part of this work. Level 10.

Nocturne in E Minor, Op. 72, No. 1 (Posth.)

Andante. Essentially consists of variations on the main idea. A beautifully undulating left-hand accompaniment provides the underpinning for the increasingly florid and impassioned melody. Level 10.

Nocturne in C-sharp Minor, Op. Posth.

Lento con gran expressione. An achingly beautiful melody above arpeggiated left-hand accompaniment. Some of Chopin's most elegant and ravishing writing. The performer needs a fine sense of inflection and the ability to execute filigree passagework.

At the top of the first edition, Chopin wrote "For my sister Louise to play, before she practices my Second Concerto." Indeed, many similarities exist between the themes and passages of this nocturne and the *Concerto in F Minor.* The four manuscripts which Chopin left contain note and rhythm discrepancies. Level 10.

Nocturne in C Minor, Op. Posth.

Andante sostenuto. Appropriate as a student's first nocturne, but not at the level of most of the other nocturnes in terms of maturity or quality of writing. Level 8.

Waltzes

The waltz was the most popular dance of the 19th century, and during Chopin's life his waltzes were among his most popular compositions. Several were published posthumously.

Waltz in A Minor, Op. 34, No. 2

Lento. Lyrical and introspective throughout, with long florid lines that need finesse and careful shaping. A good test of a player's legato. Level 10.

Waltz in D-flat Major, Op. 64, No. 1

Molto vivace and subtitled the "Minute Waltz." Right-hand rapid passagework fits the hand well. Much easier than it sounds. Suitable for working on control of fast passagework. Level 9.

Waltz in C-sharp Minor, Op. 64, No. 2

Tempo guisto. Another well-known waltz that fits the hand well. The primary difficulties may lie in the early reading stages and with the sustained right-hand legato in the central *più lento* section. A subtle rubato is needed for the opening. (Many standard editions.) Level 10.

Waltz in A-flat Major, Op. 64, No. 3

Moderato. Bold modulations and interesting writing. Best played by a mature performer. Level 10.

Waltz in A-flat Major, Op. 69, No. 1

Lento. Lyrical writing with substantial filigree in the right hand. Needs subtle rubato and finesse in phrasing. Especially appropriate for the highly expressive performer. Right-hand passagework has a "crawling" feeling. Level 10.

Waltz in B Minor, Op. 69, No. 2

Moderato. One of the least difficult of the waltzes. A touch of melancholy is found throughout the wandering melodic line. Primarily single-note writing in the A section against an oom-pah-pah accompaniment. Chopin published several editions of the waltzes simultaneously, with occasional slight differences between them. Level 8.

Waltz in F Minor, Op. 70, No. 2, Op. Posth.

Tempo guisto. Much expansion and contraction in the right hand melody. Suitable for the pianist who can inflect a long line. One of the easiest although not the most interesting of the Chopin waltzes. Level 9.

Waltz in E Minor, Op. Posth.

Vivace. Sounds more difficult than it is. Effective and brilliant in performance. Needs a fluid right-hand technique. Level 10.

Waltz in A Minor, Op. Posth.

Lento. One of the best choices for a first Chopin waltz assignment, perhaps appropriate for a performer who has already played some of the easier Haydn or Schubert dances. The large leaps and occasional ornaments need attention. ABA form. Level 7.

Waltz in E-flat Major, Op. Posth.

Sostenuto. Subtitled "To Emile Galliard" and discovered in 1941. Much shorter than any other waltz by Chopin and appropriate as a first Chopin waltz. Should not be confused with another, substantially more difficult, posthumous *E-flat Major Waltz* with many octave reaches in the right hand. Level 7.

Polonaises

The polonaise is a stately 3/4 dance with a distinctive accompaniment rhythm. Chopin imposed on the form a highly lyric and often intensely heroic character. Of the 16 polonaises of Chopin, the first 10 were published during his lifetime. An important national dance of Poland, the polonaise became a vehicle through which Chopin could express his patriotism. All of the posthumous polonaises were actually written by Chopin before he brought out the mature works such as the *Polonaises,* Op. 26.

Polonaise in C-sharp Minor, Op. 26, No. 1

Allegro. Not as difficult as it sounds. In the form of a nocturne with three sections—the polonaise proper, a trio in a slowed tempo, and finally a repetition of the first part. The passionate opening octaves and full chords need arm weight. The central contrasting *meno mosso* requires careful attention to voicing and legato, and for many this may be the most difficult part to learn. Requires a performer with a strong temperament who can also work out details. Effective in performance and one of the best of the accessible polonaises. Level 10.

Polonaise in E-flat Minor, Op. 26, No. 2

Maestoso. A somber work with suppressed rumblings. For a student with a large hand span and the ability to inflect small units. The double notes, chords and awkward key provide the primary problems here. Level 10.

Polonaise in A Major, Op. 40, No. 1

Allegro con brio. Often referred to as the "Military Polonaise." Deserving of its popularity because of its high-spirited character and strongly characteristic polonaise rhythms. Full chords need appropriate use of the arm to achieve rich sounds. A triumphant work, at times bombastic. Level 10.

Polonaise in C Minor, Op. 40, No. 2

Allegro maestro. Left-hand octave melody in the opening needs careful voicing and matching of melodic tones. Strong fingers are needed for the double notes at the end of the first part. The A-flat lyrical section requires careful voicing above the thick accompaniment. Level 10.

Polonaise in G Minor, Op. Posth.

Allegro non troppo. A short and accessible work with many different ideas closely juxtaposed. Careful attention to the various rhythmic values is essential. An intermediate teaching piece, although it should be played by a careful student who can avoid its many possible pitfalls. Level 8.

Polonaise in B-flat Major, Op. Posth.

Allegro maestoso. Right-hand passagework above left-hand broken-chord accompaniment. The trio contains interesting changes of harmony and texture. Composed when Chopin was seven years old. Sounds more difficult than it is. Level 7.

Études

The *Études*, Op. 10 and Op. 25 of Chopin are masterworks in terms of musical substance and technical value. All, however, are beyond the range of this book in level of difficulty.

Trois Nouvelles Études (1839)

These three pieces were composed for the instruction book of Moscheles and Fétis. *No. 1 in F Minor* features a right-hand melody in triplets over a left-hand accompaniment in sweeping ascending and descending broken chords. *No. 2 in A-flat* also works two-against-three with the melody in the top right-hand chords played against the bottom left-hand eighths. *No. 3 in D-flat* combines advanced voicing within a hand and is the most difficult of the three. (Many standard editions.) Level 10.

Miscellaneous Pieces

Album Leaf in E Major, KK IVb/12

One-page piece with a relatively thick texture. Appropriate for the performer able to play the waltzes but desiring a shorter Chopin work. Level 8.

Two Bourrées, KK VIIb 1/2

Historically conceived though lacking in profundity. Level 7.

Cantabile in B-flat Major, KK IVb/6

Beautiful, lyrical writing, in a work similar to an abbreviated nocturne. One of the best and most inspired of the short pieces. Level 7.

Contradanse in G Major, KK Anh. Ia/4

Good for the performer who plays chordal pieces well. Some potentially awkward voicings and chordal spacings. Two printed pages. Level 7.

Three Écossaises, Op. 72c (Posth.)

Light pieces with idiomatic technical passages. Composed when Chopin was 16. Little-known works of limited pedagogical interest. Level 8.

Écossaise No. 1

The best-known of the *Three Écossaises*, featuring many large skips about the keyboard. Dance-like character and brilliant in places. The complex, bouncing rhythms require accuracy in counting to avoid playing triplets. Finger dexterity is required. Level 7.

Largo in E-flat Major, KK IVb/5

A solemn piece in 4/4 in which one can almost detect a religious character. Primarily chordal, and slightly more difficult than the Chopin *Prelude in C Minor*, Op. 28, No. 20, but in the same vein. Level 7.

Sostenuto in E-flat Major, KK IVb/10

Short work that may precede the study of a pianist's first Chopin waltzes. Lyrical melody in single notes. More accessible than many of the preludes. Effective and rewarding. Levels 6–7.

Valse Mélancolique, KK Anh. 1a/7

Unusual work with an especially beautiful B section. Manageable for a late-intermediate or early-advanced performer. A slow work in a dance-like idiom. The key of F-sharp Minor and Major may seem intimidating. Level 8.

Fantasie-Impromptu, Op. 66

Not published in Chopin's lifetime yet now an audience favorite. Composed in ABA-Coda form with the well-known three against four passages in the A sections creating a whirlwind effect. The music fits the hand exceptionally well. The beautiful melody of the B section has been transcribed frequently for other idioms and taken out of context. Requires strong fingers and some facility. (Many standard editions.) Level 10.

Miscellaneous Volumes

Chopin: An Introduction to His Piano Works, ed. Palmer

Provides an excellent crosssection of the most accessible piano works of Chopin and includes some little-known works. Extensive prefatory material on Chopin's style, ornamentation, and pedaling as well as on the concept of *rubato*. (Alfred.) Levels 7–10.

Chopin: The First Book for Pianists, ed. Palmer

Contains the easiest selections from *Chopin: An Introduction to His Piano Works*, ed. Palmer. Three easiest preludes, three mazurkas, *Albumleaf,*

Cantabile in B-flat Major, Largo in E-flat Major and other similar works. (Alfred.) Levels 7–8.

Chopin: Selected Favorites, ed. Palmer

Includes mazurkas, preludes, waltzes, polonaises, nocturnes, études and the *Fantasie-Impromptu*. (Alfred.) Levels 7–10.

Dances of Chopin, ed. Hinson

Miscellaneous works found here include the *Waltz in C-sharp Minor*, Op. 64, No. 2, *Polonaise in A Major*, Op. 40, No. 1, *Mazurka in F Major*, Op. 68, No. 3, *Three Écossaises*, Op. 72, No. 3 and *Tarantella in A-flat Major*, Op. 43. (Alfred.) Levels 8–10.

At the Piano With Chopin, ed. Hinson

The first 22 pages of this volume consist of extensive background material on Chopin and on the pieces included here. (Alfred.) Levels 7–10.

Chopin: An Introductory Album, ed. Jones

A fine student introductory edition. Some of the most important and accessible solo works of Chopin are found here. Included are such works as *Waltz in A Minor*, Op. 34, No. 2, *Nocturne in G Minor*, Op. 15, No. 3, *Prelude in D-flat*, Op. 28, No. 15, *Albumleaf*, Op. Posth. and *Largo*, Op. Posth. Well-edited, the variety and rather uniform level of difficulty of the pieces included is desirable. (Associated Board of the Royal Schools of Music.) Levels 7–10.

Klavierunterricht mit Fryderyk Chopin, Sechs Leichte Mazurkas, ed. Walter

Six of the easiest mazurkas. Included are those in F Major, Op. 68, No. 3; B Major, Op. 7, No. 1; G Minor, Op. 24, No. 1; A Major, Op. 24, No. 3; C Major, Op. 33, No. 3; and F Minor, Op. 7, No. 3. (Breitkopf.) Level 9.

Klavierunterricht mit Fryderyk Chopin, Leichte Klavierwerke, ed. Walter

In addition to the three commonly taught *Preludes* from Op. 28, in E Minor, B Minor, and A Minor, this volume contains two very easy waltzes, a nocturne, and the "Rain-drop" prelude. (Breitkopf.) Levels 8–10.

Chopin: Master Series for the Young, ed. Hughes

Unfortunately this volume extracts portions of pieces to serve as the easiest selections in this volume. That practice and the extremely wide range in level of difficulty of the pieces included makes this volume impractical. (G. Schirmer.) Levels 6–10.

Chopin: Easiest Piano Pieces, ed. Scholtz

The selections here are printed in large type, and are obviously intended for very young talented students. Included are the *Preludes* in B Minor, A Major, and C Minor, *Mazurkas* in A Minor, Op. 7, No. 2 and E Minor, Op. 17, No. 2, and *Waltz in A Minor*, Op. 34, No. 2. (Peters.) Levels 7–10.

Masters for the Young: Chopin

Small print, some questionable alterations from originals, and a lack of sources for the pieces appearing in original form. Included are two waltzes, two mazurkas, and the *Polonaise in A Major*, Op. 40, No. 1, here transposed to C Major. (Kalmus.) Levels 9–10.

Introduction to the Cortot Editions of Chopin Works

This fine collection contains some of the best and most accessible works of Chopin from the preludes, mazurkas, polonaises, nocturnes, waltzes and ecossaises. The works included have extensive prefatory material by Alfred Cortot, including practice suggestions. Valuable for the combination of selections included and for Cortot's notes. (Salabert.) Levels 8–10.

Chopin: Selected Easy Pieces, ed. Paderewski

An excellent collection containing some of the most accessible works from the preludes, mazurkas, polonaises and waltzes. A valuable anthology of Chopin's works. (Marks.) Levels 8–10.

Chopin: Piano Music Inspired
by Women in His Life, ed. Hinson

An interesting variety of music is provided. Especially notable is the historical background provided about Louise Chopin, Emily Elsner, George Sand, Celina Symanowska, Maria Wodzínska, Baroness Charlotte de Rothschild and others. (Alfred.) Levels 7–10.

GIUSEPPE CONCONE (1810–1861) Italy

25 Melodic Studies, Op. 24

An excellent collection of tuneful technical studies for the intermediate pianist. Most are one page long and use customary Classical or Romantic-era figures. Students playing easy Burgmüller pieces might also study these works. More interesting than many of the Czerny studies. (Many standard editions.) Level 5.

No. 25 (Allegro brillante)

Requires clean and facile passagework. Filled with comfortable patterns. The phrasing requires attention to the long line. Level 7.

15 Studies in Style and Expression, Op. 25

Substantially more difficult than the Op. 24 pieces. All begin with a short prelude and are then followed by a more extended character-étude. The latter contain valuable practice in playing technical idioms of the standard Romantic repertoire. The selections are given titles such as *The Robin Redbreast*, *The Swallow* and *Triumphal March*. (Many standard editions.) Levels 9–10.

24 Brilliant Preludes, Op. 37

These are actually études in all the Major and Minor keys. They are easy to read and provide the pianist with practice in perfecting typical passagework such as scales and broken chords. The *Preludes* are short, often only 12 or 16 measures long. Valuable for study by both serious students and amateur pianists. (Many standard editions.) Level 8.

Additional Works for Study:
Op. 30 20 Studies on the Singing Touch
Op. 44 15 Studies in Expression

JOHANN BAPTIST CRAMER (1771–1858) Germany

A pupil of Clementi in London (where he lived most of his life), Cramer's greatest work is his piano method *Grosse Praktische Pianoforte Schule* (1815), which is in five parts. The last part is comprised of the 84 studies which make up the well-known *Études*.

84 Études, Op. 50

Described by Beethoven as "the chief basis of all genuine playing," the Cramer études actually predate the studies of Czerny. They are mainly used for the development of cantabile style and the playing of broken chords. Considered to be some of the most important études for the level slightly beneath that of the Chopin études.

Many editions with varying numbers of études are available. In the last edition appearing during Cramer's life, *16 Nouvelles Études* were added, making 100. Among the editions available are *Cramer-Bülow 60 Selected Studies* (Peters), *Cramer 84 Studies* (Kalmus, Schott and others) and *Cramer-Bülow 50 Selected Studies*. (Many standard editions.) Levels 9–10.

D

ALEXANDER DARGOMIZHSKY (1813–1869) Russia

Collected Piano Works

Many are salon-type pieces with special romantic appeal. (Kalmus.)

Marche in E-flat

A Russian counterpart to a Sousa march. Two pages. Full chords, square writing. Might be motivating for a student whose interest in piano study is waning. Level 8.

Française

Prevalent oom-pah-pah chords in the left hand dominate the march-like flavor of this highly patterned piece. Rich, full sounds. Level 8.

Valse Melancolique

Rich in national spirit and rhythmic verve. This writing is more entertaining than profound. Level 8.

Valse in E-flat

Sentimental, appealing writing. This could provide a good introduction to heart-on-sleeve Romantic style for those ready to play Schubert waltzes. Level 7.

Cosaque

Similar to the well-known Beethoven *Écossaise in G Major.* Full of spirit and vigor. Level 5.

Valse Brillante

Notable mostly for its general flair. Oom-pah-pah left hand and right hand repeated notes and chord passages. Might be a student's introduction to the Romantic-style brilliant playing. Level 7.

FREDERICK DELIUS (1862–1934) Great Britain

Three Preludes

Thin textures with flowing arpeggios or repeated figurations. Harp-like, within an impressionistic framework. (Oxford.) Level 8.

Five Piano Pieces

Short selections in a moderately contemporary idiom. (Boosey and Hawkes.) Levels 9–10.

GAETANO DONIZETTI (1797–1848) Italy

Donizetti wrote many solo works for piano, most of them for the upper-intermediate or early-advanced performer. Stylistically oriented toward the Classical era. A good number of these works have been recently discovered.

Allegro in F

A somewhat pretentious 10-page sonata-allegro movement containing many typical figurations and flourishes. Might be enjoyed by the adult piano enthusiast who knows the standard literature well and wants to play something unusual. (Boccaccini and Spada, Peters.) Level 10.

Adagio and Allegro in G Major

Dramatic writing with many typical figurations. Fits the hand well. (Boccaccini and Spada.) Level 10.

Allegro in C Major

Barcarolle character and sentimental mood. Requires legato octaves for the melody. (Boccaccini and Spada.) Level 10.

La Ricordanza

Sentimental, lyrical adagio movement. Easier than any of the Chopin nocturnes. (Boccaccini and Spada.) Level 8.

Larghetto in A Minor (*Una Furtiva Lacrima*)

A two-page nocturne on the famous aria *Una Furtiva Lacrima*. Melody in octaves, thirds and single notes over an arpeggiated left hand. (Boccaccini and Spada.) Level 9.

Capriccio in Sinfonia

Dramatic, operatic writing. Appropriate for the opera buff or as sight-reading for accomplished pianists. (Boccaccini and Spada.) Level 10.

Sinfonia in C Major

Displays many clichés of orchestral reductions, although composed for piano. Not for serious study. (Boccaccini and Spada.) Level 10.

Sinfonia in D Major

According to Pietro Spada, "It seems to be the rapid skeleton of an over-ture for a comic opera and is concluded by the faster ritual 'Coda' with repeated cadenzas and conclusive formulas then in use in the theater." (Boccaccini and Spada.) Level 10.

ALEXANDER DORN (1833–1901) Germany

24 Studies in all Major and Minor Keys, Op. 100

Romantic both in texture and in harmonic vocabulary. Many are too long or too repetitive to be practical. Figurations used are typical ones found in some of the best romantic period writing. See especially the *Studies in B Minor* and *C-sharp Minor*. Book 1 contains the studies in the keys of C, A Minor, G Major and on around the circle of fifths through G-sharp Minor. The remainder are in Book 2. (G. Schirmer and others.) Levels 7–10.

No. 6 in B Minor

The hands continually alternate in eighths throughout. Melodic line is played by both hands. Effective and impassioned. Worth investigating. Level 8.

No. 10 in C-sharp Minor

This work clearly reflects the volatile spirit of Romanticism, here reflected in the sweeping right-hand broken chords and arpeggios. The performer should strive for clear voicing of the left-hand melody above the tempestuous broken chords. Levels 7–8.

MARIE-AUGUSTE DURAND (1830–1909) France

Chaconne, Op. 62

The typical pianistic figurations found here will help develop facility. The A sections feature a legato single-note right hand over a staccato accompaniment. Somewhat repetitive musically. (G. Schirmer.) Level 6.

Valse in E-flat, Op. 83

An exceedingly popular and effective selection. The flourishes and figurations fit the hand to maximize the virtuosic effect with surprisingly little effort. A piece to motivate the right student. (Boston, G. Schirmer.) Level 8.

Valse in A-flat, Op. 86

Requires agile fingerwork, but rewarding for the student with a facile technique. The performer needs a natural feeling for rubato. The fast scale passages sound more difficult than they are. (G. Schirmer.) Level 8.

JEAN-BAPISTE DUVERNOY (1802–1880) France

The School of Mechanism, Op. 120

These 15 short studies were written to precede Czerny's *School of Velocity*. They embrace traditional pianistic figures—scales, arpeggios and sequential patterns—that occur in standard literature. These studies are generally two pages long and are some of the better studies available for the intermediate student who plays at the level of Kuhlau sonatinas. (Many standard editions.) Level 7.

Elementary Studies, Op. 176

Twenty-five excellent and little-known studies for the elementary pianist. These pieces could take the place of some of the less interesting Czerny études. They deal with the development of a cantabile tone, legato playing and a kinesthetic feeling for chord playing, as well as with the development of velocity. (Many standard editions.) Level 4.

No. 24 Étude

Excellent study in parallel thirds and sixths, especially helpful in developing a flexible wrist. Level 4.

ANTONÍN DVOŘÁK (1841–1904) Czechoslovakia

Perhaps the best known of the Czech composers, Dvořák's reputation rests largely on his symphonic and chamber works. He spent three years in the United States, in New York and in Iowa.

Silhouettes, Op. 8

This 1879 set consists of rewritings of pieces that Dvořák had sketched in the early 1870s. Found among these 12 character pieces are some of Dvořák's most accessible works for the early-advanced performer. Most are short, often with a folk flavor. Nos. 1, 5 and 12 share the same thematic material, but see especially Nos. 2 and 4. (Belwin-Mills, Masters Music, Supraphon and others.)

No. 1

An *allegro feroce* opening and closing surround a central *allegretto grazioso* which displays nationalistic overtones. Effective writing with strong contrast. Level 8.

No. 2

Lyrical and highly Romantic writing requiring voicing of inner parts. Level 8.

No. 4

Marked *vivace*, this selection is good for the spirited pianist. The infectious rhythms and nationalistic overtones of the middle section combine to make this an appealing piece for both listener and audience. The dramatic octaves in this selection can be motivating. Level 9.

No. 5

This selection could be a useful one for developing a kinesthetic sense for playing chords. It is a spirited *presto* with some chord changes. Level 9.

No. 7

A good precursor to full-sounding Rachmaninoff works. The patterns in this vigorous dance-like piece lie well under the hand, and the central section offers energetic octave passagework. Level 8.

No. 8

Staccato passages and characteristic five-note flourishes lend a sophisticated and playful character to this charming three-page work. Level 8.

No. 12

Marked "allegro feroce," this five-page work is another for a student who has flair. Parts of it sound Lisztian and yet the figurations fit the hand well. Big and full romantic sounds. Level 9.

Waltzes, Op. 54

Several of the eight waltzes seem to combine traits from the music of both Schumann and Chopin, although none of this is true concert material. Good stepping stones to some of Chopin's more difficult waltzes. (Masters Music.)

No. 3

Marked "poco allegro," this selection is reminiscent of the Schumann *Novelettes*. Lively rhythms and unabashedly Romantic sounds. Level 9.

No. 4

A charming Chopinesque melody is featured above a waltz accompaniment. This lively selection fits the hand well so that the performer receives maximum return for his or her effort. Winsome writing. Level 9.

No. 5

Reminiscent of the Chopin *Waltz in C-sharp Minor.* Figurations are kinesthetic and the writing is highly patterned. Level 9.

No. 7

Light and flowing. Romantic. Level 9.

No. 8

Allegro vivace. This movement requires some passion and agility but the music is not difficult to comprehend. Especially good for the student who likes "big" pieces. Level 10.

Albumleaf No. 2 (from Four Albumleaves)

Miniature Romantic tone-poem. Requires adept voicing of accompaniment and inner voices. (Peters.) Level 8.

Albumleaf No. 3 (from Four Albumleaves)

A good choice for a pianist not yet ready to play the Brahms *Rhapsody in G Minor,* Op. 79, No. 2 and needing a piece of the same spirit. Rich sonorities, effective writing. (Peters.) Level 8.

Humoreske, Op. 101, No. 7

The composer's best-known piano piece. Filled with grace-notes and Bohemian flavor. Needs a dance-like feeling and a rhythmic lilt. (Many standard editions.) Level 10.

Miscellaneous Volumes
Dvořák Selected Works

Contains some of Dvořák's best pieces for the early-advanced performer, including selections from the waltzes, silhouettes, mazurkas and humoreskes. Would be a valuable source from which to gain an overview of Dvořák's piano music. (Schott.) Levels 9–10.

Easy Original Pieces for Piano, ed. Roggenkamp

Contains some of the shorter and easier pieces. Valuable collection. (Universal.) Levels 6–10.

Works for Additional Study:
Op. 56 Mazurkas
Op. 85 Poetic Pictures
Op. 101 Humoresques

E

EDWARD ELGAR (1857–1934) Great Britain

See entry under 20th-century period.

ALBERT ELLMENREICH (1816–1905)

Spinning Song, Op. 14, No. 4

One of the most loved of all early-intermediate teaching pieces. The ascending scalewise finger patterns and the syncopations lend strong character to this effective solo. (Many standard editions.) Level 4.

F

GABRIEL FAURÉ (1845–1924) France

Most of Fauré's compositions demand musical maturity. Although Fauré never abandoned tonality, he used his own personally colored harmonic language. His music is marked by subtle emotion and often features syncopations and cross-rhythms, broken chords and verse-like melodies. Few of Fauré's works other than the *Romances Without Words*, Op. 17 and the *Piéces Breves*, Op. 84 are truly within the scope of difficulty in this book.

Romances Sans Paroles (Romances Without Words), Op. 17

Three lyrical works with patterned accompaniment. These pieces comprise some of the best of the scant amount of literature available at the upper-intermediate level for students who want to study French music of this era. See especially No. 1 (*Andante quasi allegretto*) with the melody in single notes, sustained note accompaniment, and off-beat chords and No. 3 (*Andante moderato*), a work in two voices and the most accessible of the set. No. 2 (*Allegro molto*) features a beautiful melody with broken left-hand chords, a good piece to teach longer phrases and tone quality. Should be better known. (International.) Level 8.

Eight Short Pieces, Op. 84

These pieces were given their descriptive titles by the publisher in 1903 against Fauré's wishes. See especially the *No. 1 Capriccio in E-flat* and *No. 5 Improvisation in C-sharp Minor*. (Many standard editions.)

No. 1 Capriccio in E-flat Major

Little-known work that is accessible to the early-advanced performer. Features flowing, broken arpeggios divided between the hands. A miniature impromptu. One of the best of Fauré's easier works. Level 8.

No. 2 Fantasie in A-flat Major

Displays a sensitive, dreamy and calm nature. Contains many broken chords and flowing arpeggiations. The many accidentals make the score difficult to read. Level 9.

No. 3 Fugue in A Minor

An academic study with lush harmonies. A good choice for a student who prefers literature from the Romantic period and needs to develop basic skills in contrapuntal playing. Level 8.

No. 4 Adagietto in E Minor

Contains a march-like rhythm that gives it a noble feeling. Requires a performer with the ability to sustain a melodic line. Level 9.

No. 5 Improvisation in C-sharp Minor

A highly expressive two-page work with lyrical melodies, the *Improvisation* is one of the best of the shorter pieces of Fauré. The score is difficult to read initially, but the writing is of high quality. Should be heard more frequently. Level 8.

No. 6 Allegrese

Marked *allegro giocoso*, this effective work is comprised primarily of broken chords arpeggiated between the hands and a lyrical melody. Typical of the florid arpeggiated style which many associate with the works of Fauré. Level 8.

No. 7 Fugue in E Minor

More difficult than No. 3 in this set and somewhat less profound. Three-voice writing, but homophonic as well as contrapuntal. Level 9.

No. 8 Nocturne in D-flat Major

This work in one continuous section was initially called a "Prelude" by Fauré and could easily have become another of his Barcarolles. Flowing sixteenths throughout with substantial fingerwork required. This *adagio non troppo* work in D-flat Major needs skillful control of the melodic line. Level 10.

Miscellaneous Pieces

Impromptu No. 2 in F Minor, Op. 31

Probably the most accessible and effective of the *Impromptus*. Rippling eighth-note triplets occur throughout this flowing work. For the performer with strong fingers and a strong structural sense. A fine alternative to a Chopin nocturne. Some brilliant writing in a charming work. (Many standard editions.) Level 10.

Nocturne No. 10, Op. 99

Large central climax. Lyrical writing that calls for playing a legato melody over accompaniment in the same hand. The performer needs a good sense of voicing and pacing. (Heugel.) Level 10.

Nocturne No. 11, Op. 104, No. 1

Plaintive, lyrical writing in a sophisticated harmonic framework. For the musician who can hear and project harmonic changes with finesse. Four pages, with periodic thick passagework. This nocturne was composed upon the sudden death of the wife of Pierre Lalo, a music critic of *Le Temps* and son of the famous composer. A poignant but restrained elegy. (Durand.) Level 10.

Barcarolle No. 4, Op. 44

Lush harmonies and rich arpeggiated accompanimental figures in this effective *sicilienne*. (Hamelle.) Level 10.

Barcarolle No. 10, Op. 104, No. 2

Yearning mood with a Dorian-mode theme that is treated to several variations. This piece could strengthen a student's ability to project melody over a thicker texture and to spin forward a long melodic line. Nostalgic and lyrical. Five pages. (Durand.) Level 9.

Miscellaneous Volumes

While few of Fauré's pieces can be called teaching pieces, several collections contain appropriate selections from his output.

Album of Piano Pieces

Contains some of the most widely played barcarolles and nocturnes, along with one of the *Romances Without Words*, the *Third Impromptu* and *Improvisation*, Op. 84, No. 5. (G. Schirmer.) Level 10.

Selected Piano Pieces

This volume contains perhaps the largest number of miscellaneous pieces of any of the collections. It also contains many frequently played works. (Cramer.) Level 10.

Additional Works for Study:
Op. 50 Pavane
Op. 78 Sicilienne

ZDENKO FIBICH (1850–1900) Czechoslovakia

A noted Czech composer of his time, Fibich was strongly influenced by Wagner, Liszt and Schumann.

Moods, Impressions and Souvenirs

An extensive collection of 376 pieces that were the product of Fibich's close relationship with a female student. According to Thomas Johnson in his Associated Board of the Royal Schools of Music collection, "Whenever they met, he would present her with a new piece . . . mostly constructed in ternary form. The *Souvenirs* recalled specific events; the *Impressions* highlighted Aneeka's physical features; and the *Moods,* among other things, illustrated her dresses."

These short Romantic pieces are slow and lyrical, and often filled with rich textures, calling for careful voicing. Especially appropriate for the expressive, lyrically inclined student. (Associated Board of the Royal Schools of Music.) Level 9.

JOHN FIELD (1782–1837) Ireland

A pupil of Clementi, Field was known primarily as the creator of the nocturne, a form that was perfected by Chopin a generation later. Field composed in a sweet, delicate style that served as a significant influence on Chopin.

18 Nocturnes

The nocturnes are fine preparation for those of Chopin, although a few are of equal difficulty. Liszt edited a collection of the *18 Nocturnes* which is now published by G. Schirmer, among others. Selections from the first nine are the most practical for teaching purposes. (Many standard editions.)

Nocturne No. 1 in E-flat

Sustained melody above triplet broken-chord figuration. Fluid writing in one of the better of the accessible nocturnes. Level 9.

Nocturne No. 2 in C Minor

Florid right-hand passages with skips in the bass render this nocturne more difficult than No. 1. Level 10.

Nocturne No. 3 in A-flat

This work contains busy inner voices and thick textures. More difficult than some Chopin nocturnes. Level 10.

Nocturne No. 5 in B-flat

The most popular of the Field nocturnes, perhaps due to its brevity. Contains an effective central section and an A section with a beautiful cantilena that soars above the arpeggiated accompaniment. Level 9.

Nocturne No. 7 in A Major

An appropriate piece to help improve rapid *leggiero* playing in the right hand. Lyrical writing interspersed with florid passagework. Level 10.

Nocturne No. 9 in E Minor

Soft and melancholy writing in this short adagio. Contains a triplet accompaniment that supports the unadorned melody. One of the best from the opus. Level 8.

Miscellaneous Volumes

Selected Piano Works, ed. Branson

This volume contains some minor works of Field such as *Marche Triomphale, Andante Inédit* and *Nocturne "The Troubadour"* not often found in other sources. Also found here are a sonata movement and another nocturne. (Carl Fischer.) Level 9.

Field: Nocturnes and Other Short Pieces, ed. Barsham

Interesting volume containing seven nocturnes and various other works that are hard to find such as *Marche Triomphale, Sehnsuchts-Waltzer, Waltz in A Major, Polonaise* and *Rondo: 12 O'clock*. The valuable introduction to the book discusses interpretation, fingering, pedaling, phrasing and dynamic marks, text, ornamentation and tempo in Field's music. This introduction along with the textural commentary on each piece make this volume especially valuable. (Associated Board of the Royal Schools of Music.) Levels 8–9.

STEPHEN C. FOSTER (1826–1864) USA

Complete Piano Music, ed. List

A delightful collection of Americana. The melodies are folk tunes, and the settings often feature oom-pah-pah left-hand accompaniments. Cheerful, sometimes rousing. See especially *Old Folks at Home (Theme and Variations)*, *The Old Folks Quadrilles* and *Santa Anna's Retreat From Buena Vista*. (G. Schirmer.) Levels 6–8.

CÉSAR FRANCK (1822–1890) France

Franck's music uses chromatic harmonies and often displays a Catholic religious influence in the writing. His music tends to be Germanic in sound and structure.

Three Earliest Compositions (1835)

Three small contrapuntal pieces taken from Franck's book of exercises in counterpoint and fugue. Of historical significance. (Dover.) Levels 5–6.

Twenty-Five Short Pieces from L'Organiste

Franck wrote 59 miniatures for the harmonium, an organ-like instrument without pedals. Many of them commonly appear in anthologies of piano teaching music since they also sound pleasing on the piano. Twenty-five of the best pieces were included in this practical teaching edition. The writing is highly idiomatic for the keyboard. (Associated Board of the Royal Schools of Music.) Levels 7–8.

Forty-Six Short Pieces, ed. Agay

In this volume are 46 of the pieces from *L'Organiste*, all of which were composed by Franck for the harmonium. Originally the pieces were intended to be used as preludes, postludes, voluntaries and offertories. These selections could be used by the upper-intermediate pianist to cultivate legato playing. (Presser.) Levels 7–8.

Danse Lente

A slow, sentimental waltz, with three repetitions of an eight-measure theme. (Dover.) Level 7.

The Doll's Lament (Les Plaintes d'une Poupée)

A simple work with a legato melody above an eighth-note accompaniment. Calls for refined voicing and phrasing. (Dover.) Level 4.

Polka

Composed by Franck to curb his wife's interest in dancing, this two-page solo (also arranged for piano duet) is a playful, shallow piece. Level 7.

ROBERT FUCHS (1847–1927) Austria

Children's Pieces from Op. 32 and 47

Selections from two of his albums for children. The pieces are charming in their simplicity and unashamed Romanticism. They parallel the intermediate pieces from the Schumann *Album for the Young*, Op. 68. Generally one page long, suitable for teaching Romantic phrasing and voicing. Titles of the works include *Morning Song, Soldier's March, Chatterbox, A Great Mystery* and *The Little Trumpeter.* (Associated Board of the Royal Schools of Music.) Levels 5–7.

Additional Works for Study:
Op. 8 Ländliche Szenen
Op. 31 Piano Studies

G

NIELS GADE (1817–1890) Denmark

Gade was perhaps the most significant Danish composer prior to Carl Nielsen. His style is strongly influenced by his friends Mendelssohn and Schumann.

Aquarellen, Op. 19

A set of 10 titled character pieces, several of which have become popular. Highly sentimental Romanticism. (Peters and other selected editions.)

No. 1 Elegie
Features a soaring melody with a Chopin-like bass. Level 7.

No. 2 Scherzo
Grazioso writing with some left-hand stretches and many accidentals. Level 8.

No. 5 Barkarole

Strong Romantic flavor with rolling broken chords divided between the hands. Lyrical and sweeping writing with some octave passages. Excellent preparation for the playing of Chopin. Level 8.

Children's Christmas Eve, Op. 36

Enticing set of character pieces for the intermediate performer. Includes two introductory pieces, *Christmas Chimes* and *Christmas Psalm* (without number), three pieces in a suite called *The Christmas Tree*, and a concluding movement *Good Night*. The three pieces in *The Christmas Tree*, *No. 1 Entrance March*, *No. 2 The Boys' Round Dance*, and *No. 3 The Little Girls' Dance* are the best. Little-known. (Associated Board of the Royal Schools of Music, Kalmus and other standard editions.) Level 7.

No. 2 from The Christmas Tree, The Boys' Round Dance

Lively piece that fits the hand well. Several ideas are present, linked by a single rhythmic element. Employs many chords and is effective in performance. Level 7.

No. 3 from the Christmas Tree, The Little Girls' Dance

Highly reminiscent of Chopin and excellent preparation for his waltzes. Rondo form in E Major with alternate sections in B and A Major. Enticing passagework conveys the feeling of dancing and whirling. Graceful, lyrical dance. In some respects, reminiscent of an easier version of the Chopin "Minute Waltz." Level 7.

Good Night

Needs facility in moving about the keyboard and in playing chords. Not as effective as the second and third selections in this opus. The rhythmic complexity needs careful attention. Level 6.

Miscellaneous Volumes

Aquarelles and Other Pieces, ed. Salter

Contains works taken from albums that Gade published between about 1850 and 1880 including selections from *Aquarelles*, Op. 19 and *Children's Christmas Eve*, Op. 36. This volume provides an interesting and varied overview of his piano compositions. (Associated Board of the Royal Schools of Music.) Levels 7–9.

LÉONARD GAUTIER (n.d.) France

Le Secret

At one time, this pleasant, unassuming selection appeared in all of the popular piano anthologies. Oom-pah-pah accompaniment and simple eighth-note melody. (G. Schirmer.) Level 8.

BENJAMIN GODARD (1849–1895) France

Studies for Children (Études Enfantines), Op. 149, Book 1

Godard was influenced by Schumann; in fact he orchestrated Schumann's *Scenes from Childhood*, Op. 15 in 1876. Perhaps better described as character pieces, these 10 selections for upper-intermediate students follow predictable harmonic patterns. The ideas are simple, but charming. See especially *Marche des Garconnets, Marche des Fillettes, Taquinerie* and *Peur de l'enfer*. (Associated Board of the Royal Schools of Music, Simrock.) Level 7.

CHARLES GOUNOD (1818–1893) France

Funeral March of a Marionette

This well-known work based on a single tuneful short motive was first published by Gounod as a piano solo and later orchestrated. ABA form with full solid chords in the middle section. (G. Schirmer.) Level 7.

Marche Pontificale

Pompous and chordal, but rather ordinary writing. It could be used by a student who needs to work on the kinesthetic feeling of diatonic chords, or who needs to stress rhythmic surety. (G. Schirmer.) Level 6.

Miscellaneous Volumes

Funeral March of a Marionette and Other Pieces, ed. Jones

Although Gounod wrote little for piano solo, 10 interesting selections are included in this volume. The music is strongly Romantic and sometimes sentimental. See especially *Barcarolle, The Evening, May Morning* and *Children's Dance*. (Associated Board of the Royal Schools of Music.) Level 7.

ENRIQUE GRANADOS (1867–1916) Spain

Granados lived most of his life in Barcelona, where he established his reputation as a leading piano virtuoso and teacher. He felt a strong tie with his country's past and with the paintings of Goya. Granados died as a result of World War I: he was sailing back to Spain from the United States on the British liner Sussex when it was torpedoed by a German submarine.

Stories of the Young, Op. 1 (Cuentos de la Juvenitud)

The 10 selections are lush and lyrical, and appear to be influenced by Schumann's *Scenes from Childhood*, Op. 15 and *Album for the Young*, Op. 68. See especially No. 1, *Dedication*; No. 3, *May Song*; and No. 8, *The Phantom*. (Associated Board of the Royal Schools of Music, Union Musical.)

No. 1 Dedication

One-page work dedicated to Granados' son. Lyrical and in three voices with melody and triplet accompaniment in the right hand. The texture is similar to Schumann's *About Strange Lands and People*, Op. 68, No. 1, but this work is slightly more difficult. It can provide a fine study in finger substitution. Level 5.

No. 3 May Song

Enchanting melody above an extended broken-chord accompaniment in a work that may be appropriate for those who are not yet ready to play Chopin nocturnes. Level 7.

No. 5 Coming from the Fountain

Reflective and tranquil work with a lyrical melody and an arpeggiated left hand in a Chopin-like style. The double notes in the right-hand melody make this piece seem more difficult than it initially appears. Level 8.

Valses Poeticos

One of Granados' best-known teaching works, this composition consists of a series of seven waltzes with an introduction and a concluding waltz. Preferably, the entire set should be played together. (Dover, Kalmus International, Union Musical and other standard editions.)

12 Spanish Dances, Op. 5

Effective set of pieces for the student of Spanish piano music. The titles are: *No. 1 Minuetto; No. 2 Oriental; No. 3 Zarabanda; No. 4 Villanesca; No. 5 Andaluza or Playera; No. 6 Jota or Rondalla aragonesa; No. 7 Valenciana; No. 8 Asturiana; No. 9 Mazurka; No. 10 Danza triste; No. 11 Zambra;* and *No. 12 Arabesca.* See especially Nos. 1, 2, 5 and 6. (Dover, International and other standard editions.) Levels 9–10.

No. 1 Minuetto

Broad chords and a catchy rhythmic motive may appeal to those who like works of Rachmaninoff. For the pianist able to play resonant and full chords. Level 9.

No. 5 Andaluza or Playera

Popular work, featuring a sparkling theme and a left-hand accompaniment depicting the Spanish dance idiom and castanets. Level 10.

Six Expressive Studies

Primarily lyrical pieces. Pleasant, almost naive music. See especially La Ultima Pavana and Pastoral. (Masters Music, Union Musical.) Level 8.

Bocetos

Set of four solos for upper-intermediate pianists with characteristic Spanish rhythms. See especially *Vals muy lento*, notable for its strong character, and *La Campana de la Tarde* with its native melody above a simple accompaniment. (Union Musical.) Level 8.

Escenas Poéticas, Book 1

Three movements that reflect Granados' interest in the music of Grieg, Schumann and Liszt. Inviting music, filled with Granados' unique modulations and melodic style. Titles include *Berceuse, Eva and Walter* and *Dance of the Rose*. See especially the second and third of these pieces. (Dover.) Level 9.

Escenas Romanticas

Little-known set of six pieces that sounds less Spanish than most of Granados' works. Resembles Chopin in emotional content, and occasionally in figuration; all but two of these pieces are advanced. See especially *No. 4 Allegretto*. (International and other editions.) Levels 8–10.

No. 4 Allegretto

Only 19 measures long, the shortest in the set, featuring dance-like figurations in the melody and numerous arpeggiations. This work would pair well with *No. 6 Epilogue*. Level 8.

No. 6 Epilogue

Nocturne-like work that features a beautiful lyrical melody in single notes and a left-hand accompaniment of arpeggiated chords. For a student who is not yet ready to play a nocturne. Level 8.

Sketches

Four enjoyable, brief upper-intermediate pieces. See especially *No. 2 El Hada y el Niño*. (Masters Music.) Level 8.

Carezza, Op. 38

Especially appropriate for the performer who enjoys full sonorities. Pianistic writing throughout. (Masters Music.) Level 9.

Miscellaneous Volumes

My First Granados

An interesting and useful mixture of selections from five of Granados' major works. Included are *Evening Bell, Marguerite's Song, The Hunger's Awakening, Oriental* and more. (Ricordi.) Levels 8–9.

EDVARD GRIEG (1843–1907) Norway

Grieg stands at the forefront of those composers who write in a nationalistic idiom. Much of his output is based on Norwegian folk music. The *Lyric Pieces* are some of the greatest character pieces in the teaching repertoire.

Lyric Pieces

The *Lyric Pieces* comprise the cornerstone of Grieg's teaching material for piano. They are simple pieces that are descriptive, delicate and possess a refined lyrical quality. It is believed the titles were written first. Most of the pieces are based on ABA or ABABA forms and have thin textures of rarely more than two or three voices. There are 10 books, each with a different opus number and each containing six to eight pieces.

Lyric Pieces, Opp. 12, 38, 43, 47, 54, 57, 62, 65, 68, 71

These works provide a treasure house of engaging and imaginative writing in the Romantic idiom. Annotations of various selections are below, followed by a listing of the *Lyric Pieces* by opus number. (Many standard editions.)

Arietta, Op. 12, No. 1

Features three layers of sound, with the middle voice in sixteenths split between the hands. Appropriate for control of the right-hand thumb. Expressive and beautiful writing. Good preparation for the Mendelssohn *Songs Without Words*. Level 6.

Waltz, Op. 12, No. 2

Excellent study in articulation and in inflection of melody. Right-hand melody calls for independence of fingers and the work needs a light, dance-like character throughout. Suitable preparation for Chopin waltzes. (Alfred.) Level 6.

Watchman's Song, Op. 12, No. 3

Composed by Grieg after he attended a performance of Shakespeare's *Macbeth*. The ghosts in the night and the watchman's shout are depicted in the central mysterious *intermezzo* ("Spirits of the Night"), which should prompt the student's imagination. The A sections are primarily chordal. Deserving of its popularity. Level 5.

Dances of the Elves, Op. 12, No. 4 (Elfin Dance)

A finger piece with running eighth-note figures and staccato chords. Contains two basic rhythmic motives. This mysterious work could be especially good to bring out an inhibited student. Needs right-hand dexterity to execute the runs. Hand positions are relatively stable. Level 6.

Norwegian Melody, Op. 12, No. 6

Based on a drone bass and an accented melody, with elements of a Nordic folk dance. Requires rhythmic precision. Top needs to be voiced over two- or three-note chords split between the hands. More difficult than the *Arietta*. Hand skips that are sometimes awkward. Level 7.

Album-leaf, Op. 12, No. 7

Shows Grieg's propensity for nationalistic elements in his writing. Melody with oom-pah-pah accompaniment. Requires rapid movement about the keyboard. Playful, sectional work. Level 6.

Song of the Fatherland, Op. 12, No. 8

Bold and majestic, but uses smaller intervals rather than extended chords. The dynamic contrasts help build the excitement. For the student who is adept in playing chords. Level 5.

Birdling, Op. 43, No. 4

Light, graceful character piece containing short trills notated in thirty-second notes. Requires rhythmic accuracy and finger dexterity. Much use of the upper register of the keyboard. Level 7.

March of the Dwarfs, Op. 54, No. 3

A favorite that often proves more difficult than expected. Constant repetition of broken fifths in the bass. Inherent energy and strongly contrasting themes. Requires strong octaves. Levels 8–9.

Notturno, Op. 54, No. 4

An elegant, highly expressive work for the advancing performer who is not yet ready to play Chopin nocturnes. A central *più mosso* passes through several different keys to build to a large climax. Needs sensitivity to subtle dynamic changes. Level 8.

Bell Ringing, Op. 54, No. 6

Imaginative and unique. Depicts clanging bells, with ample use of damper pedal. Dynamics range from *ppp* to *fff*. Performer needs the ability to control the gradual intensity of sound. Level 6.

Wedding Day at Troldhaugen, Op. 65, No. 6

Well-known work that begins with a memorable rhythmic drone, perhaps depicting ringing bells. Filled with fast dramatic broken octaves and large sweeping arpeggiated passages. Intense work. Level 10.

Sailor's Song, Op. 68, No. 1

Dramatic writing with big dynamic contrasts. Needs rich sound without harshness. A good study in playing chords, octaves and in executing syncopated pedaling. Short and march-like. Level 5.

Puck, Op. 71, No. 3

Mischievous, sprightly writing. A repeated four-note motive travels through different keys. The double-note passages and rapid skips help strengthen the fingers. The title refers to the famous sprite in Shakespeare's *Midsummer Night's Dream*. Level 6.

Complete Lyric Pieces

Book I, Op. 12

Arietta, Waltz, Watchman's Song, Fairy Dance, Popular Melody, Norwegian Melody, Album Leaf, Song of the Fatherland

Book II, Op. 38

Cradle Song, Folksong, Melodie, Halling, Springdance, Elegie, Waltz, Canon

Book III, Op. 43

Butterfly, Lonely Wanderer, In the Native Country, Little Bird, Erotik, To the Spring

Book IV, Op. 47

Valse-Impromptu, Album Leaf, Melodie, Halling, Melancholy, Springdance, Elegie

Book V, Op. 54

Bells, March of the Dwarfs, Norwegian Peasant March, Notturno, Scherzo, Shepherd Boy

Book VI, Op. 57

Vanished Days, Gade, Illusion, Secrecy, She Dances, Homesickness

Book VII, Op. 62

Sylph, Gratitude, French Serenade, Brooklet, Phantom, Homeward

Book VIII, Op. 65

From the Years of Youth, Peasant's Song, Melancholy, Salon, In Ballad Vein, Wedding-Day at Troldhaugen

Book IX, Op. 68

Sailor's Song, Grandmother's Minuet, At Thy Feet, Evening in the Mountains, At the Cradle, Valse melancolique

Book X, Op. 71

Once Upon a Time, Summer Evening, Puck, Peace of the Woods, Halling, Gone, Remembrances

Poetic Tone Pictures, Op. 3

Six character pieces published early in Grieg's life. See especially Nos. 1, 2 and 5. (Many standard editions.) Level 8.

No. 1 Tone Picture

Beautifully lyrical piece with many voices working independently. Due to the contrapuntal writing, this work is difficult to play well. Needs attention to appropriate fingering and to the forward flow of the melodic line. Level 9.

Miscellaneous Volumes

Grieg Easier Favorites

Amply fingered volume that contains many favorites of Grieg's works including *Notturno, March of the Dwarfs* and *Puck*. (Heinrichshofen.) Levels 8–9.

Grieg: An Introduction to His Piano Works, ed. Halford

Contains a fine foreword on Grieg's life and musical style. Some of the easier pieces. (Alfred.) Levels 5–8.

Grieg: The First Book for Young Pianists, ed. Halford

Eight of the *Lyric Pieces* are found here. (Alfred.) Levels 5–6.

Grieg: Lyric Pieces and Poetic Tone-Pictures, Op. 12 and Op. 3, ed. Morrison

A practical and scholarly edition containing the complete Op. 12 and Op. 5. The first volume of *Lyric Pieces*, Op. 12 was published in 1867 when the composer was 24. It contains some of the easiest pieces that Grieg composed. The *Poetic Tone-Pictures* were published two years earlier and are slightly more difficult. (Associated Board of the Royal Schools of Music.) Levels 8–9.

Grieg: Selected Works for the Piano, ed. Levine

Contains 38 of the *Lyric Pieces*. (Alfred.) Levels 5–10.

(FÉLIX) ALEXANDRE GUILMANT (1837–1911) France

Known primarily as an organist and organ composer, Guilmant composed only a few pieces for solo piano.

Six Short Pieces, Op. 48

These pieces were possibly composed as teaching pieces for his daughter, and are works that the young, precocious student might play well. Surprising and interesting writing. See especially *Little March* and *Tarantella*. (Associated Board of the Royal Schools of Music.) Level 7.

CORNELIUS GURLITT (1820–1901) Germany

Much of the music of Gurlitt is in the style of Schumann. Innumerable collections of his pleasantly crafted piano music survive today.

Most Frequently Used Volumes

Six Sonatinas, Op. 54

Lesser-known Romantic sonatinas, mostly in three movements. (Alfred and others.) Levels 7–8.

No. 1 Sonatina

See especially the slow movement, which is chordal and expressive. The final *Allegretto* is animated and effective, and has a big climax. Level 6.

No. 5 Sonatina

The third movement, *Vivace*, is one of the best in this set. The dance-like rhythm has strong appeal. Level 6.

Albumleaves for the Young, Op. 101

Collection of 20 short teaching pieces, relatively unknown and equal in quality to the more familiar pieces from Op. 140. Worth investigating. (Many standard editions.)

No. 2 Morning Prayer

Three-part chorale emphasizing voicing and phrase shaping. Hymn-like, peaceful. Good prelude to four-voice chorales. Level 3.

No. 5 By the Spring

More difficult than it looks. The music evokes images of rushing water. Level 5.

No. 8 The Fair

This light, elementary piece provides a good workout for the right hand through the rapid circular sixteenth-note patterns. Especially appropriate to help develop inflection of short melodic ideas. One of the best in this collection. Level 4.

No. 10 Song Without Words

Lilting and dancing work in 3/8 with a right-hand cantabile melody over broken chord accompaniment. Level 5.

No. 11 Waltz

The trite echo effects in the B section may appeal. The last section features running eighths played by the right hand over left-hand broken triads. Level 5.

No. 12 The Little Wanderer

Fragmented melody with sudden stops written in the score, as if one is lost and starting over again. The B section features staccato thirds in both hands. Level 6.

No. 13 Grandfather's Birthday

A fanfare. Extensive use of dotted-quarter sixteenth-note rhythm. The thick chords make this sound impressive. Level 4.

No. 14 Valse Noble

A cheerful waltz in miniature, only two eight-bar phrases in length. Effective contrast between the A section *grazioso* and the B section *scherzando*. Level 4.

No. 17 Free Fancies

Exhibits a wandering feeling. The left-hand accompaniment throughout is in descending broken triads, with the right-hand melody lending a lilt. Some playing of four notes against three. An excellent exercise in phrase shading and rubato. Appealing. Level 5.

No. 18 Sunday

Excellent piece for four-part harmony. The *lento* chorale-like selection helps develop a feeling for diatonic triads and voicing to the top. The A section features some right-hand movement in parallel thirds while the B section in 3/2 is in chorale style. Level 4.

No. 19 Hunting Song

Helps develop a feeling for dramatic playing especially through the *accelerando* to the climax and the fermata over the silence. Level 6.

Buds and Blossoms, Op. 107

An enchanting and little-known set of 12 Romantic character pieces, though without descriptive titles. (Many standard editions.)

No. 1 (Allegretto)

Inspiring and lyrical. Occasional left-hand descending octaves lend a touch of excitement to this two-page piece. Level 7.

No. 2 (Adantino con moto)

Expressive work with the melody generally in the left hand and off-beat syncopated chords above. Needs attention to voicing. Level 7.

No. 3 (Allegretto scherzando)

One of the easiest scherzos in this collection. The passagework fits the hand well, and does not last long. Effective writing. Level 7.

No. 4 (Allegretto grazioso)

Flowing, broken-chord passagework divided between the hands permeates this piece. An excellent study in matching melodic tones and in shaping the texture. Level 7.

No. 5 (Allegro)

A passionate work that calls for flair and facility. Level 8.

No. 6 (Con moto, quasi Allegro)

Another impassioned piece. The passagework is highly idiomatic and creates a big and resonant sound. The left hand can assist in achieving the strong *crescendos* and *diminuendos*. Level 8.

No. 7 (Moderato grazioso)

A graceful waltz with thin textures. The ascending and descending arpeggiations in the B section provide drama and sweep. Level 7.

No. 10 (Con moto)

An effective character piece with a thick texture and periodic syncopations. Tuneful, somewhat dark. Level 7.

No. 11 (Allegretto scherzando)

Repeated chord figures form the accompaniment for idiomatic double-note right-hand passages. A playful and effective two-page work. Level 8.

No. 12 (Allegro capriccioso)

A three-page *leggiero* scherzo featuring some double-note passages. Easier than it sounds. Level 8.

The First Lessons, Op. 117

Delightful little teaching pieces spanning elementary to intermediate levels. Many are frequently found in anthologies, but some are unfamiliar gems. See especially *The Clappermill, Gavotte, The Return, The Chase* and *Cradle Song.* (Kalmus.) Levels 2–6.

No. 33 The Mill

Effective work in three sections calling for even right-hand passagework. Listen for the repeated figures representing the mill wheel. Level 4.

No. 34 Song Without Words

A broken-chord study, also effective in performance. Level 4.

Album for the Young, Op. 140

A staple of the romantic teaching literature at the intermediate level. Excellent character pieces that represent the best of Gurlitt. (Many standard editions.)

No. 1 March

Rhythmic and pompous work with four-voice chords alternating with three-voice chords. Differing articulations in each hand. Rhythmic precision is needed especially in the dotted eighth and sixteenth figures. Careful articulation is required especially in measure two. Level 3.

No. 2 Morning Song

Could serve as a student's first study in voicing melody over other voices in a single hand. Limited number of measures to learn in this lyrical, chordal selection. Level 3.

No. 3 Bright is the Sky

Grazioso writing with a lyrical melody over Alberti bass accompaniment. Predictable phrase lengths. The performer has the opportunity to display a true singing tone. Level 3.

No. 4 In the Garden

Singing melody in the left hand accompanied by syncopated right-hand chords. Appropriate for students who are able to voice between the hands. One of the best in the set. Level 4.

No. 5 Murmuring Brook

The right hand plays melody and active sixteenth-note accompaniment (representing the brook), while the left hand doubles the melody. Excellent study in voicing and playing legato in a single hand. Isolation of fingers is required. Level 5.

No. 8 The Music Box

Entire piece is written in treble register, simulating a music box. Charming and engaging writing that fits the hand well. Level 3.

No. 10 The Little Norwegian

Could be an appropriate repertoire selection to emphasize clarity in passage playing. Spirited and vigorous work. Level 4.

No. 11 Longing

Expressive phrasing of the long lyrical lines is needed as the right hand features the melody throughout. This dreamy work calls for careful right-hand voicing and an especially soft thumb. Good preparation for more advanced, Schumannesque repertoire. Level 4.

No. 12 In the Church

Work in two sections, *Präludium* and *Chorale*. Continuous eighth notes appear in the *Präludium* against quarters. *Chorale* is in four parts, providing excellent preparation for hymn playing or more chordal romantic literature. Level 5.

No. 13 The Little Wanderer

Predictable phrases in a simple tuneful work featuring *grazioso* writing with an inviting melodic contour. Melody in right hand with simple accompaniment in the left. Level 4.

No. 14 Hunting Song

Uses chord inversions that are typical of horn calls. Stretches of sevenths and octaves in each hand. This is a relatively long work with much repeated material and is more difficult than most pieces in this collection. Level 5.

No. 15 Will-o'-the Wisp

A bright, light scherzo filled with repeated patterns. Sounds much more difficult than it is. Level 5.

No. 17 Scherzo

Playful work featuring chordal playing in each hand. The accent occurs on the third beat throughout until the final left-hand statement, when the accent reverts to the "proper" downbeat. May help a student learn to move freely about the keyboard. Level 3.

No. 18 Serenade

A fine study in phrasing, inflection and matching of tones. Broken-chord accompaniment. Level 4.

No. 20 Storm and Stress

A *molto vivace* and passionate work that can help develop strong fingers and evenness of passagework. Sounds more difficult than it is due to repetition and some unison passages. Called *Hurry-Skurry* in some editions. Level 5.

Little Flowers (Kleine Blumen), Op. 205

Most of these pieces are based on a rhythmic motive or have a melody and simple accompaniment. No titles were originally given to the 12 pieces, but in an Augener edition of 1936, the titles from an unknown source were used (listed here in brackets). (Associated Board of the Royal Schools of Music.)

No. 1 [Wild Mignonette]

One-page piece with a melody featuring a strong rhythmic motive. Level 4.

No. 2 [Harebell]

Simple work in ABB form. The texture generally consists of continuous eighth notes in one hand against quarter notes in the other. Level 3.

No. 3 [Lady's Smock]

Charming waltz. One of the best in this set. Level 4.

No. 4 [Ragged Robin]

Suitable preparation for easier Chopin and Schubert waltzes and effective in performance. Level 4.

No. 7 [Fritillary]

Wit and charm abound in this work permeated with a melody punctuated by syncopated chords in the accompanying voice. Good for practice in chordal playing. Level 5.

No. 8 [Rose Rock]

Perpetual-motion piece with continuous sixteenth notes in the right hand. Level 4.

No. 12 [Dandelion]

Marked *allegro con fuoco*, this piece is especially suitable for a student with energy and flair, and one who plays broken four-note chords adeptly. Level 6.

A First Book

Simple character pieces, many of which appear in modern anthologies for elementary-level students. Some of the best teaching music for the early-level student. The music in this book is more uniform in level than in Gurlitt's *The First Lessons*, Op. 117. The selections are titled. (Belwin.) Levels 4–5.

Less Frequently Used Volumes

24 Easy Melodious Studies, Op. 50

Tuneful, rather predictable character pieces or études. Not lengthy and generally highly patterned. Valuable étude material. (G. Schirmer.) Levels 7–8.

No. 5 (Allegretto)

Broken-chord study that calls for matching tone quality between the hands. Provides an opportunity to listen to harmonic progressions and to interpret accordingly. Level 3.

No. 6 (Allegretto)

Triads appear in triplets and broken between the hands to create a harp-like piece. The chords should roll from hand to hand seamlessly with the first bass note serving as a harmonic foundation. Level 4.

No. 14 (Con moto)

Triplet figuration in the right hand with the melody note heard as the first of the triplets against a single-note accompaniment mostly in eighths. Lyrical and yet exciting writing. Should be better known. Level 7.

The First Steps of the Young Pianist, Op. 82

One hundred pieces in two volumes, progressive in difficulty. These are character études, relatively short, and of strong value for the young pianist in developing the playing of passagework. Although the writing is not harmonically adventurous, the pieces contain common patterns and writing that is highly idiomatic to the Romantic period. (G. Schirmer.) Levels 3–8.

No. 65 (Allegro non troppo)

This passionate piece calls for a strongly defined bass that sings out above the repeated-note accompaniment in the right hand. Effective and exciting. Level 4.

The Easiest Studies in Velocity, Op. 83

These pieces fall into the category of pedantic studies, with many repetitions of ideas within the étude. (G. Schirmer.) Level 6.

Grateful Tasks, Op. 102

A collection notable primarily for its historical significance. Contains original pieces in all the major and minor keys, up to six sharps and flats, with the melodies confined to five notes. Both hands play the melody in most of the selections. Only the treble clef is used.

25 Easy Studies Without Octaves, Op. 130

Little-known collection that contains many interesting character pieces. Most are one page or shorter in length. The writing is enticing. See especially *Morning Song, Hymn, Rustic Dance* and *Sunshine*. (G. Schirmer.) Levels 6–7.

24 Melodious Studies, Op. 131

Some character pieces of surprisingly high quality are found here. Most are short and are more difficult than the selections in *Album for the Young*, Op. 140. Generally on the level of difficulty with the Burgmüller *25 Easy and Progressive Studies*, Op. 100. It is surprising that these are not better known. See especially *No. 8, Pleasures of the Chase; No. 13, A Steadfast Resolve*; and *No. 20, Evening Peace*. (G. Schirmer.) Levels 6–7.

No. 13 A Steadfast Resolve

The mood throughout is passionate and driving in this broken-chord piece. Effective sweep and brilliance. Worth investigating. Levels 7–8.

No. 20 Evening Peace

Andantino work with a triplet accompaniment and a lyrical right-hand melody. The left hand presents an interesting countermelody in this highly expressive and effective piece. Level 7.

School of Velocity for Beginners, Op. 141

Études in passagework that are not particularly interesting musically, but contain useful material for technical work for the elementary student. (G. Schirmer.) Level 5.

Novellettes, Op. 148

Subtitled "12 Little Salon Pieces." All are titled and some are of musical value. The most appealing are *No. 1, Morning Greeting; No. 4, Idyl*; and *No. 6, Impromptu*. (G. Schirmer.) Level 8.

Miscellaneous Pieces

Étude in D Minor

A melody is stated in the low register of the keyboard against a repeated chord right-hand accompaniment that adds tension and excitement to this dramatic character piece. Level 5.

Hunting Song in F Major, Op. 210, No. 5

Elementary piece with an infectious hunting-horn motive as the main theme. Level 3.

Scherzo in D Minor

Descending arpeggio patterns using different inversions of chords in successive order. The cross-rhythms are effective. The B section poses problems in voicing and legato. Motivating for most students and especially effective in recital and contest. Level 7.

Additional Works for Study:

Op. 51 Melodious Studies

Op. 74 (No Name)

Op. 76 Six Sonatinas

Op. 80 Rhythmical Studies

Op. 85 Studies on Scales & Arpeggios

Op. 90 50 Daily Exercises in Canon Form

Op. 113 Mimosen. 12 Characteristic Pieces

Op. 187 Very First Studies

Op. 188 Sonatinas

Op. 214 Four Sonatinas

H

STEPHEN HELLER (1813–1888) Hungary

Heller was a close friend of Chopin, Schumann and Liszt, all of whom respected and encouraged him. Heller wrote several hundred piano pieces, mostly in small forms, and generally grouped by opus. The *Études*, Op. 45–47 are among his most vital and important teaching pieces. Composed in 1866, six years after he had gone to Paris, they were written when he was at the pinnacle of his creative career. Many of the études have been assigned titles (as is the case with the *Songs Without Words* of Mendelssohn) to suggest mood or character. Some editions use these titles while others do not. Only the most significant collections of Heller are annotated here.

Études

The *Études*, Opp. 45, 46 and 47 are Heller's best-known and most useful teaching pieces. They are generally character pieces of one to four printed pages, serving to fill a gap in the intermediate teaching repertoire. The titles of the pieces are used here when available, though probably were not assigned by Heller. It is conjectured that they were added by the publisher. Heller himself is quoted as saying, "Music should be evocative rather than descriptive." (Many standard editions.)

25 Studies, Op. 45

Perhaps the best-known and most frequently played études are found here, works that are highly Romantic and sometimes sentimental. See especially *No. 1, The Brook (Étude); No. 2, The Avalanche; No. 7, Determination; No. 9, Celestial Voices; No. 10, Evening Prayer (Study); No. 14, Sailor's Song; No. 15, Warrior's Song; No. 22, The Harp*; and *No. 23, Sailing Along.* (Many standard editions.) Levels 7–8.

No. 1 The Brook

Right-hand sixteenth-note figuration throughout with a simple quarter-note accompaniment. A technical workout for fingers four and five of the right hand. Level 6.

No. 2 The Avalanche

Perhaps the most popular selection from this opus, an energetic piece that is effective in performance. Attention should be paid to producing even eighth notes in the ascending passages, and to playing resonant chords. The phrasing can become monotonous unless it is carefully worked out. Level 6.

No. 3 A Challenge

Primarily a finger study, with some twisting passages in the right hand accompanied by descending scale passages in the left. For the performer wanting to develop agile finger technique. Level 7.

No. 5 Song of May

The strong rhythm of the melody makes it memorable. Level 6.

No. 7 Determination

A bold work consisting of octaves and chords in both hands. Especially appropriate for the performer with large hands, wanting to perform a work that sounds big and yet is not technically involved. Short and effective in performance. Although the playing of four-note chords is required, no stretches of over an octave are present. Level 7.

No. 9 Celestial Voices

Undoubtedly inspired by the Chopin *Étude* Op. 25, No. 1 "Harp." The melody is played with the thumb of the right hand and the rapid broken-chord accompanimental notes are played by the other fingers. Accompanimental notes are printed in small print as in the Chopin "Harp" étude. More difficult than it appears. Level 8.

No. 14 Sailor's Song

Appears to be influenced by the Mendelssohn *Songs Without Words*, reflected in the tuneful writing with incessant repeated chords in the right hand. This work is immediately appealing but the technical difficulties of the rapid repeated chords in the right hand are significant. This piece would be especially appropriate for the student with large hands who is adept at playing chordal works. Level 7.

No. 15 Warrior's Song

Majestic chords that need arm and body weight. Features frequent movement between the registers of the piano and the playing of four-note chords in a hand. Effective writing that sounds more difficult than it is. Perhaps appropriate for the student wanting to play the Rachmaninoff *Prelude in C-sharp Minor* but who is not yet at that level. Level 8.

No. 16 Il Penseroso

A primarily lyrical work that features a singing melody in the left hand with *leggiero* arpeggiated chords in the right hand. Somewhat monotonous phrasing. Especially good for the student wanting to play Chopin nocturne-like works but not ready for that level of repertoire. Level 7.

No. 22 Song of the Harp

Features broken-chord arpeggiation divided between the hands, with the left hand crossing over the right to play many of the melody notes. Requires rapid movement about the keyboard. This is an étude of high musical quality, but one which is also more difficult than it initially appears. Level 7.

No. 25 Epilogue

A brilliant and effective work in which the central section features passagework from the opening selection of this volume, *The Brook*. Especially good for a student who plays chords and octaves with ease. Sounds more difficult than it is. Level 8.

30 Studies, Op. 46

Although the subtitle by Heller indicates that these pieces are preparatory to the *Melodious Studies*, Op. 45, they appear to be approximately equal in difficulty (if not more difficult). Often students who play these selections also could perform some of the easiest of the Mendelssohn *Songs Without Words*. See especially *No. 2, The Anvil; No. 6, The Nodding Violet; No. 7, Petite Tarantella; No. 8, Song of Courage; No. 9, The Jester; No. 14, Song of the Sea;* and *No. 22, The Queen Dances.* (Many standard editions.) Levels 8–9.

25 Studies, Op. 47

Generally much less difficult than the studies in Op. 46. See especially *No. 1, Scampering; No. 3, Autumn Song; No. 6, The Bagpipe; No. 8, The Rivulet; No. 10, The Unknown Soldier; No. 11, In the Highlands of Scotland; No. 15, Grief; No. 17, Whirling Leaves; No. 19, Lullaby; No. 20, Tragedy; No. 21, Love-Song; No. 23, Quiet Happiness.* As noted earlier, titles are not by the composer but have been associated with these pieces by tradition. (Many standard editions.) Levels 6–8.

No. 1 [Scampering]

Broken chords divided between the hands present easy coordination and natural phrasing according to the harmonic progression. Flowing and appealing to the young student. One of the most accessible and most musical of the études. A good piece to help sharpen the listening skills of a student. This should be better known. Level 4.

No. 3 [Autumn Song]

This busy piece develops pedaling, listening and voicing over thick chords. Level 6.

No. 14 [In Venice]

A beautiful barcarolle, similar to some of the Mendelssohn *Songs Without Words* but significantly less difficult. Calls for playing some double-third passages in the right hand. Requires careful voicing of the top notes in a hand as well as finesse in phrasing. Appropriate for the student not yet ready for Chopin. Level 6.

No. 19 [Berceuse]

One of the most accessible of the études. The melody is doubled a third below in the left hand to create a Schumannesque lyricism. Level 4.

Miscellaneous Collections

The Art of Phrasing, Op. 16

Heller's studies Opp. 45, 46, 47, 90, 125 and 138 were written as preparatory studies to this opus, which consists of two volumes, with 12 pieces in the first volume and 14 in the second. The works are stylistic studies with characteristic titles. See especially *No. 1, Canzonette; No. 8, Eclogue*; and *No. 9, Rondo* from Volume I; and *No. 1, Toccatina* from Volume II. (G. Schirmer.) Levels 8–9.

24 Preludes, Op. 81

Untitled pieces, nearly all of which are monothematic and quite short. Thick romantic textures and lush sonorities. Not of particular intrigue although the best are *Preludes* Nos. 2, 3, 4, 6, 7, 12, 16, 17 and 24. (G. Schirmer.) Levels 9–10.

Flower, Fruit and Thorn Pieces, Op. 82 (Nuits blanches)

Subtitled, "Restless Nights." These 18 intermediate character pieces contain some of Heller's best writing. The works display the essence of Romanticism, and have slightly stronger character and more substance than many of the études. This is a collection that deserves investigation. These works were inspired by the German novelist Jean Paul Richter, who also inspired Schumann. Note the flavor of Hungarian rhythm in Nos. 9 and 14. (G. Schirmer.) Levels 8–10.

32 Preludes (for Lilly), Op. 119

Heller referred to these preludes in a letter as "mostly simple pleasant pieces written for children, either in a facile or characteristic manner, as indicated clearly by the title." They are somewhat reminiscent of children's fairy tales. See especially *Preludes* Nos. 2, 5, 6, 9, 10, 16, 19, 23, 29 and 32. (Many standard editions.) Levels 7–8.

No. 25

An enchanting chordal work that provides an opportunity to hear the rich quality of various full harmonies. Does not require substantial finger independence. Level 6.

Valses-Reveries, Op. 122

See especially Nos. 6 and 9 (Breitkopf.)

24 Studies for Rhythm and Expression, Op. 125

Short, untitled character pieces, progressive in difficulty and especially suited for sight-reading. Romantic textures. See especially Nos. 1, 5, 7, 8, 10, 12 and 21. (Many standard editions.) Levels 7–9.

No. 8 (Allegretto)

Titled *Tolling Bell* in some editions due to the hand crossings to play treble notes, presumably representing bells. Effective writing in a short piece that calls for overlapping legato. Level 7.

No. 22 (Lento)

Highly expressive, *lento* work. The melody is usually played one sixteenth-note before the strong beats, providing a syncopated effect throughout. Should be better known. Level 8.

Album for the Young, Op. 138

Among the 25 pieces found here are several sets including five *Songs Without Words* (Nos. 1–5) and *Gypsies* (Nos. 16–20). Strong character and somewhat easier than most of the *Études*, Op. 45, 46 and 47. The well-known *Curious Story* is *No. 9* in this set. Other gems await discovery. Also see especially *No. 5, Barcarolle; No. 6, Étude; No. 14, At Evening*; Nos. 9 and 20 from *Gypsies*; and *No. 22, Oberon's Horn*. (Many standard editions.) Levels 5–8.

Abenddämmerung, Op. 138, No. 3

Calls for projection of single-line melody over a repeated-note chordal accompaniment with melody appearing in both hands. Needs sensitivity to the harmonic changes. Not complex rhythmically and not difficult to read. Levels 6–7.

Curious Story, Op. 138, No. 9

Catchy rhythms help make this piece eminently appealing. Popular work for teaching. Humorous and light-hearted. Most of the melodic material is in the right hand. Level 6.

Ses camarades le consolent, Op. 138, No. 11

Built on repeated chords and scale passages. Interesting writing with an economy of material. Level 6.

Tziganyi (Bohémiens), Op. 138, No. 17

This is the second of a set of five pieces contained in Op. 138, No. 17. This piece calls for a flexible tempo. The performer needs substantial flair and an assertive musical spirit. This work should be better known, and sounds much more difficult than it is. Level 6.

Sonatinen, Opp. 146, 147, 149

Composed as preparatory studies for the sonatas of the masters. See especially the *Finale* (Tarantella) of the *Sonatina*, Op. 147. There is a strong resemblance of the first movement of Heller's *Sonatina*, Op. 149 to the first movement of Beethoven's *Moonlight Sonata*, and it could serve as useful preparation. (Kistner.)

Miscellaneous Pieces

Tarantella in A-flat Major, Op. 85, No. 2

Rhythmically exciting, a student favorite, but also relatively difficult. The 6/8 feeling may possibly become monotonous. Highly energetic and intense. Calls for strong finger facility and much energy in the performance. Level 8.

Miscellaneous Volumes

The Heller Collection, ed. Hinson

Contains 34 études drawn from Heller's many sets of études. Valuable introductions by Hinson are provided for the interesting works found here. (Universal.) Levels 7–9.

Heller: 23 Miscellaneous Pieces, ed. Alexander

A notable collection of some of Heller's easier and more accessible works. Most are little-known selections. (Associated Board of the Royal Schools of Music.) Levels 6–8.

Heller Rediscovered, ed. Rowley

A series of five volumes of Heller's works, with the pieces grouped according to their themes. The groupings for the various volumes are *Book 1, Miniatures; Book 2, Preludes; Book 3, Mood Pictures; Book 4, Dances;* and *Book 5, Nature Sketches.* Unfortunately opus numbers are not given in the volumes and titles are of dubious nature. The lack of sources makes this volume less useful than it might be otherwise. (Alfred, Lengnick.) Levels 5–8.

Selected Progressive Études for the Piano, ed. Olson

A selection of untitled études from Op. 138, 45, 46, 47, 119 and 81. A well-conceived selection. (Alfred.) Levels 5–9.

Ausgewählte Klavierwerke-Charakterstücke, ed. Kersten

An interesting and unusual collection of character pieces by Heller. Contains some selections that are virtually impossible to find elsewhere such as those from Op. 79, 124, 128, 134 and 150. (Henle.) Levels 9–10.

Twenty Miscellaneous Studies, ed. Alexander

Includes an interesting array of pieces from Op. 45, 46, 47, 81, 90 and 125. (Associated Board of the Royal Schools of Music.) Levels 6–8.

Additional Works for Study:
Op. 134 Petit Album
Op. 150 20 Preludes

FANNY MENDELSSOHN HENSEL (1805–1847) Germany

Sister of Felix Mendelssohn, Fanny Hensel was a fine musician and composer in her own right. Some of her earliest compositions were actually published under her brother's name.

Il Saltarello Romano

Students who enjoyed playing tarantella-like pieces may be attracted to this work. Passagework can be challenging and the writing sometimes seems long-winded. Level 10.

Notturno

All cadenza-like sections are metered here and no polyrhythms (two against three, and so on) exist. Perhaps a good choice to precede Chopin nocturnes. Rich Romantic harmonies make reading somewhat difficult. Fingering needs careful work in the long, winding melodic lines. Some large chords need a span of over an octave. Level 10.

Selected Piano Pieces, ed. Elvers/Theopold

Published in 1986, this edition contains works previously unknown. Several hold strong interest for the performer and should be better known. (Henle.) Level 10.

At the Piano with Felix and Fanny Mendelssohn, ed. Hinson

Interesting combination of pieces by brother and sister is found here. The prefatory material is especially valuable, as is the accessibility of much unknown music by Fanny Mendelssohn. (Alfred.) Levels 7–10.

ADOLF HENSELT (1814–1889) Germany
Petite Valse, Op. 28, No. 1

Salon-style *grazioso* work. Calls for care in voicing the counter-melody in the alto, making this selection appropriate for the student who needs to work on melodic lines. (Musical Scope Publishers.) Level 10.

HENRI HERZ (1803–1888) Germany

Scales and Exercises

Many of the exercises are of the Pischna type, with some notes to be sustained while other fingers play. Additional selections feature patterns to be repeated up and down the scale, or double-note exercises. A substantial number of the activities begin and end around C Major position. Scales and arpeggios in written-out forms are also included. (Alfred, G. Schirmer.) Levels 8–10.

HEINRICH KARL JOHANN HOFMANN (1842–1902) Germany

Leaves From My Diary, Books 1–3

Twelve titled works in a salon-type style. Not especially profound. (G. Schirmer.) Level 8.

H. Hofmann: 17 Miscellaneous Pieces, ed. Johnson

Interesting writing. More of these intermediate teaching pieces should make their way into the piano repertoire. See especially *Melodie*, Op. 77, No. 5; *In the Evening*, Op. 88, No. 2; *Country Waltz*, Op. 117, No. 3; *Elves*, Op. 77, No. 17; and *By the Mountain Torrent* , Op. 37, No. 2. (Associated Board of the Royal Schools of Music.) Levels 7–9.

Additional Works for Study:
Op. 11 Albumblätter (Novello)
Op. 37 Nachklänge, Part II (Novello)
Op. 77 Skizzen (Rühle)
Op. 85 Lose Blätter (Challier)
Op. 87 Stimmungsbilder (Steingraber)

J

LEOŠ JANÁČEK (1854–1928) Czechoslovakia

On an Overgrown Path

A set of 15 seldom-heard character pieces expressing memories of the happy years of Janáček's youth. The writing is often lyrical and expressive. A single selection would be suitable for a high school student who enjoys expressive literature in the Romantic style. Groups of several pieces also would be effective in performance. (Masters Music Publications and other standard editions.) Levels 9–10.

Popular Moravian Dances

Folk song settings, similar in concept to those done by Bartók. Czech words are included for some selections. Traditional harmonies, often spirited settings and pianistic writing. (Ricordi.) Level 7.

Wariacje

This upper-intermediate set of variations on an opera melody "Nel cor più non mi sento" (translated as "Hope told a flattering tale") is less difficult than Beethoven's variation set on the same theme. This set, slightly longer, features strong character changes between variations (one is in the style of a polka) and idiomatic keyboard figurations. Traditional harmonic framework. (PWM.) Level 9.

ADOLF JENSEN (1837–1879) Germany

Scenes of Travel, Op. 17

Romantic character pieces that could be played by students not yet ready for the Chopin nocturnes. The writing is idiomatic although not particularly imaginative. See especially *No. 3, The Mill* and *No. 7, Peaceful Afternoon*. (Many standard editions.) Level 8.

25 Études, Op. 32, Books 1, 2 and 3

Jensen followed the Romantic tradition in writing études that also became distinct character pieces. These études are of high quality, feel idiomatic on the piano, and might benefit a talented young pianist. They are both better and easier than those by Cramer and Moszkowski. These works can serve as repertoire pieces as well as technical studies. Most are two pages long. (Peters, Presser.) Level 9.

Songs and Dances, Op. 33

See especially *No. 1, Dedication; No. 2, The Little Trumpeter; No. 3, Intermezzo; No. 4, Abendlied; No. 5, Elfin Dance; No. 8, Waltz; No. 10, Lied;* and *No. 19, Polonaise*. (Augener, Hansen.)

K

GÉNARI KARGANOV (1858–1890) Russia

Karganov composed works primarily for the piano, most of which were of a pedagogical nature.

Seven Miniatures, Op. 10

Upper-intermediate to early-advanced teaching pieces, essentially lyrical in character. See especially the first, *Souvenir*, a good predecessor to the

Chopin nocturnes. Additional titles include *Petite Valse, Reproche, Intermezzo, Scherzino, Impromptu* and *Humoresque*. (Boston Music.) Level 9.

Album for the Young, Op. 25

Eight titled character pieces, generally two pages long. Interesting repertoire choices that should be better known. See especially *No. 2, Game of Patience; No. 5, Prayer; No. 6, By the Brook*; and *No. 8, Russian Dance*. (Associated Board of the Royal Schools of Music.) Levels 6–7.

No. 6 By the Brook

The image of a brook trickling over rocks is portrayed through this perpetual-motion piece. Two-note figurations alternate between the hands. Effective writing. Level 7.

THEODOR KIRCHNER (1823–1903) Germany

Kirchner wrote a large number of short pieces for piano. Many are beautiful and of high musical quality, while others are perhaps overly sentimental.

Albumblätter, Op. 7

Nine untitled selections. Not particularly significant writing. (G. Schirmer.) Level 8.

Skizzen, Op. 11

These eight character pieces in the Heugel edition were extracted from the complete Op. 11 of Kirchner. They are shorter than many of Schumann's pieces from Op. 12 but are in the same style. (Heugel.) Level 9.

Spielsachen, Op. 35

These 14 pieces are shorter and somewhat easier than those in Op. 11 by Kirchner but are slightly more difficult than the works in Burgmüller Op. 100. The Kirchner selections are in a Schumannesque style and highly Romantic, featuring thicker textures that require voicing of inner melodies and a refined sense of phrasing. For a student with a romantic flair, or for one needing to work on Romantic playing. High-quality writing. (Schott.) Levels 7–8.

New Scenes of Childhood, Op. 55

The title reflects Kirchner's admiration for Schumann's works. First published in 1881, the 25 one-page pieces in this collection are charming, and could serve as a substitute for the frequently used *Album for the*

Young, Op. 68 of Schumann. A group of them would make an interesting recital offering. See especially Nos. 7, 17, 23 and 25. (Associated Board of the Royal Schools of Music.) Levels 6–7.

Miniatures, Op. 62

Some of the pieces found here are longer and only slightly more difficult than those in Kirchner's *New Scenes of Childhood*. These gems would be effective for high school students who want to play the big Romantic works before they are ready. Many of these pieces foster the ability to play a long melodic line. See especially *No. 7, Allegretto* and *No. 9, Allegretto, poco agitato*. (Associated Board of the Royal Schools of Music.)

No. 2 (Con moto)

Lyrical work that approaches the style of the Chopin nocturnes and Mendelssohn *Songs Without Words*. Active accompaniment which requires careful voicing. One of the best of the set. Level 7.

No. 5 (Ziemlich langsam, ausdrucksvoll)

Highly expressive writing in which each hand needs musical independence to project the character. Phrases require strong definition. Level 7.

No. 6 (Vivace)

Short piece that can be used to enhance the development of facility. One printed page with unusual modulation. Quick hand motions are needed in the last two measures to play the final chords. Level 5.

No. 7 (Nicht zu schnell, aber lebhaft)

Ländler-like feeling pervades this lively work that is short and full of sequences. The wide jumps and intervallic reaches require careful listening. The pedal needs special attention to avoid blur in this quick tempo. This work sounds impressive yet requires minimum effort. Levels 7–8.

No. 9 (Allegretto, poco agitato)

This passionate work reflects the essence of the Romantic spirit. The melody is found in the low bass register. Level 7.

No. 13 (Poco Allegro)

This short "crowd pleaser" deserves attention from the performer with natural technical facility. It requires the ability to move freely about the keyboard, attention to the complex rhythms and opposing articulations, and control of the dynamics. Levels 6–7.

No. 14 (Mässig schnell)

Broken-chord passages appear over a lyrical left-hand melody. The fingering needs special attention, but this is an excellent piece to expand a performer's ability to move freely on the keyboard. Easier than it first appears. Level 7.

No. 15 (Animato)

Schumannesque writing requiring a performer with flair and strong hands. Two pages. Level 7.

Additional Works for Study:

Op. 65 60 Preludes

Op. 70 Five Sonatinas

Op. 71 Little Studies

Op. 80 Album Leaves

CARL KOELLING (1831–1914) Germany

Fluttering Leaves, Op. 147

Three effective character pieces in a popular idiom. All are published separately. (Many standard editions.)

No. 1 (Allegro)

All fast passagework is in the right hand. Koelling has a way of writing so that the maximum effect is achieved with quite pianistic writing. Scalewise passages make this work easy to learn. Level 6.

No. 2 (Allegro molto)

The bouncy opening theme is memorable and the short amount of fast passagework fits the hand well. Effective and worth the effort. Level 6.

No. 3 (Prestissimo)

Perhaps the most difficult of the three, this work is based on descending D Major scales, broken chords in the melody, and oom-pah-pah accompaniment. Especially suitable for the student with fast fingers. Level 6.

Hungary, Op. 410

Subtitled "Rhapsodie Mignonne," this prosaic work has been a student favorite for years, due to its seeming grand effect. Filled with dramatic passagework, broken octaves and fast fingerwork. (Many standard editions.) Level 8.

LOUIS KÖHLER (1820–1886) Germany

Köhler is remembered primarily for his albums of piano studies.

First Studies for the Piano, Op. 50

Issued under one cover in two books of 10 études each, all of the études found here are in C Major, arranged in pairs, the first with passagework appearing for the right hand and the companion étude with passagework in the left hand. The longest exercises are just 24 measures. (G. Schirmer and other publishers.) Level 7.

Studies in Easy Passage-Playing, Op. 85

Rather pedantic studies, each concentrating on one particular figuration. They attempt to give equal prominence to passagework for each hand. (G. Schirmer.) Level 8.

Easiest Studies for the Piano, Op. 151

Each study is 32 measures long and in the key of C Major. The études are arranged in pairs, with the principle material first presented in eighth notes in the right hand, and then followed in the next étude by the same material in the left hand. (G. Schirmer and other publishers.)

12 Easy Studies for the Piano, Op. 157

All are 16 or 24 measures long and in the key of C Major. Found here are practical studies, mostly two printed pages, that have been popular for over a century. The composer provides performance suggestions. Appropriate reading and technical studies for the elementary student, recommended despite the uniformity of key. (Many standard editions.) Levels 4–5.

Elementary Studies in Piano Playing, Op. 163

Series of 16 one-page études, somewhat pedantic and repetitive. (G. Schirmer.) Level 7.

The Very Easiest Studies, Op. 190

The hands play together one octave apart. The short études (most are one-half of a page) progress in level of difficulty to demand the playing of melody against a broken-chord or slow Alberti-bass accompaniment. These would be relatively valuable as reading studies if finger numbers were not provided for almost every note, but that practice severely limits their use. (Kalmus.) Levels 1–3.

Children's Album, Op. 210

Thirty single-page teaching pieces that lack musical imagination. The phrase lengths are predictable and most accompaniments are oom-pah basses. These works are approximately parallel in difficulty to the Gurlitt *Album for the Young*. See, however, *No. 13, Polka* and *No. 23, Étude*. (Many standard editions.) Level 4.

Children's Exercises and Melodies, Op. 218

The short selections (often eight measures) are titled *Exercise* and *Melody* alternately throughout. The *Exercises* are written to develop agile fingers and are finger patterns to be repeated a specified number of times. The *Melodies* are written to allow a young student to work on phrasing. Although most segments are in C Major and the approach is now dated, the basic concept is good. This volume might help teachers organize their teaching of phrasing and development of facility in a methodical way. (Kalmus.) Levels 1–2.

Short School of Velocity Without Octaves, Op. 242

This volume, designed to facilitate the development of dexterity and speed, has received the widest use of all of Köhler's works. Often the hands work independently of each other with one hand imitating the scale passagework of the other in succession. Many scale passages and typical figures are found in these one- to two-page studies. Accompaniment figures often consist of two-note chords that punctuate the rhythm. Found here are appropriate and practical études for the intermediate to upper-intermediate student that can be used effectively to reinforce scale study and the development of speed in playing scales. See especially Nos. 2, 5, 10, 15 and 18. (Many standard editions.) Level 6.

The Children's Friend, Op. 243

Subtitled *60 Little Piano Pieces for Practice and Recreation*. Not his most interesting writing, although several are noteworthy. A variety of styles is found here. Could provide sight-reading material for an intermediate student. (G. Schirmer.) Level 5.

Practical Method for the Pianoforte, Op. 249 (300)

This work is actually an instruction book for beginning through advanced piano students and contains a variety of exercises and pieces. Compositions are by Bach, Handel, Haydn, Mozart, Beethoven, Schubert, Weber, and Clementi, as well as by Köhler. Selections in the upper levels become quite advanced. Some transcriptions are also included. (Boston Music, G. Schirmer.) Levels 1–9.

Additional Work for Study:
Op. 232 The First Lessons in Finger Dexterity

THEODOR KULLAK (1818–1882) Germany

Kullak, the German pianist and pedagogue, established the Neue Akademie der Tonkunst, which was a well-known, progressive piano academy. An innovator of teaching techniques, he gave his students great freedom to develop their artistic individuality.

Scenes from Childhood, Op. 62 and Op. 81

Both opuses are contained under one cover with 12 character pieces in each. Useful and little-known teaching literature, only slightly more difficult than the Gurlitt *Album for the Young*, Op. 140. Most are one to two pages. (Many standard editions.) Levels 4–7.

The Clock, Op. 62, No. 2
The music represents the ticking of a clock in this attractive programmatic work. A little-known intermediate piece of some interest. Level 4.

KONRAD MAX KUNZ (1812–1875) Germany
200 Short Two-Part Canons, Op. 14

All of these canons remain in five-finger positions, but the coordination required between the hands and the rhythmic complexity is progressive throughout this volume. Since performers need not judge movement around the keyboard, they are able to concentrate on developing coordination and on reading more complex rhythmic patterns. (Alfred, Belwin, G. Schirmer and other standard editions.) Levels 3–7.

L
THÉODORE LACK (1846–1921) France
Études Elegantes, Op. 30

Many of these selections possess a simple charm that may appeal to adult students. See especially *No. 4, Elegie*; *No. 6, Drammatica*; and *No. 9, Meditation*. Fine sight-reading material for the advancing pianist. (Presser.) Levels 8–9.

ADOLPHE-CLAIR LE CARPENTIER (1809–1869) France

Piano Method

Outmoded method for beginners, interspersing exercises, reading studies and repertoire. Rate of advancement in terms of coordination and rhythmic values studied is quite rapid. Repertoire included is by various composers in addition to Le Carpentier. Many studies and exercises (including scales in double thirds). (G. Schirmer.) Levels 1–8.

FELIX LE COUPPEY (1811–1887) France

In addition to composing piano character pieces, Le Couppey published several successful methods including *Ecole du mécanisme du piano, 24 études primaries, Cours de piano élémentaire et progressif, L'Art du piano (50 études with annotations)*, and a pamphlet *De l'enseignement du piano: Conseils aux femmes professeurs* (1865).

The Alphabet, Op. 17, 25 Very Easy Studies

Each study is preceded by a seven-measure exercise that is to be repeated several times. A variety of keys are used. The best are studies Nos. 1, 2, 5, 18 and 21. (G. Schirmer.) Level 4.

No. 6 Étude

Toccata-like legato five-finger study in which the hands seldom play together. Appropriate for the early-elementary student. Level 2.

L'Agilité, Op. 20, 25 Progressive Studies for Mechanism and Light Touch

One of the best from this opus is the *Study in No. 23 in F*. (G. Schirmer.)

15 Preparatory Studies to Czerny's School of Velocity, Op. 26

A set of fine romantic études for the advancing pianist. These works are filled with predictable figurations, but the harmonizations are relatively interesting and the patterns used are pianistically helpful. (G. Schirmer.) Level 9.

Additional Works for Study:
Op. 5 Exercises in the form of studies
Op. 6 Studies in expression

HENRY LEMOINE (1786–1854) France

A French music publisher and composer, Lemoine published methods for harmony, solfeggio and piano.

Études Enfantines, Op. 37

Two books of charming études for the upper-intermediate student. They could substitute for the Czerny-Germer études. See especially *Études* Nos. 3, 6, 8, 14, 17, 34, 35, 36 and 44. (Kalmus, G. Schirmer.) Levels 7–8.

ANATOLY LIADOV (1855–1914) Russia

Liadov composed many excellent small pieces for piano including a substantial number of preludes, mazurkas, waltzes, intermezzi and impromptus.

Musical Snuff-Box, Op. 32

Liadov's best known work, which emphasizes the high register in imitation of a music box. (Many standard editions.) Levels 7–8.

Liadov Piano Works, ed. Sasaki

An excellent cross section of the easier works of Liadov. See especially the three preludes included here as well as the mazurkas and the two bagatelles. (Zen-on.) Levels 8–10.

Additional Works for Study:
Op. 2 Miniatures
Op. 26 Petit Valse

SERGEI LIAPUNOV (1859–1924) Russia
Sechs leichte Stücke, Op. 59

Interesting romantic character pieces, most of them two pages, well-suited to the student who wants to play literature that sounds difficult. Writing that feels comfortable under the hand. These would be interesting additions to a competition list. See especially *No. 4 À Cheval sur un Bâton* and *No. 6 Ramage des enfants*. (Zimmermann.) Level 8.

HEINRICH LICHNER (1829–1898) Germany
Three Sonatinas, Op. 4

A set of neo-Classical sonatinas that could easily pass as works composed in the late 1700's. See especially *Sonatina in F*, Op. 4, No. 2, a three-movement work. The first movement, *Allegro Moderato*, contains a single-note melody accompanied by an Alberti bass and some chord patterns. The final movement, *Polonaise*, is vigorous with interesting rhythms and wit. (G. Schirmer.) Level 6.

Three Sonatinas, Op. 49

The best-known sonatina from this group is the *Sonatina in C*, Op. 49, No. 1. The last movement rondo is filled with vitality. The scale patterns need careful attention and the ending is particularly effective. (G. Schirmer.) Levels 5–6.

Sonatinas, Op. 66

These works follow in the tradition of the other sets, filled with Alberti basses and chordal accompaniments. Excellent repertoire similar in difficulty to the Clementi *Sonatinas*, Op. 36. No. 1 is the best known. (G. Schirmer.) Level 6.

Nine Sonatinas

Contains an edited version of the sonatas from Op. 4, 49 and 66. This is the most accessible collection of Lichner's sonatinas. (Carl Fischer, G. Schirmer.) Levels 4–6.

FRANZ LISZT (1811–1886) Hungary

Perhaps the greatest piano virtuoso of the 19th century, Liszt also composed a great deal of idiomatic piano music, and is known for his bold harmonic innovations. S. numbers are from the Humphrey Searle *Thematic Catalogue of the Works of Liszt* and are often included here as an added guide to identifying a work. Opus numbers are also given. Many standard editions exist of the works of Liszt. Occasionally a publisher is given when a work is perceived as somewhat difficult to locate. Works are listed in the following order: *Études, Years of Pilgrimage, Hungarian Pieces, Religious Pieces, Additional Character Pieces, The Late Years* (1870–1886) and *Miscellaneous Volumes.*

Études

Études, Op. 1, S. 136

The opus contains 12 études composed when Liszt was 16. Eleven of them were used as a basis for the 12 *Transcendental Études* of 1839 and 1852. Most are of enormous difficulty, but several are accessible to the advanced student.

Étude in F Major, Op. 1, No. 3, S. 136

A study in expansion and contraction, with parallel eighth-note motion between hand and some double-note writing in both hands. Level 10.

Étude in D Minor, Op. 1, No. 4

This étude eventually grew into the well-known *Mazeppa*. It features thirds with the hands crossing and broken-chord passagework. It is a difficult-sounding work that can be used as a motivating technical study. Level 8.

The Years of Pilgrimage

Years of Pilgrimage. First Year: Switzerland, S. 160

This set of pieces presents Liszt's impressions of Switzerland. It is a kind of musical road map, moving from *Chapelle de Guillame Tell* (William Tell's Chapel) on a mountain top, through the lake of Wallenstadt, on through various other locations, and symbolizes the strong relationship of music to forces outside of itself such as drama, poetry, landscape and so on.

No. 2 Au Lac de Wallenstadt (By the Lake of Wallenstadt), S. 160/2

Describes waves on a lake through a left-hand rolling bass with a beautiful song-like melody in the right hand. A kind of nocturne, requiring evenness and a refined legato. Level 10.

Years of Pilgrimage. Second Year: Italy, S. 161

The pieces have a philosophical connection in that they represent different artistic-literary creations by Italian masters such as Raphael, Michelangelo and Rosa. For the mature performer.

No. 2 Il Pensieroso, S. 161

Inspired by Michaelangelo's statue of Lorenzo de Medici. Highly chromatic writing in a dramatic work with frequent use of the lower register. This piece seems to create an atmosphere of meditation. Level 10.

No. 3 Canzonetta del Salvator Rosa, S. 169

A relatively light and cheerful song that is march-like. Probably a transcription of a song set to words by the painter Salvator Rosa. Level 10.

Hungarian Pieces

Five Hungarian Folk Songs, S. 245

Composed in 1873, relatively late in Liszt's life, these settings of folk songs reflect his interest in the music of his native Hungary. Highly rhythmic and containing many syncopations, the folk songs are more difficult than they appear on the page. They fit the hand well. Level 8.

Additional Work for Study:
Magyar Folk Melodies (1839–47), especially Nos. 2 and 6

Religious Pieces

The Shepherds at the Manger, S. 186

This is Liszt's solo arrangement of *Good Christian Men Rejoice*. The left hand presents an ostinato-like figure that sets the mood of a lullaby. The right hand presents the melody in diatonic chords. Level 8.

Sancta Dorothea, S. 187

Lyrical single-note melody set above a broken-chord accompaniment in both hands. Relatively easy to read, but requires careful voicing of the melody. It is representative of Liszt's body of shorter sacred piano works, composed after 1861. The "cross" motif (G, A, C) appears several times and refers to an early virgin saint who possessed much grace and tenderness, later martyred by a Roman emperor. Level 8.

Ave Maris Stella (1865)

Composed originally in 1865 for mixed choir with organ accompaniment and later arranged by Liszt for various combinations of performers, the piano solo version was transcribed by Liszt in 1868 and is based on a hymn setting in praise of Maria by the medieval poet Venatius Fortunatus. The work is sentimental and not technically involved, requiring a refined sense of fluidity of a melodic line and ease in moving about the keyboard. (Editio Musica.) Level 9.

Additional Works for Study:
Pater Noster, S. 173
The Child's Waking Song, S. 173
Ave Maria, S. 173
On The Feast of Transfiguration of Our Lord Jesus Christ, S. 188 (1880)
Recueillement, S. 204 (after 1880)

Additional Character Pieces

Consolations, S. 172

Primarily lyrical in character, all of the *Consolations* should be played more often. Many would provide fine studies to precede the Chopin nocturnes. No. 3 is the best known. (Many standard editions.)

No. 1 Consolation in E Major

Primarily chordal writing in a meditative work. Lyrical melody, lush sonorities and nocturne-like writing. One of Liszt's most accessible pieces. The right hand plays fifth-finger *tenuto* with an off-beat chord pattern beneath. Level 7.

No. 2 Consolation in E Major

A lush and Romantic song featuring a lyrical melody presented in single notes and in octaves, above an arpeggiated chordal accompaniment. Should be played more frequently. Level 9.

No. 3 Consolation in D-flat Major

The most popular work of the set features pedal problems in the beginning measures where the clearing of the pedal for changing harmonies and yet sustaining of a low tied D-flat becomes a challenge. Tied bass notes may be repeated rather than tied in the changes of harmony. This work is often studied immediately prior to the easier nocturnes of Chopin. Displays a trace of melancholy. Level 9.

No. 4 Consolation in D-flat Major

A relatively short, almost devotional piece that is slow and sustained, primarily chordal and highly chromatic. Especially suited for the performer who enjoys emotional and sentimental writing. Level 9.

No. 5 Consolation in E Major

A fine, short substitute for one of the easier nocturnes of Chopin. A singing cantilena appears above a flowing broken-chord accompaniment. Harmonic color abounds. Level 10.

No. 6 Consolation in E Major

The most demanding of the set technically, with some cadenza passagework that is highly idiomatic but contains several difficult leaps. Begins with an eerie atmosphere followed by a passionate solo. Level 10.

Wiegenlied (Cradle Song), S. 174 (1854)

Material used here is found in Liszt's last symphonic poem *From the Cradle to the Grave*. It was composed late in Liszt's life and is notable for its simplicity and transparent texture. This work is technically accessible and of high musical quality. A later version (1862) is more difficult. Level 8.

The Christmas Tree, S. 186

Later in his life, Liszt wrote this set of 12 pieces ostensibly for children. They reveal, however, Liszt's lack of familiarity with the pianistic limits of young persons, since they contain some taxing octave and double-note passages, wide stretches and so on. See especially *Shepherds of the Manger, An Old Carol, March of the Wise Men, Lighting the Candles* and *Slumber Song.* Levels 8–10.

Five (Four) Little Piano Pieces, S. 192

These works were composed toward the end of Liszt's life between 1865 and 1879 for Olga von Meyendorff, a close friend. The first four pieces were published after her death in 1926, but the last, *Sospiri!* was not published until 1969. (Some editions still publish them as *Four Little Piano Pieces.*) Intimate and warm writing. All are relatively short and lyrical. The keys in which they are written make them somewhat difficult to read. *Sospiri!* is remarkable for the 11-measure introduction with an unresolved diminished seventh chord and a development using a chromatic five-note motive. Representative of Liszt's "easiest" writing. Levels 7–8.

Later Years (1870–1886)

Nuages Gris (Gray Clouds), S. 199

Left-hand tremolos are a distinctive feature in a late work that is extraordinarily harmonically progressive. Levels 6–7.

En Rêve. Nocturne, S. 207

Written late in Liszt's life but less experimental than other works. An F-sharp pedal point in the accompaniment dominates. Some right-hand trills will need attention. A beautiful and compelling short lyrical work. Level 8.

Valses Oubliées, S. 215

The first of the set is the most frequently played, and is filled with arpeggiations and passagework running up and down the keyboard. In an impromptu style and requires delicate expression. Level 10.

Bagatelle Without Tonality, S. 216a

Composed in 1885, the year before Liszt's death, this piece was originally intended as a fourth Mephisto Waltz. A diminished seventh, the primary focal point of this composition, is left unresolved at the end. In this work

Liszt moves in the direction of free and even use of all 12 chromatic tones. Solemn yet intense, it is in two large sections, A and A'. It was not published until 1956. Level 8.

Abschied (Farewell), S. 251

Modal and mournful. Primarily chordal writing based on two Russian folk songs and conveying a feeling of deep serenity. Two pages. Level 7.

Miscellaneous Volumes

Franz Liszt: An Introduction to the Composer and His Music, ed. Banowetz

Valuable collection of interesting performance choices including many of the shorter of his late pieces. Worthy commentary as well. Editorial additions are presented in red print. (Kjos.) Levels 7–9.

At the Piano With Liszt, ed. Hinson

Engaging editorial commentary at the beginning of this easier collection. (Alfred.) Levels 7–9.

Rare and Familiar, ed. Mach

Intermediate to moderately advanced works including *En Rêve, Nuages Gris, Four Small Piano Pieces, Chanson du Bearn, Faribolo Pastour, Zum Andenken*, and four transcriptions on French national themes. (Associated.) Levels 7–9.

Liszt: Piano Music from His Early Years, ed. Hinson

Included are five études from Liszt's *12 Études*, Op. 1, works that were later transformed into the *Transcendental Études* of 1851. Also included are several additional miscellaneous early works. (Alfred.) Levels 8–10.

Liszt: Piano Music Inspired by Women in His Life, ed. Hinson

Contains *Berceuse* (first version); *Five Piano Pieces*, No. 2; *Ave Maria* and *Pater Noster from Harmonies poétiques et religieuses*, No. 5; and *Impromptu*, S. 191. (Alfred.) Levels 8–10.

Three Late Pieces

Contains the *Toccata, Carrousel* and *Sospiri!*. All three nostalgic pieces are transparent in texture. Note the wisp-like, dissipated ending of *Carrousel*. Interesting fare for the mature musician. (Bärenreiter.) Levels 8–10.

ALBERT LOESCHHORN (1819–1905) Germany

Melodious Studies, Op. 52

Contains 30 works in three books. The collection is designed to precede the Études, Op. 38. See especially *Étude No. 1 in C Major, Étude No. 2 in C Major, Étude No. 3 in G Major, Étude No. 20 in A Major* and *Étude No. 22 in E Major*. (G. Schirmer.) Level 8.

Studies for Piano, Op. 65 (For Beginners)

One-page études (or actually short pieces in different styles) for intermediate students designed for the development of technique and expression. More interesting than the Czerny studies with more kinds of figures or patterns used. Good for developing reading. Few valuable étude collections at this level exist. (G. Schirmer, Willis.) Levels 4–8.

**Studies for Piano, Op. 66
(For the Intermediate Degree)**

Provides studies on a particular figuration such as the trill, double notes, broken chords and so on. More musical validity than many étude sets and longer than those in Op. 65. See especially No. 4 in G. (G. Schirmer.) Levels 8–10.

**33 Universal Piano Studies,
Op. 169, 170, 171 (For Medium Grade)**

His best crafted musical compositions. Series of études (generally two pages) that are highly patterned, relatively interesting harmonically and easy to read. (G. Schirmer.) Level 8.

Additional Works for Study:
Op. 38 Études Mélodieuses
Op. 84 60 Melodious Practices for Beginners
Op. 96 Children's Hours

FRANK LYNES (1858–1913) USA

Lynes, who studied at the Leipzig Conservatory with Carl Reinecke, wrote at least 17 collections as well as many single pieces for piano solo although much of this music is unknown today. He was a prominent teacher, choral conductor and composer in the Boston area.

Four Analytical Sonatinas, Op. 39

These works function as Classical-style literature even though the composer's dates span the late-Romantic period. Ideal pieces to serve as a student's introduction to sonatina form. The composer provides an analysis preceding each movement to allow the student to follow the progression of themes and contrasting material. Each movement is labeled as "song form, theme and variation, rondo form, dance form or sonata form." All are tuneful and easily accessible for the upper-elementary student. (Many standard editions.)

No. 1 Sonatina in C Major

The first movement features extensive use of the C scale, broken triads and inversions, and sounds more difficult than it actually is. Most of the moving figuration appears in the right hand, accompanied by a simple and often sustained left-hand part. The second movement in dance form has an appealing melody while the third movement, a song form in 3/8, has a tricky left-hand Alberti bass. This movement might be especially appropriate for a student needing to work on facility since it does not excessively tax the hand. Bright and cheerful. Level 3.

No. 2 Sonatina in G Major

The first movement features moving right-hand passages that fit the hand well. The third movement, *Rondo*, is substantially more difficult than the first. However, its sprightly nature is infectious. Level 3.

No. 3 Sonatina in C Major

An opportunity for students to work toward proper balance of melody and accompaniment. Short motivic units need careful inflection in the tuneful and inviting first movement sonata form. The song-form second movement is perhaps the easiest movement in this opus. It is a study in the playing of blocked chords. The rondo finale is based on ascending and descending scale passages. Levels 2–3.

No. 4 Sonatina in G Major

This sonatina is the least known of the four in this opus. The first movement is characterized by the changes from eighth notes to triplets and by left-hand voicings in which a bottom note is sustained and blocked chords are played above in the right hand. Although this is the most extended movement in the set, its difficulties are minimal. The second movement consists of two minuets. Level 5.

M

EDWARD MACDOWELL (1861–1908) USA

MacDowell was probably America's best-known Romantic-era composer, and also highly regarded as a pianist. At times he also composed under the pen name of Edgar Thorne. He wrote dance pieces, character pieces, études, sketches on folk and Indian themes, and programmatic pieces prefaced with poetry. MacDowell clubs and societies have been formed in his honor in cities across the USA.

Two Phantasy Pieces for Concert Use, Op. 17

The most frequently played in this set is the *Witches' Dance*, Op. 17, No. 2 (also published separately) which is a presto finger piece that is rousing and effective. The music seems more descriptive of nymphs than witches. Motivating but difficult to read at the outset. (Many standard editions.) Level 10.

Four Pieces, Op. 24

Grieg's influence seems certain in the movement *Humoreske*. See especially the finale, *Czardas*, which is a brilliant finger piece. For the accomplished pianist. (G. Schirmer.) Level 10.

Six Poems after Heinrich Heine, Op. 31

By far the best known selection in this opus is the *Scotch Poem*, Op. 31, No. 2, which can be an effective piece for an upper-intermediate student. It vividly suggests Heine's description of waves crashing on the Scottish coast. The tempestuous figurations and large chords in the outer A sections create a mysterious and increasingly forbidding mood. This passionate piece sounds more difficult than it actually is. Appropriate for the student who enjoys big and effective pieces. (Many standard editions.) Levels 8–10.

Four Little Poems, Op. 32

These popular pieces were inspired by poems of Tennyson, Bulwer, D. G. Rossetti and Shelley. The writing here is more inspired than in MacDowell's earlier sets. (Kalmus, G. Schirmer.) Level 9.

No. 2 The Brook

This work might be used for the student who needs a short, quasi-virtuosic selection. Requires a small hand span and agile fingerwork. Fresh harmonies. Level 8.

No. 4 Winter

This piece is a musical evocation of the frozen landscape and the mourning bird. An effective two-page quasi-impressionistic piece. In the manner of *Clair de lune* by Debussy, but shorter. Level 9.

Marionettes, Op. 38

The spirit of Schumann is found in this volume of pleasant pieces evoking childhood. The titles refer to various marionettes such as *Soubrette, Lover, Witch, Clown* and *Villain*. Originally published in Germany and later reissued in this country in a revised and augmented version, it is suitable for early-advanced students who can negotiate the easiest Chopin waltzes. (Hinshaw.) Level 9.

12 Études, Op. 39

Attractive character pieces, some of MacDowell's best. Several have made their way into the modern repertoire, including *Shadow Dance, Alla Tarantella,* and *Hungarian*. One of his best known teaching collections, for the early-advanced student. (Boston, Kalmus, G. Schirmer and other standard editions.) Levels 8–9.

No. 1 Hunting Song

A vivid work in F Major, with a hornlike theme. Some unison playing as well as rapid changes in articulation and rhythmic patterns. Two pages. Level 8.

No. 2 Alla Tarantella

Exciting work in which the right hand plays rapid eighth notes in triplets against a blocked-chord accompaniment. It needs lightness to create the *scherzando* effect. Rewarding and enjoyable to play. Level 8.

No. 3 Romance

Short ABA selection featuring A sections in chorale style. The B section uses short *ppp* chords before the return to the sustained A section. Level 8.

No. 4 Arabesque

The most difficult of the studies in this collection, with many passages using double notes in both hands and a bravura ending that builds from *pp* to *ff*. Dance-like rhythm and syncopated accompaniment. Level 10.

No. 7 Idyl

Reflects MacDowell's fascination for idyllic scenes. This is a study in cantabile playing and rapid right-hand figuration which eventually turns into trills. The harmonic language is somewhat richer than in other selections in this opus. Level 9.

No. 8 Shadow Dance

A distinctive and popular work in the early 1900s. The fingery passagework is effective and not as difficult as it sounds. Short attractive introduction to the work features grace note figures. The score is not easy to read. Level 8.

No. 10 Melodie

A study in playing a *tenuto* octave melody and an accompaniment figure in the same hand. Cello-like melody in the left hand. Level 9.

No. 11 Scherzino

An effective double-note study. Contains a lyrical melody in the left hand while the right hand executes the passagework. Valuable technical study. Levels 9–10.

No. 12 Hungarian

Bravura style with strong rhythmic patterns that suggest the folk dance. Effective work that requires rapid fingerwork, leaps and trills. Level 9.

Woodland Sketches, Op. 51

Recognized as a "classic" of American music, the *Woodland Sketches* express the majesty and charm of the New England countryside. The work can be effectively performed as a set. (Many standard editions.)

No. 1 To a Wild Rose

Tender, simple and beautiful, this favorite of many deserves its popularity. Level 5.

No. 4 In Autumn

Expresses a joyous well-being evoked by the colorful trees on a clear crisp New England autumn day. The epitome of a 19th-century American character piece. Level 9.

No. 5 From an Indian Lodge

The story is left to the imagination of the interpreter, but the mood is that of a dirge, perhaps for the death of an Indian chieftain. This work is easier than it sounds and is based on thematic material sup-posedly taken from a melody of the Brotherton Indians. Rhythmic, mournful and melodic central section. An appropriate Romantic selection for a student with limited facility. Level 8.

No. 6 To a Water Lily

Evokes the beauty of the water lily against the black pool from which the lily had forced its way through to the surface. Dreamy work with many slow, sustained chords. Level 8.

No. 8 A Deserted Farm

Depicts the deserted homes left throughout New England by farm-ers who sought richer land out west. MacDowell found real inspira-tion in these neglected farm houses. Expressive melody and emo-tional writing within a texture that consists primarily of chords. Level 8.

No. 10 Told at Sunset

The composer brings back a portion of *No. 8 A Deserted Farm* and then concludes with the closing of *No. 5 From an Indian Lodge*. Level 9.

Sea Pieces, Op. 55

Many of these character pieces are reflective, while others are majestic. See especially *To the Sea, From the Depths* and *Song*. (Many standard editions.)

No. 1 To the Sea

Prefaced by the line, "Ocean, thou mighty monster." The composer reveals the weight and strength of the ocean through the use of block sonorities, octave doublings, wide use of registers and *fff* dynamic levels. This broadly conceived work employs pedal points to sustain the tension. Levels 9–10.

No. 3 A.D. MDCXX

This work pays homage to the spirit of the Pilgrims. A prefatory verse mentions a setting sun melting into the lazy sea as one looks toward a land of promise. Chromatic tones found here may be intended to create a sense of shifting of the sea in a rhythmic pat-tern. Contains a chorale, perhaps a Pilgrim hymn of thanksgiving, in the middle section to break the restless pattern of the opening. Level 9.

No. 5 Song

Lyrical melody above a thick accompaniment. This piece would appeal to those who enjoy nostalgic and sentimental writing. Level 8.

Fireside Tales, Op. 61

These later pieces from MacDowell's life (1902) display, according to Maurice Hinson in his preface to the Alfred edition, "a certain strange, far-awayness of thought and a grave tenderness [that] are not quite like anything he had composed up to this time." Some of the pieces contain a substantial number of accidentals. (Many standard editions.) Level 10.

New England Idylls, Op. 62

This work, MacDowell's last collection of short piano pieces, contains a mixture of light and serious fare. See especially *To an Old White Pine* and *From Puritan Days*. (Many standard editions.) Level 10.

Works Written under the Pseudonym of Edgar Thorn

Edgar Thorn was a name MacDowell used when he wanted publication royalties to go to the family nurse. These pieces were light, designed to sell quickly. (Ironically, MacDowell found in time that when he changed the name back to MacDowell, the pieces sold even more quickly.)

Forgotten Fairytales, Op. 4

Four romantic character pieces, charming but not easy to read: *Sung Outside the Prince's Door; Of a Tailor and a Bear; Beauty in the Rose-Garden;* and *From Dwarf-land*. See especially the first, *Sung Outside the Prince's Door*. Selections are two to three pages long. (Hinshaw.) Levels 7–8.

Six Fancies, Op. 7

Written while the MacDowells lived in their first home, a small cottage outside of Wiesbaden, Germany. Legends, elves and love of nature permeate these character pieces. Titles are: *No. 1, A Tin Soldier's Love; No. 2, To a Humming Bird; No. 3, Summer Song; No. 4, Across Fields; No. 5, Bluette;* and *No. 6, An Elfin Round*. Effective writing and highly accessible. Levels 7–8.

No. 2 To a Humming Bird

Highly programmatic writing with the darting of the hummingbird represented in chromatic scales, repeated patterns representing the hovering, and soaring arpeggiations. Level 8.

Miscellaneous Pieces

Piano Works: Woodland Sketches, Complete Sonatas and Other Pieces

Many of the important works of MacDowell are included in this single volume, which is especially good for teacher reference. Also included are the *Sea Pieces*, Op. 55, *Fireside Tales*, Op. 61 and *New England Idyls*, Op. 62. (Dover.) Levels 7–10.

GIUSEPPE MARTUCCI (1856–1909) Italy

20 Little Pieces for Piano

These pieces are in the tradition of Schumann. Many are two to three pages and often are written in keys of three or more sharps or flats. Worth investigating. (Ricordi.) Level 8.

NIKOLAI MEDTNER (1879–1951) Russia

Medtner has often been referred to as the "Russian Brahms."

Works for Study:
Op. 7 Three Arabesques (No. 1 An Idyll)
Op. 14 Two Fairy Tales (No. 2 Ophelia's Song)
Op. 51 Six Fairy Tales (No. 3 March)

FELIX MENDELSSOHN-BARTHOLDY (1809–1847) Germany

Mendelssohn, in addition to being an enormously gifted musician, was a classical scholar, athlete, artist and brilliant conversationalist. He was considered to be one of the finest organists and pianists of his day. Most of his music has a Romantic charm and a Classical predilection.

Seven Character Pieces, Op. 7

Counterpoint plays a big role in these pieces: the third and fifth are actually composed in fugal form. See especially No. 6 with its strong pathos and No. 7, a delicate and airy scherzo portrayed by rapid hands alternating passages in chords and octaves. (Many standard editions.) Level 10.

Andante and Rondo Capricioso, Op. 14

Lyrical andante opening followed by a presto in the best of Mendelssohn's scherzo style. Brilliant and effective in performance. (Many standard editions.) Level 10.

Scherzo in E Minor, Op. 16, No. 2

This well-known work is typical of Mendelssohn's use of fleet fingerwork and is reminiscent of the style of the composer's Scherzo from *A Midsummer Night's Dream*. Needs precision and coordination between the hands. Requires facility in playing repeated notes with finger changes, repeated and consecutive octaves, running passages with tricky fingering, frequent grace notes, sixteenth-note broken-chord figurations and consecutive double-thirds. Suited for the performer with a strong rhythmic sense. (Many standard editions.) Level 9.

Six Christmas Pieces, Op. 72

Often published as *Six Children's Pieces*, the title "Christmas Pieces" is the one that Mendelssohn designated for this work. These pieces came from an original set of eight written by Mendelssohn for various members of a family whom he and his wife were visiting in 1842. After Mendelssohn's death in 1847, they were published in two separate editions, *Sechs Kinderstücke für das Pianoforte*, Op. 72 and *Six Pieces for the Pianoforte*. The first edition is the preferable one and the one upon which most editions are based. These pieces are generally two to three pages. The textures are thick and the writing is highly melodic. Generally they are more difficult than many expect, sometimes approaching the difficulty of the *Songs Without Words*. No. 1, *Allegro non troppo* is the most accessible and the best known. (Alfred, Associated Board of the Royal Schools of Music, Shattinger and other standard editions.) Levels 7–8.

Prelude and Fugue in E Minor

Many know the prelude of this set as *Praeludium in E Minor*. The pairing of this prelude with a fugue has been overlooked or ignored for many years, probably due to the difficulty of the fugue in comparison to the prelude. The prelude is a rapid arpeggio étude requiring supple wrists and flexible fingers; a single-note melody is played above the accompanimental arpeggios. This piece should be better known. The fugue is an extended work in which the parts at times become homophonic. It also features jagged lines and an effective buildup of sound. (Alfred, Associated Board of the Royal Schools of Music and other standard editions.) Level 9.

Sonata in B-flat Minor

A one-movement work which dates from Mendelssohn's student years (1832) and which remained unpublished until the 1980s. First titled "sonatina" by Mendelssohn. Monothematic selection which begins with a slow introduction that returns later. Interesting writing if not profound. Ten pages. (Peters.) Level 10.

Songs Without Words

The *Songs Without Words* are a group of 48 pieces by Mendelssohn, mostly cast in a simple ternary form. He gave titles to only five of them: the three "Venetian Gondola-Songs" (Op. 19, No. 6; Op. 30, No. 6; and Op. 62, No. 5), the "Duetto" (Op. 38, No. 6) and the "Folk-song" (Op. 53, No. 5). The additional titles were not original with Mendelssohn, though they are used in the annotations as a means of helping the reader identify quickly to which work we are referring. Mendelssohn strove for unity of mood and texture within a single piece rather than for contrast within an individual work. The last two books, Books VII and VIII (Op. 85 and Op. 102) were published after his death. (Many standard editions.)

Song Without Words, Op. 19, No. 1 ["Sweet Remembrance"]

One of the most beautiful, featuring a sustained melody above broken-chord figuration arpeggiated between the hands. This is an appropriate work for a performer to study the differentiation of melody/accompaniment/bass, and to work on shaping long lines. Requires fine dynamic control. Level 9.

Song Without Words, Op. 19, No. 2 ["Regrets"]

Single- and double-note melody sustained over a sixteenth-note accompaniment. A good test of a player's legato. Voicing between the hands is a primary consideration. Somewhat more plaintive than the preceding work. Appropriate as a pianist's first "nocturne-like" piece. Level 8.

Song Without Words, Op. 19, No. 3 ["Hunting Song"]

Chords and octaves make this especially appropriate for students with large and strong hands. Energetic and full-sounding. Needs technical clarity in the tempestuous passagework. Level 9.

Song Without Words, Op. 19, No. 4 ["Confidence"]

One of the most accessible. A broken-chord introduction and postlude surround a primarily chordal body of this short piece that provides a good study in voicing chords. Slightly more difficult than the Chopin *Prelude in B Minor*, Op. 28, No. 6. Level 7.

Song Without Words, Op. 19, No. 6 ("Venetian Boat-Song No. 1")

Perhaps the most frequently taught of the *Songs Without Words*. Primary technical considerations involve the skips in the left hand and the voicing of the right-hand melody over right-hand accompaniment. The performance needs a sense of a forward motion in the musical line. Level 8.

215

Song Without Words, Op. 30, No. 1 ["Contemplation"]

Thick texture with double-note triplet accompaniment figures. This evanescent work could be a student's first work with thick Romantic textures and rapid manipulation of melody and accompaniment in a single hand. Valuable especially as a study in voicing. Level 10.

Song Without Words, Op. 30, No. 3 ["Consolation"]

Arpeggiated chords in the introduction and postlude. Otherwise, the quasi-chorale writing in the body of this work prevails. Potential problems may involve voicing the melody above the chords and playing a true legato in the right hand. One of the most accessible of the set. Level 7.

Song Without Words, Op. 30, No. 4 ("Venetian Boat-Song No. 2")

Despite its popularity, this selection is not as pianistic and idiomatic to the piano as many of the others. The left-hand skips are occasionally awkward. Level 9.

Song Without Words, Op. 38, No. 1 ["The Evening Star"]

Infrequently heard work with perpetual motion figuration throughout (as is the case with many of the *Songs Without Words*). The single-note melody needs periodic finger substitution and attention to legato. Accompaniment patterns are divided between the hands. Level 10.

Song Without Words, Op. 38, No. 2 ["Lost Happiness"]

A somewhat angular melody. The continuous off-beat chordal accompaniment makes listening for a long line essential to the successful performance of this short work. The hands remain in relatively stationary positions. Level 9.

Song Without Words, Op. 38, No. 4 ["Hope"]

Similar in form to *Confidence* and *Consolation* but more difficult. The central chordal section contains more adventurous harmonies and more movement between the voices. Level 9.

Song Without Words, Op. 53, No. 4 ["Sadness of Soul"]

Lush, Romantic sound and thick textures. This work requires skilled voicing and lyrical playing. Repeated chord accompaniment under a sustained melody. Level 8.

Song Without Words, Op. 85, No. 1 ["Reverie"]

The texture features broken chords divided between the hands with a lyrical melody above. Rhythms of two against three appear in the texture. Level 9.

Song Without Words, Op. 85, No. 2 ["The Adieu"]

The melody is doubled in the low bass and an answering accompaniment figure imitates in single notes on the off-beats. The performer needs real skill in voicing melody and accompaniment. Level 8.

Song Without Words, Op. 102, No. 2 ["Retrospection"]

Calls for shaping and projection of phrasing in a slow tempo. Sustained and moving voices appear in both hands and require many finger substitutions. A performer could easily become physically tense in an effort to maintain a legato. Level 8.

Song Without Words, Op. 102, No. 3 ["Tarantella"]

Requires fast fingerwork in the right hand and quick repeated chord playing in the left hand. Exciting writing that renders this a student favorite. Level 7.

Miscellaneous Volumes

**At the Piano with Felix and
Fanny Mendelssohn, ed. Hinson**

Interesting combination of pieces composed by brother and sister are found here. The preface is especially valuable, as is the little-known music by Fanny Mendelssohn Hensel. (Alfred.) Levels 7–10.

**Mendelssohn: The First Book
for Pianists, ed. Halford**

Contains five of the pieces from Op. 72 and three *Songs Without Words*. A practical performing collection providing an especially representative introduction to Mendelssohn's works. (Alfred.) Levels 7–8.

**Mendelssohn: An Introduction
to His Piano Works, ed. Halford**

An excellent overview of his works, including all the works in *Mendelssohn: The First Book for Pianists* and several slightly more difficult works such as the *Scherzo in E Minor* and several additional *Songs Without Words*. (Alfred.) Levels 8–10.

**Mendelssohn: Songs Without Words,
Selected Favorites, ed. Palmer**

Practical performing volume containing the most accessible and best-known of the *Songs Without Words*. (Alfred.) Levels 8–9.

Additional Work for Study:

Op. 117 Albumleaf

MORITZ MOSZKOWSKI (1854–1925) Poland

Popular in his day as a pianist, but also well-known as a teacher and composer. Moszkowski served on the faculty of Kullak's piano academy.

Spanish Dances, Op. 12

Generally highly rhythmic and animated writing in a conservative harmonic style. Could make a good sight-reading project for the advanced student. (Many standard editions.) Level 10.

No. 1

Inviting writing, with thick textures and full sounds. A sixteenth-note melody usually appears above a waltz-like bass. Level 9.

Dix Pièces Mignonnes, Op. 77 (1907)

Accessible and brief pieces that range from two to six pages. See especially *No. 2 Scherzino, No. 4 Inquiétude, No. 6 Tarantella* and *No. 8 Pantomime*. These pieces should be better known. (G. Schirmer.)

No. 2 Scherzino

A work calling for fast *leggiero* playing in both hands simultaneously. A show-piece or étude for a performer with strong fingers. Level 8.

No. 6 Tarantella

A little-known and highly effective tarantella for the advanced-intermediate student. The passagework fits the hand well, and the rollicking left hand creates an accompaniment that is memorable. Requires a performer with flair and energy. Level 8.

20 Little Études for Piano, Op. 91, Volumes 1–2

Technical studies for the advancing pianist that further the style of Schumann and Chopin. Generally one- to three-page studies, these works are less difficult than the Cramer études. Although many require fast, agile fingerwork and are filled with a single figuration throughout, others are lyrical and sustained in character, exploiting a Romantic sentimentality. Fine preparation for the study of the *Études de Virtuosité*, Op. 72. See especially the études in double notes. Numbers 1–10 are in Volume 1 and Numbers 11–20 are in Volume 2. (Leduc.) Levels 9–10.

Esquisses Techniques, Op. 97

Highy useful collection of études, idiomatic for the keyboard. Also excellent preparation for the *Études*, Op. 72. (Leduc.) Level 9.

Miscellaneous Pieces

Scherzino, Op. 18, No. 2

An excellent étude in double-note playing and a popular recital selection. (Many standard editions.) Level 9.

Serenata, Op. 51, No. 1

Popular salon-style teaching piece, with a prominent and rhythmic jumping bass. The right hand features repeated notes, repeated thirds and fast chromatic passagework. (Many standard editions.) Level 10.

Miscellaneous Volumes

Moszkowski: 13 Romantic Pieces, ed. Johnson

This anthology provides an overview of some of Moszkowski's easier piano pieces. Selections include five pieces from Op. 77, and selections from Op. 15, 18, 91 and 94. (Associated Board of the Royal Schools of Music.) Levels 8–9.

Moszkowski: 26 Pieces for Pianoforte, Volumes 1 and 2

Contains a cross-section of the most familiar works by Moszkowski. Some are quite advanced in difficulty. See especially *Mélodie*, Op. 18, No. 1; *Reverie*, Op. 36, No. 2; *Berceuse*, Op. 38, No. 2; and *Romance*, Op. 42, No. 1. (G. Schirmer.) Levels 9–10.

Moszkowski: Music for Piano, ed. Oesterle

An excellent source of the works in Op. 77 as well as the *Sparks*, Op. 36, No. 6 and several other works. (G. Schirmer.) Levels 8–10.

Additional Work for Study:
Op. 18 Fünf Clavierstücke (1878)

FRANZ XAVIER MOZART (1791–1844) Austria

Mozart's youngest son, born five months before his father died. His mature works are representative of the early Romantic period, having much in common with Hummel, Schubert and von Weber.

Four Polonaises, Op. 22

Generally in a binary minuet form with jumping bass figures and intricate rhythms. (Oxford University Press.) Level 8.

MODEST MUSSORGSKY (1839–1881) Russia

Gopak

One of his most popular works for piano, apart from *Pictures at an Exhibition*. Arranged by the composer from his opera *Sorochintsky Fair*. Strong rhythmic vitality, highly deserving of its popularity. (Many standard editions.) Level 8.

On the Southern Shore of Crimea

Several movements. The first, *Largo*, is a study in color and sonority. The second, *Capriccio*, is an ABA étude. Many right-hand passages of single notes in descending third patterns give the right hand a strong workout. The B section features folk rhythms. One of his more useful teaching pieces. (Peters.) Level 8.

Miscellaneous Volumes

Mussorgsky Album, ed. Balla

Contains two pieces from *Memories of Childhood*, written in 1865 and based on memories of his mother, his childhood, and his old nurse and her bedtime stories. One of the most interesting works in the volume is *Reverie*, a nocturne. A fine overview of Mussorgsky's piano music. (Editio Musica.) Levels 8–10.

N

CARL NIELSEN (1865–1931) Denmark

Considered perhaps the finest composer Denmark has produced, Nielsen displayed an individual style that combines traditional and progressive harmonic techniques. The music is quite rhythmic and highly melodic. Nielsen did not want to be classified with any particular stylistic school—modern or otherwise.

Five Piano Pieces, Op. 3 (1890)

Nielsen's first published composition for solo piano. These short character pieces are uncomplicated in melodic, harmonic and tonal structure, and make interesting repertoire choices. They fall between the Burgmüller *Progressive Studies*, Op. 100 and the easiest Chopin waltzes in difficulty. (Hansen, Masters Music and other editions.) Levels 6–7.

Folk Melody

> Chordal, somber writing. Easier than the Schumann *Important (Event)* but similar texture. Level 6.

Humoresque

Waltz character, playful, with a melody in eighths. Similar in character and level of difficulty to the well-known Grieg *Elfin Dance*. Level 6.

Arabesque

Exhibits sudden *sforzandi* and melisma-like figurations. Harmonically more ambiguous than the others in this set, the music contains the inscription "Have you lost your way in darkening forests? Do you know Pan?" from a verse by the Danish writer Jacobsen. Conceptually this piece is perhaps the most difficult work in the set. Level 8.

Mignon

Moderate tempo with a waltz-like character. Level 8.

Elf Dance

Marked *tempo di valse*. Level 8.

Humorous Bagatelles, Op. 11 (1894–97)

Nielsen's easiest pieces for teaching, composed between 1894 and 1897 and dedicated to his children. Light and innocent. Much of the humor comes from the figurations and the imitations of childrens' subjects. The six titles are reminiscent of scenes from a child's life: *Good Morning! Good Morning!*, *The Top*, *A Little Slow Waltz*, *Doll's March*, *Jumping Jack* and *The Musical Clock*. (Associated Board of the Royal Schools of Music, Hansen, Masters Music and other standard editions.)

No. 2 The Top

Perpetual motion work with dazzling sixteenth-note passages that fit the hand well and sound more difficult than they are. Effective glissando at the end. This selection should be better known. Level 8.

No. 6 The Musical Clock

A joking work, highly effective in performance, that depicts the regularity of a clock. The Alberti left-hand accompaniment makes this seem highly Classical in texture. Level 8.

Piano Music for Young and Old, Op. 53 (Two Volumes) (1930)

Composed a year and a half before Nielsen's death, it was written in response to a need expressed at a music educator's conference for easy new music for instructional purposes. Restricted to the range of a fifth. These untitled pieces would serve as good sight-reading material for the advancing pianist. Twenty-four pieces in all of the major and minor keys. (Hansen, Masters Music, Skandinavisk Musikforlag and standard editions.) Levels 5–9.

O

THEODOR OESTEN (1813–1870) Germany

Mayflowers, Op. 61

Subtitled "25 Easy Piano Pieces." Found here are appealing but little-known romantic character pieces of strong interest to the average student. Many are shorter than one printed page. (G. Schirmer.) Levels 3–4.

No. 10 Spanish Dance

An upbeat feeling is portrayed throughout this one-page piece. The melody appears in the right hand while the left hand features rhythmic, repeated chords. Level 3.

P

LOUIS PABST (1846–1903) Germany

Miniaturbilder, Op. 15

Romantically inspired selections. Titles include *Romaneske, Mazurka, Scherzino, Albumblatt* and *Lied ohne Worte*. Level 8.

IGNACE JAN PADEREWSKI (1860–1941) Poland

Minuet in G Major, Op. 14, No. 1 (Menuet à L'Antique)

A salon piece, highly enjoyed by the public in its day. The quasi-florid figurations and grand style may be a student's first introduction to larger-scale repertoire. (Many standard editions.) Level 10.

SELIM PALMGREN (1878–1951) Finland

Palmgren studied with Busoni and taught briefly at the Eastman School of Music, and for most of his career at the Sibelius Academy. He composed mostly piano works, especially short, lyrical pieces. (See also entry under 20th-century period.)

Album of 12 Pieces for the Piano

A fine source for introductory literature to the best of Palmgren's extensive and uneven output. In addition to the well-known *May Night*, included are *Prelude, Intermezzo, Humoresque, The Sea, The Dragon-fly, Sarabande* and others. No opus numbers are indicated. (Boston.) Levels 9–10.

ALBERT PIECZONKA (n.d.)

Tarantella

Effective writing in a highly patterned and energetic work. Quick shifts from closed to open hand positions are required. The lyrical B section may be the most difficult part to master. (Many standard editions.) Level 7.

GABRIEL PIERNÉ (1863–1937) France

Album for My Little Friends, Op. 14

Six charming, titled teaching pieces with Romantic sonorities. This music is little known but worth investigating. (Masters Music.) Level 7.

EDUARD POLDINI (1869–1957) Hungary

Poupée Valsante (The Dancing Doll)

This salon work became an international success in its day. Needs a light staccato and a refined sense of line. (G. Schirmer.) Level 7.

Album for the Young, Op. 122

Twelve charming short piano pieces. (Universal.) Level 6.

Springtime Pictures, Op. 151

Less interesting writing than in the Op. 122. Titles are *The Swallows, Frolic, Goldfinch* and *A Roundelay*. (Schmidt.) Level 6.

R

SERGEI RACHMANINOFF (1873–1943) Russia

See entry under 20th-century period.

JOACHIM RAFF (1822–1882) Germany

Sonatina, Op. 99, No. 1

Highly lyrical work with thick Romantic sonorities. The first movement resembles the look of Brahms' music on the page. The final *Tarantella* is marked to be played as fast as possible. A fine piece, though hardly subtle. (Peters.) Level 9.

Additional Works for Study:
Op. 75 12 Pieces
Op. 99, No. 3 Sonatina
Op. 130 Études Mélodiques

MAX REGER (1873–1916) Germany

The late-Romantic music of Reger shows the influence of Brahms, Grieg, Schumann and Chopin. He also revitalized Baroque polyphony and used Classical forms such as the fugue and variations. Many pieces are characterized by a certain searching quality and restless nature.

Album for Young People, Op. 17

Twenty children's pieces. In the same style Romantic-period "albums for the young." See especially *No. 5, Über Stock und Stein; No. 7, Little Dance; No. 8, Anxious Question; No. 12, Frolics; No. 18, Northern Dance;* and *No. 20, Reconciliation.* Schott publishes two volumes of seven pieces each. (Schott.) Level 6.

10 Little Instructional Pieces, Op. 44

Highly Romantic writing, much of it of high quality. See especially *No. 1, Album Leaf; No. 2, Burletta;* and *No. 3, Once Upon a Time.* (Universal.) Level 8.

10 Pieces for Piano, Op. 79a

Several surprisingly fine character pieces can be found here for the advancing pianist. Most are three to four pages and feature lush sonorities. See especially the *Impromptu, Mélodie* and *Intermezzo.* (Sikorski.) Level 10.

Dreaming at the Fireside, Op. 143

Twelve short character pieces, most of them two pages in length. An interesting alternative to better-known Romantic literature. (Peters.) Level 10.

Miscellaneous Volumes
Leichte Spielstücke für Klavier

Fine source of the easiest works of Reger. Six compositions are included. (Hug.) Levels 7–8.

Reger, ed. Schwerdtner

Contains an extensive cross-section of Reger's works including multiple selections from *Bunte Blätter,* Op. 36; *Zehn kleine Vortragsstücke,* Op. 44; *Blätter und Blüten, Zehn Kompositionen,* Op. 79a; *Traüme am Kamin,* Op. 143 and others. Polyphonic writing, lyricism and interesting harmonic colorations abound. The music is presented in chronological order to suggest the development of his style. Valuable source for anyone beginning to investigate the piano music of this composer. (Schott.) Levels 8–10.

CARL REINECKE (1824–1910) Germany

Reinecke toured Europe as a pianist and was a conductor of the famous Gewandhaus Orchestra in Leipzig. He was also a professor of composition at the Leipzig Conservatory, in addition to being a prolific composer. Reinecke was influenced by Schumann and Mendelssohn. Most of his piano output is of an instructional nature.

Three Sonatinas, Op. 47

These works can serve a special place for the talented student who is progressing rapidly and who needs "big" Romantic literature at the upper-intermediate level to introduce him to the Romantic style, sound and textures. The writing is full-blown, but still within the parameters of "teaching literature." To be specially noted are the first movement of *Sonatina No. 1*, the theme and variations of the final movement of the *Sonatina No. 2* and the entire *Sonatina No. 3*. (G. Schirmer.) Level 8.

Sonatinas, Op. 136

See especially Nos. 1, 2 and 4. The *Allegretto* from *Sonatina No. 1 in C* is one of the most playable movements from this set, although more difficult than it appears. The last two movements from this work, *Scherzino* and *Alla Polacca* are especially exciting. (Breitkopf.) Level 4.

Five Serenades for the Young, Op. 183 (1885)

These serenades are suites of three or four contrasting pieces. See especially No. 1 (*Praeludium, Song and Gavotte*) and No. 2 (*Polonaise*). The *Praeludium* of the first set is a simple broken-chord piece, somewhat in the style of J. S. Bach. This collection should be better known. (Associated Board of the Royal Schools of Music, Peters.) Levels 4–6.

Additional Works for Study:
Op. 98 Three Sonatinas
Op. 107 Notenbuch für kleine Leute
Op. 143 Dreaming at the Fireside
Op. 206 Musical Kindergarten (nine volumes)
Libre di musica per piccola gente (30 easy short pieces in the style of Gurlitt)

HUGO REINHOLD (1854–1935) Austria

Miniatures, Op. 39

Twenty-four interesting and little-known Romantic teaching pieces with strong variety and character. The textures are often thick. See especially *No. 1, March; No. 5, Savoyard Boy; No. 6, Scherzo; No. 9, Hungarian Dance; No. 13, Gypsy Song;* and *No. 24, Russian Dance.* (G. Schirmer.) Level 5.

No. 1 March

Stately work that is bold and highly rhythmic. The short notes need to be precise. Level 5.

No. 9 Hungarian Dance

Highly effective writing in a two-page selection that sounds much more difficult than it is. Requires flair and an innate sense of musicianship. Worth investigating. Level 5.

No. 13 Gypsy Song

Robust work with a staccato accompaniment in the left hand. Some double notes in the right hand call for voicing to the top. Has the potential to elicit strong audience response. Level 5.

No. 24 Russian Dance

The strong rhythmic framework and the frequent left-hand ostinato chords. This also is a rousing piece that should capture the attention of any audience. Levels 5–6.

Impromptus, Op. 28

These works are in E-flat Minor, A-flat Major and C-sharp Minor. *No. 3 in C-sharp Minor* is filled with idiomatic passagework and flourishes that make it rewarding to play and effective for an audience. This literature is more motivating than profound. (G. Schirmer.) Level 8.

Additional Work for Study:

Op. 58 Jugend-Erinnerungen

GIOACHINO ANTONIO ROSSINI (1792–1868) Italy

Most of the small body of Rossini's piano music was composed in the last years of his life.

Album for Adolescent Children

Mostly of historical interest. Selections have been republished by Masters Music in two volumes. (Masters Music.) Levels 9–10.

Rossini: Original Piano Pieces, ed. Zeitlin

A good starting place as a source of intermediate literature and for the performer who wants to know more about Rossini's piano music. His most accessible keyboard music is included here. See especially *Regret* (No. 6 from *Pièces Diverses*), an effective *Andantino* in E Major that challenges the performer to feel long phrases with voicings. Trills, inverted mordants and triplet sixteenths abound, as well as syncopation, and two-against-three appear here. An alternative to Schubert or Beethoven. (Presser.) Levels 8–10.

Additional Works for Study:
Op. 57 Rhythmic and Melodic Fingerpieces
Op. 58 Jugend-Erinnerungen

ANTON RUBINSTEIN (1830–1894) Russia

Rubinstein was the first Russian musician to be equally prominent as composer and performer. A virtuoso pianist, Rubinstein's playing was compelling and powerful.

Melodie in F Major, Op. 3, No. 1

The best-known of Rubinstein's works. Lush and lyrical but requires some flair. It is a work that is not typical of Russian music, but which sounds instead as if it could have been composed by Mendelssohn. The melody line is shared between the hands, with chordal accompaniment in the top and bottom registers. ABA Coda form. Requires skillful voicing. (Alfred.) Level 10.

S

CAMILLE SAINT-SAËNS (1835–1921) France

Two Little Piano Pieces

Berceuse and *Largo* were composed by Saint-Saëns in 1842 when he was seven. The *Berceuse* features a simple melody over an arpeggiated bass within traditional harmonic framework. The *Largo* is primarily chordal, written in two to four parts, and features a depth of pathos remarkable from a child of seven. (M.S.M. Music Publishers.) Level 5.

Six Bagatelles, Op. 3

Romantic character pieces arranged in two suites of three each. Several could provide interesting choices of repertoire as substitutes for Chopin waltzes and other similar pieces. (Peters.) Levels 9–10.

Les cloches du soir, Op. 85

A short character piece with many accompanimental repeated chords. A potential repertoire choice for a student who wants to play *Clair de lune* or one of the *Arabesques* by Debussy but is not yet ready for that music. Ostinatos resemble bells, in turn also producing interesting harmonic effects. (Peters.) Level 8.

XAVER SCHARWENKA (1850–1924) Poland

Polish Dance, Op. 3, No. 1

A piano standard, perhaps deserving of its popularity. The *Polish Dance* is in rondo form and will appeal to the performer with fire. (Many standard editions.) Level 8.

ALOYS SCHMITT (1788–1866) Germany

Schmitt was a respected composer and teacher. Most of Schmitt's compositions are heard no longer, but the *Preparatory Exercises* continue to enjoy popularity.

Preparatory Exercises for the Piano, Op. 16

Exercises for the independence of the fingers. Many of the exercises are in five-finger positions and require one or several fingers to be held while the others play a pattern. Some exercises for passing the thumb under the fingers are also included. Most of the exercises consist of one measure that is to be repeated many times. Performers must be careful to avoid tension while playing these studies. (Many standard editions.) Levels 6–10.

JACOB SCHMITT (1803–1853) Germany

Composer of numerous sonatinas in the classical style.

Works for Study:
Op. 83 Sonatinas
Op. 207 Sonatinas
Op. 248 Sonatinas
Op. 249 Sonatinas
Op. 269 Sonatinas

FRANZ SCHUBERT (1797–1828) Austria

Schubert was at the center of a circle of devoted friends and patrons, among whom were leading writers, dramatists, singers, painters and poets in Vienna. Some of these friends held evening musicales, or so-called "Schubertiaden," at which only the works of Schubert were performed. Often Schubert himself would play the piano during these evenings, either as accompanist, soloist or as part of a chamber group. Later in the evening, Schubert would sometimes play for the dancing, whereupon he would improvise waltzes, ländler and écossaises which he might later commit to paper. As a composer, Schubert is known for drawing careless slurs—in some instances it is difficult to tell where they begin and end. He used both staccato wedges and dots with the wedge probably taking its pre-Beethoven meaning of an accent (used both with and without a staccato) and the dot implying a normal staccato.

D. numbers represent the numbering established by Otto Erich Deutsch in *Schubert: Thematic Catalogue of all his Works in Chronological Order*. Opus numbers are original with Schubert. (Many standard editions.)

Dances

Most of the dances are in triple meter, and often the distinction between the various dances is difficult to define. The *ländler* is a country dance from the Austrian, Bavarian and Bohemian regions and is considered to be slightly slower than the waltz. The écossaise is similar to the *contredance* in that it is in a lively 2/4 and usually contains two eight-bar sections, each of which is repeated. The galops also are in 2/4 meter.

Dances

Schubert wrote over 400 waltzes, écossaises, German dances, Valses nobles, ländler, minuets and other kinds of dances, many of which are suitable for teaching. Many of them were left unpublished during Schubert's life. Of the most practical value are the various dance collections, rather than the volumes containing an entire opus of dances. Opuses from which dances have been extracted for anthologies are *Waltzes*, D. 365, Op. 9a and 9b; *Waltzes and Écossasies*, D. 145, Op. 18a; *German Dances and Écossaises*, D. 783, Op. 33; *Valses sentimentales*, D. 779, Op. 50; *Hommage aux belles Viennoises*, D. 734, Op. 67; *Valses nobles*, D. 969, Op. 77; *Grazer Waltzer*, D. 924, Op. 91a; *Letzte Walzer*, D. 146, Op. 127; *Ländler*, D. 790, Op. 171; *Ländler*, Op. Posth.; and *Menuette*, Op. Posth. Most of these works require some musical sophistication. (Associated Board of the Royal Schools of Music, Henle, Peters and other standard editions.) Levels 6–9.

Moments Musical

The *Moments Musical* are short, lyrical works, generally in ABA form, and somewhat reminiscent of the *Impromptus*, yet more accessible.

Six Moments Musical, Op. 94, D. 780

The title was an invention of the publisher rather than of Schubert. Strong emotional expression. Levels 8–9.

No. 1 in C Major

The opening motive could depict a "yodeler" in the Alps. Quick dynamic changes and contrasting phrase lengths and touches. Calls for refined inflection of the musical motives. Levels 9–10.

No. 2 in A-flat Major

Beautiful harmonic changes in a work especially good for the musically sensitive student. Needs legato and attention to voicing the melody. Rondo form, with both episodes made of similar material. Level 8.

No. 3 in F Minor

Considered by some to be Schubert's best-known composition. A sprightly work with consistent jumping bass figures and right-hand grace notes. The double-note passages in the right hand require clarity and demand coordination. Level 8.

No. 4 in C-sharp Minor

A finger study based on broken-chords with a perpetual motion right hand over left-hand staccato eighths. Good for building strength, although this work may be difficult for small hands. The central B section reminds one of a cheerful folk dance, albeit with irregularly accented chords. Levels 9–10.

No. 5 in F Minor

May be difficult for the performer with small hands due to the full chords and stretches. The writing is furious, and a highly repetitive rhythmic motive pervades this dance-like work. Level 9.

No. 6 in A-flat Major

Primarily chordal writing in a song-like work that contains fewer technical problems than the other chordal works in this opus. Needs careful voicing of the melody over the thicker accompaniment. One of the most accessible works in this set, especially appealing to the musically sensitive performer. Level 8.

Impromptus

The *Impromptu* is generally a character piece of intimate character, containing strong contrast of ideas. Both of Schubert's sets have become masterpieces of the standard repertoire. The label *impromptu* comes from the Bohemian composer Johann Woržischek.

Impromptus, Op. 90, D. 899

These masterful romantic character pieces show striking contrasts of texture and character in the forms. The first and third are primarily lyrical in nature while the second and fourth are more étude-like. All are in flat keys.

No. 2 in E-flat Major
This work presents a sweeping main theme consisting of scale figures, and a dramatic and strongly contrasting B section. One of the best of the *Impromptus*. Level 10.

No. 4 in A-flat Major
This work is built on flurrying broken-chord figures played in the right hand above a jumping bass accompaniment. The middle section is passionate and lyrical. Calls for mature voicing and sensitive musical playing. Level 10.

Impromptus, Op. 142, D. 935

The first, third and fourth of these pieces may have been intended to form a sonata. (Many standard editions.) Level 10.

No. 2 in A-flat Major
Serene, primarily homophonic work that begins like a sarabande with a gentle swaying rhythm. The trio section is based on triplet arpeggiations. The writing throughout calls for a strong sense of forward motion in the phrase. One of the most accessible of the Schubert *Impromptus*. Level 10.

Miscellaneous Pieces

Allegretto in C Minor, D. 915

Poetic work, somewhat shorter than the *Moments Musical* and effective for the sensitive performer. The expressive central section is marked "religioso." A justifiably popular work, appropriate to precede the *Moments Musical* and *Impromptus*. Level 8.

Andante in C Major, D. 29

Lyrical writing in a short character piece. Needs skillful voicing of thick chords and inner moving lines. Composed at approximately the same time as the Impromptus and the *Moments Musical*. Should be heard more frequently. Level 8.

Scherzo in B-flat Major, Op. Posth., D. 593, No. 1

This highly repetitive work in lilting triplets would benefit from an imaginative performer. The trio features sustained chords and moving left-hand notes. Level 7.

Fantasy in C Minor, D. 993

Maurice J. E. Brown writes in his biography that this might be called "Schubert's Fantasia on *Mozart's Fantasia in C Minor*, KV 475." In three sections, it shows strong thematic affinity with the Mozart companion work. Specified to be played on the "clavicembalo" (harpsichord), not on the piano. (Heinrichshofen and others.) Level 10.

Miscellaneous Volumes

Schubert: An Introduction
to His Piano Works, ed. Halford

The excellent foreword and the fine choice of pieces found here makes this an interesting collection for the intermediate performer. Included are *écossaises*, German dances, waltzes, scherzos and two of the *Moments Musical*. (Alfred.) Levels 3–10.

Schubert: The First Book
for Young Pianists, ed. Halford

The most accessible selections from *Schubert: An Introduction to His Piano Works* are found in this practical and useful collection. (Alfred.) Levels 3–7.

Dances of Schubert, ed. Hinson

Contains intermediate pieces by Schubert. Includes *Altzenbrugger German Dance, Galop, Eight Écossaises*. (Alfred.) Levels 8–10.

Waltzes, ed. Maier (Set 1—Eight Waltzes,
Set 2—Seven Waltzes, Set 3—Eleven Waltzes,
Set 4—Seven Waltzes, Set 5—Last Waltzes)

These volumes have long been popular teaching collections, although the scores are highly edited. In general, the waltzes provide excellent preparation for playing any Romantic music featuring a left-hand jumping bass. (Belwin.) Levels 7–9.

16 German Dances and Three Écossaises, Op. 33

Excellent edition of accessible dances of Schubert. (Henle.) Levels 7–8.

Two Minuets, D. 995

Simple, elegant pieces that show the influence of Mozart. Primarily chordal writing. (Heinrichshofen.) Level 6.

Easier Favorites

Collected with the idea of providing outstanding and characteristic works for the easy to moderate grades. The combination of works here is notable, including seven Viennese dances, two *Moments Musical,* 12 *Ländler* and two scherzos. (Heinrichshofen.) Levels 9–10.

My First Schubert, ed. Rattalino

A valuable combination of waltzes, minuets, German dances, ländler and other short pieces by Schubert presented in a scholarly edition. (Ricordi.) Level 8.

Schubert Dances for Piano, ed. Zeitlin

Thirteen dances are in chromatic succession through the 12 keys for this volume. (Presser.) Levels 6–7.

Schubert: Piano Music for Beginners, ed. Csurka

Contains many dances and also includes the Scherzo in B-flat Major and the *Moment Musical,* Op. 94, No. 3. (Editio Musica.) Levels 5–8.

33 Dances, ed. Ferguson

An excellent source of dances by Schubert for the enthusiast. (Associated Board of the Royal School of Music.) Levels 5–9.

Additional Works for Study:

D. 606 March in E Major

D. 718 Variations on a Waltz by Diabelli

D. 925 German Galop, Op. 171

D. 976 Cotillion in E-flat Major

CLARA SCHUMANN (1819–1896) Germany

Clara Wieck Schumann was an accomplished pianist and composer in her own right, despite her better-known husband. She outlived Robert by 40 years, and was the first important interpreter of his music.

Larghetto, Op. 15

A character piece in a lyric vein that features an arpeggiated bass accompaniment. It needs a flexible tempo and a singing tone. Shorter than some of the lyrical Chopin preludes or nocturnes or the Mendelssohn *Songs Without Words,* this work will be attractive to the sensitive performer. (Novello.) Level 9.

Abschied von Rom

Harmonically rich with a singing melody in the soprano voiced over a repeated chord accompaniment in a quasi-chordal texture. This work contains meter changes from 6/8 to 6/4 and complex voicing of thick textures. Level 10.

Mazurka, Op. 6, No. 3

This mazurka features an improvisatory and highly ornamented melody. Typical mazurka style with a strongly contrasting middle section. (Da Capo Press.) Level 10.

Miscellaneous Volumes

At the Piano With Robert and Clara Schumann, ed. Hinson

Especially valuable volume due partly to the inclusion of some fine works by Clara Schumann, along with some by her husband. See especially the *Romance*, Op. 16, No. 2 and the *Toccatina*, Op. 6, No. 1 of Clara Schumann. The prefatory material is especially fine. (Alfred.) Levels 7–10.

Clara Schumann: Romantische Klaviermusik, Heft 1, 2

Although some of the works are more difficult, several accessible works are included in these two excellent volumes, which feature a wide variety of literature. (Muller.) Levels 8–10.

ROBERT SCHUMANN (1810–1856) Germany

Schumann, a highly original Romantic composer, was also an influential critic. His creative and fanciful mind has produced some of the most imaginative music in the piano repertoire. His music was influenced by a strong literary background (his father was a bookseller) and Schumann himself wrote plays and poems, later founding a progressive journal that was critical of salon music and musical stagnation. His work *Musical Rules for Life and the Home* is still relevant today.

Fantasy Pieces, Op. 12 (1837)

One of Schumann's best sets of character pieces. Selections from this set can be performed separately, as opposed to the linked pieces in other Schumann sets such as *Carnaval*, Op. 9 and *Papillons* Op. 2. (Dover, Henle, Kalmus, Peters and other standard editions.)

No. 2 Soaring

A passionate work with full chords that call for resonant passage playing. Attention to clarity of voicing and refined phrasing is demanded. Many wanting to play this piece might be better served by initially studying the *Scherzino*, Op. 124, No. 3, which is quite similar in texture and character but more accessible technically. Loose rondo form with two episodes. Level 10.

No. 3 Why?

The shortest selection in this set ends in a contemplative pose. Lyrical writing. Level 9.

No. 4 Whims

Another chordal and energetic work, less difficult than *Soaring*. Needs depth of interpretation to bring off the lengthy transition section. Level 10.

Scenes from Childhood, Op. 15

Composed during Schumann's five-year period during which he concentrated on writing piano music. The metronome markings were provided by Schumann himself but are suspicious. All pieces except No. 1 were given different metronome markings by Clara in her editions. Generally her markings are slower than those of Robert. Clara's tempos are considered to be more musical, and scholars question whether Schumann checked his metronome markings when playing the music. Schumann wrote the indication *Ped.* at the beginning of each selection, but did not specifically indicate the damper pedal's release. (Many standard editions.)

No. 1 From Foreign Lands and People

Three layers of sound are present—melody, accompaniment and bass. This is a beautiful miniature calling for fine control of melodic line and bass. Level 6.

No. 2 Curious Story

The strong rhythmic framework needs attention in this brief martial work. Much repetition of material, and the pedaling can be problematic. Level 8.

No. 3 Catch Me!

Scampering sixteenths in the right hand need technical control in this *leggiero* piece. Level 8.

No. 4 Entreating Child

Three layers of sound: the melody in eighth notes presented in the soprano, a bass line in eighths and quarters, and a descending six-teenth-note passage divided between the hands in the middle. Calls for skill in voicing and refined tonal control. Level 9.

No. 5 Perfect Happiness

This selection will test the performer's skill in bringing out the top notes in the thick, moving passagework. The large left-hand leaps need refined coordination between the hands and ear for even passagework. Primarily chordal writing. Level 9.

No. 6 Important Event

This effective and popular movement needs a rich sound without excessive heaviness or a plodding feeling. The sixteenths must not be played as triplets. Level 7.

No. 7 Dreaming (Träumeri)

A popular movement, but more difficult in terms of interpretation than it initially appears. Careful attention must be paid to voicing, pedaling and continuity of the inner lines. Level 8.

No. 8 By the Fireside

This work, more difficult than it initially appears, calls for the voic-ing of melody and accompaniment in each hand. The notes in the inner voices can be redistributed between the hands for ease in play-ing accompanimental passages. Level 9.

No. 9 Knight of the Rocking Horse

The interesting syncopations accenting the third beat of the mea-sures give this piece its charm. It calls for skillful finger indepen-dence to voice and interpret the busy texture. Level 9.

No. 10 Almost Too Serious

Lyrical work that is filled with descending broken chords and a lyri-cal right-hand melody. Level 10.

No. 11 Frightening

Title of the work is depicted through strong and sudden contrasts of tempo as the different moods begin and end suddenly. Level 10.

No. 12 Child Falling Asleep

A lullaby with a dialogue between the hands interspersed in the tex-ture. Level 9.

No. 13 The Poet Speaks

This piece draws the work to a close on a spiritual and quiet ending. It is chorale-like and calls for the ability to sustain a long melodic line. More difficult musically than technically. Level 9.

Romance in F-sharp Major, Op. 28, No. 2

Popular work in a highly lyrical mode, with a beautiful duet played between both thumbs. Calls for skillful playing of legato and adept voicing. (Many standard editions.) Level 10.

Album for the Young, Op. 68

Schumann composed the *Album for the Young* in 1848 in less than a month. He later wrote, "I don't remember ever having been in such good musical form. . . . The pieces simply poured out one after another." When it was first published, it was divided into two parts that could be purchased separately. Part 1 was "for younger people" and consisted of selections Nos. 1–18 and Part 2 was "for older people." Klaus Rönnau states that, "this is one of the few works in the piano literature that successfully manages to combine pedagogic intentions with artistic demands; one might compare it with Bach's Inventions or the *Clavierbüchlein for Wilhelm Friedemann*, or in more recent times with Debussy's *Children's Corner* and Bartók's *Mikrokosmos*." (Many standard editions.)

No. 1 Melody

Simple, expressive melody over broken-chord accompaniment in eighths. Left-hand thumb must be subdued. Level 2.

No. 2 Soldier's March

The dotted eighth to sixteenth figure gives this work its charm and helps make it a favorite of elementary students. The dotted rhythm should not be played as a triplet. Level 2.

No. 3 Humming Song

Although this lyrical work is considered one of the most accessible movements in the Schumann *Album*, its hidden difficulties stem from the exchange of melody and accompaniment between the hands. The left hand or right hand usually doubles the melody at a sixth or a tenth below. Legato is necessary, but can be difficult to achieve. Similar in texture to *Little Piece*, Op. 68, No. 5, but the latter work is more accessible. Level 3.

No. 4 Chorale—Rejoice, O My Soul

In four-part chorale style, consisting primarily of half notes, this work is a study in voicing four-part chords and in syncopated pedaling. Less appealing than many other movements in this opus. Level 5.

No. 5 Little Piece (Bagatelle)

This brief, highly lyrical piece presents the melody in tenths shared between the hands. Especially suitable for developing legato phrasing for the young student. One of the most accessible movements in this collection and a deserved favorite in pedagogical circles. Level 2.

No. 7 Hunting Song

"Horn calls" and arpeggios approached from non-root positions permeate this challenging piece. The constant motion is usually parallel in both hands. Some right-hand extensions may be difficult for small hands. Especially appropriate for work on arpeggios and on developing facility. Level 5.

No. 8 The Wild Rider

A favorite with students. Needs a strong staccato and buoyant chords and rhythm. Level 2.

No. 10 The Happy Farmer (The Merry Peasant)

Jovial writing that requires careful voicing of the left-hand melody against the chordal accompaniment in the opening sections, as well as skillful voicing within each hand in the B section. Level 3.

No. 11 Sicilienne

Graceful dance with a more animated trio. Rhythmic changes from 6/8 to 2/4 back to 6/8 may need special attention. Level 4.

No. 12 Knecht Ruprecht (Knight Rupert)

Requires drama and drive, but is highly effective in performance. The simultaneous sixteenth-note passages and the rapid inner notes of measures 37–39 require attention. Knecht Ruprecht was a German legendary figure who came at Christmas to punish children for misbehaving. Some editions refer to this character as St. Nicholas, but in fact there is little similarity. Level 7.

No. 14 Little Study

This AABA, 6/8 piece with triplet eighths throughout is an appropriate selection for teaching Romantic phrasing and rubato. Broken triads alternate between the hands. This work can help a performer develop finger independence, shaping of six-note units, subtle phrasing and clean overlapping pedaling. The piece evokes the image of one whirling around. Level 4.

No. 16 First Loss

A lyrical, melancholy work with interesting motivic interplay between the hands. The double-note passages in the B section will need attention to voicing and phrasing. One of the most accessible movements in the set and one of the most popular. Level 3.

No. 18 The Reaper's Song

A notably popular and cheerful-sounding piece in C. The B section features a unison melody with unusual crossings. Level 4.

No. 19 Little Romance

Strongly contrasting B section. The A section calls for voicing of the melody in soprano and tenor over a syncopated chord accompaniment in the alto and bass. More difficult to play well than it first appears. Level 6.

No. 21 ***

Untitled work in an improvisatory style. Depicts a longing character in the singing melody over a chordal accompaniment. The right hand features a melody plus two- and three-note chords, so that careful voicing within a single hand is required. Some unusual harmonic turns require careful pacing of the phrase. Level 7.

No. 23 Horseman's Song

Strong, energetic piece with lilting sixteenth-notes, perhaps representing the galloping of a horse. One of the best in this set, and generally easier than it sounds. Level 7.

No. 25 Echoes from the Theater

Agitated work with many repeated figures that help to build the drama. Primarily chordal writing. Level 6.

No. 29 Strange Man

The appeal of this work perhaps comes from the dotted eighth-sixteenth note figure that appears in the main theme and the sound of the full chords. The B section will need careful attention to strong rhythm and to the many different note values. Level 7.

No. 31 War Song

Dynamics range from f to ff in this chordal and forceful work in which the performer needs the ability to voice well. Level 8.

No. 35 Mignon

One of the most beautiful and inspired works in the set, this piece was originally titled *Tight-Rope Dancer* in Schumann's sketchbook. It is a harmonic study, comprised of broken chords divided between the hands. A deserved favorite for the maturing performer. Level 8.

No. 37 Sailor's Song

A primarily chordal piece that requires the voicing of falling double-note passages. Level 8.

No. 38 Northern Song ("To Gade")

The last name of the Danish composer and friend of Schumann, Niels Gade is spelled in the soprano of the main theme of this short chordal work. Written in hymn-style, this work can provide preparation for reading and playing the Bach *Chorales*. Level 7.

Unpublished Pieces from Album for the Young, Op. 68, ed. Demus

Contains 17 sketches intended for inclusion in Op. 68, and other unpublished works. Many are charming and would make fine alternative Romantic literature. (Ricordi.)

No. 3 Wild Rider

Other than minor changes in the ending, this work is identical to the Op. 68, No. 8. Level 3.

No. 10 Playing Tag

An accessible work with technical requirements that are the same for both hands and the figurations often alternate between the hands. Level 4.

No. 16 Famous Melody by Beethoven

A reharmonization by Schumann of the "Ode to Joy" theme from the final movement of the Beethoven *Symphony No. 9*. This arrangement can provide students with the chance to play a familiar melody in a full, chordal sound with a harmonization that will be fresh to the ears. Consists of two- and three-note chords in each hand and requires syncopated pedaling. Level 5.

Forest Scenes, Op. 82

The nine pieces in this set are thought to be based on the literary work by Heinrich Laube, *Jagdbrevier*, written in celebration of secret hunting expeditions in Prussia. Generally this collection does not represent Schumann's most inspired writing, but even so, many are attractive and useful. (Many standard editions.)

No. 1 Entrance

Pleasant work in a moderate tempo calling for skillful voicing of the chordal textures. Slightly easier and shorter than the Chopin nocturnes. Level 9.

No. 2 Hunter in Ambush

A dramatic work for a performer with a strong temperament and good fingers. Level 10.

No. 3 Lonely Flowers

A simple piece featuring some double-note passages in the right hand and a left-hand jumping accompaniment. Level 9.

No. 6 The Wayside Inn

Enchanting melody in this pastoral work. Several simultaneously moving voices. Level 10.

No. 7 Prophet Bird

Harmonically sophisticated, and almost elusive writing. A *leggiero* work calling for real finesse in phrasing and timing. Central chordal section. Level 9.

Colored Leaves, Op. 99

Consists of a collection of 14 pieces, previously composed, that Schumann had not included in his other sets. Each work originally was to be issued with a colored cover indicating its mood. No metronome markings were present in the original edition of this work. (Many standard editions.)

No. 4 Album Leaf I in F-sharp Minor

A simple four-part work that became the subject of variation sets by Brahms and Clara Schumann. Elegant and inspired writing. Level 7.

No. 9 Novelette

Strong and energetic work, effective in performance. The triplet figures in the right hand call for skillful voicing of the melody above the double notes. Passionate B section with an effective left-hand chromatic pattern that contributes to the restless feeling. Level 9.

Three Sonatas for the Young, Op. 118

These works were composed for Schumann's daughters. Op. 118a was composed for Julie who was eight, Op. 118b was composed for Elise who was 10 and Op. 118c was composed for Marie who was 12. The difficulty level corresponds to the differences in ages. (Many standard collections.) Levels 8–9.

Sonata No. 1 ("To Julie"), Op. 118a

The first movement is perhaps the strongest, featuring primarily chordal writing and a tuneful melody. Has a spirit of naiveté. The second movement is a theme with variations. The third movement is titled *Doll's Cradle Song* and the fourth is *Rondoletto*. This final movement is spirited and sprightly, but calls for attention to fine detail in executing the many different articulations. Level 8.

Sonata No. 2 ("To Elise"), Op. 118b

The most engaging movement is the second, titled *Evening Song*, with the flowing melody placed against a triplet accompaniment in broken chords and distributed between the hands. Levels 8–9.

Sonata No. 3 ("To Marie"), Op. 118c

The third movement, *Gypsy Dance*, will catch the attention of the performer who enjoys loud, spirited works. Levels 8–9.

Album Leaves, Op. 124

Collection of 20 pieces from various periods of Schumann's life. Some may have been pieces that were rejected from *Papillons*. Interesting literature of high quality can be found among this collection. No metronome indications were present in the original edition. (Dover, Henle, Kalmus, Peters and G. Schirmer.)

No. 1 Impromptu

Continuous figurations and sixteenths throughout. It could provide a fine substitution for the longer Schumann pieces. Level 9.

No. 3 Scherzino

ABA work that can provide an excellent, similar repertoire substitution for the Schumann *Soaring*, Op. 12, No. 2. Economy of material in a work that is highly characteristic of Schumann's writing. Level 8.

No. 4 Waltz

One-page work calling for the playing of a rapid jumping bass in the left hand beneath a single-note melody. Not particularly inspired. Level 7.

No. 5 Fantasy Dance

Originally planned as part of *Carnaval*, Op. 9 but later rejected by Schumann. Perpetual-motion sixteenth figures are divided between the hands. This driving and energetic work requires facile fingers, though it is easier than it sounds. Level 6.

No. 6 Cradle Song

This selection contains melody and continuous triplets in the right hand, while the left hand imitates the melody at the interval of a tenth. More accessible than the Burgmüller *Harmony of the Angels*, Op. 100, No. 21, but this piece represents the same kind of broken-chord writing as does the Burgmüller. Level 6.

No. 8 Unending Sorrow

A performer who is innately musical would be drawn to this work that needs subtle rubato and singing grace notes. This piece will require careful voicing of the mournful melody. Level 8.

No. 12 Burla

A presto work built on an eighth- and sixteenth-note figure and modulating through several key centers. Energetic and intriguing. Level 10.

No. 16 Lullaby

Especially beautiful writing. This work features a left-hand arpeggiated accompaniment and a melody that must sing out. Central section requires adept voicing of the fifth-finger melody. Level 8.

No. 17 The Elf

Much easier than it sounds and comprised entirely of broken chords. This piece requires a leggiero touch. Level 8.

Miscellaneous Volumes

Schumann: An Introduction to His Piano Works, ed. Palmer

Contains an excellent preface with information about metronome markings, pedaling and ornamentation. Selections from Op. 15, 68, 82, 99, 118a and 124 are included here. (Alfred.) Levels 2–9.

Schumann: A First Book for Pianists, ed. Palmer

Presents the easiest pieces from *Schumann: An Introduction to His Piano Works*, ed. Palmer. (Alfred.) Levels 2–4.

Three Very Easy Pieces from the Album for the Young, Op. 68, No. 1, 8, 10

Includes facsimile editions of the pieces that are included in this volume. Scholarly edition for teaching purposes. Selections provided are *Melody, The Wild Horseman* and *The Merry Peasant*. (Schott.) Levels 2–3.

Schumann For Younger People, Part I of Album for the Young, Op. 68, ed. Ferguson

This valuable collection presents the most familiar and easiest selections from the *Album for the Young* of Schumann. It is a practical collection for teaching with excellent editing and clean text. (Associated Board of the Royal Schools of Music.) Levels 4–5.

Schumann: 16 Album Leaves, from Op. 99 and 124, ed. Ferguson

Excellent resource for Schumann's upper-intermediate to early-advanced works. This volume includes five Album Leaves from *Bunte Blätter*, Op. 99 and 11 pieces from *Album Leaves*, Op. 124. Fine selections, many comparatively unknown. (Associated Board of the Royal Schools of Music.) Levels 7–9.

At the Piano with Robert and Clara Schumann, ed. Hinson

Extensive and valuable preface. Includes such topics as Robert and Clara, Clara as Pianist, Clara and the Music of Robert, Robert's Piano Music, Interpreting Robert's Piano Music, and Robert and the Metronome. An interesting combination of literature is found here that includes works from *Album Leaves*, the *Arabeske* and selections of Clara. (Alfred.) Levels 7–10.

Robert Schumann: An Introduction to the Composer and His Music, ed. Banowetz

Contains extensive introductory material as well as selections from *Album for the Young* and *Scenes from Childhood*. (General Words and Music.) Levels 2–9.

Additional Works for Study:
Op. 21, No. 4 Fughette
Op. 32, No. 2 Gigue

Theme [and Variations] in E-flat Major (No opus number, pub. 1939)

EDUARD SCHÜTT (1856–1933) Russia

19 Romantic Pieces, ed. Johnson

These pieces are certainly worth investigating as repertoire for either study or for sight-reading. The selections contain titles such as *Confession, Village Merriment* or *Dance Tune*. (Associated Board of the Royal Schools of Music.) Levels 7–8.

LUDVIG SCHYTTE (1848–1909) Denmark

Schytte composed numerous teaching pieces, many of which sound dated but were quite popular in his day.

25 Modern Études for the Pianoforte, Op. 68

Generally ordinary pieces, although several of high quality are here, including Nos. 2 and 9. (Boston.) Level 8.

Special Melodic Studies

Series of 10 volumes, each consisting of études. Topics for the various volumes are: *Broken Chords, Shake and Tremolo, Octaves, Alternation of the Hands, Rhythmic and Polyrhythmic Studies, Legato and Staccato, Studies for the Left Hand, Thirds and Sixths, Chord-Grasps* and *Pedal Studies*. (Boston.) Levels 9–10.

25 Melodious Studies, Op. 108

The composer's most important teaching work and his most musically substantive writing. Many pieces repeat ideas often. The figurations fit the hand well. See especially Nos. 1, 3, 7, 8, 11, 12, 13, 22, 23 and 25. (G. Schirmer.) Levels 3–4.

Additional Works for Study:
Op. 69 Happy Childhood Days
Op. 76 Six Sonatinas
Op. 95 Easy Characteristic Studies
Op. 160 25 Easy Studies
Op. 174 School of Modern Pianoforte Playing

JEAN SIBELIUS (1865–1957) Finland

Romantic composer with a strong Finnish nationalist current. His work is highly lyrical.

The Solitary Fir Tree, Op. 75, No. 2

This two-page solo would especially be suitable for the mature musician. Several flourishes near the end are enticing. This piece features rich harmonies. (Chester, Hansen.) Level 8.

The Birch Tree, Op. 75, No. 4

A single-note lyrical melody makes this work not difficult to shape. Idiomatic figurations and *leggiero* passagework in the *mysterioso* section. A pleasant, energetic selection for the student not yet ready to play Chopin nocturnes. (Chester, Hansen.) Level 8.

The Aspen, Op. 75, No. 3

Highly Romantic and sentimental writing. A few technical difficulties. Easier than the Chopin waltzes. Three printed pages, with some rhythmic intricacies. (Chester, Hansen.) Level 7.

Novelette, Op. 94, No. 2

Energetic and fervent, yet the technical difficulties are few. Can be mastered quickly. (Chester, Hansen.) Level 8.

The Spruce, Op. 75, No. 5

Highly lyrical melody accompanied by oom-pah chords or broken figuration, and large arpeggiations within a single hand similar to some passages in Sinding's *Rustles of Spring*. Easier and shorter than the least difficult Chopin nocturne. (Hansen.) Level 8.

Rondino, Op. 68, No. 1

Romantic sentimentality pervades this short, nocturne-like work. The main theme resembles that of the Brahms *Intermezzo in E-flat Minor*, Op. 118, No. 6 in its intervallic structure as well as in the dreamy character. Many accidentals. (Masters Music.) Level 8.

Valse Triste

This selection is based on the incidental music, *Kuolema*, Op. 44, composed in 1903. This movement became so popular that Sibelius arranged it for piano solo. A programmatic work addressing the sickness and death of a young boy's mother. (Alfred.) Level 10.

Romance, Op. 24, No. 9

A *Song Without Words*. Primarily chordal with an effective climactic cadenza. Popular. (Alfred.) Levels 9–10.

Miscellaneous Volumes

Jean Sibelius Piano Album

Presents an excellent selection of some of Sibelius' best writing for upper-intermediate and early-advanced students. Twelve selections are found here including *The Solitary Fir Tree, The Birch Tree* and *The Aspen* from Op. 75 as well as an appealing *Dance*, Op. 94, No. 1 and *Novelette*, Op. 94, No. 2. (Chester.) Levels 8–9.

CHRISTIAN SINDING (1856–1941) Norway

Rustles of Spring, Op. 32, No. 3

An extremely popular salon piece in ternary form with numerous arpeggiated chords in both the right and left hands. Effective in performance. (Many standard editions.) Level 9.

BEDŘICH SMETANA (1824–1884) Bohemia

Smetana was plagued by ill health and financial troubles. At the height of his career a high whistling sound developed in his ears that later left him deaf. Along with Dvořák, he was a pioneer in the Czech nationalistic musical scene.

Easier Pieces

Practical collection to use as an introduction to Smetana's music. Much variety in literature is found here, including selections from his Opp. 2, 4, 5, 7, 8 and 13. (Masters Music.) Level 10.

Chanson, Op. 2, No. 2

Sentimental and sad work. Triplet accompaniment divided between both hands with the melody played by the outer fingers of the right hand. Some finger substitution is necessary for a true legato. Especially good for the performer who enjoys lyrical pieces. Level 8.

Miscellaneous Volumes

Smetana, ed. Schwerdtner

Brings together some of Smetana's best works for the early-advanced pianist. Found in this volume are four pieces from *Bagatelles* and *Impromptus*, six *Albumblätter*, and five *Bohemian Dances*. Several deserve acclaim, including the *Chanson*, Op. 2, No. 2 and the *Andante in E-flat Major*. Several might provide unusual Romantic literature for a performer not yet ready to handle the subtleties of Brahms or Chopin. (Schott.) Levels 8–9.

Additional Works for Study:
Op. 2 Albumblätter, see No. 4 Album Leaf
Op. 4 Three Pieces, see No. 2 Idyl
Op. 8 Three Poetical Polkas, see No. 2 Polka Poetique

FRITZ SPINDLER (1817–1905) Germany

Spindler is known best for his salon and character pieces in a style that is a mix of Classicism and Romanticism.

Sonatinas, Op. 157

See especially *No. 2 in A Minor, No. 4 in C Major* and *No. 8 in E Minor*. The fourth sonatina has gained popularity due to its accessible two-movement format and the thin textures. A real student favorite. Level 4.

Additional Work for Study:
Op. 281 Sonatinas

CAMILLE STAMATY (n.d.) France

Became well known as a champion of the music of Bach, Mozart and Beethoven. Stamaty composed a number of didactic works.

Singing Touch and Technique, Op. 37

Subtitled "25 easy piano studies for small hands," this collection contains little known and surprisingly fine études. See especially *Fanfare, The Ghost, The Jumping-Jack* and *The Five Notes*. (Schirmer.) Levels 4–6.

JEAN LOUIS STREABBOG (1835–1886) Belgium

Streabbog was a pianist and composer who wrote more than 1,000 light piano pieces using the pseudonym Streabbog (Gobbaerts reversed). His compositions were exceedingly popular in his day, but he is hardly known now.

12 Melodious Pieces, Book 1, Op. 63

In both this opus and in Op. 64 are found some of the easiest Romantic literature for pedagogical purposes. Each piece deals with a particular aspect of piano technique. Unfortunately, much of it is trite and set within a limited harmonic framework. The best are Nos. 1, 2, 3 and 6. (Many standard editions.)

No. 1 A Pleasant Morning

A basic study in scale and chord playing and in balance between hands. Level 3.

No. 2 Soldier's March

Stoic march-like writing with some C and G Major five-finger patterns in the left hand. Requires quick changes of inversions. Level 3.

No. 3 On the Green

An appealing, effervescent work featuring a waltz bass in the left hand and staccato repeated chords in the right hand. Primarily contains four-measure phrases based on V–I chords. Level 3.

No. 6 Distant Bells

The hand crossings to play the "bells" provide interest for the elementary performer. The broken chord accompaniment needs to be voiced beneath the melody. Level 3.

No. 7 By the Seaside

Flowing broken-chord study, with chords divided between the hands. The more tempestuous B section features more rapid harmonic changes, perhaps simulating a storm. Level 4.

No. 8 Hop-Scotch Polka

Right-hand broken octave study with a left-hand jump-bass accompaniment. Needs a light touch to prevent a ponderous sound. Level 3.

No. 9 Stubborn Rocking Horse

Left-hand rocking figure (a triplet mordant with an octave skip) needs lightness. The right hand must voice to the tops of the chords. Level 3.

No. 10 A Sad Story

Students who enjoy expressive writing will be drawn to this nocturne-like minor key piece in ABA' form. Three distinctive textures: melody in the upper part of the right hand; accompanimental chords, also in the right hand; and single-note left-hand accompaniment. Level 4.

No. 11 Chasing Butterflies

Animated writing due primarily to the lilting rhythm. Trite. Level 4.

12 Melodious Pieces, Book 2, Op. 64

Continues the presentation of practical teaching material at a slightly more advanced level than Op. 63. (Alfred, G. Schirmer.)

No. 1 Leap-Frog

Oom-pah accompaniment to a simple melody of triplet arpeggios in root position and first inversion. Level 3.

No. 2 Bees in the Clover

Legato thirds in both hands within a five-finger position. Most useful as an étude. Level 5.

No. 4 The Orphan

Sustained and lyrical melody over a broken chord, rolling accompaniment. Attention should be paid to balance between the hands. One of the best in both volumes. Level 4.

No. 6 Swaying Boughs

Sounds more difficult than it is due to the continuous triads. Right-hand staccato single-note melody. Level 4.

No. 11 The Cadets

A motivational and pedagogically fine study in scale playing. Requires strong dynamic contrast and crisp staccato chords. Level 5.

No. 12 Up and Down

This work provides good preparation for arpeggio playing in the right hand. Supple thumb crossings and flexible wrists are a necessity. Level 4.

Streabbog Album

An extensive collection of dances and short pieces for young people. (Schott.) Levels 5–6.

ARTHUR S. SULLIVAN (1842–1900) England

Piano Music

Although he is known primarily as a composer of operettas with W. S. Gilbert, Sullivan's piano music is charming. This volume contains several works that are accessible to the early-advanced pianist, including *Thoughts No. 1* and *Day Dreams* Nos. 1–6. These pieces show the influence of Schumann. (Chappel.) Levels 9–10.

MARIA SZYMANOWSKA (1789–1831) Poland

Cinq danses pour piano

Short homophonic movements in a conservative, light-hearted vein. Titles found here are *Contredanse, Anglaise* Nos. 1, 2 and 3 and *Quadrille*. (PWM.) Level 8.

T

PETER ILYICH TCHAIKOVSKY (1840–1893) Russia

While Tchaikovsky was no piano virtuoso, his fondness for the instrument is demonstrated by some 100 compositions spanning his life.

The Seasons, Op. 37b

Set of 12 pieces, one written for each of the 12 months of the year. Effective as alternative repertoire for the advancing performer. See especially *No. 4, April—Snowdrop; No. 6, June—Barcarolle*, and *No. 11, November—In the Troika*. (Editio Musica and others.) Level 10.

Album for the Young, Op. 39

Tchaikovsky probably took Schumann's *Album for the Young*, Op. 68 as a model, since both sets share the same title and consist of a succession of delightful miniatures. It took Tchaikovsky two months to write this work, drafted as three short cycles of pieces, including children's games and dances, travels throughout Russia and travels abroad. These works have a wide emotional range. The composer's original ordering is used here, followed in parentheses by the publisher's altered ordering. (Many standard editions.)

No. 1 (1) Morning Prayer

Four-part hymn style. Requires sensitivity in phrasing and in pedaling. Level 4.

No. 3 (4) Mama

The right hand and left hand play a duet. Fairly stable hand positions prevail with some double notes appearing in the right hand. Level 6.

No. 4 (3) Hobby Horse

A Mendelssohn-like perpetual motion featuring two-note chords (generally thirds, fourths and fifths) in both hands. A flexible wrist is needed in this study in rapid repeated chords. More difficult to play than it sounds. A steady eighth-note pulse should be maintained throughout. Level 8.

No. 5 (5) March of the Tin Soldiers

A somewhat delicate march in ABA form that features a single-note melody with various tricky textures in the accompaniment. Level 6.

No. 7 (6) The Sick Doll

One of the easiest pieces, composed of a texture of three clear layers. The melody notes sound on the second beat of the measure. Requires a singing tone and expressive playing. Level 3.

No. 8 (7) The Doll's Burial

Chordal work marked *grave*. One of the more popular selections from this collection. Level 4.

No. 11 (10) Mazurka

Varying rhythmic values surface as the pulse changes from duple to triple. This piece lies well under the hand with few left-hand leaps. Level 5.

No. 15 (15) Italian Song

A dance-like work with short motivic phrases. The presence of the waltz bass with relatively few leaps makes this a good precursor to the Schubert Waltzes. Level 5.

No. 17 (17) German Song

Writing reminiscent of a music box. In ABA form with a right-hand melody (single notes or in thirds) against left-hand oom-pah-pah accompaniment. Level 6.

No. 18 (18) Neapolitan Dance Song

The simple staccato polonaise rhythm in the left hand needs a light touch and an appropriate balance with the melody of the right hand. This piece portrays the mood of a rustic dance with a predominantly masculine sound. Needs technical facility in the quick left-hand leaps. Level 6.

No. 21 (21) Sweet Dreams (Daydream)

The title of the work is reflected by the mood of this gentle work. The accompaniment is comprised of off-beat chords. Pedaling could be tricky. Level 6.

No. 22 (22) Song of the Lark

Bird calls are featured high in the treble. Some right-hand rapid, delicate figures need to be balanced over the thick left hand. The reading of treble ledger lines is required. Level 6.

No. 24 (23) The Hand-Organ Man (The Barrel-Organ)

Simple waltz in the A section while the B section features an off-beat pattern in the right hand. Level 5.

No. 24 In Church

Expressive chordal selection in the form of a four- to five-part chorale with a bass pedal point in the last 20 measures, resembling a pipe organ sound. The many repeated chords make this easier to play than a traditional hymn, appropriate for work on voicing and syncopated pedaling. The phrasing is not always symmetrical. Level 4.

Chanson Triste, Op. 40, No. 2

One of the composer's most popular works, with a main theme that is haunting and plaintive. This beautiful work could be played by a performer ready to play Chopin's easiest waltzes. Level 8.

Song Without Words, Op. 2, No. 3

Originally composed for piano, but frequently heard in orchestral arrangements. Another lyrical and popular work with off-beat chordal accompaniment punctuating the texture. Somewhat reminiscent of some of Mendelssohn's *Songs Without Words*. Level 9.

Miscellaneous Volumes
At the Piano with Tchaikovsky, ed. Hinson

Valuable prefatory material precedes the selections in this collection. Many but not all are from the *Album for the Young*, Op. 39. (Alfred.) Levels 4–9.

W
RICHARD WAGNER (1813–1883) Germany
Wagner: Piano Music Inspired by Women in His Life, ed. Hinson

Extensive prefatory material on the historical background of the women can be found here. Included are *Polka, A Sonata for the Album of Mrs. M. W., Züricher Vielliebchen-Walzer, Feuille d'Album, Arrival of the Black Swans* and *Album Leaf for Mrs. Betty Schott*. Valuable for anyone investigating Wagner's piano music. (Alfred.) Levels 9–10.

CARL MARIA von WEBER (1786–1826) Germany

Weber composed a large number of dances and character pieces. His piano music has elegance and grandeur mixed with many bravura technical effects. Many of his works are quite difficult.

20 Easy Dances

Contains six German dances, six waltzes, six écossaises and two four-hand German dances. The writing is rhythmic and lively. These would provide excellent sight-reading material. (Kalmus.) Levels 6–8.

Additional Works for Study:

Op. 14 12 Allemandes (1801)

Six Écossaises

AUGUSTE (BERNARD) WOLFF (1821–1887) France

Works for Study:

Op. 195 Sonatinas

Op. 198 Sonatinas

20TH-CENTURY LITERATURE

A

KOMEI ABE (b. 1911) Japan
Sonatina No. 1 in F Major

Of the three movements, the second movement, an enchanting and imaginative theme and variations, is the best. (Zen-On.) Level 5.

Sonatina No. 2 in G Major

A work in Classical style with texture and figurations similar to those in the Clementi sonatinas. Three inviting movements. (Zen-On.) Level 5.

Sonatina No. 3 in C Minor

Slightly more difficult than the preceding two sonatinas. Interesting writing using traditional figurations. (Zen-On.) Level 6.

JEAN ABSIL (1893–1974) Belgium
Bagatelles, Op. 61

Five works, all two pages long, titled *Pastourelle, Musette, Berceuse, Gavotte,* and *Toccata.* Sophisticated pieces with unconventional harmonic writing. See especially the *Berceuse* and *Toccata.* (Schott.) Level 8.

Bulgarian Dances, Op. 102

Six strongly rhythmic dances, similar in sound but easier than those of Bartók. Driving rhythms, spirited, energetic. Effective writing. (Lemoine.) Level 8.

Sonatine, Op. 125

Interesting writing, clever harmonies and mildly contemporary sounds for the pianist wanting a piece without wide stretches. (Metropolis.) Level 9.

Humoresques, Op. 126

Rhythmic writing and thin textures in three movements, fast-slow-fast. Contemporary sounds. Appropriate for a pianist with small hands. (Lemoine.) Level 9.

SAMUEL ADLER (b. 1928) Germany

Adler immigrated to America where for many years he served as chair of the composition department at Eastman School of Music. He has composed over 200 works.

Gradus, Book I (20 Studies) (1971)

Composed with the intent, according to Adler, of "exposing the ear as well as the fingers . . . to the demands of the present and the immediate past. Each short exercise utilizes a technique of composition which has become common practice in the last half-century." Annotations are provided for each piece. This excellent compendium of contemporary devices might be studied by aspiring composers as part of their piano training. It may also be analyzed and performed by pre-college students. Compositional devices include use of the Locrian mode, irregular accents, bitonality, etc. (Oxford.) Levels 3–4.

Gradus, Book II (20 Studies) (1971)

Similar in intent but more complex than Book I. *Nos. 14* and *15* feature harmonizations of *Yankee Doodle* and *Three Blind Mice. No. 16* is aleatoric. (Oxford.) Levels 4–7.

No. 13

The temporal aspect is established by equating one unit to one second and by measuring off units on the score. Pitches are notated in relation to where the attack should come within each unit. More difficult than many other works in *Gradus Book II.* Level 7.

No. 19

The score consists of a series of continuous horizontal lines with the proportional location of the note on the keyboard judged by the performer. May also be performed with the page upside down. Level 7.

Gradus, Book III (20 Further Studies in Contemporary Techniques for Piano) (1981)

Short pieces, usually one page long, that fall between Book I and Book II in level of difficulty. Titles describe devices used in pieces such as *Two or More Simultaneous Tonalities, Strange But Fascinating Harmony* and *Hand Over Hand.* (Oxford.) Levels 6–8.

No. 18 Bells and Harps

In this 22-measure piece the left hand manipulates the inside of the piano while the right hand plays on the keys until the final measures. Also employs harmonics. An effective work. Level 6.

The Sense of Touch

Following the philosophy behind the *Gradus* volumes, this work consists of eight short pieces introducing the pianist to techniques used in 20th-century music. Compositional devices are described at the beginnings of these pieces. Similar to *Gradus, Book II* in difficulty and musical sophistication. (Theodore Presser.) Level 4.

The Road to Terpsichore

This suite of five dances provides an effective major work for aspiring pianists in a true contemporary idiom but with technical demands that talented high school students or early-level college students should be able to meet. The dissonance is sometimes biting and the writing always pianistic. This holds the possibility of becoming a major contemporary work in the standard repertory. (G. Schirmer.)

No. 1

Marked "fast and loud," this short piece features major and minor triads used in a non-diatonic fashion, with patterns often alternating rapidly between the hands in toccata-like fashion. The stretches are not wide. Level 10.

No. 2

This movement begins and ends with a quasi-*parlando* section, expressive and not interpretatively difficult. The middle section, "suddenly fast," features propulsive sixteenths in patterns, often alternating between the hands. Level 10.

No. 3

A contemporary waltz with lyrical melody and oom-pah accompaniment. Level 10.

No. 4

Marked "like a tango, with verve, and very rhythmic." Notated on three to four staves, this effective movement is easier to read than it appears. Imaginative writing. Level 10.

No. 5

A rousing tarantella finale to the suite. Figures alternate between the hands in rapid succession. Again, climactic sounds are achieved without the use of large chords. Effective writing. Level 10.

DÉNES AGAY (b. 1911) Hungary

A prolific composer for piano, Agay moved to the USA where he has held editing positions with several New York music publishing firms.

Petit Trianon Suite. 10 Easy Pieces on 18th-Century Style Dance Melodies

Charming collection of dance-like pieces for the elementary student. The works are filled with character and are highly recommended. (G. Schirmer.) Level 2.

Four Popular Diversions

Four two- to three-page character pieces, each with strong teaching appeal. Movements are titled *Little Prelude in Waltz Time, Baroque Bounce, Echoes of the Blues* and *Ragtime Doll*. They all deserve recognition. (Theodore Presser.) Level 3.

15 Little Pieces on Five-Note Patterns

These short pieces feature modal or artificial five-note patterns. Appropriate for students who need to work on reading skills as well as for development of an ear for contemporary sounds. Hand positions remain stationary. (Theodore Presser.) Level 4.

Three Recital Dances

Some "wrong-note" writing gives life to these fine movements. See especially *Mardi Gras Bolero* for a lively and effective solo. Requires flair. Level 4.

Soldiers' Hoe-Down

Off-beat rhythms. Not as significant as other music by Agay. (Boosey.) Level 4.

Serenata Burlesca

Marked *allegro scherzando*, this two-and-a-half minute piece derives its appeal through rhythmic vitality and biting sonorities. Brilliant ending. (Boosey.) Level 5.

Two Improvisations on Hungarian Folk Songs

Gypsy Tune, the second of the improvisations, is rhythmic, inviting and spirited. Motivating writing with a rousing finish. (Theodore Presser.) Level 6.

Sonatina No. 3

Spunky first movement is a favorite. Many scales and repeated chord figures. Impressionistic second movement and driving finale. Excellent. (Sam Fox Publishing.) Level 7.

Seven Piano Pieces

See especially the final piece, *Dance Scherzo*. (G. Schirmer.) Level 7.

Four Dance Impressions for Piano

Semi-popular flavor. This work is suitable for high school students with adequate fluency. (Theodore Presser.) Level 8.

Mosaics. Six Piano Pieces on Hebrew Folk Themes

For the above-average student pianist. *Number 6,* a theme and variations, is the most extended. (MCA.) Level 9.

HUGH AITKEN (b. 1924) USA

Three Connected Pieces: Thirds, Melody and Fifths

Highly contemporary writing, though reading the score is not difficult. Octave displacement and changing meters. Only four pages total. (Oxford.) Level 8.

DANTE ALDERIGHI (1898–1968) Italy

Signi Lieti

Ten short pieces for piano. Traditional harmonies, pianistic, sparkling and pedagogically sound. High quality. See especially Nos. 1, 2, 3, 6 and 10. (Curci.) Level 2.

L'Album delle Maschere

Eight short pieces, slightly more difficult than those listed above, all filled with character. (Curci.) Level 4.

HAIM ALEXANDER (b. 1915) Germany

Alexander immigrated to Israel in 1936, where he received his musical training.

Six Israeli Dances

"Written in the spirit of various folk dances but not based on any folk-material," according to the composer. Short and attractive pieces. (Israeli Music Publications Ltd.) Level 9.

JOSEF ALEXANDER (b. 1910) USA

12 Bagatelles for Piano

Occasional biting dissonance and thin textures. May be played by the pianist with small hands. (General Music.) Level 10.

Of Chinese New Year's

Dissonant writing, filled with many shifting meters. Composed for piano solo, or piano and Chinese toy cymbals or wood block. (General Music.) Level 8.

Games Children Play

Highly contemporary and sophisticated writing. Ten pieces with titles of children's games such as *Follow the Leader, See Saw, Checkers* and *Skip Rope*. (General Music.) Level 6.

Playthings for Piano

Set of 12 dissonant character pieces with titles like *Hobgoblin, Merry Go Round* and *Ballet Dancer*. Most are two pages long. (General Music.) Level 5.

ANATOLI ALEXANDROW (1888–1982) Russia

Pianist and composer who wrote many pieces suitable for teaching along the lines of Scriabin and Rachmaninoff. Much of his music is unavailable in the West.

Pieces for Children

Solid writing for early-level piano students. Eight sets of short, interesting pieces are provided under one cover. See especially the set of *Six Easy Pieces*, which is also available separately. Similar in scope to the Kabalevsky *Music for Children*, Op. 39. Levels 2–3.

Baskir Melodies, Op. 73

Set of 12 conservative yet interesting selections with nationalistic flavors. Level 8.

Petite Suite, Op. 78

Set of three pieces in a more contemporary idiom than his set of *Pieces for Children*. Pianistic. Voicing of inner melodies required. Level 8.

(PEDRO) HUMBERTO ALLENDE-SARON (1885–1959) Chile

Miniatures Grecques

Dissonant and sophisticated writing. No. 1 is played on black keys only and Nos. 2–5 on white keys only. (Salabert.) Level 7.

Deux Préludes

Sophisticated, dissonant. Marked *moderato* and *lentement.* (Salabert.) Level 8.

Tempo di Minuetto

Two pages of highly chromatic writing. (Salabert.) Level 8.

12 Tonadas de Caracter Popular Chileno

Chilean folk flavor within a highly dissonant idiom. (Salabert.) Levels 9–10.

HANS-GÜNTHER ALLERS (b. 1935) Germany

11 Bagatelles

Conceived as a cycle, though they may be performed separately, says the composer. Spirited works, contemporary in sound, and arranged in progressive order. (Breitkopf.) Levels 5–7.

HANSI ALT (b. 1911) USA

Hansi Alt was born and trained in Vienna. She now lives and works in Washington, D.C.

The Ocean

Subtitled *Deep sea explorations on the piano,* the 10 titled pieces provide high-quality supplementary literature for the pianist at the elementary level. These pieces move about the keyboard, use patterns that reappear in more advanced literature, and are musically sound. (Oxford.) Level 1.

Hot Noon on the Meadow

This work uses many contemporary harmonies in order to tell engaging stories. See especially *The Spider,* which uses the tritone to build suspense and *The Bees and Flies,* which uses constant half-steps to portray the humming. (Oxford.) Level 1.

Where the Palm Trees Grow

Six one- or two-page character pieces with titles like *Where the Palm Trees Grow, Flamingos* and *What a Strange Bird.* An appropriate and palatable introduction to contemporary idioms for the young student. Phrase lengths are predictable and patterns abound in a work that is full of charm and character. (Oxford.) Level 2.

LAURENCE ALTMAN (b. 1944) USA

Piano Pieces. 15 Studies on Different Scales

Written to familiarize students with the language of contemporary music, these pieces use such scales as a Korean scale, an Indian raga scale, and the Hungarian major scale in the writing. Well suited to analysis. (Presser.) Level 6.

WILLIAM ALWYN (1905–1985) England

Odd Moments, April Morn and Hunter's Moon

Three sets of pieces in a mildly contemporary idiom. Some interesting meters, phrasings and rhythmic patterns. (Associated Board of the Royal Schools of Music.) Level 3.

ANDRÉ AMELLER (b. 1912) France

Montréal

Slow, three-page impressionistic prelude. Only slightly more difficult than the Debussy *The Girl With the Flaxen Hair.* (Leduc.) Level 8.

FIKRET AMIROV (1922–1984) Russia

Children's Pictures

Short character studies for the early intermediate student. At this printing they were not readily available in the United States. Level 3.

Preludes

Two selections, *andante sostenuto* and *tempo di valse.* Mildly contemporary, but not especially interesting. Level 6.

12 Miniatures

More pedagogical literature at the intermediate level, again not particularly inspired. Level 7.

GARLAND LEE ANDERSON (b. 1933) USA

Three Preludes

See especially the second prelude, which is a pulsating and highly rhythmical two-page piece. Toccata-like with asymmetrical rhythms, these preludes are not terribly difficult. (American Music Edition.) Level 9.

GEORGE ANTHEIL (1900–1959) USA

Contemporary American composer who studied with Bloch. Although he was, in his earlier years, an avowed iconoclast, later his style grew more conservative and lyrical, featuring learned counterpoint. From Stravinsky, he developed an interest in using ostinati, displaced accents and consonant chords with added dissonance.

Piano Pastels

Set of 15 one- and two-page character pieces. Attractive, witty writing within a tonal framework. Mild dissonance. Not well known. Suitable for children and adults alike. See especially the *Dog-Cat Polka* and *Winter Lullaby*. (Weintraub.) Level 5.

Toccata No. 2

Chordal piece with passagework built on triads and inversions alternating between the hands. Large dynamic contrasts and big skips on the keyboard. Needs strength and brilliance. Level 10.

RAFAEL APONTE-LEDÉE (b. 1938) Puerto Rico

Tema y Seis Differencías

Short avant-garde variations. Four pages with many interval skips. (Peer International.) Level 7.

STANLEY APPLEBAUM (b. 1922) USA

American composer whose work has been widely heard.

Folk Music, Bach-Style

Twenty-one short inventions based on folk melodies of many countries. According to the composer, this collection "has been written to provide an easy, attractive and stimulating transition from the small recital pieces for the early grades to the simplest of the Bach inventions and other works of similar contrapuntal character." These pieces fill an important gap in many contemporary teaching methods by providing contrapuntal pieces at the elementary level. Some are only eight measures. Mild contemporary sounds. (Schroeder and Gunther.) Levels 2–3.

Frenzy—Toccata for Piano

Primarily consists of alternation of notes between the hands and of scale passages in the right hand. Fits well under the hand. Students with small hands could play this work. (Broude.) Level 8.

Sound World

Subtitled "a collection of new keyboard experiences for the intermediate pianist and the advanced beginner," this volume of 31 short pieces was written to "stretch the ear," as it were, of the young player. A brief description of the compositional devices used is given for each piece. Appropriate for group/individual study of contemporary compositional devices. (Schroeder and Gunther.) Level 4.

Summercloud

Lyrical, mildly dissonant and impressionistic two-page solo with an ostinato-like accompaniment. (Broude.) Level 7.

MARY JEANNE VAN APPLEDORN (b. 1927) USA

Set of Five

Strong contrast among the movements. High-school students may be drawn to the rhythmic and attractive contemporary writing in the *Ostinato* (No. 1) and the *Toccata* (No. 5). Other movements are *Blues* (No. 2), *Improvisation* (No. 3) and *Elegy* (No. 4). Deserves to be better known. (Oxford.) Level 9.

Scenes from Pecos Country

Three pieces, each one page, depicting Native American territory. Contemporary sounds are found here for the young student interested in imagining events of the early Indians. Titles are *Apache Echoes, Night on Balmorhea* and *Daybreak*. (Carl Fischer.) Level 3.

TITO APREA (b. 1904) Italy

28 Brani

Twenty-eight studies based on various structural features such as "the interval of a seventh" or "the chromatic scale." Most pieces take a contemporary pattern or figure and repeat it on various degrees of the scale, ascending, descending or both. Pianistic contemporary writing. (Curci.) Level 9.

15 Dances

Mildly contemporary, pianistic and playable by young students. The writing in general is dissonant but palatable. See especially *Columbine's Dance, Dance of the Chicks* and *Little Waltz*. (Ricordi.) Level 8.

VIOLET ARCHER (b. 1913) Canada

A great deal of her writing is linear and readily manageable by pianists with small hands. Archer, a student of Bartók and Hindemith, has taught at the University of Oklahoma, University of North Texas, McGill University and the University of Alberta.

Three Scenes

Attractive character pieces. See especially the third, *Christmas in Quebec*, which weaves melodies of familiar Christmas carols into a contemporary setting. Worth investigating for festival or contest repertoire. (Mercury.) Levels 3–4.

11 Short Pieces

Linear and dissonant. All are titled. (Peer International.) Level 5.

Minute Music for Small Hands

Three short children's pieces titled *Prayer; Waltz;* and *Hop, Skip, and Glide*, composed in a contemporary idiom. (Peer International.) Level 2.

Rondo

Spirited and pianistic 10-page piece with abundant "wrong-note" writing. (Peer International.) Level 10.

Additional Works for Study:
Four Little Studies
Habitant Sketches
Three Miniatures
Theme and Variations

RODOLFO ARIZAGA (b. 1926) Argentina

Toccata

A four-page work that is highly rhythmic and dissonant. Some octave passages. (Southern Music.) Level 10.

PAUL ARMA (b. 1904) Hungary

Pen name of Irme Weisshaus.

Round the World in 20 Minutes

Eighteen pianistic short pieces that are given such titles as *Among the Argentines, Among the Rumanians, Among the Hungarians* and *Among the Scots*. No fingering is provided in this edition. Strong writing. (Les Éditions Ouvrières.) Levels 4–5.

Two Sonatinas

The first is in three movements while the second is in one movement. Both highly rhythmic. See especially the last movement of *Sonatina No. 1* for its infectious rhythms. (Lemoine.) Level 7.

MALCOLM ARNOLD (b. 1921) Great Britain

Children's Suite

Six charming, mildly contemporary pieces, each designed as a study: e.g., "Study in legato thirds for the left hand," "Study in rhythms and colour" or "Study in touch and phrasing." (Lengnick.) Level 3.

CLAUDE ARRIEU (b. 1903) France

Promenade Mélancolique et Questionnaire

Two two-page pieces especially suited for the student with an ear for contemporary sounds. (Billaudot.) Level 3.

Les Petites filles modéles

Three chromatic pieces titled *Isabelle, Sophie* and *Verénique*. (Amphion.) Level 4.

Escapade et cerf-volant

Two two-page pieces. See especially the pianistic and driving tarantella, *Escapade*. (Billaudot.) Level 5.

Lectures pour piano, Sets 1 and 2

Two volumes containing four short character pieces each. Sophisticated, mildly contemporary writing. Set 2 is slightly more difficult. (Billaudot.) Level 7.

Musique pour piano

Five dissonant untitled movements for the sophisticated performer. (Maurice Senart.) Level 8.

GEORGES AURIC (1899–1983) France

Member of the French group "Les Six," Auric was highly influenced by Satie.

Three Impromptus

See especially *Nos. 1* and *2*. Light, rhythmic and captivating. These pieces are reminiscent of Poulenc. (Max Eschig.) Level 10.

Sonatine

Dedicated to Francis Poulenc. Rhythmic and effective. (Salabert.) Level 10.

B

MILTON BABBITT (b. 1916) USA

Playing for Time

Pointillistic writing in a short work. Highly organized musical syntax that features fragmented voices, disjunct melodic lines, many rests, and frequent dynamic, accent and tone color changes. Complex rhythmic notation. (Alfred.) Level 10.

STANLEY BABIN (b. 1932) USA

Sonatina No. 1

Dissonant, linear writing. The last movement is a toccata-like perpetual motion. (MCA.) Level 10.

Three Piano Pieces

Titles are *Musette, Fugue, Presto.* (MCA.) Level 10.

Additional Work for Study:
Dance Around the World

GRAYZNA BACEWICZ (1909–1969) Poland

Outstanding Polish female composer.

Suite Enfantine

Eight dance movements. See especially the *Burleska.* (PWM.) Level 10.

CONRAD BADEN (b. 1908) Norway

10 Bagatelles

Ten one-page dissonant pieces with titles such as *In the Evening, In the Chicken Run* and *Big Secret.* (Chester.) Level 5.

HENK BADINGS (b. 1907) The Netherlands

Arcadia

Three volumes of 10 elementary-level pieces each, arranged in progressive order of difficulty. Hands remain in set five-note positions in Books 1 and 2. The selections in Book 3 are slightly longer and more fully developed. Strong writing in a highly contemporary mode. (Schott.) Levels 1–4.

Sonatine No. 2

Forthright linear contemporary writing with thin textures. Attractive. See especially the third movement. (Donemus.) Level 7.

Reihe kleiner Klavierstücke

Eight teaching pieces. See especially the *Rondo-Finale.* (Schott.) Level 7.

Sonatine

Dissonant linear writing. In three movements. (Schott.) Level 10.

RAYMOND BAERVOETS (b. 1930) Belgium

Sonatine

Lilting first movement and a driving final toccata movement in an agreeable contemporary idiom. (Editions Metropolis.) Level 7.

Hommage á Serge Prokofiev

Interesting writing, moving from a quasi-waltz with some "wrong-note" writing in the opening to a more driving middle section, and then back again to the dance feeling. (Editions Metropolis.) Level 10.

EDUARD IVANOVICH BAGDASARYAN (1922–1987) Armenia

Humoresque and Étude-Picture

Both solos are included under one cover from this little-known Russian composer. The *Humoresque* is a biting scherzo, reminiscent of Prokofiev. The *Étude-Picture* features large chords and driving rhythms. (Soviet State Publishing.) Level 10.

ÁRPÁD BALÁZS (b. 1937) Hungary

14 Easy Pieces for Piano

Fourteen pieces in progressive difficulty. Titles include *Playing at Soldiers, A Little Invention, Arietta* and *A Sort of Rondo.* Attractive writing with contemporary sounds. Should be better known. (Boosey.) Levels 1–4.

GEORGE BARATI (b. 1913) USA, born Hungary

Rolling Wheels

Three-page solo that uses a single six-note motive which occurs throughout the music. Contemporary, sprightly writing based on two artificial scales centering on G. (Merion.) Level 10.

SAMUEL BARBER (1910–1981) USA

Love Song

This *allegretto* one-page piece is actually *No. 1* of *Three Sketches* which also includes *No. 2 To My Steinway* and *No. 3 Minuet (to Sara).* According to Maurice Hinson, "Love Song is very much a 'song without words' that slows gracefully and delights in its strong melodic emphasis." This is a little-known and highly accessible vignette of Barber. (Alfred.) Level 7.

Nocturne

Inscribed by the composer as "Homage to John Field," this beautiful work is filled with nostalgia and lyricism. A successful performance requires imagination and strong musicianship with a fine sense of timing and control of sound. Modern harmonic palette. (Schirmer.) Level 10.

SERGEY BARKHUDARYAN (1887–1972) Russia

19 Children's Pieces

Tuneful and tonal writing. These appealing pieces are pianistic and pedagogically sound. They become progressively more difficult throughout the volume. (Soviet State Publishing.) Levels 3–5.

DAVID BARNETT (1907–1985) USA

Gallery

"Nine recital miniatures for piano solo," character pieces of one and two pages in a mildly 20th-century idiom. Titles include *Village Games, Flight at Dusk* and *Galleon Under Full Sail.* Appropriate for the student who enjoys contemporary music. (Schroeder and Gunther.) Level 5.

BÉLA BARTÓK (1881–1945) Hungary

Bartók was a virtuoso pianist and an important 20th-century composer whose study of folk music, specifically Hungarian folk music, played a major influence in his writing. According to pianist David Yeomans, approximately half of Bartók's individual movements in the solo piano music use authentic peasant folk songs and dances. Bartók displayed a strong interest in writing contemporary music for less-advanced students.

Much of Bartók's piano music is published by Boosey and Hawkes, although with increasing frequency the music is also becoming available through other publishers. Opus numbers were given by Bartók only up to the *Improvisations*, Op. 20. Consequently, Sz. numbers (for scholar András Szöllösy, who numbered Bartók's works in 1957) are used throughout, especially since some titles are easily confused. While an earlier numbering system was used in Halsey Stevens's listing, the Szöllösy catalogue contains newer findings.

Three Popular Hungarian Songs (1907), Sz. 35a

Short settings based on Hungarian folk music. These short and effective pieces are more difficult rhythmically and interpretatively than technically, and would provide a good introduction to Bartók's writing through short and effective pieces. (Kalmus.) Level 8.

14 Bagatelles, Op. 6, Sz. 38 (1908)

Many original ideas, techniques and sounds. Bartók said that in these pieces "a new piano style appears as a reaction to the exuberance of the romantic piano music of the 19th century." The introduction contains instructions applicable for much of his piano music concerning accidentals, rests and tempo indications. Composed in the same year as *10 Easy Pieces*. Generally sophisticated writing, for the musically astute performer. (EBM.) Levels 8–10.

No. 1

Key signature shows four sharps in the right hand and four flats in the left hand, implying bitonality. Lyrical writing that needs adept shading of the melody. One printed page, more sophisticated musically than technically. Level 8.

No. 2

Short, toccata-like work with some hand crossings. Uses extreme registers and features biting dissonance. Appropriate for the performer who can move quickly about the keyboard. The *rallentandos* need careful pacing. Level 10.

No. 3

Chromatic right-hand ostinato figure of five notes above a single-note folklike melody in the left hand. Calls for sophisticated color and long sustained phrases. More difficult than it appears. Level 7.

No. 4

Harmonization of a Hungarian folk song. Primarily chordal writing. Level 6.

No. 5

Repeated chord accompaniment shifts between the hands, with folk melody played by the other hand. Vigorous and energetic writing that is worth investigating. Level 9.

No. 6

Dissonant lyrical writing in a one-page solo of mournful quality. For the musically sophisticated performer. Level 7.

No. 8

The many tempo changes call for a sophisticated musical interpretation. Chromatic melody with many grace-notes in the accompaniment. Level 10.

No. 9

Both hands generally play in unison, but quick melodic inflections can be tricky. Sudden changes in tempo. Much more difficult interpretatively than technically. Level 10.

No. 11

Marked *Allegro molto rubato*. Built on right-hand chords in quartal harmony. Effective if frequent tempo changes are executed convincingly. Musically sophisticated writing. Level 10.

No. 13

According to pianist David Yeomans, this piece can be interpreted as a musical reflection of Bartók's unfulfilled romance with the violinist Stefi Geyer. Low sustained triads in the accompaniment are placed under a plaintive single-note melody. Sophisticated writing. Level 7.

10 Easy Pieces, Sz. 39 (1908)

Planned as a set to complement the *Bagatelles*. Actually 11 pieces, including the introductory *Dedication*. Several are surprisingly difficult, such as the *Bear Dance*. (Alfred, Boosey, Kalmus and others.)

Dedication

Serves as an introduction to the set, and is unnumbered. Musically sophisticated despite its initial sparse appearance on the page. According to David Yeomans, a four-note motive at the opening reflects Bartók's ill-fated romance with violinist Stefi Geyer. Level 7.

No. 1 Peasant's Song

Two-voice writing in parallel motion at the octave. The music requires the playing of legato and inflection of the melody as well as the playing of different kinds of accents. The shortest note value is a quarter note, but there are many accidentals in this brief piece. Level 2.

No. 2 Painful Struggle

Left-hand ostinato in an Alberti-type figure accompanies a right-hand melody. Dissonant writing. Level 4.

No. 3 Slovak Young Men's Dance

One of the most popular of Bartók's teaching pieces. Spirited and strongly rhythmic writing with many dynamic changes. The singable melody repeats, primarily fragmented the second time. Very fast. Level 4.

No. 4 Sostenuto

Sophisticated writing, highly chromatic. Some contrapuntal interplay between the voices. Level 5.

No. 5 Evening in the Country

Perhaps the most popular movement in the set, this movement shows the freely expressive, narrative side of Bartók's writing, contrasted with the dance-like *tempo giusto* style. Bartók states that the themes are his own rather than original folk tunes but that he composed them in the style of the Hungarian Transylvanian folk tunes. The form is ABABA. Level 5.

No. 6 Hungarian Folk Song

Highly rhythmic writing in a one-page solo. The right-hand double notes require a strong hand and make it more difficult than it initially appears. Shows a strong folk influence. Level 6.

No. 7 Dawn

Sonorous work, similar in some ways to Debussy. Imaginative writing, especially good for the student with an ear for color. More difficult musically than technically (as is much of Bartók's piano music). Level 4.

No. 8 Folk Song

Ostinato accompaniment consisting of alternating chord figures. Mournful two-note slur figures separate the phrases. Level 4.

No. 9 Étude

Five-note whole tone scales ascending and descending in the right hand permeate much of the piece with a left-hand sustained melody underneath the moving soprano. Later the sixteenth-note moving passages move to the left hand while the sustained voice is played by the right hand. More difficult than many pieces in this volume. Level 4.

No. 10 Bear Dance

Much more difficult than the other movements found here. Repeated-note ostinato with chords in the right hand forms the basis of this movement. The performer needs strong fingers and the ability to move about quickly on the keyboard. Level 8.

For Children (1908–1909, revised by composer in 1945), Sz. 42, Volume 1 Based on Hungarian Folk Tunes. Volume 2 based on Slovakian Folk Tunes

Significant volumes of piano pieces for the elementary and intermediate student, purposely written without octave stretches. The melodies of all of the pieces are folk songs or folk dances. Titles in various collections are often assigned by the editors rather than the composer.

Bartók's original version contained 85 pieces, 42 in Volume 1 and 43 in Volume 2. His revised edition is slightly shorter, comprising 79 pieces in total. Bartók marked his pieces in detail, and provided fingerings and metronome markings. These are some of the best piano pieces written for beginners, occupying a similar position in the teaching repertoire to the Schumann *Album for the Young* and the Bach *Little Preludes*. The editions are as follows: Alfred (first edition), *Pieces for Children (For Children)*, Volume 1; Boosey and Hawkes (second and revised edition), *For Children*, Volumes 1 and 2; Kalmus (first edition), *For Children*, Volume 1 divided into two volumes; Kjos (first edition), Volume 1; G. Schirmer (first edition), *For Children*, Volumes 1 and 2; Universal (second and revised edition), *For Children*, Volumes 1 and 2 and divided into four volumes). Levels 3–6.

Volume 1

Based on Hungarian folk tunes. Titles were given by Bartók only in the second edition.

No. 1 Children at Play

One of the most accessible pieces from both volumes. Played only on the white keys, this work is in two voices. It is good for study of hand independence in the early levels. Well known. Level 2.

No. 3 Andante

Plaintive melody over a chordal accompaniment. Much repetition in a mournful piece. Level 2.

No. 5 Play

One of the most popular. Right-hand melody is harmonized by off-beat triads. Changes of tempo need careful attention. Level 3.

No. 6 Study for the Left Hand

Drum-like repeated eighth note accompaniment of open fifths in the left hand with melody above. Especially good for students who once enjoyed "Indian pieces" in the early years. Dynamics range from *ff* to *ppp*. Vigorous writing. Level 3.

No. 8 Children's Game

Many different kinds of articulation need attention and render this more difficult than it appears. The reverse broken chord accompaniment may be difficult at first. Deservedly popular but the tempo changes need careful pacing. Brilliant writing. Level 4.

No. 12 Allegro

Folklike melody with broken chord accompaniment and double-note figures that need strong fingers. Some tricky passages in the second part, but immediately appealing. Level 4.

No. 15 Allegro

This selection is another of the highly accessible, popular pieces in this volume. Features an off-beat chordal accompaniment to a catchy melody. Level 2.

No. 17 Round Dance

Plaintive and questioning character. Right hand is in five-finger patterns with repeated notes. Left-hand chords alternate between the octaves. The melody needs careful inflection of nuance. Level 5.

No. 21 Allegro robusto

A boisterous drinking song that appears in many anthologies. An excellent study in voicing thick, chordal textures. Needs a student with a strong hand. Level 5.

No. 29 Allegro (omitted from second edition)

Theme with two variations and a Coda. Short but concentrated writing with several tempo changes. Level 6.

No. 31 Pentatonic Tune (No. 29 in second edition)

Grace-note figurations may present problems. This one-page piece is effective in performance but is more difficult than it first appears. Jesting character. Level 5.

No. 32 Jeering Song

Well-known work consisting of a melody and primarily triadic accompaniment. According to David Yeomans, the repeated-note chords in the 2/4 measures accompanied the shouts of "Whoopee!" in the original folk song. Level 5.

No. 35 Allegro non troppo (No. 33 in second edition)

Wide left-hand skips in the oom-pah accompaniment. Excellent preparation for playing similar figurations that occur in Schubert and Chopin waltzes. Many different articulations are employed. Level 5.

No. 38 Drunkard's Song (No. 36 in second edition)

This spirited, boisterous short selection appears in many anthologies. The quick repeated four-note chordal passages need supple wrists. Level 5.

No. 40 Winter Solstice Song

Consists of four variations and a Coda. Left-hand ostinato of four notes descending stepwise pervades much of this two-page work. More difficult than it appears. Level 6.

Volume II

Based on Slovakian folk tunes, but similar in musical style to Volume I. Titles in Volume II are original with Bartók.

No. 3 Allegretto

Off-beat chordal accompaniment in the left hand requires coordination. Marked *scherzando*, the writing is playful and animated. Level 3.

No. 6 Rondo (first edition); Round Dance I (second edition)

Left-hand single-note accompaniment could be tricky. Level 4.

No. 7 Rogue's Song (first edition); Sorrow (second edition)

Plaintive single-note melody over simple chordal accompaniment. A naturally expressive performer would play this well and the coordination between the hands is not difficult. Level 3.

No. 18 Jeering Song (first edition); Teasing Song (second edition)

Melody appears first in the left hand, then in the right, and returns again to the left. The off-beat triads in the accompaniment should not be rushed. Needs careful changes of tempo. Level 4.

No. 24 Poco andante (No. 23 Andante tranquillo in the second edition)

Simple expressive melody with off-beat chordal accompaniment. Many changes of tempo and dynamics. Level 4.

No. 35 Highwayman's Tune (No. 31 Highway Robber in the second edition)

Alternates a drum-like motive with a short melody. The melody is varied in each recurrence. Vigorous writing. Level 5.

Sketches, Op. 9/b, Sz. 44 (1908–1910)

Set of seven intimate pieces, more for mature musicians. Many changes of tempi and rhythmic intricacies. More difficult musically than technically. Sometimes referred to as *Equisses*. The fourth and seventh are beyond the scope of this book in difficulty. (Boosey, Kalmus.) Level 10.

Allegro Barbaro, Sz. 49 (1911)

A turning point in Bartók's writing and in keyboard writing of the early 20th century, since the piano is used here primarily as a percussion instrument. Performers often refuse to pay attention to the numerous details inscribed in the score by Bartók. Driving, dissonant and barbaric. Contains large chords and wide leaps and needs careful voicing and attention to the dynamic range, from *fff* to *pppp*. (Boosey and others). Level 10.

Piano Method, Sz. 52 (1913)

Written by Bartók and Sándor Reschofsky, a colleague of Bartók at the Budapest Academy and specialist in elementary piano instruction. Bartók scholar B. Suchoff reports that five volumes were completed and that Nos. 2 and 5 were by Reschofsky, No. 4 was by Sándor Kovács, and No. 3 consisted of Bartók's edition of 13 pieces from the *Anna Magdalena Bach Notebook*. In this first volume, Reschofsky wrote the basic instructional material and exercises while Bartók wrote the original music (some pieces by Czerny, Duvernoy and Lemoine also appear). The method includes 125 examples of technical exercises interspersed with teaching pieces. Valuable information is contained in the method concerning the proper execution of touch for slurs, *portato, tenuto,* dynamics and accents. Levels 1–3.

First Term at the Piano (1913)

The pieces here were taken from the *Bartók-Reschofsky Piano Method* and published as an independent set of 18 pieces for the elementary student. David Yeomans in his book on Bartók piano music suggests that they could be used as an introduction to the *Mikrokosmos* and provides a pairing of works from the *First Term* and the *Mikrokosmos,* Volume I for possible study. The more difficult pieces in the *First Term* do not surpass *Mikrokosmos,* Volume III. Numbers 1–10 of the *First Term* keep both hands in the same five-note position. These pieces, like many pieces by Bartók, help develop contrapuntal playing skills. See especially No. 10, *Hungarian Folk Song* and No. 11, *Minuet,* which helps develop a kinesthetic feeling for sixths. No. 17 (untitled) is composed of asymmetrical phrase lengths. Most of these 18 pieces appear in various modern teaching methods and anthologies. This literature is some of the easiest writing by a major composer that is specifically aimed toward the beginning student. (Boosey, EMB, Kalmus and other standard editions.) Levels 1–3.

No. 1 [Untitled]

Hands remain in five-finger C position and play in parallel motion two octaves apart. Only quarter, half and whole notes are used. Level 1.

No. 2 [Untitled]

Hands remain in a five-finger G position and play in parallel and contrary motion. Fine introduction to contrapuntal playing. Level 1.

No. 3 Dialogue

Features an A Minor five-finger position in the right hand and E Major position in the left, providing an early example of bitonal writing. Hand positions are stationary and note values are basic. Level 1.

No. 4 Dialogue

Contrapuntal writing at the elementary level, much of it in contrary motion. Accents are introduced. Level 1.

No. 5 [Untitled]

Staccato writing and eighth notes are introduced. Largely parallel motion at the octave. Level 1.

No. 6 [Untitled]

Rapid notes in the right hand help develop facility. Drone-type accompaniment. In general the hand position is stationary. Level 1.

No. 7 Folk Song

Both an Alberti bass in a reversed pattern and the presence of two-note slurs and other detailed articulations require the performer's attention. Eight measures long. Level 1.

No. 8 [Untitled]

An elementary contrapuntal study, longer and slightly more complex in terms of coordination than the preceding examples. Level 2.

No. 9 [Untitled]

Two-voice contrapuntal study with contrasting dynamics indicated between the hands. Level 2.

No. 10 Hungarian Folk Song

Ostinato accompaniment with occasional double notes against a folk melody. Might be a student's first study in playing a moving melody against an accompaniment. Level 2.

No. 11 Minuet

Study in parallel sixths in one hand. Several different kinds of accents are used and detailed coordination is required. This piece appears in many anthologies. Level 3.

No. 12 Swineherd's Dance

Contains sustained notes in each hand with an inner or outer voice playing different note values and various articulations. Complex writing for this level in this four-voice piece. Level 3.

No. 13 Hungarian Folk Song

Sixteen-measure work featuring melody and double-note accompaniment. Some contrapuntal passages appear. Equal in difficulty to the easier pieces in *For Children*. Level 3.

No. 14 [Untitled]

Contrapuntal writing in a work featuring sixteenth notes and syncopations throughout. Level 3.

No. 15 Wedding Song

Chordal accompaniment and melody, both using different articulations. Reminiscent of some of the easier selections in *For Children*. Level 3.

No. 16 Peasant's Dance

Melody against a chordal accompaniment. Level 2.

No. 17 [Untitled]

Four-voice writing in a primarily chordal, boisterous selection. Many different kinds of touch are used. Level 3.

No. 18 Waltz

Melody and oom-pah-pah accompaniment. Level 4.

Sonatina, Sz. 55 (1915)

Based on five Rumanian folk tunes that Bartók collected from the peasants and gypsies in Transylvanian villages. The writing is effective throughout. (Many standard editions.) Level 8.

I. Bagpipers

Robust, peasant dance character, with changing meter, for a performer with a strong sense of rhythm. Some accents on weak fingers will need special work. Appealing and representative of Bartók's best writing. Bartók stated that this work is comprised of two dances played by two bagpipe players. ABA form, ending on a dominant chord. Levels 7–8.

II. Bear Dance

Bartók heard an elderly gypsy play this melody on the violin, all the while accompanied by a two-string guitar. Attractive melodic ornamentation over a lumbering left hand. Several different kinds of accents are used. Level 7.

III. Finale

According to Bartók, "The last movement also contains two folk melodies played by peasant violin players." B. Suchoff further relates that it depicts a dance in the Christmas season by a man wearing a bird costume. The most difficult movement of the set, dazzling in its effect. Level 8.

Rumanian Folk Dances, Sz. 56 (1915)

Six highly effective movements based on folk melodies representing different dance forms and dances from four regions in Transylvania. Fresh and original effects surface in this popular set. Effective performed as an entire set. These pieces also exist in many arrangements for the mature performer. (Boosey.) Level 9.

No. 1 Joc cu Bătă

This is a "stick" dance, performed by a boy. Lively and energetic writing with a strong syncopated melody. Level 8.

No. 2 Brâul

The word refers to a cloth belt worn by men and women. A round dance. Bartók heard it being played on the peasant flute. Level 7.

No. 3 Pe loc

This "stamping dance" is danced by a couple standing in one spot. The man dances with his hands on his hips and the woman with her hands on his shoulders. Level 8.

No. 6 Măruntel

This dance, the lively Rumanian polka, alternates even and uneven beats and uses very small steps. Level 10.

Three Hungarian Folk Tunes, Sz. 66 (1914–1917)

Simpler and more straightforward settings than the 1907 set *Three Popular Hungarian Songs*, which are much more complex rhythmically. The *Three Hungarian Folk Tunes* are effective and similar in style and texture to those in the *15 Hungarian Peasant Songs*. They should be better known. This short collection will provide an excellent introduction to Bartók's writing for the advancing student. (Boosey.) Level 9.

Rumanian Christmas Carols, Sz. 57 (1915)

Two series of 10 settings each, both contained in one volume, and progressive in difficulty. Rhythmic, often animated and generally short. Easier than the *Fifteen Hungarian Peasant Songs* but similar in nature and style. The Boosey edition provides the words to the tunes on which the settings are based. (Boosey.) Level 10.

Nine Small Piano Pieces (1926)

A little-known collection with surprising teaching pieces by Bartók. The pieces are different from those in *For Children* in that they are more difficult, some are longer, the variance in the levels of difficulty is wider, they are not directly based on settings of folk tunes, and the dissonances are stronger and more pronounced. Presented in three volumes of contrapuntal studies (Volume I, Nos. 1–4), character pieces (Volume II, Nos. 5–8) and a brilliant, difficult concert piece (Volume III, No. 9). (Boosey.) Levels 5–10.

Volume I

Nos. 1–4 Four Dialogues
Dissonant linear writing. Level 4.

Volume II

No. 5 Menuetto
Dissonant seconds throughout. Level 4.

No. 6 Air
Attractive three-page piece, strong rhythms and folk-like melody. Would be a suitable repertoire choice to substitute for the well-known *Evening in the Country*. Level 4.

No. 7 Marcia delle bestie (March of the Animals)
Pianists who enjoy the repeated rhythms and chords of Bartók will be attracted to this primitive, pulsating writing. Kindred in spirit to the first movement of the Bartók *Out of Doors*. Little finger facility is needed. Levels 7–8.

No. 8 Tambourine
Rhythmic playing of repeated chords to resemble the effect of the tambourine. *Fortissimo* ending. Effective work that is not difficult and should be better known. Level 7.

Three Rondos on Folk Tunes

Infectious writing. Based on seven Slovakian folk tunes. Frequently more than one folk tune forms the basis for a single selection. Based on three themes and in three sections, No. 1 is perhaps the most effective and the most accessible. Effective use of silence is necessary for a successful performance. Requires flair. (Boosey.) Level 10.

Mikrokosmos, 153 Progressive Piano Pieces in Six Volumes, Sz. 103 (1926–1937)

Bartók himself best describes the didactic purpose of his monumental work: "The first four volumes of *Mikrokosmos* were written to provide study material for the beginner pianist—young or adult—and are intended to cover, as far as possible, most of the simple technical problems likely to be encountered in the early stages. The material in Volumes 1–3 has been designed to be sufficient in itself for the first, or first and second, year of study. These three books differ from a conventional 'piano method' in that technical and theoretical instructions have been omitted, in the belief that these are more appropriately left for the teacher to explain to the student. . . . Work on Volume 4 may—indeed should—be combined with the study of other compositions such as the *Notebook for Anna Magdalena Bach* by J. S. Bach, appropriate studies by Czerny, etc. To facilitate the teacher's task, exercises are included in an appendix to each of the first four volumes. The metronome markings and indicated duration should be regarded only as a guide. Particularly in Volumes 1–3; the first few dozen pieces may be played at a faster or slower tempo as circumstances dictate. As progress is made, the tempi should be considered as less variable, and in Volumes 5 and 6 tempo indications must be adhered to." (Taken from the preface by the composer, found in the *New Definitive Edition of the Mikrokosmos*, p. 8 published by Boosey and Hawkes.) Research for the 1987 edition included the comparison with the original printed versions of all known manuscript sources and the correction of any errors. Aptly named, this microcosm presents many of the compositional techniques used in the first part of the 20th century. (Boosey and Hawkes.) Levels 1–10.

Volume 1

Written almost entirely in simple five-finger positions with simple rhythms. The 36 pieces deal with playing in unison, dotted notes, repetition, question and answer, imitation and inversion, canon at the octave, Dorian mode, Phrygian mode, counterpoint, and other devices. Ten exercises are found in the appendix. Nos. 1–6 are rudimentary unison studies to foster legato. Contrapuntal writing commences in No. 10.

No. 10 With Alternate Hands

> The phrases are in dialogue and each begins on the last note of the previous phrase. Contrapuntal playing at the earliest level. Generally single-note melodic textures. Level 1.

No. 14 Question and Answer

> Hands play in parallel motion at the distance of an octave. Only half and quarter notes are used. This work contains two five-measure phrases and two four-measure phrases, noted in the form of question-answer phrasing. Level 1.

No. 15 Village Song

> Unison playing, modal writing. Primarily a study in position moves. Especially good for helping a student hear modal writing. Only quarter and half notes are used. Level 1.

No. 23 Imitation and Inversion

> Simple study in contrapuntal playing. Contains single-note melodies in both hands. Level 1.

Volume 2

Mostly in five-finger positions with many of the same compositional and technical devices as in the first volume. Devices include canon, pentatonic melody, chromatic writing, triplets in Lydian mode, Mixolydian mode, Hungarian style, etc. The appendix contains 14 exercises.

No. 38 Staccato and Legato

Two-voice writing, primarily in contrary motion, focusing on the alternation of staccato and legato articulation. Mainly eighth and quarter notes. Level 3.

No. 47 Big Fair

The first piece to use pedal in *Mikrokosmos*. Hands play fourths contrapuntally. Difficult coordination for this level. Level 4.

No. 51 Waves

Played primarily on the black keys. The title *Waves* suggests that the composer wants melodic inflection of the two independent lines. Hands remain in set positions throughout, allowing total concentration on the intricate counterpoint. Level 4.

No. 57 Accents

Two-voice canon with accents occurring at different places in the measure for each hand. Four key changes. Level 4.

No. 63 Buzzing

One of the most captivating movements in this volume. Melody is played above a "buzzing" ostinato. Level 4.

Volume 3

Rhythmic and technical difficulties gradually increase. The pieces are more musically satisfying in this volume than in the earlier volumes, while the use of folk material is as prominent as before. Devices include thirds, sixths and triads, melody against double notes, variations, chromatic invention, five-tone scale and others.

No. 69 Chord Study

Engaging selection based on parallel triads played in a catchy rhythmic pattern against a single-note melody. The melody and accompaniment change hands later in the piece. Level 4.

No. 71 Thirds

Parallel thirds in each hand play against each other in contrary motion patterns. Some shifting meters and mirror images. Good for strengthening fingers. Four-voice writing. Level 4.

No. 72 Dragons' Dance

A captivating *pesante* one-page work based on the tritone and shifting accents within the bar. This is one of the first pieces to expand the hand beyond a five-finger position. Level 4.

No. 79 Hommage à J.S.B.

Features the same rhythmic patterns and texture of some of the Bach *Short Preludes* that use broken chords. Major thirds alternate with minor thirds. Level 4.

No. 82 Scherzo

The shifting meters (7/8 and 2/4) give this its strong appeal. Primarily chordal writing that needs a performer with a strong sense of pulse. Level 5.

No. 84 Merriment

Presenting exotic oriental sounds, this work begins with two measures of strong chordal syncopations, gradually moving to a long line with pedal effects that create mysterious sonorities. Canonic patterns appear. Level 5.

No. 90 In Russian Style

Recurring rhythmic motives in this folk-like melody. Many small slurrings. *Pesante* writing. Level 5.

No. 94 Tale

Based on simple melodic dialogue with changing meters. The sound is a contrapuntal one. Level 5.

Volume 4

Beginning with this volume, the pieces seem to stand readily on their own as significant musical compositions. Devices include Bulgarian rhythms, diminished fifths, harmonics, clashing sounds, crossed sounds and others.

No. 97 Notturno

Haunting and lyrical piece. Requires fine tonal control and balance between the melody and accompaniment. Texture characteristic of the Romantic period, with an arpeggiated accompaniment and a lyrical melody. Level 6.

No. 99 Crossed Hands

Clever piece that offers colorful dialogue between the two voices. Different key signatures for each hand. Level 6.

No. 102 Harmonics

This is Bartók's only use of harmonics in his piano music. Here the use of overtone effects and percussive chords occurs in a relatively simple and generally lyrical piece. The left hand silently depresses the chords while accented triads elicit sympathetic vibrations. These accented triads interrupt an otherwise lyrical melody. Level 7.

No. 104 Through the Keys

The music remains in one key for no more than six measures. Two-voice parallel writing at the distance of an octave. Level 6.

No. 107 Melody in the Mist

Excellent short introduction to varied sonorities and colors through chord clusters and blurred pedaling. The texture consists of the alternation of right- and left-hand chord clusters in a *piano* dynamic range interrupted by *forte* unison passages. A good piece for exploring visual and aural relationships in music. Level 6.

No. 108 Wrestling

Could be a technical study to help the performer develop independence of the fingers, since a sustained note is held in each hand while the other voice in the hand is active. Both hands play in parallel motion at the distance of one octave. Vivid *marcatissimo* touches, frequent *sforzando*, and dissonant intervals. Level 6.

No. 109 From the Island of Bali

Three short sections are presented—*Andante, Risoluto* and *Andante*—with the *Risoluto* section consisting primarily of unison passages. Prolonged pedaling and many opportunities for tone color in an exotic-sounding work. Level 6.

No. 110 Clashing Sounds

Much repetition of ideas in a highly dissonant selection. Level 6.

No. 112 Variations on a Folk Tune

Bartók varies the melody by adding sixths, using canon and imitation, and adding melodic chromaticism and chromatic harmonies. Fine example of variation technique. Level 7.

No. 113 Bulgarian Rhythm

Good introduction to 7/8 irregular rhythmic patterns in an immediately appealing work. The left hand presents a legato ostinato pattern. An appropriate prelude to the *Six Dances in Bulgarian Rhythms*. Level 7.

No. 120 Fifth Chords

Passages of parallel triads are played by both hands. Major, minor and diminished triads. Level 7.

Volume 5

Eighteen compositions for the advancing performer. Compositions are written on such devices as alternating thirds, fourths, major seconds broken and together, whole-tone scale, etc. Several selections could be profitably grouped for recital performance.

No. 121 Chords Together and Opposed

Pan-diatonic sound and a highly syncopated character with some subtle changes in chord notes. Primarily chordal writing, good for the performer with strong hands. Level 7.

No. 125 Boating

Study in quartal harmony that requires careful attention to slurring and balance between the hands. The swaying rhythmic patterns need inflection. Level 8.

No. 126 Change of Time

Meter changes occur in practically every measure during half of this short work. Folklike qualities lend a compelling character. Level 8.

No. 128 Peasant Dance

Obvious appeal due to the conspicuous folk element and *pesante* quality. Melody is varied throughout. One of the most attractive selections in this volume. Level 8.

No. 129 Alternating Thirds

Harmonic thirds are alternated in various rhythmic patterns. A fine study in coordination between the hands. Vivacious writing. Level 8.

No. 130 Village Joke

Seems to present a stumbling villager in the humorous writing. Strong appeal to both listener and performer. Level 7.

No. 131 Fourths

Serves as a study in quartal sounds as well as a double-note étude. Uses the fourth finger frequently. Filled with humor and wit. Level 8.

No. 133 Syncopation

Exciting writing that can also help develop a strong sense of rhythm. Uses many double-notes and as such is especially good for the performer with strong hands. Effective in performance. Level 8.

No. 138 Bagpipe

Features a syncopated drone and three-bar phrases. Later the drone is varied and embellished. Interest and momentum are maintained to the end partly through the improvisatory character of the B section, the added harmonies in the A' section and the unusual rhythmic combinations. Level 9.

No. 139 Merry Andrew

Appealing character piece in which the melody is first divided between the hands and then presented in each hand. Level 8.

Volume 6

Fourteen major works, the last six of which are the well-known and difficult *Six Dances in Bulgarian Rhythms*.

No. 142 From the Diary of a Fly

The staccato major and minor seconds in this piece create a vivid buzzing effect. Hands play in exceptionally close proximity. Excellent writing in a contemporary example of program music. Level 10.

No. 144 Minor Seconds, Major Sevenths

Study in dissonant sonorities in which the performer must develop a sensitivity to blurring. A good choice in preparing a student for the larger works of Bartók. Level 10.

No. 146 Ostinato

Driving rhythms, effective in performance. Needs a performer with strong hands. Primarily chordal writing. Level 10.

Miscellaneous Volumes

Play Bartók!

Twenty-one progressive selections from the Bartók *Mikrokosmos*, Volumes 1 and 2. The hands remain stationary in most of the pieces found here, although the level of contrapuntal difficulty in these selections increases rapidly. Bartók's original titles are not given at the beginning of the pieces. Also not provided are their original numbers. (Boosey.) Levels 1–2.

Bartók is Easy! ed. Agay

Short collection of 15 of Bartók's works from *For Children* and *10 Easy Pieces*. Fine variety and appropriate leveling of the pieces chosen. (Presser.) Levels 4–5.

43 Little Pieces and Studies for Piano, ed. Agay

Contains pieces selected from the Bartók-Reschofsky *Piano Method*. Arranged in progressive order, as in the method. Interesting pieces usually not found in other collections. This book provides a practical way for the modern teacher to incorporate Bartók's pedagogical philosophy into present-day instruction. Deserves further investigation. (Presser.) Levels 1–3.

Béla Bartók: An Introduction to the Composer and His Music, ed. Banowetz

Contains valuable prefatory information on Bartók's life and the history of Hungarian music. This volume contains *For Children*, Volume I. (Kjos.) Levels 2–5.

16 Pieces for Children, ed. Philipp

A fine teaching collection that is not too long. Features pieces from *For Children, 10 Easy Pieces* and others. All are at approximately the same level and a short group could be created for recital or festival. This is a practical book to use for teaching. (International.) Levels 2–4.

Bartók: An Introduction to His Piano Works, ed. Palmer

Thirty-one pieces. A valuable addition is the commentary written by Bartók on wrist and finger action, touch schemes, accents and syncopations. Performance suggestions also appear for each piece. (Alfred.) Levels 3–8.

Bartók: The First Book for Young Pianists, ed. Palmer

Contains the easier pieces from the *Bartók: An Introduction to His Piano Works*, ed. Palmer. Valuable for pianists beginning their study of Bartók. (Alfred.) Levels 1–3.

Béla Bartók: Selected Children's Pieces for Piano, ed. Palmer

Thirteen miscellaneous pieces, similar to *Bartók: An Introduction*, ed. Palmer. Levels 2–5.

Young People at the Piano, Volume I and II

Two short volumes, each containing 12 and 10 pieces, respectively, from *For Children.* Excellent for teaching. (EMB.) Level 2.

JAN ZDENĚK BARTOŠ (1908–1981) Czechoslovakia

Bagatelles

Six tuneful teaching pieces with primarily traditional harmonies. These are little-known selections by a rather obscure composer, yet are of surprisingly high quality and strong pedagogical potential. Titles are *Ukolébavka (Berceuse), Scherzando, Melodie, Barcarolla, Marcia funebre* and *Slováčká.* (Praha.) Level 5.

Bagatelly, Op. 3

Fresh writing throughout the eight untitled selections. Strong characterization and nationalistic overtones. (Praha.) Level 10.

Vánoce

Six character pieces for the intermediate-level pianist. More dissonant than the *Bagatelles* or *Bagatelly.* Level 6.

NEVETT BARTOW (1934–1973) USA

Six Character Pieces

High-quality writing is found in these six sparkling short pieces. Mild contemporary dissonances. (Shawnee.) Level 5.

Toccata for Piano

Interesting, effective and unusual, with several changes of mood within the six pages. Rhythmic and syncopated with a large buildup to a big climax. Some full-hand clusters and a few large chords are found here. Effective writing. (Shawnee.) Level 10.

LEONID BASHMAKOV (b. 1927) Finland

Six Preludes

Engaging writing if not profound. This set would be especially effective performed as a whole. It presents strong contrast between the movements and mildly contemporary harmonies. About 10 minutes in total length. (Fazer.) Level 10.

LESLIE BASSETT (b. 1922) USA

Mobile

Lyrical two-page work. According to Maurice Hinson, it is "constantly unfolding, rich in color and range. Its chromatic language is enhanced by several varied repetitions that, as it were, assume new perspectives as they turn in the wind." Expressionistic writing. (Alfred.) Level 8.

JAMES BASTIEN (b. 1934) USA

Toccata

Marked and energetic, with many chords and driving rhythms that never let up. Motivational literature for the young advancing student. Has a *fff* ending. (General Words.) Level 9.

STANLEY BATE (1913–1959) Great Britain

Seven Pieces

Consider programming the entire set of these agreeable, light works as part of a recital. Strong contrast between the seven character pieces. Reminiscent of the Shostakovich preludes. Most are only two pages long. (Schott.) Level 10.

RAYMOND BAUER (n.d.) USA

Sonatina in G Major

Mildly contemporary, reminiscent in sound, and piano figurations of the Kabalevsky *Sonatina in A Minor*. In three movements with mostly linear writing, this piece deserves to be better known. Can be played by students with small hands. (Carl Fischer.) Level 7.

CECIL BAUMER (n.d.) Great Britain

Four Keys. Album of 16 Short Pieces

Fresh, mildly contemporary short pieces. All are in one of four keys—A Minor, C, F or G. (Lengnick.) Level 4.

IRWIN BAZELON (b. 1922) USA

Suite for Young People, Parts I and II

Dissonant writing meant, according to the composer, "to acquaint young pianists to the style and character of contemporary music as early as possible in their musical training." Part I is easier than Part II. See especially Part II: *The Clown and Puppet, Circus Parade* and *Goblins and Ghosts.* (Peer International.) Part I, Level 8. Part II, Level 10.

DAN BEATY (b. 1937) USA

Woodsprite and Waterbug Collection

Twelve very short and imaginative pieces in contemporary idioms, with titles such as *Red Dog, Mists, Pagoda* and *Morning Song.* These pieces should be better known. (General Words and Music.) Level 5.

Seven Bagatelles

Strong contemporary writing that is palatable, often rhythmic. The short pieces are titled *Seconds, Thirds, Fourths,* and so on up through the *Octave.* (General Words and Music.) Level 8.

JOHN BECKWITH (b. 1927) Canada

Six Mobiles, Sets 1 and 2

Highly dissonant and primarily linear writing. Three solos are contained in each set. (Berandol.) Levels 1–2.

Interval Studies

Three short pieces built on *Fourths and Fifths, Seconds and Ninths* and *Thirds.* (BMI.) Level 3.

Suite on Old Tunes

Mildly contemporary settings with generally thin textures and some changing meters on the tunes *Vive la Canadienne!, Cockles and Mussels, Jingle Bells* and *O Can Ye Sew Cushions?* Perhaps best for the precocious child. (Berandol.) Level 5.

ARTHUR BENJAMIN (1893–1960) Great Britain

Jamaican Rumba

Its immense popularity stems in part from its highly rhythmic nature and the tunefulness of the writing. The right-hand counter melody is not as easy as it sounds. Perhaps a motivational or recreational supplement to a student's standard fare. (Boosey.) Level 7.

Three New Fantasies

Composed by Benjamin specifically to introduce students "to the use of both pedals to obtain colour and atmosphere" in the *Dance at Dawn* and *Drifting*. Impressionistic works, easier than Debussy. (Boosey.) Level 8.

Additional Works for Study:
Tambourin
Let's Go Hiking
Chinoiserie

RICHARD RODNEY BENNETT (b. 1936) Great Britain

Diversions

Seven one-page pieces for the intermediate student, composed in a contemporary idiom. (Universal.) Level 7.

A Week of Birthdays

Titled *Monday's Child, Tuesday's Child* and so on, these pieces each have strongly defined, distinct characters. For a student who enjoys contemporary music. See especially *Thursday's Child* and *Saturday's Child*. (Belwin.) Level 7.

CLIFFORD BENSON (b. 1946) Great Britain

Three Pieces for Piano

Three character pieces, *Little March, Rondo* and *Spanish Dance*, any of which may be played separately. See especially the *Little March* or *Spanish Dance*, a short and relatively flashy piece. (Novello.) Level 6.

NIELS VIGGO BENTZON (b. 1919) Denmark

Seven Small Pieces, Op. 3

Short, sophisticated pieces in a dissonant idiom. (Hansen.) Level 5.

JEAN BERGER (b. 1909) Germany

Berger studied music at the University of Heidelberg, and in 1941, immigrated to the USA where he taught and composed.

Country Sketches

Character pieces with titles such as *Mountain Meadow, In Days Past* and *Cross Country*. Some of the rhythms in these pieces are more difficult to realize than they first appear. (General Words and Music.) Levels 4–5.

Diversions

Fresh, mildly contemporary writing. Titles include *On the Trail, Half-forgotten Tune, Skipping Through Woods* and *Dance*, among others. These pieces should be heard more often. (General Words and Music.) Level 5.

Seven Inventions

Surprisingly palatable contemporary linear writing. Effective inventions in two voices, not as difficult as they sound. They would be especially good for students who do not have a large reach, for students needing to work on the development of contrapuntal playing skills, or for development of independence of the hands. (Shawnee.) Level 6.

More Diversions

Slightly more difficult than the earlier set, *Diversions*. High-quality writing in a contemporary idiom that students can comprehend. One or several selections from this volume would be interesting repertoire additions to a contest or festival list. Representative titles are *Through the Woods and Fields, Things Past and Remembered* and *Tumble*. (General Words and Music.) Level 7.

Sonatina

The outer movements are animated and lively, especially well suited for a pianist who enjoys vigorous playing. Mild contemporary writing. (Shawnee.) Level 7.

SVERRE BERGH (b. 1915) Norway

Gubben Noah

Theme and variations based on the story of Noah's Ark. Features engaging writing with strong variety and character between the variations. A performance of this work will attract attention from the audience. It should be played by a performer with some flair. (Norsk Musikforlag.) Level 9.

LUCIANO BERIO (b. 1925) Italy

Erdenklavier (1969)

Pointillistic writing in a thin texture with a different dynamic marking for each note. This work is much more difficult musically and interpretatively than technically. (Universal.) Level 10.

Wasserklavier (1965)

Extensive rolled arpeggiations and expansive chordal writing with relatively thick textures. Also more difficult musically and interpretatively than technically. (Universal.) Level 10.

SIR LENNOX BERKELEY (b. 1903) Great Britain

Five Short Pieces

Mild contemporary sounds and lyrical writing. These pieces are pianistic and might be played as a set by a serious student. (Chester.) Level 9.

Three Piano Pieces

Titled *Étude, Berceuse* and *Capriccio*, these pieces are in a lyrical idiom and the writing is highly pianistic. Dissonant writing and contemporary sonorities. (Galliard.) Level 10.

Three Mazurkas

The neo-Classicism of Berkeley is revealed in these three homages to Chopin. Contains textures and mazurka rhythms similar to those found in Chopin's music. The harmonic language is fully contemporary. (Chester.) Level 9.

SOL BERKOWITZ (b. 1922) USA

Nine Folk Song Preludes

Fresh adaptations of folk tunes in writing that is alive and embracing. Titles include *All the Pretty Little Horses, The Drunken Sailor* and *The Birds' Song*. One or two selections from here would be welcome and fresh additions to contest or festival repertoire. Often used themes from American folk songs. (Frank Music Corporation.) Level 7.

12 Easy Blues

This collection should be known better. Pianistic and motivating writing. (Boston.) Level 5.

Four Blues for Lefty

Although both the right and left hands are used, these short blues pieces emphasize passagework and melodies in the left hand to help develop dexterity. The writing is more chromatic than in the set of *12 Easy Blues*. (Theodore Presser.) Level 7.

MIGUEL BERNAL JIMÉNEZ (1910–1946) Mexico

Antigua Valladolid (The Ancient City)

Pleasant teaching pieces, generally tuneful with a mildly contemporary flavor. The four movements include *Toccatina for the Right Hand Alone, Double Minuet, Gavotte* and *Pleasantry.* (Peer International.) Level 5.

Pastels

Attractive teaching pieces which definitely reflect a Mexican influence. Stronger writing here than in *The Ancient City.* Rhythmic, tuneful, full of vitality. See especially *Mayan Dance, Merry Go Round, Folk Dance* and *Fiesta.* (Peer International.) Levels 6–7.

LEONARD BERNSTEIN (1918–1990) USA

Better known as a composer and conductor, Bernstein was also a virtuoso pianist. His piano style as a composer is obviously American, with influences of Stravinsky, Copland, Shostakovich, jazz and 12-tone techniques.

Four Movements from West Side Story, arr. Smit

These arrangements are pianistic and well-conceived. A student able to play the *Muczynski Preludes* could enjoy these pieces for supplementary recreational playing. Included are *Jets, Jump, Cha-Cha* and *Cool.* (Amberson.) Level 9.

Seven Anniversaries (1943)

A set of portrayals of people who had been close to Bernstein during his formative years. This is the least difficult of the sets of *Anniversaries* as a group. (Warner Brothers.)

I. For Aaron Copland

Sweet and singing melody, often doubled at the third. Some of Bernstein's warmest and most singable piano writing. Level 9.

II. For My Sister, Shirley

Staccato left-hand eighths form a rhythmic figure that lends a carefree, lighthearted character to the octave melody above. Effective cross-rhythms. Bernstein's relationship with his sister was one of the most important and meaningful in his life. Level 10.

III. In Memoriam: Alfred Eisner

Bernstein's Harvard roommate and close friend, who died of cancer at the age of 23. Beautiful melodic writing offset in the middle by stark *fortissimo* chords. Effective in performance. Level 10.

IV. For Paul Bowles

Bowles was a composer and close friend of Bernstein. Tightly knit movement presenting five thematic variations over five consecutive appearances of a walking ostinato. Carefree spirit is epitomized. Level 10.

V. In Memoriam: Nathalie Koussevitsky

Bernstein undoubtedly knew Mrs. Koussevitsky well because of his close relationship with the Boston Symphony conductor Serge Koussevitsky. This is perhaps the most beautiful movement in all of the *Anniversaries*. Highly expressive, and built on consonant intervals, with thirds and triads abounding. The linear emphasis and the effective writing make this a convincing elegy. Level 10.

VI. For Serge Koussevitsky

Conductor Serge Koussevitsky held a striking position in the musical development of Bernstein. Bernstein looked upon Koussevitsky as a father figure and a mentor. Dramatic and dissonant outbursts, and changing meters. Thirteen measures long, with many dynamic indications. Level 8.

VII. For William Schuman

Schuman was a gifted American composer and, at that time, a friend of Bernstein. This movement is a mini-toccata based on broken chords between the hands and repeated chords. Similar to some of Ginastera's driving writing, but much easier. Insistent rhythms drive the work to a *fff martellato* ending. Level 10.

Four Anniversaries (1948)

This group works especially well as a set and is probably the most frequently played. It is also the shortest, comprising only nine pages of music. Tempos of the pieces alternate slow, fast, slow, fast. (Jalni.)

I. For Felicia Montealegre

Written for Felicia Montealegre before Bernstein's marriage to her in 1951. She was a Chilean actress who had come to New York to make it on the Broadway stage. Simple and lyrical. Voicing of the inner parts needs attention. Level 10.

II. For Johnny Mehegan

Johnny Mehegan was a jazz pianist in New York. At one point in his life, Bernstein frequently went to a club in Greenwich Village to hear

Mehegan play. Strong jazz influence in this scherzando work. Sudden silences, angular lines and unexpected motivic entrances. Attractive and short. Needs a strong rhythmic command. Level 10.

III. For David Diamond

Diamond, an American composer, became one of Bernstein's closest friends. A two-page work, with every measure on the first page having a different time signature. Lyrical, with wide skips in the melody. Level 9.

IV. For Helen Coates

Coates was Bernstein's first important piano teacher and continued to provide stalwart support and encouragement for Bernstein throughout his life as his personal assistant. A spirited and rhythmic piece. *Sforzando* chords and quick passagework. Level 10.

Five Anniversaries (1949–51)

Written at about the same time as the two other sets but published later. The characters portrayed here seem to hold a less obviously central position in Bernstein's musical and professional development. (Jalni.)

I. For Elizabeth Rudolf

A contemporary version of a "parlor piece." A certain nonchalance is combined with simplicity and warmth. The rhythmic motive unifies this entire *grazioso* selection. Level 9.

II. For Lukas Foss

The composer Lukas Foss studied in the same composition class as Bernstein at Tanglewood in the summer of 1940. Imitative, with irregular phrase lengths and some cross-rhythms. Easy-going and effective with a *scherzando* undercurrent. Level 9.

III. For Elizabeth B. Ehrman

Effusive movement that sparkles with accents on off-beats and quick, nimble sixteenth-note passages in both hands. Strong jazz influence. Some large reaches. Level 9.

IV. For Sandy Gellhorn

Dedicated to the daughter of a friend. Carefree and lighthearted, this piece is permeated by a single, infectious rhythmic motive. Moves from a *pp* opening to a *ff* goal and climax, returning to a *pp* ending. Level 8.

V. For Susanna Kyle

Susanna Kyle was the daughter of Betty Comden, a good friend who collaborated with Bernstein on some musical theater productions. Lyrical and consonant, very brief. The melody sings out over a simple, unadorned accompaniment to pose a peaceful and warm conclusion to the set. Level 8.

13 Anniversaries (1990)

This set follows in the tradition of the earlier sets. Movements are composed both *In Memoriam* and for contemporaries. Various movements are *For My Daughter, Nina; In Memoriam: Helen Coates;* and *In Memoriam: William Kapell.* (Jalni.) Level 10.

SEYMOUR BERNSTEIN (b. 1927) USA

Seymour Bernstein is a noted East Coast composer of children's pieces, a distinguished pedagogue and a concert pianist.

Birds, Set 1

Perhaps the best of his sets. Some pieces are highly impressionistic while others are almost avant-garde. These selections require sensitive pedaling and listening for color, and should be heard more often in performance. See especially *The Purple Finch, The Hummingbird, The Woodpecker, The Penguin* and *The Vulture.* (Schroeder and Gunther.)

No. 1 The Purple Finch

Impressionistic and evocative with some crossed-hand playing. Especially appropriate for a musical student with a strong musical imagination. Level 7.

No. 2 The Hummingbird

Easier than it sounds, and easier to read than it initially appears. Marked *Fast and shimmering,* this effective piece with crossed hands is strongly rhythmic. Perhaps the best in this set. Level 5.

No. 3 The Woodpecker

Short and appealing work with changing meters and rapidly alternating seconds. Level 6.

No. 4 The Sea Gull

Uses a wide keyboard range and requires playing with the fist on grace-note clusters. Dramatic writing, aggressive in character and highly patterned. Level 6.

No. 5 The Chickadee

Biting rhythms and effective passagework with an effective glissando at the end. Level 5.

No. 6 The Vulture

Uses a wide range of the keyboard and dramatic effects. Tone clusters. Level 7.

No. 7 The Penguin

Tuneful and appealing, with an inventive left-hand ostinato that waddles beneath the melody. Level 5.

No. 8 The Eagle

Dramatic work, using a wide range of the keyboard and changing meters. Level 7.

Birds, Set 2

Nine works titled after various birds, and slightly more difficult than Set 1.

No. 1 Myna Bird

A canonic work in which the hands mimic each other. The exact imitations somehow go wrong, especially at the end, where the attempt to "sing" in unison results in strong, amusing dissonance. Level 7.

No. 2 The Swan

The accompaniment figure and the melodic elements are derived from Saint-Saëns' famous selection by the same name. The first six notes of that theme appear backward in the left-hand arpeggio. Contains an effective full-keyboard glissando. Level 8.

No. 3 The Robin

A robin tugs at a worm, only to find out that it is much longer than he anticipated, and that the music almost runs off the keyboard. Alternating-hand passagework and large flourishes appear throughout. Level 7.

No. 4 The Owl

A grace-note slide and its variations represent the bird's hoot. Spooky and effective in performance. Sophisticated writing. Level 7.

No. 5 Roadrunner

A study in finger staccato. The composer states his intention of mimicking the well-known Warner Bros. cartoon character, with the "beep, beep" signature represented by clusters. The performer is called on to tap on the wood of the piano. Level 7.

No. 6 Condor

Needs a big, resonant sound for the large chords and dramatic octave playing. A spell-binding cadenza concludes this majestic and intense two-page piece. Level 8.

No. 7 The Nightingale

Directed to be played as an "old-fashioned love song," this work is permeated with trills and warbling flourishes. A contemporary nocturne, with expansive writing in a relatively slow tempo. Level 8.

No. 8 The Guinea Hen

This piece, like its namesake, is unpredictable and full of wild contrasts. Features clusters played by slapping palms on the keyboard and moving up and down the keyboard. Rapid scale passagework is divided between the hands. Much easier than it sounds. Level 7.

No. 9 Phoenix

One of the most effective movements in the set. Contains a dramatic cluster that is played by slapping the palms on the piano, and concludes with the performer striking the bass strings inside the piano with a pen and then slamming down the keyboard lid while holding the pedal. Ominous left-hand ostinato throughout. Uses the piano as a resonance or echo chamber. Level 7.

Insects, Book 1

This book, as well as *Birds*, Sets 1 and 2, grew out of events of the composer's summers in coastal Maine. Some pieces feature avant-garde effects. (Tetra Music/Broude.)

The Carpenter Ant

This work is a study in coloristic effects. Tone clusters, changing meters and crossed hands. Level 6.

The Mosquito

A highly effective perpetual motion with buzzing effects created by the written-out trills. Much easier than it sounds. Level 6.

The Cockroach

An étude in turning under the thumb. Scale passages. Level 7.

The Centipede

A quick and light work with sixteenth-note passages throughout. Brilliant writing with effective glissandos. Level 9.

Insects, Book 2

Continuation of the series begun in *Insects*, Book 1. (Tetra Music/Broude.)

The Black Fly

This piece evokes the amusing scene of a fly pestering a pianist. The notation omits the barline, and indications in the score call for changes of tempo in keeping with the fly's changing movements. A humorous work with a great deal of extra-pianistic activity including clapping hands, slapping the leg, slapping the neck and so on. Level 8.

The Dying Moth

More difficult than the surrounding movements, calling for a mature musician. The music simulates the death-flutters of a huge moth. Level 8.

The Humbug

Scherzo-like with two ideas that alternate. Level 7.

The Praying Mantis

Numerous fluctuations of tempo. Conveys the story of a preying mantis that lures smaller insects into its clutches. Level 7.

Racoons, Book 1

The story of the composer's "acquaintance" with a racoon during a summer in Maine. The score contains the story in prose, in music and in photographs. The nine single-page pieces include *Swoosh and Crash, Silvery Path, Waiting in the Dark, Beth, Friendship, Crunch! Smack!, Gulp! Gulp!, All Together, Sticky Marshmallows* and *Farewell*. These effective works are appropriate for the sophisticated mind as well as for the nature lover. (Tetra Music.) Level 3.

Racoons, Book 2

The story of the racoons as told through music, text and photos, all by the composer, continues in this volume of 10 one-page pieces. The racoons return to visit the composer during the next summer after the experiences related in *Racoons*, Book 1, and the pieces found here once again describe feelings of the animals and activities they experience. Mildly contemporary writing. The music is at the same level of difficulty as in Book 1. (Tetra/Broude.) Level 3.

Belinda, The Chipmunk

The 12 one-page lower-intermediate pieces in this volume collect observations of the composer about a befriended chipmunk during one Maine summer. An enthralling story accompanied by photos by Bernstein himself prepare the young player for the scene represented in the music. Especially appropriate for the student with a vivid imagination. (Schroeder and Gunther.) Level 4.

Köchel and Sheila

The five solos were inspired by two cats named Köchel and Shiela. The caricatures of their activities depicted in the one-page solos are accompanied by photographs and verbal descriptions of their activities. The pieces are witty, musical, mildly contemporary, and satisfying to play and to hear. (G. Schirmer.) Level 4.

Trees

Subtitled "Five hymns and poems to the miracles of nature," these single-page pieces are accompanied by fine illustrations and short poems. The writing is naive and appealing. Titles include *The Young Maple, The Willow, The Magnolia, The Dying Birch* and *The Sequoias*. Characterized by an often linear yet romantic style, these pieces would be accepted well by the adult student playing at this level or by children interested in nature. (G. Schirmer.) Level 6.

Warbles and Flutters

Volume I of the Earth Music Series, subtitled *An Introduction to the Trill*. Found here are pieces relating directly to the trill, specifically composed to give elementary students trill practice. The trills are often written out and are relatively simple to execute. Detailed explanation precedes the music. The selections become progressively more difficult. Titles include *The Smiling Parakeet, The Good-Natured Blue Jay, The Venetian Swan* and *Fluffing Feathers*. (Broude.) Levels 3–5.

Out of the Nest

Volume II of the Earth Music Series and subtitled *An Introduction to the Mordent*. Pieces found here were composed specially to give elementary students practice in playing mordents, with the ornaments both written into the figuration of the music and indicated by the sign. Detailed and valuable explanation precedes the music. The selections here also become progressively more difficult. Titles include *Out of the Nest, The Waltzing Cow Bird* and *Hymn of the Birds*. (Broude.) Levels 3–5.

Early Birds

Book III of the Earth Music Series, this volume in the set was written to be a young pianist's introduction to the appoggiatura. Extensive preface and commentary precede the ten one-page pieces that present numerous examples of appoggiaturas. The preface thoroughly explains the appoggiatura in language that a young student can understand. Best used in its entirety. Tuneful linear writing. (Schroeder and Gunther.) Level 2.

The Pedals

Book IV of the Earth Music Series. A valuable 15-page introduction to the pedals and their uses on the piano precedes the eight short pieces. This book is valuable for the informative introduction it contains as well as for the pedaled, tuneful writing. (Schroeder and Gunther.) Level 3.

Dragons. The Contemporary Idiom

Book V of the Earth Music Series. The composer whets the imagination of the student for contemporary sounds through a series of pieces about different kinds of dragons. *The Magic Bells* explores sympathetic vibrations, *The Grumpy Dragon* is built on the interval of the fourth, *The Snoring Dragon* features clusters and *The Moaning Dragon* uses chromatic scales. Valuable prefatory material describes the compositional devices and explains their use in each piece. (Schroeder and Gunther.) Level 4.

WALLACE BERRY (b. 1928) USA

Eight 20th-Century Miniatures

Mildly dissonant writing. For the sophisticated ear. Titles found here include *Melody, Folk Song, Polka* and *Ostinato*. (Carl Fischer.) Level 7.

FRANK MICHAEL BEYER (b. 1928) Germany

Avanti

Subtitled *15 Piano Pieces for Young Players*, this collection presents worthy musical writing. This highly contemporary idiom includes unbarred selections and atonal sounds. Chiefly linear, and seems to elicit experimentation with color and sonority from the performer. Not difficult to read. Most selections occupy one to two printed pages. (Schott.) Levels 5–8.

SERGIO BIANCHI (n.d.) Italy

L'Album di...

Contemporary Italian teaching pieces, some of which contain clusters and feature changing meters. (Bèrben.) Levels 5–7.

ANTONIO BIBALO (b. 1922) Italy

Fire Miniaturer

Four short contemporary pieces written in traditional phrase groups. Reflects the influence of Bartók. (Hansen.) Level 8.

JOHN BIGGS (b. 1932) USA

Three Short Pieces

Waltz, Little Fugue and *Polka,* each two pages long. Thin textures, pianistic, mildly contemporary. (Consort Press.) Level 4.

12 Little Études

The hands remain in set positions. Each étude emphasizes a different interval such as the minor second, augmented fourth, perfect fifth, etc. Contemporary sounds with some bitonal writing. The edition is a reproduction of a manuscript copy. (Consort Press.) Level 7.

Three Sonatinas

Subtitled "In the spirit of Clementi." The writing is contemporary within a tonal framework. Reprinted manuscript, and difficult to read. (Consort Press.) Level 7.

GORDON BINKERD (b. 1916) USA

Piano Miscellany

Set of five short upper-intermediate pieces in a contemporary idiom. Fine writing that might be more attractive to adults rather than young students. Titles include *Lake Lonely, Rough-and-Tumble, Something Serious, For the Union Dead* and *Country Dance.* (Boosey.) Level 8.

Entertainments

Character pieces filled with personality and set in a contemporary idiom. Many display gaiety with dissonance that is often biting. Titles include *Brief Encounter, The Trumpet, The Tuba and The Metronome, Tristan and the Magic Broomstick* and *Graceful Exit.* (Boosey.) Level 10.

The Young Pianist

Delightful tonal character pieces. Selections from this set could appear on a competition or festival list for young students and provide fresh teaching repertoire. Titles of some of the 10 pieces include *The Flying Nun, Eaves-Dropping, Busy by One's Self* and *Look-alikes*. (Boosey.) Level 6.

KEITH BISSELL (b. 1912) Canada

Three Preludes for Young Pianists

The first and last prelude are characterized by linear writing, thin textures and mildly dissonant sounds. Level 7.

JEAN BIZET (b. 1924) France

Le Singe Vert

Two-page piece with changing meters and contemporary harmonies in a rhythmic framework. Biting character. (Amphion.) Level 9.

BORIS BLACHER (1903–1975) Germany

Two Sonatinas, Op. 14

Primarily linear writing with thin textures and biting harmonies. (Bote and Bock.) Level 8.

Three Pieces for Piano, Op. 18

Each is two pages and highly individual. These pieces would work well for a student needing light contemporary selections. Highly rhythmic, with signs of jazz influence. (Universal.) Level 9.

HOWARD BLAKE (b. 1938) Great Britain

Eight Character Pieces

Sharply defined characters and palatable harmonies. This volume makes the choice of an effective combination of three or so pieces for a recital possible since so many short pieces are included. See especially the *Rag, Ballad, Toccatina* and *Berceuse*. (Novello.) Level 9.

ARTHUR BLISS (1891–1975) Great Britain

Two Piano Pieces

Inspired by jazz idioms, found here are light character pieces. Titled *"Bliss" One-Step* and *The Rout Trot*, both selections require a performer who can span a tenth. A progressing student who needs light music to help him maintain interest in serious music study might enjoy playing these pieces. (Novello.) Level 9.

ERNEST BLOCH (1880–1959) Switzerland

Bloch began teaching at the Mannes School of Music in New York 1917, and in 1924 became a US citizen. He was a central figure among early 20th-century Jewish composers. His compositional style takes French Impressionism as a point of departure.

Enfantines (1923)

Written for the composer's daughters Suzanne and Lucienne. Each piece represents a moment in a child's experience. They date from the time during which Bloch was serving as director of the Cleveland Institute of Music. Eight of the pieces are dedicated to Cleveland piano teachers and the other two (*Lullaby* and *With Mother*) are dedicated to his daughters. (Carl Fischer.)

No. 1 Lullaby

A work in a serious mood featuring an Aeolian melody with the omitted third. A study in legato playing, this piece requires the holding of one finger while the other fingers of the same hand play a melody above it. Highly expressive. Level 3.

No. 2 Joyous Party

Allegro giocoso theme in Dorian mode permeated with two-note slurs. Requires distinction between various types of accent markings, as well as *portato* playing. Frequent changes of meter. Level 4.

No. 3 With Mother

Expressive melody with a seeming tinge of reminiscence. Study in phrasing requiring legato playing and smooth changing of fingers on a held note. Level 5.

No. 4 Elves

Many swirling arpeggio-like figures. The performer must work to play evenly the divided arpeggio figures that occur between the hands. Left-hand melody needs projection. Level 5.

No. 5 Joyous March

Alternating meters (4/4 and 3/4) need a performer with a strong sense of pulse. Rapid finger changes on the same notes. This work features contrast of legato and staccato touches, as well as chordal playing and energetic writing. Level 6.

No. 6 Melody

Romantic work with sustained *crescendos* and *decrescendos*. A left-hand expressive theme is stated three times, each statement occurring a third lower than the preceding entry. Later the theme is stated three times in the right hand above a chordal accompaniment. Aeolian/Lydian modality. Level 4.

No. 7 Pastorale

Syncopated rhythmic patterns and a somewhat carefree and jovial theme in F Major. Level 4.

No. 8 Rainy Day

Repeated ostinato in the right hand that is reminiscent of rain drops. Melody and accompaniment interchange between hands. Requires the holding of a finger while the other fingers of the same hand are playing. Features *legato* in one hand with different touches in the other. Level 5.

No. 9 Teasing

Programmatic, jovial work, with disjunct writing. Based on a tune built of two descending fourths. Use of dotted rhythms, *portato*, off-beat accents, different types of accent markings and different touches at the same time. Level 5.

No. 10 Dream

An impressionistic tone picture in 9/8 meter using crossed hands. Refined legato playing is needed in both hands. Dorian melody with a series of repeated G Minor chords and some playing with the hands crossed. Level 6.

Ex-Voto (1914)

Bloch's earliest published piano piece. The title refers to a votive offering. Two-page atmospheric solo for a student not ready to play the impressionistic music of the Debussy *Preludes*. (Broude.) Level 9.

Poems of the Sea (1922)

Set of three pieces inspired by verses of Walt Whitman. The titles of the movements evoke pictorial images. Titles include *Waves, Chanty* and *At Sea*. Modal folk-song atmosphere. The final movement is the most difficult. One of the few multi-movement works by Bloch that is not cyclic. (G. Schirmer.) Level 10.

Five Sketches in Sepia (1925)

Dissonant, impressionistic works, all of which are short and expressive. They require musical maturity and control more than technical facility. Effective as a cycle. In five movements, with the *Epilogue* drawing upon themes from the four preceding movements. (G. Schirmer.) Level 10.

Additional Work for Study:
Nirvana

MICHEL BLOCK (b. 1937) Belgium

While born in Antwerp, Block grew up in Mexico where he made his debut with the National Orchestra there. He then studied at the Julliard School of Music and currently resides in the USA.

Un Beau Jour (One Fine Day)

An enticing set of six late-intermediate to early-advanced pieces depicting French scenes and reflective moods. The writing is tuneful in a mildly contemporary idiom. Worth investigating. Movements include *Dis-moi (Tell Me)*, *Te souviens-tu? (Do You Remember?)*, *Autoroute du sud (Highway to the South)*, *Rendez-vous manaué (The Rendezvous We Missed)*, *Viens . . . (Come . . .)* and *L'heure reveé (The Perfect Hour)*. (Alfred.) Levels 9–10.

ESTA DAMESEK BLOOD (b. 1933) USA

Balkan Suite

These four movements are based on the "aksak" rhythms of Balkan folk music. Coming from a Turkish word meaning "uneven," the "aksak" rhythms give these pieces uneven rhythms such as 11/8, 10/8 and so on. These rhythms are infectious, and a student who is drawn to strongly rhythmic motives that are somewhat similar to the repetitive rhythms in some popular music, might enjoy studying one of these pieces. *Macedonian Rhythm* and *Krk* are somewhat easier than the third and fourth pieces, *Syrtos Polyphonikos* and *Bulgar*. (G. Schirmer.) Level 10.

WILLIAM BOLCOM (b. 1938) USA

Monsterpieces (and Others)

Subtitled "An adventure in contemporary music for the piano student," some of these selections are character pieces about monsters and some are about other activities that provoke the imagination. The titles include *The Mad Monster* and *The Sad Monster* as well as *A Boating Tune* and *The Bitty Town*. The pieces are appropriately short to keep the student's attention, yet allow the progressing performer to experience contemporary sounds. The writing is palatable, sometimes almost predictable. The first five are mildly contemporary while the last five explore many more aggressively contemporary techniques.

These fine pieces should appear regularly on lists of required music for competitions and festivals for young students. (Marks.) Level 2.

Seabiscuits Rag

Six pages in cakewalk tempo. This work does not require substantial facility, but the many accidentals may make the reading difficult. (Marks.) Level 9.

BRUNO BONTEMPELLI (b. 1948) France

Miniatures

From the French pedagogical school, a collection of teaching pieces for beginners. The hands remain in set positions and the rhythms are straightforward. These works seem quite dry. (Billaudot.) Level 1.

Touches, Volumes 1 and 2

Volume 1 contains pieces 1–10 while Volume 2 presents pieces 11–18. Primarily linear writing in a mildly contemporary idiom. (Billaudot.) Level 6.

ENZO BORLENGHI (b. 1908) Italy

Sei Pezzi Pianistici

Six character pieces, for the progressing student pianist. Titles include *Preludio, Capriccio, Valzer, Intermezzo, Noveletta* and *Studio*. (Curci.) Level 6.

SIEGFRIED BORRIS (b. 1906) Germany

Bagatelles, Op. 83

Nine pieces with mildly contemporary sonorities. Short, with appeal to the more sophisticated performer. (Heinrichshofen.) Level 7.

SERGEY EDUARDOVICH BORTKIEVICH (1877–1952) Russia

Post-Romantic pianist and composer who lived in both Russia and Austria.

Mélodie. Menuet-Fantasie, Op. 7, No. 1

Traditional writing in the Romantic style. In three sections, slow-fast-slow. This is the kind of piece that might be studied by a student who can play the easiest Chopin waltzes. Lyrical writing that is pedagogically sound and inviting. This might be a good substitute for the often-played Rubinstein *Mélodie*. (Ries and Erler.) Level 9.

Mélodie. Menuet-Fantasie, Op. 7, No. 2

Highly patterned and more extended than the *Mélodie*, No. 1. This selection would be good for a performer needing more experience in developing flair for the Romantic style. The writing is pianistic and of high quality. Nine printed pages in this edition. (Ries and Erler.) Level 9.

The Little Wanderer, Op. 21

Excellent and imaginative collection of teaching pieces similar to the Burgmüller selections in Op. 100. Highly Romantic, and pianistically idiomatic writing. These selections should be better known. (D. Rahter.) Level 5.

A Musical Picture Book, Op. 30

Subtitled *After Andersen's Fairy Tales*, this collection contains 12 titled character pieces in a highly conservative harmonic language. The most interesting are *No. 4, The Angel; No. 9, The Butterfly;* and *No. 12, The Metal Pig*. (D. Rahter.) Levels 7–8.

Marionettes, Op. 54

Nine Russian delightful character pieces. Pianistically solid and potentially valuable for helping young students to develop a flair in Romantic playing. These works deserve a position beside the major teaching works of other Russian composers such as Tchaikovsky and Kabalevsky. (Simrock.)

No. 2 The Cossack

Chordal writing with much repetition and simple melodic ideas that are immediately appealing. A suitable piece for an energetic performer. Level 5.

No. 3 The Spanish Lady

Appealing, Spanish-sounding literature at the elementary level. The *habanera* left-hand accompaniment and the syncopations in the right hand give it strong flavor. Accompaniment that spans a tenth. Calls for an expressive performer. Level 5.

No. 4 The Tirolese

Dance-like, light work with wide jumps and some double notes. This work is appropriate for building strength. Level 6.

No. 5 The Gypsy

Vibrant writing that is immediately appealing, due largely to syncopated, biting appoggiaturas. The performer should adhere to the off-
beat accents in the accompaniment. Effective and little-known.
Level 6.

No. 6 The Marchioness

This *tempo di minuetto* work is a lively and dance-like selection with
single-notes in both hands. Effective contrapuntal writing that
needs projection. Level 5.

No. 9 Punch-Harlequin

Another lively, dance-like work that features various mood changes,
some with tricky rhythmic ideas. Technical coordination of the
hands and the rapid changing of moods may be difficult for some
students. Level 7.

Additional Work for Study:
Op. 14 From My Childhood

KURT BOSSLER (1911–1976) Germany

So bauen wir ein Zwölftonhaus

Highly contemporary set of pieces using set pitches to build a "12-tone
house," gradually increasing the members of the pitch-set for each suc-
ceeding piece. Take-off on Hindemith's *Let's Build a City.* (Impero Verlag.)
Level 8.

WOLFGANG BOTTENBERG (b. 1930) Germany

Moods of the Modes

Five modal teaching pieces based on the theory that each different mode
should have a different character or mood. The writing is some of the
best pedagogical material available for the teaching, hearing and understanding of modes. These pieces are rhythmic, vital and often vigorous,
making the collection one that students will enjoy. It deserves investigation. See especially *Intrada, Dance in Bulgarian Rhythm* and *Rondo.*
Several of these selections would be welcome additions to festival lists.
(Waterloo.) Level 5.

LILI BOULANGER (1893–1918) France

Trois Morceaux pour Piano (1914)

Elegant Impressionistic pieces composed by the sister of Nadia
Boulanger. Especially good for the sensitive student and for the per-

former not yet ready to play the Debussy *Preludes*. Titles are *D'un vieux jardin, D'un jardin clair* and *Cortège*. See especially the first and the second movements. (G. Schirmer.) Level 8.

DEREK BOURGEOIS (b. 1941) Great Britain

Bits and Bytes, Op. 105

Six pieces for the more advanced pianist, written in a pianistic manner within a contemporary idiom. (Fentone.)

Scherzo Grottesco

"Wrong-note" writing in a witty piece. A fine selection for a high school student, and one of the most immediately appealing movements from this set. Level 9.

Arabesque

Slow and graceful work with many arpeggiations divided between the hands. Level 9.

Lugubre

Dissonant, lyrical writing. Level 9.

Frolic

Agile fingerwork is required in this 6/8 romp. The central section presents a mock fugue. One of the most appealing in the set. Level 10.

Things that Might Have Been

Lyrical *adagio mesto* movement, pensive and longing in character. Level 9.

March of the Kilobytes

A mechanical march with "wrong-note" writing and some octave passages. Reminiscent of Shostakovich. Level 10.

PAUL FREDERIC BOWLES (b. 1910) USA

Folk Preludes

Enchanting arrangements of high-quality American folk tunes. Captivating, vivacious and highly pianistic. (Presser.) Level 4.

El Bejuco

Two-page chordal piece based on a folk song. Highly rhythmic and in a "strict, mechanical tempo." (Mercury Music.) Level 10.

Sonatina

Highly rhythmic and containing a driving final movement. (Elkan-Vogel.) Level 10.

Six Preludes

Contemporary dissonant linear writing that is idiomatic to the keyboard. (Mercury.) Level 10.

Additional Works for Study:
El Indio
Huapango Nos. 1 and 2
Two Portraits

ATTILA BOZAY (b. 1939) Hungary

Medailles

Thirty-six exceedingly short avant-garde pieces. Originally intended as a study in the mechanics of composition, and for that reason performers also interested in composing will be interested in these works. Many are only six to eight measures long. (Boosey.) Levels 3–5.

EUGÏENE BOZZA (b. 1905) France

Esquisse

Three-page piece presenting a simple melody and frequently featuring a reverse broken-chord accompaniment. (Leduc.) Level 6.

Promenade dans le parc

Melody with broken chord left-hand accompaniment in a moderate tempo. Thin textures and two printed pages. (Leduc.) Level 4.

MERRILL BRADSHAW (b. 1929) USA

Bradshaw has taught at Brigham Young University in Utah.

Sympathies

Silently depressed right-hand clusters produce overtones while the left hand plays a melody. This kind of innovative writing can enhance a student's listening skills. The long rests must be held their full value. Level 3.

SUSAN BRADSHAW (b. 1931) Great Britain

Eight Hungarian Melodies

Interesting and different literature that is highly rhythmic and which features changing meters. Each piece is approximately one page long. (Chester.) Level 10.

WILLIAM BRANDSE (b. 1923) The Netherlands

Postcards from Holland

Eight imaginative solos, mostly one page long, depicting picture postcards of an interesting Dutch locale frequented by tourists. Moderately contemporary and well-written for the young pianist. These pieces should be better known. Titles include *An Old Abbey, Field of Tulips, The Blue of Delft, Sailing on the Lakes* and *An Old Church*. (G. Schirmer.) Level 4.

HENRY DREYFUS BRANT (b. 1913) Canada

Brant was born in Montreal to American parents, and lived most of his life in the USA.

Four Short Nature Pieces

Thin textures and dissonant melodic writing. (MCA.) Level 6.

CESAR BRESGEN (b. 1913) Italy

Impressions I and II

Though published in 1973, these *Impressions* originated between 1928 and 1930 and were written down improvisations. Some of the pieces which were written in 1929 were collected under the title *November Music* and were used for dancing by Leslie Burrowes under the title "Dances of the Dawn." The pieces have little to do with program music other than No. 17, which was derived from the idea of the motion of a bicycle and No. 21 in 5/8 which was written immediately after a bicycle tour in the North Tyrol. Contemporary writing, often highly rhythmic. Worth investigating. (Gerig/MCA.) Levels 6–8.

Additional Work for Study:
Studies VII Romanesca

HOUSTON BRIGHT (b. 1916) USA

Four for Piano

Upbeat, rhythmic pieces that might captivate the student who thinks he does not like contemporary music. Some tongue-in-cheek writing. *Notion, Invention on a Ground, Quick Dance* and *Finale*. (Associated.) Level 10.

SIR BENJAMIN BRITTEN (1913–1976) Great Britain

One of England's foremost composers.

Walztes [sic], Op. 3 (1923–25)

Five works within a tonal framework. (Faber.) Level 8.

Sonatina Romantica (1940)

Composed for an amateur musician in an attempt to encourage Britten's friend to practice different repertoire. It seems that Britten was tired of hearing him practice the Weber *Invitation to the Dance* over and over. Originally structured in four movements, Britten was dissatisfied with the finale and undertook revisions. Ultimately he left that revision unfinished and rejected the work as a whole. Trustees of the composer's estate felt that the first two movements, *Moderato* and *Nocturne* could be charming and successful and, in 1986, allowed their publication. (Faber.)

Nocturne

> *Cantilena* melody in the A sections is confined to a narrow melodic range. The accompaniment figure consisting of broken chords in the left hand is similar throughout. Two printed pages. Easier than the Chopin nocturnes. Requires the ability to inflect very soft sounds. Level 7.

Moderato ma drammatico

> The sound is highly diatonic, but the zest of Britten's writing is at the forefront. The performer needs flair to bring it off, as well as fluid arpeggios and the ability to contract the hand with ease. Difficult voicing within the hand on the last page. Level 8.

FRANTISEK BRÓZ (1896–1962) Czechoslovakia

Three Capriccios

Generally brilliant writing in a mildly contemporary idiom. No. 1 features effective rhythmic writing in the toccata-like piece. No. 2 is free and passionate. No. 3, *presto giocoso*, is rhythmic and driving and features repeated chords. Motivating writing. (Artia.) Level 10.

DAVE BRUBECK (b. 1920) USA

Themes from Eurasia

Seven pieces written by Brubeck for his young son and based on themes from Brubeck's improvisations on music from different parts of the world. Dissonant contemporary writing. (Shawnee.) Level 7.

Reminiscences of the Cattle Country

A reminiscence of the composer's early days on a ranch. Freely changing meters and many seventh chords, even if not in a full-scale jazz idiom. Written when Brubeck was a student of Milhaud. Titles include *Sun Up*, *Breaking a Wild Horse* and *Dad Plays the Harmonica*. A wide span is needed for some of the stretches. (Associated.) Level 10.

COLIN BRUMBY (b. 1933) Australia

Harlequinade

Set of six pieces named after characters from the Italian *commedia dell'arte*. The background of the *commedia dell'arte* is explained and a description is provided for its characters. Titles are *Arlecchino, Columbina, Dottore Gratiano, Pulcinella, Pantalone* and *Il Capitano*. Spirited contemporary writing within a tonal framework. (Fentone.) Level 10.

ALAN BULLARD (b. 1947) Great Britain

Air and Gigue

Mildly contemporary sounds in a work composed for the clavichord or piano. The *Gigue* fits the hand especially well. (Oxford.) Level 5.

RICHARD BUNGER (b. 1942) USA

Two Pieces for Prepared Piano

Some of the easiest and shortest pieces for prepared piano available. The piano is prepared by inserting a credit card, felt strip, clothespin wedges, screws, rubber erasers, dimes, a bamboo wedge, and vinyl tubing between strings of a piano. Study of these pieces would motivate a student to appreciate new sounds. Effective and imaginative writing. (Highgate Press.) Level 8.

Three Bolts Out of the Blues

Three short, attractive prepared piano pieces (the entire set takes 3 minutes, 40 seconds). Once the strings are prepared, the playing takes place entirely on the keyboard. Felt strips, clothespins, erasers, screws, dimes, and vinyl tubing are used in this appealing set. (Highgate Press.) Level 8.

WILLY BURKHARD (1900–1955) Switzerland

Was die hirten alles erlebten

Modal arrangements of Christmas tunes for children. Manuscript reproduction in this edition. (Bärenreiter.) Level 1.

Eight Easy Piano Pieces

Short, linear and dissonant pieces for elementary-level pianists. (Bärenreiter.) Level 3.

11 Little Pieces for Piano, Op. 31

Neo-Classical, dissonant and linear. (Bärenreiter.) Level 5.

Additional Work for Study:
Kleine Toccata

GEOFFREY BUSH (b. 1920) Great Britain

Toccata

Highly patterned, lively and tuneful writing in an accessible toccata with the rhythm of a gigue. Worth investigating. (Galaxy.) Level 8.

FELIKS BYBICKI (b. 1899) Poland

I Begin to Play

Tonal pieces for beginning students. Many finger numbers are included. This music stresses the development between the independence between the hands and features writing that is idiomatic to the keyboard. Bold, colorful pictures make this volume attractive for the young student. The one-page selections are titled. (PWM.) Levels 1–2.

C

JOHN CAGE (1912–1993) USA

Cage was an experimental composer/philosopher, highly regarded in avant-garde circles. The importance of his innovations may exceed the compositions themselves.

A Valentine Out of Season

Subtitled "Music for Xenia to play on a Prepared Grand Piano." Found here are three very short pieces, in sparse notation and with thin textures, to be played on prepared piano. The preparation includes the use of rubber, weather stripping, slit bamboo, pennies, bolts and wood. Much more sophisticated musically than technically. (Henmar/Peters.) Level 2.

Additional Work for Study:
Suite for Toy Piano

R. CALABRESE (n.d.) Italy

Miniature

Four short pieces in a highly contemporary neo-Classical idiom. (Curci.) Level 8.

LOUIS CALABRO (b. 1926) USA

Five for a Nickel Pie

Perhaps Calabro's most appealing pedagogical writing. Some dissonance. (Elkan-Vogel.) Level 2.

Young People's Sonatine

Three short movements of moderately dissonant writing. The third movement features changing meters, often with every measure. (Elkan-Vogel.) Level 4.

Suite of Seven

Seven short pieces, mostly one page long. Lyrical writing within a dissonant framework. (Elkan-Vogel.) Level 5.

Diversities

Well-written selections for the advancing pianist, composed within a dissonant framework. These selections contain some intricate rhythms and wide stretches. (Elkan-Vogel.) Level 8.

CHARLES CAMILLERI (b. 1931) Great Britain

Berceuse and Out of School

Pedagogically sound pieces for the beginner. Berceuse deals with legato playing while *Out of School* features staccato playing and some two-note slurs. (Robertson.) Level 1.

Petite Suite

Three movements, the first of which leaves the duration of the notes to the performer. The second movement has no barlines and is marked "gently flowing." The last movement is playful and strongly rhythmic, with some biting seconds. In a much stronger contemporary idiom than other teaching works by Camilleri, this short suite can be a feasible introduction to various avant-garde compositional techniques. (Robertson.) Level 3.

Sonatina Classica

Tonal writing in a work that is highly melodic. This sonatina would be especially appropriate for the student who enjoys predictable phrases and light music. Its study could precede the easiest sonatinas by Clementi. (Robertson.) Level 4.

Pieces for Anya

Light, traditional harmonies, rhythmic buoyancy, and enjoyable music. These selections would be interesting additions to a contest or festival list. Titles include *A Carol of Charms, A Sad Folk-Song, Morning Playtime* and *A Tender Melody*. (Robertson.) Level 5.

Little African Suite

Inspired by African music and based on traditional melodies, the movements of *Little African Suite* generally feature strong rhythms and appealing writing. Deserves to be played more often. (Robertson.) Level 5.

Due Canti

Two selections. *Cantilena* would be suited for a student wanting to play nocturne-like pieces but not ready for the standard literature. Romantic tonal framework. *Arabesque* is filled with flourishes and "turns." A student will need a good sense of pulse. (Robertson.) Level 7.

Three African Sketches

Strong rhythms and animated writing in attractive pieces. The third piece, *Lament for an African Drummer*, is based on a left-hand ostinato in 5/8. (Robertson.) Level 7.

Additional Works for Study:
Op. 9 Five Children's Dances
Little English Suite
Four Pieces for Young Pianists
Chemins

HENRI CAROL (n.d.)

Drôleries, Set 1

Twelve short teaching pieces, reminiscent of the Tansman *Pour les Enfants*. Predictable phrase lengths abound in these generally light-hearted pieces. (Delrieu.) Level 6.

Drôleries, Set 2

Twelve further pieces, all composed within a tonal framework and more difficult than those in the first set. Many are light and dance-like, if insubstantial. (Delrieu.) Level 8.

ROBERT CASADESUS (1899–1972) France

Six Enfantines, Op. 48

Lyrical teaching pieces. The writing is pianistic, but the harsh dissonances could discourage some early-level performers. (Durand.) Level 5.

ALFREDO CASELLA (1883–1947) Italy

Casella studied with Fauré and taught piano at the Paris Conservatory, at Santa Cecilia in Rome, and in Siena. He also founded the Italian Society for Modern Music in 1917. Debussy, Stravinsky and Mahler influenced Casella. He writes in a neo-Classical style.

Children's Pieces (Pièces Enfantines), Op. 35 (1920)

Pieces in varying levels of difficulty, with some in an Impressionistic idiom and more highly contemporary in sound. Most are in fast tempos and several employ ostinatos. See especially *No. IV, Bolero; No. VI, Siciliana;* and *No. IX, Carillon. No. III, Canone* and *No. VI, Carillon* are the most difficult. (Universal.)

I. Preludio

Appealing, bitonal writing with the right hand playing the black keys and the left hand playing on the white. Ostinato fourths provide the left-hand accompaniment to the simple *grazioso* right-hand melody. Level 5.

III. Canone

Two-voice canon, highly sectional, played entirely on the black keys. This work requires a competent legato. Level 5.

IV. Bolero

Highly rhythmic writing with ostinato patterns. The left-hand ostinato lends a strong and appealing Spanish flavor to one of the best pieces in this set. Level 5.

VI. Siciliana

Rhythmic and lyrical selection with a melancholy melody. The chords in the accompaniment repeat often. Level 4.

VII. Giga

Energetic writing in Lydian mode. Needs a pianist with flair. Driving rhythm in a work worth investigating. Level 6.

IX. Carillon

Ostinato accompaniment figures and bitonal writing with the right hand playing the white keys, and the left hand the black. Mostly *pp* and *ppp* playing in a work that calls for strong finger independence. Interesting and different. Level 7.

X. Berceuse

Care needs to be taken to sustain the long phrases in this Lydian work. Ostinato fifths in the accompaniment and long right-hand phrases. Level 5.

XI. Galop Final

A brilliant movement that calls for strong finger facility and concludes with a large chord. Effective and unusual in performance, especially appropriate for the student with flair. Level 6.

Additional Works for Study:
Op. 32 Inezie

JACQUES CHAILLEY (b. 1910) France

Sketchbook

Subtitled "20 Easy Pieces for Piano," the first 10 pieces are based on French folk songs while the last 10 are original works. Pianistic, mildly contemporary and strong writing. Study of these pieces would be appropriate especially for someone needing extra practice in working with thicker textures such as four-part harmonies. Tuneful and upbeat. (Salabert.) Level 5.

CLAUDE CHAMPAGNE (1891–1965) Canada

Quadrilha Brasileria

Rhythmic and exciting. The repeated chords help sustain the drive necessary for the build-up at the end. (BMI Canada.) Level 10.

Prelude et Filigrane, Op. 4 and Op. 5

Mildly contemporary writing that is pianistic and somewhat neo-Romantic. No fast fingerwork appears. (BMI Canada.) Level 9.

THEODORE CHANDLER (1902–1961) USA

A Child in the House

A set of 10 titled movements in a mildly contemporary idiom, some of which feature changing meters. See especially *No. 2, Mooning* with its unusual phrases that seem to wander as if the performer is in a daze. *No. 6, Being Naughty* is a humorous work filled with "wrong-note" writing, false starts and surprises in a ABA' form. (Mercury.) Level 7.

Toccata

Running passages that are sometimes awkward require dependable fingers. Often the writing presents sixteenth-notes against eighths in the other hand in a two-voice framework. An appropriate choice for a student who wants to play a toccata, but who cannot maintain the endurance of one where the passagework is incessant. Here the alternation between the hands eliminates this problem. (Mercury.) Level 9.

CARLOS CHÁVEZ (1899–1978) Mexico

Mexico's most famous composer is also well-known as an orchestra conductor. Many of his works are experimental.

Valses Moderato

These two pleasant pieces might be performed by a pianist able to play the easiest Chopin waltzes. Both waltzes are two pages long and worthy of performance. (Carlantia/G. Schirmer.) Level 9.

Cakewalk

This two-page piece is suited for a pianist who would like to play rags but who is not quite ready for music with many left-hand skips. Fractional harmonic framework. (Carlantia/G. Schirmer.) Level 8.

10 Preludes

The writing is highly linear and dissonant, often modal. Fine for a pianist with a small reach. (G. Schirmer.) Level 10.

Early Piano Pieces, Volume 1 (1918–1920), ed. by Lifchitz

Contains early-advanced pieces that are, according to the editor, "rooted in the Romantic 'salon' tradition." See especially *Esperanza Ingenua, Pensamiento Feliz, Berceuse, Inocencia* and *Berceuse*. (Carlantia Music Co.) Levels 8–9.

ERIC COATES (1886–1957) England

Six Short Pieces (without octaves)

These highly romantic selections would work well with adults. They fit the hand well and are an interesting change from better-known fare. See especially the first, *Prelude*, which is a good right-hand finger study in sixteenth-notes. (Masters.) Level 6.

SAMUEL COLERIDGE-TAYLOR (1875–1912) Great Britain

British composer of African descent.

Negro Melodies, Op. 59

According to the composer, Coleridge-Taylor tried to do for these Negro melodies "what Brahms has done for the Hungarian folk music, Dvořák for the Bohemian, and Grieg for the Norwegian *tema con variazioni*." (Da Capo.)

No. 2 The Stones Are Very Hard

Perhaps the easiest of the selections included in this volume, this piece might be played by students almost ready to play Romantic literature like the Chopin waltzes. Features skips in the left hand and full chords. Level 8.

No. 8 The Bamboula

Rhythmic, highly diatonic and motivating. This would be appropriate for a student who plays chordal pieces well. *The Bamboula* sounds more difficult than it is and features a *fortissimo* ending. Level 9.

No. 10 Deep River

In the Romantic tradition, this effective version of the well-known spiritual builds to large climaxes and uses the full resources of the piano. Level 10.

No. 23 Steal Away

Full-blown arrangement, skillfully paced with impressive climaxes and resonant piano sounds. Level 10.

FRANZ CONSTANT (b. 1910) Belgium

For the Youth

Five easy, mildly contemporary pieces, full of character. Titles include *A Little Tale, Dreaming, Dance, Little Steps* and *Folk Song*. (Metropolis.) Level 3.

ARNOLD COOKE (b. 1906) Great Britain

Suite in C

Neo-Classic writing in a three-movement work, *Capriccio, Sarabande* and *Finale.* (Oxford.) Level 9.

Dance of the Puppets

Attractive selection in a quasi-Shostakovich style, featuring unexpected harmonies and an interesting rhythmic layout. (Ricordi.) Level 8.

JAMES FRANCIS COOKE (1875–1960) USA

Mastering the Scales and Arpeggios

An extensive compendium of scales and arpeggios in their written-out versions. Includes double thirds, double sixths, octaves, arpeggio variants, chromatic scales with various fingerings, and so on. Extensive commentary is provided, but quite dated. (Presser.) Level 9.

PAUL COOPER (b. 1929) USA

Cycles

Twelve short pieces for intermediate students, featuring contemporary techniques such as spatial notation, indeterminate repetitions, clusters, etc. Expressive miniatures with much of the writing indicated in the soft dynamic range and requiring a sensitive ear. Especially appropriate for university composition students. Writing of high quality and strong inspiration. (Chester.) Level 7.

Additional Work for Study:
Changes (1973)

AARON COPLAND (1900–1991) USA

Copland may be the quintessential American classical composer of this century. He exerted a strong influence on American music, creating a unique sound that blends folk, jazz and classical idioms.

Down a Country Lane

Composed by Copland specifically for young piano students and first published in *Life Magazine* in 1962. Two pages of gently flowing music, and modest in demands. Might be studied by a performer who wants to play Impressionistic music. Has a nostalgic quality. (Boosey.) Level 4.

The Young Pioneers

Strongly rhythmic writing, deriving much of its interest from the 7/8 meter, with occasional metrical shifts. To be performed with sparkle and vitality. (Carl Fischer.) Level 4.

Sunday Afternoon Music

Two-page intermediate solo built around two harmonies, and slow in tempo. Impressionistic. (Carl Fischer.) Level 5.

In Evening Air

This piece came about when the Scribner Music Library commissioned a piece from Copland in 1966. He used a leftover tune from the documentary film *The Cummington Story*, arranged it for piano, and titled it *In Evening Air* after a poem by American poet Theodore Roethke.

Contains key shifts, parallel motion in open fifths and syncopation. Because Copland liked the poem so much, he chose a few lines to have printed in the score. This work needs rhythmic control and careful attention to the frequently changing meters. (Boosey.) Level 5.

Midsummer Nocturne

A two-page mood piece with some double notes in the right hand and right-hand skips near the end. Marked *"Slowly and poetically (and somewhat thoughtful)."* (Boosey.) Level 7.

Midday Thoughts

According to the composer, *"Midday Thoughts* is based on sketches for the slow movement of a projected *Ballade* for piano and orchestra."* Strains of the folk idiom in Copland here sound somewhat akin to parts of *Appalachian Spring*. (Boosey.) Level 7.

Proclamation

This work is more dissonant than *Midday Thoughts*. Thick textures abound, leading to a *fff* ending. Some tempo changes. (Boosey.) Level 7.

Our Town

This work contains three excerpts from the film score Copland wrote to *Our Town*. Copland arranged these movements himself. (Boosey.) Level 7.

Sentimental Melody

Subtitled *Slow Dance*, this two-page piece is bluesy and not difficult. Seldom played, and potentially motivating. (Schott.) Level 7.

The Cat and the Mouse (Scherzo Humoristique) (1920)

One of Copland's best-known piano pieces. The music depicts such activities as stalking, scampering, a mocking dance and more. Effective program music for the high school student. Requires a fluid keyboard technique. Copland's first published composition. (Boosey and Hawkes.) Levels 8–9.

Three Moods

Strong contrasts in these works make the entire set effective in performance. A fine introduction to Copland's writing. *Embittered* features dissonant chords and rhythmic writing, aptly reflecting that emotion. *Wistful* is nostalgic and lyrical. *Jazzy* is in a fox-trot tempo and gives an animated conclusion to the set. (Boosey.)

I. Embittered

An animated work building to a powerful climax. Many short sections and charged with emotion. Level 8.

II. Wistful

Somewhat impressionistic, with a repetitive left hand. A pleasant and atmospheric work for the performer who is not yet ready to play Debussy. Meter changes from 4/4 to 3/4. Level 8.

III. Jazzy

For performers attracted to jazz and who have a strong sense of rhythm. The work is filled with dotted syncopated rhythms, triplets and interval reaches of a seventh. The lyrical section reminds one of Gershwin. The left-hand chords jump quickly from the bass to treble register. Level 9.

Four Piano Blues

A work of moderate length and difficulty. Full harmonies and strong syncopations. Movements are titled *Freely Poetic, Soft and Languid, Muted and Sensuous* and *With Bounce*. (Boosey.)

No. 1 (Freely Poetic)

Appealing improvisational writing that is lyrical. Contains some wide stretches. Level 8.

No. 2 (Soft and Languid)

Spiced with "wrong notes." The grace notes in the thirds of the main theme lend a lazy feeling to this summer-day, bluesy piece. Level 9.

No. 3 (Muted and Sensuous)

Subtle metric changes from 4/4 to 7/8 to 6/8 and so on. Dedicated to American pianist William Kapell. Level 8.

No. 4 (With Bounce)

The only really fast movement in this set, featuring syncopated passages that lend a true jazzy flavor. Left-hand chords span a tenth. Flatted seventh ending. Level 9.

Passacaglia (1922)

Eight-bar theme treated in a variety of textures. Effective in performance. Lyrical writing with a huge climax. Dedicated to Copland's composition teacher Nadia Boulanger. (Salabert.) Level 10.

Miscellaneous Volume

Piano Album

A valuable collection, especially for instructor reference, containing many of the easier pieces by Copland. Includes *Petit Portrait, Down a Country Lane, Midsummer Nocturne, In Evening Air, Sentimental Melody, The Resting Place on the Hill, The Young Pioneers, Sunday Afternoon Music,* etc. (Boosey.) Levels 4–9.

ARMANDO ANTHONY (CHICK) COREA (b. 1941) USA

Children's Songs (20 Pieces for Keyboard)

Composed by the American jazz-rock pianist between 1971 and 1980 to convey, in Corea's words, "simplicity as beauty as represented in the spirit of a child." Probably not intended to be played by children, but to evoke childhood. Sections 1–15 were composed for the Fender Rhodes electronic keyboard and 16–20 for the acoustic piano. Traces of jazz and a strong rhythmic structure pervade in this mesmerizing repertoire. (Schott.) Levels 8–10.

JEAN COULTHARD (b. 1908) Canada

A native of Vancouver and a distinguished Canadian composer, Coulthard has made significant contributions in educational music.

Pieces for the Present

Character pieces, many of them only two pages long. Some are quasi-impressionistic and might be profitably studied before Debussy. (Waterloo.) Levels 7–8.

Four Piano Pieces

Much easier than *Pieces for the Present,* these miniatures with strongly contrasting personalities are fine contemporary pieces that should appear on a contest or festival list to help encourage their performance. (BMI.) Level 4.

Additional Works for Study:
White Caps

STEPHEN COVELLO (b. 1924) USA

The Little Avant-Garde, Books 1 and 2

A beginning method using a unique system of pictorial notation and an abbreviated staff. The reading moves to traditional notation at the end of Book 2. (Schroeder and Gunther.) Levels 1–2.

Echoes and Images, Book 1

A series of pieces for the beginner, with each piece covering a specific problem in an overall plan to encourage students to read proficiently. The well-constructed works are arranged in pedagogical order. An excellent introduction to contemporary music. (Schroeder and Gunther.) Level 1.

Echoes and Images, Book 2

Composed to expose the piano student to a wide range of musical styles, textures and harmonies, the pieces contain various compositional devices such as bitonality, modality, counterpoint and harmonies based on whole tones, fourths, fifths and tone clusters. The writing is tuneful within a mildly contemporary idiom. These pieces deserve more recognition. (Schroeder and Gunther.) Level 2.

HENRY COWELL (1897–1965) USA

Often considered one of the American fathers of 20th century music, Cowell's many innovations for piano include the use of tone clusters and ways to manipulate the piano strings directly.

The Irishman Dances

Two-page solo featuring highly rhythmic writing and some dance-like skips in the left hand. (Carl Fischer.) Level 4.

Two Woofs

Two one-page bitonal pieces. These selections would be suitable ones to use to introduce bitonality. (Merion.) Level 6.

Amerind Suite

The title represents "American Indian" and the suite is built around customs and ceremonials of Indian tribes. In three movements: *The Power of the Snake, The Lover Plays His Flute* and *Deer Dance*. This piece holds many possibilities for different methods of performance. (Shawnee Press.) Levels 7–10.

The Snows of Fuji-Yama

Three-page piece that features tone clusters played with the flat of the hand or with the forearm, depending on the length of the cluster. One hand outlines an *andante* melody in octaves while the other hand plays the melody in octaves with the clusters filled in. The primary difficulty stems from correctly defining the melody while playing the clusters. (Associated.) Level 9.

Piano Music, Volume 1

Perhaps his best-known collection of pieces. Several of these pieces would make effective recital fare. (Associated.)

The Tides of Manaunaun (1912)

Features clusters played with the palm and the forearm in the bass underneath the melody played by the right hand. Big, dramatic climaxes. The coordination of the clusters and the melodic playing is not as easy as it first appears, but the work is effective and playable. Dynamics range from *ppp* to *ffff* within the two-page piece. Mananaun was the Irish god of motion, who supposedly sent tremendous tides sweeping through the universe. Based on the Irish mythological poems of John O. Varian. Level 10.

The Banshee (1925)

This "ghostly" piece is played on the open strings of the grand piano with the player standing in the bend of the instrument. Calls for an ear for different sonorities and vivid imagination in interpretation. Requires a second person or an object to hold down the damper pedal. A banshee is a ghost-like woman who comes at the time of a death to take back the soul into the inner world. Level 10.

Aeolian Harp (1923)

To be played by strumming the strings of the piano with one hand while the other hand silently depresses chords indicated in the score. This piece requires the performer to listen carefully to sonorities. An Aeolian harp is a tiny wind harp that children make of silk threads stretched across an arched twig. The silken strings provide faint sounds, according to the force of the wind. Level 9.

Additional Works for Study:

Anger Dance

Bounce Dance (Merion)

The Irish Minstrel Sings

Sway Dance (Merion)

Pegleg Dance

PAUL CRESTON (1906–1985) USA

Creston was a pianist and organist, serving during much of his career as a church organist in New York City. He later taught at Central Washington State College. His music is characterized by strong melodic lines and frequent use of dissonance.

Five Little Dances, Op. 24

Set of short important pieces with only one or two ideas explored in a given dance. Folklike quality, use of modes and ostinato basses. (G. Schirmer.)

No. 1 Rustic Dance

Marked by Creston to be played "heavily," this piece is one of the most appealing of the set and features extreme and sudden changes of tempo. This work is composed in ABA form with detached and rugged A sections contrasting with the more lyrical B section. Captivating ostinato in the A section consisting of open fifths. Both hands are limited to the stretch of a sixth. Level 4.

No. 2 Languid Dance

Syncopated rhythms with a flowing left hand. Level 4.

No. 3 Toy Dance

The right-hand melody is staccato with frequent slurred measures, while the left hand plays staccato quarter notes outlining triads throughout. Extreme and sudden changes of dynamics. Level 4.

No. 4 Pastorale Dance

Berceuse-like work with an extended legato and an arpeggiated bass line that makes it a good pre-nocturne study. One of the most lyrical of the set. Requires fine control of soft sounds and legato in both hands. The largest interval in the right hand is a seventh. Level 4.

No. 5 Festive Dance

In a lively, rhythmic 9/8. Left hand maintains the same rhythmic pattern throughout. This selection is appropriate for a performer who does not move around the keyboard with ease, since the position shifts are limited. Level 5.

Five Two-part Inventions, Op. 14

Filled with highly dissonant linear writing, these works should be studied by performers who can play the Bach inventions with ease and who have an ear for contemporary dissonance. (Seesaw Music.) Level 9.

Six Preludes, Op. 38 (1949)

Diatonic melodies with some bichordal harmonies. Frequently found are harmonically complex ostinato accompaniment figures. This set of preludes studies various methods of rhythmic structure. (MCA.) Level 10.

Prelude and Dance No. 1, Op. 29, No. 1 (1942)

Prelude begins majestically with the melody in the left hand ornamented with lush chords and flamboyant gestures. Marked "Liltingly," the *Dance* begins softly, increasing in loudness and tempo, and then relaxes. The *Dance* is in an expressive jazz style, and much rhythmic drive and flair are required. Strongly rhythmic, powerful and effective writing. (Mercury Music.) Level 10.

Prelude and Dance No. 2, Op. 29, No. 2

Dramatic composition that opens with a meditative *Prelude* preceding the impassioned *Dance*. Marked "with passion," the rhythmic and melodic ideas are repeated often. This would be an effective work to conclude a recital. (Mercury Music.) Level 10.

Romanza, Op. 110

Lyrical neo-Romantic writing. A fine contemporary nocturne. (Music Graphics.) Level 10.

D

JEAN-MICHEL DAMASE (b. 1928) France

Toccatine

A little-known toccata which features chords alternating between the hands similar to those in Pinto's *Run! Run!* but slightly more difficult. *Pianissimo* ending. Effective and not as difficult as it appears. (Lemoine.) Level 8.

Pièces Brèves

Interesting literature with strong contrasts between the four untitled movements. The first movement is a dance-like selection, the second lyrical, the third is a *scherzando* presto movement and the fourth a driving *allegro vivo*. This volume provides a fine choice of contemporary literature for a student needing a short set or wanting to choose selected movements. (Lemoine.) Level 9.

PETER MAXWELL DAVIES (b. 1934) Great Britain

Stevie's Ferry to Hoy

Three one-page pieces: *Calm Water, Choppy Seas* and *Safe Landing.* The writing is mildly dissonant and the music highly descriptive. (Boosey.) Level 4.

Farewell to Stromness and Yesnaby Ground

According to the composer, these pieces "are piano interludes from 'The Yellow Cake Revue,' a sequence of cabaret style numbers . . . ." Stromness and Yesnaby are both villages in the rugged North Sea Orkney Islands. *Farewell to Stromness* features a rocking, syncopated accompaniment and lyrical melody offset by a central syncopated triadic section. *Yesnaby Ground* is built on a six-measure ground with a florid soprano melody. (Boosey.) Level 8.

CLAUDE DEBUSSY (1862–1918) France

One of the most original and influential musical geniuses, Debussy essentially created a one-person revolution. Debussy's music epitomized the concept of Impressionism in music, with the origin of Impressionism stemming from the Impressionistic art of Monet, Manet, Renoir and others. Impressionistic music tended to hint at an idea rather than state boldly, and to feature color and atmosphere over Germanic clarity. Almost all that he composed for piano is of high quality and is still played.

Danse Bohémienne (1881)

An early neo-Classical work. Agile fingerwork is required to negotiate the right-hand movement on the keyboard and the voicing of melody and accompaniment in that same hand. Does not require the musical maturity equal to some later Debussy works. (Many standard editions.) Level 9.

Two Arabesques (1888)

These pieces were among the earliest and most popular works composed by Debussy. Debussy was known to use the term "arabesque" loosely, even applying it to his own *Prélude à l' après-midi d'un faune*. (Many standard editions.)

Arabesque No. 1 in E Major

Lyrical writing characterized by elegance, continually a favorite with performers of all ages. The fingering for the right hand in the three-against-two passages needs careful planning. The concept of an arabesque is revealed in the curving patterns that are repeated throughout the work. Excessive sentimentality should be avoided. Level 8.

Arabesque No. 2 in G Major

An appealing scherzo with a Mendelssohnian wit and featuring many rapid changes of melodic contour. Requires agile finger facility and a delicate touch. Level 9.

Rêverie (1890)

Contains an elegantly beautiful melody that is set in a Chopinesque texture. It was published without Debussy's approval, and Debussy considered it a work of little quality. The melody has a certain ageless charm. An appropriate substitute for the *Claire de lune*. Left-hand arpeggiations require a fine control of nuance. The final A' section will need attentive listening so that the alternation of melodic pitches between the hands is indiscernible. (Many standard editions.) Level 9.

Suite Bergamasque (1890)

The inspiration for this work probably came from a group of poems entitled *Fêtes galantes* by Verlaine. The word "bergamasque" appears in the poem and there indicates the use of grotesque, colorful costumes. This represents Debussy's attempt to recapture the elegance, charm and delicacy of the music of bygone days of the French court. Infrequently played as an entire set, though its movements have achieved popularity as separate pieces. Movements are *Prélude, Menuet, Clair de lune* and *Passepied*. (Many standard editions.)

Prélude

Brilliant and improvisatory in the opening but requires careful attention to rhythmic intricacies. This movement is in standard sonata
form. Suitable for building strong fingers through the right-hand passagework and double-note figures. Level 10.

Clair de lune

Probably Debussy's most popular piano work, more difficult than
many perceive. Needs careful attention to voicing, color, rhythmic
accuracy and the many markings in the score. Many different ideas
within the piece. Has been sentimentalized for years, but is deserving of its popularity. Level 10.

Passepied

Constant activity in an accompaniment consisting of non-legato
eighths throughout. Requires substantial skill in inflecting short
motives and in varying the color. Level 10.

Nocturne in D-flat (1890)

Romantic writing with many different ideas to mold into a whole. The
work is flowing, with many arpeggiations, some rhythmic intricacies
and voicing within a single hand. The closing measures are particularly
powerful. Should be performed by those students already adept at voicing and control of rhythmic subdivisions. Grand writing if not particularly inspired. (Marks and many standard editions.) Level 10.

Ballade (1890)

Somewhat repetitious melodically, but contains traces of arpeggios later
found in the *Toccata* of *Pour le piano*, and an early form of a theme the composer later used in *La plus que lente*. (Many standard editions.) Level 10.

Valse Romantique (1890)

A very early work of Debussy, not among his most profound works. Uses
many seventh and ninth chords. Chopinesque. (Peters and other editions.) Level 9.

Pour le Piano (1901)

In three movements: *Prélude, Sarabande* and *Toccata*. The final movement is much more difficult than the two other movements, and is
omitted from discussion here. (Many standard editions.)

Prélude

Highly rhythmic, perpetual-motion writing that features a syncopated chordal middle section with glissandos. Strong fingers and an awareness of color are required. Level 10.

Sarabande

Slow and somber writing in a work with thick textures and parallel chords. Requires fine control of nuance. Level 10.

Morceau de Concours (1904)

This little-known work was composed for the French periodical *Musica*. Six unknown pieces by different composers were printed in the magazine, and readers were invited to guess each composer.

Marked "somewhat animated and quite rhythmic," the short piece is playful and lively. It would be an interesting addition to a contest list or for a festival. (Durand.) Level 9.

Children's Corner (1906–1908)

These pieces were inspired by childhood, but are not necessarily meant to be played by children. The simplicity masks quiet humor, fantasy and a sense of play. Debussy uses reduced textures, and clear, open sounds. His daughter Chouchou was only three at the time this set was dedicated to her. She had an English nanny and this could be a reason for the English titles. Several of the movements were inspired by Chouchou's toys. (Many standard editions.)

Doctor Gradus ad Parnassum

Calls for brilliant fingerwork and an ear for color. This work is full of humor and makes fun of the finger exercises in the Clementi *Gradus ad Parnassum*. Debussy wrote that it "should not be thought of as a virtuoso piece, nor should the touch necessarily be brittle or percussive." Effective in performance and extremely popular. Level 8.

Jimbo's Lullaby

Jimbo, an elephant, was one of Chouchou's favorite stuffed toys. Jimbo is supposedly being told a bedtime story through this music. Debussy uses the low registers of the keyboard, and seems to reveal the soul of the elephant more than to portray the elephant's physical being. The first phrase of a popular children's lullaby appears in quotation. His daughter Chouchou and Debussy's bad English ("Jumbo," not "Jimbo") influenced the title of the lullaby. Level 8.

Serenade of the Doll

Open fourths and fifths seem to depict the mechanical movements of a doll. This work portrays a song sung to Chouchou's doll. Features hand crossings and sharp dynamic contrasts. Level 8.

The Snow Is Dancing

A kind of *pp* toccata in which a dry touch is called for to capture the pointillism of the figuration. Much of this is to be played quite softly and staccato, and the entire dynamic range of the piece is *ppp* to *mp*. The many sixteenth-notes in this piece may represent dancing snowflakes. Level 9.

The Little Shepherd

Alternates a free, quasi-improvised panpipe tune section with a more rhythmic dance-like section. Contains many mood changes and some difficult rhythms. Level 8.

Golliwog's Cakewalk

Shows the influence of jazz on European music. Golliwog was a humorous black doll that was popular in Europe at this time, as also were American minstrel songs and ragtime. The jazzy rhythm with many syncopations needs to be strict in the first section. This work contains Debussy's parody quotation from Wagner's opera *Tristan und Isolde*, beginning in measure 61. Here is found a motive from the introduction to Act I of the famous opera, accompanied by the notation "avec une grande émotion" (with great emotion). The jerky dance-like movements, sudden stops and starts, strong accents and extreme dynamic contrasts provide abundant humor in a highly effective work. (Alfred.) Level 8.

Le petit Nègre (1909)

A miniature version of *Golliwog's Cakewalk* and perhaps the most accessible of Debussy's piano pieces. Two strongly contrasting moods, with an appealing syncopated opening theme. Witty and good-natured writing, with roots in American jazz. Outmoded, unfortunate title: "The Little Negro." (Alfred and other standard editions.) Level 8.

Hommage à Haydn (1909)

Composed in response to a call for pieces to honor the centenary of Haydn's death. The theme is based on the letters of Haydn's name, as devised by Debussy. The piece has a slow introduction followed by a quicker section. (Many standard editions.) Level 10.

La plus que lente (1910)

Composed in 1910, Debussy actually wrote this piece to poke fun at a popular song titled *La valse lente (Slow Waltz)*. Debussy's result, even with humorous intentions, is this delightful and slow (i.e., "slower than slow") waltz. The score appears to be more difficult to read than the music is to play. Needs careful work in voicing the thick texture and in following the subtle rubato written into the score. (Curci and other standard editions.) Level 10.

Preludes, Book 1 (1910)

Significantly, Debussy placed the title at the end of each of the 12 preludes. It is thought that he preferred to reveal the titles only at the end so as not to intrude upon the music. (Many standard editions.)

Danseuses de Delphes (Dances of Delphi)

Inspired by a group of three dancers as seen on a sculpted fragment from a Greek temple. Debussy saw the reproduction in the Louvre. He first performed this Prelude in 1910, playing it slowly. The step-wise chromatic melody in the alto should always be played as legato as possible. The atmosphere should be one of solemn dignity. Level 10.

Des pas sur la neige (Footsteps in the Snow)

Great calm pervades this melancholy piece. Two elements permeate the work: a rhythmically consistent ostinato representing the footsteps in the snow, and a melodic theme, unchanging in its mood of stillness. Strong contrast exists between these two elements. Level 10.

La Fille aux cheveux de lin (The Girl with the Flaxen Hair)

Study in tempo flexibility and inspired by a poem of the French Romantic Leconte de Lisle. The tonal level never rises above *forte*. Level 9.

La Cathédrale engloutie (The Engulfed Cathedral)

In composing this piece, Debussy recalled the legend of the village of Ys on the coast of Brittany. Because of the evil deeds of a sorceress there, the island was engulfed, but tradition says that during bad weather sailors still hear singing in the church. Debussy creates representations of submerged chimes at the beginning, allows the cathedral to begin to rise out of the mist, presents a sonorous chorale, reminiscent of antique *faux-bourdon* musical practice with parallel modal chords, and then allows the sonority of the church bells to become submerged again under the sea.

An enigma concerning the rhythm in this piece exists. If played as written, the tempo seems to slow down and speed up at several points. Debussy actually recorded this prelude: at bar seven in his performance, the preceding quarter-note equals the forthcoming half-note. At bar 13, the preceding half-note equals the coming quarter-note. At bar 22 the preceding quarter-note equals the coming half-note which represents the pulse from bar 22 through bar 83. At bar 84 the preceding half-note equals the coming quarter-note, and finally at bar 86 the preceding quarter-note equals the coming half-note. While this is incorrect according to the printed score, Debussy's performance indicates that this is the way he wanted it to sound. Level 10.

Minstrels

The title apparently refers to a vaudeville group of musicians, comedians and dancers, either blacks or, more often, white entertainers made up in black face and masquerading as blacks. The minstrel show migrated to Europe from America around Debussy's era.

Debussy's jazzy minstrels have darting movements and playful dance rhythm. Level 10.

Preludes, Book 2 (1913)

These preludes are slightly more advanced in their harmonic language and are slightly more difficult to play than those in the first volume. (Many standard editions.)

Brúyeres (Heather)

Atmosphere of the heaths, covered with shrubs whose pink and purple flowers lend breathtaking hues to the countryside. Pastoral atmosphere is present in this simple work that expresses happiness and melancholy at the same time. The dynamic level never exceeds *mezzo-forte*. Level 10.

Berceuse héröique

Many parallel chords in a grave and sustained work. Short and relatively unknown. (Durand, Peters and other editions.) Level 9.

Page d'Album (Album Leaf) (1915)

A simple, elegant and effective representation of Debussy's style in a two-page miniature with occasional pedal points. Perhaps Debussy's easiest piano work both technically and musically. Composed for a fund-raising auction for a war relief organization in 1915. In a moderate tempo with a waltz-like feeling. (Many standard editions.) Level 8.

Élégie (1915)

Chromatic writing. The phrase structure is not easily determined. Debussy's last piano solo. (Jobert.) Level 9.

Miscellaneous Volumes

Debussy: An Introduction to His Piano Music, ed. Halford

An excellent performing edition containing the complete *Children's Corner, Clair de Lune, Le Petit Nègre, Reverie, Sarabande* and *Arabesque No. 1.* Extensive material provided in the forward including information on Symbolist poets, Impressionism and musical matters. (Alfred.) Levels 8–10.

Dances of Debussy, ed. Hinson

Includes *Menuet* and *Passepied* from *Suite Bergamasque, Golliwog's Cakewalk, Danse, Danse Bohémienne* and others. Interesting foreword includes information about Debussy's ideas on the dance. (Alfred.) Levels 8–10.

At the Piano With Debussy, ed. Hinson

Provides an interesting cross-section of pieces by Debussy including *Album Leaf, The Girl with the Flaxen Hair, Hommage á Haydn, Valse Romantique, Danse* and others. (Alfred.) Levels 9–10.

Claude Debussy: An Introduction
to the Composer and His Music, ed. Banowetz

A valuable volume containing *Two Arabesques, Rêverie, Suite Bergamasque, Valse Romantique* and *Mazurka*. Editorial suggestions are indicated in red. Extensive and valuable prefatory material. (Kjos.) Levels 8–9.

Claude Debussy, Easier Favorites

Included are Debussy's less-difficult selections such as *The Little Shepherd, Jimbo's Lullaby, The Girl With the Flaxen Hair, Arabesque No. 1, Valse Romantique, Clair de lune, Golliwogg's Cakewalk* and *Doctor Gradus ad Parnassum*. (Peters.) Levels 7–9.

Debussy: Selected Favorites, ed. Olson

Presents selections from *Suite Bergamasque, Children's Corner, Pour le Piano* and others. (Alfred.) Levels 8–10.

HELMUT DEGEN (b. 1911) Germany

Kleine Klavierstücke für Kinder

Tuneful pieces for beginners. Rhythmic and animated, and not nearly as dissonant as the *Spielmusik für klavier*. Thin textures with substantial work given to the left hand. (Süddeutscher Musikverlag.) Level 2.

Spielmusik für Klavier

Short intermediate teaching pieces in a linear contemporary idiom reminiscent of Hindemith. Study of these works can help develop independence between the hands. (Süddeutscher Musikverlag.) Levels 3–4.

Three Sonatinas

Neo-Classic writing with mildly contemporary sonorities. These works could take the place of a sonatina by Clementi or Kuhlau in a student's plan of study. (Süddeutscher Musikverlag.) Levels 5–6.

NORMAN DELLO JOIO (b. 1913) USA

Dello Joio is a Pulitzer Prize-winning composer who has written a great deal for young performers. Descended from three generations of Italian organists, Dello Joio writes with exuberance, an engaging sense of melody, and idiomatic pianistic technique. For many years Dello Joio taught at Boston University. Most of his piano music was composed in the 1940's. Jazz, dance and the Roman Catholic liturgy were the greatest influences on his writing.

Suite for the Young

Ten short pieces that provide a good introduction to some aspects of 20th-century harmony and melody. A classic. (Marks/Belwin-Mills.)

No. 2 Invention

Based on a major and minor triadic melody, this selection features highly imitative and linear writing in which both hands are truly independent of each other. Level 3.

No. 3 Little Sister

Tender, lyrical work, played mostly in the treble range. Level 2.

No. 4 Little Brother

Bouncy and rhythmic selection that is especially good for teaching independence of the hands. The offbeats in the left hand can create problems in coordination. The melody changes from the right hand to the left hand. Level 4.

No. 5 Lullaby

Double-note thirds in the right hand that call for voicing of top and strict legato in a lyrical work. Level 4.

No. 6 Echoes

Many changing rhythms and patterns in a piece that could serve as a student's introduction to improvisatory style. Echoes are found between the hands. Level 4.

No. 7 Bagatelle

A one-page work that is filled with sequences, two-note slurs and staccato passages. Requires a performer with flair and energy. Level 4.

No. 9 Small Fry

A driving work that is especially suitable for a talented student who understands syncopation. This work, sometimes exhibiting a "boogie" feeling, needs careful attention to articulation. Level 4.

No. 10 Chorale Chant

Setting of the Lord's Prayer in a rather traditional chordal version. Level 4.

Lyric Pieces for the Young

Six superior teaching pieces that exhibit highly pianistic writing. The score is not fingered. All of these pieces should be better known. Especially appropriate for the talented student. (Marks/Belwin-Mills.)

No. 1 Boat Song

Crossed hands are used occasionally in this quiet and gentle piece. The dotted figures perhaps represent the flow of the water. Level 7.

No. 2 Prayer of the Matador

Spanish-style writing that needs an expressive performer. The left hand provides an ostinato throughout the piece. Level 7.

No. 3 Street Cries

An energetic and effective work with many double-note passages that require strong fingers. A passage in measures 27–30 pokes fun at the parlor song "East Side, West Side." Level 7.

No. 4 Night Song

A slow and sustained work with rich harmonies. The least frequently played of the set. Level 7.

No. 5 Village Church

The character changes throughout from the simulated quick-tempo hymn tune to the sustained chords evoking an organ. Appropriate for a sensitive performer. Adult students especially will be drawn to this piece. Level 6.

No. 6 Russian Dancer

Appropriate especially for the energetic performer although the tendency may be to play this too fast. Requires flair and voicing within a hand. Textures contain alternating chordal passages between the hands. Effective and dramatic, and a decided student favorite. Level 7.

Diversions

Five pieces titled *Preludio, Arietta, Caccia, Chorale* and *Giga.* The *Chorale* is a refreshing arrangement of "Good Christian Men, Rejoice" and the final *Giga* presents a dancing and energetic variation of that same tune. The *Caccia* is especially effective in performance. Mildly contemporary writing. (Marks/Belwin-Mills.)

1. Preludio

A fugue-like piece that is more difficult than it appears. Level 6.

2. Arietta

Sustained and nocturne-like piece with thick textures and lyrical writing. Contains a hauntingly beautiful melody. Level 7.

3. Caccia

Allegro animato work that features chromaticism, bitonality, triads, seventh chords and open harmonies. Requires strong hands. Highly effective in performance. Level 7.

4. Chorale

Features the Christmas carol "Good Christian Men Rejoice" which is heard in its entirety against a counter-theme. Appropriate preparation for more advanced chorale playing. Level 5.

5. Giga

A quick 6/8 movement based on the popular Christmas carol "Good Christian Men Rejoice." Bubbling and animated, especially suited for the student who plays Baroque dances well. Effective neo-Baroque writing with a dramatic close. Levels 7–8.

Suite for Piano

Four movements, the first and third of which are slow. Second movement, *Bright*, is strongly syncopated and features alternating meter but contains some wide reaches and octave passages. The last movement, a driving finale marked *"Fast, with ferocity,"* is a quasi-toccata with dynamic levels that range from *f* to *ffff*. Interesting writing for the advancing performer. (G. Schirmer.) Levels 8–10.

I. (Moderato)

Slow and lyrical work with a mild blues flavor that serves as an introduction to the entire suite. The hands cross to present the melody in the lower register of the piano. Level 8.

II. (Bright)

Strongly rhythmic and syncopated work with alternating meter as well as wide reaches and octave passages. Canonic passages featuring some quartal writing are present. Opening contains jazz syncopation in the right hand. Level 9.

III. (Calm)

Spacious ABA work with some stretches of a tenth. Requires the holding of inner notes that are sustained. Level 8.

IV. (Fast, with ferocity)

A toccata. Most difficult of the four movements. Effective writing with dynamic levels ranging from *f* to *ffff*. Level 10.

Nocturne in E (1946)

Lyrical three-page work in a neo-Romantic vein. Not his most inspired work. (Carl Fischer.) Level 8.

Nocturne in F-sharp Minor (1946)

Lyrical work, with an especially thick texture and a dance-like central section. Relative absence of thirds is countered by the frequent use of fourths, fifths, seconds and sevenths. (Carl Fischer.) Level 10.

Prelude: To a Young Musician (1943)

Pianistic writing with varied rhythms and filled with seconds and sevenths. Exploits changing meters and an ostinato-like bass. Contains a paraphrase of the well-known motif from Beethoven's *Fifth Symphony*. ABA' form. (G. Schirmer.) Levels 9–10.

Prelude: To a Young Dancer (1943)

C-sharp Aeolian melody within a dissonant contrapuntal texture. Alternates between 6/8 and 9/8 meter, building to a large climax and then falling back to a *pianissimo* ending. More extended than the *Prelude: To a Young Musician.* (G. Schirmer.) Level 10.

Short Intervallic Études

Dissonant pieces built on various intervals in varying moods. Titles include *1/4's and 1/5's, 1/3's, 2nds, 1/6's, 1/7's* and *Octaves and Unisons.* The set would be an unusual and effective set on a recital program. (Associated.) Level 10.

Salute to Scarlatti (1981)

A suite of four single-movement "Sonatas" for piano or harpsichord that readily reveal Dello Joio's predilection for both the old and the new in his writing. The texture, keyboard figurations, cross-handed acrobatics and the rhythmic vitality remind one of Scarlatti, yet the harmonic language is thoroughly contemporary. Phrases often are of irregular lengths, with unpredictable harmonic twists.

The sonatas seem to belong to one larger work, with the second sonata clearly a pastorale and the third sonata a *grazioso* movement that precedes the final perpetual motion movement. The bipartite form of the Scarlatti keyboard sonatas is abandoned here. Instead Dello Joio follows a loose ABA form, always returning to the opening material near the close. No repeat signs appear in the entire work. (Associated.) Level 10.

EDISON DENISSOV (b. 1929) Russia

Bagatellen

Seven short pieces featuring mildly contemporary writing with strong contrast among the pieces. Rhythmic, animated playing is frequently required. As a set or in separate movements, this music would be effective in contest or as part of a solo recital. Should be better known. (Peters.) Level 10.

YVONNE DESPORTES (1907–1993) France

12 Piècettes

Teaching pieces in a dissonant lyrical style. Titles include *Tango, Canon, Tic-tac* and *Petite Danse.* (Billaudot.) Level 4.

GONTRAN DESSAGNES (b. 1906) France

Le Cashier de Frédéric

Six teaching pieces, similar in concept to the Dello Joio *Lyric Pieces for the Young*. Linear writing, thick passagework and mild dissonances. Text is in French. (Delrieu.) Level 7.

NATHANIEL DETT (1882–1943) Canada

Juba (from In the Bottoms)

A popular piano piece representing foot-stomping and pats of the hands in 2/4. (Summy.) Level 10.

The Collected Piano Works of R. Nathaniel Dett

Includes the complete sets of Magnolia, In the Bottoms, Enchantment, Cinnamon Grove, Tropic Winter and Eight Bible Vignettes. (Summy.) Levels 8–10.

ALBERT KENNETH DE VITO (b. 1919) USA

Piano Sonatina No. 1

Popular flavor permeates several passages. (Kenyon.) Level 7.

WALERY DIACZENKO (n.d.)

Miniatures for Piano

Indicative of the wealth of fine contemporary teaching literature from Poland. Mildly contemporary with spirited rhythms. The pianistic writing lies well under the hand. Bold color pictures may attract the attention of children. (PWM.) Level 5.

DAVID DIAMOND (b. 1915) USA

Alone at the Piano, Volumes 1–3 (1967)

Subtitled "pieces for beginners," the strongly dissonant writing found here might discourage some students who had not been adequately prepared for the sounds of contemporary music. These very easy pieces progress through the three volumes with well-graduated pacing. The volumes contain 10, 11 and 13 one-page pieces respectively. (Southern Music.) Levels 1–4.

Album for the Young (1946)

Ten elementary character pieces with agreeable contemporary sounds. Should be heard more frequently in festivals and on recitals. (Elkan-Vogel.)

I. Little March

Effective and interesting writing which overall needs a steady march tempo and full tone. Requires large gestures to play the detached and accented notes. Level 2.

III. Happy-Go-Lucky

Short, bright work with an open-fifth accompaniment and accents in the left hand. Level 2.

V. A Gambol

Energetic, spirited piece, appropriate for work on independence of the hands at an elementary level. Linear writing, mostly in eighths and quarters. Level 2.

VI. Christmastide

Four-part writing in a sustained work with interesting dissonances. Level 5.

IX. Jostling Joe

Short and effective work in 5/4 with some double-note writing. Level 2.

Eight Piano Pieces

Less dissonant than some of Diamond's other pedagogical writing. A strong rhythmic foundation is implicit in many of these pieces. All are one page long, and most have nursery rhyme references. These are some of Diamond's most attractive teaching pieces. (G. Schirmer.) Level 3.

Then and Now

Subtitled "11 Pieces for Very Young Pianists," these character pieces are composed in a strongly contemporary harmonic framework. Diamond's music is always pianistic. See especially *A Desperate Toy*. (Southern Music.) Level 5.

Sonatina for Piano (1935)

Three movements, Slow-Moderate-Fast. See especially the last movement with its "wrong-note" writing and its rhythmic vitality. (Mercury.) Level 6.

A Private World (1954–1959)

Thirteen titled character pieces that feature dissonant sounds and primarily linear writing for the sophisticated intermediate student with small hands. Representative titles include *Sifting and Sorting, At the Bottom of the Sea, Quickened Time* and *A Sad Story.* (Southern Music.) Level 7.

Prelude and Fugue in C Minor

According to Maurice Hinson, "The *cantando* lyric lines of the *Prelude* go their graceful individual way and finally arrive at a colorful cadence. The three-voiced *Fugue* is basically tonal but uses chromaticism freely and builds to a strong emotional climax. A rhythmic subject with strong off-beat accents add excitement to this forceful work. . . ." (Alfred.) Level 8.

EMMA LOU DIEMER (b. 1927) USA

Four Piano Teaching Pieces

Gavotte, Gigue, Invention, Serenade are titles of these elementary-level solos, all available separately. These are spirited and motivating pieces for the young student and should be heard more frequently. See especially *Gigue* with its buoyant rhythm and tone clusters. *Serenade* is filled with "wrong-note" writing in an irregular meter of 5/4. (Boosey.) Level 2.

Time Pictures

Four two-page pieces in a mildly contemporary idiom. The technical features for each piece are discussed at the bottom of the first page of each. See especially *Gavotte* and *Gigue*. Each of these pieces is also published separately. (Boosey.) Level 3.

Sound Pictures

Perhaps Diemer's best-known teaching set, these 10 short selections are written in a highly contemporary idiom, yet are very comprehensible. (Boosey.) Level 7.

Space Suites (1989)

Subtitled "12 Short Pieces for Solo Piano Using Idioms and Techniques of the 20th Century." Contains 12-tone technique, playing on the strings, changing meters and quartal chords. (Plymouth Music.)

JOHN HENRY DIERCKS (b. 1927) USA

12 Sonatinas for Piano, Volumes I and II (1978–80)

Contemporary writing requiring agile movement about the keyboard. The title "sonatina" here refers more to the length of these works rather than to their difficulty. Six sonatinas are contained in each volume. (Crystal Spring Music Publishers.) Level 10.

HUGO DISTLER (1908–1942) Germany

Elf kleine Klavierstücke

Engaging set of 11 contemporary intermediate teaching pieces. Harmonies and melodies are interesting and well-crafted. The entire set should be better known. (Bärenreiter.) Levels 4–6.

No. 1 Kindlwiegen

Tender, melodic writing in ABA form with an entrancing ostinato accompaniment of open fifths. Level 6.

No. 2 Trommeln und Pfeifen

Driving and bold with changing meters. Level 4.

No. 3 Walzer

Lyrical writing revealing a flavor of surprising harmonies and "wrong-note" writing. Level 5.

No. 4 Hirtenmusik

Sophisticated and effective work that requires agile fingerwork and a strong rhythmic sense. Level 5.

No. 5 Echo

Rhythmic writing with echoes occurring in repetitions in different registers of the keyboard. Primarily chordal. Level 5.

No. 6 Alte Spieluhr

All is played in the upper register in this one-page selection. The right-hand trills may need attention. Level 5.

No. 7 Pankraz, der Schmoller

Strong rhythms with shifting meters in a work that is primarily chordal. Highly effective and inviting. Level 6.

No. 8 Fanfaren

Primarily chordal with a straight-forward rhythmic framework. Would be an effective addition to a contest list. Level 5.

No. 9 Die Zigeuner

Shifting meters and thick textures in this selection require careful attention. Level 6.

No. 10 Perpetuum Mobil

Rapid figurations divided between the hands, but sounds more difficult than it is. Performer needs a strong rhythmic drive. Level 6.

No. 11 Aria

Cantabile, one-page piece with written-out ornamentation and flourishes in the right-hand melody. Inspired writing. Level 6.

ERNST von DOHNÁNYI (1877–1960) Hungary

Ernst von Dohnányi, a contemporary of Kodaly and Bartók, composed in a highly Romantic 19th-century style. Dohnányi came to the USA in 1949 and taught at Florida State University.

Albumblatt (1899)

Two-page solo, especially appropriate for an adult wanting a melodic, expressive and reflective work with lush harmonies. Little known. (Editio Musica.) Level 7.

Intermezzo in F Minor, Op. 2, No. 3

Sustained, expressive, lush Romantic harmonies with a Brahmsian texture and a large central climax. (Doblinger. Also Kalmus, complete opus.) Level 10.

Four Rhapsodies, Op. 11

Virtuosic pieces, generally beyond the scope of the literature in this volume. No. 1 is the most difficult. No. 2 needs the flair and temperament of a performer capable of handling *Hungarian Rhapsodies*. No. 4 is predominantly lyrical but has a *grandioso* ending. (Marks.) Level 10.

No. 3 Rhapsody in C Major

The most popular, perhaps due to the enchanting and catchy second theme. Spirited, full sonorities, emotional writing, especially appropriate for the performer with flair. Level 10.

Winterreigen, Op. 13 (Winter Rounds)

Subtitled "10 Bagatelles" and prefaced by a poem of Heindl, this collection contains Dohnányi's most accessible selections for early-advanced pianists. All of the pieces refer to specific persons or events in Dohnányi's life. (Doblinger, Master.)

No. 1 Widmung

Features an arpeggiated left-hand figure beneath a melody in single notes or octaves. *Widmung* could provide an interesting choice of Romantic literature for a student not quite ready to play the Chopin *"Raindrop" Prelude*, Op. 28, No. 15. Level 8.

No. 2 Marsch der lüstigen Brüder

Appropriate for the pianist enjoying full-sounding works but who is not inclined to learn a work of the scope of the Brahms *Rhapsody in G Minor*, Op. 79, No. 2. Full chords, octaves, rich sonorities and large climax. Level 10.

No. 3 An Ada

The pitches A D A are used throughout in the soprano in the melody, while melodic and harmonic interest are maintained through the contrapuntal lines and chordal arpeggiations beneath the ostinato melody. A good piece for study in voice-leading. Level 8.

No. 4 Freund Victor's Mazurka

Salon music, more effective than profound, and similar in texture to some of the Chopin mazurkas. Requires the ability to play arpeggiations and right-hand flourishes. Level 10.

No. 7 Um Mitternacht

Agitated four-page piece with patterned ascending and descending figurations that fit the hand well. A motivating finger piece with repetition. Level 9.

No. 9 Morgengrauen

Marked *Andante, quasi Adagio* and in an ominous mood, this two-page lyrical work features an expressive melody over a recurring syncopated octave-C motif. Especially appropriate for studying voicing within thick textures. Level 10.

No. 10 Postludium

The most frequently played piece in the set, driving and passionate. The left hand features an ascending and descending broken chord as accompaniment, while the right-hand melody soars. Level 9.

Ruralia Hungarica, Op. 32/a (Hungarian Landscapes)

Seven little-known pieces in a generally lyrical and poetic style. No. 4 is beyond the technical scope of music covered in this book. (Editio Musica.) Level 10.

Six Piano Pieces, Op. 41

Pleasant, alternative teaching selections. These works are more demanding technically than musically. (Lengnick.)

No. 1 Impromptu

ABA form with florid left-hand arpeggios in the central sections and lyrical writing with close harmonies in the outer sections. Level 9.

No. 2 Scherzino

Well-suited for the pianist adept in playing *leggiero*. Continuous sixteenth-note motion. Level 10.

No. 3 Canzonetta

Lush miniature. Level 8.

No. 5 Ländler

A *scherzando* character piece, appropriate for a pianist able to play the easy Chopin waltzes. Level 10.

SAMUEL DOLIN (b. 1917) Canada

Little Toccata

A short, effective toccata for the student who has agility in playing repeated notes. (BMI Canada.) Level 5.

A Slightly Square Round Dance

Some "wrong-note" writing lends a playful flavor to this already rhythmic selection. Attractive writing. (BMI Canada.) Level 6.

Sonatina

Mildly contemporary writing with a lyrical melody punctuated with various triadic harmonies. Two pages. (BMI Canada.) Level 6.

ROBERT DONAHUE (b. 1931) USA

Five Chromatic Sketches

Subtitled "Musical portrayals of colors," this little-known set is effective and might stir the imagination of a student to relate color to expression in music. Titles include *Purple, Scarlet, Cocoa, Blue Green* and *Yellow*. Mildly contemporary sounds, well-written score. These short pieces could be mastered quickly. (Willis.) Level 6.

ANTHONY DONATO (b. 1909) Czechoslovakia

Although he was born in Czechoslovakia, all of Donato's education and teaching positions have been in the USA.

Recreations

Mildly contemporary writing in pieces that are filled with animation and spirit. For a young student. Titles include *The Surfboard, The Motorboat, A Whim, Table Tennis* and *The Squirrel Cage.* (Southern Music.) Level 7.

MADELINE DRING (1923–1977) Great Britain

12 Pieces in the Form of Studies

Intriguing, little-known pieces. (Marks.)

Additional Work for Study:
Three Dances (Cambria)

MIECZYSKAW DROBNER (b. 1912) Poland

The Lane of Master Watchmakers for Piano

The structure is perfectly planned, the feeling on the keyboard highly idiomatic, and the sound effective in these eight short teaching pieces. Titles include *The Sundial, The Water Glass, The Candle Clock, The Pendulum Clock* and *The Alarm Clock.* Color illustrations are included in this attractive short volume. (PWM.) Level 3.

PIERRE-MAX DUBOIS (b. 1930) France

Voulez-vous jouer? Au cirque, Volumes 1–3

Three volumes of short teaching pieces from the French pedagogical school. The volumes are progressive in difficulty, with Volume 1 featuring linear pieces with open sonorities. The literature in Volume 2 is slightly more difficult and features open sonorities and mildly contemporary sounds. Volume 3 perhaps contains the most appealing pieces. See especially *Patinoire* (a toccatina) and *Le Défilé* (a march). (Billaudot.) Levels 1–4.

GENEVIEVE DUCHESNE (1943–1985) France

Pièces faciles pour piano

Strongly contemporary writing for the elementary student. Five short selections. (Durand.) Level 4.

HENRY DUKE (b. 1920) Great Britain

So Easy

Fourteen tuneful and predictable linear pieces for beginners. These pieces can help a beginner develop independence between the hands. (Fentone.) Level 1.

Nursery Sing-Song

Almost all of the 10 nursery tunes found here are arranged into eight-measure selections. The melody is found in the right hand, and the left hand features simple single-note accompaniments. Good for the very young student. (Fentone.) Level 1.

THOMAS DUNHILL (1877–1946) Great Britain

First Year Pieces

Based on traditional harmonies, these 12 teaching pieces for beginners are of high quality. The writing contains strong character changes between the pieces, and is pianistic and primarily lyrical. All of the selections are tuneful. These pieces, mostly one page long, would be a good supplement to a method. (Associated Board of the Royal Schools of Music.) Level 1.

LOUIS DUREY (1888–1979) France

Dix Inventions

Two-voice inventions in a contemporary idiom. Sophisticated writing. (Musicales Transatlantiques.) Level 9.

ZSOLT DURKÓ (b. 1934) Hungary

Dwarfs and Giants

Avant-garde teaching pieces featuring clusters, the absence of barlines, mixed meters, etc. (Editio Musica.) Level 9.

Kindermusik

Contemporary writing is found in these quality teaching pieces, some of which use avant-garde features. May spark a student's imagination. (Editio Musica.) Level 8.

ANDRZEJ DUTKIEWICZ (b. 1942) Poland

Dutkiewicz now resides in the USA.

The Puppet Suite

Short character pieces with strong rhythms and mildly biting dissonances. Titles include *A Mysterious Story, Playing Ball, On the Trampoline* and *Bouncing Along*. Some of the best contemporary music for children available and should be much more widely known. See especially *Tick-Tock Dream*. (Kjos.) Level 4.

Seascapes

A set of 11 character pieces in which the writing strongly depicts the title in a contemporary idiom that is highly pianistic. Each of the pieces is preceded by practice suggestions. Titles include *Racing the Wind, Sandpipers, Walking on the Sand* and *Dancing in the Waves*. (Kjos.) Levels 5–6.

MARIA DZIEWULSKA (b. 1909) Poland

Inventions

Two-voice atonal contrapuntal writing. (PWM.) Level 7.

E

PETR EBEN (b. 1929) Czechoslovakia

Die Welt der Kleinen (Young People's World)

Twenty short piano pieces that cover all the basic elements of "orthodox" technique but which also contain musical poetry. Attractive contemporary teaching pieces, most of which are slightly less than one page in length. (Schott.) Level 7.

MAX EISIKOVITS (n.d.) Hungary

Miniatures

Generally linear writing in a highly contemporary idiom. The pieces are filled with character and energy as well as strong dissonance. (Editio Musica.) Level 6.

HANNS EISLER (1898–1962) Germany

18 Petits Morceaux, Op. 31

Character pieces in a highly contemporary idiom. Nos. 1–11 consist of a theme and 10 short variations. Fine writing in a series that should be better known. (Heugel.) Levels 2–4.

7 Petits Morceaux, Op. 32

Untitled character pieces featuring thin textures. This music should take its place beside the best contemporary piano-teaching literature. (Heugel.) Levels 5–6.

EDWARD ELGAR (1857–1934) Great Britain

Dream Children

Two lush solos for piano, *Andante* and *Allegretto piacevole*. Interesting alternatives for the upper-intermediate student who enjoys the Romantic literature. Thin textures, not difficult to read. (Faber.) Levels 7–8.

Additional Work for Study:
Music for Piano

OSCAR ESPLÁ (1886–1976) Spain

La Pájara Pinta

The Spanish flavor combined with passages of "wrong-note" writing makes these three pieces for the early-advanced performer intriguing. Substantially more difficult than the Pinto *Scenas Infantis*. The entire set would be effective in recital. (Union Musical Española.) Level 10.

Lyrica Española, Op. 54, Set 4

Atmospheric writing conveying a strong Spanish flavor. Strong rhythmic sense required of the performer. (Union Musical Española.) Level 10.

F

RICHARD FAITH (b. 1926) USA

Pipes

Many harmonic and subtle effects appear throughout. See especially *V. (Allegro)* and *VII. (Allegretto)*. (Belwin.) Levels 6–7.

Four Cameos

Waltz, Toccatina, Lullaby and *Ronding*. Thin textures and contemporary writing. (Shawnee.) Levels 5–6.

Travels

Set of seven travelogue pieces with occasional biting dissonances. Frequent lyrical writing. Titles include *The Highlander, Provence, Express* and *Caravan*. (Shawnee.) Level 5.

Dances for Piano

Five movements with strongly defined character differentiation between dances. See especially Nos. 1, 3 and 5. Some of his best writing for teaching. (Shawnee.) Level 6.

Finger Paintings

Primarily lyrical writing with mildly contemporary sounds requiring color, tonal voicing and sensitive pedaling. A group from this imaginative set of character pieces would represent American composers well in a contemporary festival. Titles include *Country Scene, Medieval Gardens, Celebration, Spinning* and *End of the Day*. (Shawnee.) Levels 6–7.

Three Sonatinas

Strongly rhythmic outer movements. Tongue-in-cheek works that are amusing, whimsical and sophisticated. Each in three movements. (Shawnee.) Level 4.

Moments in a Child's World

Set of seven works that require fine coordination between the hands. Titles include *Prancing Pony, Traffic, Moonlight Dreams, The Old Mill, Treasure Chest, Winter* and *Harvest Dance*. (Shawnee.) Levels 6–7.

Sketches

Subtitled *Miniature Piano Pieces in 12 Keys*. Colorful works containing interesting rhythms. Some of the selections are more difficult than they appear. See especially *The Chase, Bickering, Romance* and *Bustling City*. (Belwin.) Level 7.

Carousels

Three movements, each two to three pages long. Outer movements in a lively neo-Classical style and a slow movement that features flowing arpeggios and broken chords as accompaniment to a lyrical melody in longer note values. The last movement, with a repeated-note motif and catchy rhythms, is perhaps the most effective. Idiomatic. One of the strongest of the set. (Belwin.) Level 9.

Night Songs

May be played separately. The first is an expressive song, ending with mysterious chords. The second is rich in sonority and requires much rubato. (Shawnee.) Level 9.

Five Preludes and a Nocturne

The *Preludes*, contemporary in idiom, differ strongly from one another in character. The *Nocturne* is slightly more difficult. Not especially significant works. (Shawnee.) Levels 8–9.

Recollections

Nine imaginative intermediate works in a contemporary style. The textures are thin and the scores are generally easy to read. Titles include *Monastery, The Hunt, Fountains, Reflection, Autumn* and others. Most are short. (Shawnee.) Level 8.

Souvenir

Three-page linear *andantino* work. According to Maurice Hinson, "Bitonal shifting from A Minor to F Major is colored with chromatics that add interest to the following." Interesting writing in a single work from Faith. Highly expressive. (Alfred.) Level 8.

Additional Works for Study:

Masquerades

Russian Folk Tales

Tableaus

YURI FALIK (b. 1936) Russia

10 Pieces for Piano

High-quality contemporary teaching literature from the Russian school. The music is tuneful, mildly contemporary and rhythmically interesting, and the writing fits the hand well. (VAAP/G. Schirmer.) Levels 5–6.

MANUEL DE FALLA (1876–1946) Spain

Homenaje

Arranged by the composer from his rhythmic guitar piece. A recurring arpeggiated flourish punctuates the texture throughout. Although it is one of de Falla's more accessible piano pieces, a pianist needs a strong grasp of rhythmic subdivisions to play it. (Chester.) Level 8.

Danse du Meunier

De Falla's arrangement for piano of the *Dance of the Miller* from *The Three-Cornered Hat* is highly rhythmic, stimulated in part by the repeated chords. Exciting climax. Three pages. (Chester.) Level 10.

Nocturno

Sentimental, Romantic writing in a five-page work containing an expansive arpeggiated left-hand accompaniment. Its appeal stems from its emotional and sentimental qualities. (Union Musical.) Level 10.

Andaluza *from* Pieces Espagnoles

Highly exciting and rhythmic work based on a Spanish folk motif. Somewhat Impressionistic. (Many standard editions.) Level 10.

GUIDO ALBERTO FANO (1875–1961) Italy

Rimembranze di Padova, 1892

Neo-Romantic writing with lush sonorities and some rhythmic subdivisions, in a suite of five medium-length pieces. For the seasoned performer. Titles include *Preludio, Mestizia, Valzer Improvviso, Intermezzo* and *Fuggevole Visione*. (Curci.) Level 10.

FERENC FARKAS (b. 1905) Hungary

Three Fantasias (originally composed by Bakfark, arr. Farkas)

Arrangements based on three pieces originally composed for lute in which Farkas has retained the modal sounds but has added octave doublings and has filled in some chords. (EMB.) Level 8.

Additional Works for Study:
Five Hungarian Danses
Holiday Excursions
Hybrids

ARTHUR FARWELL (1872–1952) USA

American Indian Melodies, ed. Hinson

Authentic American Indian melodies harmonized for piano. Pianistic settings and some flexible rhythms within a Romantic harmonic framework. (Hinshaw.) Level 8.

HOWARD FERGUSON (b. 1908) Great Britain

Five Bagatelles, Op. 9

Highly effective, mildly contemporary writing for the early-advanced student. Strong and vibrant rhythms, and strong character differentiation between movements. *Allegro con fuoco, Andantino amabile, Allegro scherzando, Molto moderato, Allegretto non troppo*. Study of these works would provide a fine substitute for the Tcherepnin *Bagatelles*. A set worth investigating. (Boosey.) Level 9.

OSCAR LORENZO FERNANDEZ (1897–1948) Brazil

Fernandez' teaching pieces are tuneful and convey a nationalistic spirit. Innately rhythmic writing.

Suite on Five Notes

The music remains in relatively stationary positions in the eight movements of this suite, in which selections often sound more difficult than they are. One or a group of these would be effective for a beginner in a recital or in a festival. (Peer International.) Levels 1–2.

Dolls

South American rhythms, traditional melodies in pieces that sound much more difficult than they are. Simple melodies and vibrant rhythms abound. See especially *Spanish Ballerina, Italian Peasant Girl* and *Chocolate Cake Girl Vendor*. (Peer International.) Level 2.

First Brazilian Suite

Three movements, *Old Song, Sweet Cradle Song* and *Serenade*, all published separately. Lyrical, Romantic writing that requires a refined legato. (Peer International.) Level 7.

Children's Visions

The three movements, all published separately, are titled *Little Cortege, Nocturnal Round* and *Mysterious Dance*. See especially the first movement, with its cheerful melody and big central climax. (Peer International.) Level 8.

Second Brazilian Suite

Three movements, *Prelude, Song* and *Dance*. The inspired *Prelude* is pensive and expressive, calling for a legato melody. This especially fine two-page movement could help a student master finger independence necessary for voicing. *Song* contains some double-note passages within a South American rhythmic framework. *The Dance*, in a rumba rhythm throughout and sounding more difficult than it is, displays intriguing syncopations and full chords that fit the hand well. Large effective climax. (Peer International.) Levels 7–8.

Third Brazilian Suite

Three movements, *Song, Serenade* and *Negro Dance*, all published separately. See especially the third movement, which is in the same vein as

Bartók's *Allegro Barbaro*, but shorter and less difficult. It features driving rhythms and percussive use of the piano. (Peer International.) Level 9.

IRVING FINE (1914–1962) USA

At some point in his life Fine studied or was associated with Koussevitsky, Copland, Stravinsky and Boulanger. He wrote in a neo-Classical style.

Lullaby for a Bady Panda

Two-page teaching piece in which tonality shifts between several keys. Filled with two-note slurs. (Presser.) Level 1.

Victory March of the Elephants

A vigorous and jolly march with changing modes and some dissonances. (Presser.) Level 1.

Hommage à Mozart

Marked *allegretto grazioso*, this two-page piece features florid right-hand passagework. Phrase structure and tonal center are sometimes ambiguous. (Boosey.) Level 5.

ROSS LEE FINNEY (b. 1906) USA

Ross Lee Finney was a student of Nadia Boulanger, Alban Berg and Roger Sessions. His style is generally characterized by tonal writing, although the 12-tone influence has been prevalent in the writing of Finney since 1950.

32 Piano Games (1969)

According to the composer's preface, the purpose of this volume is to lead children "to a freer and more musical concern for the instrument." The 32 studies promote familiarity with the geography of the keyboard through symmetry, two-and-three-note black groupings, extreme registers, etc. Works are in both conventional and modern notation. (Peters.)

I. Middle, Bottom and Top

No barlines in a work featuring new notation. Level 1.

II. Five Fingers

Mirror writing in a five-finger pattern with both thumbs on middle C. Level 1.

III. Thirds

Mirror writing with both hands playing diatonic double thirds. No hand position changes occur. Level 1.

IV. Three White-Note Clusters

Same patterns as in *III*, but all is played here using three-note clusters. Level 1.

VI. Moving Three White-Note Clusters

Elementary playing in three-note clusters, with some skips about the keyboard. Level 2.

VIII. Everything Everywhere

Clusters and simple double-thirds in both hands. Various registers of the keyboard are explored. Level 3.

IX. Five White-Note Clusters

Right-hand clusters of five notes, with the left hand playing a repetitive melody on the lowest notes of the piano. Level 2.

XI. Three White-Note Clusters, High and Low

Using the entire range of the keyboard, this work is a study in sonority. The pattern changes only at the end. Level 1.

XIII. Mirror Mimic

Mirror writing between the hands in eighth-note values. Contains a passage that should be freely improvised. Level 3.

XIV. Tightrope Walker

Rapid alternation of repeated patterns between the hands. Level 3.

XVII. Up and Down

Explores the ranges of the keyboard through the playing of single notes and glissandos up the keyboard. Level 4.

XIX. Berceuse

Lyrical writing within a quartal framework. One page. Level 4.

XX. Argument

A work that is effective in performance and which features rapidly alternating C's, with quick stops and starts, and free tremolos. Level 4.

XXI. Thumb Tricks

Exciting writing with patterns that repeat often. Should be better known. Level 4.

XXII. Black Notes and White Notes

Features three-note clusters, indeterminate pitches, repetitions from slow to fast to slow, and no barlines. Requires expressive playing. Level 5.

XXIV. Running

Effective writing for the performer with strong fingers. Eighth-note passages permeate the score. Level 7.

XXVII. Mirror Waltz

Primarily chordal writing featuring the same rhythmic values in both hands. Level 4.

XXVIII. Mountains

Absence of barlines and indeterminate repetitions. One of the best of the collection. Level 5.

XXIX. Windows

Free rhythms and no barlines. This work especially needs an imaginative performer. Level 4.

XXX. Mobile

Indeterminate repetitions of a figure while a barless melody is played. Level 6.

XXXI. Arapaho

Driving work with clusters and strong rhythms. *fff* climaxes. Level 4.

XXXII. Winter

Free rhythms and opportunities for expressive playing. Contains glissandos, clusters and strong, dramatic, dynamic contrasts. Level 3.

25 Inventions

Composed in 1956, the *Inventions* is an intriguing collection of pieces in which each contains a musical puzzle or game. Mr. Finney states in the preface, "The names of the pieces rarely give any clue as to the game that is being played with the notes. Only by studying the notes themselves can one solve the puzzle." The puzzles pertain to scales, the relation of the notes in one hand to the other, inversions, retrogrades and other devices. All but one of the short linear pieces employ 12-tone techniques.

These are especially appropriate pieces to use to interest students in the analysis and discovery of patterns in music, and as such could be used in a camp or in a group-study situation. See especially *No. 1 Hot; No. 2 Rocking; No. 5 Crossing Over; No. 8 Almost Opposites; No. 15 Dancing;*

No. 17 Dawn; No. 19 Holiday; No. 21 Twilight; No. 22 A Sad Song; No. 23 Playing Ball; and No. 25 Shadows. (Peters.) Levels 5–7.

No. 23 Playing Ball

Fanfare-like work with many triads. Fingerings and left-hand melody need attention. Not easy to read at the outset. Level 5.

Youth's Companion

Five pieces that reflect upon events from Finney's childhood in North Dakota. Each piece is based on a group of six notes that may be repeated symmetrically later in the piece on another pitch to give all 12 tones of the scale. However, Finney prefers that his technique not be called a 12-tone technique since pitch polarity is always present. Titles include *Hawk over the Prairie, Pasque-flowers on the Hill, Jack Rabbit, The Town Dump* and *Riddle Song.* Students interested in compositional techniques should especially look at this volume. (Peters.) Level 8.

Melody

Three-page harmonic work subtitled "Campfire on Ice." Expressive writing with several tempo changes. Based on "Red River Valley" and "Dinah, Won't You Blow Your Horn?" Melodies move from one hand to the other and ultimately are combined in this ABA' work. (Alfred.) Levels 7–8.

JACOBO FISCHER (b. 1896) Argentina

March in File

Humorous march style with some "wrong-note" writing. Students who like popular-sounding literature might enjoy this chordal piece. (Peer-Southern Music.) Level 8.

Polka

Highly rhythmic work composed in a popular vein. (Peer-Southern Music.) Level 8.

Cancion Triste

Pensive, lyrical writing with a thick texture that needs careful voicing. (Southern Music.) Level 8.

NICHOLAS FLAGELLO (b. 1928) USA

Petits Pastels

"Seven [musical] drawings for young pianists" to introduce them to contemporary writing. (General Music.) Level 3.

Episodes for Piano

Some of his most attractive teaching pieces. Vibrant rhythms in the *March*, lyrical writing in *Lullaby* and agile fingerwork in *Pulcinella*. (General Music.) Level 7.

Three Dances

Abstract Dance, Ceremonial Dance and *Tarantella* contain modern sonorities and linear writing. (General Music.) Level 9.

CARLISLE FLOYD (b. 1926) USA

Episodes, Volume 1

Mostly one-page intermediate teaching pieces from a leading contemporary American composer. Found here is linear writing that is highly pianistic within a tonal but contemporary idiom. Titles include *An Ancient Air, Marching Hymn, Chorale* and *Arietta*. (Boosey.) Level 4.

Episodes, Volume 2

These 12 selections with strongly defined characters are slightly more difficult and somewhat longer than those in Volume 1. See especially *Processional, Jig, Impromptu, Fanfare* and *Dance*. Better of the two volumes. (Boosey.) Level 7.

LUKAS FOSS (b. 1922) Germany

Foss immigrated to the USA in 1937.

Four Two-Part Inventions

More difficult than the Bach inventions, these pieces would be suitable for a performer especially adept in contrapuntal playing. They would be interesting performed as a complete set. (Carl Fischer.) Level 10.

JEAN FRANÇAIX (b. 1912) France

10 Pieces for Young People

These pieces follow the development of a boy from the newborn child to manhood. The selections become gradually more difficult as the mythical gentleman becomes older. Strong characterization of the various life stages in an interesting set of pieces. (Schott.) Level 10.

The Françaix Collection, ed. Hinson

Presents 17 piano works that are refreshing and rewarding to play. Pieces are presented in graded order. Highly recommended. (Schott.) Levels 1–10.

Additional Works for Study:
In Praise of the Dance
Five Portraits of Young Girls
The Promenade of an Eclectic Musicologist
Five Encores

ISADORE FREED (1900–1960) USA

Waltz on White Keys

Two-page work with an oom-pah-pah accompaniment featuring changes between Dorian and Aeolian modes. The modes are indicated. (Presser.) Level 2.

Toccatina (The Wind)

Exciting writing that uses various modes and scales for a non-functional, harmonic feeling. The modes and scales are explained in the score. (Presser.) Level 4.

Additional Works for Study:
Pastorales
Sonatina No. 1

PETER RACINE FRICKER (b. 1920) Great Britain

Diversions

Six interesting character pieces. Dissonant contemporary writing that is effective. See especially *Fast and Light* and *Parade*. (Fentone.) Level 9.

RUDOLF FRIML (1879–1972) Bohemia

Well-known as an operetta composer, Friml lived much of his life in the USA.

Chanson

Popular and sentimental writing with a long singing melody punctuated with off-beat left-hand chords. (G. Schirmer.) Level 8.

ANIS FULEIHAN (1900–1970) Greece

Fuleihan lived primarily in the USA, serving on the staff of G. Schirmer and teaching at Indiana University.

Around the Clock

Subtitled "12 preludes for young pianists." Interesting combinations of several pieces can be made for recital or contest performances. Several perpetual-motion pieces good for the student with agile fingers. Mildly contemporary, sometimes modal. (Southern Music.) Level 6.

Ionian Pentagon

Modal and pianistic writing for the sophisticated musical ear. (Southern Music.) Level 6.

From the Aegean

Four-movement work with biting dissonances and rhythmic passage-work. Titles include *Serenade, Tango, Sicilienne* and *Greek Dance.* (Southern Music.) Level 9.

Additional Works for Study:
Harvest Chant
15 Short Pieces
Five Very Short Pieces for Talented Young Bipeds
Not for Squares
A Foot in the Door (Boston)

G

BLAS GALINDO (DIMAS) (b. 1910) Mexico

Five Preludes

Linear writing in a work that is rhythmically vibrant. These pieces may be played by a pianist with small hands. (Ediciones Mexicanas.) Level 10.

RUDOLPH GANZ (1877–1972) Switzerland

Ganz came to the USA from Switzerland in 1901 and became Professor of Piano at Chicago Musical College. Later he became director of that school. Ganz became well known as a teacher but also made a number of concert tours of the USA and Europe.

Animal Pictures

Twenty interesting and little-known miniatures composed in a modern idiom. The writing is tuneful, often humorous, filled with character. Most selections are one page long, and humorous indications in the music enliven the study of these pieces for students of any age. Titles include *Galloping Horses, Bumblebees, A Squirrel, Fleas* and *Listening to the Cuckoo*. Motivating literature. (Carl Fischer.) Levels 4–5.

The Clock from Over There

Programmatic work with staccato figures in the right hand representing the ticking clock and a buoyant melody in the left hand. This piece requires strength in the right hand for the alternating double notes and coordination of staccato and legato in opposing hands. Fresh writing. (The Composers' Press.) Level 5.

Miscellaneous Pieces

The Mosquito (from Three Little Piano Pieces)

Playful work with repeated trill figures representing the buzzing of a mosquito. Restless piece punctuated with humorous staccatos. (Carl Fischer.) Level 6.

JANINA GARCIA (b. 1920) Poland

Two Sonatinas

Contemporary writing to which young students could be drawn due to the rhythmic flavor and biting dissonances. (PWM.) Level 5.

Bagatelles

Engaging short pieces with clearly defined phrases, mildly dissonant harmonies, tuneful writing and strong character definition. Although these pieces can help develop basic pianistic skills, they do not sound like "study pieces." (PWM.) Level 4.

Miniatures for Piano

Titled character pieces with vivid color illustrations. A large number are lively and animated, and almost all are strongly rhythmic and buoyant in nature. (PWM.) Level 6.

ROBERTO GARCÍA-MORILLO (b. 1911) Argentina

Tres Piezas, Op. 2

Energetic pieces and driving rhythms requiring forceful playing. These pieces would be motivating for students who enjoy flamboyant and big-sounding works. Level 10.

Cuentos para Niños Traviesos, Second Series

These three pieces will provide inviting study material for the advocate of South American music. Rhythmic, biting dissonances. (Ricordi.) Level 10.

TERENZIO GARGIULO (b. 1903) Italy

Prima Sonatina

Rhythmic writing in an accessible piece, the last movement of which is a perpetual motion. Strong writing that often sounds more difficult than it is. (Curci.) Level 7.

Cinque Bagatelle Pastorali

Music in the Spanish idiom for the intermediate pianist. Despite the thin textures, the nationalistic character and strong rhythms create interesting literature that is filled with jollity. (Curci.) Level 6.

GEORGE GERSHWIN (1898–1937) USA

Merry Andrew, Three-Quarter Blues, Promenade

These three pieces are probably Gershwin's easiest piano works. The first and third selections feature oom-pah left-hand accompaniments with intricate and syncopated rhythms. *Merry Andrew* needs a strong rhythmic sense, careful phrasing, and the ability to play staccato in the left hand against legato in the right. *Promenade* was written for a film sequence titled "Walking the Dog." It alternates between a casual saunter and a faster pace. *Three-Quarter Blues* is primarily chordal and slow-moving. The thumb holds dotted half-notes while the other fingers play staccato. These pieces are sometimes awkward. (Chappell Music.) Levels 7–8.

Impromptu in Two Keys

Syncopated, bitonal work with a jazz-like melody centered in D above left-hand pulsations in E-flat. (Warner Brothers.) Level 7.

Two Waltzes in C

Each is first played individually, and then the two waltzes are superimposed on one another. Requires a large hand. (New World Music.) Level 7.

Preludes for Piano

Highly popular works filled with elements of jazz. Highly motivating writing, although these selections are not easy. (New World Music.)

I. (Allegro ben ritmato e deciso)

Rhythmic, filled with syncopations. The music is boisterous, permeated with fast passagework and changing rhythmic values. Effective in performance. Level 9.

II. (Andante con moto e poco rubato)

Gershwin referred to his second prelude as a "sort of blue lullaby." The left-hand minor tenths of the A sections may be rolled, with the first note coming before the beat. Level 8.

III. (Allegro ben ritmato e deciso)

Vivacious work with a strong rhythmic foundation and many syncopations. Requires flair and energy. Level 9.

GYORGY GESZLER (b. 1913) Hungary

Works for Study:
Sonatina in C (EMB)
Sonatina in G (EMB)
Wasser treibt die Mühle

LUIS GIANNEO (b. 1897) Argentina

Villancico

Lyrical melody above a simple, dance-like accompaniment. Chromatic writing, for the sophisticated musical ear. (Peer-Southern Music.) Level 4.

Music for Children

Ten selections with titles including *Argentinian Rustic Dance, The Juggler, Prelude and Fugue* and *Zapateado*. Folk influences pervade some of these selections, and many are strongly rhythmic. Interesting teaching material. (Peer-Southern Music.) Level 6.

The Little Road to Bethlehem

Folk-like tune is stated in the tenor under a pulsating chordal accompaniment. Rhythmic. (Peer-Southern Music.) Level 3.

Seven Children's Pieces

Attractive, energetic pieces for young students. Many require agile fingerwork. See especially *Tango, Rustic Dance, Small Drum* and *Little Hat*. (Peer-Southern Music.) Level 2.

Additional Works for Study:
Cinco Pequeñas Piezas
Three Argentine Dances

ALBERTO GINASTERA (1916–1983) Argentina

Ginastera's vigorous style tends to be tonal and neo-classical, with many works presenting driving rhythms and folkloric themes from South America.

12 American Preludes, Volume 1 (1944)

Strong contemporary writing for the upper-intermediate to early-advanced student. Ginastera described the *Preludes* as experimental studies composed while he was searching for new musical idioms. Many are based on Creole folk music. (Carl Fischer.)

No. 1 Accents

Based on a Creole dance, this bitonal work is a study in the placement of accents within a *vivace* setting in 6/8. Consists totally of broken chords and arpeggios. The syncopated feeling comes from the occurrence of the downbeat on the second of the triplets. The hands play simultaneously through most of this work in a selection that sounds more difficult than it is. Levels 8–9.

No. 2 Triste

The title "Triste" is used in Argentina to refer to a type of folk song that is a slow and melancholy love song. This short work may appear easy technically, but requires tonal control and shaping of the long nocturne-like phrases. The dissonances evoke a "far-away" feeling. Level 6.

No. 3 Creole Dance

Based on the *gato*, a popular Argentine dance in 6/8. Powerful and *marcato* writing with a driving four-measure rhythmic motive throughout. Features polychordal clashes which give this ABACA work a restless, violent quality. Quartal harmony permeates this primarily chordal work, which is a brilliant showpiece sounding more difficult than it is. Level 8.

No. 4 Vidala

The "vidala" is a slow Argentine folk song which shows Italian and Spanish influences. This selection is a somber *adagio* work in 3/8 with dynamics ranging from *p* to *ppp*. Less dissonant than other movements. Level 7.

No. 5 In the First Pentatonic Minor Mode

An austere canon in 7/8 for two voices, the second voice entering at the octave in the fourth measure. Single-line writing in both hands with rhythms that are relatively complex. Level 7.

No. 6 Tribute to Roberto García-Morillo

Presto writing with continuous sixteenth throughout. The right hand plays in D-flat Major while the left hand is in C in a short, toccata-like piece with rapidly alternating hands. Sounds much more difficult than it is. The dynamic range spans from *f* to *fff*. The patterns here fit well under the hand. Large clustered chords at the end build by adding one more note in each measure to the repeated right-hand chords until eventually five-note cluster chords are used. García-Morillo is an Argentine composer. Level 8.

No. 7 Octaves

Excellent and effective study in octave playing, with both hands playing simultaneous eighth-note octaves throughout. The performer needs a strong rhythmic sense and a good sense of continuity. Level 9.

No. 8 Tribute to Juan José Castro

Tempo di tango work with a fairly complex rhythm and a chromatic tenor line. A phrase is repeated four times in the melody, with variation and a different harmonization each time. The dynamic range is from *pp* to *mf*. This work has a sentimental, melancholy mood. Juan José Castro is an Argentine composer. Level 8.

No. 9 Tribute to Aaron Copland

Prestissimo with passagework alternating between the hands in a breathless vignette. Ginastera is imitating Copland's jazz style. Bravura passage playing with wide leaps and glissandi. Levels 8–9.

No. 10 Pastorale

Lento. The bass plays open fifths, the alto presents an ostinato, and the *lento* soprano features the melody. Effective harmonies. Level 8.

No. 11 Tribute to Heitor Villa-Lobos

Vivace and continuously loud in wild, syncopated writing that is sempre *forte*. Based on a repeated rhythmic pattern stated in chords, above which the right hand plays sixteenth notes in a perpetual-motion work. Level 9.

No. 12 In the First Pentatonic Major Mode

Study in sonority, with wide spacings on the piano. Dynamic levels range from *mf* to *ffff* in a bell-like work with changing meters and large reaches for both hands. Based on an Inca descending pentatonic scale. A bass octave C is used as a pedal point throughout. Level 9.

Milonga (1948)

When Ginastera was asked to compose a piano piece for students, he transcribed his song *Canción al árbol del olvido* as *Milonga*. It is a languid two-page piece, with a left-hand rhythmic ostinato and a tuneful and syncopated melody. Some of the rhythmic subdivisions are complex. A student with solid rhythmic and musical abilities but with less technical fluency might play this piece well. The texture is generally thin throughout. (Ricordi.) Level 7.

Rondo on Argentine Children's Folk Tunes (1947)

Ginastera said that he decided to base this spirited work on specific Argentine children's folk tunes to entertain his own children. Form is ABACA with a short introduction and a Coda. Various Argentinian folk tunes with biting accompaniments reappear within the sections of the rondo. Variations in tempo between the different tunes in the sections need careful pacing. Brilliant climax. (Barry.) Level 9.

Malambo (1940)

A toccata based on the *gaucho* contest for men. The *malambo* begins with one dancer performing intricate steps alone, followed by a succession of dancers who try to outdo each other. An introductory guitar chord opens the entire piece, followed by the *malambo* proper in a rapid 6/8. Driving work filled with ostinatos, repetitions and sequences. (Ricordi.) Level 10.

REINHOLD GLIÈRE (1875–1956) Russia

Professor of composition at the Moscow Conservatory from 1920–1941, Glière often appeared in performance both as conductor and pianist. His style was influenced by the 19th-century Russian Romantic tradition.

12 Student Pieces, Op. 31

Nine of these pieces are essentially songs for piano. The other three are dances: a waltz, a mazurka and a ballet dance. Especially good for developing a cantabile tone. (Leeds.)

No. 1 Prelude

Study in playing arpeggiated chords divided evenly between the hands. Lush romanticism and chromatic melody lines that evoke nostalgia. Level 8.

No. 2 Nocturne

Requires independent voicing between the two hands. Easier than the Chopin or Field nocturnes. Left-hand accompaniment is primarily linear and chromatic. Emotional writing. Level 7.

No. 3 Lullaby

Both hands play in the upper register of the piano in a work that requires less technical facility than most pieces in this volume. Levels 7–8.

No. 7 Romance

One of the most successful compositions in this collection. Contains long melodic lines accompanied by an arpeggiated left hand. Level 8.

No. 8 Étude

Downward broken arpeggios divided between the hands help to give this a lush feeling. Sounds more difficult than it is and the writing fits the hands well. Level 8.

No. 11 Album Leaf

Another tranquil, lyrical work, highly sentimental in nature. Thick chords need voicing for clarity. Level 8.

Eight Easy Pieces, Op. 43

Graceful and expressive examples of the Russian Romantic tradition. They could provide relief from the standard Romantic teaching literature of Gurlitt and Burgmüller. (Associated Board of the Royal Schools of Music.)

No. 1 Prelude

Flowing chords arpeggiated between the hands give this work a sweep that makes it exciting for intermediate pianists. Chromatic harmonies. Level 7.

No. 2 Prayer

A short, tender selection that needs a sensitive interpretation. The harmonic framework of this chordal work should awaken the ears of the intermediate performer. Level 7.

No. 3 Mazurka

This mazurka might be suitable for a performer wanting to study a dance-like piece and not quite ready for Chopin mazurkas. Interesting writing that fits the hand well. Level 7.

No. 5 Evening

Repetitive work with a left-hand ostinato in the A section. Level 7.

No. 6 Rondo

This work with skipping figures feels good under the hand, although it requires facility in moving about the keyboard. Levels 7–8.

12 Sketches, Op. 47, ed, Johnson

Lush and romantic sounds, directly out of the Russian Romantic school. Untitled selections that are slightly more difficult than the works in Op. 46. Almost all are two printed pages. (Associated Board of the Royal Schools of Music.) Level 8.

Additional Work for Study:
Op. 34 24 Characteristic Pieces

ALEXANDER GOEDICKE (1877–1957) Russia

Some sources spell his name *Gedike.*

60 Simple Pieces for Beginners (60 Klavierstücke), Op. 36

Two books of 30 pieces for teaching. Contains dances, Russian songs and similar pieces in a Romantic style. (Peters.) Levels 2–5.

A Happy Tale

Repeated patterns in the ABAC structure. Right-hand melody calls for facility over left-hand chordal accompaniment. Appealing writing for the beginner. (Frederick Harris.) Levels 1–2.

Additional Works for Study:
Op. 22 Four Études in Octaves
Op. 32 Melodic Études
Op. 46
Op. 58

DIANNE GOOLKASIAN-RAHBEE (b. 1938) USA

Pictures, Op. 3

Contemporary writing that is imaginative and fits the hand well. Performance directions are included and creative instructions for improvisation on the given score are sometimes included. Should be better known. (Boston.)

No. 2 Chase

Right hand plays continuous sixteenth notes while the left hand is in staccato eighth notes. This work depicts someone being chased so closely that his heels are being stepped on. Effective in performance. Level 3.

No. 3 Roaming

Depicts someone roaming thoughtfully along a quiet country road. Features an expressive melody in half notes with accompaniment in quarter notes and based on an A pedal point. Levels 1–2.

No. 4 Frolicking

The right hand plays continuous triplets up and down the keyboard. Accessible left hand ostinato. Level 2.

No. 6 Parade

Avant-garde work using the inside of a grand piano. The work depicts a parade off in the distance, the bass drum faintly heard and gradually becoming louder and closer. When it arrives, trumpets blare and echo until the parade passes and goes off into the distance. The construction of the work must be established by the performer from a series of instructions which include reaching inside the piano and striking as many of the lowest strings of the piano as possible with the flat underpart of the fingers as if playing a drum, as well as traditional playing on the piano keyboard. Highly imaginative writing. Level 3.

No. 8 Mosquito

An energetic dance with some pentatonic playing and repeated notes and intervals to create the pesky buzz of a mosquito. Level 4.

No. 10 What Do I Hear?

Left-hand accompaniment is played on the keyboard, during which overtones of a silently depressed chord are heard. The right hand simultaneously strums the strings, producing a harp-like sound. Level 3.

Essays for the Piano, Op. 4

A strong set of contemporary works for the advancing elementary student. See especially *No. 1 Allegretto; No. 9 Changing Meters; No. 11 Marcato;* and *No. 12 Modular Improvisation*. (Musicalligraphics.)

MORTON GOULD (b. 1913) USA

Americana

Subtitled "Five mood sketches for piano," these solos are all in a popular idiom. Based on traditional harmonies, these solos exploit the feeling of Americana and would serve more as leisure-time reading than for serious pedagogical study. See especially *Music Hall*. Other titles include *Corn-Cob, Indian Nocturne, Hillbilly* and *Night Song*. (Carl Fischer.) Level 10.

Pavane

A popular flavor pervades a syncopated work that seems to amble and saunter. This piece would be especially appropriate for adults playing at the intermediate level since the chord structures are basic and the theme and accompaniment are simply stated in single notes. (Belwin.) Level 6.

PERCY GRAINGER (1882–1961) Australia

The music of Grainger is direct, uncomplicated and prone to good humor. Although he lived half of his life in the US and was born in Australia, many assume that Grainger was a Briton because he began his professional career in England.

Three Scotch Folk Songs

Settings of folk songs inspired by a visit to Scotland. Full chords, dotted rhythms, upbeat settings. Worth investigating. (Peters.) Level 9.

The Young Pianist's Grainger, ed. Stevenson

Fifteen pieces by Grainger. The melodic material of six of the pieces (Nos. 4, 6, 8, 9, 10 and 14) is Grainger's own with no borrowing from folk-music sources. Seven of the pieces are easy arrangements by the editor of Grainger's originals. Notes on the music are provided. (Schott.) Levels 8–9.

Percy Grainger Piano Album

Contains 16 of the best-known pieces by Grainger including *Country Gardens, Handel in the Strand, Children's March "Over the hills and far away"* and *Shepherd's Hey*. Wide range of difficulty levels found here. A good introduction to Grainger's works. (G. Schirmer.) Levels 8–10.

Additional Works for Study:
Mock Morris (Room-Music Tit-Bits)
Three British Folk-Music Settings

ARTHUR GREENE (b. 1945) USA

Seven Wild Mushrooms and a Waltz

A set of intriguing pieces for prepared piano. The simple preparations for a grand piano include the use of wood screws and pencil erasers, with the same preparation used for all pieces in this book. The works are skillfully written to utilize interesting sounds and to fascinate the ears of the elementary student. See especially *Three Blind Mice Rollin' Along Toccata (R.A.T.)*, *Chain Gang*, *Hot Pursuit*, *Dies Irae* and *Hypnosis Special*. Use one or several of these to enliven lessons and to effectively introduce avant-garde idioms. (Galaxy.) Level 6.

ALEXANDER GRETCHANINOFF (1864–1956) Russia

Gretchaninoff taught at the Moscow Conservatory. He moved to Paris in 1925 and then came to the USA in 1939, later becoming an American citizen. The influence of Tchaikovsky can be heard throughout his music. A highly prolific composer, Gretchaninoff composed a great deal of music for children.

Five Little Pieces, Op. 3

More difficult than many of his teaching pieces. Highly lyrical writing, if not especially inspired. (Kalmus.) Level 8.

Children's Album, Op. 98

Gretchaninoff's best-known set of teaching pieces. Fine writing in a set of titled character pieces in a harmonically conservative idiom. (Alfred, International, G. Schirmer and others.) Level 3.

No. 2 In Camp
Playful work with melodies built on various chord inversions. ABA form with horn-call introduction and Coda and echo effects. Level 3.

No. 3 March
March-like piece in three voices, suitable as preparation for later chordal pieces. Level 3.

No. 4 Farewell
Contemplative work with question-and-answer phrases. This also may serve to prepare students for chordal textures. Level 3.

No. 5 Horse and Rider (Riding the Hobby Horse)

Animated piece with vivid depiction of the title in the music. Rapid staccato scale passages and different articulations. Hands alternate to give a rocking feeling. Level 3.

No. 6 In a Woodland Glade

Evokes the feelings of children playing out of doors. The texture is comprised of a running staccato melody split between the hands and repeated chords in the left hand. It can help develop facility, lightness of touch and finger strength. Level 4.

No. 8 A Tiresome Tale

This piece contains an especially humorous passage with deliberately tiresome musical repetitions. Many short phrase groupings. Level 3.

No. 10 Dance

This graceful dance has some awkward leaps and may require special attention to fingering. Level 4.

No. 11 A Terrible Tale

Dramatic, almost spooky writing with tempo changes to help create the dramatic effects. Most of the melodic work occurs in the low register where voicing may need attention. Level 4.

No. 12 Étude

Rapid repeated chords and thirds alternate between the hands in a work that helps develop coordination between the hands and the feeling of both hands playing close to each other. Uses primarily the treble range of the piano and looks more difficult than it is. This short, playful work is effective in performance. Level 4.

No. 14 A Lingering Song

Especially good to teach the playing of a three-part texture. May help develop chordal playing as well as the balance of melody and accompaniment. Level 3.

A Child's Day, Op. 109

Ten titled selections composed around the events in a child's day such as *Morning Prayer, At Work, My Little Horse, A Visit to Grandmother, Nurse's Fairy Tale* and *Bed Time*. Most are one page. This book contains writing of higher quality than many of the other Gretchaninoff collections. See especially *My Little Horse* and *A Visit to Grandmother.* (Marks, Schott.) Level 5.

Sonatine in G Major, Op. 110, No. 1

Three-movement work, *Allegretto, Largo, Finale-Allegro* with some large stretches. The double notes and full chords in all three movements make this not the most effective for young hands. Many grace notes appear in the first and second movements. The mildly contemporary sonority is more modern than in many of Gretchaninoff's works, but the writing is still fundamentally conservative. (Schott.) Level 8.

Sonatine in F Major, Op. 110, No. 2

This sonatina seems better suited for the mature pianist. Sophisticated musical language is found and the piece is more difficult than it first appears. In three short movements. (Schott.) Level 9.

Grandfather's Book, Op. 119

Many of the selections are shorter than one printed page and several are quite attractive. See especially *My Mother, Old Romance, Holidays, March* and *A Happy Meeting*. (Marks.)

No. 1 My Dear Mother

Sentimental work with repeated chords in the accompaniment and a lyrical melody. Enchanting writing. Level 3.

No. 8 Nurse Tells a Story

A pleasant remembrance from childhood can be depicted through the performance of this lyrical work. The performer should strive for skillful and appropriate voicing of melody and accompaniment. Economy of material. Levels 3–4.

No. 17 Holidays

A zestful work that calls for a strong rhythmic sense and a bold interpretation. Level 3.

Glass Beads, Op. 123

One of Gretchaninoff's best-known collections. These easy character pieces are tuneful and fit the hand well. (Many standard editions.)

No. 1 Morning Walk

Modulates from major to relative minor and back to major. A technical challenge appears in a passage that requires the holding of the thumb or fifth finger while other fingers within the hand play. Tuneful writing that contains many repetitions in each of the lines, making it easy to learn. Level 2.

No. 2 The Little Beggar

Patterned piece, with the pleading of a beggar represented by descending slurred intervals. In the three sections of this piece, the short B section repeats the A section in the major mode for a change of mood before it returns to a repetition of the original material in minor. Effective programmatic writing. Level 3.

No. 5 On the Bicycle

In 3/8 with accompanimental chords appearing on the second beat and the melody played in eighths on the first and third beats in the right hand. Refreshing and interesting. Level 3.

No. 6 Waltz

Lyrical writing in the right hand and off-beat chords in the left. A good introduction to the waltz style. Level 3.

No. 7 Difficult Work

A study in slurred double thirds and sixths. Level 3.

No. 8 My First Ball

Two-part writing in both hands within the A section. Level 4.

No. 10 In the Fields

The many short, slurred phrases need careful attention regarding articulation. Expressive B section with alternating major and minor phrases. Levels 4–5.

No. 12 On the Harmonica

Imitates a person playing a harmonica. Contains grace-notes and a strong rhythmic framework. Excellent, sparse writing. Level 3.

Dew Drops, Op. 127a

Some of Gretchaninoff's most enchanting writing for the elementary student. This volume compares favorably with the Gretchaninoff *Children's Book*, Op. 98 in terms of quality and practical usefulness for study. The nine pieces are tuneful and imaginative, and based on traditional harmonies. These selections should be part of a student's basic study. (Schott.) Level 4.

Album de Nina, Op. 141

Ten easy miniatures, all one page in length. Tuneful writing. (Max Eschig.) Level 4.

Miniature Suite Op. 145

Ten works for the upper-intermediate student. Uninspired. (Kalmus.) Level 7.

12 Little Sketches for Children, Op. 182

The writing is more contrapuntal than that found in many of Gretchaninoff's selections. The titles of the one-page pieces render them most appropriate for study by children. Some of his easiest writing. (International.) Level 3.

No. 5 A New Friend

Rubato indications within the piece help depict two friends becoming acquainted. Interesting and different writing, in 9/8. Level 4.

Gouaches, Op. 189

Three one-page pieces, *At Joyful Work, In Solitude* and *Encounter,* for the early grades. See especially the third, *Encounter,* which features the hands alternating. (Leeds.) Level 4.

Five Miniatures for Piano, Op. 196

Titles are *Étude, Mazurka, Little Rhapsody, Insistence* and *Ballad.* See especially *Little Rhapsody,* featuring strong rhythms in a primarily staccato piece. *Ballad* is marchlike and especially appropriate for the student who is adept at playing chordal pieces. (Marks.) Levels 4–5.

Suite, Op. 202

Contains eight short, early-intermediate selections in one of Gretchaninoff's most interesting but little-known collections. (Marks.)

No. 1 Little Prelude

Effective writing. Processional-like, with a stately mood. Sounds more difficult than it is. Level 4.

No. 3 Come On, Let's Go!

A martial feel, with repeated notes that suggest trumpet calls. Thirty-second notes make the rhythm of the piece seem difficult. Level 5.

No. 8 Ballad

Lyrical and interesting writing, with legato thirds in the right hand. Level 5.

Additional Works for Study:
Op. 61 Eight Pastels
Op. 138 Brimborions
Op. 146 Aquarelles (Five Pieces) (Augener, Schott)
Op. 156 Eight Easy Pieces (Belaieff, Schott)
Op. 170 Four Pieces for Children (Schott)
Op. 183 By the Fireside (10 Pieces) (Boosey)

Miscellaneous Volumes

The Gretchaninoff Collection, ed. Hinson

A volume of 20 varied selections representing a wide range of difficulty levels. Works are included from Op. 98, Op. 99, Op. 109, Op. 115, Op. 119, Op. 123 and Op. 127a. The pieces are introduced and discussed briefly by Hinson. (Schott.) Levels 3–7.

CHARLES TOMLINSON GRIFFES (1884–1920) USA

Griffes was a true American Impressionist. During his early student days in Europe, it was Humperdinck who steered him away from a career as a concert pianist and into composition instead. Mussorgsky and Scriabin were important influences on Griffes, as were Debussy and Ravel.

Three Preludes

Three two-page works, with no tempo indications marked. Effective and more accessible than Griffes' other piano works. (G. Schirmer and others.) Levels 8–9.

The Lake at Evening, Op. 5, No. 1

An atmospheric work calling for refinement of color. Repeated bell-like octaves permeate the texture. (G. Schirmer and others.) Levels 9–10.

Clouds, Op. 7, No. 4

Filled with planed sonorities and full chords. Much of the playing uses primarily the black keys. (G. Schirmer and others.) Level 10.

GABRIEL GROVLEZ (1879–1944) France

A Child's Garden

Six pieces, some of which are quasi-Impressionistic. This is music about children that probably will be played by older students due to its sophistication. Poems accompany each piece. (Chester.) Level 8.

DAVID WENDELL GUION (1892–1981) USA

Mother Goose

Based on familiar nursery rhyme tunes. Within the 17 movements are a number of jazz-flavored pieces, hints of Impressionism, some witty musical jokes and even a parody of polytonality. (G. Schirmer.) Level 8.

Arkansas Traveler

A popular folk tune. Virtuosic version, often played by Percy Grainger. (G. Schirmer.) Level 10.

Piano Album

The best source of much of Guion's piano music. Contains 24 pieces: the entire *Mother Goose Suite* as well as *Arkansas Traveler, Harmonica Player, Scissors Grinder, Sheep and Goat* and other pieces. This music is charming, but by no means easy. (G. Schirmer.) Levels 9–10.

H

JOSEPH HAAS (1879–1960) Germany

Frohe Launen (Good Humour)

Subtitled "Humoresques for Piano," this set of pieces is attractive and should be better known. Titles include *Glad, Roguish, Wanton, Witty, Amiable* and *Talkative.* (Rahter.) Levels 7–8.

Additional Work for Study:
Op. 16 Lose Blätter (Flying Leaves)

ANDRÉ HAJDÚ (b. 1932) Hungary

Sonatine

Both of the outer movements are driving, featuring repeated chords and highly rhythmic passages, appropriate for the energetic student. The *tranquillo* middle movement is bitonal and atmospheric. None of the movements are difficult to read. (Editio Musica.) Level 9.

RODOLFO HALFFTER (b. 1900) Spain

Halffter left Spain in 1939 for Mexico where he became a Mexican citizen.

11 Bagatelles, Op. 19

Short works with haunting harmonies and some contrapuntal writing. Elegant pieces for the sophisticated musical ear. (Union Musical Española.) Level 9.

HOWARD HANSON (1896–1981) USA

Native of Nebraska and long-time director of the Eastman School of Music. Hanson composed in a highly Romantic style.

Three Miniatures

All three are predominantly slow pieces and present ponderous, pensive writing in a modern lyrical idiom. Titles of the movements are *Reminiscence, Lullaby* and *Longing*. (Carl Fischer.) Level 9.

For the First Time

Subtitled "12 Impressions in a Child's Day." Each movement uses a different technical medium and a limited yet diverse tonal vocabulary. The child awakens to the sound of *Bells*. Then he watches the play of two Irish terrier puppies, *Tamara and Peter Bolshoi*. He explores a *Deserted House*, meets an *Eccentric Clock*, wanders through a *Deep Forest*, meets a group of *Clowns* going to the circus. In time the child observes a happy *Dance* in Polish style and takes part in *Serious Conversations*. He hears the Russian fairy tale of *Kikimore*, sees the *Mists* of evening rising, watches *Fireworks*, and finally goes to sleep to gentle *Dreams*. The music is imaginative and captivating and should be much better known. See especially *The Eccentric Clock, Bells, Dance, Fireworks* and *Tamara and Peter Bolshoi*. (Fischer.) Level 8.

No. 1 Bells

> Requires large span in this *lento* work featuring both 7/4 and 5/4 time signatures. Syncopated pedaling is required as well as the playing of octaves. Voicing in the B section will need attention. Level 7.

No. 2 Tamara and Peter Bolshoi

> Especially good for a student with fast fingers and a natural flair. Requires clean staccatos and a contracted hand for the sixteenth-note patterns. Level 8.

Enchantment

Mood piece in ABA form with melody and sustained notes in the right hand. (Carl Fischer.)

Dance of the Warriors

Rhythmic and spirited, sounding more difficult than it is. (Carl Fischer.)

The Bell

Unusual harmonic structure in an expressive work. Graceful, flowing music based on a fragment of a theme from Hanson's *Fourth Symphony*. Requires a refined legato. Based on the Aeolian and Dorian scales. Two pages. (Carl Fischer.) Level 6.

Clog Dance

Rhythmic interest abounds in a work with large leaps and octaves. (Carl Fischer.)

CUTHBERT HARRIS (n.d.) Great Britain

Introduction and Fugato in D Minor

Somewhat pompous writing, but effective in performance. Large chords and majestic sonorities in the *Introduction* are followed by a tuneful, almost jazzy *Fugato*. Brilliant alternating octaves and *con forza* passage-work occur at the conclusion of the fugue. (Warren and Phillips.) Level 8.

ROY HARRIS (1898–1979) USA

Little Suite

Conscious use of contemporary compositional techniques in the inter-mediate literature. Quartal harmony, free meter, irregular meter, non-traditional harmonies. The four short, titled movements are *Bells* (notated on three staves), *Sad News, Children at Play* (in 7/8 with tricky phrasing) and *Slumber*. (G. Schirmer.) Level 7.

American Ballads

Five miniature tone poems based on familiar American themes. The works feature colorful harmonies and diatonic melodies. Titles include *Streets of Laredo, Wayfaring Stranger, The Bird, Black is the Color of My True Love's Hair* and *Cod Liver Isle*. (Carl Fischer.) Levels 7–8.

Streets of Laredo

This contemporary-sounding arrangement is filled with accidentals. It can be played by a performer with a smaller hand. *Streets of Laredo* uses both the damper and sostenuto pedals. Level 8.

Wayfaring Stranger

This attractive piece is easier to play than to read. The bitonal writing features the right hand in B-flat Major and the left hand in E-flat minor. Both the damper and sostenuto pedals are used. The left hand alternates between the lower and middle registers. Level 8.

Toccata

Bravura, effective and little-heard work calling for resonant sonorities. Based on a pair of motives that are transformed extensively within the work. Some structural tempo changes. (Carl Fischer.) Level 10.

LOU HARRISON (b. 1917) USA

Reel—Homage to Henry Cowell

Shows the influence of Harrison's teacher Henry Cowell on his writing. Black key right hand and arm clusters in similar notation to that of Cowell in his work *The Lilt of the Reel.* A single-note melody is heard between sections with clusters. An effective and accessible work using large clusters on the keyboard. (Alfred.) Level 8.

Homage a Rameau

One-page lyrical selection featuring "a musette-like left hand part [that] supports and interacts with a flexible archaic melodic line that produces a charming medieval polyphony," according to Maurice Hinson. (Alfred.) Level 7.

JACK HAWES (b. 1916) Great Britain

Three Whimsical Pieces

Lyrical, neo-Romantic and expressive writing within a mildly contemporary idiom. Requires playing a long, sustained line. Titles include *Let's Play, Jane's Air (Lullaby)* and *Samantha's Dance.* (Robertson.) Level 6.

Toccata

Rapid passagework in continuous sixteenths, featuring passages that alternate between hands, driving rhythms and exciting climaxes. Effective in performance. (Carl Fischer.) Level 10.

Nocturne

Dramatic writing in a two-page piece that fits the hand well. Non-traditional harmonic framework using a primarily chordal texture. (Carl Fischer.) Level 8.

JOHN HEISS (b. 1938) USA

Four Short Pieces

One-page atonal pieces in a sound and style similar to that of Schoenberg. These works could provide an introduction to atonal writing. (Boosey.) Level 9.

EVERETT HELM (b. 1913) USA

New Horizons

Twelve pieces composed as an introduction to contemporary styles in piano music, with the intent of serving as a bridge between the past and present. The pieces are progressive in order of difficulty presented but are meant to be musical entities in themselves rather than pedagogical studies. Selections deal with such techniques as change of meter, free use of dissonance, harmony used for color rather than functionally, and bitonality. (G. Schirmer.) Level 8.

MICHAEL HENNAGIN (1936–1993) USA

American composer and recipient of various awards from the National Endowment for the Arts, the MacDowell Colony, ASCAP and others. Hennagin was the former head of composition at the University of Oklahoma.

Children's Suite (1961)

Fascinating writing in a tonal framework. Based on reflections of the life of children, this is music that can be played by adults or talented pre-college students. Most of the movements are in ternary form. (Walton Music.)

No. 1 Tag

Sounds of children on the playground. Major and minor seconds used throughout. Level 8.

No. 2 Broken Doll

Almost continuous sixteenth-note texture. Features three-note figure in one hand with rhythmic inventions in the other hand. Level 8.

No. 3 Hopscotch

Begins with a big jump in which the child hops to a new square. In 5/8 alternating with 6/8 and 3/8. Level 8.

No. 4 Hobby Horse

Irregularity of a child rocking on a horse. The music is sometimes fast and sometimes slow, as if the child is lost in a reverie. No formal barlines, although dotted barrings are used. Level 8.

No. 5 Chocolate Soda

Swinging rhythms throughout and a simple idea presented in different keys. *Chocolate Soda* features many seconds, sevenths and ninths. Level 8.

No. 6 Feathers

Light and delicate brief work, reminiscent of Claude Bolling and Copland. Level 7.

No. 7 Parade

Reminiscent of Kabalevsky or Shostakovich, with meter shifts, pandiatonicism, and chords based on fourths and fifths. Short motifs are developed at length. Features extended lyric lines and bitonal passages. Level 8.

HANS WERNER HENZE (b. 1926) Germany

Six Pieces for Young Pianists

These works are excerpts from his opera for children *Pollicino*, which he arranged for piano. Strong contemporary writing, for the mature performer. Movements are *Ballade, Allegro con grazia, Allegretto barbaro, Moderato cantabile, Allegro mostroso* and *Anhang: Margaretenwalzer.* (Schott.) Levels 9–10.

EDUARDO HERNÁNDEZ MONCADA (b. 1899) Mexico

Cinco Piezas Bailables

Light-hearted pieces, for the fans of Mexican music. Strongly rhythmic writing. (Ediciones Mexicanas.) Level 9.

WILLY HESS (b. 1906) Switzerland

Notebook for Sandra, Op. 109 (1982)

"Twenty-Four Easy Pieces for Piano," composed for the first lessons of a gifted little girl. Hess states the aim of these pieces is to encourage musical phrasing. No indications of tempo are provided except for the last piece. Most are composed in two voices, and the linear writing encourages independence between the hands. Excellent. (Amadeus.) Levels 1–3.

PAUL HINDEMITH (1895–1963) Germany

Hindemith was a neo-Classical and highly contrapuntal composer with a personally conceived theory of tonality and harmonic relationships. He left Germany in 1938 to teach at the Yale School of Music for many years, eventually returning to Europe. Hindemith composed for almost every conceivable solo instrument and combination of instruments. His concepts about tonality are explained in his book *The Craft of Musical Composition.*

Kleine Klaviermüsik (1929)

Twelve short teaching pieces, some of Hindemith's best. Although the hands remain in relatively stationary positions, the dissonance and highly contrapuntal writing render this music more difficult than it first appears. For a pianist who has an ear for dissonant counterpoint, or for composition majors. (Schott.) Levels 4–8.

Let's Build a City (Wir bauen eine Stadt) (1931)

These six pieces were adapted from Hindemith's cantata of the same name. Each piece centers around a different key. The writing, although typical of Hindemith, is more palatable than in *Kleine Klaviermüsik.* Pianistic writing with textures that are often contrapuntal. Titles include *1. March, 2. Let's Build a City, 3. New Arrivals are Shown the Town, 4. I'm a (Train) Conductor, 5. Gossiping* and *6. Cops and Robbers.* (Schott.) Level 5.

Foxtrot (1922)

Subtitled "Dance of the Wooden Dolls" and taken from the Christmas play *Tuttifäntchen,* this is a dance that mixes ragtime and foxtrot. Syncopation, many octaves and oom-pah accompaniment. (Schott.) Levels 9–10.

Miscellaneous Volumes
The Hindemith Collection

An excellent and practical collection for the performer. Included are the set of pieces *Let's Build A City,* three pieces from *Kleine Klaviermüsik, Foxtrot,* a fugue and interlude from the *Ludis Tonalis,* a movement from *Sonata No. 2* and others. (Schott.) Levels 4–10.

GUSTAV HOLST (1874–1934) Great Britain

Two Pieces for Piano

The *Nocturne* is a quasi-Impressionistic selection featuring a double-note figure in the right hand alternating between octaves, with passagework in the left hand. The middle *animato* section provides strong contrast through rapid fingerwork in both hands. The *Jig* is a lively dance calling for agile fingers. (Faber.) Level 10.

ARTHUR HONEGGER (1892–1955) France

Souvenir de Chopin

Chopin-like texture with a single-note melody. Perhaps Honegger's least difficult piece for solo piano. (Choudens.) Level 8.

Hommage à Albert Roussel

Mysterious, chordal, two-page piece based thematically on the spelling of composer Albert Roussel's name. Requires a large span. (Salabert.) Level 9.

Le Neige sur Rome

This selection was arranged by Honneger from his incidental music for *L'Impératrice aux Rochers*. It is a two-page piece in a lamenting mood. (Salabert.) Level 9.

ANTHONY HOPKINS (b. 1921) Great Britain

Sonatine

This piece could substitute for the Kabalevsky *Sonatina in A Minor* and thus provide an interesting change for the teacher. Strong writing in the outer movements with a slow movement that requires keen sense of the timing of phrases. Inviting contemporary writing. (Oxford.) Level 8.

For Talented Beginners, Books 1 and 2

Featuring highly pianistic writing for the elementary student in a mildly contemporary idiom, these books contain titled programmatic character pieces. Titles include *Interrupted Melody, Trumpets, Ghosts* and *The Last Dance*. Ten pieces are in Book 1, nine in Book 2. (Oxford.) Levels 2–4.

ALAN HOVHANESS (b. 1911) USA

Hovhaness' works generally are mysterious and somewhat exotic, and can often be categorized as Impressionistic. His is an individual style with an evolved musical language of his own, characterized by blending of both Eastern and Western artistic influences.

Mystic Flute, Op. 22

Three-page solo in 7/8 with melody above a repetitive accompaniment. Modal inflections including augmented seconds give it a mystic quality. (Peters.) Level 5.

12 Armenian Folk Songs, Op. 43

Based on Armenian mountain village tunes, and generally one page or shorter in length. The settings contain the melody stated in a straight-forward manner with simple accompaniments. Some of his best writing. (Peters.) Level 4.

Moonlight Night, Op. 52a

Four-page solo, delicate and wistful, that derives its character from four inter-changeable Near-Eastern scale forms. The left-hand accompaniment gives the effect of a paired drum accompaniment. (Merion Music.) Level 4.

Pastoral No. 1, Op. 111, No. 2

Requires strumming on the inside of the piano, as well as on the keys. A marimba stick and a timpani stick are required. (Peer International.) Level 10.

Macedonian Mountain Dance Op. 144b

Rhythmic, repetitive music requiring agile fingers. Six pages. Not particularly inspired. (Peters.) Level 10.

Bare November Day, Op. 210

A prelude and five short hymns with generally thin textures. Written for any keyboard instrument. (Peters.)

Sketchbook of Mr. Purple Poverty, Volumes I and II, Op. 309

Mr. Purple Poverty is an idiotic, clownish poet who dreams of being in love with Lady Purple, a great and beautiful poetess who lived 1,000 years ago. The pieces are generally short, sparse in texture (often two voices) and contemporary. Representative titles include *Purple Rags, Sleeping Cat, Mr. Purple, a Poor Poet* and *Love Song to Lady Purple*. Thirteen selections in each book. (Broude.) Level 2.

Lullaby

A simple one-page piece with a simple melody and left-hand cluster. (Marks.) Level 8.

Mountain Idylls

The first and third in this set of three are sad, while the second features a lively melody with a repetitive phrase rhythm. *Moon Lullaby, Moon Dance, Mountain Lullaby.* (Associated.) Level 5.

HERBERT HOWELLS (1892–1983) Great Britain

Country Pageant and A Little Book of Dances

Howells wrote little for piano, but these two sets of pieces reflect his feeling for the English tradition. *Country Pageant* contains four intermediate works: *Merry Andrew's Procession, Kings and Queens, There was a most beautiful lady* and *The Mummers' Dance*. *A Little Book of Dances* is slightly more difficult, with all pieces in dance forms, including *Minuet, Pavane, Galliard* and *Jig*. Conservative harmonic vocabulary. (Associated Board of the Royal Schools of Music.) Levels 7–9.

BERTOLD HUMMEL (b. 1925) Germany

10 Piano Pieces for Children, Op. 56b

Well-written kinesthetically for the piano. Moderately contemporary. See especially *Puffing Bill, Ball Game* and *Dance in the Moonlight*. (Simrock.) Levels 5–6.

Sonatina

Dissonant linear writing. The last of the three movements is decidedly the most difficult. (Simrock.) Level 7.

MICHAEL HURD (b. 1928) Great Britain

Bagatelles

Six brief, titled pieces for the elementary pianist. Occasional sections of bitonality are cleverly handled. Interesting and different. (Novello.) Level 4.

I

MICHAEL ANTHONY IATAURO (b. 1943) USA

Children's Pieces for Adults

Mildly contemporary solos with titles such as *A Stuffed Lion Called Jonathan, Italian Pony Cart, The Toy Donkey* and *Traffic*. (Peer International.) Level 8.

JACQUES IBERT (1890–1962) France

Histoires

Set of 10 character pieces. A significant collection, especially since there is a lack of high-quality teaching pieces at this level from the French school. These pieces are more difficult to read than to play. The writing is highly pianistic. In addition to the movements listed below, see *La marchande d'eau fraiche* and *Le Cortège de Balkis*. (Leduc.)

Le petit âne blanc (The Little White Donkey)

Humorous depiction. Left-hand staccato needs clean definition. Suitable piece to work on finger independence and articulation. A student favorite and the best-known of the set. Level 9.

A Giddy Girl

Visually difficult to read, but less difficult to play. Highly patterned and idiomatic to the keyboard. Marked to be played, "In the style of a sentimental English romance." Students ready for their first Debussy preludes might find this selection to be a good alternative. Humorous and playful writing. Level 8.

La cage de cristal (The Crystal Cage)

Animated, with several tempo changes in a good-natured selection featuring light glissando-like figures and lyrical melodic lines and light chordal accompaniment. Level 9.

La marchande d'eau fraiche

Witty writing featuring a rhythmic ostinato with fragmented melody. The hands are positioned on top of each other much of the time. Worth investigating. Level 10.

Petite Suite en Quinze Images (1943)

High-quality writing in 15 intermediate pieces that are substantially easier than those from *Histoires* and generally shorter. See especially *Le gai vigneron, Le cavalier sans-souci, Parade, Romance, La machine à coudre* and *Premier bal.* These selections should be better known. Level 8.

Scherzetto

Spirited and patterned, built primarily on the same theme throughout. The economy of material makes this a delightful piece for recreational study. (Leduc.) Level 9.

VINCENT D'INDY (1851–1931) France

Tableaux de Voyage, Op. 33

Thirteen travel portraits. Pleasant and appealing within a neo-Romantic idiom. See especially *En Marche, Paturage, Le Glas, Halte, au Soir* and *Lermoos.* (Leduc.) Level 9.

CHARLES IVES (1874–1954) USA

A signal American composer, but nearly all of his music is too difficult for study by the intermediate or early-advanced performer.

Invention

Two-page work with large reaches. Often one voice moves in sixteenths against eighths in the other two voices. (Hinshaw.) Level 8.

J

KAREL JIRÁK (1891–1972) Czechoslovakia

12 Pieces for Children, Op. 62, Books 1 and 2

Interesting writing. (Associated.) Levels 3–5.

OTTO JOACHIM (b. 1910) Germany

Joachim left Germany in 1934, eventually settling in Canada where he played with the Montreal Symphony and taught at the Montreal Conservatory.

12-Tone Pictures

All pieces are based on a single row presented at the beginning of the volume. Twelve pieces, mostly one page long. Titles include *Snowy Morning, March, Bless You, Full Moon* and *Plastic Soldier.* (BMI/Canada.) Level 5.

GRANT JOHANNESEN (b. 1921) USA

Improvisation on a Mormon Hymn "Come, come, ye saints"

This well-known Mormon hymn is given a two-page setting that features full chords and effective use of the piano sonority. Several hymn adaptations are found here. (Oxford.) Level 7.

MAGNUS BLÖNDAL JÓHANNSSON (b. 1925) Iceland

Four Abstractions

Brief atonal sketches, easier than Schoenberg *Six Little Piano Pieces,* Op. 19 and featuring thin textures and wide melodic leaps. For the contemporary music enthusiast who plays at the intermediate level. (Elkan.) Level 5.

K

DMITRI KABALEVSKY (1904–1987) Russia

Kabalevsky made an invaluable contribution to the teaching repertoire for the piano. He had a flair and talent for writing children's music, working in a style that is melodic and harmonically conservative. Most of the selections in *24 Little Pieces,* Op. 39 can be considered to be early elementary literature. The *30 Pieces for Children,* Op. 27, *Five Easy Sets of Variations,* Op. 51, and *Four Rondos,* Op. 60 are among those works that are of intermediate level. The *Sonatinas,* Op. 13 and the more accessible of the *Preludes,* Op. 38 can be viewed as early-advanced.

Im Ferienlager, Op. 3/86

Set of six medium-length pieces. The writing is more highly contemporary than in many of Kabalevsky's pieces. Mature character pieces, strongly motivic. (Sikorski.) Level 8.

Four Preludes, Op. 5

Thick textures, and short in length. Interesting neo-Romantic pieces that foreshadow the later *Preludes,* Op. 38. Could be considered as an introduction to the two *Sonatinas,* Op. 13. Infrequently heard. (G. Schirmer, MCA.) Level 9.

Sonatina in A Minor, Op. 13, No. 1 (1930)

This sonatina should not be confused with the one-movement *Sonatina in A Minor,* Op. 27, No. 18. Both the first and third movements are based on sonata-allegro form. The first movement is energetic, opening with three fanfare-like chords and ending with a splash. The second movement, *Andantino,* is an ABA song-form. The third movement is a real showpiece, requiring fast movement in 6/8 meter. Contains a great deal of triplet passagework. (Alfred, Kalmus, MCA, International and G. Schirmer.) Level 8.

Sonatina in G Minor, Op. 13, No. 2 (1933)

Four movements in a work that is longer and more serious than the *Sonatina in A Minor,* Op. 13, No. 1. See especially the vigorous and march-like first movement, which requires fine rhythmic control of triplets and the playing of double notes. The fourth movement is also notable for its brilliant opening and passagework. Calls for the playing of consecutive thirds. (Alfred, MCA, Kalmus.) Level 9.

Children's Pieces, Op. 27

Thirty pieces which have become standards in the 20th-century teaching literature. Imaginative titles, striking rhythms and interesting melodies. Many publishers issue a selected number of pieces from this opus. Numbering used here is that appearing in the VAAP edition, which contains the complete set of 30 pieces revised by Kabalevsky and in progressive order of difficulty. (VAAP, Alfred, MCA in two volumes. Also International, Kalmus, etc.)

No. 1 Waltz

> A study in the playing of two-note slurs that overlap between the right and left hands. An expressive, cantabile piece. Level 3.

No. 2 A Little Song

> Beautiful, lyrical melody, which is set against a sustained double-note accompaniment in slower note values. Appropriate for developing evenness of tone and finesse in tonal control at the early elementary level. Level 3.

No. 3 Étude in A Minor

> Dazzling in performance. The primary difficulties are in the right-hand descending B-flat scale and left-hand coordinating figuration. Especially good for the student with fast fingers. Level 6.

No. 4 At Night on the River

> Simple lyrical work, similar in texture to No. 2, but slightly more complex. Enchanting writing that is seldom heard. Needs skill in pacing the rubato. Level 3.

No. 5 Playing Ball

> Repeated notes in rapid passagework. Alternate hands play throughout and a rhythmic ostinato unifies the work. Appropriate for the student able to play fast passages. Level 4.

No. 6 A Sad Story

> Tender piece in which the right hand plays a melody above a chordal accompaniment. Level 4.

No. 7 An Old Dance

> Reminiscent of a Baroque minuet. The quick trills and varied articulations may pose problems. One of the least frequently heard pieces in this set. Level 4.

No. 8 Cradle Song (Lullaby)

Descending broken seventh chords, perhaps simulating a rocking motion. The right and left hand exchange melody and accompaniment. Programmatic writing in a cantabile work. This selection can help develop a feeling for seventh chords as well as a balance of melody and accompaniment. Level 6.

No. 9 Little Fable

Generally the hands play in unison, calling for strong inflection of the melody. Level 4.

No. 10 Clowning

Continuous eighths throughout this brilliant 6/8 piece are divided between the hands and create a driving rhythmic effect. Single-note passagework requires evenness. Level 5.

No. 11 Rondo

Generally in two voices, occasionally with some parallel legato thirds in the right hand. Kabalevsky surprises the listener by varying the melody each time it returns. Mysterious in character. Level 7.

No. 12 Toccatina

An excellent work for developing the feeling of first inversion triads in the right hand. Study in legato melody in the left hand and staccato chords in the right hand. Requires balance of left-hand melody over right-hand accompaniment. Perhaps the most popular selection in this collection. Level 3.

No. 13 A Little Joke

Rapid ascending or descending five-finger patterns permeate the lean, staccato texture. Effective in performance and enjoyable to practice. Vivacious character. Level 5.

No. 14 Scherzo

Calls for voicing of melody and the playing of a scherzando accompaniment. Requires a *leggiero* touch and strong fingers. Level 6.

No. 15 March

Primarily staccato work in march tempo. Contains ascending and descending passages in eighths with hands in parallel motion. Level 6.

No. 16 Lyric Piece

Calls for a mature performer to shape the expressive lines in this neo-Romantic work. Level 6.

No. 17 Meadow Dance

Continuous left-hand triads skip between octaves under a lyrical melody in the upper register. Level 6.

No. 18 Sonatina

One-movement work in A Minor, march-like with dotted rhythms throughout. Three distinct key areas. The left hand provides blocked chord accompaniment. Snappy rhythms. Level 5.

No. 19 Warlike Dance

Aggressive writing, effective in performance, and requiring a performer with strong fingers and the ability to play double notes. Strong rhythms. Level 7.

No. 20 Fairy Tale (A Short Story)

Melody with left-hand broken chord accompaniment, often in second inversion chords broken from the top. Sensitive writing, for the mature performer. Level 7.

No. 21 The Chase

A 6/8 work filled with triplets and accidentals, with some surprising modulations. Level 6.

No. 22 A Tale

Seldom heard, perhaps due to the many accidentals. Interesting modulations create unusual harmonic tension. Level 7.

No. 23 Snow Storm

A *presto* work built on two- or three-note slurs with the passagework alternating between the hands. Level 7.

No. 24 Étude

A splendid F-Major study in the playing of arpeggios and in expansion and contraction of the hand. Rapid arpeggios are played note-against-note against rapid descending/ascending scale passages. Effective in performance. Level 7.

No. 25 Novelette

One of the most popular works in this collection, perhaps due to the haunting melody and the effective building of tension through the harmonic writing. Marked *molto sostenuto*, this work could serve as a student's first study in playing right hand double-note passages. Level 4.

No. 26 Étude

This A-Major work is the least well-known of the three works titled "Étude" in this volume. Contains simulated "horn calls" and requires strong fingers. Level 6.

No. 27 Dance

A study in double thirds, this Russian dance features staccato passages which alternate between the hands. Some unpredictable harmonic turns. Good for developing finger strength. An energetic piece. Level 7.

No. 28 Caprice

Much of the piece consists of sustained and tied half notes with staccato passagework played above or below the held note written in a single hand. Requires finger independence. Level 7.

No. 29 Cavalry Gallop (Song of the Cavalry)

Persistent rhythms portray the charge of a cavalry brigade. Requires refined voicing. Off-beat chords pervade the thick texture. Written primarily on the black keys. Level 7.

No. 30 Dramatic Episode

Slow, sober work, perhaps intended as a satiric commentary on serious music. The dotted rhythms and resonant chords in the middle section create a pompous conclusion to this opus. Level 7.

Jugendleben, Op. 14 (1931/1968)

These two-page character pieces are filled with fresh ideas and musical vitality. Titles include *A Brisk Game, The Drummer, In the Gymnasium* and *Soldiers' March*. (MCA, Sikorski.) Level 7.

24 Preludes, Op. 38

The *Preludes,* dedicated to his teacher Nikolai Miakovsky and composed in 1943, are among Kabalevsky's more serious and abstract works. They display characteristics of his style, including a fondness for parallelism, mediant relationships and extended pedal points. The key arrangement follows that of Chopin, and progresses through the circle of fifths in major and minor pairs. The final *Prelude* begins in D Minor, ending in D Major. Although not always obvious, each of the *Preludes* has a folk song as a generating point. A surprising high number of the *Preludes* begin with an outline or repetition of the tonic triad. See especially Nos. 1, 2, 8, 9, 15, 20 and 23. (International, Kalmus, MCA and many others.)

No. 1 (Andantino)

Displays a lyricism that reveals full-blown Romanticism. Much of the accompaniment is comprised of repeated chords. One of the best of the *Preludes*. Level 9.

No. 2 (Scherzando)

Probably the most popular *Prelude* in the set, this scherzo-like work in A Minor requires a crisp touch and a strong rhythmic sense. Light staccato triads, fast *leggiero* passagework, biting chords and dissonant effects are found throughout. Level 9.

No. 8 (Andante non troppo. Semplice e cantando)

Features a slow accompaniment in quarter notes above which a cantilena melody is heard. Somewhat reminiscent of Satie. Level 9.

No. 12 (Adagio)

An adagio work in arch form ABCBA, highly dramatic and arresting in its intensity. Segments of a folk-tune are separated by original interludes. Level 10.

No. 15 (Allegretto marcato)

Similar to a Prokofiev march, with clockwork rhythms and daring harmonic progressions. Level 8.

No. 20 (Andantino semplice)

A deep work with some harmonic ambiguity. Level 9.

24 Pieces for Children, Op. 39

Some of the easiest music by a major composer. Each selection presents a particular technical problem, and many can be played in the first or second year of study. Worthy of an integral place in the standard teaching repertoire. (Alfred, International, Kalmus, MCA and others.) Levels 1–6.

No. 1 A Little Tune

Melody in quarter and half notes over whole-note accompaniment. Level 1.

No. 2 Polka

Legato quarter-note melody in the left hand and off-beat staccato chords played by the right hand. Level 1.

No. 5 Playing (A Game)

A staccato piece using primarily quarter notes. Emphasizes large motions and alternation between the hands. Should be played with one pulse per measure rather than three. Level 1.

No. 6 A Little Joke

Highly patterned piece in which both hands remain in relatively stationary positions on the keyboard. Level 2.

No. 7 Funny Event

Sometimes titled *Conversation,* quite appropriately, since this piece is largely a dialogue between the hands. Humorous and light piece filled with patterns. Level 1.

No. 8 Song

Lyrical contoured melody, played in unison at the distance of two octaves between the hands. Appropriate to teach inflection and phrasing of a musical line in the first year. Level 1.

No. 9 Dance

Staccato passagework and chords, with little movement of hands on the keyboard. Appealing dance for beginning students who have strong hands. Level 1.

No. 10 March

Snappy rhythms lend a flair that can appeal to beginning students. The passagework is based totally on broken chords. Level 2.

No. 11 Song of Autumn

The hands play in unison at the distance of two octaves. Lyrical writing with some hand shifts. Good for the development of phrasing. Level 2.

No. 12 Scherzo

A pattern piece that can easily be taught by rote early in a student's study. Much easier than it sounds, and effective in performance. Level 1.

No. 13 Waltz

Graceful writing with a simple right-hand melody, and left-hand accompaniment punctuated by double thirds. Level 1.

No. 14 A Fable

Three-part piece in the form AA'A with the central A' section being a minor version of the two outer A sections. Easier than it appears and one which should be better known. Level 2.

No. 15 Jumping

An appealing piece in which both hands play the same notes an octave apart, although one hand lags behind the other to create musical interest. Level 1.

No. 16 A Sad Tale

Two-voice writing, with a lyrical melody and an accompaniment moving in quarter notes. Level 1.

No. 17 Folk Dance (Country Dance)

Playful, canonic work with constantly shifting five-finger patterns and rapid staccato eighths. A light touch is needed. Level 3.

No. 18 Galop

Buoyant work in which the large right-hand leaps, though effective, make this more difficult than some of the earlier selections. Level 3.

No. 19 Prelude

This busy piece features five-finger patterns and scales, often in G Minor and C Minor keys. Requires independence between the hands. Level 3.

No. 20 Clowns

The continual shift from major to minor and back to major and the inversion of the melody throughout are all types of musical clowning. A light left-hand touch is needed for this deservedly popular selection. Level 3.

No. 22 A Short Story

Serious work that uses the high register of the piano. Level 4.

No. 23 Slow Waltz

Perhaps a portrayal of someone who is awkward and learning to dance. Features wide leaps of register. More difficult. Level 5.

No. 24 A Happy Outing

Interesting writing with some jump-bass left-hand passages. More difficult than most of the pieces in this collection and seldom heard. Level 6.

Variations, Op. 40 (1944)

Two fine variation sets for the upper-intermediate student. (Kalmus, International, MCA.)

No. 1 Variations

Continuous set of 12 character variations beginning with a four-measure introduction and concluding with a Coda. The theme is based on a descending D Major scale. Level 8.

No. 2 Variations

Theme and five variations in A Minor. Little-known work which displays a sadness and simplicity throughout. Not his most inspired writing. Level 8.

Five Sets of Variations on Folk Themes, Op. 51 (1952)

Strong writing that needs a performer with flair and the ability to achieve sharp contrast. All based on folk songs. Students who enjoy energetic and driving literature will enjoy playing these works. Available separately. (MCA, Masters Music and others.) Levels 4–8.

No. 1 Variations on the Theme of a Russian Folk Song

Sometimes known as *Five Happy Variations on a Russian Folk Song,* this is the most accessible variation set in this collection. Thin textures here call for skillful inflection of the melodic lines and careful detail to articulation. Robust and effective ending. Three pages. Level 4.

No. 2 Variations of the Theme of a Russian Folk Song

Sometimes known as *Merry Dance Variations on a Russian Folk Song,* this set contains an eight-measure theme and six variations. The rhythmic values and the coordination between hands are more complex. Three pages. Level 6.

No. 3 Variations on the Theme of a Slovak Folk Song

Titled *Gray Day Variations on a Slovakian Folk Song* in several collections, this set is one of the most effective in Op. 51. The lyrical theme that opens this set is soon displaced by lively and animated variations that build to a sparkling climax in variation five before the return of the opening cantabile theme in variation 6. Level 6.

No. 4 Variations on the Theme of a Ukrainian Folk Song

In some collections this set is titled *Seven Good-Humored Variations on a Ukrainian Folk Song.* A *scherzando* theme opens this lively set of seven variations. Requires a student with flair for the virtuoso sound. Five printed pages. Level 6.

No. 5 Variations on the Theme of a Ukrainian Folk Song

Sometimes known as *Six Variations on a Ukrainian Folk Song.* Opening with a *cantando* theme, this little-known variation set gradually builds to an effective peak before subsiding at the close of the set. Perhaps the most lyrical of the variation sets. More difficult than it appears. Level 7.

Variations on Folk Themes, Op. 87

Three seldom-heard variation sets on themes of America, France and Japan. More difficult than the earlier sets. (Masters Music.) Levels 8–9.

No. 1 Variations on an American Folk Song (1966)

Six variations on "All the Pretty Little Horses." Spunky writing in a version that is not childish. Note the *tranquillo* restatement of the theme at the conclusion. Level 9.

No. 2 Variations on a French Folk Theme (1968)

A sustained theme opens this work in 4/4 and closes it in 3/4. A good-natured selection with effective writing filled with capricious passagework. Level 8.

No. 3 Variations on a Japanese Folk Theme (1969)

The most technically involved of the sets in this opus and perhaps the most effective. Broken-chord passagework is found throughout. *Pesante* ending. Level 9.

Four Rondos, Op. 60

These works may be performed separately or as a set. (Associated, International, MCA and others.)

No. 1 March

The *March* presents the theme in sixths in the right hand with a punctuating accompaniment low in the bass. The appeal stems in part from the catchy dotted rhythm of the main theme. Martial character, enjoyable to play. Level 8.

No. 2 Dance

A lilting work in 3/8 with buoyant rhythms. This amiable and graceful movement needs a light elegant touch. The lively staccatos and the predictable rhythms give it the dance-like character. Levels 7–8.

No. 3 Song

Requires a rich, singing tone in the melody. Plaintive melody with triadic passages needs skilled inflection. Kabalevsky says that this piece should remind one of a lullaby. Levels 7–8.

No. 4 Toccata

Spirited and humorous, and highly effective in performance. Levels 7–8.

Preludes and Fugues, Op. 61

Six neo-Baroque preludes and fugues with thin textures. The preludes are relatively short and all are accessible. These selections could be played prior to some of the Bach *Sinfonias* or fugues from the *Well-Tempered Clavier*. Especially suitable for developing contrapuntal sight-reading. The set contains one four-voice fugue, with the remaining fugues composed in two or three voices. See especially No. 2, with its gigue-like fugue, as well as No. 6. (International, Leeds and others.) Levels 7–8.

Six Pieces for Piano, Op. 88 (Children's Dreams)

These works, composed relatively late in Kabalevsky's life, show the continuation of his interest in writing music for children. The pieces display less rhythmic vitality than some of his earlier works. Titles include *Dreams, Who'll Win the Argument?, Tale of an Old Organ-Grinder, Contrast, Queer Waltz* and *Naughty Boys*. (Zen-On.) Levels 6–7.

Spring Games and Dances, Op. 81

A free-form suite in a playful, dance-like character with frequent return to the main theme, thus imparting the character of a rondo. Should be played continuously as a set. (MCA, VAAP.) Levels 9–10.

Children's Adventures, Op. 89 (1972)

In many respects this collection of 35 easy pieces can serve as a parallel collection to *24 Pieces for Children*, Op. 39. Found here are very easy pieces, some only 16 measures long. Significant collection. See especially *No. 8, A Little Porcupine; No. 15, The Trumpeter and the Echo; No. 20, The Trumpet and the Drum; No. 21, The Little Juggler; No. 26, A Merry Tune; No. 34, A Melancholic Rain;* and *No. 35, At the River.* (Sikorski.) Levels 2–3.

Lyric Tunes, Op. 91

Slavic music consisting of a series of movements connected by *attacas*. Opens with a prelude, followed by a waltz, variations and Coda. Improvisatory writing that requires supple phrasing. Should be better known. (Hal Leonard.) Level 9.

Miscellaneous Volumes

Kabalevsky: An Introduction to His Piano Works, ed. Palmer

A practical teaching collection containing some of Kabalevsky's most accessible works from *Children's Pieces*, Op. 27 and *24 Pieces for Children*, Op. 39. (Alfred.) Levels 1–8.

Kabalevsky: The First Book for Young Pianists, ed. Palmer

Presents the most accessible pieces from the book *Kabalevsky: An Introduction to His Piano Works, ed. Palmer*. (Alfred.) Levels 1–6.

At the Piano with Kabalevsky, ed. Hinson

An interesting variety of pieces is found here including *Four Rondos*, Op. 60; *A Brisk Game*, Op. 14, No. 1; selections from Op. 27; and two variation sets. (Alfred.) Levels 3–8.

25 Piano Pieces by Dmitri Kabalevsky, ed. T. Dubrovskaya and M. Kabalevskaya

Contains a wide variety of pieces by Kabalevsky including selections from Opp. 27, 30, 39, 51, 61, 88 and 89. Edited by Kabalevsky's daughter in consultation with Tatiyana Dubrovskaya, a teacher at the Moscow Central Musical School. Worth investigating. (Hal Leonard.) Levels 2–9.

PÁL KADOSA (1903–1983) Hungary

Kadosa, a once-prominent composer and a piano professor at the Franz Liszt Academy in Budapest, composed piano works of consistently high quality.

Epigrams, Op. 3 (1923–34)

Contains eight short titled pieces. The writing is folk-like and highly expressive, calling for dramatic mood changes. Should be better known. Some selections use alternating triads, harmonics, indeterminate repetitions and gypsy-like idioms. (Editio Musica.) Levels 3–5.

Al Fresco, Op. 11/a

Three short pieces, highly reminiscent of Bartók. Driving rhythms, folk vitality and strong characterization mark these movements. Movement titles are *Capriccio in modo ongharese*, *Allegro robusto* and *Allegro giocoso*. Level 10.

Sonatina, Op. 11/b

In two movements. The first movement with biting dissonance, rhythmic vitality, and shifting meters is akin to the music of Bartók. The brief finale spans a dynamic range from *fff* to *ppp*. (Boosey.) Level 9.

Folk Song Suite, Op. 21

Strong and vibrant rhythms in a work that should be better known. Folk song flavor, similar in many respects to the Bartók *Suite*, Op. 14. (Boosey.) Levels 8–9.

Five Studies, Op. 23/f

Rarely do we find contemporary études written by contemporary composers for the upper-intermediate to early-advanced student. Short and musically inspired. (EMB.) Level 8.

55 Small Piano Pieces, Volumes 1–2

Similar in concept to the Bartók *Mikrokosmos*, these are fine progressive teaching pieces, of folk inspiration. Less dissonant than some Bartók. Reflects the native folk idiom of Hungary. Volume 1 contains 31 pieces and volume two contains 24 works. Should be better known. (EMB.) Levels 1–7.

No. 25 Toccatina

A perpetual motion, *molto vivo*, in eighths, effective and little known. Requires evenness and steady rhythm but generally remains in five-finger patterns. Sounds more difficult than it is. Level 4.

Kaleidoscopes, Op. 61

See especially No. 3 *Allegro* and No. 4 *Poco lento*. (Boosey.)

Snapshots, Op. 69 (1971)

Five short pieces featuring frequent meter changes and much dissonance. Strong writing for the mature performer. (EMB.) Level 8.

No. 3 (Tempo diminuetto)

Excellent writing in the contemporary idiom. Needs strong changes of character. Level 7.

Sonatina in B flat

In one movement, four pages long. Features thin textures, linear writing and biting dissonance. The phrase structure is not readily evident. Requires much use of forearm staccato. (EMB.) Level 4.

24 Easy Technical Études

Intriguing and accessible études in a contemporary Hungarian folk idiom, for the early-intermediate performer. The music is readable and the studies are relatively short (often less than one page). (Boosey.) Level 4.

Additional Works for Study:
Op. 18/a Three Easy Sonatinas
Op. 23/d Sonatina on Hungarian Folk Songs
Op. 35/b 12 Short Pieces for Children
Three Little Piano Pieces
Sonatina (in C)

HANS KANN (b. 1927) Austria

Sonatine für Klavier

Short contemporary work in four movements featuring writing that is predominantly rhythmic. Effective, highly pianistic. Good for a performer with small hands. (Doblinger.) Level 7.

PÁL KÁROLYI (b. 1934) Hungary

24 Piano Pieces for Children

Continues in the strong Hungarian tradition of producing worthy modernist teaching materials for young pianists. The pieces here are progressive in difficulty and filled with spirited rhythms, modal folk writing, and sparkling passagework. Somewhat reminiscent of Bartók *For Children.* (EMB.) Levels 2–4.

WALLY KARVENO (b. 1914) France

Étude Impressioniste

Beautiful writing in a two-page solo that is especially appropriate for the student not yet ready to play Debussy Preludes but wanting to play Impressionist literature. (Lemoine.) Level 7.

ULYSSES SIMPSON KAY (b. 1917) USA

10 Short Essays

Mildly contemporary writing with linear textures. Easy to read and pianistic. (MCA.) Level 5.

Four Inventions

Neo-Baroque writing, especially effective performed as a set. *Andante moderato* is lyrical and contrapuntal with gracious melodic contours. *Scherzando* in 5/8 is a humorous invention, full of gaiety. *Larghetto* features expanding intervals and strongly melodic writing. The last invention, *Allegro,* is full of energy, surprising syncopations and sweep. Grows to a dramatic climax. (MCA.) Level 9.

MILKO KELEMEN (b. 1924) Yugoslavia

The Donkey Walks Along the Beach

Nine pieces in a rhythmic and highly dissonant contemporary idiom with melodic writing that communicates well. (Peters.) Levels 4–5.

KENT KENNAN (b. 1913) USA

Three Preludes (1938)

A staple in the contemporary teaching repertory. The first is a playful, humorous *Allegro scherzando* in which the passages in double notes need attention. The brief second Prelude is in the style of a modern chorale. The concluding Prelude, *Allegro con fuoco,* is a loud and vigorous toccata with repeated octaves. Deservedly popular. (G. Schirmer.) Level 9.

Two Preludes (1951)

Neo-Romantic works with thick textures and chromatic writing. These have not gained the popularity of the first set of preludes. (G. Schirmer.) Level 10.

ARAM KHACHATURIAN (1903–1978) Russia

Khachaturian studied at the Moscow Conservatory and later taught there. He made his American debut in 1968. The writing of Khachaturian is highly melodic. The *Children's Albums, Volumes 1 and 2* and the *Sonatina (1959)* comprise Khachaturian's intermediate writing and only one or two of the selections in the *Children's Album* are truly elementary.

Children's Album, Volume 1

These 10 pieces are much more widely known than those in the second volume. This first set was first published in the late 1940s, though the pieces were composed over a period of many years. Listeners of all ages can appreciate them. The pieces often known as the *Adventures of Ivan* are part of Volume 1. Alfred, edited by Palmer, issues Book One of the *Children's*

Album in its complete form. Other publications containing *Adventures of Ivan* include Kalmus, MCA, and G. Schirmer. Annotations below are based on the complete set issued by Peters. (Alfred, Peters.)

No. 1 Andantino (Ivan Sings)

The best-known selection in this collection. This melancholy piece in an ABA' Coda form features a right-hand cantabile melody above left-hand blocked thirds and syncopated sixths descending chromatically. Voicing of the left-hand moving parts below the melody needs attention. Level 5.

No. 2 No Walking Today

Could be a student's first introduction to double-note playing in one hand. Fine writing for the child committed to serious study. Level 4.

No. 3 Ivan Is Sick

Interesting harmonies in a primarily chordal setting. Good for voicing the tops of chords and for studying contemporary harmonic procedures. Level 4.

No. 4 The Birthday

Dance-like and festive in character. The unpredictable sounds and the movement about the keyboard render this piece harder than it sounds. Level 6.

No. 5 Étude

Refined coordination between the hands is required in this exciting and effective selection. Precision is needed to play the repeated notes and alternating figures. Level 6.

No. 6 A Musical Picture

A beautiful and seldom-heard movement. Those with an affinity toward Romantic music will enjoy the lush sounds and powerful climaxes. The phrasing needs natural pacing. A gem still waiting to be discovered. Level 7.

No. 7 Invention

Somewhat academic. Level 6.

No. 8 Fugue

One of the few two-voice fugues in the standard literature. Highly dissonant. Level 6.

No. 9 Horseman's March

A repeated rhythmic figure provides the feeling of a horse galloping. A relaxed arm is necessary for the repeated figures. Appealing. Level 5.

No. 10 A Folk Song

An ostinato rocking rhythm pervades the piece. Lies well under the hand, although the harmonies are relatively dissonant. Level 5.

Children's Album, Volume 2 (1964)

These pieces are less well known than those in *Volume 1,* but the quality of the writing is high. (Peters, VAAP.) Levels 3–9.

No. 4 Little Leopard on the Swing

Impressionistic writing in a selection that would provide excellent preparation for the more advanced music of Debussy. Levels 7–8.

No. 5 Snare Drum

Straightforward work filled with humor and strong character. "Wrong-note" writing. Level 8.

No. 6 Two Ladies Gossiping

Joking writing in a dance-like, toccata framework. Calls for quick right-hand playing of passagework. One of the most difficult pieces in this volume, but a real showpiece. Level 8.

No. 9 Toccata

This work is as exciting as the much more famous *Toccata* of Khachaturian, and equally difficult. Levels 9–10.

Two Pieces (1926)

The movements are *Valse-Caprice* and *Dance,* both energetic. For many years *Dance* was a popular examination piece for the Trinity College in England. (Kalmus and others.) Level 8.

Sonatina (1959)

Brilliant and rhythmic writing that students enjoy. The first movement is the most popular due to the mild clashes and tuneful writing in the melody over broken or blocked left-hand octaves. The seldom-played second movement features a sad, singing melody over a basically chordal accompaniment. The last movement suffers from being too long to balance the other movements. It is nevertheless virtuosic and exciting. Level 8.

I. Allegro giocoso

Exciting movement calling for fast fingers and a strong sense of rhythm. Left-hand octaves, broken and blocked, need to be detached and never heavy. The central cantabile section is more difficult than many performers realize. Level 7.

II. Andante con anima, rubato

Expressive work in 3/4 with long lines and many changes of character. Dissonances lend a contemplative quality. Requires musical maturity. Level 7.

III. Allegro mosso

By far the most difficult movement of the *Sonatina*. Containing many meter changes, this is a toccata in rondo form that requires strict rhythmic control and evenness. Harp-like sixteenth-note passages between the hands demand rapid hand shifts and fine coordination. An extended movement with an effective ending. (Alfred, Kalmus, MCA, Peters and others.) Level 9.

Toccata (1932)

This war horse has gained its popularity through the brilliant passage-work and surging drive. It was composed when Khachaturian was in his third student year at the Moscow Conservatory. Apparently Khachaturian wrote it in one night, working late into the night so that the first performer could have a couple of hours of practice on it before its premiere.

The passages contain idiomatic and athletic patterns that lie well in the hand. The propulsive rhythms enhance the drama and flair required. Strong fingers are needed. The main pitfall appears in the middle section with the cross-rhythms that are difficult to count. (Alfred, Kalmus, MCA, Peters and others.) Level 9.

LEON KIRCHNER (b. 1919) USA

Kirchner studied with Schoenberg and Sessions, and his academic teaching career has been at Harvard University. His work shows some relation to the Classical tradition, while his tonal palette features dissonant and chromatic harmonies.

Little Suite for Solo Piano (1949)

Short one-page sketches featuring no particular tonal framework. Changing meters and lyrical writing. Movement titles are *I Prelude, II Song, III Toccata, IV Fantasy* and *V Epilogue*. (Mercury.) Level 8.

GISELHER KLEBE (b. 1925) Germany

Neun Klavierstücke für Sonja, Op. 76

Nine untitled, highly contemporary movements for piano. For the sophisticated performer. More difficult than they appear on the page. (Bärenreiter.) Level 8.

JOHN KOCH (b. 1920) USA

From the Country

Subtitled *Pictures for the Young Pianist,* these pieces are mildly contemporary and contain thin textures. They would be good for the young student who does not read well since the spacing on the page is clean. Fine supplementary material for elementary students. Titles include *A Beautiful Morning, The Moon Rises, Snow Falling* and *Rondino for a Quacking Duck.* (General Music Publications, Inc.) Level 2.

ZOLTÁN KODÁLY (1882–1967) Hungary

Kodály's style stems from the Hungarian folk idiom, with the music characterized by a kind of nationalistic Impressionism. He has exerted a strong influence on the teaching of music to school children and was a close colleague of Bartók.

Nine Piano Pieces, Op. 3 (1910)

Kodály's most important work for piano students. For its day, it presented a novel blend of folk elements and progressive sounds. Best suited for the performer with a sophisticated musical ear and a feeling for improvised folk music. (MCA and others.) Level 10.

Valsette (1907)

Originally a part of the *Nine Piano Pieces,* Op. 3. A short work with introduction in the form ABA' and Coda. Contains an ostinato accompaniment, hemiola and some emphasis on the interval of the third. Modal writing. (EMB, Masters.) Level 8.

24 Little Canons on the Black Keys

Originally composed as part of the Kodály *Choral Method* in 1945. The first 16 canons include the solfège syllable abbreviations written under the rhythmic notation. Only one line is provided and the student plays the second hand in canon an octave higher or lower, reading the solfège indications and note values. Canons 17–24 are written on two staves and are to be played a semitone higher. These pieces would likely be used most successfully by a Kodály-method teacher. (Boosey.) Levels 4–5.

Children's Dances (for the Black Keys) (1945)

Group of 12 dances somewhat similar to the Bartók *For Children*. No key signatures are provided. Nos. 1–8 are to be played a semitone higher than written. Nos. 9–12 are to be played a semitone lower or higher as indicated. All are written with no accidentals or no key signatures and are based on Hungarian folk tunes. Musical maturity is required. (Boosey.)

1. (Allegretto)

Binary form work with ostinato rhythms in melody and accompaniment, which consists of blocked fifths and thirds. Level 1.

2. (Allegretto cantabile)

Imitative work with variation. Both hands move in eighth-note motion. Level 2.

3. (Vivace)

Quartal sounds and parallelism are present. Level 2.

4. (Moderato cantabile)

Left hand melody. Contains large chords with added seconds, metric changes and chordal melodies. Level 3.

5. (Allegro moderato, poco rubato)

Chords with added seconds and a strongly syncopated accompaniment, which lends excitement. Thicker texture than in the preceding movements. Level 3.

6. (Vivace Hornpipe)

Ostinato accompaniment and drone writing in one of the most immediately inviting selections in this collection. Level 3.

7. (Vivace, quasi marcia)

Off-beat chordal accompaniment, with melody appearing in both hands. Level 3.

8. (Friss)

Work in ternary form with an exciting *presto Coda*. The term "friss" refers to the faster of two dances paired in the Hungarian "csardas." Ostinato accompaniment of broken chords. Worth investigating. Level 4.

9. (Allegro marcato)

Emphasis on unison playing and on fourths and fifths. Strong rhythmic drive and *fortissimo* ending. Level 4.

10. *(Allegretto leggiero)*

Off-beat accompaniment and chords spanning the octave with the third omitted. Strong rhythmic vitality. Level 4.

11. *(Vivace)*

Features some unison writing between the hands and an emphasis on fourths and fifths. Ostinato accompaniments. Level 5.

12. *(Allegro comodo)*

Work in ternary form with grace notes and ostinato accompaniment. Strongly contrasting sections. Level 5.

12 Little Pieces (1973)

Very easy pieces, most in eight measures, for the beginner. Some of the left-hand accompaniments feature two-note chords while others are linear. All except two (which center around D) are notated using the white keys but are to be played on the black keys only. Very simple pieces with pentatonic sounds. (Boosey.) Level 1.

CHARLES KOECHLIN (1867–1951) France

Koechlin was a student of Massenet and Fauré. Some feel that he is one of the finest composers of the 20th century. He is known for his beautifully flowing melodic ideas, modal harmonies and ear for sonority.

12 Petites Pièces Faciles, Op. 208

Most are contrapuntal, primarily two voices, although several homophonic pieces are included. The writing is sometimes modal. This is serious music by a major composer that is accessible to the elementary student. (Heugel.) Level 3.

Nouvelles Sonatines, Op. 87

Four sonatinas, each in three movements and published separately. These pieces are filled with subtle nuances. (Salabert.) Levels 8–9.

Additional Works for Study:

Op. 41 Esquisses

Op. 61d 12 Petites Pièces

Op. 77 12 Pastorales

Op. 140 A Portrait of Daisy Hamilton

Op. 298 Preludes

LEO KRAFT (b. 1922) USA

Easy Animal Pieces

Subtitled "A First Book for the Piano," found here are 20 very easy pieces. Some are bitonal and would provide young students with a good introduction to contemporary sounds. The rhythmic values are basic and the textures relatively thin. Titles include *Two Zebras, The Lion* (with an effective drone bass), *The Hungry Aardvark* (an inverted canon in two keys), *Monkeys at Play* and *Rabbits*. (General Music Publishing.) Level 1.

10 Short Pieces for Young Pianists

Much more difficult than the *Easy Animal Pieces*. Palatable contemporary writing at the elementary level. See especially *Busy Day* (with alternating hands), *Spiritual* and *Thumbs Under* (requiring fast fingers). Worth investigating. (General Music.) Level 5.

Music for a Day

A set of eight titled pieces, of which the best are *Good Morning, Raindrops, At Evening* and *Happy Day*. (General Music.)

ZYGMUNT KRAUZE (b. 1938) Poland

Easy Pieces for Piano

A collection of avant-garde pieces featuring traditional notation. Textures are generally thin, with much disjunct movement. (Universal.) Level 8.

Additional Works for Study:
Ohne Kontraste (1960)
Funf Klavierstücke (1957–58)
Sieben Interludien (1958)

ERNST KRENEK (1900–1991) Austria

12 Short Piano Pieces, Op. 83 (1938)

Twelve–tone pieces, all composed on the same tone row, which is stated with its various permutations at the beginning of the volume. An excellent introduction to serial technique. Titles include *Glass Figures* and *The Sailing Boat Reflected in the Pond*. (G. Schirmer.) Level 9.

Echoes from Austria (1958)

Seven pieces within a tonal framework. (Rongwen.) Levels 8–9.

GAIL KUBIK (1914–1984) USA

Celebrations and Epilogue

Set of 10 short, titled and highly contemporary pieces. Dissonant harmonies, strong rhythmic character. Most appropriate for the mature student. (Southern Music.) Level 9.

JULIASZ KUCIUK (n.d.) Poland

Improvisations for Piano (1963)

Short avant-garde pieces for young people featuring such devices used as indeterminate notation, clusters, free repetitions, spatial notation, use of harmonics, free ordering of sections of a piece and others. Colorful drawings add interest to the volume, although the scores themselves will be fascinating to many. The brevity of these selections makes their study feasible. (PVM.) Levels 8–9.

MEYER KUPFERMAN (b. 1926) USA

14 Canonic Inventions for Young Composers

Presented with a detailed analysis of each canon given on the same page. The analytical material includes scrutiny of the contrapuntal methods used. (General Music.) Level 7.

GYÖRGY KURTÁG (b. 1926) Hungary

Work for Study:
Jékok, Spiele für Klavier, Books I–IV (EMB)

MILAN KYMLICKA (b. 1936) Czechoslovakia

Kymlicka immigrated to Canada, where he did most of his composing.

Sonatina No. 1

Boisterous and spirited writing in a mildly contemporary idiom. Effective and easy to read. A student able to play the Khachaturian *Sonatina (1959)* likely would be drawn to this work also. Worth investigating. (Leeds.) Levels 7–8.

L

WIKTOR LABUNSKI (1895–1974) Poland

Second Impromptu

Two–page work filled with large full chords in a texture similar to that of the Chopin *Prelude in C Minor*, Op. 28, No. 15. Large hand span required. Level 7.

Four Variations on a Theme by Paganini

Deserving of its popularity. The variations are filled with vitality, strongly idiomatic figures and mildly modern sounds. (Carl Fischer.) Level 8.

HELMUT LACHENMANN (b. 1935) Germany

Child's Play

A cycle of seven avant–garde pieces featuring new notation, clusters and other devices. The texture is not thick, and interesting sonorities are elicited here. A good introduction to avant–garde literature and a fascinating score to decipher. All instructions are in German. (Breitkopf.) Level 9.

JOHN LA MONTAINE (b. 1920) USA

This distinguished composer was the recipient of two Guggenheim fellowships and a Pulitzer Prize. La Montaine was pianist for the NBC Symphony under Arturo Toscanini for four years.

Copycats

Canons in five–finger positions, providing fine preparation for contrapuntal study. All of the canons are at the octave, except for one that is at the fifth. (Summy-Birchard.) Level 3.

Questioning

A two-page solo, adapted by the composer from his *Sonata for Flute Solo*. Thin texture. Sophisticated, though not difficult. (Oxford.) Level 4.

12 Relationships, Op. 10

Each of the canons is at a different interval. Most are one page long and all, except the canon at the octave, are bitonal. Titles include *Bold and Plain, Teasing, Sprightly, Piquant* and *Spirited*. (Carl Fischer.) Levels 8–9.

A Child's Picture Book

Significant contemporary writing for the intermediate student. Interesting sonorities in a contemporary idiom that features generally free use of all 12 tones. Titles include *Story for a Rainy Day* (tender writing calling for a singing tone), *Jack Frost* (calling for crisp staccato and featuring *sforzando*) and *The Giant Has a Hobby-Horse*. (Broude.) Level 7.

No. 1 Even Coolies Watch the Sunset

A serene piece permeated by open fifths and seconds with some two-part writing in the right hand. The left hand has large leaps to navigate. Attractive. Levels 6–7.

No. 3 Story for a Rainy Day

Expressive work with hidden subtleties. A work for a sensitive student. Should be better known. Level 7.

No. 5 Pageant

Vigorous and dramatic work. The many accidentals make the chords somewhat difficult to read. Levels 6–7.

Toccata, Op. 1

Driving work in 6/8, built on many open fifths, with hand-alternating passagework and a bravura ending. Some awkward sections, but effective and motivating. (Broude.) Level 9.

FILIP LAZAR (1894–1936) Romania

Later in his life, Lazar lived and worked in France.

Pièces minuscules pour les enfants, Op. 16

Contemporary teaching literature of exceptionally high quality and strong characterization in these vignettes, often 16 to 20 measures. All selections are untitled. Two books of six pieces each. Would provide a refreshing addition to contest lists. (Durand.) Level 7.

ERNESTO LECUONA (1896–1963) Cuba

Granada

Smaller hands could handle this, and the musical interpretation is not involved. (Marks.) Level 9.

Andalucia

From his Spanish suite of the same name, this work features a simple melody, full chords and appealing Spanish rhythms. Deserving of its popularity. (Marks.) Level 10.

Danzas Afro-Cubanas

Six highly rhythmic and colored pieces. Not easy. See especially the last, *La Comparsa,* which is the best known in this volume. (Marks and others.) Level 10.

19th-Century Cuban Dances

Set of 10 pieces on Cuban dance rhythms, most of which are two pages long and slightly easier than the *Danzas Afro-Cubanas.* Would be good for high school students who may need motivation. See especially *La Mulata.* (Marks.) Level 9.

ROMAN LEDENEV (b. 1930) Russia

Little Things, Op. 9, No. 1

Twenty-four very short pieces with thin textures for beginners. Some mild dissonances, and often humorous. The printed score is clean and well-spaced. Fine pedagogical writing for the early elementary student, which hopefully will make its way into the standard teaching repertoire. Printed in the same volume with *Mixed Pages* by the same composer. (Ricordi.) Level 2.

Mixed Pages, Op. 9, No. 3a

Eighteen excellent short pieces, with strong character. Most are one page long and follow *Little Things* in level of difficulty. No fingering. (Ricordi.) Levels 3–4.

BENJAMIN LEES (b. 1924) USA

Lees was born in China to Russian parents. He was brought to the USA in his infancy. Lees was the recipient of two Guggenheim fellowships and a Fullbright. He taught at many conservatories and music schools, including Julliard.

Kaleidoscopes (1959)

Subtitled "10 Pieces for Students," found here are excellent contemporary selections for the talented intermediate student. Most are one page long, and a group of several programmed jointly is effective. The writing is energetic, dissonant and musical. Significant contemporary teaching literature by an American composer. See especially Nos. 2, 3, 5, 6, 7, 9 and 10. (Boosey.) Levels 7–8.

No. 3 (Risoluto)

Brilliant writing, perhaps a good recital opener. The large chords call for a performer with a wide reach. Level 8.

No. 9 (Alla marcia)

Exciting work that makes full use of octaves, accents and changing meters. Good for the student who enjoys the rich sonorities of the piano. Performer needs accomplishment in octave playing. Level 8.

Fantasia (1954)

Striking, driving work, bold and dissonant. Pianistic writing, appropriate for students who play bravura writing well. (Boosey.) Level 10.

JEAN LEGROS (b. 1903) France

Trois Preludes

These works, while not profound, could serve as effective repertoire study for students wanting to play modern Impressionistic literature. The music is patterned, easy to read and pianistic. Each of the preludes is two pages long. The full chords provide resonant passages, for effective contrast with the more lyrical writing. (Musicales Transatlantiques.) Level 8.

KENNETH LEIGHTON (b. 1929) Great Britain

Sonatina No. 1

Lyrical writing, often featuring repeated chords in the accompaniment. The movements may feel drawn out, and consequently require endurance. Three movements. (Lengnick.) Level 7.

Sonatina No. 2

Extended work permeated with dissonance that resolves. (Lengnick.) Levels 7–8.

Household Pets, Op. 86

Character pieces with titles such as Cat's Lament, Bird in Cage, Squeaky Guinea-Pig and Animal Heaven. Highly contemporary, expressive writing that requires a mature pianist. (Novello.) Level 8.

Additional Work for Study:
Op. 47 Pieces for Angela

YURI LEVITIN (b. 1912) Russia

Levitin was a pianist and composition student of Shostakovich.

Pipes of Pan: 24 Pieces for the Beginning and Intermediate Piano Student

Pieces in all keys up through five sharps and six flats, some with compound meters. No fingering is provided. (G. Schirmer.) Level 5.

NORMAN LLOYD (b. 1909) USA

Episodes

Five contrasting pieces exhibiting jazz influence as well as strong rhythms and vibrant characters. Inherently lyrical writing. Should be better known. (Elkan-Vogel.) Levels 9–10.

Three Scenes from Memory

Mildly contemporary and appropriate for the intermediate pianist. No fingerings are provided. Titles are *Winter Landscape, Sad Carrousel* and *City Street*. (Elkan-Vogel.) Level 5.

TOM LONG (b. 1948) USA

Alea, Music by Change

Excellent collection of short elementary chance pieces using a variety of imaginative notational systems (many resemble graphs of geometric figures). The printed score is aesthetically appealing and is easy to interpret. An interesting and unique introduction to chance music for the elementary performer. Level 2.

NIKOLAI LOPATNIKOFF (1903–1976) Russia

Lopatnikoff immigrated to the USA where he became a citizen in 1944. His works are primarily neo-Classical and economical.

Intervals, Op. 37

Outstanding contemporary writing for the upper-intermediate pianist. Creative and resourceful selections with some biting dissonance. Pianistic works built on different intervals from a second through an octave. (Leeds.) Level 8.

Dance Piece

Rhythms frequently alternate between 5/8, 6/8 and 7/8. Mild dissonances and bitonal writing. This would be an appropriate piece to familiarize a student with alternating meters. Requires a strong sense of rhythm. (Presser.) Level 8.

OTTO LUENING (b. 1900) USA

10 Pieces for Five Fingers

Pieces for beginners featuring predictable phrase lengths and a tonal framework that is more conservative than in other works by this composer. Excellent writing for beginners who can coordinate the playing of both hands together. Level 1.

Eight Preludes

Dissonant writing with a variety of textures in the various one-page pieces. For the sophisticated musician who is interested in 20th-century music. (Merion.) Level 10.

WITOLD LUTOSLAWSKI (b. 1913) Poland

Lutoslawski is a leading Polish contemporary composer. Some of his music is based on Polish folk melodies.

Folk Melodies (1945)

Although conceived primarily as teaching pieces, these *Folk Melodies* have made their way into the concert repertoire. Fine native settings that deserve to be heard more often. (PWM.) Level 6.

Invention (1968)

Two voices with lyrical writing and shifting meter in almost every measure. Two pages. (PWM.) Level 7.

Bucolics (1952)

Evidences of folk music elements abound in these five pieces. Sparkling rhythms and melodic writing in a set that should be better known. Reminiscent in some ways of the Bartók *Rumanian Folk Dances*. (PWM.) Levels 7–8.

Three Pieces for the Young (1953)

Titled *Four Finger Exercise, An Air* and *March*, these pieces have strong pedagogical value. Appropriate for the sophisticated musician. (PWM.) Levels 8–9.

M

JOHN McCABE (b. 1939) Great Britain

Afternoons and Afterward

Set of contemporary character pieces. Solid writing. See especially *Swans at Stratford* and *Forlane*. (Novello.) Level 7.

Five Bagatelles (1964)

Serial writing especially appropriate for the sophisticated musician. (Elkin.) Level 10.

TEO MACERO (b. 1925) USA

Flower Pieces

Mildly contemporary selections, one page or less in length, which describe flowers such as the *Golden Marguerite, Butterfly Weed, Japanese Anemone* and *Japanese Pearly Everlastings*. (Broude.) Level 3.

MARY MAGDALEN MAGEAU (b. 1934) USA

Australia's Animals

Pianistic and colorful writing in a sophisticated contemporary idiom for the elementary pianist. Highly recommended. Titles include *Sleepy Koala, Wandering Wombat, Ponderous Platypus, Silver Swan, Capering Kangaroo* and *Elegant Emu*. (G. Schirmer.) Level 2.

Forecasts

Four short pieces without meter and without key signatures. *Clouds* features clusters, while *Feathery Fog* is written in free notation. (G. Schirmer.) Levels 2–3.

MILOSZ MAGIN (b. 1929) France

Images d'enfants

Interesting contemporary writing in this short set of seven pieces. The music is filled with color and features biting harmonic language. See especially *Le Chinois en porcelaine* and *Arlequin*. (Durand.) Level 10.

MARTIN MAILMAN (b. 1932) USA

Martha's Vineyard

A set of seven titled pieces with fascinating sounds and myriad contemporary approaches including the use of clusters. The pieces are generally one page long. Especially good for introducing contemporary trends to young students. (Presser.) Level 4.

Petite Partita

A six-movement suite in which the short movements display strongly contrasting characters. The writing is idiomatic to the piano. (Mills.) Levels 7–8.

GIUSEPPE MANZINO (n.d.) Italy

Five Easy Pieces

Inviting set of teaching pieces that feature linear writing in an attractive, mildly contemporary idiom. The writing is tonal but features some biting dissonances and captivating rhythms. Highly pianistic. (Ricordi.)

Preludio

> Scale figures in sixteenth notes abound. Étude-like, suitable for developing finger dexterity and strength. Level 6.

Ninna-nanna

> This lyrical, one-page piece could be an upper-elementary student's first work in playing right-hand double notes, primarily double thirds. Atmospheric and expressive work which can be learned quickly. Requires attention to legato playing. Level 4.

Carillon

> The entire piece is played in the treble register. Left-hand broken-chord accompaniment supports the high melody. Level 6.

Danza

> Rhythmic vitality pervades this winsome two-page solo with predictable phrase lengths. Tonal writing. Level 5.

Scherzo

> Rapid pattern figures played in several registers provide the main theme for the concluding movement of the set. The performer will need a clean, well-articulated touch. Level 6.

WLADYSLAWA MARKIEWICZÓWNA (n.d.) Poland

Colored Pictures

Strong rhythms, biting dissonance, and highly contemporary writing based on non-functional harmonies. (PWM.) Level 7.

Zoo Time

These attractive rhythmic pieces each describe different animals in the zoo such as *Two Baby Elephants, A Monkey Jumping, A Fierce Lion* and *A Polar Bear*. (PWM.) Level 8.

Sonatina

Linear writing and contemporary sounds in a three-movement work. See especially the last movement *Vivace leggiero*, with its finger patterns and witty demeanor. (PWM.) Level 9.

Tema con variazioni

Clear textures, biting dissonance, easy to read and features writing of high quality. (PWM.) Level 10.

RUDOLF MAROS (1917–1982) Hungary

East European Folk Song Suite

Nine elementary pieces from Slovakia, Austria, Hungary and Croatia. Straightforward writing and thin textures. (Southern Music.) Level 6.

BOHUSLAV MARTINŮ (1890–1959) Czechoslovakia

Martinů is one of Czechoslovakia's most important 20th-century composers. He made substantial contributions to the piano repertoire, although his works are somewhat uneven in quality. The music of Martinů, often folklike at least in inspiration, generally has well-defined key centers and features many repetitions of an idea.

Puppets, Books 1, 2 and 3 (1912–1914)

Delightful early-advanced teaching pieces that should be better known. Titles describe various aspects of a puppet's life or personality. Each movement portrays the puppet in a new characterization (such as *The Shy Puppet* or *The Puppet's Dance*). The writing is strongly tonal with some traces of chromatic progressions. Many of these will have strong student appeal. Book 1 is perhaps the best. (Masters Music, Supraphon.) Levels 8–9.

Book 1

Columbine Dance. Valse

> This work needs to be played with a suave and fun-loving character. In ABA form, fits the hand well and is easily learned. Columbine was the sweetheart of Harlequin in Italian Renaissance popular comedy, which was often presented in pantomime. One of

the most interesting and most amusing movements to play in all of the books. Level 8.

The New Puppet. Shimmy

Study in voicing double notes within a hand. Sarcastic character. Effective. Level 8.

The Shy Puppet. Chanson

Lyrical, chordal texture. *Allegretto* section adds vitality before the return to the *Andante moderato*. Level 8.

Fairy-Tale

Requires flair and suave phrasing. A student who plays Chopin well would also enjoy this selection. Levels 7–8.

The Puppet's Dance

Perhaps the most brilliant movement of the set, concluding with an especially effective Coda. This work fits the hand well, especially in the chromatic passages. This selection should be better known. Level 9.

Spring in the Garden (1922)

These pieces are similar to the Dello Joio *Lyric Pieces for the Young* in that they are longer than many intermediate teaching pieces (three to four pages), and contain strong character definitions. Some of Martinů's better material for teaching. (Masters Music.) Levels 6–7.

Fables (1924)

Five extended character pieces, uneven in quality, for upper-intermediate students. See especially *The Poor Rabbit*, with its use of consecutive seconds; *The Angry Bear*, featuring percussive sounds on the piano; and *The Monkeys*, with its use of consecutive fourths. These pieces are appropriate for festivals or competitions. (Masters Music.) Levels 7–8.

Film en Miniature (1925)

Six titled pieces, from one to three pages, featuring interesting dissonances. (Masters Music.) Level 8.

No. 1 Tango

"Wrong-note" writing over a tango bass. Isolated double-note passages will need careful attention. Interesting and different. Level 8.

No. 2 Scherzo

Strong rhythms and biting dissonance. Needs sparkle and energy. Effective in performance. Level 8.

No. 3 Berceuse

Expressive writing in a contemporary idiom. Levels 7–8.

No. 4 Valse

Animated and humorous. Level 9.

No. 5 Chanson

The shortest work of the set, this effective selection with its economy of material could be learned quickly. Level 7.

No. 6 Carillon

Strong rhythms and a sing-song effect lend character and flair to this appealing movement. Level 8.

Fenêtre sur le Jardin (1938)

Contemporary sounds are more pronounced than in the Martinů *Puppets* but these pieces lack the character definition of the *Puppets*. (Leduc.) Level 8.

Dumka (1941)

Two-page piece based on quartal harmonies. (Max Eschig.) Level 8.

Les Bouquinistes du quai Malaquais (1948)

Strongly rhythmic, almost folk-like writing. Much of the writing is in unison at the octave. This work is especially appropriate for a student who wants a contemporary piece that requires energy and flair, but which is not technically demanding. This should be better known. (Heugel.) Level 8.

Four Movements

Four two-page pieces which are especially convincing performed as a set. Good recital fare. (Supraphon.) Level 10.

CELESTINA MASOTTI (b. 1956) Italy

Il Cigno Blu (The Blue Swan)

Designed for beginning piano study and co-authored with Carlo Panetta, this volume of pieces contains 12 four-measure exercises for reading and 50 short pieces. The hands play together throughout except in the preliminary short exercises, which are all written on the treble staff only and are to be played half with the right hand and half with the left. The rate of progression within the single volume is rapid. A strong emphasis is placed on developing contrapuntal playing skills (14 canons are included). Most of the pieces are in C Major and many finger numbers are included. This book reflects a dated approach to teaching beginners. (Bèrben.) Levels 1–2.

ALEXI MATCHAVARIANI (b. 1913) Russia

Matchavariana taught at Tbilisi State Conservatory in Soviet Georgia.

Children's Album (1950)

This set of pieces holds an important place in the Russian teaching literature. The works are mildly contemporary, highly pianistic and worth investigating. Titles include *Fairy Tale, Dance, In the Garden* and *Morse Code*. (G. Schirmer.) Levels 7–8.

WILLIAM MATHIAS (b. 1934) Great Britain

Toccata alla Danza

Short, brilliant toccata requiring strong agile fingerwork and featuring driving rhythms. This highly pianistic work in a tonal framework is effective as an encore or program closer. Three minutes long. (Oxford.) Level 10.

SAMUEL MAYKAPAR (1867–1938) Russia

Maykapar was a professor at the Leningrad Conservatory. He composed in a highly Romantic style such as that of Tchaikovsky, and was known for writing a wealth of fine teaching literature.

Kleine Geschichten, Op. 8 (Little Novelettes)

The rhythms are somewhat complex for the technical level of these 18 Romantic character pieces. Intricate coordination between hands. Levels 7–8.

No. 1 Toccatina

Needs a performer with good fingers since it calls for clarity of articulation and evenness of passagework. Level 8.

Trifles (Biriulki), Op. 28

Many of these 26 character pieces are brilliant. The key progression in the set is from major to the relative minor. A significant teaching collection.

See especially *The Shepherd, Passing Fancy, Short Story, The Moth (Butterfly), In the Garden, The Music Box, Funeral March, Sailors' Song, Prelude and Fughetta* and *Echo in the Mountains.* (Associated, PWM, Soviet State Publishing and others.) Levels 2–5.

No. 1 In the Garden

Built on rhythmic patterns, repeated tones and sparkling staccatos. Appropriate as an early-level chord study. Level 2.

No. 2 The Orphan

Expressive work primarily in the upper register of the piano. Triplet accompaniment in the left hand and lyrical right-hand melody. Level 3.

No. 12 The Butterfly

Programmatic work filled with patterns that can facilitate the learning. Levels 2–3.

No. 13 The Music Box

Uses very high register of the piano. The repetition of the theme, with variation in the accompaniment, renders this piece easy to learn. Levels 2–3.

Miniatures, Op. 33

In addition to *No. 1 The Turbulent Waters*, mentioned below, see especially *No. 8 Étude, No. 12 Dew Drops* and *No. 14 A Witch's Story.* (Soviet State Publishing.)

No. 1 The Turbulent Waters

An impassioned, perpetual-motion work that needs an even technique for the sixteenth notes. Level 7.

Pedal Preludes

Twenty brief Romantic pieces composed for the development of pedal technique. Captivating and enchanting writing that should be better known. Highly patterned throughout and sound harder than they are. See especially Nos. 1, 4, 5, 11, 12, 17 and 19. (Summy-Birchard.) Level 6.

Miscellaneous Volumes

Selected Miniatures from Op. 33

Several are brilliant and demand agile fingerwork. (Soviet State Publishing.) Level 7.

18 Selected Pieces for Students, ed. Mirovitch

Most of the pieces included here are from the collection *Trifles*, Op. 28, although works from other volumes also are included. Brief notes are presented for many of the pieces. (MCA.) Levels 6–7.

KIRKE MECHEM (b. 1925) USA

Whims

It is surprising that the teaching pieces of this fine American composer are not played more often because his work is fresh and pianistic. Selections from *Whims* would be attractive on any festival or competition list for intermediate students. Mechem writes in a diatonic or modal framework. Titles of movements include *Country Dance, Fanfare, Dialogue, March* and *Classical Dance*. (E. C. Schirmer.) Level 5.

TILO MEDEK (b. 1940) Yugoslavia

Adventskalender

Twenty-four pieces for Advent, with strong character definition. High quality. (Hansen.) Levels 9–10.

GIAN CARLO MENOTTI (b. 1911) Italy

Born in Italy, Menotti came to the USA in 1928. Recently, he's been dividing his time between the two countries.

Poemetti

Set of 12 short and effective works in which meters change frequently. No fingering is provided. (Belwin.)

Giga

Fresh and seldom-heard work, calling for a light touch and ability to make quick shifts on the keyboard. Changing meter and bucolic character. Level 5.

Bagpipers

Allegretto one-page piece. Melody with an ostinato accompaniment. Level 4.

The Brook

An energetic piece with many right-hand double-notes and two-note phrases. A light touch is needed. Level 4.

Nocturne

Expressive work with inner melodies that require voicing. The left-hand part demands careful attention to fingering as a result of the wide skips and shifts. The double-note writing in the right hand needs careful voicing. Level 5.

The Stranger's Dance

Featuring diatonic right-hand triads in root position and in inversions, this piece is a good study in chord playing, especially appropriate for the student with a strong hand and a good rhythmic sense. Various rhythmic complications. More difficult than it appears on the page. Level 5.

Winter Wind

Rapid, swirling sixteenths provide this piece with its distinctive rush of sound. Shifts of hand position and hand crossings also may need attention. Effective writing. Level 6.

War Song

Filled with rich sonorities and octaves. Sounds difficult. Effective writing. Level 6.

Amahl and the Night Visitors

Excerpts from Menotti's well-known opera, which he arranged for piano solo. Words are included. (G. Schirmer.) Levels 7–9.

OLIVIER MESSIAEN (1908–1992) France

Messiaen often looked to the music of the Catholic church and to the sounds of bird calls and songs for inspiration and musical ideas.

Vingt Regards sur l'enfant Jésus

A major 20th-century work in which the composer expresses his thoughts of Christ. Several themes (God, the star and the cross) circulate between the various movements. Chordal textures are also prevalent. Only several of the works, those listed below, are accessible to the upper-intermediate player. (Durand.)

II. Regard de l'étoile (View of the Star)

Based on the theme of the star and the cross and expressing the shock of grace. Levels 9–10.

VII. Regard de la Croix (View of the Cross)

Based on the theme of the star and the cross. Texture contains open octaves and four-note chords in both hands. Levels 9–10.

IX. Regard du Temps (View of Time)

Based on the mystery of the fullness of time. Primarily chordal writing in a moderate tempo. Levels 9–10.

GÉRARD MEUNIER (b. 1928) France

Les Animaux Magiques

Clever teaching pieces for elementary students. The pieces concern animals and their escapades. The writing is tonal and pianistic. Titles include *The cat's lullaby, The millepede who had sore feet, The elephant who wanted to be slim, The crocodile who had a tooth-ache* and *The giraffe with a bow-tie.* (Lemoine.) Level 2.

Le Chateau du Temps Perdu

All of the pieces invoke the imagination of tales from a castle. Titles include *Mists, The Guard's Hall, The Troubadour, Moon Reflection, Merry Jests* and *Nostalgia.* Impressionistic and colorful sounds in the best of Meunier's pedagogical writing. (Lemoine.) Level 8.

LÁSZLÓ MEZÖ (b. 1939) Hungary

Works for Study:
Sonatina (EMB)
Leichte Klavierstücke (EMB)

NIKOLAI MIASKOVSKY (1881–1950) Russia

Four Little Fugues, Op. 43, 78

Linear works in two voices that can provide excellent study in contrapuntal playing using Romantic sounds. Idiomatic to the keyboard. (Kalmus.) Level 7.

Yellowed Pages, Op. 31

Seven short pieces, mostly two pages long. Mildly contemporary writing with a dark Russian Romantic sound. Abundant use of the lower register of the piano. See especially *No. 1 in E Minor* and *No. 2 in C Minor.* (Soviet State Publishing.) Level 8.

Children's Pieces, Book 1, Op. 43

Subtitled "10 Very Easy Pieces" (1938). See especially *No. 1, Spring Mood; No. 6, Carefree;* and *No. 7, In Waltz Style.* (Soviet State Publishing.)

Children's Pieces, Book 2, Op. 43

Subtitled "Four Little Polyphonic Pieces." Titles include *No. 1, Elegiac Mood; No. 2, Hunter's Call; No. 3, Small Duet;* and *No. 4, In Ancient Style.* (Soviet State Publishing.)

Sonata in F Major, Op. 84

Appropriate for junior high or high school students, this pleasant sonata is tuneful and pianistic. Much of the writing in the first movement is chordal, but it fits a small hand well. The third movement is an energetic rondo in 6/8. (Kalmus, Peters.) Levels 8–9.

FRANCISCO MIGNONE (1897–1986) Brazil

Seven Piano Pieces for Children

Each two pages long. Although they are similar in character, style and inspiration to the Pinto *Scenas Infantis,* they are substantially easier. The strong rhythms and dance-like characters will appeal to many students. Titles include *Sleep, Little Baby Doll, Little Japanese Toy* and *Country Dance.* (Marks.) Level 6.

Four Sonatinas

Generally in two movements, primarily slow-fast. The writing is highly rhythmic and sometimes driving. Published separately. The performer needs a strong rhythmic sense and good sense of flair. (Ricordi.) Levels 9–10.

Additional Works for Study:
Quasi Modinha
Miudinho
Criancas Brincando

GEORGES MIGOT (1891–1976) France

Sonatine sur les touches blances

Three short movements, *Prélude, Berceuse* and *Fugue.* Strong lyrical writing in a thin and mildly dissonant linear texture. Literature of high quality. (Leduc.) Level 5.

LEONORA MILÀ (b. 1942) Spain

Images from Count Berenguer IV of Catalonia's Court, Op. 39 (1982)

Combines a mildly contemporary harmonic idiom with an Iberian flair. Representative titles from the 14 selections include *Peronella, My Land!* and *Catalans, Let's Fight for Liberty*. (International.) Level 8.

DARIUS MILHAUD (1892–1974) France

Milhaud wrote an immense amount of music for piano. A member of "Les Six," his music is basically lyrical. Milhaud was a pioneer in the use of jazz in art forms. Polytonality is frequently found in his music.

Accueil Amical

Seventeen very easy one-page contemporary teaching pieces that do not require a large hand. Wide variety of rhythmic values and wide range of the piano used in some of the selections. This collection should be better known. (Heugel.) Level 2.

One Day (Une Journée)

Lyrical writing in a contemporary idiom aimed toward the sophisticated student at an earlier level. Easy reading, but requires musical intuition. Organized musically by the parts of the day, *Dawn, Morning, Noon, Afternoon* and *Twilight*. Adults might be drawn especially to these pieces. (Mercury.)

I. Dawn

Requires a delicate touch, lyrical phrasing and refined shading. Octaves appear in the right hand. Level 4.

II. Morning

Broken-chord pattern in the left hand with some contrary motion playing and polymeters. An excellent study in phrasing. Level 4.

III. Noon

Requires expressive playing. Some double thirds. Level 3.

IV. Afternoon

Exciting and cheerful work requiring some virtuoso playing. Sixteenth-note figurations and short two-note slurs. Level 4.

V. Twilight

Lullaby feeling. Features polytonality combined with traditional sound. Level 3.

Touches Blanches

Simple melody and broken chord accompaniment, all on the white keys. Short phrases throughout in a short piece for the sophisticated student. Level 4.

Touches Noires

Played on the black keys. Appropriate for the musically sensitive student. Requires simple balance between the hands, syncopated pedaling, and shading of phrases. In the mood of Debussy's *The Girl with the Flaxen Hair*. Level 4.

Friendly Welcome

This set of 18 short pieces for children offers an introduction to polytonality, and several places contain tricky rhythms, wide leaps, chromaticism and multi-note chords. Titles include *Red Pajamas, Hello, Dominique, Elma Plays, Marie Sleeps, The New Tooth* and *Marion Paints*. (Heugel and Cie.) Level 5.

A Child Loves (L'Enfant Aime)

Five solos with titles indicating the "loves" of a child's life such as *Flowers, Candy, Toys, Mother* and *Life*. The writing is chromatic and primarily linear. These strongly contemporary pieces for the elementary student require an ear for dissonance. (MCA.) Level 5.

L'Album de Madame Bovary

Set of 17 short character pieces, ranging from two lines to eight lines. Some of Milhaud's most tonal writing. (Enoch.) Level 6.

The Household Muse (La Muse Ménagere) Op. 245

These 15 short pieces depict "household" activities such as *The Awakening, Household Cares, Poetry, Cooking, Flowers in the House, Laundry, Music Together, The Son Who Paints, The Cat, Fortune Telling, Nursing the Sick, Reading at Night* and *Gratitude to the Muse*. Restrained and lyrical writing with mildly dissonant sounds. Most are in ternary form and only one page long. Phrase lengths are often irregular. A work often referred to but seldom heard. Worth investigating. (Elkan-Vogel.) Levels 7–8.

Four Romances Without Words (1933)

Primarily lyrical and linear writing, perhaps best suited for the mature student with limited facility. Emotionally akin to the Mendelssohn *Songs Without Words*. The first and second are lyrical, the third is fast and playful and the fourth features frequent right-hand octave work. Highly syncopated, many large chords and numerous repeated eighth-notes impart the feeling of drive. The entire set encompasses four pages of music. (Salabert.) Level 8.

The Joys of Life

Set of six titled pieces composed in "Homage to Watteau" and taking its title from Watteau's painting "Les Charmes de la Vie." The set portrays scenes suggested by six of the artist's paintings. Titles of the pieces are *Pastoral, The Indifferent, Rustic Pleasures, Serenade, Bagpipe* and *Masquerade*. The writing is pleasant and accessible to the student able to play the easiest Chopin nocturnes. These pieces deserve to be heard more often. They would be especially appropriate as competition repertoire. (Belwin.) Level 9.

Four Sketches

See especially *Alameda,* which is given the indication "mouvement de habanera" and *Sobre la Loma,* "mouvement de rumba." The strong rhythms and dance-like flavor enhance their appeal to the early-advanced performer and their brevity makes them easily accessible. (Mercury.) Level 9.

Le Printemps (1915–1920)

Two volumes, each containing three untitled pieces that are lyrical, atmospheric and intriguing. These sophisticated pieces would be especially appropriate for a mature musician and would work well as part of a recital program. (Eschig.) Levels 9–10.

FEDERICO MOMPOU (1893–1987) Spain

Mompou's music combines elegance and charm with simplicity. He is known for his introspective, personal, sometimes song-like and dance-like music that seems often to be tinged with sadness. The music is sometimes dreamy and Impressionistic but full of color. Mompou is the master of the miniature, and most of his piano works are collections of such miniatures. One of Spain's best-known composers.

Impresiones Intimas (1911–1914)

Nine short, charming pieces, especially suited for the expressive performer. Spanish Impressionistic writing. (Union Musical.)

No. 5. Sad Birds

Imitates the sounds of birds warbling. Harmonized with seventh, ninth and eleventh chords. Level 7.

No. 8. Secret

Monothematic work in AAA' form requiring melodic projection and a strong legato. Expansive accompaniment with wide stretches in the left hand. The key signature, C-sharp Major, makes the score appear difficult to read. Technical demands are minimal. Level 8.

No. 9. Gypsy

Close in some ways to the atmosphere of Albeniz and Granados. Mixolydian mode. Levels 7–8.

Pessebres (1914–16)

The three pieces depict the rustic Catalan landscape. The first, *Danza*, is highly rhythmic with many modulations. The second, *L'Ermita (The Hermitage)*, a lyrical intermediate "impressionistic-sounding" work, is in a moderate tempo. The final movement, *El pastor (The Shepherd)*, is modal and contains some wide reaches. A folk-like rhythmic ostinato prevails. (Union Musical.) Level 8.

Scènes d'Enfants (1915–18)

Effective suite of pieces with unmeasured writing. Titles include *1. Cris dans la rue (Cries in the Street), 2. Jeux sur la plage (Beach Games), 3–4. Jeu (Play)* and *5. Jeunes filles au jardin (Girls in the Garden)*. (Salabert.)

Cris dans la rue

Strongly rhythmic, effective in performance and seldom heard. Contains the notable indication midway through to "sing a little vulgarly." Level 9.

Jeunes filles au jardin

Highly Impressionistic writing in which the melody stems from a popular song in Barcelona. It has been conjectured that Mompou wanted to show that a cheap melody could become extremely refined. Some accompaniment chords span a ninth and a tenth. The second melody is extremely beautiful and also appears in *Cris dans la rue*. Level 9.

Suburbis (1916–17)

Contains five pieces which depict scenes from the outskirts of Barcelona. The first, titled *The Street, The Guitar Player* and *The Old Horse*, infuses Spanish melodies and brilliant passages in cadenza-like passages. See also the fifth piece, *The Man from Ariston*, which is a Spanish dance that contains some freely barred passages. (Salabert.) Level 10.

Fêtes Lointaines (Distant Festivals) (1920)

Contains six untitled pieces. Most of them are dance-like Spanish music. Very few dynamic markings are provided. (Salabert.) Level 8.

Three Variations (1921)

Theme is stated simply (only half and quarter notes values are used) and without accompaniment. Modest technical demands, strong contrast between the short variations. Especially appropriate for the older student who enjoys creating imaginative interpretations. (Eschig.) Level 7.

Preludes 5–10 (1930–44)

See especially *Prelude No. 5,* the most accessible of the preludes, with its slow lyrical introduction and *animato* dance-like postlude. *Prelude No. 6,* a *moderato—cantabile espressivo* work displaying an absence of barlines and composed for the left hand alone, would be appropriate for a creative performer. *Prelude No. 9* is a thin-textured and highly lyrical work. It especially deserves note as a beautiful miniature of warm emotions and elegance. (Salabert.) Levels 8–9.

Paisajes (Landscapes) (1957)

Set of beautiful character pieces. See especially *I. The Fountain and the Bell* which is a slow and hauntingly beautiful work. This could precede a student's study of the Chopin nocturnes. *II. The Lake* is a lyrical work with a sustained melody on top and broken chords divided between the hands throughout. It is highly programmatic in content and easy to read. The third and final piece is titled *Carts of Galicia.* (Salabert.) Level 7.

Musica Callada, Books 1–4 (pub. 1959, 1962, 1966, 1974)

Set of 28 pieces, mostly one or two pages long. These works are eminently accessible and would be fine choices for students wanting to play Impressionistic music but not yet ready for the piano works of Debussy. See especially Book 4, perhaps the best. (Salabert.) Levels 7–8.

Canciones y Danzas

The 14 *Songs and Dances* were composed between 1921 and 1971. They are miniatures, in pairs consisting of a song and a dance that is usually in the slow/fast order. The sets are short, display a Spanish flavor, and are not particularly demanding from a harmonic and rhythmic standpoint. Many are based on Catalonian folk tunes, providing a directness, simplicity and lyricism as found in most of the songs. Nos. 1–4 are published by Union Musical, Nos. 5–12 by Salabert, and Nos. 13–15 by Salabert or remain unpublished.

Cancion y danza No. 1 (1921)

Perhaps Mompou's most famous piano piece. An earlier edition of this piece does not include barlines or time signatures. In the first edition the composer had indicated the words, "In the mist of darkness." (Union Musical.) Levels 7–8.

Cancion y danza No. 2 (1924)

The *lento* song is created from two-note lyrical figures. The texture of the dance is thin, and features primarily sustained chords in the left hand while the right hand plays the rhythmic dance passages. This is one of the easiest of the Mompou *Songs and Dances*. (Union Musical.) Level 6.

Cancion y danza No. 3 (1926)

More sophisticated musically than the *Cancion y danza No. 2*, this *Song and Dance* is unbarred, as is much of the piano music of Mompou. Noted for the dotted rhythms that lend a lilting effect. (Union Musical.) Level 8.

Cancion y danza No. 4 (1928)

More straightforward than the earlier *Songs and Dances*. The *Song* is based on a Spanish folk melody. Requires a strong rhythmic sense in both movements. Many right-hand double notes and chords. Students who play chords well would be attracted to this work. (Union Musical.) Level 8.

Cancion y danza No. 8 (1946)

Along with No. 2, this is one of the most accessible of the *Songs and Dances*. Consists of a lyrical *Song* portion, sentimental in character, followed by a two-page *Dance* featuring diatonic chords. Displays economy of material, *fortissimo* climax, and predictable phrasing. One of the most appealing of these works for teaching. (Marks.) Level 7.

DOUGLAS MOORE (1893–1969) USA

Suite for Piano

Work in six contemporary dance movements, *Prelude, Reel, Dancing School, Barn Dance, Air* and *Procession*, each of which is also published separately by Carl Fischer. (Carl Fischer.)

Prelude

Permeated with a rhythmic, vivacious melody supported by a staccato supporting bass. Reminiscent of American folk music. (Carl Fischer.) Level 10.

Dancing School

Humorous, flowing, enjoyable for the listener. Displays jumping bass in left hand, left-hand octaves, and changing meters. (Carl Fischer.) Level 10.

Barn Dance

Spirited writing that is primarily chordal and features jumping bass. Forthright and rhythmic writing. (Carl Fischer.) Level 10.

Procession

Chordal writing with more dissonance than other movements. Marked to be played "with steady menacing beat throughout." Double notes and full chords in the right hand appear. (Carl Fischer.) Level 10.

ANGUS MORRISON (b. 1902) Great Britain

Work for Study:
Pieces for Clio

ROBERT MUCZYNSKI (b. 1929) USA

Well-regarded American pianist-composer, based for many years at the University of Arizona.

Fables, Op. 21

Collection of nine short untitled pieces for the young. Muczynski states that he wrote *Fables* with intermediate students in mind. He tried to use strong patterns with the idea of liberating one hand by assigning it a repeating rhythmic or melodic figure. Excellent literature. (G. Schirmer.)

No. 1 (Allegro)

A study in question-and-answer playing between the hands. Fast but flowing, with hand crossings, intriguing syncopations and infectious rhythms. Sparse texture. Level 5.

No. 2 *(Andante moderato)*

Expressive and mysterious. The angular melody needs careful shading. The feeling of two pulses per measure should be maintained. Level 5.

No. 3 *(Allegro molto)*

Spunky piece with strongly defined rhythmic patterns requiring fine coordination between the hands. Surprise ending with *forte* double thirds in contrary motion. One of the most attractive in this set. Level 6.

No. 4 *(Waltz tempo)*

A waltz featuring interesting syncopations and irregular melodic patterns, somewhat sentimental in character. Level 5.

No. 5 *(Adagio)*

Haunting work that needs skill in voicing melody over chordal texture. Highly expressive writing. Level 5.

No. 6 *(Presto)*

Lively, dancelike work, especially good for students with a strong rhythmic sense. One of the most interesting pieces in the set due to the changing metric accents. Difficult ending. Level 6.

No. 7 *(Moderato)*

Berceuse-like imitative writing. Presents a dialogue between the hands, especially good for helping students develop lyrical playing and control of softer dynamic ranges. Level 5.

No. 8 *(Allegretto)*

Sprightly and folklike, with changing meters. Level 7.

No. 9 *(Allegretto)*

This 5/8 work is exciting and driving. Students with a strong sense of pulse will enjoy this assertive work. Appropriate perhaps for an older student who is not as advanced as his contemporaries but who needs a flashy piece. Level 6.

Diversions, Op. 23

Nine short, untitled, contemporary pieces, varying in meters and tempi, and first published in 1970. Clear-cut forms, usually ABA. Emphasis on rhythmic control, lyricism, and articulation. Less difficult than the *Fables*. They generally do not require a large hand. (G. Schirmer.)

No. 4 (Allegro moderato)

Whimsical and lyric writing in 3/8 for the musically and rhythmically secure student. Sparse texture but sophisticated rhythms. Level 7.

Preludes, Op. 6

Composed when Muczynski was 25, this set of six preludes features a wide keyboard range, ostinato figures, clusters and bitonal writing. Requires some agility. (G. Schirmer.)

I. (Vivace)

Short lively ABA work with Coda, needing tight rhythm and musical vitality. The leaps and the wide dynamic range used here make this movement sound difficult. Based on a triadic melody in right hand and left-hand staccato chords played in middle and upper registers. Features triads with added sixths, seventh chords and quartal sonorities. Forceful *crescendo* to the end. Needs crisp rhythm and some finger substitution. Level 9.

II. (Lento)

Expansive and nocturne-like work with wide left-hand leaps. The only truly slow prelude of the set. Hauntingly reflective work that requires deliberate control of rubato, matching of tones and the sustaining of a long melodic line. Angular right-hand melody that distorts the regular pulse. Mysterious. Level 8.

III. (Allegro giocoso)

Playful work requiring a crisp sound and fast fingerwork. Changes of meter and rhythmic patterns add interest. Features scale passages in the right hand against staccato eighths in the left hand. The close hand positions are not as difficult as they appear initially. Level 9.

IV. (Allegretto meno mosso)

Bright and toccata-like, with five-note clusters forming an almost constant tremolo in the right hand. Perpetual motion sixteenth-note chords alternating with single notes in the right hand against a left-hand syncopated melody and quick hand crossings. Levels 8–9.

V. (Moderato)

More freely expressive than the other preludes, with portions of the work notated on three staves. Level 9.

VI. (Allegro marcato)

Needs stark intensity. *Marcato* writing within an ABA form. Low left-hand octaves add sonority. A student favorite. Level 9.

A Summer Journal, Op. 19

Suite of seven pieces concerning Muczynski's recollections of a warm summer's day in the West. (G. Schirmer.) Levels 8–9.

Morning Promenade

Originally conceived for harpsichord. Lyric melodic passages in the first part with a chorale-like central section. Level 8.

Park Scene

Work in 7/8 featuring a left-hand ostinato and a right-hand isorhythmic pattern. Level 8.

Midday

An ABA blues. Levels 8–9.

Birds

An effective *leggiero* perpetual motion piece. The central motive contains repeated notes. Levels 9–10.

Solitude

Reflective work with an ambiguous harmonic structure and changing meters. Level 9.

Night Rain

Muczynski calls this "a Japanese watercolor." Ostinato in the left hand throughout, perhaps suggesting the sound of droplets falling after a night's shower. The music uses only three different pitches in the left hand. Level 10.

Jubilee

Exuberant work with almost constant running sixteenth notes. Level 10.

Sonatina

A three-movement work in a spirited and vivacious style. The first movement calls for large hands to avoid rolling the many tenths in the accompaniment at the opening. The writing is mildly dissonant. See especially the last movement. (Associated.) Level 9.

N

ZVI NAGAN (b. 1912) Germany

Nagan immigrated to Israel where he did most of his work.

A Town Is Awakening. Five Bagatelles for Piano

Linear, dissonant writing in a collection of mostly one-page pieces. Titles include *The Grasshopper, Boating, Quarrel and Reconciliation* and *A Town Is Awakening*. (Israel Music Publications/Broude.) Level 5.

YOSHIANO NAKADA (b. 1923) Japan

Currently Nakada is professor in Feliz Women's College and director of the Japanese Society of Rights of Authors and Composers.

Japanese Festival

Set of 17 attractive teaching pieces with titles that appeal to children, such as *Lively Children, Ballet by the Little Flower, The Speedy Car* and so on. Selections are progressive in difficulty throughout the volume. In addition to movements annotated here, see *Five Lively Children, Children's Song* and *Étude Moderato*. (MCA.) Levels 4–6.

The Speedy Car

Requires a rapid left-hand Alberti bass. Passages of "wrong-note" writing humorously simulate honking horns while rapid sixteenth-note passages simulate a car rushing through traffic. For a student with flair and fast fingers. Level 5.

Étude Allegro

The most popular selection of the set. Bravura toccata that requires agile fingerwork and rapid alternation of the hands. Sounds more difficult than it is. Level 6.

Suite for Piano "Time" (1952)

Six-movement work. The composer titled it *Time* to express a progression from the Classicism in the *Prelude* and *Harpsichord* through Romanticism to Modernism. This work should be better known. Movements include *I. Prelude, II. Harpsichord, III. Piano, IV. Étude, V. Romanticist* and *VI. Toyopet. Toyopet* is the nickname of an automobile produced by Toyota in Japan. (Ogaku No Tomo Sha.) Level 8.

Suite for Piano "Light and Shadow" (1957)

Six-movement work, found in the same volume with the *Suite for Piano "Time."* First, third and fifth movements are tonal or modal while the second and fourth are 12-tone or atonal. The sixth features both tonal and atonal passages and the contrast between the two is indicated in the title *"Light and Shadow."* Titles of movements are *I. Highlight, II. A Story of Ocean, III. The Girl Playing the Koto, IV. Computer, V. Dirge* and *VI. Labor.* Found in the second movement, *A Story of Ocean,* are fragmentary melodies from the Japanese national anthem and several naval marches. (Ongaku No Tomo Sha.) Level 8.

Additional Works for Study:
Piano Pieces for Little Hands

VACLAV NELHYBEL (b. 1919) Czechoslovakia

After studying composition and conducting in Prague, Nelhybel worked in radio in Europe. He moved to the USA in 1957 and became a citizen in 1962.

Kaleidoscope for Young Pianists, Volumes 1 and 2

These untitled 133 tiny pieces are mildly contemporary in idiom. Designed to introduce elementary pianists to contemporary sounds. Less dissonant than some of Bartók's teaching music and on the order of the Pál Kadosa *51 Piano Pieces.* High-quality writing, easy to read, generally diatonic. Several selections would be effective as contest repertoire for a young student. (General Music.) Level 3.

WALTER NIEMANN (1876–1953) Germany
The Children's Delight, Op. 58, Volume 1

Subtitled *Easy Melodic and Instructive Pieces for Piano,* these pieces are short upper-elementary character pieces for the young student. Twelve selections, traditional writing. (Kahnt.) Levels 2–3.

The Children's Delight, Op. 58, Volume 2

Continuation of the style of pieces in Volume 1. Slightly more difficult and slightly longer. See especially *Chasing the Butterfly, Ride a Cock-horse to Banbury Cross, The Magic Little Bell* and *The Hunt's Up!* Twelve selections. (Kahnt.) Levels 3–4.

Table-Music, Op. 125

Charming collection of neo-Romantic teaching pieces, most of them one page. Titles include *Intrada, Pavane, Inventione Fugate, Allemande, Courante, Sarabande, Rigaudon* and *Gigue.* (Kahnt.) Level 6.

BARBARA NIEWIADOMSKA (b. 1938) Poland

Children's Miniatures

Sophisticated and imaginative writing. Strongly idiomatic for the piano. Might also appeal to adults. (PWM.) Levels 7–8.

JOAQUÍN NIN-CULMELL (b. 1908) Germany

Nin-Culmell, son of the pianist-composer Joaquín Nin, developed a strong interest in Spanish folk music. His music has a strong rhythmic energy and is filled with syncopation, frequent triplet figures and vigorous dance rhythms.

Tonadas, Volumes 1–4

Four volumes of 48 short titled pieces (12 per volume). A *tonada* is a Spanish word meaning anything sung, played or danced. Rhythmic writing, mild dissonances, at the same approximate level as Turina *Miniatures*. The works are tonal and frequently use ostinatos containing tonal and modal variety. The performance of an entire volume by an advancing pianist would be interesting. They evoke the richness of Spanish folk music. These pieces might substitute for the teaching works of Granados, de Falla, Monpou or Turina. (Rongwen.) Level 8.

12 Cuban Dances

Strong syncopations add to the appeal of these delightful short selections. The writing is mildly contemporary, and the dance flavor is pervasive. (Max Eschig.) Level 8.

HERBERT NOBIS (b. 1941) Germany

Hommage à Jelinek

Five short, thin-textured works based on a tone row. Few technical difficulties inherent in the writing. Less complex than the Schoenberg *Six Little Piano Pieces*, Op. 19. The writing is technically accessible. Movement titles include *Invention, English Waltz, Siciliano, Bolero* and *Epilog*. (Moeck.) Level 8.

O

CARL ORFF (1895–1982) Germany

Klavier-übung

Short pieces for beginners. The first pieces in the collection have moving notes in one hand and sustained notes in the other. No titles or tempo indications are provided although Nos. 22–40 contain metronome indications. (Schott.) Levels 1–2.

LEO ORNSTEIN (b. 1892) Russia

Ornstein immigrated to the USA with his family in 1907.

Memories of Childhood

Collection of eight elementary titled pieces in a dissonant contemporary idiom. Highly pianistic, suited for the sophisticated pianist. (Joshua.)

A Tale from the Moon

> Wistful, languid melody is played by both hands two octaves apart. Level 4.

The Organgrinder and the Monkey

> A fine example of the use of dissonance to create humor in music. Some bitonal writing in an appealing waltz-like work. Level 3.

In Grandpapa's Big Rocker

> Dissonant chords are set in a rocking ostinato rhythm reflecting the character of the title. Level 4.

The Funny Story

> Open fifths in the right hand are set against a swaying dissonant accompaniment. Level 3.

An Arabian Fable

> Bitonal writing, ostinato accompaniment against a chromatic melody. Level 3.

In the Swing

> Swaying accompaniment against linear, dissonant melody in the right hand. Level 4.

The Sleeping Doll

> Legato melody over flowing left-hand accompaniment. Dissonant. Level 3.

March of the Tin Soldiers

> Strong rhythmic motive. Level 3.

JUAN ORREGO-SALAS (b. 1919) Chile

Diez Piezas Simples, Op. 31

Two volumes of intriguing character pieces from the South American school. (Barry.) Level 4.

P

JÓSEF PÁLFALVI (b. 1928) Hungary

Four Pieces for Piano

Interesting, mildly contemporary writing. These pieces would be appropriate for the sophisticated high school or early-level college pianist. *Lullaby, March, Air, Waltz.* (EMB.) Levels 7–8.

SELIM PALMGREN (1878–1951) Finland

Palmgren studied with Busoni and taught briefly at the Eastman School of Music, and for most of his career at the Sibelius Academy. He composed mostly piano works, especially short, lyrical pieces. (See also entry under Romantic period.)

Five Sketches from Finland, Op. 31

Pleasant character pieces. Titles include *Karelian Dance, Minuet, A Guilty Conscience, Waltz* and *Finlandish Dance.* (Boston.) Level 7.

May Night, Op. 27, No. 4

Impressionistic writing requiring melodic projection in the left hand. Parallelism and rolled chords are present. Requires color in the playing. Level 8.

Palmgren Album

Source of some of Palmgren's best-known works including *Prelude, Intermezzo, Waltz, Berceuse, Sarabande, The Sea* and *May Night.* (Boston.) Levels 9–10.

Additional Work for Study:

Op. 28 Six Lyric Pieces

ANDRZEJ PANUFNIK (1914–1991) Poland

Panufnik left Poland for Great Britain where he did most of his work. He became a British subject in 1961.

Six Miniature Studies, Volumes I and II

Contemporary well-crafted études. One or several would provide fine repertoire choices for a contemporary music festival. (Boosey.) Level 10.

YORAM PAPORISZ (b. 1944) Poland

Paporisz immigrated to Israel where he did most of his work.

Discoveries, Volumes 1–3

Graded contemporary studies featuring a fascinating variety of influences. One piece is based on a 14th-century Alleluia, another on an ancient Chinese song, another on a Hindu raga, etc. The pieces are short and exhibit distinctively individual characters. (Peer International.) Levels 2–8.

LAJOS PAPP (b. 1935) Hungary

Papp is one of the many Hungarian composers who have written a great deal for the elementary pianist. He is primarily known for his chamber music.

27 Small Piano Pieces

Mildly contemporary writing for early elementary students. Most of the short pieces remain in five-finger positions. Tuneful, with the underlying folk element always present. These pieces would be especially good for teaching independence of the hands and contrapuntal playing skills to an average elementary student. (EMB.) Levels 1–2.

Story Scenes (1987)

Twenty short pieces with imaginative titles and creative writing. These works make an excellent introduction to contemporary music for beginners, and most are less than one page long. Some writing is avant garde although many of these selections are highly traditional.

See especially *The Gold-Ball in the Well*, which calls for left-hand notes to be silently depressed and held while the right-hand melody is played. Other notable selections include *Rumpelstiltskin, The Dragon, The Frog* and *Rumpelstiltskin Spins Gold out of Straw*. (EMB.) Levels 2–4.

Six Bagatelles

Highly contemporary and pointillistic writing. Accessible avant-garde writing. (Boosey.) Level 10.

CLAUDE PASCAL (b. 1921) France

Portraits d'Enfants

Twelve one-page pieces in a contemporary idiom. The writing is primarily linear and these pieces can help develop the independence of the hands. Mild dissonances. Bold writing. (Durand.) Levels 2–3.

FLOR PEETERS (1903-1986) Belgium

10 Bagatelles, Op. 88

Short, fresh pieces in varied styles. Dissonant, but tonal writing. Many are in neo-Romantic styles. (Peters.) Level 6.

No. 1 Intrada

Many nonfunctional triads in block position. Energetic, this piece requires a performer with a strong rhythmic sense. Level 6.

No. 2 Menuet

Graceful and one of the easiest of the set. Palatable contemporary sonorities in a work that is especially good for a student who plays classical articulations well. Rhythmically and musically straightforward. Level 5.

No. 4 Tarantella

Single notes and root position triads in the right hand. Repeated and patterned figures in the left hand. Appropriate for the student with fast fingers. Level 6.

No. 5 Valse lente

Neo-Romantic writing that fits the hand well and contains few left-hand skips. Rhythmically straightforward writing. Level 6.

No. 9 Tango

The catchy tango rhythm pervades the simple accompaniment in a modal work. Level 6.

No. 10 Rondo

Right-hand scale passages are played against a simple eighth-note accompaniment in the outer A sections. One of the most brilliant selections in the volume. Level 6.

Additional Works for Study:
Op. 45 Sonatina I
Op. 46 Sonatina II

BARBARA PENTLAND (b. 1912) Canada

Music of Now, Books 1–3

A piano method based on contemporary techniques, with highly organized presentation. Steps for practice and for learning pieces are given for many selections. Several ways of performing the various selections are given. The author has a strong concern for the development of a sensitivity to rhythm and line. Best used with a gifted or older piano student. Book 1 introduces intervals, rhythms and playing in relatively stationary hand positions. Book 2 features additional use of the black keys, dotted notes, tone clusters, more complex rhythms and meters. Fixed finger positions remain in this volume. Book 3 introduces some simple part playing, some double notes and triads. The hand positions shift slightly. (Waterloo.) Levels 1–4.

Additional Works for Study:

Maze-Puzzle

Space Studies

VINCENT PERSICHETTI (b. 1915) USA

American composer, pianist and conductor. Persichetti uses modal, tonal and polytonal structures in his music. The variety of harmonic devices produces a wide range of textures within the writing. His music generally fits the hands well.

Little Piano Book, Op. 60 (1953)

These 14 short pieces are all dedicated to different students, and feature displaced harmonies, pandiatonicism and irregular phrase lengths. Requires hand extensions beyond a major sixth. Neither fingering nor pedaling is given. These works have become a classic in the standard teaching repertory and provide a good introduction to 20th-century sonorities and writing styles. Persichetti has said that these pieces may be performed separately or in groups. They were premiered by Persichetti's 10-year-old daughter Lauren in 1954. (Elkan-Vogel.) Levels 2–3.

No. 1 Berceuse

Lyrical writing with motivic interest and counter-melodies in the texture. Simple two-part accompaniment with many inner ledger lines. The nontraditional harmonies may provide a challenge. Level 3.

No. 2 Capriccio

Repeated staccato notes give this quick and spirited piece vitality. Bitonal writing with recurring rhythmic motive. Texture features sixteenth-note passages in one hand while the other is silent or moves in slower rhythmic values. Level 3.

No. 3 Dialogue

The charm is in the irregularity of the 5/4 measures (2+3). Melodic work appears in the right hand and then in the left, creating a dialogue between the two hands. Level 3.

No. 4 Masque

Lively *presto* work of 10 measures in which the hands remain in relatively stationary positions. Slurred melody in sixteenths over accompaniment of second and seventh intervals. Level 2.

No. 5 Statement

Lively, declamatory writing built from a right-hand two-measure motive. Level 2.

No. 6 Arietta

The absence of barlines allows free interpretation of this recitative. Florid right hand is totally independent from the left-hand thirds that descend through an octave. An appropriate piece to introduce a student to the concept of recitative. Level 3.

No. 7 Humoreske

Zestful writing with off-beat accompaniment. Bizarre harmonies and a memorable melodic motive. Level 3.

No. 8 Fanfare

Polychordal writing with many root-position triads. Marked *allegro con spirito*, this selection is one of the most vigorous and winsome of the set. Level 3.

No. 9 Interlude

Lyrical writing, *adagietto* tempo and featuring the upper register of the piano. Level 2.

No. 10 Prologue

Adagio pesante writing in blocked triads. *Fortissimo*, bichordal and dissonant. Much of the notation is in half notes. Level 2.

No. 11 Canon

Strict two-voice canon with the same material used in C, then in B, then again in C. Dissonant counterpoint. Level 2.

No. 12 Epilogue

Chordal writing with melody in soprano and an absence of rhythmic complexities. Level 2.

No. 13 Fugue

Strong detached subject in quarter and eighth notes. Bold, dissonant writing with few rhythmic intricacies. Dissonant. Level 4.

No. 14 Gloria

Primarily chordal writing in a work marked *allegro risoluto*. Joyful and cheerful in character. One of the most effective of the entire set. Level 3.

Little Mirror Book, Op. 139 (1983)

Studies in symmetrical inversion. The five elementary solos are written as mirror music so that the black and white key patterns reflect each other. Strong dissonances, simple rhythms. The titles are *Magnifying Mirror* (broken chords and triads), *Makeup Mirror* (contrast between staccato and legato), *Magic Mirror* (staccato and legato on broken chords), *Mirror Lake* (water image created through grace notes) and *Rearview Mirror* (some offbeat rhythms). See especially *Rearview Mirror*. (Elkan-Vogel.) Level 3.

Parades, Op. 57 (1952)

Three dissonant movements, *March, Canter* and *Pomp*. Persichetti's most accessible teaching material featuring rhythmic variety and frequent repetitions. Striking use of polychords, modal shifts, ostinatos and various articulations. Some rhythmic variety without extreme complexity. Should be heard more frequently. Fits small hands well since these works require only the span of a fifth. Light-hearted and infectious. Premiered by Persichetti's son Garth in 1956. (Elkan-Vogel.)

March

Staccato passages and dotted rhythms appear in this rhythmic and spirited work. Ternary form with a G tonal center and some bichordal passages. Melody and blocked root-position triads in right hand above repeated (quasi-ostinato) left-hand thirds. Level 3.

Canter

Allegretto, song-like writing with continuous left-hand staccato eighths in the accompaniment. The performer needs to subtly inflect the melody. From G Lydian through various modes to a conclusion in A Ionian. Level 2.

Pomp

Filled with root-position blocked and broken triads in both hands. Bichordal writing in a work that is bold and rhythmic. Level 2.

Four Arabesques, Op. 141 (1979)

Highly pianistic writing, primarily linear. Dissonant harmonic framework. No. 1, featuring major sevenths, is perhaps the most accessible. It features frequent clef changes for the left hand and elegant broken chords. Nos. 2–4 feature some imitative, linear textures. All require attention to nuance and careful pedaling. (Elkan-Vogel.) Level 3.

Serenade No. 2, Op. 2 (1929)

Three short pieces, *Tune, Strum, Pluck,* that are witty and interesting. Tonal, although the composer uses all 12 tones freely with occasional unexpected chords. *Tune* features double notes with major sevenths in the accompaniment. *Pluck* includes striking syncopations and dynamic changes. Six pages. (Elkan-Vogel.) Level 7.

Serenade No. 7, Op. 55

Six short pieces limited to two octaves and requiring finger legato. Most are suitable for children, but could also appeal to older performers. Titles are *Walk, Waltz, Play, Sing, Chase* and *Sleep.* (Elkan-Vogel.)

Walk

Melody switches between Phrygian and Dorian modes on A. Level 2.

Play

Features quickly alternating hands with strong *accelerando* and *crescendo.* Level 3.

Sleep

Slow chromatic descent with a slow trill in the left hand. Level 3.

Variations for an Album, Op. 32

Theme and five short variations in a lyrical and convincing work. Strong character definition between variations. Similar to some of the Kabalevsky variation sets. (Elkan-Vogel.) Level 7.

Sonatinas Volume 1, Nos. 1–3, Op. 38, 45 and 47 (1950)

Dissonant writing, with an underlying rhythmic vitality. No. 1 is in three movements. The complete sonatinas are published in two books of three sonatinas. Nos. 4–6 are easier than the first three. (Elkan-Vogel.) Level 7.

Sonatina No. 1

In three movements, *Flowing, Quietly* and *Briskly.* See especially the last movement, with the sudden dynamic changes and strong rhythmic interest. Level 8.

Sonatina No. 2

Composed in one movement, this is the most difficult of the three sonatinas. The opening features a canon in double notes. The middle section is humorous and fast, featuring jazz and polyharmonies. Levels 7–8.

Sonatina No. 3

In two movements. The first features two-voice texture and is marked "warmly" and "singing." The second movement is filled with double notes. Levels 7–8.

Sonatinas Volume 2, Nos. 4–6, Op. 63–65 (1957)

Melodies are primarily diatonic with moderate chromaticism and tonal harmonies that often move in parallel motion. Traditional rhythms and textures. (Elkan-Vogel.) Levels 3–4.

Sonatina No. 4

In three movements with five-finger melody alternating between the hands in the opening *Allegretto*. Finger substitution required in the second movement. The third movement features descending broken seventh chords. Levels 3–4.

Sonatina No. 5

In two movements, *Poco adagio-Moderato* and *Vivace*. See especially the second movement, which contrasts *marcato* and *dolce*. Folk-like melody in the second section, with chordal accompaniment. Level 3.

Sonatina No. 6

Five sections in this one-movement work with changing meters. Levels 3–4.

Reflective Keyboard Studies, Op. 138 (1981)

Exercises designed to develop both hands simultaneously by using mirror music. *D* and *G-sharp* are used as pivotal points, and the black and white keys are distributed equally, graphically reflected between the hands. Three sets of 48 contemporary studies. Preparatory studies for the *Mirror Études*. (Elkan-Vogel.) Levels 9–10.

Poems for Piano, Volumes 1 and 2, Op. 4 and 5 (1939)

Titles of these works are derived from 20th-century poets. Set of 11 pieces, all two to three pages except No. 11. The first six are included in

Volume 1. Wide range of moods and characters, presenting a variety of technical and interpretative challenges. Especially appropriate for the sophisticated performer. (Elkan-Vogel/Presser.)

Volume 1

Unroll the flicker's rousing drum

March-like, *marcato* writing with asymmetrical rhythms. Wide dynamic range. Level 9.

Soft is the collied night

Long melodic lines with a wide range of the keyboard used. *Andante* work with some wide stretches. Level 8.

Gather for the festival bright weed and purple shell

One of the most appealing, marked to be played *brightly*. Repetition of an interesting rhythmic figure. Level 9.

Wake subtler dreams, and touch me nigh to tears

Expressive one-page work calling for attention to voicing, phrasing and inflection. Level 8.

Ravished lute, sing to her virgin ears

Con mosso work calling for the playing of three-against-two and alternating meters. Level 9.

Whose thin fraud I wink at privily

Playful *Allegro* with some changing meters, but otherwise straightforward rhythms. Many double notes and tertian harmonies spiced with many accidentals. Needs quick fingers. One of the most appealing. Level 9.

Poems for Piano, Volume 2, Op. 5 (1939)

Five additional poems, similar in style and difficulty to those in Volume 1. (Elkan-Vogel.)

And warm winds spilled fragrance into her solitudes

Leaping melody with left-hand descending chords. Level 8.

To whose more clear than crystal voice the frost had joined a crystal spell

Frequent meter changes. Widely spaced melodic line with thick chordal accompaniment. Level 8.

Sleep weary mind: dream heart's desire

Crossing hands with melody featured in both hands. Melody spans a wide range with an accompaniment comprised of thirds and sixths. Levels 7–8.

Dust in sunlight, and memory in corners

Wide leaping melody with seventh chords throughout. Dynamic range from *p–ff*. Levels 7–8.

Make me drunken with deep red torrents of joy

One of the most successful. Features disjunct melody in sixteenth notes against eighth notes. Wide dynamic range. Level 9.

Poems for Piano, Volume 3, Op. 14 (1981)

Set of five works with long musical lines requiring nuance. Somewhat more difficult than the previous volumes. Technical and interpretative challenges. (Elkan-Vogel.) Level 10.

Three Toccatinas, Op. 142 (1979)

Neoclassic style is prevalent in this brilliant short group that requires agile fingers. Passagework divided between the hands. (Elkan-Vogel.) Level 10.

MORRIS PERT (b. 1947) Great Britain

Voyage in Space

According to the composer, these 20 evocative contemporary works are intended "to introduce some of the freedoms of contemporary notation, expression and sound production to the adventurous and imaginative piano student." (Boosey.) Levels 6–8.

IRENA PFEIFFER (b. 1912) Poland

Piano Miniatures

Mildly contemporary, strongly rhythmic works at the upper-elementary level. Predictable phrase lengths. (PWM.) Level 5.

NICOLE PHILIBA (b. 1937) France

Évocations, Volume 1

Linear writing for the beginning student. Not particularly interesting. (Lemoine.) Level 2.

Évocations, Volume 2

Linear writing in this set of six teaching pieces. (Lemoine.) Levels 3–4.

Six Pieces, Volume 2

Titles of these primarily lyrical pieces include *Étude I, Invention I, Final I, Étude II, Invention II* and *Final II*. More interesting than the *Évocations*. (Billaudot.) Level 4.

OCTAVIO PINTO (1890–1950) Brazil

Children's Festival (Fiesta de Criancas)

Worthwhile, mildly contemporary teaching literature for the elementary student. Short pieces, generally one page. Movements are progressive in level of difficulty. See especially *No. 4 Serenade* and *No. 5 Playing Marbles*. (G. Schirmer.)

No. 1 Prelude

Simple two-voice writing. Level 2.

No. 2 Minuet

Two-voice writing, slightly more complex rhythms. Level 3.

No. 3 Little March

Infectious motive, strong march rhythms. Level 4.

No. 4 Serenade

Lyrical melody with sixteenth-note five-finger flourishes over a left-hand broken-chord accompaniment alternating between C Minor and D-flat Major. Level 4.

No. 5 Playing Marbles

Patterned and fast, marked to be played *allegro brillante*. Rapid right-hand passagework, repeated notes, chromatic scales and a brilliant concluding glissando. A highly effective work for the student with agile fingers. This piece is more difficult to read than it is to play. Level 5.

Scenas Infantis (Memories of Childhood)

Important work featuring imaginative and interesting writing. Especially effective performed in its whole. (G. Schirmer.)

Run, Run!

An attractive and flamboyant piece in which the rapid alternation of triads between the hands creates a flurry of sonority. The B section, much slower than the *brilliant and rapid* opening, needs careful voicing and phrasing. The concluding glissando needs careful pacing. Level 7.

Ring Around the Rosy

An energetic and spirited bitonal work with a playful melody line. Left hand changes registers quickly. Levels 6–7.

March, Little Soldier

Features left-hand moving triads in the bass while the melody uses grace notes, appoggiaturas and glissandos. Should be heard more frequently. Levels 6–7.

Sleeping Time

A descriptive work with many suggestions provided by the composer. Level 6.

Hobby Horse

Sectionalized work with changing meter. Uses the entire keyboard. Requires wide stretches and fine coordination. Level 7.

Marcha do Pequena Polegar (Tom Thumb's March)

This is an appealing piece for a performer with flair. The many register changes require the ability to move freely about the keyboard. (G. Schirmer.) Level 9.

WALTER PISTON (1894–1976) USA

Piston was a neo-Classical composer who employed linear contrapuntal textures and adventurous harmonies. He was the author of important texts on music theory.

Passacaglia

Builds to a sonorous climax. Powerful contemporary writing in a four-page piece. (Mercury.) Level 10.

THOMAS PITFIELD (b. 1903) Great Britain

Studies on an English Dance Tune

Six mildly contemporary movements on the first section of "Jenny Plucks Pears." Rhythmic and inviting writing that is palatable and patterned. The entire set would be effective in performance. Worth investigating. (Elkin.) Level 9.

MANUEL MARÍA PONCE (1886–1948) Mexico

20 Easy Pieces

Short tonal pieces, often slightly shorter than a page. Highly rhythmic and tuneful, many are based on Indian folk dances or songs. (Peer International.) Levels 2–4.

Four Variations on a Mexican Theme

Interesting writing that is pianistic and Romantic in sound. (Peer International.) Levels 9–10.

Four Mexican Dances

Generally animated and strongly rhythmic. Pianistic and accessible to the advancing performer. The dances are approximately two pages each. (Southern Music.) Level 10.

CLIFFORD POOLE (b. 1916) Canada

Fleas

Alternation of melody pitches between the hands, with jumps divided between the hands. Interesting. (Frederick Harris.) Level 2.

MARCEL POOT (1901–1988) Belgium

Six Petites Pièces Récréatives

Enticing writing in a strong rhythmic framework. Requires strong depiction of character. These mildly contemporary pieces should be better known. Titles include *Joyeux Départ, Idylle, Soleil Printainer, Berceuse, Valse Lente* and *Parade*. (Max Eschig.) Level 3.

Six Pièces Faciles

Mildly contemporary collection of pieces that reveal the influence of folk elements from England, France, Spain and Russia. Thin textures, tuneful writing. (Max Eschig.) Level 5.

In All Directions

An attractive collection of two-page pieces with titles that refer to different areas of the world such as England, France, Spain and Russia. Titles in addition to those listed here are *1. Across the Channel, 2. Towards Avignon* and *5. Reeling Home.* (Universal/Boonin.)

No. 3 On the Spanish Border

Spirited rhythms lend an air of festivity. This piece would be effective on a contest list. Level 4.

No. 4 From Omsk to Tomsk

Strong, humorous writing with biting chords. *Allegro violento* with *fortissimo* cluster chords. Meter changes. Level 3.

FRANCIS POULENC (1899–1963) France

Poulenc is the best-known member of the French group of composers known as "Les Six." At one point his music was considered to be too popular in style to be taken seriously. His is a generally light style with masterful craftsmanship, filled with pianistic figurations and sentimental harmonies.

Mouvements Perpétuels (1918)

A deservedly popular work that needs strong character differentiation between the movements. The first movement is the best known, featuring large skips in the melody and mild dissonances. The left-hand accompaniment is ostinato-like. The main idea of this movement is derived from the fifth piece in Beethoven's song cycle *An die ferne Geliebte*, Op. 98. The second movement is short and lyrical, comprised of many motives. The vigorous final movement is spirited, with tenths in the accompaniment. (Chester.) Level 9.

Valse (1919)

Appealing three-page work that can provide a fine introduction to Poulenc's style. Light, appealing and rhythmic. Waltz accompaniment. (Eschig.) Level 8.

Suite in C (1920)

Three short, contrasting and energetic movements, *Presto, Andante, Vif.* Appealing writing. Should be heard more often. (Chester.) Level 9.

Pastourelle (1927)

A lyrical transcription from the ballet *L'Eventail de Jeanne.* A folk-song-like quality pervades. (Heugel.) Level 8.

Three Novelettes (1927–1959)

Interesting and attractive set. The lyrical first piece is by far the most popular, displaying a pastoral quality. Students enjoying lush Romantic sonorities would be drawn to this work. The second movement is brilliant, filled with biting dissonances and surprising cadences. It is the most difficult of the three movements. The final movement was written 32 years later than the other movements and is lyrical, filled with pungent harmonies and widely spaced left-hand arpeggiations. (Chester.) Level 10.

Villageoises (1933)

One of Poulenc's most accessible works. All but the last movement are in ABA form. Poulenc indicated at the beginning of the score that "preferably one will play these pieces in succession." Subtitled *Petites Piéces Enfantines,* the entire set is infused with good nature. This work is indicative of the interest in children's piano music in the early 20th century by Debussy, Bartók, Ravel, Prokofiev and Poulenc. (Salabert.)

Valse Tyrolienne

Lively and melodic waltz. The wide left-hand jump bass can present problems. Level 7.

Staccato

Sharp staccato chords requiring a loose wrist. Lively work in a march-like tempo. Level 7.

Rustique

The tempo makes this more difficult than expected. A haunting melody permeates. Level 7.

Polka

Fast repeated notes in a bouncy and appealing movement. Level 7.

Petite Ronde

Although this is the simplest technically of the set, it is in a way the most difficult musically. The many repetitions in this rhythmic work call for variety in interpretation. Level 6.

Coda

Presents material from the earlier three movements in a kind of a summation of the suite. Another spirited and effective movement. Levels 7–8.

Badinage (1934)

Playful writing. Spans a ninth and requires a fine legato. (Salabert.) Level 9.

Suite Francaise (1935)

Reflection of the idiom of French Renaissance composer Claude Gervaise is seen through Poulenc's use of modal cadences and progressions, 16th-century dance rhythms and Renaissance dance forms. Pentatonic writing and dissonant harmonies. (Durand.) Levels 9–10.

Bransle de Bourgogne
> Appealing repeated cadential figures in a lively and dissonant work. Highly rhythmic. Level 10.

Pavane
> Simple chordal work, consisting predominantly of blocked chords. Sophisticated writing. Level 7.

Petite marche militaire
> Primarily chordal. Repeated rhythmic figures. Level 8.

Complainte
> Calm and melancholy writing in a simple texture. Level 8.

Bransle de Champagne
> Sing-song effect with appealing repeated rhythms, especially appropriate for the student with larger hands. Level 10.

Sicilienne
> Elegant work, primarily chordal. Performer will need an acute sense of a long line. Level 8.

Carillon
> Bright and energetic chordal work. Level 9.

Improvisations

Nos. 2 and 12 are the most accessible and are both influenced by Schubert: No. 2 begins like a Schubert waltz, and No. 12 is a waltz subtitled "Hommage á Schubert." No. 12 is especially brilliant. (Salabert.) Levels 9–10.

Additional Works for Study:
Feuillets d'Album
Bourée au Pavillon d'Auvergne

Miscellaneous Volumes

Album of Six Pieces for Piano

Contains such works as *Mouvement Perpetuel No. 1, Presto from Suite in C, Impromptu No. 3, Novelette No. 1 in C* and others. (Chester.) Levels 8–10.

ANDRÉ PREVIN (b. 1929) Germany

André Previn immigrated to the USA where he became a citizen in 1943. Something of a child prodigy, he became an orchestrator at MGM studios in Hollywood while still in high school. In addition to classical music, Previn has composed jazz, popular music and film scores, but is known primarily as a conductor.

Matthew's Piano Book

Subtitled "10 Piano Pieces for Advanced Students," these are somewhat abstract character pieces in a mildly contemporary idiom. (Hansen/ Chester.) Levels 7–8.

Impressions

Significant addition to the contemporary teaching literature. Most of the 20 pieces are one page long. Mild dissonances and a variety of styles. (MCA.)

No. 1 Good Morning
> A one-page waltz featuring "wrong-note" writing. Wide melodic range. Cheerful and pianistic. Level 4.

No. 2 Polar Bear Dance
> Bitonal thirds are heard from register to register in a humorous work that is a vivid depiction of the title. A wide range of keyboard is used. Level 4.

No. 3 Promenade in the Park
> Graceful lyrical writing. 5/4 meter. Level 3.

No. 4 Poodles
> Scale passages and alternation of motives between the hands. Level 4.

No. 5 By a Quiet Stream
> Flowing, lyrical, reflective writing with a left-hand ostinato. Some wide skips in the right hand can be navigated by those with small hands. One of the best in the set. Level 5.

No. 6 Parade of the Penguins

Changing meters add interest and unpredictability. Repeated notes and two-part writing in a work that requires finger independence. Level 5.

No. 7 Trees at Twilight

Simple and lyrical writing that is based on seventh and ninth chords. Level 4.

No. 8 Mechanical Toy

Simple but syncopated right-hand melody against constant left-hand accompaniment that outlines open fifths. Engaging writing. Level 4.

No. 9 Procession with Lanterns

Dotted rhythms permeate the texture and offer stateliness. Level 4.

No. 10 In Perpetual Motion

Brilliant and effective work that needs good fingers, but sounds more difficult than it is. Based on triads and scales and written primarily in sixteenth notes. Should be better known. Level 4.

No. 11 Roundup

Energetic work with a syncopated melody and accompaniment that give it a "western" flair. Level 4.

No. 12 A Piece of Lace

Melodic writing with double notes in the right hand. Level 4.

No. 13 The Out-of-Tune Band

Effective and humorous work with "wrong-note" writing. Level 4.

No. 15 Miniature March

Bold writing that calls for the playing of octaves, strong depiction of the march theme and flair. Level 5.

No. 16 A Gentle Thought

Hemiolas make this flowing, melodic piece interesting. Level 5.

No. 17 Mimicry

Needs agile fingers. Level 5.

No. 20 Scherzo

Spirited boisterous writing with skips of a ninth and tenth. Level 5.

Additional Work for Study:
Birthday Party

SERGEI PROKOFIEV (1891–1953) Russia

Prokofiev was admitted to the St. Petersburg Conservatory at the age of 13, where he studied conducting, composition and piano. His style was somewhat cramped by the Soviet regime in the later part of his life. Music for children was of special interest to Prokofiev, and the piano was Prokofiev's favorite instrument. Much of the music is sophisticated, suited best to the mature musician.

Music for Young People, Op. 65 (1935)

The 12 works in this opus provide Prokofiev's most accessible music for the pianist. Long lyrical lines and "wrong-note" writing. The selections are filled with *scherzando* qualities and unexpected turns of the harmonic framework. Adult pianists will also enjoy performing many of these works. (Alfred, Boosey, International, Kalmus, Ricordi, G. Schirmer and others.)

No. 1 Morning

A dreamy, impressionistic study using a wide range of sonorities on the piano. Deservedly popular as a study in color. Appropriate for a student drawn to the sound of Debussy. Level 6.

No. 2 Promenade

Primarily chordal textures. Contains "wrong-note" writing and melodic passages with many unusual turns. Requires the ability to inflect short motifs. More difficult than it appears on the page. Level 7.

No. 3 A Little Story

Less effective than most of the other pieces in the set, perhaps due to the awkward rhythmic framework. Levels 6–7.

No. 4 Tarantella

A fine finger study that is highly effective in performance. Level 7.

No. 5 Regrets

A true Impressionistic study, especially appropriate for the sensitive and musical performer. Level 6.

No. 6 Waltz

Highly effective in performance and strongly typical of Prokofiev's style. The displacement of the melody between various octaves produces humor. For the sophisticated musician who can move with agility on the keyboard. Level 8.

No. 7 March of the Grasshoppers

Popular and effective due to the graphic depiction of the title. Represented in the music are the hopping movements of a grasshopper as well as a kind of promenade. Since this work moves rapidly around the keyboard, it is best performed by an individual with a strong kinesthetic feeling. Level 7.

No. 8 The Rain and the Rainbow

Another atmospheric and Impressionistic work, shorter than most of the other pieces in this collection. Uses the entire keyboard and requires the reading of ledger lines. Many clef changes and hand crossings. Level 7.

No. 9 Playing Tag

A vigorous finger study that dances up and down the keyboard. Requires agile fingerwork and a strong rhythmic sense. Less known. Level 8.

No. 10 March

Most immediately familiar work in the set. Somewhat more difficult than it appears on the page due to the rapid crossing of hands, shifting of registers for the octave displacements and the detailed attention required for the articulation. Level 7.

No. 11 Evening

A hauntingly beautiful work. Requires a fine sense of the flexibility of a line and a good legato. Tender, lyrical writing in a highly expressive and sophisticated work. Level 7.

No. 12 The Moon Strolls in the Meadows

Less familiar than many of the selections in this collection. The *andantino* melody is exchanged between the hands. Requires agile movement about the keyboard. Primarily lyrical in nature. Level 7.

Sonatina Pastorale, Op. 59, No. 3 (1934)

A sonatina in one movement with a "musette" bass. Strict form with a Lydian melody. Moderate tempo, primarily lyrical writing. (Boosey, Kalmus and others.) Level 8.

Tales of the Old Grandmother, Op. 31 (1918)

Composed in New York City when Prokofiev was 27 years old, these works are generally slow and enchantingly lyrical Russian pieces. (Boosey, MCA, International, Kalmus and others.)

No. 1 Moderato

Expansive hand crossings and sophisticated pedaling are required. Somewhat involved harmonic framework. One of the best in the set. Level 8.

No. 4 Sostenuto

Complex dotted-rhythm ostinato over a left-hand melody. Harmonically static. Level 9.

Four Pieces, Op. 32 (1918)

Elegant neo-Classic dance suite and one of his lightest sets of pieces. (Boosey, International, MCA and others.)

No. 1 Dance

"Wrong-note" writing in a work with crisp staccato and leaps. Easier than it sounds. This piece journeys through several unlikely keys with an organized rhythmic pattern that permeates the entire work. The opening is rhythmically similar to Debussy's *Minstrels*. Level 10.

No. 2 Minuet

Two-page ABA' form with off-beat rhythms. Levels 8–9.

No. 3 Gavotte

The best known work in this set with a wry, march-like feeling. Constructed harmonically almost completely with triads. The trio is primarily in two voices with each of the voices doubled at the octave. Level 9.

10 Pieces, Op. 12

Light and witty opus of neo-Classical works. Movements especially appropriate for study at the earlier levels include *No. 1 March, No. 2 Gavotte, No. 6 Legende* and *No. 7 Prelude.* (International, Kalmus, MCA, Peters and others.)

No. 2 Gavotte

Charming and intriguing writing. The piece calls for a large left-hand span. Use of chromatic scale is frequent here. Level 10.

No. 4 Waltz

More Impressionistic than neo-Classic. It is a slow waltz that abounds in augmented-sixth chords. Level 10.

No. 6 Legende

Scriabinesque harmonies in a lyrical work that requires mature interpretative skills. Essentially a dramatic recitative, and especially suited for the person with an affinity toward sensitive lyrical writing. Dynamic range drops to *ppp*. Many parallel fifths. Levels 9–10.

No. 7 Prelude

This perpetual-motion work, filled with right-hand broken chords, is somewhat reminiscent of the Chopin *"Harp" Etude*. Composed by Prokofiev for harp or piano. Contains effective *glissandi* passages. Level 10.

Miscellaneous Volumes

Prokofiev: Selected Works, ed. Baylor

Contains an interesting cross section of works by Prokofiev including *Tales of the Old Grandmother*, Op. 31, *Pastoral Sonatina*, Op. 59, No. 3, *Episodes* from *Romeo and Juliet*, Op. 75 and *Prelude*, Op. 12, No. 7. (Alfred.) Levels 8–10.

R

JAN RÄÄTS (b. 1932) Russia

Toccata

Energetic 14-page work, for the talented upper-intermediate student. Driving rhythms, large repeated *fortissimo* chords, and some *glissandi* all help create excitement. Highly pianistic and effective in performance. (Associated.) Level 8.

SERGEI RACHMANINOFF (1873–1943) Russia

Born in Russia to a musical family (his grandfather was a pianist who had studied with John Field), Rachmaninoff left his homeland for Europe after the 1917 Bolshevik Revolution. He often toured America during these years, and in 1939 he immigrated to America. His music contains strong Russian Romantic expression with an often melancholy cast. Rachmaninoff's compositions remain as some of the most popular literature for the piano, and the composer himself was one of the great piano virtuosos of the 20th century.

Preludes

Rachmaninoff wrote 24 preludes in all the major and minor keys, although they were not published this way. The well-known *Prelude in C-sharp Minor*, Op. 3, No. 2 was considered to be the first of the 24, and to this Rachmaninoff added the 10 preludes of Op. 23 and the 13 preludes of Op. 32. Most of the preludes require musical maturity and are beyond the difficulty level of this book. (Many standard editions.)

Prelude in G Minor, Op. 23, No. 5

Ternary-form work that suggests the sound of a military march in the opening and closing sections. The central section contains a broad lyrical melody and expansive arpeggiations. This piece is more difficult than it initially appears. Vigorous and aggressive writing with wide jumps. Note the countermelodies throughout the central section. Level 10.

Prelude in G Major, Op. 32, No. 5

Serene and elegant work that focuses on the upper register of the piano. A murmuring accompaniment is heard against a contemplative and lyrical melody that needs careful dynamic control. Performance of this work requires rhythmic flexibility. Left-hand quintuplets permeate the languid texture. Level 10.

Prelude in G-sharp Minor, Op. 32, No. 12

The continuous *obligato* should remind the listener of bells. Contains a melody in the baritone register that needs careful voicing and shaping. For the mature performer. Level 10.

Miscellaneous Works

Fantasy Pieces, Op. 3

These works were dedicated to Arensky. The second in the set, *Prelude in C-sharp Minor*, is undoubtedly Rachmaninoff's most popular work. (Alfred, Belwin, VAAP and other standard editions.)

No. 1 Elégie

Rhapsodic work constructed on a passionate theme. Uses dark, rich sonorities and a wide expressive range. Level 10.

No. 2 Prelude in C-sharp Minor

Rachmaninoff was motivated to write this immensely popular prelude by the thought of the profit of forty rubles (about $20 at that time)! Requires skilled control of sonority. Rachmaninoff said that he did not have a descriptive mood in mind when he wrote this work. The music is melancholy, with an impassioned central section and a grand climax. Avoid achieving loudness without resonance. Level 10.

No. 3 Mélodie

Contains a cello-like melody, typical of Rachmaninoff, presented successively in four voices. This work was later revised into a much more elaborate setting. Levels 9–10.

No. 4 Polichinelle

Represents a puppet's dance, full of humor and irony. The name refers to *Punch*, a character in the Punch and Judy puppet shows. An ABA' work that is more difficult than many realize. Brilliant writing with wide leaps and thick octave chords. Dramatic with varying textures and many ideas. Makes a large splash. Level 10.

No. 5 Sérénade

Opens with a statement of the theme and four bars of introductory material. Seems to depict the atmosphere of Spain (perhaps a love song sung to guitar accompaniment). Level 10.

Salon Pieces, Op. 10

See especially *No. 1, Nocturne; No. 2, Valse*; and *No. 5, Humoresque*. (Many standard editions.) Level 10.

No. 2 Valse

Beautiful writing in a work with a lengthy Viennese theme and lush suspensions. Level 10.

No. 5 Humoresque

A delightful work with abundant jesting. The dotted rhythms and sudden loud chords make it inviting and unusual. Its opening theme echoes the *First Symphony*, and the wit and light-hearted character found here are unusual for Rachmaninoff. Level 10.

Two Fantasy Pieces

Published in 1951 without opus number. The first is a passionate work with rapid right-hand passagework. The second piece dates from the early 1890s and probably was dropped from Op. 3. (Hinshaw.) Level 10.

Fantasy Piece No. 1

A two-page selection with rapid passagework in sixteenths found usually in the right hand over a rocking accompaniment in 6/8. Level 10.

Fantasy Piece No. 2

Marked *moderato*, this work is a 12/8 study with continuous eighth notes in both hands. Requires careful attention to fingering. Not Rachmaninoff's most profound writing. Unlike its companion, this work was left untitled by the composer. Level 9.

Three Nocturnes

The first contains elements of real dramatic flair. *Nocturne No. 3* can be seen as a forerunner to the *Prelude in C-sharp Minor*. (Hal Leonard.) Level 9.

Four Improvisations

These pieces are based on melodic fragments of Arensky, Glazunov, Taneyev and Rachmaninoff, respectively. This is some of Rachmaninoff's most accessible writing. Each of the improvisations is one page in length. (Hinshaw.) Levels 7–8.

Miscellaneous Volumes

Rachmaninoff Album of Piano Works, ed. Hinson

Contains the *Four Improvisations*. Interesting choices for alternative literature. (Hinshaw.) Levels 8–9.

Rachmaninoff Album for the Piano

For many years, this was one of the most popular anthologies of Rachmaninoff's works due to the presence of the Op. 3 pieces such as the *Polichinelle, Elégie* and *Mélodie*. An arrangement of the third movement of the *Second Piano Concerto* is also included here. (G. Schirmer.) Level 10.

NIKOLAI RAKOV (b. 1908) Russia

From Morning to Evening

This collection contains 24 pieces in all keys with widely varying levels of difficulty represented. Mildly contemporary writing. See especially *No. 1 Morning, No. 5 Promenade, No. 13 Swallow, No. 19 Trumpeters*. The first piece in the collection is titled *Morning* and the last, *Evening*. (Associated.) Levels 8–9.

GYÖRGY RÁNKI (b. 1907) Hungary

Works for Study:
König Pomades neue Kleider
Leichte Klavier-Variationen über ein ungarisches Volkslied
Sieben leichte Klavierstücke über vietnamesische Melodien

SAM RAPHLING (b. 1910) USA

Six Tiny Sonatas

Short works in three or four movements each characterized by sparse textures and appealing contemporary sounds. Especially appropriate for talented young elementary-school students. Highly pianistic. (General Music.) Level 3.

12 Indiscretions

Woven into these short character pieces are themes from well-known classical melodies such as the main theme of the Chopin *Polonaise in A Major* and the habanera theme from *Carmen*. These pieces might be used well with an adult who likes light music and has a well-based knowledge of classical music. (General Music.) Level 8.

Seven Mobiles

Dissonant, rhythmic selections especially appropriate for the contemporary enthusiast or the sophisticated performer. Excellent writing. (General Music.) Level 9.

American Album

A fine collection of "Americana" in eight mildly contemporary solos. This collection is somewhat reflective of the Barber *Excursions*, but is less advanced. It is a collection that surely should be better known. See especially *Square Dance, Harmonica* and *Jitterbug*. (Mercury.) Levels 9–10.

Additional Works for Study:
At the Movies
Children's Special

MAURICE RAVEL (1875–1937) France

Ravel was essentially a neo-Classicist composer of Impressionistic tendency. His music is objective, filled with original sonorities and is highly pianistic.

Prélude (1913)

Fine introduction to Impressionistic style in one of Ravel's most accessible works. It was composed as a sight-reading piece for the Paris Conservatory competitions. Contains some unexpected harmonies, hand crossings and interlocking passages, and can work well as a bridge between intermediate and advanced literature. (Alfred, Durand and others.) Level 8.

Menuet sur le nom de Haydn (1909)

Binary form work based on a theme using Hadyn's name with the pitches determined by renaming the letters when Ravel thought necessary. Ravel indicated the music anagram in the score, and used the five notes in mirror inversion, cancrizans (backward), transposed form and other various permutations. The work was composed to commemorate the centenary of Hadyn's death.

The second page becomes much more complex than the opening. Thick textures. Not Ravel's best writing. (Durand.) Levels 9–10.

Pavane pour une Infante defunte (1899)
(Pavane for a Dead Princess)

This was the first of Ravel's works to achieve real popularity. Ravel told the Princess Polignac, to whom it was dedicated, that it ". . . is not the funeral mourning for a girl who has just died, but the evocation of a pavane which could have been danced by a small princess in days of old, at the court of Spain." The accompaniment resembles a lute at times. Ravel preferred that it be played calmly and without too much passion or sentimental *rubato*. It is in a rondo form. (Alfred and others.) Level 10.

Miscellaneous Volumes

At the Piano With Ravel, ed. Hinson

Excellent foreword and notes on the individual pieces precede the musical text. Works included are the *Menuet Antique, Pavane for a Dead Princess, Jeux d'eau, Sonatine, Menuet on the Name of Haydn, Sad Birds* and *The Valley of the Bells*. Some of these works are quite difficult. (Alfred.) Levels 9–10.

Ravel: Selected Favorites, ed. Hinson

Contains many less well-known pieces of Ravel as well as the more commonly heard works. Includes *In the Style of Borodin-Valse, In the Style of Chabrier* and several of the *Noble and Sentimental Waltzes*. (Alfred.) Level 10.

VLADIMIR REBIKOV (1866–1920) Russia

Rebikov's work was influenced by Debussy and his writing features whole tones, consecutive fourths and fifths and unresolved dissonances. Rebikov's works often can be considered Impressionistic.

The Christmas Gifts

Significant collection of 14 short elementary pieces. The sounds are often Romantic and the writing fits the hand well. These pieces are filled with strong characterization and are probably Rebikov's easiest pieces for students. They are only slightly greater in difficulty than the Kabalevsky *Music for Children*, Op. 39. See especially *No. 1 Children Gather Around the Christmas Tree* and *No. 4 The Bear*. (Belwin.) Levels 2–3.

Pictures for Children, Op. 37

Seven Impressionistic character pieces. See especially: *Preparing the Lesson,* which is a take off on someone practicing the first movement of the Mozart *Sonata in C Major*, K. 545; *Promenade of the Gnomes,* which depicts two gnomes taking a walk and meeting a frog; and *A Joyous Moment.* These brief works should be better known. (International.) Level 4.

Silhouettes, Op. 31

Subtitled "Nine Pictures from Childhood," this opus provides a kind of children's album in a mildly contemporary vein. (Alfred, International and others.) Levels 4–6.

No. 4 Playing Soldiers

Ostinato right-hand melody of two measures gives this motivating one-page solo with mild dissonance its martial character. The hands play in close proximity. Level 4.

No. 7 Rocking

Impressionistic writing for the expressive intermediate student. Four layers of sound need voicing. Cantabile melody in the soprano. Level 6.

Pieces for Piano

Miscellaneous and accessible teaching pieces from Rebikov's collections Opp. 2, 5, 8, 9, 21, 28 and 29. Most of these pieces are unknown, but many are interesting. (Soviet State Publishing.) Levels 6–7.

Miscellaneous Volumes

Rebikov: Miscellaneous Short Pieces, ed. Johnson

Provides an overview of Rebikov's extensive output and a source for some of his best teaching pieces. (Associated Board of the Royal Schools of Music.) Levels 3–6.

Additional Works for Study:

Op. 2 Six Pieces

Op. 8 Reveries d'automne

Op. 15 Mélomimiques I

Op. 50 Trois Idylles

ALAN RIDOUT (b. 1934) Great Britain

Portraits

Set of eight pieces composed for various friends who are only identified by their initials. Contemporary harmonies, thin textures, readable score. Brief sketches, similar to those by Virgil Thompson and Leonard Bernstein except that these selections are more accessible. (Weinberger.) Level 8.

WALLINGFORD RIEGGER (1885–1961) USA

Riegger's music displays a 19th-century Romantic style until sometime after 1920, when his writing became Impressionistic, and later, even more contemporary.

New and Old (12 Studies) (1944)

Each piece uses a specific compositional or musical device prominently in its structure such as *The Augmented Triad, Shifted Rhythm, The Tritone* and *Tone Clusters.* Analysis and explanation of the contemporary terminology are included for each piece. Significant contemporary volume. (Boosey.)

No. 1 The Augmented Triad

Based on the B-flat augmented triad and its inversions. Complex rhythms, strong dissonance and frequent imitation between the hands. Level 8.

No. 2 The Major Second

Seconds alternate between hands (almost in toccata style) within this one-page piece that sounds more difficult than it is. Level 8.

No. 3 The Tritone

A patterned figuration is the basis of the progressions. No key signature. Fits the hand well. Level 7.

No. 4 The 12 Tones

Lyrical one-page work featuring simple use of the 12-tone scale. Level 8.

No. 5 Shifted Rhythm

Built on the same row as in No. 4 but in original and inverted forms. A rhythmic pattern shifts position in later measures. Primarily linear writing and angular melodies in a two-page piece. Level 8.

No. 6 12 Upside Down

The tone series used in earlier pieces is inverted. Features melodic writing over an ostinato-like accompaniment. Level 8.

No. 7 Seven Times Seven

Patterned figurations fit the hand well in this 7/4 selection. The central recitative gives variety from the *vivo* perpetual motion. Level 8.

No. 8 Chromatics

Linear, chromatic writing with one line in each hand. Level 8.

No. 9 Dissonant Counterpoint

Begins as a two-voice fugue. Level 8.

No. 10 Tone Clusters

Probably the most immediately appealing and tuneful of the set. Strong rhythms, syncopated and frequent use of fourths. Central recitative needs careful timing and pacing. Level 8.

No. 11 Polytonality

Highly dissonant work that alternates between B Major and E-flat Major. Level 8.

No. 12 Fourths and Fifths

Toccata-like alternation between hands, with black notes played by the left hand and white notes by the right. Dissonant writing. Level 8.

Petite Étude

Polytonal writing with the left hand playing on the black keys and the right hand on the white keys. Rapidly alternating patterns of eighths in each hand. Three pages. (Merion.) Level 7.

VITTORIO RIETI (1898–1994) Egypt

Rieti spent most of his life in Italy and the USA. Although he is primarily self-taught, Reiti acknowledges Stravinsky to be a prime influence on his compositional style. His music tends to be lean, neo-Classical and tonal. Often the element of dance is found in his works.

Six Short Pieces

Neo-Classical tendencies within a mildly contemporary idiom are portrayed in these pieces. The music is alternately rhythmic and lyrical, holding possibilities especially for the performer who has a strong tendency toward playing linear music. Titles are *Preludio, Invenzione, Elegia, Momento Musica, Barcarola* and *Saltarello*. (General Music.) Level 8.

Five Pieces for Young Pianists

See especially the *Silly Polka*, with its "wrong-note" writing and its carnival-like atmosphere. (General Music.) Level 7.

Chironomos

Short character pieces with strong character delineation. Primarily linear writing in a dissonant idiom. Titles include *Preludio, Allegro Volante, Intermezzo, Mazurka, Improviso* and *Epilogo*. (General Music.) Level 9.

12 Preludes

Thin-textured, accessible works. Many of the preludes are dance-like, and rhythmic buoyancy is inherent in Rieti's style. Phrase lengths are often symmetrical. See especially *Nos. 2, 7* (Prokofiev-like), *10* (a witty and humorous work) and *11* (a brilliant toccata requiring some bravura). (General Music.) Levels 9–10.

Contrasts (1967)

Five titled movements in a mildly contemporary idiom. Movements are *Preludio, Variazioni, Bagatella, Elegia* and *Girandola*. Perhaps his most popular collection. (General Music.) Level 9.

GEORGE ROCHBERG (b. 1918) USA

Arioso

A two-page solo written in three voices with the middle voice alternating between the hands. It is built around G as a tonal center using a Phrygian mode with the lowered second step. Rather esoteric writing. (Presser.) Level 8.

JOAQUÍN RODRIGO (b. 1901) Spain

Sonada de Adios

Five-page lyrical work marked *Andante sostenuto* and featuring a dramatic climax. Appropriate for the student playing Chopin nocturnes. Mournful writing calling for a fine concept of rich sonority. (Eschig.) Level 10.

NED ROREM (b. 1923) USA

Rorem studied at the Curtis Institute and the Juilliard School and is best known as a composer of songs, which he writes almost entirely in extended cyclical structures.

A Quiet Afternoon (1948)

Set of nine short character pieces. Sensitive, lyrical writing in a simple and communicative work perhaps best performed by more mature performers. Key signatures through five sharps and three flats. See especially *No. 8 A Trick.* (Peer International.) Levels 6–7.

Barcarolles (1949)

Three movements ("Romances sans paroles") in 6/8 and dedicated to American pianist Leon Fleisher. Rorem states that they were written in Morocco in 1949 during a very wet season and that he was playing a great deal of Chopin's 6/8 music at the time. (Peters.) Level 10.

WALTER ROSS (b. 1936) USA

Six Shades of Blue. Preludes for Piano

Written to be a set of piano works similar to the Gershwin *Preludes*. Blues character is maintained throughout the six preludes. According to the composer in the preface: "the first and fourth are 'cool,' while the third and fifth are 'hot.' The second is 'slick' and the last is 'down.'" (Boosey.) Level 9.

ALEC ROWLEY (1892–1958) Great Britain

A leading composer of educational piano music, known better in Great Britain than in North America.

Elves and Fairies

Fourteen titled pieces in five-finger positions with complex coordination required between the hands despite the lack of movement about the keyboard. Dated writing without profundity. (Peters.) Levels 1–2.

Five Miniature Preludes and Fugues

Probably Rowley's most important and useful teaching collection. The highly patterned selections fit the hand well, making them especially appropriate for students with small hands. Each prelude features a single figuration throughout such as broken-chord arpeggiation. Easy, two-voice fugues. (Chester.) Level 2.

From My Sketch Book, Op. 39

Ten short pieces, primarily diatonic. Dated. (Peters.) Level 2.

12 Little Fantasy Studies, Op. 13

A specific technical challenge is emphasized in each study. See *Study in C*, which features broken third patterns, *Songs Without Words*, which employs broken chords and *Little Stream*, which exploits the trill. Most pieces are in the keys of C, G, F and D. Predictable writing. (Boosey.) Levels 2–3.

10 Miniatures From a Paris Window

Tuneful writing, thin texture and harmonically conservative in two books each of five pieces. (Chester.) Level 4.

Happenings

These 17 studies feature five-finger patterns in major and minor keys. *Wasp* is bitonal with the right hand playing in G and the left in F-sharp. Other titles include *All On a Summer's Day, Marching, In the Aeroplane, Chase Me, Imitation* and *Sailor Bold*. (Banks.) Level 4.

From Dell and Hillside: Five Outdoor Pieces for Piano

Cycle of descriptive pieces featuring folk elements indigenous to England. See especially *Mysterious Hollow*, which is a study in nocturnal sonorities. (Banks.)

Jolidays

Four untitled pieces in ternary form. (Banks.)

Marionettes

Overture followed by five pieces, each of which depicts a particular marionette. See especially *Drummer Boy* with its "rat-a-tat-tat" rhythm, *Ballet Dancer, Clown, Spanish Dancer* and *Sailor*. (Banks.)

Sonatinas, Op. 40

The entire set is subtitled *Seasons* and the four individual sonatinas are given subtitles which are the names of the seasons of the year: Op. 40, *No. 1 (Spring)*, Op. 40, *No. 2 (Summer)*, Op. 40, *No. 3 (Autumn)*, Op. 40, *No. 4 (Winter)*. Most of the first movements are in sonata form and three of the four sonatas conclude with rondos. See especially the finale of *Winter*, which interpolates the themes of "The Mulberry Bush" and "The First Noel." Limited harmonic language, conservative writing. (Peters.) Level 6.

30 Melodious and Rhythmic Studies, Op. 42, Volume I and Op. 43, Volume II

Comprehensive collection of miniature character pieces, somewhat similar to the Mendelssohn *Songs Without Words*. Such generic titles as *Invention, Prelude, Fugue, Scherzo, Mazurka, Impromptu* and *Nocturne* are found throughout the two volumes. (Peters.)

Etudes in Tonality, Op. 44

Eight selections in 20th-century idioms. Titles are *Prologue* (jazz influence), *Modal, Pentatonic, Atonal, Diatonic, Whole-Tone, Chromatic* and *Polytonal*. Each étude features a specific technical skill. (Peters.) Levels 9–10.

Polyrhythms, Op. 50

Seven titled selections featuring a different meter for each hand: *Canzonetta*, two notes against three; *Idylle*, three against two; *Vignette*, six against three; *Preambule*, 12 against six; *Impromptu-Appassionato*, three against four; *Nocturne*, five against three; and *Tango*, irregular groupings. (Peters.) Level 10.

EDWIN ROXBURGH (b. 1937) Great Britain

Les Miroirs de Miró

Four pieces for piano based on four paintings by Miró. See especially *Spanish Dancer*, a one-page contemporary flamenco piece. (United.) Level 7.

MIKLÓS RÓZSA (b. 1907) Hungary

Rózsa left his native Hungary in 1931, and eventually settled in the USA.

Bagatellen, Op. 12

Pianistic and mildly dissonant. Strong rhythmic feeling. See especially *Kleiner Marsch* and *Capriccietto*. (Breitkopf.) Level 8.

Kaleidoscope, Op. 19 (1945)

Subtitled *Six Brilliant Recital Pieces. Kaleidoscope* presents contemporary writing for the elementary student. The style is highly rhythmic and generally sparkling. Titles include *1. March, 2. Zingara, 3. Musette, 4. Berceuse,*

5. Chinese Carillon and *6. Burlesque.* See especially the vigorous *March.* It would be especially good for a student with strong hands and a vibrant rhythmic sense. Also effective is the *Chinese Carillon* with its left-hand ostinato, played high in the treble register. (Associated.) Level 6.

S

PIERRE SANCAN (b. 1916) France

Pièces Enfantines, Volume 1

Little-known suite of six interesting teaching pieces filled with vitality. Movements include *Tendre Souvenir, Promenade, Sans histoire, Jouet mécanique, Princesse lointaine* and *Sur les chevaux de bois.* (Durand.) Level 7.

DOMINGO SANTA CRUZ (1899–1987) Chile

Imagenes Infantiles (Childhood Images)

Two sets of four pieces each found under one cover and presenting sophisticated contemporary writing for the upper-intermediate student. Bitonal selections. See especially *Na Pancha's Song* and *The Mischievous Boy.* Level 8.

CLAUDIO SANTORO (b. 1919) Brazil

Sonatine No. 2

Attractive and highly rhythmic writing. Thin textures make this suitable for the advancing student with small hands. Requires energy and strong rhythmic sense. An unusual and yet readable contemporary work. Level 10.

TIBOR SÁRAI (b. 1919) Hungary

Works for Study:
Rondoletto
Sonatina

ERIK SATIE (1866–1925) France

Satie, often referred to as an eccentric and a genius, had an enormous influence on 20th-century music. He is often known for the bizarre or whimsical titles he gave to many of his works, perhaps to parody the evocative moods of Impressionist music. Satie's works are characterized by transparent texture, simple melodies, fresh harmonies and avoidance of all complexities. Much of the music by Satie is published by Associated, Dover, Eschig, Peters or Salabert.

Sarabandes (1887)

These works anticipated a harmonic language that was later adopted and developed by Debussy and Ravel. These three works initially must have sounded strange with their unprepared seventh chords and unresolved ninths. (Salabert.) Level 7.

Gymnopédies (1888)

These three simple and charming works foreshadow the linear style that he later used. The first and third are perhaps Satie's best compositions and were probably inspired by a decoration on a Greek vase. "Gymnopedia" was a yearly festival mentioned by the ancient Greek historian Herodotus in honor of those who fell at the battle of Thyrea. The three selections perhaps represent the stately dance performed by youths before statues of the gods. All are sad and beautiful pieces. Debussy later orchestrated two of these works. (Many standard editions.)

First Gymnopédie

Lyrical work, opening with a four-bar introduction. Calls for the sustaining of a melodic line with long note values and a left-hand accompaniment with wide jumps. Extremely popular. Level 8.

Second Gymnopédie

Similar in texture to the *First Gymnopédie*. Lyrical melody over bass chords presenting a dreamy character. Relaxed writing in five sections. Level 7.

Third Gymnopédie

Compelling lyrical writing in a work with a relaxed tempo. Very well known. Level 8.

Gnossiennes (1890)

Three two-to-three-page works that were inspired by archaeological excavations at Knossos' palace in Crete. The orientalism might be a result of Japanese and other exotic music Satie heard at the Paris Exhibition in 1889. Barlines and key signatures are absent. These are the first compositions in which he gives humorous directions to the performer. Although they are often published with the *Three Gymnopédie*, these works are different in sound and style. Reading them as if they were in 4/4 time may facilitate the initial learning. (Alfred, Salabert, G. Schirmer and others.) Level 8.

Sonneries de la Rose-Croix (Rosicrucian Fanfares) (1892)

Movements include *Air of the Order, Air of the Grand Marshal* and *Prelude of the Heroic Gate of Heaven.* (Dover, Salabert.) Level 8.

Le fils des étoiles (The Song of the Stars) (1892)

In three movements, *First Act Prelude (The Calling), Second Act (The Initiation)* and *Third Act (The Incantation).* (Dover, Salabert.) Levels 7–8.

Poudre d'or (Gold Dust) (c. 1901)

Waltz with numerous artificial ritards. Not as successful as the other waltz *Je te veux.* (Dover.) Level 8.

Véritables préludes flasques (Pour un chien) (Genuine Flabby Preludes [for a dog]) (1912)

No barlines or key signatures in these *Flabby Preludes* with humorous Latin instructions. Movements are *Severe reprimand, All alone at home* and *Playing.* (Eschig.) Level 6.

Nine Children's Pieces (1913)

Includes three groups of three pieces, all written in 1913. The works included are *Childish Small Talk (Menus Propos Enfantins), A Child's Quaint Ways (Enfantillages Pittoresques)* and *Tiresome Pranks (Peccadilles Importunes).* Sparse textures and uncomplicated pieces with running commentary on events concerning the life of a child such as "Get used to seeing a slice of bread and jam without wanting to steal it." Sophisticated writing, most appropriate for adult humor. (Associated Board of the Royal Schools of Music, Novello.) Level 2.

Croquis and Agaceries d'un Gros Bonhomme en bois (Sketches and Temptations of a Big Wooden Man) (1913)

Titles are *Mountain Song of the Turkish Tryol, Skinny Dance* and *Espanaña.* No barlines or key signatures. (Cramer.) Level 7.

Descriptions automatiques (Automatic Descriptions) (1913)

These pieces begin to show Satie's imitation of Impressionism. Movements are *About a boat, About a lantern* and *About a helmet.* Part of *Voici les tambours* imitates a portion of Debussy's *Minstrels.* (Eschig.) Level 8.

Chapitres tournés en tous sens
(Matters Thoroughly Discussed) (1913)

Movements are titled *The Woman Who Talks too Much, The Rock Carrier* and *The Shut-Ins' Laments.* Sophisticated writing, musically challenging. (Eschig.) Level 8.

Embroyns desséchés (Dried Up Embryoes) (1913)

An imaginary crustacean described in a preface to each movement is portrayed in the three movements. The second piece *d'Edriophtalma* includes a version of the Chopin *Funeral March.* (Eschig.) Level 10.

Enfantillages pittoresques (Picturesque Child's Play) (1913)

In three movements, *Little Prelude to the Day, Lullaby* and *March of the Great Staircase.* (Eschig.) Level 3.

Je te veux (I Long for You)

A waltz, traditionally notated and moving through many keys. Conservative and appropriately sentimental. Level 8.

Menus propos enfantis (Childish Small Talk) (1913)

More sophisticated musically than technically. Movements include *The War Chant of the King of Beans, What the Little Tulip Princess Says* and *Waltz of the Chocolate with Almonds.* (Associated Board of the Royal Schools of Music, Eschig.) Level 3.

Peccadilles importunes (Annoying Offenses) (1913)

Titles of movements are *Being jealous of your friend who has a swelled head, Eating up your friend's piece of bread* and *Taking advantage of the corns on his feet to grab his hoop.* (Eschig.) Level 3.

Heures seculaires and instantanées
(Times of Day, Then and Now) (1914)

Musically sophisticated. Movements include *Venomous obstacles, Morning light [from noon]* and *Stampeding boulders.* (Eschig.) Level 9.

Vieu sequins et vielles cuirasses
(Antique Gold and Ancient Armor) (1914)

Musically sophisticated. Movements include *At the Gold Merchant's House, Armored Dance* and *The Defeat of the Cimbres.* (Eschig.) Level 8.

Sports and Divertissements (1914)

Set of 20 one-page miniatures with witty commentary and no barlines and preceded by a mock chorale. Masterpieces of wit and irony. Topics deal with such diversions as golf and tennis. Much more difficult musically than technically. Needs a sophisticated performer. (Dover, Salabert and others.) Level 10.

Sonatine bureaucratique (1917)

The last of Satie's humorous pieces, this sonatina is closely based on the Clementi *Sonatina in C Major*, Op. 36, No. 1. Teachers and adults especially will enjoy the parody on this well-known teaching piece of Clementi. (Many standard editions.) Level 8.

Five Nocturnes (1919)

These short pieces represent Satie's return to formal writing. Absent are the humorous titles and unconventional commentary and directions to the performer. He intended the set of five to be his final solo piano works. These selections reflect the simplicity of Satie that is often overlooked amidst his need to shock or amuse. The first three are most frequently heard. (Eschig, Salabert.) Level 10.

AHMED ADNAN SAYGUN (1907–1991) Turkey

Inci's Book

Short teaching pieces for children in which much of the writing is on the white keys and is sometimes modal. Well-crafted with titles that include *Inci, Playful Kitten, A Tale, The Giant Puppet, A Joke, Lullaby* and *A Dream*. (Southern Music.) Level 4.

PETER SCHICKELE (b. 1935) USA

Composer, pianist and musical humorist. Schickele is mostly known by the stage name, P.D.Q. Bach.

Small Serenade

Suite of six movements titled *Song, Riff, Rumba, Tango, Dream Waltz* and *Stomp*. Intermediate level with thin textures and an easy-to-read score. *Song* is modal while *Stomp* and *Riff* touch on a popular style. A diverse set of pieces. (Elkan-Vogel.) Level 5.

Epitaphs

This set embodies a series of stylistic tributes to five major composers, while remaining fully contemporary as well. (Elkan-Vogel.)

Orlando di Lasso

The composer notes this as "a transfigured memory of two-part motets." Level 5.

Michael Praetorius

This boisterous selection with changing meters is highly rhythmic, and features broken-octave accompaniment. Level 5.

Domenico Scarlatti

The figuration that opens and predominates in this selection is clearly an offshoot of a well-known Scarlatti sonata with its rapid, descending five-note step-wise figures. The most difficult of the set, but reflects the exuberance of Scarlatti's music. Level 8.

Frédéric Chopin

A long cantabile melody with a wide range is set to a simple chordal accompaniment. Level 5.

Igor Stravinsky

A bright two-page movement with large chords and changing meters. Mildly contemporary harmony. Level 5.

In My Nine Lives

All of these elementary contemporary pieces are based on themes concerning cats. The writing is some of Schickele's best. See especially *With Closed Eyes, Kittenhood, Good Hunting, Parenthood* and *Coming of Age.* (Elkan-Vogel.) Levels 3–5.

Little Suite for Susan

Originally conceived as a birthday gift of little piano pieces that Schickele's wife might be able to play. Seven short titled pieces with changing meters and some tricky passages. Titles include *Dulcimer Tune, Blues Etude, Tango, Strut, Hymn, Fanfare* and *Dusk Song.* (Elkan-Vogel.) Level 7.

Razzle-Dazzle Triptych

The three movements *Prelude, Razzle-Dazzle* and *Afterthought* are all written with a humorous spirit. The entire set takes only three minutes. These would be most appropriate for the adult student with sophisticated taste and a strong rhythmic sense. (Elkan-Vogel.) Level 7.

Hollers, Hymns and Dirges

Although subtitled by the composer as *Eight Folk Song Settings*, these pieces are anything but traditional settings. Textures are lean and sparse, and this contemporary writing is sophisticated. For each old American folk song, Schickele describes his thoughts or feelings concerning a time in his past when the folk song moved him. Adult students may be interested in this collection. Titles include *Go Tell Aunt Rhody, Amazing Grace, Darlin' Corey* and *Ruby*. (Elkan-Vogel.) Level 7.

Additional Works for Study:
Three Folk Settings
Little Suite for Josie

JULIUS SCHLOSS (n.d.) Germany

Schloss spent most of his life in the USA.

23 Pieces for Children in 12-Tone Style

All are short (some only seven or so measures) with classical rhythms and many accidentals. Imaginative titles and many expression marks. Many recurring figures and imitation between the hands. Titles include *Spook, The Soloist, Raindrops, Odd, Feeling Blue* and *Chimes*. (Peer International.) Level 5.

12-Tone Suite

Strong character definition between movements. The rhythmic framework is neo-Classical but the harmonic language is 12-tone. Sophisticated writing that an early-advanced student should handle well. The writing reflects the influence of Schloss' teacher, Alban Berg. The movement titles in this short suite are *Prologue, Scherzo, March, Interlude, Air, Chaconne, Étude* and *Epilogue*. (Peer International.) Level 10.

FLORENT SCHMITT (1870–1958) France

Schmitt was a student of Fauré and Massenet. Many of his salon-style works were immensely popular in their day.

Pupazzi, Op. 36

Subtitled *Petite Suite pour Piano*, this work contains eight early-advanced works. (Mathot.) Level 8.

ARNOLD SCHOENBERG (1874–1951) Austria

Schoenberg, a great innovator, composed in an atonal style and initiated the 12-tone system that resulted in a reversal of previously existing theoretical concepts of harmony.

Six Little Piano Pieces, Op. 19

Found here are short, compact works that are thin in texture. The longest of the six atonal pieces comprises 17 measures, and three of the pieces are only nine measures long. The last is perhaps the most moving, with its two bell-like chords that sound throughout. (Universal.) Level 9.

RUTH SCHONTHAL (b. 1924) Germany

Schonthal immigrated to the USA.

Potpourri

A collection of solos for the elementary student, featuring contrasting characters and primarily thin textures. (Carl Fischer.) Level 3.

Near and Far

Subtitled "13 Musical Scenes for the Older Student," these pieces might be best for older students who are interested in contemporary writing. Sonority often takes precedence over melody, and students who enjoy atmospheric literature will be interested in these pieces. (Carl Fischer.) Level 3.

Sonata Breve

An eight-minute work in one movement with many tempo and mood changes. It is a study in warm sonorities and color from the *tranquillo* opening through large climaxes to the final decay of sound resulting from indeterminate repetitions of a motive at the end. (Oxford.) Level 10.

WILLIAM SCHUMAN (1910–1992) USA

Schuman, a student of Roy Harris, later served as president of The Juilliard School from 1945 to 1962. Exerting a strong influence on Persichetti, Mennin, Bergsma and Ward, Schuman's style is tonal, highly lyrical and melodic.

Three Piano Moods

Three brief movements, published separately. According to the composer in a note on the scores, "may be performed separately [but] it would be more effective to play them as a group." (Merion Music.)

Lyrical

An ostinato bass consisting of a descending four-note motive pervades most of this movement. The right-hand melody is freely tonal. For the sophisticated ear. Level 9.

Pensive

Highly chromatic lyrical writing in a primarily chordal work. Calls for a mature musician. Level 8.

Dynamic

In three sections, each starting piano and growing to an intense *forte*, this work exhibits strong rhythms and much syncopation, with mirror construction between the two voices in the middle section. Dramatic writing with a tinge of jazz flavor makes it the most appealing movement of this set. Level 8.

Three Score Set

Three-movement work. The first is gigue-like and is in 6/8 with a moving melody. The second is a bitonal chord study, written almost entirely in blocked triads. The final movement is a dance, highly rhythmic, bringing the work to a rousing close. Excellent contemporary literature for the early-intermediate student. (G. Schirmer.) Levels 7–8.

CYRIL SCOTT (1879–1970) Great Britain

Scott was a master of the musical miniature and his writing portrays his respect for French Impressionism. Even though much of his music sounds dated today, some of the most popular teaching pieces retain their appeal.

Zoo

Subtitled "Animals for Piano," this work is a collection of highly descriptive pieces about the various animals at the zoo. Engaging writing, easy to listen to and highly descriptive. These pieces need imaginative interpretations and should be better known. All selections are intriguing, but see especially *The Elephant, The Bear, The Monkey* and *The Giraffe.* (Schott.) Level 4.

Miscellaneous Pieces

Lotus Land, Op. 47, No. 1

Perhaps his best-known piano work and rewarding to play. *Lotus Land* is filled with atmospheric passages, rich and sonorous chords, brilliant cascades and arpeggiations, all of which contribute to its effectiveness. (Many standard editions.) Level 9.

A Song from the East, Op. 54, No. 2

Appealing mostly for its evocative atmosphere. A staccato broken-chord bass in eighth notes stretching over a tenth forms the accompaniment during much of this Romantic piece. (Many standard editions.) Level 9.

Danse Nègre, Op. 58, No. 5

A tonal and tuneful piece, filled with energy and brilliant right-hand passagework. Useful as supplementary literature to a student's standard fare. (Galaxy.) Level 10.

Additional Works for Study:
For My Young Friends
Miniatures

ALEXANDER SCRIABIN (1872–1915) Russia

Although his first works were highly influenced by Chopin, Scriabin's style went through extreme changes during his life. During his later life he was preoccupied with mystical phenomena, and his later works exhibited harmonic experimentations that led to a highly personal style of writing. The music is filled with emotionalism in a basically Romantic idiom. (Many standard editions.)

Selected Preludes

Prelude in B Major, Op. 2, No. 2 (from Trois Morceaux)

Subdued work with three-voice textures and triplet figurations. Highly expressive writing. Level 8.

Prelude in A Minor, Op. 11, No. 2

Calls for skillful use of rubato. Linear writing, highly Romantic. Level 9.

Prelude in E Minor, Op. 11, No. 4

Lyrical work with enchanting left-hand descending melodic motives. Calls for refined voicing and a good sense of rubato. Enchanting melancholy work. Scriabin first began this as a ballade. Level 8.

Prelude in D Major, Op. 11, No. 5

One of the most elegantly beautiful of the early works of Scriabin. Calls for a flexible left hand and a refined sense of pacing rolled chords. Level 10.

Prelude in E Major, Op. 11, No. 9

Andantino work, highly lyrical. Left hand contains interesting counter-melodies to the chordal right hand. Level 9.

Prelude in G-flat Major, Op. 11, No. 13

Long lines prevail throughout this lyrical work that calls for a refined ability to voice the busy texture. Level 10.

Prelude in D-flat Major, Op. 11, No. 15

A lovely and simple work with a melody over a slowly moving accompaniment. The performer must sustain the forward movement of the phrases. Level 8.

Prelude in G Major, Op. 13, No. 3

Beautiful harmonic colors in a work with triplet accompaniment figures and two- and three-note chords in the right hand. Expressive writing. Level 8.

Prelude in G Minor, Op. 27, No. 1

Marked *patetico*, this resonant and sonorous work uses augmented sixths and many delayed resolutions of nonchord tones. Level 10.

Three Pieces, Op. 45

Titled *Feuillet d'album, Poème fantasque* and *Prélude*, these selections display chromatic writing within a tonal framework. More difficult musically than technically. Level 8.

Miscellaneous Volumes

2 Preludes for the Intermediate Pianist

A highly practical collection of works from throughout Scriabin's life for the upper-intermediate student pianist. (Presser.) Levels 8–10.

Scriabin: Selected Works, ed. Baylor

A practical performing edition containing a compilation of many genres including several poems, preludes from Op. 11, Op. 16, Op. 48, Op. 74, several études from Op. 42, Op. 65, the *Fourth Sonata*, an album leaf, several poems and other works. The variety of works found here makes it especially interesting. (Alfred.) Levels 9–10.

KAZIMIERZ SEROCKI (1922–1981) Poland

The Gnomes (Krasnoludki)

A set of seven significant children's miniatures featuring strong writing that is mildly contemporary and quite pianistic. These works should be much better known and more frequently performed. Vividly illustrated. See especially *Dance, Mazurka, Cradle-song* and *Oberek*. (PWM.) Level 7.

ROGER SESSIONS (1896–1985) USA

Waltz

Wide skips and a disjunct melody in this dissonant three-page work for early-advanced pianists. The sometimes complex rhythms in the accompaniment will need careful study. (Merion.) Level 9.

Additional Works for Study:
March (Carl Fischer)
Scherzino (Carl Fischer)

RALPH SHAPEY (b. 1921) USA

Seven Little Pieces

Brief, untitled movements in which each piece presents certain pianistic problems, noted at the top of the piece. Dissonant writing for the sophisticated musician. (Presser.) Level 10.

RODION SHCHEDRIN (b. 1932) Russia

Notebook for Young People

Shchedrin consciously wrote teaching pieces based on Soviet character and content. This work, a piano cycle for youth, much in the same vein as the Schumann *Album for the Young* and the Tchaikovsky *Children's Album*, contains 15 character pieces in a contemporary idiom. Highly pianistic. Interesting writing, of high quality. See especially *No. 9 Fanfares, No. 13 Chase* and *No. 15 Etude in A*. This *Notebook* is widely heard in Russia. (Sikorski.) Levels 7–8.

DMITRI SHOSTAKOVICH (1906–1975) Russia

Greatly gifted composer whose career was at times hampered by the restrictions placed on Soviet artists during the reign of communism. His music often exhibits examples of satire, as well as unexpected turns of harmony or of rhythm.

Six Children's Pieces, Op. 69 (1944–45)

This set of pieces was composed in one day by Shostakovich for his daughter Gayla when she was eight years old. Generally in two voices, these pieces can be highly effective in performance. Unfortunately many performers may shy away from them due to their disjunct lines and numerous accidentals. (Many standard editions.) Level 3.

No. 1 March

The best-known movement of the set, with "wrong-note" writing that pervades the texture and adds interest. The last three measures need careful work in fingering. Level 2.

No. 2 Waltz

Two-voice waltz in which both hands rarely move simultaneously. Many shifts of hand position. Level 2.

No. 3 The Bear

Again, two-voice writing, with predominantly disjunct melodic lines. The non-legato playing of quarter notes can create a lumbering effect while the big gestures help develop freedom of arms. Some unison playing. Level 3.

No. 4 A Funny Story

The movement about the keyboard and the use of distant keys makes this selection more difficult than it appears on the page. Filled with quick shifts and many accidentals, but effective when played up to tempo. Level 5.

No. 5 A Sad Story

Lyrical writing. Provides a fine study in voicing and inflection of melodic lines. Level 3.

No. 6 The Mechanical Doll

This selection and the *March* are the best-known movements. Rapid passagework for both hands, "wrong-note" writing, and thin textures. Calls for fine attention to articulation. Level 4.

Puppet Dances (Dances of the Dolls) (1952–62)

Collection of intermediate pieces, less contemporary in sound than some of Shostakovich's other works. Uneven in quality, but several are quite charming. Titles are *No. 1 Lyrical Waltz, No. 2 Gavotte, No. 3 Romance, No. 4 Polka, No. 5 Waltz-Scherzo, No. 6 Hurdy-Gurdy* and *No. 7 Dance.* (Alfred, MCA and many standard editions.)

No. 1 Lyrical Waltz

Graceful work with an oom-pah-pah accompaniment. Provides preparation for Chopin playing. Not especially easy to read, calling for many different kinds of articulation within the piece. Harmonies change frequently and unpredictably, and the fingering is sometimes tricky in the right hand. For the sophisticated musician. Levels 7–8.

No. 6 Hurdy Gurdy

Ostinato oom-pah bass, repeated in each measure except the last. The right-hand melody with its wide melodic range is varied throughout, forming a kind of continuous variation set. Cheerful. Level 5.

No. 7 Dance

Giocoso work for the student with good fingers and a strong sense of pulse. Quirky. Level 6.

Events of a Day

This set includes 21 pieces. Titles include *The Break For Rest, Making Peace, At the River, Dance, Evening Country, Lullaby* and *Dream*. Effective writing. (Sikorski.) Levels 6–8.

25 Pieces for Piano

Collection of intermediate character pieces. Infrequently heard, but a gold mine for the performer looking for fresh modern literature in a conservative vein. (Sikorski.) Levels 7–9.

Three Fantastic Dances, Op. 5 (1) (1922)

These works were originally published as Op. 1 and are humorous, sparkling pieces and filled with imagination. Unexpected harmonic changes and unusual turns of melody all add character and personality. (Many standard editions.)

I. (Allegretto)

A saucy march in ABA form with dotted rhythms and sarcastic melodic phrases. Level 8.

II. (Andantino)

A "wrong-note" waltz in ABA form. Levels 7–8.

III. (Allegretto)

A humorous polka with strong changes of mood and interesting key changes. This jovial work requires careful voicing and technical control in the double-note passages. Level 8.

Five Preludes (1920–21)

Early pieces completed when Shostakovich was 14. Movements include *No. 1 Allegro moderato e scherzando, No. 2 Andante, No. 3 Allegro moderato, No. 4 Moderato* and *No. 5 Andantino. No. 1* is written entirely in the upper register of the keyboard. *No. 2* is in Mixolydian mode with a drone bass. (MCA, Sikorski.)

Prelude in F Minor

For the musically sophisticated student, this folk-like piece with a haunting mysterious effect provides preparation for fugal playing. Highly contrapuntal with many accidentals. Levels 8–9.

Aphorisms, Op. 13

A little-known collection of 10 titled pieces, seldom heard, but providing substantive fare for the performer able to play the Bach *Inventions*. Primarily linear writing and thin textures characterize a work that should be better known. (VAAP.) Levels 8–9.

24 Preludes, Op. 34

Modeled after Chopin's set. Many are humorous and employ Shostakovich's much-used "wrong-note" writing techniques, and each prelude has a clearly defined mood or character. They follow the cycle of ascending fifths. Many have been transcribed for other mediums. See especially *Preludes* Nos. 7 (A Major), 13 (F-sharp Major), 16 (B-flat Minor), 17 (A-flat Major), 19 (E-flat Major), 22 (G Minor), and 24 (D Minor). (Boston, International, Kalmus and other standard editions.)

No. 1 (Moderato)

A haunting and somewhat nostalgic prelude that opens with an Alberti figure in the right hand that then moves to the left. Wide keyboard range and contrapuntal interplay in this linear and moving work. Level 9.

No. 2 (Allegretto)

Brilliant chromatic scales and a light, dance-like nature mark this work. The rhythmic interest often falls on the third beat of the measure in the accompaniment. Cheerful. Level 10.

No. 3 (Andante)

Contains an almost Impressionistic effect in a serenely lyrical piece. Nocturne-like two-page piece with a dramatic intrusion near the close. Three-voice texture. Worth investigating. Level 9.

No. 4. (Moderato)

A serious three-voice fugue in 5/4 that is on the technical and musical level of some of the Bach *Sinfonias*. Level 9.

No. 6 (Allegretto)

Found here is an appealing satiric polka featuring dissonance, bitonality, wide interval skips, halting accompaniment and abrupt shifts of key. Level 9.

No. 9 (Presto)

Perpetual-motion piece with biting dissonances in two voices and featuring a whirling accompaniment in 6/8. Continuous triplet rhythms, bitonal dissonant effects and use of the extreme upper register of the piano characterize this effective tarantella. Two printed pages. Level 10.

No. 10 (Moderato non troppo)

A lyric processional with a typically Russian melody in a tender, poignant mood. The melody is made of some wide stretches. Requires a sensitive performer and a delicate touch and subtle dynamic control. Level 10.

No. 13 (Moderato)

A tiny but highly effective march with fife and drum effects. Uses the wide ranges of the keyboard. Level 9.

No. 14 (Adagio)

A weighty and somber work, perhaps the best of the set. Orchestral writing, requiring resonant sonorities, rich tone and featuring wide melodic intervals. Rises to a *fff* climax before ending *ppp* within the 36-measure piece. This effective work has been orchestrated by Stokowski. Level 9.

No. 15 (Allegretto)

One of the most humorous and appealing of the Preludes, this waltz-like work is filled with "wrong-note" writing. The oom-pah-pah accompaniment appears in the right hand and the melody in the left in the opening. Thin textured, witty. Level 9.

No. 16 (Andantino)

A stately march with amusing "wrong-note" writing and humorous twists of the phrase. The dotted rhythms in the accompaniment give this work its unique character. Bold and interesting. Level 9.

No. 19 (Andantino)

Lyrical writing in a 6/8 work, similar to one of Mendelssohn's barcarolle-like pieces from the *Songs Without Words*. Filled with harmonic richness. Level 10.

No. 23 (Moderato)

An Impressionistic piece with a chant-like melody appearing in the middle register of the piano and a triplet accompaniment figure in the upper part. Level 10.

No. 24 (Allegretto)

A satiric gavotte, highly effective as a close to this set of pieces. Level 10.

ELIE SIEGMEISTER (1909–1991) USA

Folk-Ways U.S.A., Volumes 1–5

Siegmeister wrote a series of volumes subtitled "A Progressive Series of American Song Scenes and Sketches" as a corrective to his own uninteresting childhood experience studying piano with unmotivating literature. He tried to think of his own children in writing these volumes and to imagine the kind of music they would like to play. According to the preface, the composer bases this series on American folk and popular sources due to "the beauty of the music; because of its strong appeal to the American imagination; because it presents certain technical and musical features of great interest to the modern mind (i.e., modal scales, changing meters, syncopation, etc.); and because it is a means of introducing the child to the point of view of the American composer." Volume 1 is designed for the beginner and the pieces are based on folk songs such as *Ev're Night, Down in the Valley, The Mocking Bird* and *One, Two, Three O'Leary*. The arrangements are tonal. (Presser.) Levels 1–7.

A Set of Houses

Descriptive elementary pieces that depict different kinds of houses including *No. 2 Two-Story House, No. 3 City House, No. 5 Monkey House, No. 6 Old Stone House, No. 7 Penthouse*, as well as others. This set of pieces should be much better known. The writing is mildly contemporary and quite pianistic. (Carl Fischer.) Levels 3–4.

The Children's Day

Strong writing appears in these six character pieces. The harmonic palette is mildly contemporary and the works will be attractive to the performer and audience alike. This collection should be better known. See especially *No. 1 Sunny Morning, No. 2 Skipping Rope, No. 3 Playing Clown* and *No. 5 Catching Butterflies*. (MCA.) Levels 4–5.

American Kaleidoscope

Twenty strong pieces in a variety of moods, especially appropriate for small hands. See especially *No. 3 Song of the Dark Woods, No. 5 Street Games, No. 15 The Chase, No. 17 Marching* and *No. 19 Sunny Day*. (Sam Fox.) Levels 4–5.

NICHOLAS SLONIMSKY (b. 1894) Russia

Slominsky immigrated to the USA where he became a citizen in 1931.

51 Minitudes for Piano

Mini-études for piano, often humorous. Each one illustrates some quirk of thematic, melodic, canonic or harmonic manipulation. They are, according to the composer, "curt, terse and quick" with some of them only four measures long. The unusual titles include *Bach x 2 = Debussy, A National Anthem in Search of a Country, Czerny Shmerny* and *Blitzpartie*. Novelties. (G. Schirmer.) Level 8.

YURI SLONOV (1902–1978) Russia

28 Easy Pieces

These tonal, pianistic pieces are progressive in difficulty, spanning the elementary to intermediate levels. The character differences between movements are distinctive and these works fit the hand well. Titles include *Conversation, Czech Folksong, Jolly Etude, Dance, Morning Prelude* and *Mazurka*. Fine writing from the Russian school. (Associated.) Levels 4–6.

LEO SMIT (b. 1921) USA

Five Pieces for Young People

Primarily linear writing, often modal, in a set of pieces that sound more difficult than they are, perhaps as a result of the interesting use of rhythms. See especially *Finger Play* and *Little Fanfare*. (Carl Fischer.) Level 2.

Martha Through the Looking Glass

Three pieces with contemporary sonorities and angular writing. Titles are *The White Knight, It's My Own Invention* and *The Upside-Down Deal Box*. (Boosey.) Level 8.

A Visitor's Album

Four short pieces in a highly contemporary style. Titles are *In Sohmertime, The Dog Star (Lullaby), The Dancing Lesson (Rondo)* and *Madrigal*. (Boosey.) Level 9.

Dance Card

The four movements are neo-Romantic takeoffs on dances. This is music that would be especially appropriate as "light American music" to end a program. Traditional harmonic framework with some dissonance. Titles include *Tango Bolshoi, Diabelli Polka, Valse Tristan* and *Prater Rag*. (Merion.) Level 10.

HALE SMITH (b. 1925) USA

Faces of Jazz

Twelve titled pieces in original jazz idioms for the intermediate pianist. See especially *Off-Beat Shorty, That's Mike* and *Goin' in a Hurry*. Should be better known. (Marks.) Levels 7–8.

Evocation

Twelve-tone work with strong character, flexible rhythms and full sonorities. Level 9.

JULIA FRANCES SMITH (1911–1989) USA

Episodic Suite

See especially the movements titled *Yellow and Blue, March* and *Toccata*. Biting contemporary sounds in a palatable style. (Mowbray/Presser.) Levels 7–8.

JÓZSEF SOPRONI (b. 1930) Hungary

Note Pages, Volume I (1974)

This set of 44 brief avant-garde piano pieces contain titles such as *Chasing About, Beckoning* and *Autumn Poem*. Contemporary techniques include notation for free repetitions, clusters, free accelerandos and ritards and playing with the side of the hand. Should be better known. (EMB.) Levels 5–7.

Note Pages, Volume II (1976)

These 23 avant-garde pieces are slightly more difficult than those in Volume I. The range of works extends from slow, one- or two-line compositions to longer pieces that are rapid, lively and transparent. Each piece is based on a single musical thought and the forms are concise and clear. (EMB.) Levels 7–9.

Additional Works for Study:
Note Pages, Volume III
Note Pages, Volume IV

ROBERT STARER (b. 1924) Austria

Prolific composer whose style is a synthesis of several nationalistic elements. Born in Austria, Starer immigrated to the USA after World War II and taught composition in New York at The Juilliard School and Brooklyn College.

12 Pieces for Ten Fingers (1963)

Literature for beginners by a major contemporary American composer. The first ones use only quarter and half notes, and all are progressive in difficulty. Contemporary idioms are explored at the beginning level, including pentatonic writing and changing meters. All selections are titled. (Sam Fox.) Levels 1–2.

Games with Names, Notes and Numbers (1979)

A set of 12 contemporary pieces for the elementary student. Each piece is constructed to be a game, providing some permutation or representation of the title to be discovered in the music by the student. These would be especially good for the student who has a mathematical mind or who enjoys contemporary sounds. (MCA.)

ABE, GABE, ADA, FAE and ED
　　All of the notes in the piece (the letter-names of the notes) consist of the five names in the title. Level 1.

In the Mirror
　　Each hand plays a mirror image of the other. Only quarter and half notes are used and hands remain in relatively stationary positions. Somewhat academic, but the form is clear. Level 1.

Echo-Chamber
　　Sustaining pedal is held for long periods causing blurring of sonorities. Written primarily with long sustained note values. Level 1.

Turn-Me-Round

A short piece that can be played upside down or in retrograde. Exact mirror images are used. Starer states in his preface that this is "a game for people who like puzzles . . . [like] 'Madam I'm Adam.'" No eighth notes are used. Level 1.

Countdown

Each consecutive bar has one beat less than the one before. The player is to speak a number, from nine to one, to "blastoff" at the beginning of each measure as the piece progresses. No eighths are used. Level 1.

Evens and Odds

The meter changes in each measure from even to odd numbers of pulses such as from 4/4 to 3/4 to 4/4 to 5/4 and so on. Blocked thirds in the left hand. Level 1.

Up and Down, Right and Left, Over and Across

This selection asks the student to change fingers on the same note and to cross hands. Level 2.

Darkness and Light

The music contrasts low with high, threatening sounds with pleasing sounds, dissonance with consonance. Many sustained sonorities. Level 2.

Adding and Taking Away

Notes are added to form clusters and are then taken away, one by one, to return to a single note. One of the most effective selections in this volume. Level 2.

Walking with Two Fingers

Played with the second and third fingers only. Many 3-2 and 2-3-2 eighth-note fragments appear between the hands. Level 2.

Sliding Into the Keys

Demonstrates the concept of modulation. Attractive bouncing rhythm throughout. Level 2.

12 Notes 12 Times

This one-page selection shows 12 ways of presenting all of the 12 notes: in fourths, fifths, the chromatic and the whole-tone scale and in chords. Dense texture. Level 2.

Seven Vignettes (1950)

Short character pieces in contemporary idiom, filled with color. See especially *Fanfare, Chorale* and *Toccata.* (MCA.) Level 7.

Four Seasonal Pieces (1985)

Contemporary reflections. Titles include *As the Gentle Wind, Orange Sun, Leaves are Falling* and *Leaves on the Frozen Pond.* (MCA.) Level 7.

Sketches in Color, Set One (1963)

A set of seven pieces in varying moods and colors, and employing 20th-century techniques. An especially good introduction to contemporary music. (MCA.)

1. Purple

Expressive, polytonal work to be played *slow with intensity.* Subtle dynamics are required. Levels 6–7.

2. Shades of Blue

Jazz rhythms fill this bluesy piece, a favorite from the set. Some syncopations appear throughout. Diatonic melody with left-hand accompaniment of parallel fifths. Perhaps the easiest piece in the set. Level 5.

3. Black and White

Folk-like melody in a polytonal setting. Pentatonic scale on black keys is played by one hand and diatonic scale on white keys is played by the other. The two hands alternate these tonalities. Level 5.

4. Bright Orange

This jazzy piece, good for a student with flair, is marked to be played fast and light. The use of jazz syncopations makes it especially appealing. Many students may be inclined to rush the rhythm. Levels 6–7.

5. Grey

Built on four forms of a 12-tone row and marked *slow, without expression.* Generally soft dynamic level with some patterns (and many intervals of the seventh). Level 6.

6. Pink

Tonal writing that is song-like and sentimental, especially appropriate for the expressive performer. The melodic leaps should be played expressively. A favorite. Level 6.

7. Crimson

Based on asymmetrical divisions of 7/8 meter. This fast and driving work contains dynamic ranges from *pp* to *ff*. Appealing writing for the energetic performer with fast fingers and a light touch. Level 7.

Sketches in Color, Set Two (1973)

More advanced than Set One, both in the technical demands made on the performer and in the compositional techniques employed. The pieces do not need to be played as a set or in the order in which they appear. The composer states that things can be played without indications of their titles. (MCA.)

1. Maroon

This piece is almost pure color; the melody is difficult to find, if not absent, and the rhythm is not especially memorable. Cluster chords, register shifts and sudden dynamic changes. Levels 7–8.

2. Aluminum

Rhythmical work marked to be played *fast and even*. Combines added-note chords in parallel motion with polytonality. Level 8.

3. Silver and Gold

A slow, reflective and expressive work with left-hand ostinato. "Silver, the ostinato accompaniment in the left hand, constantly repeats its 12 notes, like a row," Starer said. "Gold is threaded against it, with D as tonal center—a point of departure and return." Levels 7–8.

4. Khaki

Sounds of drum rolls, bugles and rifles. Crisp and energetic writing featuring cluster chords, changing rhythmic patterns and a wide dynamic range. Levels 7–8.

5. Pepper and Salt

Chords built of identical intervals playing against clusters. The three basic ideas on which this work is built include the widely spaced eighth notes alternating between hands, the repeated-note rhythmic pattern and the cluster chords in several ranges. Unpredictable and non-melodic. Levels 7–8.

6. Aquamarine

Bluesy and mellow, this work features quintuple meter, jazz rhythms, a left-hand accompaniment with blocked and broken chords and a right-hand melody with subtle dynamic changes. Levels 7–8.

7. Chrome Yellow

Highly rhythmic with nonsymmetrical rhythms, marked to be played in a "brittle" manner. Level 8.

Three Israeli Sketches (1957)

In three varied and contrasting movements. Tonal works which freely use all 12 tones. (MCA.)

1. Pastorale

Marked to be played lento, *un poco rubato,* this work is highly improvisatory and features a quasi-oriental flavor. Students with a vivid imagination will enjoy this work. Level 8.

2. Little White Sheep

Opens with seven staccatos, repeated treble Cs, in a two-page piece with much repetition. Effective rhythms and thick texture. This work is in a playful vein. Level 7.

3. Dance

This *Allegro giocoso* work uses a wide keyboard range and features interesting and unexpected syncopations in a contemporary harmonic framework. Interesting writing and quite pianistic. Level 8.

At Home Alone (1980)

In the preface, Starer has said that "these pieces are dedicated to people who play the piano when they are at home alone. This does not mean that they cannot be played for others, in private or in public; of course they can. It only means that the images, views, sounds, and thoughts will come, as they did to me, when you are at home alone." These character pieces for advancing performers by this American composer should be better known. (MCA.)

1. Dialogue with the Self

Marked *Deliberate.* Many different tempo and character changes are present. The different registers suggest two different personalities. Level 8.

2. Opening Petals

Flowing and elegant writing. Clusters expand to wider intervals in this lyrical two-page piece which should be played with slight rubato. Level 7.

3. Dreams of Glory

A march featuring triplets, chordal accompaniment and dotted rhythms. Sharp dynamic contrasts and use of all registers of the keyboard. Level 8.

4. In the Birdcage

Imitations of bird songs in the right hand. Dreamy work requiring freedom and rubato. Level 8.

5. A Faded Old Photograph

An elegant waltz in a contemporary idiom, with changing meters. Level 8.

6. Pop-Time

Energetic work in a jazzy idiom. One of the favorites from this collection. Needs sharp rhythms and attention to articulation. Level 9.

7. Herman The Brown Mouse

A one-page scherzo, delicate and impish. Marked to be played *cautiously, delicately.* Level 8.

8. A Small Oriental Vase

Emphasizes lyrical playing and tone production. Marked *gently flowing, with intensity.* Level 8.

9. Steps to the Attic

Tone clusters in a quick, march tempo. Needs sharp staccatos and bite. Level 8.

10. Shadows on the Wall

Marked *slowly, creepily.* Changing meters and mysterious writing. Level 8.

11. Deep Down the Soul

Serious chordal piece to be played *with dignity.* A somber, probing work. Level 8.

12. Dancing Next Door

Quick and light piece in mixed meters, shifting from 10/8 to 7/8 to 9/8 and so on. Effective in performance and good for the performer who enjoys *scherzando* works and has a strong sense of rhythm. Level 9.

Hexahedron (A Figure Having Six Faces) (1971)

Six contrasting pieces presenting fine contemporary writing for the advancing performer. Titles are *1 Musingly, 2 Gurglingly, 3 Coolly but not chilly, 4 Doggedly, mulishly, almost pig-headedly, 5 Philosophically* and *6 Frantically.* These pieces should be heard more often. (MCA.) Levels 9–10.

Miscellaneous Volumes

Robert Starer Piano Solos

A volume containing a wealth of solo piano music by Starer including *Games With Notes and Numbers, At Home Alone,* both sets of *Sketches in Color* and *Four Seasonal Pieces.* (MCA.) Levels 1–10.

EVERETT STEVENS (1916–1959) USA

Six Modal Miniatures

Different and little-known teaching pieces, each built on a different mode. The modes are explained at the beginning of the volume. This collection could also be used for analysis in a student theory class. (Oliver Ditson.) Level 4.

Additional Works for Study:
Above, Below and Between
Bugle, Drum and Fife
Syncopated Serenade
The Telegraph
Lullaby for Amittal
Mountain Calls
Nofiah, Gadya, Mahol

HALSEY STEVENS (1908–1989) USA

Halsey Stevens was for many years chair of the composition department at the University of Southern California. He is also remembered as a prominent biographer of Bartók.

Six Little Pieces for the Piano

Two-voice modal writing, totally on the white keys, with most of the pieces approximately eight measures long. The score is published in manuscript form. (American Composers Alliance.) Level 1.

Five Little Five-Finger Pieces (1954)

Hands remain in stationary positions. The writing is modal or bitonal, and predominantly contrapuntal. Several are canonic. No note values smaller than the quarter note are used. For the sophisticated beginner. (Helios.) Level 1.

Music for Ann (1953)

Prelude, Trumpet Tune, Chorale, Quiet Song and *Piece for Skipping*. Modal writing, sophisticated tonal framework. (Helios.) Level 2.

Five Portuguese Folksongs (1968)

Folk songs transcribed by Halsey Stevens for piano and placed in simple arrangements for the elementary student. Interesting settings, with some octaves and ninths. Worthy competition repertoire for elementary performers. (Peer International.) Levels 3–4.

Five Swedish Folk Tunes (1961)

Some of Stevens' most appealing pieces. Adults especially will enjoy playing this music. (Helios.) Level 5.

17 Piano Pieces

Brief character pieces for the intermediate student. Dissonant writing best suited for the sophisticated musical ear. Representative titles include *Erratic Rhythms, Palindrome II* and *From a Roman Sketchbook*. (Westwood.) Level 8.

Sonatina No. 1 (revised version, 1959–67)

Neo-Classical linear writing that is pianistic and mildly contemporary. Adult students might be more drawn to this literature. *Allegro giusto, Tempo di menuetto* and *Allegro*. (American Composers' Alliance, Helios.) Level 8.

Sonatina No. 2 (1959)

Absolute music, better played by seasoned musicians than by young students. The interpretative considerations outweigh the technical problems. *Allegro moderato, Canon, Rondo*. (Helios.) Level 9.

Sonatina No. 3 (1950)

Linear writing that is more dissonant than the other sonatinas. The second movement is an *Elegy* that concludes the sonatina quietly. (Helios.) Level 9.

Notturno—Bellagio Adagio

According to Maurice Hinson, this piece is "characterized by beautiful singing lines, concise and clear form (ABA), eloquent chromatic motifs, and logical transfer of the line between the hands. Dynamic indications are sparse but the natural dynamic fluctuation is highly expressive." Three pages. (Alfred.) Level 8.

Additional Works for Study:
Ah, mon beau château (1959)
Christmas Songs from Hungary (1955)
Three Czech Folktunes (1958)
Seven French Folksongs (1953)
10 French Folksongs (1953)
Three Hungarian Folksongs (1957)
Jumping Colts (1961)
Lyric Piece (1955)
Moto perpetuo (1961)
Four Romanian Folktunes (1952–56)
Six Russian Folktunes (1955)
11 Ukrainian Folksongs (1956)
Three Ukrainian Folksongs (1960)

RICHARD STOKER (b. 1938) Great Britain

Fireworks

Chordal outlines often prevail in this contemporary nonfunctional harmonic writing for the liberated musical ear. Titles include *Sky Rocket, Jumping Jacks, Volcano, Silver Spray* and *Roman Candle*. (Fentone.) Level 7.

VESELIN ANASTASOV STOYANOV (1902–1969) Bulgaria

20 Piano Pieces for the Young

Vibrant, engaging writing and generally Romantic sonorities. These would be interesting to investigate for a contest listing. (Peters.) Level 6.

IGOR STRAVINSKY (1882–1971) Russia

Stravinsky left Russia for Paris in 1919 right as the communists were coming to power. He toured Europe and America until the outbreak of World War II, when he moved permanently to the USA. Stravinsky exerted a profound influence on 20th-century music, although his piano music is relatively minor when compared with the vastness of his output.

Les Cinq Doigts (1921)

Eight very easy tunes on five notes. According to the composer, "the five fingers of the right hand once on the keys, remain in the same place . . . while the left hand which is destined to accompany the melody, executes a pattern either harmonic or contrapuntal of the utmost simplicity . . . I found it rather amusing, with these much restricted means, to try to awaken in the child a taste for melodic design in combination with a rudimentary accompaniment." See especially Nos. 1, 2, 4, 6 and 7. (Many standard editions.)

No. 1 Andantino

An excellent study in legato, with both hands remaining in the C position. Also stresses independence between the hands. A justifiably well-known beginner selection to work on phrasing and musicianship skills. Level 1.

No. 2 Allegro

Helps develop coordination between the hands and facility in passage playing in the right hand. No black keys are used, but the left hand must voice lower notes of accompaniment figures as melodies. Level 1.

No. 3 Allegretto

Comes across almost as a drone since the range of pitches is so narrow. Modal sounds. Only white keys are used. The coordination between the hands is somewhat difficult here. Level 2.

No. 4 Larghetto

A *siciliano*, this work is a study in playing a legato melody and in voicing a melody above double notes in a single hand. Difficult musically and technically compared to the other pieces in the volume. Level 3.

No. 5 Moderato

This short piece also requires voicing a melody above double notes in the right hand as well as "voicing down" an insistent repeated-chord accompaniment. Level 3.

No. 6 Lento

Strongly modal writing with some shifting hand positions. Level 3.

No. 7 Vivo

Modal writing. Broken-chord accompaniment. Level 3.

No. 8 Pesante

Syncopated chords, though the harmonic language is not that of jazz. Perhaps the most immediately appealing of the set. Level 3.

SOULIMA STRAVINSKY (b. 1910) USA

Pianist-son of Igor Stravinsky, who taught at the University of Illinois.

Piano Music for Children, Volume I, II

Uses various devices to expand one's concept of tonality. The titles generally limit them to study by children and include *Stepping Stones, Wandering, Swaying, Daddy Is Home, For the Kid Next Door, Pals, Carefree, On the Way to School* and *Mama and Papa Are Talking*. Generally short pieces that do not quite reach their potential. Volume I contains 19 pieces. (Peters.)

Three Fairy Tales

Three suites of pieces on the fairy tales of *Cinderella, Jack and the Beanstalk* and *The Sleeping Beauty,* all contained under one cover. The movements of the various pieces, featuring thin textures and mild dissonances are titled and indicate the progress of the story through the music. Sophisticated writing and effective characterization of the stories. These pieces should be heard more often. (Peters.) Levels 7–8.

15 Character Pieces for Piano

While these pieces are not technically difficult, the musical understanding necessary to play and enjoy them far surpasses the technique required. Linear dissonant writing, thin textures. (Peters.) Level 8.

Six Sonatinas For Young Pianists, Nos. 1–3

The first three of the series are included under one cover. All are contemporary and feature dissonant writing. (Peters.)

Sonatina No. 1

The last of the three movements, *Rondo,* with unexpected rhythmic shifts and bucolic character, make it among the most appealing of Soulima Stravinsky's works. Students with small hands could play this work. Level 8.

Sonatina No. 2

This sprightly work consists of two fast movements, *Allegro moderato* and *Tarantella (vivace).* Agile fingerwork is needed for the fast figures in the tarantella. May be played by a student with small hands and strong fingers. Level 7.

Sonatina No. 3

The first movement, *Fantasia piccola corrente,* is a solo movement for the right hand, written on one staff and consisting of a single melody. The last movement, *Epilogue tranquillo,* is a left-hand solo, also written on one staff and containing only a melody. A contemporary march with linear writing and strong rigorous rhythms joins the two movements. Musical sophistication is called for in interpreting this sonatina. Level 8.

Six Sonatinas for Young Pianists, Nos. 4–6

Continuation of the first set of three sonatinas. (Peters.)

Sonatina No. 4

Fanfare, Plainchant, Bourrée d'Auvergne. The *Fanfare* has the most immediate appeal with its strong, energetic rhythms and tuneful motives. Level 7.

Sonatina No. 5

The first movement, *Quodlibet,* features melodic dialogue between the hands. The tuneful final *Rondino* is perhaps the most immediately appealing movement of the set. Level 7.

Sonatina No. 6

Composed on themes by the 14th-century composer Machaut. The first movement is a theme and variation, the second an inviting *Fughetta* and the third a lively rondo, obviously modal in character. One of the best of the set. Level 8.

Piano Variations, First Series

Several sets of variations appear within each volume. Linear writing, contemporary harmonic framework. The dissonance would be appreciated by an experienced musician whose musical aptitude might be ahead of his technical ability. Each movement is in a specific variation form such as sectional variations, continuous variations or ground bass variations. Movements include *Prelude, Forlane, Stanza, Piccolo Divertimento, In Modo Russo* and *Les Valses.* (Peters.) Level 8.

Piano Variations, Second Series

Similar to the *First Series* of variations by S. Stravinsky. Titles include *11 Tones, Metrics, 12 Tones* and *Pavana.* See especially the *Pavana.* (Peters.) Level 8.

The Art of Scales

According to the composer, this volume contains 24 "exercises set in the form of short preludes, whereby the phrasing of a scale in one hand is always governed by the musical content of the other hand." More of intellectual interest. (Peters.) Level 9.

Three 3-part Inventions

Contemporary contrapuntal studies in a mildly dissonant fashion. (Peters.) Level 10.

REZSÖ SUGÁR (1919–1988) Hungary

Hungarian Children's Songs

These 25 Hungarian melodies are arranged for the elementary pianist. Melodies were taken from the *Collection of the Hungarian Folk Music, edited by Bartók and Kodály*. Fine arrangements, should be more widely used. (Boosey.) Levels 3–5.

Sonatine für Klavier, No. 1 (1919)

The tuneful first movement is highly motivic while the *andante molto* third movement is folk-like and features interesting syncopations. (EMB.) Level 6.

Additional Works for Study:
Sonatine für Klavier, No. 2
Sonatina Baroque

FERNANDO SULPIZI (b. 1936) Italy

Album Secondo Per Daniela

Highly contemporary writing with new notation utilized for several of the short pieces. Accessible avant-garde literature. (Bèrben.) Level 7.

LEPO SUMERA (b. 1950) Estonia

Three Piano Pieces for Children

Published in 1989, these are some of the most current teaching materials available for piano from the former Soviet Union. Mildly contemporary idiom with thin textures and "wrong-note writing." Appealing literature. (VAAP.)

The One Who Is Wiser Concedes

Rollicking *vivo* in 6/8 requiring agile fingerwork and a strong rhythmic sense. Level 7.

The Sad Toreador

An amusing takeoff on the *Toreador's Song* from *Carmen* with "wrong-note" accompaniment. Level 8.

The Butterfly Who Woke Up in Winter

Reflective, swaying piece with delicate figurations in the right hand. Marked *larghetto*. Level 8.

TOMÁŠ SVOBODA (b. 1939) Czechoslovakia

Tomáš immigrated to Boston during World War II. After the war, he lived and studied music in Prague until the 1960s, when he returned to teach and compose in California and Oregon.

A Bird, Op. 1

Two-page solo with mixed meters. An accompanimental motive depicting a mournful bird recurs under a sorrowful melody played by the right hand. (Strangeland.) Level 8.

Prelude in G Minor, Op. 3a

Quasi-Baroque. A good study for a student to precede the Bach inventions or Handel fugues. (Strangeland.) Level 7.

Children's Treasure Box, Volume 1

This group of 20 short pieces is written to introduce various aspects of contemporary piano technique to the first- or second-year student. Both hands remain in stationary five-finger patterns throughout each piece. (Strangeland.) Level 1.

Children's Treasure Box, Volume 2

The 17 pieces found here continue to develop the various aspects of contemporary piano technique introduced in Volume 1. The level of difficulty is slightly greater, and the student is required to play outside stationary hand positions. These are less contrapuntally oriented than in Volume 1. (Strangeland.) Level 2.

Children's Treasure Box, Volume 3

Additional group of 12 piano pieces. The works feature broader contrasts in tempos, key signatures and dynamics and more extended hand positions. (Strangeland.) Level 3.

Children's Treasure Box, Volume 4

This is the last in the series. (Strangeland.) Levels 3–4.

FELIX SWINSTEAD (1880–1959) Great Britain

Work and Play

Short character pieces for beginners, each tuneful and enchanting. True musical miniatures with few notes for the beginner. Traditional harmonies. (Associated Board of the Royal Schools of Music.) Level 2.

FERENC SZABÓ (1902–1969) Hungary

Selected Piano Pieces, I

Pedagogically sound, musically inviting and exciting character pieces of high quality. Similar in quality to the Bartók teaching pieces in *For Children* but these would be even more accessible musically. The folk tune basis is not as strong here as in the Bartók pieces. Volume I includes 11 short pieces. (EMB.) Levels 4–5.

Selected Piano Pieces, II

These pieces are slightly more difficult than those in Volume I. Titles include *Sonatina, All' Concerto, Prelude and Fugue, Rondo* and *Spring Wind.* (EMB.) Levels 6–7.

ENDRE SZERVÁNSKZY (1911–1977) Hungary

Piano Compendium

During his life, it appears that the composer planned to write a number of practice-oriented books on the theory of composition. István Barna and Mátyás Kovács have compiled this *Piano Compendium* from sketchbooks found after Szervanskzy's death. The writing is based on the modern Hungarian school of composition of Kodály and Bartók. These 33 selections are primarily of historical interest. (EMB.) Levels 6–8.

KAROL SZYMANOWSKI (1882–1937) Poland

Work for Study:
Some Polish Songs (PWM)

T

GERMAINE TAILLEFERRE (1892–1983) France

3 Sonatines pour piano

All three are in three movements of one page each and the writing is sparse in texture and straightforward. See especially the third movement of *Sonatina No. 1* based on children's playground mocking themes. Little-known and interesting writing. The manuscripts of these works were discovered in the 1970s. (Lemoine.) Levels 2–3.

Fleurs de France

Pleasant if dated elementary pieces depicting various flowers of different regions of France in one- or two-page vignettes. Primarily linear writing with a tonal basis. (Lemoine.) Level 6.

Additional Work for Study:
Enfantines

MARKO TAJČEVIC (b. 1900) Serbia

Lieder von der Murinsel

Included here are folksongs from the Medumurje region in Yugoslavia, arranged for piano by the composer. The melodies are based primarily on modes, most often the Dorian, and the settings are similar to some of Bartók's. Rhythmic and inviting. No titles are given for the folksongs. (Henle.) Levels 3–4.

Serbian Dances

Similar in concept to the Bartók *Rumanian Folk Dances*. Folk melody basis, rhythmic, modal with a harmonic underpinning. (Rongwen.) Level 8.

JENÖ TAKÁCS (b. 1902) Hungary

Takács taught piano for many years at the Cincinnati College–Conservatory of Music before returning to his homeland.

Little Sonata, Op. 51

Pianistic and interesting contemporary two-movement sonatina at the intermediate level that is worth investigating. (Doblinger.) Levels 5–6.

Sounds and Colours, Op. 95

This collection of 15 intriguing miniatures which extend from the tonal sounds of Liszt and Bartók to more avant-garde colors. Selections include *Study in Sounds* (muted strings, free notation), *Sounds and Colours* (spacial notation), *Echo* (spacial notation, clusters, cardboard muting of white and black keys), *Chinese Chimes* (new notation, improvisation within a note group, free ordering of sections) and *Sounds of the Night* (spacial notation, free repetitions, strumming inside the piano). (Doblinger.) Levels 7–9.

No. 3 In a Great Hurry

Changing meter in this *presto scherzando* and humorous work that calls for a staccato technique in a fast tempo. Level 8.

No. 12 Toccatina

Patterned piece featuring black keys in one hand and white in the other. Requires playing with alternating hands and rapid hand-to-hand scale passages. This staccato study needs fast fingers and attention to even sounds. Level 9.

For Me, Op. 76

Delightful little recital pieces for the upper-elementary student. The harmonic palette is mildly contemporary and the writing especially fine. See especially *No. 14 Raindrops* and *No. 21 The Little Fly*. Should be heard more often. (Doblinger.) Levels 3–4.

From Far Away Places, Op. 111

The 21 pieces found here vary in tonal framework from diatonic writing to a few selections that emphasize more contemporary devices. Based on melodies or idioms from such countries as Norway, Hungary, Austria, North America, Tatar Republic of the former USSR and Israel. The writing is primarily linear and most appropriate for students performing at the level of easier sonatina literature.

Highly recommended 20th-century pedagogical literature. (Universal.) Levels 5–6.

When the Frog Wandering Goes

Delightful and little-known set of six imaginative and energetic pieces. All movements are strong, but see especially *Merry Andrew, Tsheremis Dance, When the Frog Goes Wandering* and *March*. (Doblinger.) Levels 7–8.

Sonatine

The second movement is a one-page ornamented *Nocturne* and the final movement is especially effective with lively folk-like writing. (Doblinger.) Level 10.

Toccata, Op. 54

Primarily continuous sixteenth notes in a rousing and effective toccata. A *Lento rubato, quasi Fantasia* section immediately prior to the final Coda breaks the momentum slightly. Requires attention to evenness of passage-work and pacing of large *crescendos*. Convincing and brilliant writing. (Doblinger.) Level 10.

Additional Works for Study:
Op. 37 From Far and Wide
Op. 51 Little Sonate
Double-Dozen for Small Fingers

LOUISE TALMA (b. 1906) France

Talma and her family immigrated to the USA while she was still a child. A recipient of two Guggenheim fellowships, she was the first woman composer to be elected to the National Institute of Arts and Letters.

Soundshots

Twenty intriguing character pieces in a biting contemporary style. Titles include *Run, Rabbit, Run!, Strolling, Pitter-Patter, Jumping High, End of Day* and *The Clocks.* Strong writing by an American female composer, suitable for festivals of American and contemporary music. Selections are generally one to three pages. (Hinshaw.) Levels 5–7.

ARIKA TANAKA (b. 1947) Japan

Do-Ré-Mi de coucours

Eight short pieces, several of which are of strong musical interest. See especially *Rècit, Fanfare* and *Silhouette.* Appropriate for the student playing his or her first "classics." (Lemoine.) Level 3.

Concert en famille

Twelve-tonal teaching pieces, tuneful and varied. See especially *Promenade dans les bois,* a march-like piece that builds to a brilliant climax before subsiding. Especially suitable choices for contest repertoire. Strong writing. (Musicales Transatlantiques.) Level 6.

Pages pour la Petite ëtoile

Melodious writing with traditional harmony used in a nontraditional way. Primarily linear, suited well for the sophisticated musician. The four short pieces are titled *Chaconne pour l'étoile, Berceuse, Le Papa* and *Ballet de Fées.* (Lemoine.) Level 5.

ALEXANDER TANSMAN (1897–1986) Poland

Tansman lived in the USA during World War II, but otherwise was based in his adopted Paris. He composed many excellent collections of piano pieces for young students.

Happy Time, Book 1 (Primary)

The three volumes in *Happy Time* include some of the most accessible contemporary literature available by a major composer for an early-elementary pianist. Often the pieces are somewhat contrapuntal, making them especially suitable for students needing to develop independence between the hands. All books provide original music that is interesting and musically alive while teaching technique progressively. Book 1 includes 15 pieces for the early-elementary student and the level is approximately the same level as the Kabalevsky *Music for Children*, Op. 39. (MCA.) Level 2.

Both Ways

Slow lyrical piece that is a good repertoire choice to work on developing legato in a young student, and on developing independence of the hands. The melody shifts to the left hand in the middle of the piece while the accompaniment is comprised primarily of a descending chromatic scale in whole notes. Level 2.

Little Gavotte

Animated and decisive, appropriate especially to help students work on moving out of stationary hand positions. Correct fingering and finger crossings need special attention. Level 2.

Common Tones

Early hands-together playing in a piece that could serve as a student's first work in bringing out a left-hand melody "over" a right-hand accompaniment. Excellent material for study or for sight-reading. Level 2.

Arabia

The exotic flavor of *Arabia* renders it perhaps the most popular selection in this volume. A legato melody sounds above a bass two-bar ostinato. The modal writing may catch a student's interest. Level 2.

Shadow

Contrapuntal writing in this canon at the octave. Level 2.

Sailors' Dance

One of the most tuneful and energetic pieces in the volume. Coordination between hands will be a primary technical consideration. Level 3.

Melody

Highly lyrical work comprised of broken descending chords divided between the hands. Requires voicing within a single hand. Melody sounds more difficult than it is. Level 2.

Popular Air

The patterned left hand will make this one-page piece accessible to most young students. Appealing melody with nontraditional accompaniment, all within a tonal framework. The first section features a simple melody and the second features double notes. Level 3.

Happy Time, Book 2 (Elementary)

The selections here are decidedly more difficult than those in Book 1. Included are 13 selections, most of which are one page. (MCA.) Levels 4–5.

Dancing Air

Vigorous dance, with an ostinato left-hand accompaniment played staccato throughout. Animated work that may provide coordination problems in rhythm and articulation between the hands. Challenging. Level 5.

Caravan

Left-hand ostinato might depict the slow lumbering of a caravan in the midst of its trek. Lyrical melody is stated first in single notes and then as a duet. Level 4.

Perpetual Motion

This work is in some ways a single long *crescendo*. Melody in left hand in half notes and quarters occurs underneath the perpetual motion patterned sixteenths in the right hand. Contains little musical value, but could be dazzling. Level 4.

Pursuit

Marked *allegro con moto,* this brief selection provides a fine study in coordination between the hands. Highly motivic, vigorous music. Level 5.

Chorale and Variation

Three-voice chorale requiring skillful pedaling and providing good preparation for the playing of four-part writing such as that in modern hymnals. The fingering is well-marked but not easy. Levels 3–4.

Swedish Dance

Open fifths alternating between registers give this its boisterous dance-like feeling. Level 5.

Happy Time, Book 3 (Intermediate)

Perhaps the strongest book in the series. Many of the pieces are reminiscent of other composers' styles. It seems strange that this exceptionally fine collection of pieces is so little known. (MCA.) Level 6.

A la Schumann

One-page piece with a thick texture and voice leading moving from hand to hand as in the writing of Schumann. Voicing of melodies and even control of the texture is needed here. Level 7.

Organ

Primarily chordal writing, especially good for practice in playing in four-part harmony and in voicing thick textures. Exceptionally effective melodic writing. Level 6.

Little Game

Fast broken-chord passages in the right hand are set off by a stable half-note accompaniment figure. Brilliant. Level 5.

Light Waltz

Perhaps appropriate for the student who wishes to play Debussy and is not ready for that music. Level 7.

Night Mood

Another Impressionistic one-page vignette, expressive and accessible for the average student. Worth investigating. Level 6.

Arioso, alla J. S. Bach

Largo movement in overture style with dotted rhythms and full chords. Sounds big. Level 6.

Oriental Dance

Rhythmic and driving with repeated tone clusters. Not as effective as some of the other selections in this set. Level 7.

Iberian Mood

Short, Spanish-sounding piece. Little movement on the keyboard in the left hand. Level 6.

In Memory of George Gershwin "1925"

Shows Gershwin's international influence at the time when the Tansman pieces were composed. Blues tempo, ornamented right-hand melody. Level 7.

Finale, Solo-Piece

Lively work that could serve as a recital piece for a talented elementary school student. Level 7.

Piano in Progress, Volume 1

Tansman intended the two volumes in the series to be a kind of "Gradus ad Parnassum" geared to the early years of piano study. Volume 1 is easier than Volume 2, but the selections within each book are not necessarily arranged in progressive order. The writing is pedagogically strong, using patterns that appear commonly in standard piano literature. See especially *No. 2 Romance, No. 4 Modulation, No. 7 Tango, No. 9 Étude* and *No. 10 Joking Mood*. (Marks.) Levels 2–3.

Piano in Progress, Volume 2

Excellent elementary literature in a mildly contemporary, almost neo-Romantic idiom. Selections Nos. 11–19 are contained in this volume. See especially *No. 12 Descending, No. 13 Rustic Dance, No. 16 Intermezzo, No. 18 Spleen (Tempo di Blues)* and *No. 19 Going Ahead*. (Marks.) Level 4.

Pour les Enfants, Set 1

Subtitled "Little Pieces for Piano." The leveling indications of the four sets of *Pour les Enfants* may deter some from playing them, since the pieces are more difficult than the indications indicate. Each of the collections contains 12 pieces except the last which contains 10 pieces. The writing is appealing and these are uniformly strong pieces. (Eschig.)

Set 1

Representative titles of movements include *Old Song, The Doll, The Bouncing Ball, The Dancing Bear, Russian Dance, Dresden China Figures* and *Conclusion*.

No. 1 Old Song

Right-hand double notes with a lyrical left-hand melody. Neo-Romantic writing in a beautiful work that should be better known. Level 3.

No. 3 The Bouncing Ball

One-page perpetual motion figure with continuous sixteenths in the right hand and a bouncing eighth-note figure in the left hand. Energetic and highly effective in performance. Level 3.

No. 4 The Dancing Bear

Pesante work with a lugubrious left hand and heavy chords. The rhythm of the right hand adds interest. Level 2.

No. 6 Russian Dance

Needs rhythmic vitality without rushing and contains several off-beat accents. One of the most effective in this collection, sounding more difficult than it really is. Level 3.

No. 7 Dresden China Figures

Suitable for a performer who needs to work on playing with finesse and polished articulation in the context of a short piece. Needs a "proper" minuet style, graceful slurs and gentle staccatos. Level 4.

No. 9 Skating

The performer who needs to develop scale facility might benefit from working on this short piece that features both ascending and descending scales as well as broken thirds and octave stretches. Level 3.

Pour les Enfants, Set 2

The majority of the 12 highly Romantic pieces in this volume are lyrical. Musically they are sophisticated and would be appropriate for adults, although the child-like titles may deter some. Generally these pieces are less contrapuntal than the selections in *Happy Time*, Books 2 and 3 and often they are easier. (Eschig.)

No. 1 Stroll

Could be mistaken for one of the easier pieces by Gurlitt. The writing is highly lyrical and requires a fine legato. Level 4.

No. 2 In the Garden

Song-like, with melody in the right hand and accompaniment in the left. The disjunct melody makes the matching of the sound of each note to the one previously played especially important. Level 4.

No. 3 Mazurka

Melody with many directional changes above repeated two-note accompaniment chords. Tuneful, lively and appealing work. Level 4.

No. 4 The Arithmetic Lesson

The attractive melody with its catchy tune may camouflage the fingering difficulties in the left-hand crossings. The writing is almost sing-song. Should be appealing to many. Level 5.

No. 5 Meditation

Beautiful, lyrical writing depicting a reflective mood. Accompaniment that consists of broken descending triads. Worth investigating. Level 5.

No. 7 Spinning Top

Highly effective perpetual-motion piece with continuous sixteenths throughout. Level 5.

No. 10 Arabian Nights

Requires imagination in interpretation for this slow, mysterious work. Level 4.

No. 12 Parade

March-like with repeated notes in both hands. Somewhat repetitive, but the rhythmic patterns are enticing to both performer and listener. The performer needs a strong rhythmic sense. Level 5.

Pour les Enfants, Set 3

Although this set is designated by the composer as "Fairly easy," the pieces are more appropriately labeled as "Intermediate" in difficulty. Of the four sets, this one may have the largest number of motivating selections. Several pieces grouped in performance from this set (or any of the sets) would be highly effective. The proportion of slow and fast pieces is approximately equal. (Eschig.)

No. 1 Awakening

Most of the playing is done in C Major and in the center of the keyboard, which gives it a bright feeling with the close voicings. The right hand features a good bit of double-note passagework. Level 6.

No. 2 The Warbler

One of the most effective pieces in the four sets, this work is a perpetual-motion piece with a right-hand melody depicting a warbler and a left-hand accompaniment in repeated chords, necessitating a light touch. Less difficult than it sounds. Level 5.

No. 3 Noël

Naive simplicity in a melody heard against a repeated-chord accompaniment. Fits the hand well. This is the most accessible selection in this set. Level 4.

No. 4 Petite reverie

The performer should avoid interrupting the lyrical and expressive melody in the right hand with the left-hand rocking accompaniment figures. For the musically sensitive performer. Level 5.

No. 5 Tin Soldiers

Parallel thirds and double notes in the right hand with left-hand accompanimental syncopations that give vitality. The countermelodies in the short B section will need careful attention to voicing and coordination within the hand. Energetic and motivating writing. Level 5.

No. 6 Rest

Calm mood depicted through a repeating left-hand accompaniment and a lyrical melody. Level 6.

No. 9 A Difficult Problem

A fast finger-twister, especially appropriate for a student who likes to decipher patterns. This piece fits the hand well, but the key of E Major makes it appear more difficult than it is. Level 6.

No. 12 Ping-Pong

A quick but short perpetual-motion work that depicts the bouncing back and forth of a ping-pong ball. Requires fine coordination of double-note passages that nevertheless fit the hand well. Effective writing. Level 7.

Pour les Enfants, Set 4

As with the other sets, these selections are not heard often enough. High-quality modern writing that is idiomatic to the hand. (Eschig.)

I. An Old Tale

Slow and melancholy writing with some chromaticism and dissonance. A fine piece for developing voicing and for studying continuity of line and phrasing. Can easily be over-pedaled. Levels 6–7.

II. Rocking Horse

Highly pianistic work in A Minor with a left-hand accompaniment spanning a tenth. Musical writing, energetic tempo and easier than it looks on the page. The first and third phrases feature the Natural Minor mode while the second and fourth phrases feature the harmonic and Melodic Minor forms. Can help in developing left-hand wrist rotation, coordination between two hands, clarity and quick chordal changes. Level 7.

III. A Serious Moment

An expressive piece with delightfully colorful harmonies, especially good for developing chordal playing in the right hand and for voicing melody over thick texture. Should be better known. Level 6.

IV. Hide and Seek

The energy in this spunky piece is generated from the repeated chords and figures. Right-hand passages in double-fourths need a supple wrist. Most of the piece is staccato. Large *fortissimo* climactic ending. Level 7.

V. In a Venetian Gondola

Quiet legato left-hand figure in an ostinato rhythm that spans an eleventh and requires careful fingering in the crossings and attention to shaping. The right hand frequently sustains one voice while another is moving. More difficult than it sounds. Level 7.

VI. Blues Record

The most accessible work in this volume. Bluesy and short, with fairly stable hand positions. Suitable for a student needing motivation. Level 6.

VII. Valse lente

Slow chromatic waltz with an unpredictable harmonic framework. An appropriate early 20th-century choice for the student who enjoys Romantic styles and textures. Short and effective. Level 7.

IX. Berceuse

Mostly played on the black keys, this delicate and graceful piece features various recurrence of the main theme in variation. Each four-bar phrase adds or subtracts countermelodies or chordal reinforcement in the right hand. Excellent study in voicing for both hands. Level 7.

X. Marche Militaire

Dry and rhythmic, especially appropriate for a performer who can play large chords. Descending left-hand octaves provide a full effect. Theme and variations with the theme reappearing in different guises against the left-hand ostinato accompaniment. Level 7.

Recreations

Worthy neo-Romantic writing at the upper-elementary level. Six little-known pieces that should be much more widely performed and are worth investigating. See especially *Walk, Game* and *Étude.* (Summy.) Level 5.

10 Diversions for the Young Pianist

See especially *Spanish Mood, Merry Go Round, Rainy Day, Speeding Along, Mischief* and *Toccata.* For the student with flair. (Associated.) Level 7.

Five Impressions (1934)

Especially suitable for the student who enjoys playing works in the style of Debussy. Interesting harmonies, pianistically conceived. Entire set of strongly contrasting pieces consists of six pages. Titles include *Calm, Burlesque, Triste, Animé* and *Nocturne.* (Eschig/Associated.) Level 9.

Quatre Danses Polonaises

Little-known. See especially *No. IV Oberek.* (Eschig.) Level 10.

Additional Works for Study:
Album d'amis. Neuf Miniatures (1980) (Eschig)
Four Nocturnes (1952) (Universal)

ANTONIO TAURIELLO (b. 1913) Argentina

Toccata

Dedicated to Ginastera, this bold work sounds more difficult than it is. Especially suitable for the performer with flair and the ability to move quickly about the keyboard. May be considered as a precursor to the Bartók *Allegro Barbaro.* (Barry.) Level 9.

Additional Work for Study:
Four Sonatinas (Barry)

ALEXANDER TCHEREPNIN (1899–1977) Russia

Tcherepnin was a respected Russian-born American composer, conductor and pianist. Displaying the influence of Mussorgsky and Prokofiev, the music of Tcherepnin is a fascinating amalgam of early 20th-century styles, principally French and Russian, and features some passages of thin textures with the lines spaced far apart, parallel movement of chords and modal lines, driving rhythms, an irregular rhythmic style, harsh dissonance and repetition to create hypnotic effects. Rhythms are vital in his work, and ostinatos and/or motor rhythms are often used. All articulation markings are especially important (staccato, wedge staccato, dash, accent mark). "W. numbers" of Tcherepnin's works in chronological order are taken from *Alexander Tcherepnin, A Bio-Bibliography* by Enrique Alberto Arias.

Bagatelles, Op. 5

Ten exciting and sonorous works that have become staples in the repertoire. Tcherepnin himself described them as "absolutely anti-Impressionistic and anti-eclectic, rather like Prokofiev, but with chromaticism." This work exists in several editions.

The Bagatelles were first composed by the teenage Tcherepnin as Christmas and birthday presents in his household in St. Petersburg. Isidor Philipp, Tcherepnin's piano teacher in Paris, suggested that he compile the pieces into the present set. Approximately eight editions of the Bagatelles exist, though the composer himself seems to have preferred the 1964 Heugel edition. (Alfred, Heugel, International, MCA, Leeds and others.)

No. 1 (Allegro marciale)

> The best known and most popular of the set. Martial, driving rhythm and *martellato* octaves with the hands in close range. Effective ending. Level 7.

No. 2 (Con vivacita)

> Alternating meters, and staccato playing with parallel eighth-note motion between both hands. Some left-hand tenths may need to be rolled. Level 8.

No. 3 (Vivo)

> A staccato dance with biting vitality. Parallel melody and staccato chords. Level 9.

No. 4 (Lento con tristezza)

A sad work with a left-hand ostinato that pulsates through much of the piece. Incorporates an aria from one of Tcherepnin's own works. Expressive and effective writing, especially appropriate for the performer who enjoys Romantic literature. Level 8.

No. 5 (Dolce)

Sensitive harmonic coloring within a nocturne-like work. Tcherepnin stated that the extended chords in tenths may be played instead in closed position to avoid the rolls. Needs refined voicing of tops. One of the best in the collection and especially good for the sensitive student. Level 8.

No. 6 (Allegro con spirito)

Easier than it sounds or appears on the page. The left-hand broken-chord accompaniment creates a swirling effect beneath a slower melody in this perpetual-motion work. Tcherepnin says that this was composed on a cold Russian winter day when, in the middle of winter, the sky was blue, it was sunny and his thoughts turned to spring. Level 8.

No. 7 (Prestissimo)

Effective in performance for a performer with competent facility. Calls for strong fingers. Much of the staccato playing is highly patterned. Level 8.

No. 8 (Allegro)

A seldom-heard chordal march filled with zest and energy. Level 9.

No. 9 (Allegretto)

Calls for fine fingerwork in playing the staccato passages. One of the more popular selections from this volume. Level 8.

No. 10 (Presto)

Exciting work built on chromatic scales and other passages in eighths against a chordal accompaniment. Fits the hand well. Level 8.

Pieces Without Title, Op. 7, W8

Eight character pieces, most of them in three-part forms. See especially *1 Allegro, 5 Allegro molto, 6 Sostenuto* and *8 Impetuoso.* (Durand.) Level 9.

Canzona, Op. 28

The sections of this four-page work are *slow, fast, slow, fast* in a subdued piece with thin textures. Interesting writing that uses extreme registers. (Simrock.) Level 8.

Four Romances, Op. 31

Pieces are in free form, with each dedicated to a friend. Piano writing is based on an invented nine-step scale. These short pieces are to be considered as four movements of one work. (Universal.) Level 8.

Histoire de la Petite Thérèse de l'Enfant Jésus (The Story of the Little Theresa of the Infant Jesus), Op. 36b

In 1925 while in Liseux, France, Tcherepnin was impressed by the crowds praying that Theresa would be made a saint. He read her book and visited places connected with her. In this series of children's pieces, Tcherepnin wanted to show the stages of her life. The 13 pieces are written to show the simplicity of her faith. A folk-like tune, quoted at the beginning of the book, is used in several additional pieces including Nos. 3, 8, 9 and 13. (Durand.) Levels 7–8.

Piano Method on the Pentatonic Scale, W141

This was composed as a result of Tcherepnin's visit to China in 1934 during which he became aware of the need for a piano method in Chinese. The method uses the pentatonic scale and was completed in Beijing in 1935. (Shanghai-Commercial Press.) Levels 1–6.

Autour des Montagnes Russes (Around the Russian Mountains), W142

A single piece composed for a collection to which various composers each contributed one piece. The subject of the piece is the scenic railway. (Eschig.)

Chinese Bagatelles, Op. 51, No. 3

Consists of 12 one- to two-page pieces with strong rhythmic vitality and open harmonies, reflecting an Oriental flavor. Dedicated to 10 young pianists who took part in a concert of the *Bagatelles*, Op. 5 in a concert in Beijing. This work is the third part of Tcherepnin's work *Piano Études on the Pentatonic Scale*. (Heugel.) Level 7.

For Young and Old, Op. 65,
Volumes 1 and 2 (Pour Petits et Grands)

Twelve moderately difficult pieces in two volumes of six. Character pieces, generally in three-part forms. These pieces are notably popular in France. See especially *4 Les Contrastes, 6 La Babillarde, 7 L'Affligée, 11 Les Plaisirs du Toutou* and *12 Le Belle au bois dormant.* (Durand.) Levels 5–7.

Expressions, Op. 81

Composed when an American publisher suggested that he wanted some pieces similar to the *Bagatelles,* Op. 5. In the composer's explanatory remarks on the inside front cover of *Expressions,* Tcherepnin wrote, "The title *'Expressions'* indicates that the music is subjective, dynamic and meant to give scope to a performer's expression of his own feeling in relation to the musical content of the pieces." Neo-Romantic and more rhythmically complex than the *Bagatelles,* Op. 5. Ten pieces with titles printed at the ends of the pieces. See especially *Entrance,* which is Stravinsky-like and contains broken octaves and marcato playing; *At the Fair,* which is a witty polytonal work with changing meters; and *At Dawn,* which features shrill bird calls and bird chirps. (MCA.) Level 8.

Episodes (Priskasi) (Short Stories)

These pieces, written in his early childhood and youth, are in a mildly contemporary idiom, and would provide fine study material from the 20th century for a performer able to play the more advanced works from the *Anna Magdalena Bach Notebook.* Worth investigating. (Heugel.) Levels 5–7.

A Sunny Day, Op. Posth. (1915)

Composed in 1915, Tcherepnin found and recopied this work on the day of his death in 1977. This two-page solo is filled with parallel triads and is marked *moderato tranquillo* with several tempo changes. (Theodore Presser.) Level 4.

Trois Préludes en forme de Blues

The sophisticated blues feeling here makes these pieces more appropriate for adults who know swing style and popular music than for young students. Primarily chordal and a large span is required. The blues feeling is unmistakable. (Max Eschig.) Level 9.

Songs Without Words, Op. 82, W 98

Two- and three-page works in Romantic forms with a contemporary sound. Titles are at the ends of the pieces rather than at the beginning.

These works avoid repetition and extremes of dynamics and range. See especially *No. 4 Skomorokh* which is based on syncopations. The final work, *No. 5 Schmkhar-Venokhe* is a kind of processional based on medieval chant and presenting a long *crescendo* from the beginning to the end in *fff*. (Peters.) Levels 9–10.

17 Easy Pieces in Contemporary Piano Literature, W 175

These pieces were composed in 1954 and are included in six volumes titled *Contemporary Piano Literature*, selected by Frances Clark and Louise Goss, and published by Summy-Birchard. They reveal Tcherepnin's talent for composing with limited technical resources. A strong contribution to the elementary contemporary teaching literature. The pieces are *Book 1: March, Joy and Tears, Relays; Book 2: Melody, To and Fro, Chimes; Book 3: Prelude, The Clock, Hide and Seek; Book 4: Valse, Merry-Go-Round, Old Tale; Book 5: Escapade, Frolics, Ivan's Accordion; Book 6: Happy Stowaway, Mic and Mac.* (Summy-Birchard.) Levels 3–5.

Quatre Nocturnes

These four gentle one-page nocturnes are wistful and nostalgic. The linear writing has a natural shape and flow. Generally featuring few technical difficulties. The first movement is lively and animated while the third movement, *Allegretto,* is reminiscent of a music box and contains a recurring melody. (Universal.) Level 9.

Vingt Pièces Faciles

These short untitled teaching pieces have thick textures with many accidentals. (Salabert.) Level 8.

Album D'Amis

The sophisticated harmonic language and overall style of this later work of Tansman make it most effective for the mature musician with a strong imagination. Nine miniatures are found here, requiring less in the way of technique than in musicianship. (Max Eschig.) Level 9.

IVAN TCHEREPNIN (b. 1943) France

Son of Alexander Tcherepnin. He spent most of his life in the USA.

Four Pieces from Before

Composed in 1957 by Ivan at the age of 19 as a Christmas gift for his father. *Riding the Clouds* is in a contemporary idiom and contains no barlines. (Boosey.) Level 7.

SERGE TCHEREPNIN (b. 1941) France

Brother of Ivan, another son of Alexander Tcherepnin. He spent most of his life in the USA.

Inventions (1961)

Composed to represent three different treatments of the two-part invention. No. I builds on the idea of fluid chromatic horizontal continuity. No. II is in a 12-tone idiom and uses two five-note motives. No. III is constructed diagonally, and the writing is quite angular. (Belaieff.) Level 10.

MARIANNE TEÖKE (n.d.) Hungary

Tarka-Barka, A Microcosmic Collection of New and Extraordinary Pieces for Piano

Collection of about 90 true avant-garde miniatures for piano, some only two lines long. The wealth of techniques used includes contemporary notation (a detailed key to the signs used is provided at the beginning of the collection), various techniques inside the piano, the use of the fist, palm and forearm, various cluster formations and a variety of pedal techniques. Excellent introduction to avant-garde music for the intermediate performer. (EMB.) Levels 7–8.

VIRGIL THOMSON (1896–1989) USA

Virgil Thomson is known for the hundreds of personal musical *Portraits* that he composed beginning in 1928. They are scored for piano as well as for other solo instruments and combinations of instruments. The subject of a Thomson portrait would sit for his or her likeness just as if for a painter, and Thomson usually composed the work in front of the individual, often in one sitting. The musical styles varied with the personality of the subject, sometimes harmonious, sometimes dissonant, sometimes tuneful, sometimes contrapuntal. Many of these solo piano portraits are accessible for the lower-advanced performer. More appropriate for the adult pianist.

Portraits, Album 2

See especially *Aria: A Portrait of Germaine Hugnet; Portrait of R. Kirk Askew; Portrait of Ramon Senabre; Sea Coast: A Portrait of Constance Askew;* and *Meditation: A Portrait of Jere Abbott.* (Mercury.) Level 9.

Portraits, Album 3

See especially *Toccata: A Portrait of Mary Widney, Pastorale: A Portrait of Jean Ozenne* and *Souvenir: A Portrait of Paul Bowles.* (Mercury.) Level 10.

Nine Portraits (1974)

Sparse textures and easy to read. See especially *Madame Dubost chez elle, Russell Hitchcock, Reading* and *Ettie Stettheimer.* (Southern Music.) Level 8.

13 Portraits

See especially *Clair Leonard's Profile; Florine Stettheimer: Parades; Jamie Campbell: Stretching; Peter Monro Jack: Scottish Memories;* and *Persistently Pastoral: Aaron Copland.* (Boosey.) Level 10.

19 Portraits for Piano (1981)

Many of the portraits in this volume are one page long, slightly shorter than in other volumes. See especially *Bill Katz: Wide Awake; Norma Flender: Waltzing; Richard Flender: Solid: Not Stolid; Barbara Upstein: Untiring;* and *Craig Rutenberg: Swinging.* (Boosey.) Levels 9–10.

17 Portraits for Piano (1982–84)

See especially *Dennis Russell Daiver: In a Hammock; Rodney Lister: Music for a Merry-go-round;* and *Louis Rispoli: In a Boat.* (G. Schirmer.) Level 10.

Prelude

Slow three-page work that builds to an effective climax. Many open chords and parallel fifths. (McAfee.) Level 8.

Additional Works for Study:
Sonata No. 1
Sonata No. 2
Sonata No. 3
Sonata No. 4
Five Two-Part Inventions
10 Easy Pieces and a Coda

ERNST TOCH (1887–1964) Austria

Viennese émigré composer who became a film composer in Hollywood, and taught André Previn, among others. In the piano music of Toch, one notes a fondness for simplicity in texture, with much of the writing in two voices. He rarely uses key signatures, and changes of meter are common. Much of the playing takes place in the middle register. Toch has written a series of études for all levels.

Burlesques, Op. 31

Set of three jovial pieces. The harmonic palette displays biting dissonances and the rhythms are generally exciting. The second is the most
accessible, and only the third is titled. (Schott.) Level 10.

No. 3 The Juggler
  By far the most popular. A sparkling concert piece calling for facile
  fingerwork and the ability to control a rapid tempo. Easier than it
  sounds and effective in performance. (Schott.) Level 10.

Three Piano Pieces, Op. 32

The first piece is delicate, almost Impressionistic at times. The second is
a pastoral work, while the third moves about the keyboard using a full
range of dynamics. This last work is a restless piece and the most difficult of the three. (Schott.) Level 10.

Five Caprices, Op. 36

Interesting works at the intermediate level. See especially No. 2 with running passagework and No. 5, an exuberant piece. (Associated.) Level 9.

Echoes of a Small Town, Op. 49 (Kleinstadtbilder)

Set of 14 attractive and relatively short intermediate character pieces, all
of which require strong characterization and feature biting dissonances.
This set could be considered as an excellent modern counterpart to the
Debussy *Children's Corner* and Schumann *Scenes from Childhood*. See especially *No. 5 The Organ-Grinder,* which features changing meters and syncopated melodic lines, *No. 6 Marching Geese* in which the geese strut
along in an almost mechanical manner, *No. 12 In the Marketplace,* which
depicts movement and rushing people and *No. 14 Street Song,* the
longest, and carefree. (Schott.) Levels 7–8.

Diversions, Op. 78a

Five sophisticated one- or two-page pieces that are primarily linear and
which require detailed attention to articulation. No. 3 features changes
in meter in a quiet duet while No. 4 is light and fast with touches of
humor. (Leeds.) Level 7.

Sonatinetta, Op. 78b

Extroverted work, generally in two voices. The first movement, "allegro
and gay," contains percussive added-note chords. See especially the witty
third movement, a miniature march. (Leeds.) Level 9.

Three Little Dances, Op. 85

The first is written to be played only on the black keys, the second on the white keys and the third on both. See especially the third dance, notable for its lively, vigorous rhythm and biting sonorities. Dissonant and robust writing, even flamboyant. (Belwin-Mills.) Level 10.

Reflections, Op. 86

Five one-page pieces. These neoclassic pieces are relatively easy to read, but seem to lack the depth of some of his other collections. The textures are not thick. (Belwin.) Level 7.

Études—Five Times Ten

Five series of 10 études, progressive in difficulty through the series. Only the first three volumes are within the scope of difficulty included in this book. These études form the core of Toch's piano writing. The more difficult études are more effective than the easier ones. Accidentals apply only to the notes directly after them. (Schott.)

10 Studies for Beginners, Op. 59

Linear writing with many open intervals. Good studies in hand independence but the writing is somewhat dry. (Schott.) Levels 2–4.

10 Easy Studies, Op. 58

Most are in two parts and highly linear. Excellent studies in 20th-century contrapuntal writing. (Schott.) Levels 5–7.

10 Studies of Medium Difficulty, Books 1 and 2, Op. 57

At times more in the vein of character pieces than études. Predominantly linear, with some fingerings provided. (Schott.) Levels 8–10.

Additional Work for Study:
Op. 40 Tanz und Spielstücke

TRYGVE TORJUSSEN (1885–1977) Denmark

To the Rising Sun, Op. 4, No. 1

Atmospheric character piece. It builds to a brilliant climax, portraying the noonday and afternoon sun, and then closes gently and quietly as the sun sets. Passionate and sustained writing. Melody is found first in the left hand and later in the right hand. (Alfred.) Level 8.

JOAQUIN TURINA (1882–1949) Spain

Turina was a Spanish composer and pianist who drew his inspiration from scenes of Spanish life. Part of a foursome of early 20th-century major Spanish composers that included Albeniz, Granados and de Falla, Turina was known for lyrical melodies that are primarily tonal.

Niñerias, Set 1 Op. 21, (1919)

Eight titled selections that are slightly more difficult than those in the *Gypsy Dances*. Titles include *Jeux, Berceuse, Danse des poupées* and *A la mémoire d'un bébé*. Interesting and little-known works. (Salabert, Rouart.) Level 10.

Miniatures, Op. 52 (1930)

These eight Impressionistic pieces are slightly easier than the *Circus* by Turina. Most are filled with color and vitality, but the musical ideas are often disjunct. An ear for color and the ability to inflect short motives is important especially in playing these pieces. All selections need careful attention to fingering. (Schott.)

I. Caminando (Strolling)

Rather brief *Andantino* movement appropriate for the performer needing additional experience playing chords and octaves. Requires careful voicing of chord tops and melody over chordal accompaniment in the same hand. The performer needs a strong inner sense of rhythm. Level 8.

II. Se acercan soldados (Soldiers coming)

Fanfare-like work containing many different ideas. Appealing, but more difficult than it appears on the page. Essentially a march with low, rich basses and some double-note playing in the right hand. Level 8.

III. La aldea duerme (The village sleeps)

Impressionistic work, appropriate for the performer able to play Debussy *The Little Shepherd*. Effective cadenza in the middle of this *lento* work. More difficult musically and interpretatively than technically. Level 7.

IV. Amanecer (Dawn)

One of the most effective pieces in this collection, beginning *pp* and growing to an effective, full-chorded *fff* climax at the majestic close. Warm sonorities. Level 7.

V. El mercado (The Market Place)

Bustling with energy portrayed in the continuous sixteenth notes heard throughout. Invention-like imitative writing. Requires careful attention to fingering. Level 7.

VI. Duo Sentimental

Flowing work that features dialogue between voices. Frequent shifts from eighths to triplets. Calls for finger independence. Dynamic range is primarily *p* to *ppp*. Level 7.

VII. Fiesta

The most effective work in the set. Highly rhythmic and festive in character. Should be heard more frequently. Level 7.

VIII. La Vuelta (The Return)

Recalls themes from other movements in a disjunct two-page work. Needs inherent musicality to bring it off. After several tempo changes, the work concludes with a quiet ending. Level 8.

Gypsy Dances (Danses Gitanes), Set 1, Op. 55

The *Danses Gitanes (Gypsy Dances)* appear as two five-piece sets, with Op. 55 being the most popular. The pieces in both volumes will be attractive to the advancing student who has flair. (Salabert.)

No. 1 Zambra

Slow introduction followed by an energetic dance with percussive "strums" that suggest the guitar. Primarily chordal and rhythmic. Level 10.

No. 2 Danza de la Seduccion

Flowing and expressive ternary-form work that reveals the influence of the Impressionists. Many altered and seventh chords, sparse textures and changing rhythms. The most accessible movement in this volume. Level 8.

No. 3 Danza ritual

Repetitive work in minor with some ninth chords. Contains fewer skips than other movements in this set. Two pages. Level 8.

No. 4 Generalife

Describes what was originally a summer palace of the Moors in Granada, near the Alhambra. Based on an actual gypsy dance, a *polo*, this movement features frequent hemiola-type syncopations, fast broken arpeggios and parallel triads in imitation of a guitar. One of the best movements in the set. Level 8.

No. 5 Sacro Monte

Gypsy dance, opening with imitations of dancers clapping their hands and stomping their feet. This work depicts the fury of a dance from the famous caves at the Sacro Monte near Granada. The entire movement is a gradual *crescendo* through two-note figures, then triplets and finally sixteenths. Figuration fits the hand especially well but finger strength is required. Demands rapid movement about the keyboard. The guitar idiom is always present here. Level 8.

Niñerias, Set 1, Op. 56

A second set of eight titled works in the same idiom as the earlier set. Titles include *Entrée de Conchita, A l'école, Divertissement, Parade* and *Carnaval des enfants.* (Salabert.) Level 10.

The Circus, Op. 68 (1931)

Six character pieces that are unified by motives presented in the opening movement. These themes are further developed in subsequent movements. This format is similar to the way a circus highlights all acts briefly at the beginning followed by subsequent spotlighting of individual acts. The final movement rounds off the set by referring back to the first movement. A good alternative to the Debussy *Children's Corner.* (Schott.)

Fanfare (Trompeteria)

Filled with imagery including a march, trumpets and drum rolls. Introduction, ABA sections and Coda. Rapidly repeated triads, leaps and sequential writing. Levels 8–9.

Jugglers (Equilibristas)

Note repetition, broken-chord patterns and skips over the keyboard describing various juggling acts. Contains an eight-measure introduction followed by passagework in which alternating hands play repeated sixteenth notes in sequential figuration. Demands a light, bouncy sound. Level 9.

The Bareback Rider (Amazona)

Begins with introductory material from *Fanfare.* The music could be interpreted as suggesting a horseback rider in a trot, moving to a gallop represented by the continuous use of sixteenth-note figurations. Spirited writing. Level 9.

The Trained Dog (El perro sabio)

Technically the easiest movement of the set. Playful work, at times pentatonic and Impressionistic. Note the dog bark in measures 13–14 and 17–18. Exploits high registers and calls for a light touch overall. Levels 7–8.

Clowns (Payasos)

Perhaps the most effective movement of the work. The tempo changes several times between *Allegro* and *Andante* and returns to *Allegro*. A favorite with students, perhaps due to the quick shifts of mood and a highly effective *glissando*. The chord sequences suggest a boisterous mood. Level 9.

The Aerialists

Hand-over-hand arpeggios set the mood for this work. A later contrasting section with Debussy-like harmonic color over a slowly moving bass separates the lyrical statements of the theme. The theme of the Coda is from the *Fanfare* movement. Level 9.

Danses Gitanes, Set 2, Op. 84

Five pieces that follow in the style and character of the better-known *Danses Gitanes*, Op. 55. (Salabert.)

No. 1 Fiesta de las Calderas

Tempo changes call for a fine improvisatory flair. Rhythmic *allegretto* middle section and strong Spanish flavor. Level 8.

No. 4 Danza Rítmica

Reminiscent of the popular *Sacro Monte* from *Danses Gitanes*, Op. 55. Dazzling. Level 9.

No. 5 Seguiriva

Rhythmic and exciting. The several measures of consecutive fourths in the right hand need attention. This movement requires flair and drive. Level 9.

Viaje Marítimo (1930)

Three highly descriptive character pieces that provide interesting writing for the advancing student wanting to play Spanish music. Titles are *Luz en el mar, En fiesta* and *Llegada al puerto*. (Schott.) Level 9.

Radio Madrid (1931)

Contains three sets consisting of a prologue and three pieces each. The pieces can be played separately. Strongly rhythmic writing and straightforward harmonies. Worth investigating. See especially *Fêtes à Séville* and *Carrentra Castellana*. Shorter than the pieces in *Viaje Marítimo*. (Schott.) Levels 8–9.

Postcards (1931)

Set of five pieces, each representing a snapshot of a different place in Spain. See especially the suave *Madrid* and the *Basque Dance,* composed in 5/8 and chordal and strongly rhythmic. A fine collection of high quality and technically accessible Spanish music. (Schott.) Levels 7–8.

At the Shoemaker's (1933)

Set of six character pieces with strong characterization. See especially *The Peasant's Boots, The Shoes of the Ballet Dancer* and *Shoes of the Toreador.* Should be better known. Intriguing works that require flair. (Schott.) Level 7.

The Turina Collection, ed. Maurice Hinson

Collection of 20 piano works including selections from *At the Shoemaker's, The Circus, Miniatures, Postcards, Radio Madrid* and *Sea Voyage.* An interesting, varied collection. (Schott.) Levels 6–9.

Additional Work for Study:

Op. 80 Préludes

V

MICHAEL VALENTI (b. 1942) USA

Five Sonatinas

Appealing works utilizing popular idioms in classical forms. References to ragtime, rock, blues and folk music. Should be better known. (Associated.) Levels 7–8.

RALPH VAUGHN-WILLIAMS (1872–1958) Great Britain

A Little Piano Book

Titles include *Valse Lente, Nocturne, Canon, Two-part Invention in F, Two-part Invention in E-flat* and *Two-part Invention in G.* In general the music is not particularly inspired. (Oxford University Press.) Level 4.

HEITOR VILLA-LOBOS (1887–1959) Brazil

The first composer from Brazil to achieve truly world-wide fame, Villa-Lobos' reputation was gained primarily by using melodies and subjects from his native land. Primarily self-taught, he seemed to be intrigued by the world of childhood, and many children's folksongs occur in his writing, as well as pieces descriptive of children's activities.

Cirandinhas

Twelve folk song arrangements that are published separately and in collection. The accompaniments are simple, and the scores are relatively easy to read. These harmonically agreeable works are filled with the spirit of Brazilian folk music. Excellent teaching pieces and ones that should appear more frequently on competition lists. (Eschig.) Level 7.

Circle Game (Brinquedo de Roda)

Simple piano adaptations of popular Brazilian children's songs. Titles include *The Poor Little Country Girl* and *My Mother Used to Sing a Lullaby Like This*. (Peer.) Level 6.

Francette et Pià

A group of 10 short piano pieces intended for the famous French pianist Marguerite Long to use in her teaching studio. In this set of pieces, the composer follows the adventures of a Brazilian boy and a French girl. The story encompasses the boy Pià's arrival in France, the moment when he first sees Francette, their initial conversation, their playing together (in the fourth piece) and their arguing in the fifth piece, *Francette is Angry*. In the sixth piece, *Pià Went to War,* he leaves, and in the eighth piece Francette shows how lonely she is without him. In the seventh piece, the opening is a Brazilian theme in march tempo, although as the work progresses, Francette's own French theme is heard. Pià returns and Francette is happy to see him again. In the ninth piece, *Francette is Happy,* the composer alters the previously used children's themes and depicts their happy reunion. The set closes with a four-hand duet titled *Francette and Pià Play Together Forever.* (Eschig.) Levels 7–8.

Guia Pratico (Practical Guide)

The *Guia Practico* was composed during the period when Villa-Lobos was deeply involved with music education in Brazil. It is a delightful piano method, an anthology of teaching pieces based on popular Brazilian children's songs, and can be as satisfying as the Bartók *For Children.* The nationalistic touches in the music make the it especially inviting. Of the 11 volumes, not all are available in the United States. (The following is a partial list of volumes and publishers: Volumes I, VIII, IX—AMSCO; Volumes II, III—Associated; Volume XI—Peer Southern.)

Volume I

Contains five well-written selections on Brazilian children's songs. Titles are *Dawn, Full Tide, The Rose Bush, Little Lame Girl* and *On the Strings of a Viola.* (Consolidated.) Levels 7–8.

Volume III

Five works. See especially *I. O Pastorzihno* with an ostinato and a highly rhythmic bass, *III. A Freira* and *IV. Garibaldi foi a Missa*. Effective writing. (Eschig.) Level 6.

Volume VIII

Works found here include *Oh Lemon, Goodness!, Poor Blind Woman, Fly, Little Bird, Farmer's Daughters* and *Little White Dress*. (Mercury.)

Volume XI

Additional works from Villa Lobos' *Practical Guide* are in this volume. Strongly rhythmic, generally animated and require flair. Several require a wide span. Especially absorbing selections are *Little Dove, Tiny Dove, Circle Dance, Constant* and *The Castle*. (Southern Music.) Level 10.

Petizada (Little Children)

Six beginning children's pieces, published both separately and as a collection. Strong rhythmic interest with much use of repeated patterns and thematic groupings. (Peer International.)

No. 1 The Right Hand Has a Rose

The right hand has a catchy ostinato rhythm. Can help develop evenness of passage playing for both hands. Level 5.

No. 2 My Mother Used to Sing a Lullaby Like This

Fine example of tone painting is found in this nostalgic piece with a tango rhythm. Voicing the beautiful melody out against the chordal accompaniment is a primary concern. Level 5.

No. 3 The Poor Little Country Girl

Lyrical melody above syncopated left-hand accompaniment in the A sections. Repeated chords in the right hand provide variety in the B section. Level 5.

No. 4 The Little White Dress

Ragtime style is recalled with the sixteenth-note motives and syncopated patterns. Features a predominance of broken thirds. For students with small hands. Level 4.

No. 5 Sacy

Samba rhythm imparts an unmistakably Latin American feeling. Two voices in each hand. Captivating writing. Level 5.

No. 6 The Story of Caipirnha

Unusual syncopated rhythmic ideas. Comprised of a repeated figure which uses the two hands as a single unit. The double notes require strong hands. Level 5.

10 Pieces on Popular Children's Folktunes of Brazil

Two volumes of short, simple settings of popular Brazil folktunes. (Mercury.)

The Three Maries

Three pieces written on a Brazilian children's story about "The Three Maries of Earth" who play in the countryside of Brazil. They are cheerful and the best of friends. The movements are also published separately. (Carl Fischer.)

No. 1 Alnitah

Requires facility for the perpetual-motion sixteenth found in both hands throughout the piece. Glittering music that uses a modal scale of nine notes and features phrases of irregular length. Level 7.

No. 2 Alnilam

Lyrical ABA work. A treble G forms a kind of pedal point for the entire piece. Calls for playing in thirds. Level 6.

No. 3 Mintika

Substantially more difficult than No. 1 or No. 2. This work needs appropriate balance between the hands. Features a left-hand melody with a melancholy sound despite the cheerful quality of the right-hand passages. Interesting harmonic progressions. Difficult to read due to numerous accidentals. Level 8.

The Toy Wheel

Set of six pieces based on children's folk tunes. (Peer International.)

No. 1 Put Your Little Foot Out

Two-page rhythmic solo, based on folk tunes and featuring several tempo changes. (Peer International.) Level 5.

No. 2 The Carranquinaha Mode

Latin flavor. The texture is thin and the writing highly tuneful and harmonically conservative. Can be played by small hands. (Peer International.) Level 4.

No. 3 The Three Little Caballeros.

Tuneful writing that fits the hand well. Worth investigating. Level 3.

No. 4 One, Two Angolinhas

The double notes, accents and syncopations make this more difficult than the preceding movements. Rhythmic and driving, with Latin sound. Level 5.

No. 5 Garibaldi Went to Mass

The reversed left-hand Alberti bass is awkward. The B section contains a folk-like melody, reminiscent of Bartók. (Peer International.) Level 5.

No. 6 Let Us All Go to Dance

Simple melody in quarter notes with eighth-note accompaniment comprising the outer A sections. The B section features more complex rhythms and strongly contrasting material. Two tuneful pages. (Peer International.) Level 5.

Twice Five Pieces

Contains several pieces from the sixth and seventh albums of *Guia Pratico*. See especially *The Child's Dream, The Little Doves* and *The Crab*. (Mercury.)

The Little Dove Flew Away (A Pombinha Voou)

The opening is based on a jazz-like harmony that appears six times in the work and serves as a unifying device. The texture is relatively thin and features a chordal accompaniment that is subservient to the simple melody. Level 7.

The Baby's Family, Volume I

A set of pieces depicting dolls. Exciting writing, based on Brazilian children's themes. Rapid figurations. These pieces characterize eight different dolls. (Many standard editions.)

Branquinha (The Porcelain Doll)

Sweet and tender. This doll introduces the family. A melody that imitates a bell is heard first in the middle register and then in the high treble. Level 10.

Moreninha (The Paper Doll)

Debussy-like quality with a fresh melody on the black keys. Left-hand tremolos appear beneath triplet figures in the right hand. Level 10.

Caboclinha (The Clay Doll)

A decidedly strong character pervades this work. A vivid musical depiction of a clay figure, rather immobile and cumbersome. Some double-note passages. Level 10.

Mulatinha (The Rubber Doll)

A rhythmic piece in which the music seems to bounce joyously. Level 9.

Negrinha (The Wooden Doll)

A restless piece with many sixteenths and strong dissonances. Hands-alternating passagework. Level 10.

A Probresinha (The Rag Doll)

A plaintive work of two pages, based on a folk-like melody. Perhaps the most accessible movement. Level 8.

O Polichinelo (Punch)

This popular selection is a musical caricature of the puppet Punch, who is full of zany antics. Rapid hands-alternating passagework. A favorite for recitals and encores. Level 9.

Bruxa (The Witch Doll)

In this piece, the Witch Doll sings her song of doom, frightening the children. Difficult but exciting. Level 10.

Additional Works for Study:
Carnaval das Criancas Brasileiras
Guia Prático, Volumes II, IV, V, VI, VII, IX, X
Simples Coletanea—Three Pieces

W

DAVID WARD-STEINMAN (b. 1936) USA

Three Miniatures

Attractive set with movements that include *Rustic Dance*, featuring sudden dynamic changes, *Song*, a legato study in 5/4 and *City Sketch*, which features irregular rhythms. The final movement is the most difficult. (Lee Roberts.)

Improvisations on Children's Songs

Modern versions of such songs as *Twinkle, Twinkle Little Star* and *Happy Birthday*. (Lee Roberts.)

DONALD WAXMAN (b. 1925) USA

The New Recital Pageants, Books 1–4

Progressive series of excellent contemporary teaching pieces. With titles such as *Two Chickens, Sly Fox, The Bear, Lone Firefly* and *Grasshopper on the Go*, the pieces are spirited and effective. They feature mild contemporary sounds and fit the hand well. Similar in concept and quality to Dello-Joio's *Lyric Pieces for the Young*. (Galaxy.) Levels 4–7.

50 Études, Books 1–4

Series of contemporary études with strong teaching value. Each focuses on a certain figuration or technical pattern. Highly pianistic and idiomatic to the hand. Subtitles appear at the end of pieces and include *Étude in Finger Staccato, Étude of Glissandos, Étude of Thumb Holds, Étude of Alternating Double-Notes, Étude of Consecutive Thirds* and *Étude in Phrased Double Notes*. Several are published separately. (Galaxy.) Book 1—Level 7; Book 2—Level 8; Book 3—Level 9; Book 4—Level 10.

ANTON VON WEBERN (1883–1945) Austria

Kinderstück (1924)

This 12-tone piece could provide an excellent introduction to serialism. Webern intended to write a series of pieces for children, but this is the only one that was finished. Seventeen measures long. (Carl Fischer.) Levels 7–8.

LEO WEINER (1885–1960) (Hungary)

Three Hungarian Rural Dances

See especially the *Fox Dance*, the first of the set, an effective and virtuosic work. It is polka-like in character and requires a staccato technique, a big sound, freedom at the keyboard and physical strength. (EMB.) Level 9.

31 Hungarian Peasant Songs, Volumes 1 and 2

Volume 1 contains Nos. 1–19 while Volume 2 contains Nos. 20–31. Strong settings of Hungarian folk tunes, progressive and generally much more difficult than the Bartók *For Children*. Some of the later ones would be effective for study by advanced performers. (General Music.) Levels 8–10.

Additional Work for Study:
10 kleine leichte Stücke (EMB)

FREDERICK WERLÉ (b. 1914) USA

Vignettes

Set of 10 pieces of high quality. A student should understand hemiola and be able to voice a left-hand waltz accompaniment to perform *Two for Three*. The *Auto-Harp* emphasizes arpeggiated major-minor seventh chords and triads, ascending and descending. Other selections to note include *Romanza, A Royal Procession* and *Gavotte*. (Schroeder and Gunther.) Level 5.

The Color Wheel

Pieces in all of the major and minor keys. Each piece has a color for its name, and the works are arranged first through the sharp keys and back through the flat keys. (Schroeder and Gunther.) Level 6.

Variations on a Theme of Paganini

Delightful writing for the upper-intermediate student. This well-known tune takes on new twists in a mildly contemporary setting with ingenious turns of harmony, creating a colorful setting that is pianistic and effective. (Schroeder and Gunther.) Level 7.

Six Fancies

Less inspired than the *Vignettes*. These six two-page character pieces include *She Dances, Popular Song* and *Water Bells*. (Alexander Broude.) Level 7.

Additional Works for Study:
Pastorale
Sarabande
Piano Sports

ALEC WILDER (1907–1980) USA

Pieces for Young Pianists, Volumes 1 and 2

Accessible harmonic idiom. The selections feature a variety of compositional forms and techniques such as canon, fugue, duet, melody and accompaniment and so on. The music is of high quality. In Volume 2 see especially *No. 2 Summer Song, No. 3 Butterfly, No. 9 Invention* and *No. 13 An Old Picture Album*. (Margum Music.) Levels 2–3.

12 Mosaics

Arranged into groups of four by the composer, these pieces feature mildly contemporary sounds, upbeat rhythms and predictable phrase lengths. The *Minute March, Thirds on the Run* and *Pattern in Color* are especially attractive. All pieces are one page or shorter. (Presser.) Level 3.

DARWIN WOLFORD (b. 1936) USA

Suite à la Mode

In this set of 14 short modal pieces for piano, the composer portrays a variety of moods. Pianistic and rhythmically vibrant. See especially *Escapade, Witches' Hoedown, Madame Chatterbox, March* and *Fanfare for Trumpets and Tubas*. (Boosey.) Level 5.

STEFAN WOLPE (1902–1972) Germany

Wolpe immigrated to the USA in 1938.

Early Piece for Piano (1924)

A four-section work, *Andante con moto, Allegro, Meno mosso* and *Andante con moto*, of about 13 pages. The second part, *Allegro*, reveals traces of American folk dance and jazz. Many syncopations and much linear writing are present throughout. Should be performed as a whole. Worth investigating. (McGinnis and Marx.) Level 10.

GERHARD WUENSCH (b. 1925) Austria

Wuensch now resides in Canada.

Mini-Suite No. 2

In three movements, *Prelude, Berceuse* and *Burlesque*. Light-hearted. (Leeds.)

Shades of Ivory

Subtitled "Excursions through Popular Dance Rhythms," these selections all have a popular flavor. Titles include *Blues, Swing Rock, A Sentimental Ballad, Beguine* and *Viennese Waltz*. (Waterloo.) Level 9.

Ping Pong Anyone? Op. 91

Composed for Canadian festivals. The pieces present a variety of styles and are progressive in difficulty. See especially *No. 4 Ping Pong Anyone?* and *No. 9 Perpetuum Mobile*. (Harris.)

Z

HAROLD ZABRACK (b. 1929) USA

Preludes

These works deserve to be better known since they display an appealing contemporary sound and often exhibit a finely honed melodic contour. Slightly easier than the well-known Muczynski *Preludes*. Motivating writing. See especially No. 2. (Kenyon.) Levels 8–9.

Scherzo-Hommage á Prokofiev

Witty and brilliant writing in a piece that sparkles with energy and sudden changes. Contains frequent passages in which the hands cross, also many keyboard shifts. (Boosey.) Level 10.

MIKHAIL ZIV (b. 1921) Russia

Ziv was a student of Kabalevsky at the Moscow Conservatory.

Piano Album for Children

Set of 30 pieces in a neo-Romantic and highly expressive style. No fingerings are provided. (G. Schirmer.) Level 7.

BOGUSLAW ZUBRZYCKI (b. 1929) Poland

Sketches

A fascinating set of character pieces, reminiscent of Turina's *Miniatures*. Contemporary writing that would appeal both to children and adults. See especially *The Spanish Guitarist, Great Grandmother Goes Skating* and *Postlude*. (PWM.) Level 7.

APPENDIX

Index of Music Publishers

The constant changes in and shrinking of the classical music publishing industry makes entirely accurate listings difficult, and so the following are intended more as a guide. Often a local music store will prove helpful in the attempt to acquire difficult-to-obtain materials. For the most complete information available, consult the Music Publishers Sales Agency List, issued periodically by the U.S. Music Publishers' Association, the National Music Publishers' Association and the Church Music Publishers' Association as a service of the music industry. Information found here was submitted by the publishers listed below.

Administrating Parent Companies, Distributors and Music Publisher's Imprints

Parent Companies Indicated in Parentheses for Imprints
Country of Foreign Publishers Usually Indicated in Parentheses

Alfred Publishing Co., Inc., P.O. Box 10003, Van Nuys, CA 91410

Amadeus, Edition (Foreign Music Distributors)

Amberson Enterprises, Inc. (Boosey & Hawkes, Inc.)

American Composers Alliance, 170 West 74th Street, New York, NY 10023

American Music Editions, 263 East 7 Street, New York, NY 10009

Amphion (Kerby)

Ars Nova (Theodore Presser Company) (Brodt Music Co.)

Artia (Boosey & Hawkes, Inc.)

Associated Board of the Royal Schools of Music (U.K.) (Theodore Presser Company)

Associated Music Publishers (Hal Leonard Publishing Corp.)

Augener (E. C. Schirmer Music Company)

Augsburg Fortress Publishing House, 426 South 5th Street, Box 1209, Minneapolis, MN 55440

Bärenreiter-Verlag (Foreign Music Distributors)

Barry & Co. (Argentina) (Boosey & Hawkes, Inc.)

Belaieff (Germany) (C. F. Peters Corp.)

Belwin-Mills Publishing Corp., 3808 Riverside Dr., Suite 408, Burbank, CA 91505

Berandol Music Ltd. (Associated Music Publishers)

Bèrben, Edizioni (Italy) (Theodore Presser Company)

Billaudot, Editions (Theodore Presser Company)

Boccaccini & Spade Editori (Italy) (Theodore Presser Company)

Boosey & Hawkes, Inc., 52 Cooper Square, New York, NY 10003

Bornemann, Editions (Paris) (Theodore Presser Company)

Boston Music Company, 116 Boylston St., Boston, MA 02116

Bote & Bock (Germany) (Hal Leonard Publishing Corp.)

Bourne Company, 5 W. 37th Street, New York, NY 10018

Breitkopf & Härtel (Broude Brothers) (Foreign Music Distributors) (Hal Leonard Publishing Corp.)

Brodt Music Company, Box 9345, 1409 E. Independence Blvd., Charlotte, NC 28299

Broekmans & Van Poppel (Oxford University Press)

Carlanita Music Company (E. C. Schirmer)

Chappell (Mark Foster Music Company)

Chester Music (Music Sales Corporation)

Choudens (France) (C. F. Peters, Theodore Presser)

Colombo, Franco, Publications (CPP/Belwin Music)

Composers' Press (Seesaw Music Corp.)

Concordia Publishing House, 3558 South Jefferson Avenue, St. Louis, MO 63118

Consolidated Music Publishers (Music Sales Corporation)

Consort Press, Box 50413, Santa Barbara, CA 93150

CPP/Belwin Music, 15800 N.W. 48th Ave., Miami, FL 33014

Cramer Music, London (Boosey & Hawkes, Inc.)

Curci, Big 3 Music Corp., 729 Seventh Avenue, New York, NY 10019

Curwen, J., & Sons, Ltd (UK) (Hal Leonard)

Delrieu & Cie (France) (E. C. Schirmer)

Ditson, Oliver, Company (Theodore Presser Company)

Doblinger Verlag (Austria) (Foreign Music Distributors)

Donemus (Holland) (Theodore Presser Company)

Dover Music (Alfred Publishing Co., Inc.)

Durand (France) (Theodore Presser Company)

E. C. Schirmer Music Company, 138 Ipswich St., Boston, MA 02215

Eaton Music, Inc., 11330 Ventura Blvd., Studio City, CA

Editio Supraphon (Foreign Music Distributors)

Editions Musicales Transatlantiques (France) (Theodore Presser Company)

Edward B. Marks Music Company, 1619 Broadway, New York, NY 10019

Edwin F. Kalmus & Company, Inc., P.O. Box 5011, Boca Raton, FL 33433

Elkan, Henri Publishing Co., Inc, P.O. Box 7720, FDR Station, New York, NY 10150

Elkan-Vogel, Inc. (Theodore Presser Company)

Elkin & Co., Lt. (E. C. Schirmer)

EMB (Hungary) (Boosey & Hawkes, Inc.) (Theodore Presser Company)

Enoch & Cie (France) (Theodore Presser Company)

Enoch & Sons (Boosey & Hawkes, Inc.)

Eschig, Editions Max (France) (Hal Leonard Publishing Corp.)

European American Music Dist. Corp., 2480 Industrial Blvd., Paoli, PA 19301

Faber Music, Ltd. (Hal Leonard Publishing Corp.)

Fazer, Mussikki (Helsinki) (M M B Music, Inc.)

Fentone Music, Ltd. (UK) (Theodore Presser Company)

Fischer, Carl, Inc., 62 Cooper Square, New York, NY 10003

Fischer, J. & Bros. (CPP/Belwin Music)

FJH Music Company, Inc., 20432 Northeast 16th Place, North Miami Beach, FL 33179

Foreign Music Distributors 13 Elkay Drive, Chester, NY 10912

Foster, Mark Music Company, 28 E. Springfield Avenue, Champaign, IL 61820

Fox, Sam (Music Sales Corp.) (Plymouth Music Company, Inc.)

Frank Music Corp. (Hal Leonard Publishing Corp.)

Frederick Harris Music Company, Ltd., 340 Nagel Drive, Buffalo, NY 14225

G.I.A. Publications, Inc., 7404 South Madison Avenue, Chicago, IL 60638

Galaxy Music Corp. (E. C. Schirmer Music Company)

Galliard, Ltd. (U.K.) (E. C. Schirmer Music Company)

General Words and Music Company (Neil A. Kjos)

Gray, H. W., Company (CPP/Belwin Music)

Hal Leonard Publishing Corp., 7777 West Bluemound Road, Milwaukee, WI 53213

Hamelle et Cie. (France) (Southern Music Company) (Theodore Presser Company)

Hansen (Music Sales Corporation) or (Hansen House)

Harris, Frederick Music Company, Ltd., 340 Nagel Drive, Buffalo, NY 14225

Heinrichshofen Edition (C. F. Peters Corp.)

Helios (Plymouth Music Company, Inc.)

Henle, G. USA, Inc., 2446 Centerline Industrial Drive, Maryland Heights, MO 63043

Henmar (C. F. Peters Corporation)

Heugel et Cie. (France) (Theodore Presser Company) (Southern Music Company)

Highate Press (E. C. Schirmer)

Hildegard Publishing Company, Box 332, Bryn Mawr, PA 19010

Hinrichsen Edition (U.K.) (C. F. Peters Corp.)

Hinshaw Music, Inc., P.O. Box 470, Chapel Hill, NC 27514

Hoffmeister, Friedrich (Foreign Music Distributors)

Hudenbni Matice, Ve Smeckach 30, Prague 1, Czechoslovakia

Hug (Magnamusic Distributors) (Southern Music Company)

Impero-Verlag (Germany) (Theodore Presser Company)

International Music Co. (Bourne Company)

Islip Music Publishing Co., 120 W. Bayberry Road, Islip, NY 11751

Israeli Music Publications (Theodore Presser Company)

Jalni Publications, Inc. (Boosey & Hawkes, Inc.)

Jerona Music Corp., P.O. Box 5010, S. Hackensack, NJ 07606

Kahnt, C. F. (Germany) (C. F. Peters Corp.)

Kalmus, Edwin F. & Company, Inc., P.O. Box 5011, Boca Raton, FL 33433

Kenyon Publications (Hal Leonard Publishing Corp.)

Kerby, E. C. Ltd., 198 Davenport Road, Toronto, Ontario, Canada MR5 IJ2 (Hal Leonard Publishing Corp.)

King, Robert, Music Sales, Inc. 28 Main Street, Shovel Shop Square, North Easton, MA 02356

Kistner & Siegel (Concordia Publishing House)

Kjos, Neil A., Music Company, 4382 Jutland Drive, San Diego, CA 82117

Leduc, Alphonse (Theodore Presser Company) (Southern Music Company)

Leeds Music Corporation (Hal Leonard Publishing Corp.)

Lemoine, Henry, ed Cie. (France) (Theodore Presser Company)

Lengnick, Alfred, & Co. (UK) (Music Sales Corporation)

Littolf (C. F. Peters Corp.)

M C A Music Ltd. (Hal Leonard Publishing Corp.)

M C A Music Publishing, 1755 Broadway, 8th Floor, New York, NY 10019

M M B Music, Inc., 10370 Page Industrial Blvd., St. Louis, MO 63132

Magnamusic Distributors, Route 41, Sharon, CT 06069

Margun Music, Inc. (Jerona Music Corp.)

Marks, Edward B., Music Company, 1619 Broadway, New York, NY 10019

Martin, Editions Robert (France) (Theodore Presser Company)

Masters Music Publications, Inc., P.O. Box 810157, Boca Raton, FL 33481

Mathot (France)

Maurice Senart (Salabert)

McAfee (CPP/Belwin Music)

McGinnis & Marx Music Publishers, 236 West 26th St., #11 S, New York, NY 10001

Mercury Music Corporation (Theodore Presser Company)

Merion Music, Inc. (Theodore Presser Company)

Metropolis Editions (Henri Elkan Publishing Co.)

Mexicanas de Musica, Ediciones (Theodore Presser Company)

Mills, Irvin, Music, P.O. Box 10372, Sedona, AZ 86336

Moeck (Germany) (European American Music Dist. Corp.)

Mowbray Music Publishers (Theodore Presser Company)

Music Graphics Press, 121 Washington Street, San Diego, CA 92103

Music Sales Corporation, 5 Bellvale Rd., Chester, NY 10918

Musica Antiqua Bohemica (Supraphon)

Musical Scope Publishers, Box 125, Audubon Station, New York, NY 08401

Musicales Transatlantiques

Myklas Music Press, P.O. Box 929, Boulder, CO 80306

New School for Music Study (Warner Bros., Inc.) (Summy Birchard, Inc.)

Nosrsk Musikforlag A/S (Oslo) (Robert King Music Sales, Inc.)

Novello & Company (UK) (Theodore Presser Company)

Ongaku-No-Tomo-Sha (Japan) (Theodore Presser Company)

Orbis (London)

Oxford University Press, 200 Madison Avenue, New York, NY 10016

Peer International Corp. (Theodore Presser Company) (Peer-Southern Concert Music)

Peer-Southern Concert Music, 810 Seventh Avenue, New York, NY 10019

PeerMusic, 810 Seventh Avenue, New York, NY 10019

Peters, C. F., Corp., 373 Park Avenue South, New York, NY 10016

Plymouth Music Company, Inc., 170 Northeast 33rd Street, Fort Lauderdale, FL 33334

Polskie Wydawnictwo Muzyczne (Hal Leonard)

Presser, Theodore Company, Presser Place, Bryn Mawr, PA 19010

PRI Music Publishing Companies, 810 Seventh Avenue, New York, NY 10019

Rahter, D. (U.K.) (Theodore Presser Company)

Ricordi, G. Co. (Boosey & Hawkes, Inc.)

Ries & Erler (Germany) MH (C. F. Peters Corp.)

Robert King Music Sales, Inc. 28 Main Street, Shovel Shop Square, North Easton, MA 02356

Roberts, Lee (Hal Leonard Publishing Corp.)

Robertson, Don, Music Corp., P.O. Box 4141, Thousand Oaks, CA 91359

Rongwen Music (Broude Brothers Limited)

Rork Music, Ltd. (Theodore Presser Company)

Rouart, E. Lerolle & Co. (Salabert)

Salabert, Editions (Hal Leonard Publishing Corp.) (G. Schirmer, Inc.)

Sassetti & Cia., R. Nova do Almada 60, Lisbon 2, Portugal

Schirmer, E. C., Music Company, 138 Ipswich St., Boston, MA 02215

Schmidt, Arthur P., Company (Warner Bros., Inc.)

Schmitt, Hall & McCreary (CPP/Belwin Music)

Schott Music Corporation (European American Music Dist. Corp.)

Schroeder & Gunther (Hal Leonard Publishing Corp.)

Seesaw Music Corporation, 2067 Broadway, New York, NY 10023

Shanghai-Commercial Press

Shattinger International Music (Hansen House)

Shawnee Press, Inc., Waring Drive, Delaware Water Gap, PA 18327

Sikorski, Musikverlage Hans (Augsburg Fortress Publishing House)

Simrock, N. (U.K.) (Theodore Presser Company)

Southern Music Company, P.O. Box 329, 1100 Broadway, San Antonio, TX 78215

Stainer & Bell, Ltd. (U.K.) (E. C. Schirmer Music Company)

Steingräber Verlag, Auf der Reiswiese 9, Offenbach, Germany

Studio P/R, Inc. (CPP/Belwin Music)

Süddeutscher Musikverlag (C. F. Peters Corp.)

Summy-Birchard Inc., 265 Secaucus Road, Secaucus, NJ 07086

Supraphon (Foreign Music Distributors)

Tetra/Continuo Music Group (Plymouth Music Company)

Tonos Editions (Seesaw Music Corp.)

Transcontinental Music Publications, 838 Fifth Avenue, New York, NY 10021

Union Musical Española (Music Sales Corporation)

United Music Publishers (U.K.) (Theodore Presser)

Universal Edition (London & Vienna) (European American Music Dist. Corp.)

VAAP (Soviet Music) (Hal Leonard Publishing Corp.)

Vanguard Music, 357 W. 55th Street, New York, NY

Vienna Urtext Edition (European American Music Dist. Corp.)

Walton Music Corp., 170 N.E. 33rd Street, Fort Lauderdale, FL 33334

Warner Brothers Publications, Inc., 265 Secaucus Road., Secaucus, NJ 07096

Waterloo Music Co. (Alexander Broude, Inc.)

Weinhberger, Josef, Ltd. (UK)

Weintraub Music (Music Sales Corporation)

Willis Music Company, 7380 Industrial Road, Florence, KY

Yorktown Music Press (Music Sales Corporation)

Zen-On (European American Music Dist., Corp.)

Zerboni, Edizioni (Italy) (Boosey & Hawkes, Inc.)

COMPOSER'S INDEX

A

B